A MILE SQUARE OF CHICAGO

By

Marjorie Warvelle Bear

A MILE SQUARE OF CHICAGO
by MARJORIE WARVELLE BEAR

Published by
TIPRAC
P.O. Box 4941
Oak Brook, IL 60522-4941

ISBN-10: 0-9633995-4-3
ISBN-13: 978-0-9633995-4-0

Library of Congress Control Card Number: 2007904963

Book covers were designed by George Bolger, with Tatiana M. Orawski contributing the initial design of the photo montage appearing on the front cover. All photos included in the montage were selected from those illustrating pages of this book. The back cover photo comes from the author's family album.

First Edition, 2007; first printing, 2007.

To my great-uncle, Abraham Hanson, appointed by Abraham Lincoln in 1860 as United States Counsel General to Liberia, Africa, where he died serving the Black people.

To our family name giver, Brissot de Warville, member of the Legislative Assembly of France, who organized the <u>Societe des Amis des Noirs</u> for the world-wide abolition of Black slavery. Brissot de Warville was a humanitarian who paid for his hopes of <u>Liberte et Egalite</u> for mankind at the guillotine in 1793.

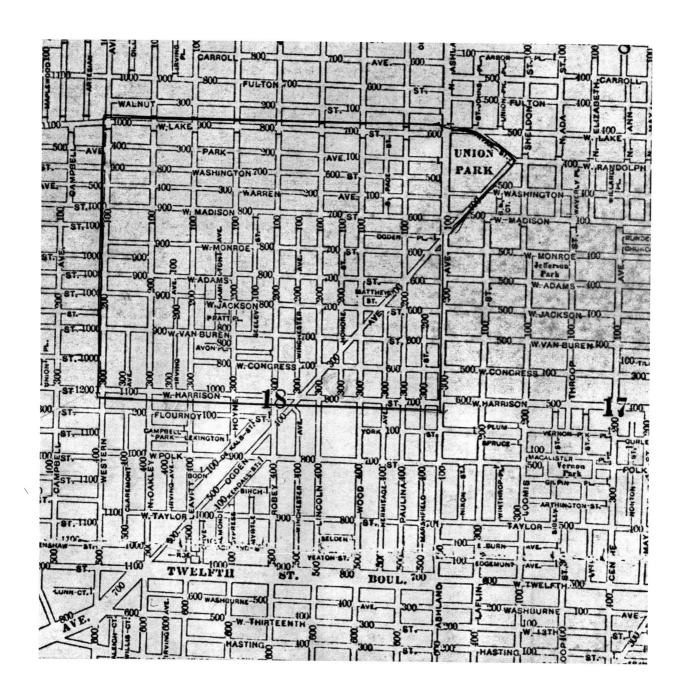

1. Map of Mile Square of Chicago. From: "Blanchard's Map of Chicago with the New Street Names," Rufus Blanchard (146 Lake Street, Chicago, IL), published jointly by R. Blanchard and G. F. Cram, 1901. Call Number: map3C G4104.C6 1901 .B5a. Photo Courtesy of The Newberry Library, 60 West Walton Street, Chicago, Illinois 60610.

"--I have turned for consolation to the past, gathering up the fragments of my early recollections, and putting them in a form that might live. It is thus, that when we find our personal and substantial identity vanishing from us, we strive to gain a reflected and substituted one in our thoughts; we do not like to perish wholly, and wish to bequeath our names at least to posterity. As long as we can keep alive our cherished thoughts and nearest interests in the minds of others, we do not appear to have retired altogether from the stage, we still occupy a place in the estimation of mankind, exercise a powerful influence over them, and it is only our bodies that are trampled into dust or dispersed to air. Our darling speculations still find favour and encouragement, and we make, as good a figure in the eyes of our descendants, nay, perhaps a better than we did in our life-time."

William Hazlitt, 1778-1830
From: "On the Feeling of Immortality in Youth"

ACKNOWLEDGEMENTS

The history of <u>A Mile Square of Chicago</u> would not have been possible without the interest and gracious help of many persons and organizations. The list is long, too long to name all, and some of the kindest friends have passed on, such as Dr. Karl A. Meyer, former Superintendent of Cook County Hospital for fifty years. Predominantly, the following listed have made this work possible over the many years of preparation.

They are Robert E. Kelley, Director of Administrative Research for the Chicago Board of Education; David Patek, Research Analyst for the Illinois Medical Center; The Chicago History Museum (formerly The Chicago Historical Society), with Helen Chase of the Library and Mary Rhymers of the Photography Archives; The Newberry Library with Diana Haskell, Curator of Modern Manuscripts and Amy Nyholm now retired; Chicago Public Library with Joseph Lutz and also Katharyn Kenyon and Jessie Howes, now retired; Rush-Presbyterian-St Luke's Hospital Center with Helen Ernest Dosick and Ivy M. Leventhal; Max I. Light, Director of University of Illinois at the Center for public information with Catharine W. Conover; and Santa Barbara Public Library with John Hart. Also, the author is grateful for materials from the Wisconsin State Historical Society, Illinois State Historical Society, and the Chicago Theological Seminary.

Among the many individuals who have recalled so generously with nostalgic memories of the old Mile Square are Valerie Walker Hoffman, Alura Goff Rogers, Dorothy Fitch Schaefer, Dorothy Kent Toms, John Johnston, Alfred Marks and two who have left this world, Dr. George Orseck and Helen Frohmuth Bray. Above all to my daughter, Marjorie Harbaugh Bennett, who has urged me on during many of our interrupted days.

7

TABLE OF CONTENTS

9

10

11

TABLE OF ILLUSTRATIONS

14

FOREWORD

Marjorie Warvelle Bear wrote her manuscript in the 1960's and 1970's. At the time she was living in California. When she was finishing it, she wanted to bring the manuscript back to Chicago, but by then Alzheimer's was preventing her from being fully in control of her life. Her daughter, Marjorie Harbaugh Bennett, offered to mail it to publishers, but, as Eric Zorn of the Chicago Tribune reported in his column on July 24, 1994, Marjorie Bear wanted "to be there to explain it herself."[1] After Marjorie Bear died on May 28, 1982, her daughter, Marjorie Bennett, and her family, sorted through the papers and stored them in boxes in a closet. Upon her retirement from a career in teaching, Dr. Marjorie Bennett came to Chicago with the manuscript in the hopes of fulfilling her mother's wishes to have it published there. While she may not have found any publishers, she did meet with a "curious newspaper columnist"[2] who wrote about it. It thus came to the attention of an intrigued editor who made contact, and the result is seen in these pages.

Marjorie Warvelle Bear was born in Chicago in 1897. She was the daughter of the noted lawyer and educator, George Warvelle, author of numerous books and Dean of the Chicago Law School. She attended Chicago public schools and graduated from the Academy of the Lewis Institute in 1916. After receiving a B.S. degree from Milwaukee-Downer College in 1921, she obtained her M.S. degree from the University of Wisconsin in 1925 in Horticulture and Landscape Architecture.[3]

Marjorie Bear spend a life in artistic and horticultural endeavors, lecturing on gardening, contributing regularly to publications such as Horticulture magazine, designing and developing gardens, perennial beds and borders, working in metal (e.g., she made and sold pewter art work and jewelry while a young wife of Marion Dwight Harbaugh in Madison, Wisconsin, "designed and made the brass processional cross for All Saints Episcopal Church"[4] in Miami, Oklahoma, where she lived from 1929 until moving to Hudson, Ohio in 1938), made quilts, paintings, sculptures, etc. She continued to live in Hudson for five years post the death of her first husband in 1952, after which she lived in Santa Barbara, California until her death. She also outlived her second husband, Captain Herbert Stanley Bear, who died in 1977. She was a charter member of the Western Reserve Chapter of the Herb Society of America, a member of

---

[1] Eric Zorn, "Love Story Told in Pieces of Past," Chicago Tribune, Chicagoland Section, July 24, 1994, p. 1.

[2] Ibid.

[3] "Former Hudsonite Marjorie Bear dies at 84," The Hudson Times, Hudson, Ohio, June 9, 1982, p. 19. Permission Record Publishing Co., P.O. Box 1549, 1619 Commerce Drive, Stow, Ohio 44224-0549.

[4] Ibid.

the Preservation for the Historic Trust and the Theosophical Society. As her obituary stated: she

> "...will be remembered by many as a "Renaissance woman" who was skilled in many fields and ever eager to share her talents with others. During her lifetime of nearly 85 years she pursued interests enough for a dozen people."[5]

Arthur T. Orawski
Editor

---

[5]Ibid.

PREFACE

Just as Chicago, which like many other American cities, is re-evaluating its architecture and social history, so too, this text revalues and recalls the earlier population and its social history. This book, titled A MILE SQUARE OF CHICAGO, covers the period from 1860 to 1914, and beyond. The exact area included is from Ashland to Western Avenues and from Lake to Harrison Streets.

The manuscript contains 121 excellent rare photographic reproduction (from various museums, libraries, and personal collections) of this particular region. The total volume is divided into three books or sections: Before My Day, In My Day, and a closing section, Today and Tomorrow.

In Book II, I give my own personal memories of this Mile Square, since I was born there and attended its public and private schools. My father was a well-known Chicagoan and professor of law for fifty years.

Book III ends with hope and knowledge of all the late restorations now in progress. The development of the Illinois Medical Center, the largest in the world, and the later schools and colleges, are considered.

Interspersed in the three books are brief biographies of some of those national leaders who came out of this Mile Square in which most of them had their early education. I have been in personal contact with some of these persons now living, and they seem very interested in this work.

This is the essence of A MILE SQUARE OF CHICAGO.

Marjorie Warvelle Bear
1976

INTRODUCTION

Great cities, such as Chicago, are composed of lesser communities, little worlds of places, events and people. Many who grew up in a large city, even though they may have long since moved away, vividly recall their childhood neighborhood.

In this time of change in American cities, it seems a challenge to recall details of an old Chicago neighborhood before sources of information and memorabilia are lost in the onrush. This book is about a small section of Chicago where my family resided and I went to neighborhood schools. The area roughly spans a square mile of Chicago's west side. It is bounded by Lake Street on the north, Ashland Boulevard on the east (with an extension along Ogden Ave and Bryan Street to include Union Park), Harrison (with an extension to West Polk Street) on the south, and Western Avenue on the west. The description extends beyond this area for some events, as the Great Fire of 1871 and the World's Fair of 1893. The time considered is from 1850 to about 1920; the period from the World's Fair through World War I is treated in greater detail since more facts are available.

A greater part of this book is a history of the neighborhood's schools from first grade to college level, where those who attended were surrounded by a larger world of preparation and experience as citizens of Chicago. Schools recalled are Brown Grammar School, Central High School and its descendants, West Division High School and William McKinley High School; also considered are Lewis Institute and the Illinois Medical Center with its colleges and hospitals. Other humanitarian, religious and commercial organizations complete the saga of this neighborhood's institutions.

This study is based on facts from official school records, historical materials, my own memory of childhood events and other persons' recollections of this neighborhood. Names, events, places, dates and descriptions are as authentic as records could reveal. Many scenes and circumstances are reviewed through a child's eye, not as an adult mind might have remembered them. Youthful impressions, both preschool and later, of houses, gardens, Madison Street stores, parks, passing traffic, and grammar school activities in the early 1900's are part of the vignette. The reader may recognize himself, his forebears or kith and kin among these mutual ruminations.

A former resident of the West Side from 1891 to 1938, John W. Johnston, frequently helped me in recalling names of persons, places and events once associated with the old Mile Square. He may be said to have a photographic memory for details of buildings and scenes with their architectural qualities as well as of people with their visual habits and physical appearances.

When he offered to help me with his great reservoir of West Side memories he gave two reasons for his accumulations of family names and dates. First, his father had been a maintenance man for over twenty years for many businesses as well as homes on Ashland Avenue and vicinity until his death in 1912.

Second, young John W. Johnston, starting in school days, worked twenty years for Paul C. Eiler who owned a high class grocery store on Van Buren and Laflin Streets. The job at first was delivering groceries to many residents and original builders of the old mansions, especially on the boulevards. Mr. Johnston wrote in his sincere recapitulation of those years:

"In a way this puts me in a category with the Chicago novelist, Arthur Meeker, who wrote about the families of Prairie Avenue, with the exception that he had access to the front door whereas I went in the back door; he also had a journalistic background which I did not."[1]

A large number of famous persons came from this Chicago area, most of whom had part of their education in the local schools. Biographies are given which may interest older readers, as well as contemporary students. As the lives of these persons are traced, one feels they are cradled in the definition of history given by Alfred North Whitehead in Adventures of Ideas:

"...History includes the present and the future together with the past, affording a mutual elucidation and wrapped in common interest."[2]

In this study for A Mile Square of Chicago, historical records were searched which would reveal information on the "growing years," namely from childhood to maturity, of the persons recalled. Surely those years, roughly about twenty, are important building stones for the individual and are usually happy days. It is a fact that the average encyclopedia or reference on famous persons furnishes little information on the youthful period of their subjects. Luckily, school records, newspapers, printed programs and high school annuals help preserve some of the thoughts and actions of adolescence while scribbled diaries are a rich treasure chest.

The world today is becoming a world-city; we are becoming urban but unfortunately neither sufficiently neighborly, nor humanitarian; this will be a long struggle. In the meantime, we look ahead, and we also look back to see how it was; that too is difficult. Marcel Proust in his search for the past wrote:

"It is a labor in vain to recapture it... The past is hidden somewhere beyond the reach of intellect, in some material object which we do not suspect, and as for that object, it depends on chance whether we come upon it or not before we ourselves die."

Leonardo da Vinci wrote as eloquently:

"Men do wrong to lament the flight of time complaining that it passed too quickly and failing to perceive its period is sufficiently long; but a good memory,

---

[1] Correspondence between John W. Johnston and the author.

[2] Whitehead, A.N., Adventures of Ideas, MacMillan Publishing Co., Inc, New York, 1933, p. 3. Copyright renewed by Evelyn Whitehead, 1961. Considered fair use by Simon and Schuster.

with which nature endowed us, causes everything that is long past to appear to us as present."

My old neighborhood has suffered change and decay as in areas of other American cities. Such blight is not just recent but rather an insidious, gradual affliction, one of the alarming aspects of modern civilization.

Yet, there is hope; a renaissance is coming to our cities. Where Chicago's old hospitals and clinics were, the Illinois Medical Center has become the world's largest, extending over three hundred and fifty acres. In 1969, the Rush Medical College charter was reactivated and Rush-Presbyterian-St. Luke's Medical Center was formed, all part of this great humanitarian region.

A new Chicago City College, Malcolm X College, opened in 1971 on a twenty-eight acre campus, one building alone costing twenty-two million dollars and serving 10,000 students. New public school buildings, recreation centers, high rise apartments and town houses are replacing obsolete structures - urban renewal is a promise being kept, though proceeding slowly.

Philosophers have expressed the mystery of life in countless metaphors. Living men find themselves reliving many recorded experiences of thought and action by persons who preceded them; yet such later experiences are not intentionally imitated nor truly identical, so the conclusion is simply - "a strange coincidence."

A strange coincidence - a <u>new</u> Mile Square is in the making. The present neighbors in this <u>old</u> Mile Square have recently organized and become the <u>Mile Square Federation.</u> This area embraces most of the region of this book - this oldest Square, too, was a federation of neighbors.

Eleanor Roosevelt wrote of what a Mile Square could be to anyone, anywhere:

"Where, after all, do universal human rights begin? In small places, close to home - so close and so small that they cannot be seen on any map of the world. Yet they are the world of the individual person: the neighborhood he lives in, the school or college he attends, the factory, farm or office where he works.

Such are the places where every man, woman and child seeks equal justice, equal opportunity, equal dignity without discrimination. Unless these rights have little meaning anywhere."[3]

"History is really the stuff of all men's lives, inalienably woven into the places they lived, the paths they walked, the activities they pursued, and the scenes they loved."[4]

---

[3]Rusk, M.D., Howard A., "A Void At Christmas," <u>New York Times</u>, Sunday, December 26, 1965, p. L71. This quotation was asked by Eleanor Roosevelt when she was the Human Rights Commission chairperson; it appears on the web site of: Office of the High Commissioner for Human Rights: Universal Declaration of Human Rights, http://www.unhchr.ch/udhr/miscinfo/carta.htm, published by the United Nations Department of Public Information, DPI/1937/A–December 1997.

[4]Wrenn, Tony P., "Conservation, Preservation and the National Registry." <u>Historic Preservation</u>, Vol. 18, No.4, Published by National Trust for Historic Preservation, Washington, D. C., 1966, p. 169.

BOOK ONE

BEFORE MY DAY

CHAPTER ONE: BROWN SCHOOL AND SOME OF ITS DISTINGUISHED STUDENTS

BROWN SCHOOL

"'Tis man's worst deed
To let things that have been run to waste
And in the unmeaning present sink the past,
In whose dim glass even now I faintly read
Old buried forms and faccs long ago."

Charles Lamb, 1775-1834

On this pilgrimage, recalling a certain time, through a special place and among many persons, it is well to begin at the time when a school bell was first heard at Brown School, Chicago's second oldest existing grammar school, built on the prairie west of the Chicago River in 1855, at what is now Warren Boulevard and Wood Street. The original school buildings are gone; modern structures replace the old on the site of the original buildings.

In twenty years between 1817 and 1837, far-reaching changes occurred in a village near Fort Dearborn in Illinois. This would become the site for Chicago, eventually to be the second largest city in United States.

In 1803, Fort Dearborn had been built by the United States Army in a most propitious location near Lake Michigan and the mouth of the Indian-named river, Checagou.[1] This region was popular with both native Indians and the trader settlers. In the War of 1812, Fort Dearborn was destroyed, its troops and civilians massacred by the Indians. In 1817, Fort Dearborn was rebuilt, and trading posts of John Kinzie and others were established. The area from Lake Michigan to the banks of the meandering river became known as Chicago, a village of a few hundred inhabitants.

By 1837, the village received its charter and became the City of Chicago. The inrush of settlers, over 4,000 by the 1837 census, spread north, south, east and west of the Chicago River

---

[1]Editor's Note: It was called "Chicagou" or "skunk" after a mild-tasting native garlic, allium tricoccum, which grew in the shade of Maple trees and is "known for its big, broad leaves that, when stepped upon, emit in skunk-like manner a pungent perfume," not after a bad smelling onion which was incorrectly taught in Chicago schools for many years, a fact rediscovered by John Swenson, Glencoe, IL (Barbara Mahany, "Chicago's roots: Garlic lover sniffs out the real story of the city's name," Chicago Tribune, Tempo Section, Sunday, July 10, 1994, pp. 1, 4).

and its branches. A public school was established in 1837, and others soon followed. As each school was built, it was given a number, not a name. So it came about that School #8 was built in 1855.

In February, 1852 a group of citizens in the western portion of Chicago secured a seventy-five dollar appropriation for a teacher; in December, 1852 a site was purchased at Wood and Page Streets for $2,800. Here, by 1855 stood a two-room frame structure, "one room up and one room down," costing $2,500, and housing 150 children. It was surrounded by a grove of shade trees, and was known as old School #8.[2]

In 1857 a twelve-room, three-story brick building costing $25,000, stood on the same site and became known as the Brown School. It had steam heat, a new heating system for public buildings. Henry Keith was principal, and there were five teachers and 693 students.

In the interim of 1857 to 1870 it became necessary to open branches, such as the basement of First United Presbyterian Church, on Monroe and Paulina, to accommodate 300 primary students, who had half day sessions. By 1871, another twelve-room building, accommodating 768 students, was built alongside the earlier structure. The new building was known as the primary building, while the upper grades used the older school.

A ROLL CALL OF EARLIEST STUDENTS

Among the early trader-settlers living near Fort Dearborn was Colonel John Beaubien, who established a fur trading post as an agent for John Jacob Astor. John Beaubien's son, Alexander, was the first white male child to be born in Chicago, in 1822. Alexander's youngest daughter, Frances Beaubien, became one of Brown School's earliest pupils. She married Richard S. Beaubien, her third cousin, the youngest son of Mark Beaubien, who built the first frame house, which later became known as Sanganash Tavern. Frances Beaubien owned her grandfather's sword, which she gave to the Chicago History Museum.

In 1945, she and her husband were still living and recalled their early school days and the Chicago Fire for an inquiring reporter. When a pupil at Brown School, Frances Beaubien's family lived on Grand Avenue and Wood Street. Sunday's activities, as for many early Chicagoans, included a walk to Union Park, where they fed peanuts to Old Bob, the bear - the same animal to which Mayor Carter H. Harrison II, as a boy, remembered feeding peanuts.[3]

Harriet N. Dunn, of a pioneer family and a genealogist, wrote a history of Brown School, and compiled a list of its early students for Chicago's centennial celebration of free public schools in 1937. Today, more than a century after Brown School's beginnings, Chicago names are recalled here, which live on in the city's history and in the hearts of their descendants.

---

[2]From its early number, Brown School was the eighth successive school to be built. However, today "Old Number 8" or Brown School, is considered Chicago's second oldest school existing in its original location.

[3]Gilbert, Paul T., "Old Chicago Comes To Life Once More In Beaubiens' Tales," Chicago Sun, May 20, 1945, p. 21.

23

Among the earliest pupils were Lulu, Nellie, Bell and Mamie Boyington, children of William Boyington, Chicago's first architect, who was self-taught and came to Chicago in 1853. He is best remembered for his Water Works and Tower on Michigan Avenue, among the only buildings in the vicinity to survive the fire of 1871. Other names were Helen, Ernest and Myrtle Heath, children of Monroe Heath, Mayor of Chicago from 1876 to 1878, and a partner in the Heath and Mulligan Paint Company. Some names of girl pupils are best recalled through their married names, such as Louise Buchanan, whose husband, James A. Patten, was Northwestern University's benefactor, and Eva Butler, who became the wife of James W. Ellsworth, promoter of the World's Fair of 1893.[4]

The school is old, the list is long; brothers and sisters came trooping while many a name has a familiar Chicago ring, yet dating back well into the 1860's, '70's and '80's. Space and patience permit giving only the surnames which to someone, somewhere, may be recalled. At random, some are: Moore, Kimball, Hoadley, Isham, Michaels, Hellman, Boughan, Crandall, Ludington, Griswold, Gardener, Goodsmith, Kettlestrings, Walker, Still, Sykes, Woodruff, Rathaker, Mortormer, Finney, Chamberlain, Rice, Oakley, Skinkle, Willard, Ryerson, Shumway, Babcock, Leonard and Booth.[5]

Among the many thousands who attended Brown School, there were those who pinnacled to national and international fame, as well as becoming household names among Chicago neighbors. Again, the list is long, and must be shared in many instances with schools of higher education, both public and private. They, too, claimed these progeny as their sons and daughters. Since almost all the educational institutions in our Mile Square are reviewed, it becomes apparent how many of these excellent students continued on in these regional schools from kindergarten through college.

Among the boys recalled were Barry Hodge, a perfect gentleman, and Chris Vardis, a charming Italian boy who sent me a Valentine of an ambiguous meaning:

"Roses are red, and violets blue
No knife can cut our love together."

There were Alphonse La Belle, blond and rosy-cheeked, Auburn Rector with a shining pompadour, and the quiet Irving Brand. There were two heart-breakers: handsome Merrill Smith and Edwin Stott who had the makings of a diplomat.

Within a span of sixty years of Chicago's historical existence, there were three great happenings which were the heritage of all the citizens, no matter where they lived or who they were. All Mile Square neighborhoods, the city's three sides, were concerned with these red letter events. First, was the City of Chicago's documented birth or charter of 1837. Here, in a

[4]Dunn, Harriet N., "Well Known Names in List of Brown School's Early Pupils," Oak Leaves, Oak Park, IL, June 28, 1945, p. 9.

[5]Ibid., p. 9.

region leading out from the old Fort Dearborn site, to the north, south and west, was a sprawling community numbering less than 8,000 persons.

The second happening was the Great Fire of 1871, which, at the time, was tragic: a population of 500,000 had 100,000 of its people left homeless. But after the fire, a still small voice so inspired the people that, after the clean up, the period from 1880 to the World's Fair of 1893 was the greatest building era in Chicago's history.

The third happening was the climaxing World's Columbian Exposition. By then, Chicago's population had increased to over a million people who in turn would be hosts to 27,000,000 visitors to its Fair. This event has been considered Chicago's finest hour.

There was a fourth happening which would come later in our city's history and would concern only a minority of Chicago's citizens, yet it was a most dramatic and nostalgic event. On November 18, 1932, Brown School celebrated its Diamond Jubilee in the old building at Warren Avenue and Wood Street.[6]

Among the names of the oldest alumni who returned were Elliott S. Goodsmith, Class of 1864; Charles P. Walker, '66; Fannie S. Reeder, '69; Harry Greenbaum, '73; and Al. W. Booth,'73, whose early job was to ring the school bell. The class of 1874 had Cyrus H. McCormick II, Charles Michaels, reporter for the Tribune, and John Bougham of the Associated Press. Carolyn B. Tyler, granddaughter of William H. Brown, gave a sketch of his life. Here on the third floor, where two rooms could become one with a disappearing wall, the old desks, then of an outdated style, were filled with hundreds of alumni. What memories, like spirits, must have entranced that venerable audience.[7]

It is interesting to note the long tenures of Brown School teachers and the great love that was shown them. During my sisters' years at Brown, they had Mrs. Helen Waite, Miss Elizabeth Sneed, Mrs. Sara G. Perce, Miss Josephine Kirkley, who became Mrs. Greene, her sister, Miss Sarah E. Kirkley, and Miss Isabel F. Gould. All these teachers were still holding the fort, and strongly too, twenty-five years later when the last of the Warvelle Sisters graduated in 1912.

This long service of teachers at Brown, while characteristic of other schools of the period, seems unusually meritorious, especially when considering what a later student, Charles A. Anderson, recalled about his teachers when he graduated from Brown in 1921. There were still Mrs. Waite and Misses Gould, Sneed, Black, Ryan, Appleyard, and the principal, Miss Niehaus. Bless all these dear souls who were the alma mater for so many thousands of students.

Of all the teachers at Brown School, the one I recall most vividly and one I probably never encountered more than a half dozen times in the eight grades, was our principal, Miss Matilda Niehaus. Our meetings were never a matter of discipline, probably studies or personal

---

[6]Editor's Note: The City of Chicago's flag has four red stars on its center horizontal white strip; the first three commemorate the first three events the author refers to above, while the fourth star symbolizes the Century of Progress Exposition of 1933 (Wikipedia, The Free Encyclopedia, "Flag of Chicago," http://en.wikipedia.org/wiki/Flag_of_Chicago#Stars; accessed 12-3-07).

[7]"Alumni of Brown School Stage a Rousing Reunion," Chicago Daily Tribune, November 19, 1932, p. 3.

problems. Why her face should remain so alive to me is a mystery. She was first, a statuesque person, tall, broad shouldered and heavily set; she appeared strong enough to whip or wrestle any wayward boy. She was quiet spoken, deep voiced and her face was serene, almost passive, yet sometimes stern. Her eyes were light faded blue, with reddish brows, while her hair was a fading auburn, tightly drawn back from her face. Her skin was very white with small freckles. Today, she might be described as appearing more masculine than feminine, partly because her clothes did nothing to compliment her. A large, gold watch rested on her left shoulder. In conversation, she was a kind and patient listener although she could become a thundering, commanding officer, and one withered under her orders. In all these childhood years, I humbled in her presence and yet I loved her but could not tell her so.

For seniority, the primary teacher, Mrs. Helen Waite, took the honors; having joined the faculty in 1876, she was still there in the early twenties - a half century of teaching with love and patience, such as both Ella Flagg Young and Maria Montessori stressed.

One Alumna of 1924 remarked that while present day pupils and parents complain that the

"gymnasium needs new equipment, whose auditorium paint is peeling, or whose library is not as up-to-date as it might be. At old Brown School [built in 1857] we had no gymnasium, no assembly hall, no library..." [and] "despite all these "disadvantages," we managed to get a good education. There has to be a moral there, somewhere."[8]

A hundred years later, in 1956, it was necessary to erect a new school on the old #8 site, and in 1957, there was need for an addition, due to added neighborhood high-rise apartment buildings. The new school in 1956 embraces the best of modern institutional and architectural principles in a two-story, twenty-four classroom building, with two kindergartens, adjustment room, clinic, office suite, library, home mechanics room, assembly-gymnasium, and lunch rooms. Here in this splendid modern complex, this century-old grammar school lives on proudly bearing the name, not Brown School, but the William H. Brown School. His biography follows later.

During the demolition period of old Brown School in 1956, many memories were invoked and found their way to city newspapers. The Chicago Daily News ran a series of letters. One from Meta Schadel Smith of 1892, recalled that Alice Nevers McCauley was class poet; and how one newspaper ran a popularity contest for city teachers. The prize, a trip to Europe, went to Miss Sneed.[9]

---

[8]Dorothy Kent Toms, "Old Days at Crane Recalled," in the column: "Your View of the News," Chicago Daily News, Jan. 26, 1970, p. 8. Quote comes from letter sent to the Chicago Daily News by Dorothy Kent Toms, who communicated numerous other pieces of information to the author, which the author included in this book.

[9]Editor's Note: Despite a lengthy search, the 1956 editions of the Chicago Daily News that supposedly contain the information in this paragraph and the next, including the poem by the anonymous "Jealous," were not identified by the Editor; therefore the sources of this

Another student, moved by the publicity of Brown School's renaissance, simply signed "Jealous" to this verse:

> "O what fate has let us down
> We that ne'er went to Brown
> We might have been matured under another color,
> Say Hyacinth, Primrose, Green or other.
> But after all is said - don't frown,
> We confess, we did not grad from Brown.
> Had predestination only favored thus
> Future generations might acclaim us.
> To get into print and be known about town
> We'd only to say: "We're from the Brown."
> Pray pity one poor sinner
> Who has to confess he went to Skinner."

As we weave in the last remaining threads, one recalls the expression, old school ties. It means what it infers, ties and bonds with past school associates. It is probable that Eton and Rugby started the custom of distinguishing ties or insignia, a form of heraldry. This blazonry, now a worldwide tradition, carries on in commerce with its trademarks, while all levels of the military, religious, and especially the scholastic, have their insignia.

From grammar school to college, class or school colors are nostalgic to all. They are seen in shoulder ribbons at grade school graduations, or as college pennants displayed on dormitory walls or waved at stadium games. Old school ties are seen in their colorful ceremonies when faculty and students assemble for a baccalaureate procession, each wearing his cap, gown and hood, representing a particular alma mater and its degree. Quite as dramatic is a vested religious recessional, with candles and choir; or the pomp of royalty marching with crowns and ermine robes, while heralded by guards in medieval splendor.

A master from Western Reserve Academy, Harlan Parker, scholarly defined this bond - old school ties: "A mental ligation coming from having dwelt among certain surroundings or sat under common teachers."[10] In a larger sense it could be said that all who have ever been a part of the old Mile Square neighborhood of Chicago's west side, have old school ties.

---

information and poem are not known to the Editor.

[10]Correspondence between Harlan Parker and the author, August 1971.

2. Old Brown School. Chicago Public Schools Photograph. Courtesy Chicago Board of Education.

3. New William H. Brown School. Chicago Public Schools Photograph (Mr. Gartski, photographer). Courtesy Chicago Board of Education.

WILLIAM H. BROWN

Through the years, American students of all ages have abbreviated too many distinguished names until they have become anonymities and no longer bring the intended honor to the memory of great souls. In some cases, the uniqueness of a name gives a better chance for memorable survival, but with a name like Brown, what chance is there after a generation or two?

In this decade the name of William H. Brown looms as great as in 1857 when School #8 became known as Brown School. William H. Brown, lawyer, banker, philanthropist, and friend of public education, was more than these. After Abraham Lincoln, he was Illinois' foremost statesman in the cause for the abolition of Negro slavery.

In the light of present day publicity of Afro-Americans, or the colored population who have migrated from the rural south to northern industrial cities such as Chicago - and of its public schools, such as the William H. Brown School - his name should be a remembered friend. As a child I never knew who Mr. Brown was; we children jokingly said that Red School, not Brown, should be our name since the two buildings were kept a painted bright red. Students enrolled today in that school do know his history.

William H. Brown was born in 1796 in Colchester, Connecticut and came to Illinois as a young lawyer in 1818. He had chosen Illinois because it had a free constitution. He settled in Kaskakia, then the state capital; he was appointed Clerk of the United States Court, which office he held for sixteen years in Vandalia, Illinois. He purchased a half interest in the newspaper, The Illinois Intelligencier, of which he was editor and partner of William Berry who was a member of the State Legislature.

A resolution was passed in the Legislature to alter the Illinois constitution with a view to the introduction of slavery in the State of Illinois. Mr. Brown opposed the movement in his paper; some of his editorials were stolen from his office and he was censured for such an indignity to the Legislature. Here, he cited the Constitution and the freedom of the press. The resolution remained an unfinished business: Mr. Brown sold his interest in the paper, which continued to be pro-slavery, and he now pushed efforts into securing the final Illinois verdict. This was passed by a large majority - the establishment of slavery was forbidden forever in the State of Illinois.

In 1835, Mr. Brown moved to Chicago where he became associated with the State of Illinois Bank. In 1840, he was appointed school agent for Chicago's public schools; this involved care of all funds. He continued to serve the schools for thirteen years and declined any remuneration. He was one of the original organizers of the Chicago Historical Society in 1856 and became its first president in 1857. The purpose of the Society was to establish a library and cabinet of antiquities, relics, manuscripts, documents, and to encourage research on the aboriginal remains within the State of Illinois.

In 1860, Mr. Brown was elected to represent Cook County in the Illinois General Assembly; he was a supporter and friend of Abraham Lincoln. During the Civil War, he supported measures to sustain the government and the federal troops. William H. Brown died, June 17, 1867 and is buried in Chicago's Graceland Cemetery.[1]

---

[1]"William H. Brown," <u>Biographical Sketches of Some of the Early Settlers of the City of Chicago</u>. Brochure, Fergus Printing Co., Chicago, Illinois, 1876.

4. William Hubbard Brown (1795-1867). Courtesy Chicago History Museum, Clark Street at North Ave, Chicago, Illinois 60614.

TAD LINCOLN

The nearest our family ever came to knowing Abraham Lincoln was in August, 1856, when he toured the northern states. My mother, than three years old, went with her father to Kalamazoo, Michigan, to hear Lincoln speak on the evils of slavery.[1] Here she was to shake hands with Lincoln. There is no affidavit for such a statement, only her cherished memory of a great man's being. Now her children, and their children, continue to sense the immortality of this great man and the cause he espoused. Later, when her children went to Brown School, where his son Tad had gone before them, there was another link in memory's appeal to human sympathy for our greatest American.

The story of Tad Lincoln's life, which lasted only eighteen years, reveals incidents common to many American childhoods; it also brings the human side of Abraham and Mary Lincoln closer to later generations of readers. While it is said that time heals, it also reveals. After the passing of a century and more, truths saved in written letters, which were kept inviolate through family inheritance or government protection, now shed new light on the Lincoln Family and refute erroneous or intentional acts of man's inhumanity to man as found in some printed histories of Abraham and Mary Lincoln.

To know Tad, we must know his parents and brothers. We recall briefly that Abraham Lincoln was born February 12, 1809 in a log cabin in the backwoods of Kentucky to Thomas Lincoln, a poverty-stricken farmer and his wife, Nancy Hanks Lincoln. This mother would die early, and the stepmother, Sarah Bush Johnston, would be kind to her step-son. The family would next live in Indiana, and then move on to Macon County, Illinois.

In the meantime, young Abe would grow to be a raw-boned, lanky man of great strength and a so-called homely face. He was a rail splitter as well as a hungry scholar seeking some book learning. Next, settling in New Salem, Illinois, he worked in a store, was village postmaster, studied and practiced surveying and read law books.

In 1834 he was elected to the Illinois State Legislature and served four terms; in 1836 he was licensed to practice law. He moved to Springfield where, in turn, his law partners were J. T.

---

[1]An excerpt of that meeting in Kalamazoo says in part: "The speaker (Lincoln), although a shrewd man, could advance scarcely a single proposition that would command the entire concurrence of his hearers... If he proclaimed the durability of the Union through patriotic endeavors of both northern and southern men, the sentiment met no favor at the hands of the ultra abolition element of his audience... The occasion more than ever convinced us of the utter discordancy of our opponent's (Lincoln's) sentiment in regard to Slavery alone" ("The Kalamazoo Meeting," Michigan History Magazine, Michigan Department of State, 717 West Allegany St., Lancing, MI 48918-1805, 1921, Vol. 5, p. 288) (p. 287 indicates that the article first appeared: "The Kalamazoo Meeting," Daily Enquirer, Vol. I, 229, Grand Rapids, September 1, 1856). According to a communication to the author from James I. Hickney, Curator Lincoln Collection, January 27, 1969, Illinois State Historical Society, Centennial Building, Springfield, IL 62706, Abraham Lincoln was one of five speakers at a Republican meeting at Kalamazoo, Michigan on August 27, 1856.

Stewart, Stephen T. Logan and William H. Herndon. The latter, years later after Lincoln's death, wrote a biography of the President and his wife which would become the nemesis of the Lincoln family.

In 1842 Lincoln married Mary Todd of Lexington, Kentucky. She was charming, well bred and educated, coming from an aristocratic family who did not approve of her marriage to Lincoln. They would live in Springfield at the Globe Tavern; Lincoln was a member of the Illinois Circuit Court which required periods of traveling and absence from home. He also had an interest in the Wig political party.

In August, 1843, Mary Lincoln bore her first child, Robert Todd Lincoln. The family prospered and purchased a house in Springfield which would be their home until 1861. A second son, Edward Baker Lincoln, was born in 1846; he was always called "Eddie." This child would die in 1850, probably from diphtheria; this was a crushing sorrow to the young family. Lincoln had just served in Congress from 1847 to 1849 and had returned to Springfield.

Less than a year later, in 1850, a third son, William Wallace Lincoln, was born; he was always called "Willie." And again in 1853, a fourth son, Thomas Lincoln, was born. He was called "Tad" because as a baby he had a large head and his father called him "Tadpole."

The years passed; Lincoln became a nationally known lawyer serving in the United States District Courts of Springfield and Chicago, in appeals to the Illinois State Supreme Court and the United States Supreme Court. He became a spokesman for the emerging Republican party which succeeded the Wig organization. When in Chicago, Lincoln stayed at the Tremont House, where most of the country's leading politicians made their headquarters. Sometimes he took members of his family with him.

In 1858 Lincoln was nominated at the Republican Convention in Springfield as their candidate for the U.S. Senate. Stephen A. Douglas was the Democratic nominee, who campaigned for re-election to a third term. Lincoln's famous premise - "A house divided against itself cannot stand"[2] - echoed in both the North and South, and would high-light the famous Lincoln-Douglas debates.

While Douglas won re-election to the Senate, Lincoln had been introduced to a national audience, and was considered a potential Presidential candidate.

Willie went to Chicago with his father in June, 1859, and was thrilled over the hotel accommodations at the Tremont House. He wrote in a letter to a young friend:

> "...two little pitcher(s) on the washstand. The smallest for me and the largest for father... me and father went to two theatres the other night."[3]

At an earlier trip to Chicago Mrs. Lincoln had sent a message to Lincoln that Tad was having an attack of "lung fever." This was one of Tad's early evidences of weak lungs.[4]

---

[2]Angle, Paul M., The Living Lincoln, 1854-1861, Rutgers University Press, 1955, p. 223.

[3]Willie Lincoln to Henry Remaun, Chicago, June 6 (?), 1859. Original in University of Chicago Library.

[4]Mary Lincoln to Azras M. Halch, Feb. 1859. Photostat, Lincoln National Life Foundation.

By fall, Robert Lincoln went east to Phillips Exeter Academy, and his parents missed him at home: "...it almost appears as if light and mirth had departed with him."[5]

The momentum of events increased at unimagined speed. Lincoln was now vigorously stumping in the campaign for the Presidency. Mary Lincoln accompanied him on some trips, and loved the excitement and the people, while the two boys, Willie and Tad, were safe at home. There were speeches at Cooper Union in New York, and at Phillips Exeter, in New Hampshire, where Robert was now a student. There, in spite of baggy knees and awkward body, Lincoln was accepted for his oratory.[6]

By April of 1860 Lincoln wrote Lyman Trumbull, "The taste is in my mouth a little..."[7] By May 18 at the Republican Convention in Chicago at Tremont House[8], Lincoln was nominated on the third ballot as the Republican candidate for President.

In the November election, Lincoln's electoral vote was 180, and the popular vote of the people, 39.8%, as compared to the Democrat's, where the combined electoral vote for Douglas, Breckenridge and Bell was 118, and the people's vote, a combined 30.8%,

As the committee of well-wishers reached Lincoln's doorstep in Springfield, there were two little boys sitting there in order not to miss any of the excitement. The oldest boy was asked, "Are you Mr. Lincoln's son?" "Yes, sir," replied Willie with a handshake. Tad then spoke out, "I'm a Lincoln too." The gentleman shook Tad's hand with equal esteem and rang the doorbell.[9]

With the Presidency won, the Lincoln family left Springfield to journey by train to Washington. As the family bade farewell to the people of Springfield, President Lincoln said:

> "Here I have lived a quarter of a century, and have passed from a young man to an old man. Here my children have been born, and one is buried. I now leave, not knowing when or whether ever I may return, with a task before me greater than that which rested upon Washington... Trusting in Him who can go with me, and remain with you, and be everywhere for good, let us confidently hope that

[5]Mary Lincoln to Mrs. Shearer, Springfield, Oct. 2 (1859), Journal Illinois State Historical Society, Spring, 1951, pp. 16-17.

[6]Randall, Ruth Painter, Mary Lincoln, Little, Brown & Co., Boston, 1953, p. 179.

[7]Lincoln to Lyman Trumbull, Springfield, April 29, 1860. Photostat. It is to be found in the COLLECTED WORKS OF ABRAHAM LINCOLN at the Illinois Historical Preservation Agency, 1 Old State Capitol Plaza, Springfield, IL 62701-1507. Reprinted with Permission.

[8]Editor's Note: The Republican Convention was held at the Wigwam, a convention center that was built for $5,000. in five weeks with a capacity of 10,000 (Ciccone, F. Richard, "Century of Kingmakers," Chicago Tribune, Section 1A, Sunday, August 25, 1996, pp. 1, 8).

[9]"Mr. Lincoln and the Official Committee," New York Tribune, May 25, 1860, p. 6 (credited to: Special Correspondence of the Chicago Journal, Springfield, IL, May 9, 1860).

all will yet be well. To his care commending you, as I hope in your prayers you will commend me, I bid you an affectionate farewell."[10]

It is from the White House period in the lives of Willie and Tad that we learn to know them. Of the three sons it has been said that Willie was the brightest, perhaps precocious. He resembled his father, with light brown hair and blue eyes. Tad was the least developed mentally, and as a child was handicapped by a speech defect. He had his mother's dark brown hair and eyes. Noah Brooks wrote of him,

> "...Tad, although he doubtless had his wits sharpened by being in such strange surroundings, was never anything else... but a boisterous, rollicking, and absolutely real boy."[11]

Robert, in the White House days, was a grown man and away at Harvard University. He impressed some as reserved and aristocratic, and was often termed "his mother's son" or "a Todd". Ida M. Tarbell interviewed Robert Lincoln in later years:

> "I searched his face and manners for resemblances (of President Lincoln). There was nothing. He was all Todd, a big plump man perhaps fifty years old, perfectly groomed..."[12]

Robert was the only son to live out a normal life span. He became a prominent corporation lawyer in Chicago and president of the Pullman Company; he was Minister to Great Britain. He married Mary Harlan and there were two daughters and a son, Jack (Abraham), who died in childhood. Hope passed for a male Lincoln descendant.

"Let the children have a good time," Mrs. Lincoln often said to Julia Taft[13], who with her younger bothers, Bud and Holly, was a frequent visitor at the White House. Here, Julia, at sixteen, helped look after this romping quartet of boys. In 1861 Mrs. Lincoln engaged a tutor

---

[10]Transcription of Farewell Address, Feb. 11, 1861; Series 1. General Correspondence. 1833-1916. The Abraham Lincoln Papers at the Library of Congress.

[11]Angle, p. 431. (Can also be found in: Noah Brooks, Washington In Lincoln's Time, Rinehart & Co., Inc., New York, Toronto, 1958, p. 248; originally published in 1895.)

[12]Tarbell, Ida M., All in the Day's Work, MacMillan Company, New York, 1939, p. 166. (Book is no longer controlled by Simon and Schuster. According to University of Illinois Press, which reprinted the book in 2003, it is in public domain.)

[13]Bayne, Julia Taft, Tad Lincoln's Father, Little, Brown & Co., Boston, 1931. (Can also be found in: University of Nebraska Press (First Bison Books), Lincoln and London, 2001, p. 47.)

for Willie and Tad, and invited the Taft boys to join the class.[14] Tad was not an eager student, and President Lincoln would say, ""Let him run... there's time enough yet for him to learn his letters and get pokey.""[15]

Tad was a loving, impetuous child, and when looking for some object in the library,

> "having found it, he threw himself on his father like a small thunderbolt, gave him one wild, fierce hug, and, without a word, fled from the room before his father could put out a hand to detain him."[16]

Lincoln took Tad to various meetings and one, a meeting with the Cabinet in attendance, proved boring to the restless child; and he climbed into his father's lap -

> "as the long bony hand spread over the dark hair, and the face above rested the sharp chin upon it, it was a pleasant sight. The head of a great and powerful nation... soothing with loving care the restless creature so much dearer than all the power he wields..."[17]

The boys had the run of the White House, from the roof to ground floor. On the roof they had a circus, with Tad having a charcoal blackened face and singing, ""Old Abe Lincoln came out of the wilderness."" Tad was wearing his father's spectacles which were rescued by John Hay, the President's secretary. Willie wore his mother's lavender, long gown; both boys were heavily swabbed with the beauty aid, "Bloom of Youth."[18]

Julia was apprehensive of the boys wearing Mrs. Lincoln's wardrobe: ""Boys,... does the President know about this?""

""Yep," said Tad. "Pa knows and he don't care neither. He's coming up when those generals go away.""[19] The President attended the circus, paying five cents admission and having a good laugh.[20]

---

[14]Ibid., p. 65 in 2001 edition.

[15]Brooks, Noah, <u>Washington In Lincoln's Time</u>, Century Company, New York, 1895, p. 281. (Can also be found in: Rinehart & Co., Inc., New York, Toronto, 1958 edition on page 249.)

[16]Ibid.

[17]Klement, Frank, "Jane Grey Swisshelm and Lincoln," <u>Abraham Lincoln Quarterly</u>, Dec. 1, 1950. Quoting St. Cloud <u>Democrat</u>, April 9, 1863, p. 236.

[18]Bayne, pp. 43-44 in 2001 edition.

[19]Ibid., p. 44 in 2001 edition.

[20]Ibid., p. 46 in 2001 edition.

One day Tad was heard singing at Julia's house:

> ""Old Abe Lincoln a rail splitter was he,
> And he'll split the Confederacee."
> "Willie asked, "Ought Tad to sing that song, Mrs. Taft? Isn't it real disrespectful to Pa?"""

Julie's mother agreed it was

> "bad taste for the President's son."
>   "Why, Mama Taft," said Tad. "Everybody in the world knows Pa used to split rails..." "Well, I s'pose I can sing "John Brown's Body"."" [21]

Julia Taft Bayne recalled:

> "President Lincoln liked to play with the boys whenever he had a little time from his duties. Willie used to say mournfully, "Pa don't have time to play with us now." Once I heard a terrible racket in another room, and opening the door... beheld the President lying on the floor, with the four boys trying to hold him down. Willie and Bud had hold of his hands, Holly and Tad sprawled over his feet and legs, while the broad grin of Mr. Lincoln's face was evidence that he was enjoying himself hugely. As soon as the boys saw my face at the door, Tad called, "Julie, come quick and sit on his stomach."" [22]

Another time, Tad had eaten all the ripe "strawberries being forced for a state dinner." Julia went out to see the ravaged plants; Willie told his mother. "" Major Watt was fuming..." "The Madam's wildcat," snarled the head gardener." [23]

The Lincoln boys had many pets given to them. Tad had a goat named Nannie. When Tad and his mother were visiting in Philadelphia, the President wrote that the goat "had been found in the middle of Tad's bed, chewing her cud." Then the animal disappeared; it was conjectured that perhaps the gardeners knew something of the goat's fate because it had damaged the flower beds. [24]

On one occasion Tad accidentally broke a mirror by carelessly throwing a ball in the vestibule where the Marine Band played at receptions. Tad said,

---

[21] Ibid., p. 165.

[22] Ibid., pp. 109-110 (p. 48 in 2001 edition).

[23] Ibid., p. 111 (p. 48 in 2001 edition).

[24] Ibid., pp. 113-114 (p. 49 in 2001 edition).

""Well, it's broken... I don't b'lieve Pa'll care."

"It is not Pa's looking glass," objected Willie. "It belongs to the United States Government.""[25]

Then Holly Taft

"added: "Aunt Kitty says if you break a looking glass you'll have bad luck for seven years 'less you throw salt over your left shoulder and say the Lord's Prayer backwards.""

Tad rushed out and brought salt and threw it over his left shoulder on to the carpet.[26]

""How do you begin? Amen first, I s'pose, n'ever n'ever--oh, I'll have to get Pa's Bible to do it.""[27]

On another occasion Willie and Tad were allowed to attend a state dinner. When asked about it,

""I tell you," boasted Ted, "those 'bassadors were all tied up with gold cords; they glittered grand."

Willie added, "Pa looked pretty plain with his black suit, but Ma was dressed up, you bet.""[28]

On Sundays Willie and Tad went to church, sometimes with Julia and her brothers. Mrs. Lincoln wondered why her boys preferred Julia's church. Julia answered,

"answered, "I reckon our church is livelier...""

"Oh, yes," answered Willie. "Lots livelier. Only, maybe it won't be as lively any more." And he told of the coming of the provost guard and the effect the lieutenant's threat upon the pew-door banging secessionists."[29]

Tad had

---

[25]Ibid., pp. 111-112.

[26]Ibid., p. 112 (pp. 48-49 in 2001 edition).

[27]Ibid., p. 113 (p. 49 in 2001 edition).

[28]Ibid., p. 70 in 2001 edition.

[29]Ibid., pp. 33-34 (pp. 13-14 in 2001 edition).

"expressed his scorn of the "Secesshes,"... [after the service].

"If I was Secesh," said Tad, "I wouldn't let him stop me banging pew doors.""[30]

""And, Pa," demanded Tad... "why do the preachers always pray so long for you, Pa?"

"Well Tad," said Mr. Lincoln... "I suppose it's because the preachers think I need it... I guess I do.""[31]

In February 1862 Willie was taken suddenly ill on the evening of an entertainment at the White House. Days passed, the boy's fever rose and fell. It was typhoid or "bilious fever" as the newspapers called it. Mrs. Lincoln did not leave his bedside after his condition became serious. Tad also felt ill, and the President had a sore throat and headache. On February 20, Bud Taft, Willie's dear friend, held his hand and he seemed better; by five o'clock Willie was gone.[32]

Willie's death stunned the parents; the father already burdened with the unspeakable anxiety for the whole nation, now faced his own personal grief. Mary Lincoln collapsed both physically and mentally. Later she wrote to a friend:

"Since I last saw you, I have sometimes feared that the <u>deep waters</u>, through which we passed would overwhelm me. Willie, darling Boy!, was always the idolized child of the household. So gentle, so meek, for a more Heavenly Home... My position requires my presence, where my heart is <u>so far</u> from being."[33]

Lincoln found great consolation in Tad after Willie's death; he took the boy with him where possible, and the President's office became Tad's sanctuary. Tad, now a lonely child, reached out to other children - hungry urchins he might find on Washington's streets - and had them fed in the White House kitchen. He was an ardent Unionist, and always wanting to send books and fruit to the lonely soldiers. He told his father of his plans:

"Yes, my son, send a big box; ask Mother for plenty of warm things and... pack in... good eatables... and mark the box "From Tad Lincoln"."[34]

---

[30]Ibid., p. 30 (p. 12 in 2001 edition).

[31]Ibid., p. 34 (p. 14 in 2001 edition).

[32]Ibid., p. 200.

[33]Luthin, Reinhard H. <u>The Real Abraham Lincoln</u>, Prentice Hall, N.Y., 1960. p. 416.

[34]Delano, James S., "Recollections of the Home Life of Abraham Lincoln," <u>Washington Evening Star</u>, Feb. 7, 1915, Section 1, p. 6, col. 1.

At Lincoln's second inaugural at the east front of the Capitol, on March 4, 1865, he gave his famous appeal:

> "With malice toward none; with charity for all; with firmness in the right, as God gives us [power] to see the right, let us strive on to finish the work we are in; to bind up the nation's wounds; to care for him who shall have born the battle, and for his widow, and his orphan--to all which may achieve and cherish, a just and a lasting peace, among ourselves, and with all nations."[35]

After the inaugural ceremony, Lincoln returned to the White House accompanied by his son Tad. Walt Whitman, who had observed the proceedings, wrote:

> "March 4th: I saw him return... He was in his plain two-horse barouche and look'd very worn and tired; the lines, indeed of vast responsibilities, intricate questions, and demands of life and death, cut deeper than ever upon his brown face; yet all the goodness, tenderness, sadness and canny shrewdness, underneath the furrows... By his side sat his little boy of ten years..."[36]

Lincoln, as the war-time President, made visits and inspections at the military camps, and had many conferences with the officers. While these trips were burdens of state, they also were a change from the White House routine. On such trips, Mrs. Lincoln and Tad often accompanied the Presidential party. One such trip was in April 1863, to inspect the Army of the Potomac before the Battle of Chancellorsville.

On such occasions the President preferred to travel by horseback rather than by ambulance, as the exercise gave him both mental and physical relief -

> ""I don't know about "the rest" as you call it. I suppose it is good for the body. But the tired part of me is <u>inside</u> and out of reach.""[37]

Noah Brooks, who frequently accompanied the President, said:

---

[35]The Abraham Lincoln Papers at the Library of Congress. Series 3 General Correspondence. 1837-1897. Abraham Lincoln, March 4, 1865, Second Inaugural Address; endorsed by Lincoln, April 10, 1865. Transcribed and Annotated by the Lincoln Studies Center, Knox College, Galesburg, Illinois.

[36]Whitman, Walt, <u>Complete Prose Works</u>, Small, Maynard & Co., Boston, 1892, p. 57.

[37]Browne, Frances Fisher, <u>The Everyday Life of Abraham Lincoln</u>, The Northwestern Publishing Co., Minneapolis, 1887, p. 590.

""He rode a great deal while with the army, always preferring the saddle to the elegant ambulance which had been provided for him. He rode his horse well, but he rode hard, and during his stay I think he regularly used up at least one horse each day. Little Tad invariably followed in his father's train; and mounted on a smaller horse, accompanied by an orderly, the youngster was a conspicuous figure, as his gray cloak flew in the wind while we hung on the flanks of Hooker and his Generals.""[38]

On this review it was recalled:

"...the brilliant cavalcade of the General-in-Chief... being escorted by the Philadelphia Lancers, a showy troop of soldiers... as the horses galloped afar, the form of Lincoln, conspicuous by his height and his tall black hat. And ever on the flanks of the hurrying column flew, like a flag or banneret, Tad's little gray riding cloak. The soldiers soon learned of Tad's presence... The men cheered... when they saw the dear face and tall figure of the good President, then the best beloved man in the world; but to these men of war, far away from home and children, the sight of that fresh-faced and laughing boy seemed an inspiration. They cheered like mad."[39]

The President's family accompanied him on the River Queen to City Point in March, 1865. Here, in this vessel's cabin, the memorable conference of President Lincoln, Generals Grant and Sherman, and Admiral Porter was held on March 28.[40] The war was ending; within days Petersburg and Richmond fell to the Union troops.[41] [42]

The President wished to go to Richmond, since it was the symbol of the Confederate capital. Now traveling on the Malvern flagship, President Lincoln, Admiral Porter, Tad, and guard Crook were then rowed ashore in "a twelve-oared barge."[43] Here an elderly man recognized Lincoln.

""Bress de Laud," he said, "dere is *de great Messia!* I knowed him soon as I seed him. He's bin in my heart fo' long yeahs, an' he's cum at las' to free his chillun from deir bondage!. Glory Hallalujah!" And he fell on his knees..."

---

[38]Browne, pp. 590-591.

[39]Ibid., pp. 643-644.

[40]Ibid., p. 679 (1954 edition).

[41]Ibid., p. 682 (1954 Edition).

[42]Sandburg, Carl, Abraham Lincoln, War Years, Vol. IV, Harcourt, Brace & Co., 1926, pp. 174.

[43]Ibid., p. 176.

as did other Negroes.

> "Don't kneel to me," he <the President> said, "that is not right. You must kneel to God only, and thank Him for the liberty you will hereafter enjoy."[44]

> "Yes, Mars," said the old man, "but after bein' so many yeahs in de desert widout water, it's mighty pleasant to be lookin' at las' on our spring of life. 'Scuse us, sir; we mean no disrepec' to Mars Lincoln; we means all love and gratitude."[45]

Then "they reached hands toward him in greeting,"[46] and the black folks filled the place with singing and shouting.

"...With twelve armed sailors forming a guard,"[47] six in front and six in the rear, Rear Admiral Porter and Captain Penrose on the left of the President, and "Crook holding Tad by the hand" on the right, the procession marched through crowds of both black and white spectators for two miles to the abandoned Confederate Executive Mansion,[48] now headquarters of Generals Weitzel and Shepley (George F. Shepley was the Union military governor[49]).

After the conference, on April 5 Tad and his father rode to the wharf in the officers' ambulance, then in the waiting row boat to the waiting <u>Malvern</u>[50], and returned to City Point.[51] On April 9, the Presidential family returned to Washington.[52]

The Civil War ended on April 9, with General Robert E. Lee's surrender at Appomattox at the McLean house.[53] On April 11, the President appeared in the early evening at the window of the White House facing the semi-circular avenue. Here, thousands of persons were to hear him deliver a speech on reconstruction and welcoming the South back into the Union.

---

[44]Browne, p. 691.

[45]Ibid., p. 692.

[46]Sandburg, p. 176.

[47]Ibid., p. 177.

[48]Ibid., p. 178.

[49]Ibid., p. 180.

[50]Ibid.

[51]Ibid., p. 182.

[52]Ibid., p. 194-195.

[53]Ibid., p. 199.

Shortly before Lincoln was to appear, he heard a yell inside the house mingling with merriment of the throng outside. It was Tad, "tumbling down the stairs and bursting with anger." He had, in one of his life's greatest moments, just leaned far "out of a second-story window waving a captured rebel flag" to the vast cheering crowd. The door keeper caught "Tad by the seat of his breeches and" pulled him to safety. The father comforted the boy and had a good laugh; then the President went upstairs to the balcony window to give his message to the people.[54]

Concealed by the drapery at the window, Noah Brooks held a candle for the President to read by. On the floor at his father's feet was Tad, who caught each page of the manuscript as the President finished reading it, and told his father to send down another.[55] In those last war-torn and heart breaking years, it was said that Tad "gave to the sad and solemn White House the only comic relief it knew."[56]

It was during this oration that among those on the White House lawn were two men; John Wilkes Booth whispered to Lewis Thornton Powell (alias "Paine"): "That is the last speech he will ever make."[57]

The fifth day after the end of the Civil War is a black page in American history. On Good Friday night, April 14, 1865, President and Mrs. Lincoln, with their young guests, Miss Clara Harris and Major Henry R. Rathbone, attended Ford's Theatre to see Tom Taylor's Our American Cousin. It was a relaxing comedy, and the President in his horsehair rocker relaxed, as did his cheerful Mary Lincoln beside him. Fate, in the person of John Wilkes Booth, the actor, stealthily entered the Presidential box, barred the door, aimed his Derringer pistol at the President's head, fired, and then jumped onto the stage, out a back exit, on to a waiting horse, and raced up F Street, heading for Maryland.

The unconscious President was taken across the street to the Peterson home. Here the sobbing Mary Lincoln and weeping Captain Robert Lincoln watched the labored breathing of the martyr, while the doctors and dignitaries stoically stood by. Mrs. Lincoln wanted Tad brought in because "...she knew Lincoln would speak to him, because he loved him so well". Near morning, a young reporter heard Mrs. Lincoln say, "Oh my God, and I have given my husband to die." Never had he heard "so much agony in so few words."[58]

Abraham Lincoln died at 7:22 the morning of April 15, 1865. Secretary of War Edwin M. Stanton closed the simple bedside prayers with these immortal words - "Now he belongs to the ages."[59]

---

[54]Ibid., p. 219.

[55]Luthin, p. 605; (also in Browne, p. 698).

[56]Browne, p. 642.

[57]House Report. No.7, 40th Congress, 1st Session, p. 674.

[58]J. P. Usher to wife, Washington, April 16, 1865, Copy in Library of Congress.

[59]Editor's Note: it is noted in assorted books and websites that Edwin Stanton may have said "to the angels" rather than "to the ages", but the Editor was not able to locate an original source for this claim.

44

Thomas Gray in his <u>Elegy in a Country Churchyard</u> still speaks for the obsequies of famous men as well as for "the short and simple annals of the poor":

> "The boast of heraldry, the pomp of pow'r,
> Await alike the inevitable hour:
> The paths of glory lead but to the grave."

On April 18, in the East Room of the White House, thousands viewed the casket, which rested upon a canopied catafalque with greens and flowers. At the funeral ceremony, Robert and Tad Lincoln represented the family; Mrs. Lincoln was too ill to attend.

After the service, the casket was driven in a special hearse to the Capitol. Following the hearse were Robert Lincoln, President Johnson, Cabinet members, Supreme Court Justices, Diplomatic Corps and government officials. Here the casket was viewed by thousands until Friday, April 21, when the cortege by special train, stopping frequently, travelled slowly to Springfield. With this coffin was the small coffin of Willie Lincoln, who had died three years earlier in Washington. Among the many stops was Chicago, where the body of Lincoln lay in state in the old Court House, truly a place of nostalgia for the many who recalled the lawyer Lincoln. General Sheridan stood at the head, and General Logan at the foot, of the coffin; while looking down the center steps, one saw several hundred men with torches and music books singing a requiem for the dead.

The cortege finally reached the Oak Ridge Cemetery in Springfield, where the funeral oration was given by Bishop Matthew Simpson. He said in part:

> "More persons have gazed on the face of the departed than ever looked upon the face of any other departed man. More have looked upon the procession for 1600 miles or more, by night and by day, by sunlight, dawn, twilight and by torchlight than ever before watched the progress of a procession."[60]

And so a kind father and his little son were laid to rest in their home town, Springfield, Illinois.

Mrs. Lincoln remained in seclusion in the White House. Robert and Tad were her only comfort. Tad would hear her sobbing at night and go to her room:

---

[60]The Editor was not able to confirm the author's source for this quote. However, it is widely quoted in books and on the web. The Beck Center, Robert W. Woodruff Library, Emory University, Atlanta, GA 30322 has the "Funeral Address Delivered at the Burial of President Lincoln" (http://chaucer.library.emory.edu/lincoln/data/simpson.txt), that was delivered on May 4, 1865, on its Lincoln Sermons website, and informed me that the quote is in the public domain. Other sources have the word "people" or "eyes" in place of "persons" as the second word of the paragraph, and/or use dashes, instead of commas, before and after "by night and by day".

"Don't cry, Mamma; I cannot sleep if you cry. Papa was good and he is gone to heaven. He is happy there. He is with God and my brother Willie. Don't cry, Mamma, or I will cry."[61]

On May 22, 1865 Mrs. Lincoln, Robert, and Tad, accompanied by Mrs. Keckley and Dr. Henry, left the White House for Chicago. They arrived with many satchels, boxes and trunks, and became part of the railroad station traffic. After a brief stay at Tremont House, Mrs. Lincoln moved to a less expensive location in Hyde Park.[62]

Letters were now her main contact with friends; love, grief and reverence for her dead husband, and her obsession about her lack of money, were the subjects she wrote on. She had incurred great debts in Washington, which included extravagant and unnecessary purchases of clothes and jewelry. President Lincoln left a comfortable estate which would be divided between the widow and sons. The government gave Mrs. Lincoln the President's salary for the last year, amounting to $22,000, plus smaller gifts. This Mrs. Lincoln used to purchase and furnish a large stone house in Chicago on 375 West Washington Street near Ann Street. She could ill afford this house, but wanted the security of a home.[63]

Here Tad would enter a new world; he was now twelve years old. After his father's death Tad had said: "I am not a President's son now. I won't have many presents anymore. Well, I will try to be a good boy."[64] He would attend a Chicago public school, Brown School, starting in the fall of 1865. Previously, in August, Mrs. Lincoln had written to a friend:

"Taddie is well and sends you a photograph of himself, just taken. He is growing fast, and I am sorry to say, he does not apply himself to his studies with as much

---

[61]Clark, Robert D., _Life of Matthew Simpson_, MacMillan, New York, 1956, pp. 247-248. Considered fair use by Simon and Schuster.

[62]Keckley, Elizabeth, _Behind the Scenes_, Oxford University Press, New York, 1868, 1988, pp. 190-196. Ghost written story by Mrs. Lincoln's mulatto modiste.

[63]Pratt, Harry E., _Personal Finances of Abraham Lincoln_, The Abraham Lincoln Association, Springfield, IL, 1942, p. 184. Evans, William A, _Mrs. Abraham Lincoln_, Alfred H. Knopf, p. 188, refers to 375 West Washington; Carl Sandburg, _Mary Lincoln: Wife and Widow_, Harcourt Brace, New York, 1932, p. 280, refers to 460 West Washington. The author's notes indicate: Mary Lincoln purchased the house at 375 West Washington on May 22, 1866; but in May, 1867, she rented the house and moved to Clifton House; in October she boarded at 460 West Washington, the Daniel Cole home almost opposite Union Park. Then in 1871, after returning from England, where she had gone in 1868, she lived with son Robert at 653 Wabash and then moved back to Clifton House.

[64]Keckley, p. 196.

interest as he should. We intend that he shall attend school, regularly after the 1st of September."[65]

Brown School was about seven blocks away from his home. Twice a day he would pass through Union Park, which had many attractions for children, and it would become Tad's playground. It is conjectured that this green woodland influenced Mrs. Lincoln in the purchase of the Washington Street house; also, Ashland Avenue, nearby, was where several prominent Southern families were living. Tad also attended church with his mother. Sometimes it was the old First Congregational Church; and sometimes, the old Third Presbyterian Church. Both were on Washington Street near his home. By January, 1866, in another letter to the same friend, Mrs. Lincoln wrote:

> "Dear little Taddie goes to school and does not miss an hour. He already is very much beloved in C, his teacher speaks of him in the highest and most affectionate terms."[66]

In Tad's brief stay at Brown School, he was to leave a lasting remembrance of his enthusiasm and industry. He and a classmate, Sterling P. Rounds, Jr., originated and printed the first elementary public school paper in the United States. The issue, <u>Brown School Holiday Budget</u>, printed in December, 1866, has survived. If there were other editions, they have not been found. This paper, with its century old humor, still emerges with youthful warmth. A few excerpts follow: under "GREETINGS" is one of the editorials:

"Many of us have spoken the good old "piece," as our fathers did before us -
"You'd scarce expect one of my age,
To speak in public on the stage;
And should I chance to fall below
Demosthenes or Cicero -
Don't view me with a critic's eye,
But pass my imperfections by."
And so, if our first steps into the world of Newspaperdom are weak, please grant us the same indulgence the young orator asks.
We make our 'bow,' kind Teachers and pleasant playmates, and present you our "*Holiday Budget*," wishing you, one and all, a "Merry Christmas" and lots of them."

---

[65]Sandburg, Carl, <u>Mary Lincoln: Wife and Widow</u>, Harcourt Brace and Co., 1932, p. 237. Excerpt from MARY LINCOLN, WIFE and WIDOW, copyright 1932 by Harcourt, Inc. and renewed 1960 by Paul M. Angle and Carl Sandburg, reprinted by permission of the publisher.

[66]Ibid., p. 255.

In the editors' "Card of Thanks" perhaps Tad's personal memories of the battle grounds he had so recently witnessed with his father, the General-in-Chief, are echoed:

> "Oh, if they could only *talk*, what stories could they tell! The blood and carnage of the field - the charge - the shout - the stout heart bearing the flag aloft, and the thousand eyes watching it, to see where it waves - that it does not falter and that it *never* goes down! Let us hope that never more will these little presses be required to tell the tale of disaster or ring out the paeans of victory, but ever be employed in some more genial occupation, like printing our *Budget*."[67]

We learn from the Budget that a cylinder press was given to the editors, S. P. Rounds, Jr. and Thomas Lincoln, by Charles Wells, Esquire, of the Cincinnati Type Foundry. It was called a Wells Army Press and used during the Civil War at different Headquarters. In the column of "Card of Thanks," the editors mentioned the firm of Rounds and James, Printers and Printers' Warehouse, 46 State Street "who provided us the Type and material for our little sheet, as well as much kindly assistance and advice, will also please accept our acknowledgements." Sterling's father was the printer who helped the boys.

The Sterling P. Rounds family lived at Robey and Park Avenue, now known as Damen and Maypole; the printing press was set up "in the basement of the residence" where Mrs. Lincoln and Tad were living on north side of Washington Blvd, east of Elizabeth Street.[68]

While some of the little paper's contents are influenced by pedagogic help, one column definitely echoes Tad's own humor and would have given his father a good laugh:

> "Telegrams per GREASED Lightning.
>
> ...
>
> ---
>
> Bridgeport, Dec. 25, 1866.

Weather exceedingly cold, clear and unpleasant - and we miss the balmy and *odorous* breath of Summer. Illinois Canal closed, but the Alimentary Canals open and doing a brisk business. Ten Thousand lives lost yesterday - all hogs."

> ---
>
> ...
>
> BY THE CABLE.
>
> ---
>
> London, England, Christmas.

---

[67]Rounds, S.P. and Thomas (Tad) Lincoln, Editors, Brown School Holiday Budget, Vol. 1, No. 1, West Chicago, Christmas, A.D., 1866. qF38QB B81. Chicago History Museum.

[68]Letter given to Chicago History Museum by Norman D. Fraser, March 9, 1922. Hugunin, Henry Matthew, 1827-1905. In: QF38QB B81. Brown School Holiday Budget 1866 and Miscellaneous Material. Chicago History Museum.

48

The Queen having indulged too freely in Plum Pudding and Roast Beef at Dinner - is seriously indisposed. The Court Physicians are in consultation.

Paris, France, Christmas.

Eugenie has discarded the use of Crinoline, and invented a substitute therefor called the Gossamer Expander. Vendors of the old style of hoops are bankrupt and in despair.

...

Washington, Christmas, 1866.

All quiet on the Potomac."[69]

There would be interruptions in Tad's school life as his afflicted and restless mother roamed the country and the world. In May 1867 Mrs. Lincoln rented her house on West Washington Street (which was eventually sold) and moved to Clifton House on Madison and Wabash. Tad would attend the Chicago Academy at 216 Wabash Avenue.[70] That summer Mrs. Lincoln went to Racine, Wisconsin to consider a boarding school for Tad. But "the air of restraint" and the rows of white cots chilled the mother's heart - "so far away from loving mothers, who would at any moment almost give their life to see them."[71]

Events in the winter of 1866 and the year of 1867 would be cruel to Mary Lincoln. Even a hundred and more years later, the reader of Lincolnian history is sickened by the pettiness, deceitfulness and inhumanity shown to Mrs. Lincoln. The first to make untrue insinuations in her widowhood was William Herndon, who had known Lincoln only during their early law practice in Springfield; he now decided to write a history of Abraham Lincoln. Herndon's lectures on Ann Rutledge in the fall of 1866 would start this vicious work. The nebulous and fictionalized Ann Rutledge story, as it concerned Abraham Lincoln, has now been discredited by Lincoln scholars, as well as some of the Herndon-Weik history of Lincoln which followed.

The next assault, in 1867, was the desperate "old clothes scandal" of Mrs. Lincoln's futile attempts to sell her excessive wardrobe and jewelry in New York City to help pay her debts. Here the firm of Brady and Keyes acted as agents, and Mrs. Keckley was her representative. The results were that the agents published Mrs. Lincoln's tragic letters in the World newspaper, to the Lincoln family's embarrassment. The agents then returned the bulk of her unsold garments and charged eight hundred dollars for their expenses. Elizabeth Keckley tried to help Mrs. Lincoln by writing a ghost-written Behind the Scenes volume, but only caused Mrs. Lincoln to be further ridiculed, and ended their friendship.[72]

---

[69]Rounds and Lincoln.

[70]Evans, Williams A., Mrs. Abraham Lincoln, Alfred A. Knopf, New York, 1932, p. 189.

[71]Randall, p. 416.

[72]Ibid., pp. 412-415.

Tad's school period at the Chicago Academy would be very brief, as by October, 1867, Mrs. Lincoln took rooms at 460 West Washington Street, boarding with the Daniel Cole family.[73]

Little information of Tad's academic progress in 1867-1868 has come to light. W. A. Evans in his <u>Mrs. Abraham Lincoln</u> wrote that:

> "...a correspondent writing in the <u>Chicago Tribune</u>, said that Tad attended the Elizabeth Street school (now the Tilden) in 1867; that he was very nervous; that he stuttered and was called "Stuttering Tad" by the children. His mother, a woman in black, brought him daily to school. Another correspondent wrote: "Tad did not stutter... but had a slight deficiency in speech... The writer... sometimes protected him from pests who teased him because of his manner of speech and his timidity. He was a bright boy, slight and delicate in health - too advanced for a primary school.""[74]

Mrs. Keckley, who had been a seamstress in the White House as well as a companion for Mrs. Lincoln for part of her troubled Chicago period, wrote that Tad was not able to read in the Spring of 1865.[75] He was then about twelve years old.

While there has been considerable discussion through the years on both Tad's and his mother's personal problems, in today's more scientific, and more sympathetic appraisals, the claim that Tad was deficient mentally has been disproved. His physical handicaps of speech problems, his delicate lung condition, starting in early childhood, plus the turmoil of the period while he lived in the White House, and the inevitable lack of discipline - all this aggravated Tad's rebellious temper tantrums, his slow learning to read and his aggressiveness in his likes and dislikes.

In defense of Tad, Noah Brooks of White House days and a keen observer of Tad wrote:

> "Even when he could scarcely read, he knew much about the cost of things, the details of trade, the principles of mechanics, and the habits of animals, all of which showed the activity of his mind and the odd turn of his thoughts."[76]

Julia Taft Bayne's estimate of Tad, given from her close association with the boy, recalled:

> "Tad had a quick fiery temper, very affectionate when he chose, but implacable in his dislikes. A slight impediment in his speech made it difficult for strangers to understand him."[77]

---

[73]Evans, p. 189.

[74]Ibid., p. 58.

[75]Keckley, p. 216.

[76]Brooks, p. 281 (p. 249 in 1958 edition).

[77]Bayne, p. 8 (p. 3 in 2001 edition).

It is known that in 1868 Robert Lincoln tried to have Tad's speech problem corrected by having special lessons. Also, at the same time, Tad had dentistry, an early form of orthodontia. This only aggravated his speech defect and was discontinued.[78] In view of Tad's dental and speech problems, the length of such a period at Tilden School is speculative. In that early period of Chicago's public schools, attendance records were not always kept.

In September, 1868 his brother Robert was married to Mary Harlan, and by October first Mrs. Lincoln and Tad sailed for Europe since Mrs. Lincoln was in failing health and sought a change in climate and scenery, settling in Frankfort on the Main in Germany. This would be the beginning of Mrs. Lincoln's wanderings in Europe, always living in cheap lodgings, being subject to respiratory infections, headaches and rheumatism. She was obsessed by poverty notions and hoping for a government pension. Tad was her star of hope, and she tried to give him the best education in her power. Tad was a loving son to his mother, as his father had been a loving husband to Mary Lincoln. A letter written from Germany when Mrs. Lincoln was ill recorded:

"Taddie, is like some old woman, with regard to his care of me - and two or three days since - when I was so very sick - his dark loving eyes - watching over me, reminded me so much of his dearly beloved father's - so filled with deep love."[79]

In Germany Tad studied at the "Institute" of Dr. Hohagen, where there were both German and English boys. He was there for two years; during that time Tad was able to overcome his speech defect by reading aloud as a regular exercise. Robert later added details: "...he is... articulating perfectly, but in English, owing to his practice in reading, he had a slight German accent."[80]

During Tad's vacation in the summer of 1869, Mrs. Lincoln and Tad visited Scotland for seven weeks. That autumn there was great joy in the birth of Robert's and Mary's daughter in Chicago. The little girl was named after her grandmother, Mary Todd Lincoln. In July a pension of $3,000 per year was finally granted to Mrs. Lincoln.

She went to Leamington, England and Tad was placed under "a very fine English tutor" as she wrote to a friend in October, 1870,

"... who comes highly recommended, a fine scholar and a gentlemanly, conscientious man. He recites his lesson with his tutor seven hours of each day,

---

[78]Evans, p. 60.

[79]Mary Lincoln to Mrs. Arne, Frankfort, December 29, 1869. Manuscript. Call number: HM 25209. This item is reproduced by permission of *The Huntington Library, San Marino, California.*

[80]Randall, p. 424.

so you can imagine that I see very little of my dear, good son. If he improves as he is doing I shall be satisfied."[81]

Mrs. Lincoln, in early 1871, on the advice of her physician, left Tad in school while she went to Italy in an attempt to ease her rheumatism and a bad cough. By May both son and mother were so homesick to see Robert and the new baby that they returned to Chicago. They were welcomed by Robert and his family, who were in good health.[82]

After a brief visit at Robert's home, Mrs. Lincoln and Tad moved to Clifton House. Tad was ill with a cold after their arrival in Chicago. His illness persisted; on June 8 his mother wrote Mrs. White: "My dear boy has been <u>very, very</u> dangerously ill... I have been sitting up... constantly for the last ten nights..."[83] His condition worsened with a dropsical condition in his chest, possibly tuberculosis. After six weeks of suffering Tad's weakened heart and lungs ceased to function. He died July 15, 1871.

The exhausted mother was too ill to journey to Springfield where Tad's body was placed beside his father.

"I feel that there is no life to me without my idolized Taddie. One by one I have consigned to their resting place my idolized ones and now in <u>this</u> world there is nothing left me but the deepest anguish and desolation."[84]

There would be still other blows. Herndon was pursuing his biography of Lincoln, which labelled him as illegitimate, and lecturing on "Lincoln's religion," calling him an infidel. This caused Lincoln's widow great humiliation as well as further disturbing the desolate mother's mind. She ended up having to appear in court; the outcome of a trial in Cook County Court in May 1875 was a verdict of insanity. Mrs. Lincoln who fully understood all that went on, faced her son: "O, Robert, to think that my son would ever have done this."[85] Her son, with the best of medical and legal advice, was doing his duty. After less than a year Mrs. Lincoln was declared "restored to reason." But she continued to be estranged from her son, Robert.

---

[81]Sandburg, 1932, p. 302. (Also found in: Helm, Katherine, <u>The True Story of Mary, Wife of Abraham Lincoln</u>, Harper & Bros., N.Y., 1928, p. 287).

[82]Helm, Katherine, <u>The True Story of Mary, Wife of Abraham Lincoln</u>, Harper & Bros., N.Y., 1928, p. 290.

[83]Mary Lincoln to Mrs. White, Chicago, June 8, 1871. Original in University of Chicago Library.

[84]Mary Lincoln to Elizabeth Todd Grimsley Brown, Chicago, April 12 & March 12, 1872. Originals owned by Mrs. Mary Grimsley Donaldson, Springfield.

[85]Chicago <u>Inter Ocean</u>, May 20, 1875.

Mrs Lincoln's sister's grandson, Edward Lewis Baker, Jr., then eighteen, about Tad's age, became a sympathetic and helpful friend to Mrs. Lincoln. When she decided to seek medical help, and "an exile," Lewis escorted her to her ship in New York where she sailed for Pau, France, a health resort.

By 1880, in further deteriorating health, she returned to the United States and, again, Lewis was her kind helper. Finally, back in Springfield, her Robert, with his little daughter Mary, asked his mother's forgiveness. The child melted her heart. In these shortened days, living in a darkened, cloistered room, Mary Lincoln died on July 16, 1882.

As the news flashed over the country, an old friend, Jane Swisshelm spoke out:

> "I have mourned with her often, and why should I not rejoice with her now?" "
> Mrs. Lincoln had once told her: "Ah, my dear friend, you will rejoice when you
> know that I have gone to my husband and children!""[86]

The years passed; in 1937 a bronze plaque was placed on the old Brown School building:

> "Tad" Lincoln's School
> In 1866-67, while living on West
> Washington Street,"Tad" Lincoln,
> son of Abraham and Mary Todd
> Lincoln, attended the Brown School.
>
> Erected by
> Chicago's Charter Jubilee
> Authenticated by Chicago History Museum
>
> 1937[87]

In the years which have followed, many children's hands, both black and white - some of them probably descendants of those slaves in Maryland - now touch this plaque with affection and questioning.

In the aftermath of Tad's tragic childhood, two questions remain unanswered. How much of the Brown School Holiday Budget was Tad's work? What had been written by Sterling P. Rounds? How generous had been the contribution of adult advisors?

And strangely, up to the present day, no hand-written efforts of any description by Tad have been found by researchers in Lincolnian; there is only hope that in a future day some treasure chest may be opened, and yellowed papers will speak for Tad Lincoln and his precious humor.

---

[86]Jane Grey Swisshelm letter to Editor, "Tribute to the Dead from Mrs. Jane Grey Swisshelm To the Editor of the *Chicago Tribune*", Swissdale, PA, July 17, 1882, Chicago Tribune, July 20, 1882, p. 7.

[87]From photo provided the author by the Chicago Sun-Times. Since the quote is from a plaque on a public building, the quote would be in the public domain.

5. Thomas "Tad" Lincoln Portrait. Courtesy Illinois Historical Society, Springfield, Illinois.

BERTHA HONORE PALMER

One of the earliest students who attended Brown School was Bertha Honore. When she was six years old, the family of Henry H. Honore moved from Louisville, Kentucky in 1855 and settled on Reuben Street, later known as Ashland Boulevard. The period in this house was brief, as by 1866 the Carter H. Harrison family, also from Kentucky, were living on the property formerly owned by the Honore family who had moved to a palatial home on Michigan Avenue. While Bertha Honore Palmer's most recent biographer does not mention Brown School as an early school for either Bertha or her sister, Ida, it is a century's tradition, if not fact, which has not been refuted, that Bertha Honore attended Brown School. Being a family with southern traditions, it can be understood why a reference to a public school of that early period might be insignificant in this family's annals. It is known that the Honore sisters also attended St. Xavier's Academy on the West Side.[1]

In 1870, Bertha Honore was married to Potter Palmer, merchant prince, landowner and builder of the Palmer House Hotel. Ida Honore married Colonel Frederick Dent Grant, son of President Ulysses S. Grant in 1874. These two families set society standards in Chicago where an increasing percentage of the population was polyglot as well as unsophisticated in earning an urban livelihood. Such society consciousness has never been repeated in Chicago and probably never will. That period of American ostentation was a phase in our nation's growing up.

After the Chicago Fire of 1871, there was need to rebuild a fair, new city. The Palmer family gave unstintedly of their time and wealth to the reclamation of the city and in the promotion of the World's Columbian Exposition of 1893. The careers of both Potter Palmer and Bertha Honore Palmer created two of America's most spectacular biographies which found their way across the world, as well as known by Chicago's school children, even today.

One of Mrs. Palmer's greatest contributions to Chicago was as Director of the Board of Lady Managers for the Exposition and presiding over the women's exhibits in the Woman's Building; here domestic and artistic efforts of women were shown, being sent from all over the world.

Mrs. Palmer spoke of herself as "the nation's hostess and the nation's head woman servant."[2] She was indeed, the queen of the fair with her natural beauty and its adornment of regal jewels and gowns as well as her gracious poise. Back of all this was her great intelligence and executive ability.

In those years of Chicago's recovery and continual preparations for the World's Fair, both Mr. and Mrs. Potter Palmer were frequent visitors to the European capitals. Their American presence helped interest the European elite, both socially and artistically, in the prospective World's Fair. Mrs. Palmer had developed a sincere appreciation of the fine arts, especially in

---

[1]Ishbel Ross, Silhouette in Diamonds, Harper & Brothers, New York City, New York, 1960, p. 13.

[2]Ibid., p. 100.

painting, and with an unlimited purse, she could purchase many European treasures as well as influence the various countries to send exhibits to the Fair. France interested her with its new painters emerging with the Impressionist school. These ambassadorial visits to Europe made possible many loans of paintings which Mrs. Palmer personally selected for the Fair.

Some of these French paintings loaned to the Exposition were from the Palmer "castle" gallery and others would be given to the Art Institute. These today are one of the Art Institute's proudest possessions, since this Impressionist collection is among the best in the United States.

A late remark by an eminent, visiting Frenchman to the Art Institute asked its then president of trustees, Mr. Chauncey McCormick, how they could afford all of those marvelous Impressionist pictures. The host answered that they didn't buy them: they inherited them from their grandmothers.[3]

Today, Mrs. Palmer is still recalled as Chicago's Society Queen or more affectionately, grande dame. Anna Morgan in her small but expressive book, My Chicago, quotes in 1918 a charming history of three Chicago women, each of whom had contributed much to Chicago's welfare. Speaking of Mrs. Potter Palmer she wrote:

> "Her reign synchronized the career of another Chicago woman, unlike her in everything but prominence. What the "first lady" was to the undefined realm that included social functions on one hand and presidency of the board of lady managers of the Columbian Exposition on the other, Frances E. Willard was to a very definite movement of which we are just now seeing final strokes. It is doubtful if any other of our cities can boast in their history of three women contemporaries, so diverse, so widely known, so influential as Mrs. Palmer, Miss Willard and Jane Addams... In their various ways they have left their impress upon our age, an impress not exceeded by that of any politician or captain of industry of their era and locale."[4]

Incidentally, all four women, including the writer, Anna Morgan, were once part of the old West Side. Mrs. Palmer was the "hostess with the mostest" as the trite saying goes, while Frances E. Willard was a comforting visitor to the Frances E. Willard Hospital for Women and Children in the old Medical Center, and Jane Addams was the motherly helper to thousands of immigrant children at Hull House.

---

[3]Time, "Illuminating the Impressionists," Dec. 1, 1967, p. 96.

[4]Morgan, Anna, My Chicago, Ralph Fletcher Seymour, Chicago, 1918, pp. 145-146.

MYRTLE REED MCCOLLOUGH

The saying by Henry Havelock Ellis in <u>The New Spirit</u>: "Every artist writes his own biography" could be said of Myrtle Reed McCollough who holds an esteemed place in Brown School's history as a prolific and beloved writer.

She was born in 1874 and graduated from Brown School in 1889. The traditional graduation program in 1889 gave the class motto: "Character is Higher than Intellect." The debate was "Resolved that a country owes more to its statesmen than to its warriors."

Myrtle Reed graduated from West Division High School in 1893 where she was beginning her writing career, being editor and contributor to the monthly publication, <u>Voice</u>. She became a free lance journalist and much of her works were tinged with sentimental longings as evidenced in their titles - <u>Love Letters to a Musician</u> (1899), <u>The Spinster's Book</u> (1901) and <u>Lavender and Old Lace</u> (1902). This last book went through nine printings and was made into a popular play which continued to be produced by amateur theatre groups and is her best known work.

As well as writing sentimental titles she took a pen name of <u>Olive Green</u> and wrote a practical volume <u>What to have for Breakfast</u>, a cook book, and <u>The Myrtle Reed Year Book</u> (1911) which was on the press at the time of her death. Unhappily married to James Sidney McCollough, she ended her life by an overdose of drugs in August 17, 1911.[1]

---

[1]"Dictionary of American Biography," Vol. VIII, Charles Scribner and Sons, New York, 1955.

LILLIAN RUSSELL

Another early student at Brown School was Nelly Leonard, or more correctly, Helen Louise Leonard, later to be known as the glamorous Lillian Russell. She was born with pulchritude, a singing voice and ambition. Her father was Charles E. Leonard, a printer; her mother was Cynthea Leonard who also had a voice as an advocate for woman suffrage. She provided editorial materials for eager reporters, since her subject was then so controversial.

When Nelly Leonard went to Brown School, the family lived at Lake and Robey Streets. Harry A. Smith was also a student at Brown School. This was after the Great Fire of 1871 when his family were refugees and moved into one of Carter H. Harrison's houses on Monroe Street. At Brown young Harry had his first meeting with the potential singer whom he would know later in the theatrical and musical world as Lillian Russell.

Harry B. Smith would become a renowned playwright of such well known light operas as Robin Hood, the music by Reginald De Koven, and The Serenade, with music by Victor Herbert. Later his book, First Nights and First Editions, would become a standard authority on American operas, in many of which Lillian Russell was the star performer.

Besides attending Brown School, and also Skinner School, for a brief period, it is known that she attended the Convent of the Sacred Heart. This was probably located on Oakleys Boulevard and Huron Street, the school having been in existence until 1868. Lillian Russell had written:

"At fourteen, when I was properly "finished" at the correct finishing school, the Park Institute, on the West Side, I sang at my first concert."[1]

Park Institute, a private school, was located at 203 (old number) Ashland Avenue and listed in the Chicago City Directory, 1879. This school was not far from Union Park which may have accounted for the Institute's title since the vicinity was then a fashionable district with imposing mansions.

The "first concert" was at Kimball Music Hall - here Helen Louise Leonard, no longer plain Nelly, recalled: "I sang Sullivan's "Let Me Dream Again" and "Hast Thou E'er Seen the Land" from Mignon. Shortly after that my great adventure began - and Helen Louise Leonard became Lillian Russell."[2]

At this period Florenz Ziegfeld remarked about Lillian: "Destiny and the cornfields of Iowa shaped her for the stage."[3] He had probably seen and heard the very young singer when she sang at Kimball Hall where his Chicago Musical College was located and where Mr. Kimball sold pianos.

---

[1]Morell, Parker, Lillian Russell, the Era of Plush, Random House, N.Y., 1914, p. 20.

[2]Ibid., p. 20.

[3]Burke, John, Duet in Diamonds: the Flamboyant Saga of Lillian Russell and Diamond Jim Brady in America's Gilded Age, G. P. Putnam's Sons, N.Y., 1972, p. 23.

Young Lillian next studied in New York under Leopold Damrosch. Tony Pastor was her early promoter in <u>Olivette</u>, and soon to follow was a cross country trip via the new transcontinental railroad to San Francisco. Here in the rough but rich mining west, she captivated her audience with her singing of <u>Babes in the Woods</u> and <u>Fuss in a Photograph Gallery</u>. She was a comedian as well as a singer. She is remembered as the Princess in <u>Nadjy</u> and <u>The Grand Mogul</u> in 1881.[4]

In 1883 she made her debut in London in <u>Virginia and Paul</u>. From 1889 to 1904 her greatest triumphs were with Weber and Field Burlesque Company.

Old timers in Chicago recalled hearing her sing at the Star and Garter and the Bijou Theaters on Madison Street near Halsted. While these theaters deteriorated with the influx of pedestrians from Skid Row, there were periods when excellent vaudeville programs were given.

This was the age of alliteration which Weber and Field started in 1889 and was associated with Lillian Russell. There was <u>Whirl-I-Gig</u> which featured David Warfield and Lillian Russell. By 1900 came the <u>Fiddle-De-Dee</u> with a cast of De Wolf Hopper, David Warfield, Fay Templeton and Lillian Russell. By 1901 came <u>Hoity-Toity</u>, in 1902 it was <u>Twirly-Whirly</u>, the music for which was written by Robert Smith, brother of Harry B. Smith who wrote musical plays for forty-seven years. In 1903 it was <u>Whoop-De-Doo</u> with Lillian and cast.[5]

John Stromberg, who also wrote the words for many of the songs during this period, committed suicide with his last and best song in his pocket - "Come Down My Evenin' Star." Lillian Russell broke into tears when she sang this song; it would become her theme song in the years which followed.[6]

Later alliteration shows were <u>Higgelty-Piggelty</u> in 1904, <u>Twiddle-Twaddle</u> in 1906; <u>Hip-Hip Horary</u> in 1907; and <u>Hokey-Pokey</u> in 1912; this last one included Lillian Russell.

While in Weber and Field burlesque, Lillian's voice was not considered as ravishing as her beautiful body; one critic said her voice was like a ""teakettle.""[7]

In an interim of 1890 during this rash of alliteration comedies, Lillian Russell played in <u>The Grand Duchess</u> in New York's Casino. This production later went on tour and was considered one of the nation's top attractions.

There was the great interlude of Chicago's World Fair in 1893 when interesting events occurred in Lillian Russell's old "hometown," some of which became a side show for the visiting public. James Buchanan Brady, known as "Diamond Jim," was Lillian Russell's escort for many events, both in Chicago and New York.

He had pyramided a sizable fortune in the business world and remained a bachelor all his life. He had two dominating eccentricities: he loved food accompanied by his gargantuan appetite which was evident in his overweight torso; and he loved diamonds which he always wore, hence his name, "Diamond Jim."

---

[4]Srang, Lewis A., <u>Famous Prima Donas</u>, L. C. Page & Co., Boston, 1906, pp. 41-42.

[5]Ewen, David, <u>American Musical Theatre</u>, Henry Holt & Co., N.Y., 1958, p. 555.

[6]Burke, p. 163.

[7]Ewen, p. 555.

He once said:

> "Now I take it that I am considered a handsome man and one who could be called well dressed. Never by any chance do I permit more than seventeen colors to creep into the pattern of my waistcoat. Moreover, I consider that twenty-eight rings are enough for any man to wear at one time. The others may be carried in the pocket and exhibited as occasion requires. A similar rule applied to cuff buttons and shirt studs. My favorite stud is a petrified prune. Three of them may be worn without entirely covering the shirt bosom. Diamonds larger than door knobs should never be worn except in the evening."[8]

When Lillian and Jim vacationed during the World's Fair, they dined together most every day on the Midway Pleasance where they were the delight and curiosity of the other visiting public. It was like a series of theatrical scenes with the changing of the courses, from soup du jour, swallowing live oysters, quantities of corn on the cob drenched in butter, French titled lamb or beef dishes, to rich desserts as crepe suzettes. Jim did not drink any alcoholic beverages but did consume pitchers of orange juice.

Here were two persons, who had been termed "the Beauty and the Beast," over-loading their bodies. She, of whom it has been said, touched the scales at 186 pounds and he, given a courtesy weight of 200 pounds. She, who had a contrived or tortured waistline of 27 inches and a 42 inch bust - while he could be termed a Santa Claus with his oversized measurements and diamond ornaments.[9]

It is recalled by Jacques Bustanoby, a restaurant keeper in New York, that Jim Brady bet Lillian Russell "a diamond ring that he could eat more than she could. Before the contest began," Lillian went "to the ladies' room and returned with a" bundle which she asked Bustanoby "to keep for her until the next day." After she returned to the table she ""ate plate for plate with Brady, and beat him fair and square."" The next day she returned for her corset.[10]

While in Chicago during the Exposition, Lillian rented a South Side mansion complete with horse and carriage. However, Chicago Society, as the Palmers, Armours, Swifts and McCormicks, snubbed her - regarding "her as being more notorious than famous."[11]

After the earlier years in Weber and Field's alliteration burlesque shows, a more classical period followed when Lillian Russell was with the McCaull Opera Company at the Bijou Opera House in New York. This was where she formed her own company.

---

[8]Smith, Harry Bache, <u>First Nights and First Editions</u>, Little, Brown & Co., Boston, 1931, pp. 192-193.

[9]Morell, pp. 128-9.

[10]Burke, p. 175.

[11]Burke, pp. 84-85.

In the early years, Lillian Russell had three marriages which were associated with the theatrical world, and all were short lived. In 1879 she married Harry Braham and divorced a few years later. The second was to Edward Solomon in 1883. From this marriage, Dorothy Solomon was born; in 1885 this marriage was annulled because of bigamy. The third was to Giovanni Perugani in 1894; he was the leading man in Lillian's "Princess Nicotine;" this ended in divorce in 1898.

The friendship with Jim Brady lasted through the years. He possessed personal honesty, gentility and money and with such he remained a friend to Lillian until his death in 1917, which was caused by gastric ulcers. The bulk of his large estate went to charitable institutions, especially for children and to hospitals for research on urological disorders.

In 1904-1905, Lillian Russell acted in the stage plays, School for Scandal and Barbara's Millions; the latter was not a success. Her forte was definitely not serious acting.[12] In 1912 she joined Weber and Field's Jubilee Company for her last vaudeville and retired from the theater.

The last ten years of her life were spent as the wife of Alexander P. Moore, editor of Pittsburg Leader, and were filled with gracious and cultured activities as Red Cross work, helping with the Liberty Loans during World War I and interest in political and national problems.

The only exception, related to activities of a former beauty queen, was her beauty column for the Chicago Daily Tribune. Fanny Butcher, a veteran newspaper writer and critic wrote in her book, Many Lives, One Love:

"When the love and beauty editors were away, I wrote their column. Lillian Russell, famous for her hour glass figure, was our authority on imperishable beauty, and there arrived from her regularly a bulky envelope filled with seven days' advice, for her words of wisdom and experience embellished the Sunday as well as the daily paper. Miss Russell's literary efforts were almost illiterate, and her column had to be rewritten from scratch."[13]

Lillian Russell died June 6, 1922, and like other charming women, she had never disclosed her age. She was born in Clinton, Iowa on December 4, 1861.

After Lillian Russell's death, her husband, Alexander P. Moore, represented United States at the Court of Spain. Mayor Carter H. Harrison wrote: "Had she but lived what a figure as ambassadress to a stately court the fair Lillian would have cut!"[14] Earlier in the Mayor's boyhood he had expressed envy for his friends who went to Skinner School and were classmates of the beautiful Nelly Leonard.

---

[12]Dumas, Malone, Dictionary of American Biography, Vol. VIII, Part I, Charles Scribner & Sons, N.Y., 1955, pp. 246-247.

[13]Butcher, Fanny, Many Lives - One Love, Harper & Row, N.Y., 1972, pp. 110-111. Quotation from MANY LIVES - ONE LOVE by Fanny Butcher. Copyright (c) 1972 by Fanny Butcher. Reprinted by permission of HarperCollins Publishers Inc.

[14]Harrison II, Carter H., Growing Up with Chicago: Sequel to "Stormy Years", Ralph Fletcher Seymour, Chicago, IL, 1944, p. 91.

6. Lillian Russell (1861-1922). Falk, 14 & 16 West 33rd St., New York City, photographer, copyrighted 1889. Courtesy Chicago History Museum.

FLO ZIEGFELD

Flo Ziegfeld was given the abbreviated and affectionate form of his name to distinguish father from son and it would serve later as an attractive theatrical name. His father, Dr. Florenz Ziegfeld, was director of Chicago Musical College, one of the best known schools of its kind in the Middle West. Flo Ziegfeld, Jr. was born in Chicago March 21, 1867. His father was born in Germany and his mother in France.

During the Great Fire of 1871 the Ziegfeld family, like many thousands, fled their home to safer ground. Young Flo, then four years old, with his mother and the two other children, hid under a bridge while the father searched for them for two days. Billie Burke described this story and added:

> "It was an exciting vantage point for a small boy to view the holocaust... perhaps this staggering show had some influence on Flo Ziegfeld... it became his habit in later years to create the vastest and most colorful spectacles possible, whatever the cost."[1]

Flo was thirteen years old when the family moved in 1882 to the long-lived-in home on Adams Street between Loomis Street and Ashland Avenue. Earlier the family had lived on East Chicago Street where Flo was born. Their next move was to Wabash Avenue. Here Flo's father joined with W. W. Kimball who sold pianos and George Root who composed Civil War songs. The men combined forces, settling in the Crosby Opera House. Here, for every piano sold, the buyer was given a pound of published sheet music. This advertised George Root's business and hopefully brought future students to Dr. Ziegfeld's Chicago Musical College.

In the meantime young Flo went to schools on the South Side, one of which was the old Ogden School. There are no records of his attending any public schools after the family moved to West Adams Street. While some biographies of Flo Ziegfeld state that he attended old West Division High School, there is no authentic record of him in the Chicago Board of Education files.

As the Ziegfeld residence on Adams Street was near the old West Division High School on Monroe Street, it was natural that Flo would have many friends among the students there. He enjoyed the social life of the neighborhood cotillions, many of which were held in the ballrooms of four-story homes on Ashland Boulevard, just a block away from the Ziegfeld home. At that time there was no indication of the spectacular career Flo would develop as, up to the World's Fair period, he helped his father in the management of the Chicago Musical College.

There was an incident in that youthful period when Flo went to Buffalo Bill's "Wild West" show on Halsted Street. After a demonstration of marksmanship, Buffalo Bill challenged

---

[1]Burke, Billie, <u>With a Feather on My Nose</u>, Appleton-Century-Crofts, Inc., N.Y. 1949, p. 136. From WITH A FEATHER ON MY NOSE by Billie Burke and Cameron Shipp, copyright 1949 by Billie Burke and Cameron Shipp. Used by permission of Dutton, a division of Penguin Group (USA) Inc.

anyone in the audience to duplicate his performance. Flo accepted the challenge, stepped to the stage, and shot a bull's eye in the target. Buffalo Bill was impressed and hired Flo on his travelling show. He was gone three weeks, earning fifty dollars a week, when his worried parents located him and brought him back to the Adams Street home.[2]

In the coming years Flo helped his famous father at the Chicago Musical College, and probably had piano lessons, although in later life he never played anything more than a few dramatic but interrupted arpeggios in an evening of gaiety.[3] However, unwittingly young Flo had exposure to theatrical staging and acting scenes in his father's School of Opera, as well as learning the rudiments of orchestral instrumentation and the business side of such an establishment. The College in its earlier period was located in Central Music Hall on Van Buren and Michigan Avenue, near the Auditorium Theater Building. This was the center of Chicago's musical world with its flourishing orchestras and operas.

Also, the College was near theaters of every caliber, from those of legitimate stage performances to burlesque shows. This was Flo's theatrical schooling in both the beautiful and the bawdy. He would first use this stage door knowledge for importing bands and other musical features for the World's Fair of 1893 as well as being manager for four years for Sandow, the strong man, who was featured in the Trocadero Theater on Michigan Avenue near Monroe Street. This was Flo's first success in his theatrical career which began in Chicago.

Later in England he saw Anna Held on the stage and persuaded her to come to America for a then non-existent show for which he would find financial help to create. A Parlor Match opened in New York in 1896 starring Anna Held, and in 1897 she would marry Flo Ziegfeld. She appeared in other later comedies such as Miss Innocence and The Little Duchess.

My sisters, who admired Flo as one of the neighborhood boys who "had gone into the stage business," also were anxious to see Anna Held; so they took me along to a Chicago theater where she was playing. The name of the play is not recalled but Anna Held's face was beautiful to a seven year old. The play may have been Parisian Model or Papa's Wife since both were gay, colorful and evidently, not too sophisticated for children.

While it has been written that Flo Ziegfeld's idea for the Follies was inspired after his seeing the Folies Bergeres in Paris where feminine pulchritude and sex appeal were the viewers' chief enjoyment, it was Anna Held, his own wife, who suggested his creating in New York an equivalent or better of the Folies Bergeres of Paris.[4]

And so the Follies of 1907 were presented at the Jardin de Paris on the rooftop of a New York theater. The title was derived from a newspaper column, "Follies of the Day."[5] The girls

---

[2]Drury, John, Old Chicago Houses, The University of Chicago Press, Chicago, 1941, p. 183.

[3]Burke, p. 154.

[4]Ibid., pp. 144-145.

[5]Ewen, David, New Complete Book of the American Musical Theater, Holt, Rinehart and Winston, N.Y., 1970, p. 587.

in that extravaganza had Ziegfeld's label as all "Anna Held Girls" but Anna Held herself was not in this cast.

Digressing a bit, the story is told of Anna Held who in 1904 was described as ""...the epitome of Gallic spice and naughtiness," what with her dark luminous eyes, baby face, eighteen-inch waist, and piquant French accent."[6] She and Flo would remain married until 1913 when they were divorced. A year later, on April 11, 1914, Flo would marry the charming actress who was the toast of London and Broadway, Billie Burke.

Anna Held continued her theatrical career in England and United States under Ziegfeld management and later under Shubert. In 1918 at age forty-five she became fatally ill. One of her last statements to her confreres was: "It is the last curtain. It is to die - that is easy. How much more difficult to live."[7]

Ziegfeld's life story was so popularized in the movie The Great Ziegfeld, which even today has re-runs, that most persons know Flo Ziegfeld's history. It is almost synonymous with the word Follies. His Follies began in 1907 and were continued by him for over twenty years, always "glorifying the American Girl." In addition to the Follies, among his productions, Sally, Show Boat, Bitter Sweet, Kid Boots, Rosalie and Rio Rita are recalled.

In the theatrical world each actor lives two lives. One is possibly a star-studded, glamorous, ostentatious, self-seeking existence; the other often is an introverted life yet still clinging intensely to a human, loving passion for parents, wife and child, home and garden, a dog and a few dear friends in that innermost circle which he has managed to keep inviolate. This was true of Flo Ziegfeld of whom Emerson might have written:

> "A man is a bundle of relations, a knot of roots, whose flowers and fruitage is the world."

Flo's marriage to Billie Burke on April 11, 1914, took place in the time period between Billie's matinee and evening performance of Charles Frohman's Mind the Paint Girl in a New York theater. They had time to go to Hoboken, New Jersey with Mrs. Burke as a witness for a simple ceremony and later to be joined by mothers Ziegfeld and Burke as well as Dr. Ziegfeld at the old Brevort Hotel for a wedding dinner. A few days later this happy five went to Long Beach, California.[8] This could have been called an "All in the Family" wedding trip.

Upon their return Billie's new show Jerry was sent to Chicago. Here, also, Billie learned to know both Dr. and Mrs. Ziegfeld more domestically at their home on Adams Street. Mother Ziegfeld brought out her favorite cook-book full of recipes for French and German dishes of

---

[6]Ibid., p. 556.

[7]Source of quote is not know to Editor.

[8]Burke, pp. 131-132.

strudels, sauces, fritters - all which Flo had enjoyed as a boy.[9] Billie was par excellence as an actress but not as a cook.

In October, 1916 Patricia Burke Ziegfeld joined the family and would be a stabilizing member for her parents, bringing joy and hope. While in her mother's widowhood, Patricia became a pillar of strength just as Billie's mother had been for her daughter from Billie's youthful days to her disenchanted periods. Life repeats itself over the generations.

In the years with Flo Ziegfeld's continually increasing spiral of his Follies and other stage productions and the unbelievable cost of such to produce in terms of Flo's demanded acme of perfection, there were pages on the debit side which could never be balanced on the credit side. The worst came with the stock market crash in 1929. The Roaring Twenties were now over. From then on the once extravagant as well as generous Flo was pinched for pennies even though the show went on and Billie Burke continued her trouping in her own successful performances.

The years suddenly were drawing to a close for Flo Ziegfeld. In March, 1932 he fell ill with influenza while introducing a new show Hot Cha! By April he was doing a national radio show on the Chrysler Hour. Show-Boat was having a revival and was a hit. In June his newest Follies were a sell out in Pittsburg and Flo felt it would be the best show he had ever done.[10] But Flo was ill - mentally and physically exhausted. Rest was the doctor's only answer. Billie brought Flo home by train to California and to the hospital for a check up and rest.

In the final hours of Flo's life in the hospital he roused himself and called to his faithful attendant and valet, Sidney: "Let the curtain go up. I want some fast music." Sidney understood the illusion and turned on the radio with dance music and Flo continued his directing... "All right, boys, you'll have to stop the scene. I want to look at the girls..." Then almost as if mesmerized he saw the Follies' beauties standing by his bedside while Sidney stared at the emptiness in the room through his tears...

Then Flo went on: "The seats in this theater ought to be fixed... This is a dress rehearsal. We're opening tomorrow night. Hurry up. The Finale!" Sidney turned to stronger music on the radio and Flo, getting out of bed with vigor, threw on his bathrobe and walked across the room as if he were leaving the theater. This was the last rehearsal. The next day Florenz Ziegfeld died, July 22, 1932.[11]

After Flo's death the Follies were presented by Mrs. Flo Ziegfeld in 1934 and 1936. In 1937 and 1943 the Shuberts were in charge. In 1957 Kroll and Conway presented the Follies. Of this last attempt Louis Kronenberger reported: "The spirit all but vanished: the songs had no tunefulness, the lyrics no bounce, the sketches no crackle..."[12]

---

[9]Ibid., p. 162.

[10]Ibid., p. 288.

[11]Cantor, Eddie and David Freedman, Ziegfeld, The Great Glorifier, Alfred H. King, N.Y., 1934, pp. 162-163.

[12]Ewen, p. 603.

In 1945 the movies started producing <u>Ziegfeld Follies</u> with good material starring Fred Astaire, Judy Garland, Lena Horne and Fannie Brice - but this was a new age.

During Ziegfeld's glamorous years, his parents continued living in the old home on Adams Street and his father directed Chicago Musical College until his death in 1923; the other son, Carl, took over the management for a time. The college was later reorganized and Rudolph Ganz, the world renowned pianist, became the President, and later President Emeritus, of Chicago Musical College. After several relocations of this famous institution, it is now affiliated with Roosevelt University in the Auditorium Theatre Building - back to its earliest neighborhood which Flo knew so well.

Flo never forgot his old home on Adams Street, nor his parents who continued living there, and visited them when his travels permitted. In 1915 he was there for his parents' golden wedding anniversary. When his father died in 1923 at the age of eighty-two, Flo was at the bedside. After his mother was left alone he wanted her to move away from the old neighborhood but she preferred to stay with her memories and treasures. In 1932 Mother Ziegfeld died at age eighty-four in the old Adams Street home without knowing that her son had preceded her in death a few months earlier.

The house for some years had developed an aura about it, as many old homes of the great and near-great seem to acquire. This continued on in this Adams Street home, as the caretakers, Guy Carlton Williams and his wife, Lillian, lived in the old Ziegfeld home for about ten years watching over the old ruin. They, too, became part of the neighborhood, learning of its past gracious days and witnessing its growing deterioration period. These sights, Guy Carlton Williams put in a descriptive novel, <u>The Street of Death</u>, published in 1939.

Mrs. Williams recalled the pathos of that old Chicago home when its contents were sold at auction a few weeks after Mother Ziegfeld died:

> "All of the articles and furnishings she loved so much - things like marble-topped tables, rugs, glassware and china, tapestried chairs, statuettes, books and the autographed pictures, were all placed under the hammer. It was among these things... that Flo Ziegfeld grew up to manhood."[13]

As one recalls the life and times of Flo Ziegfeld, one realizes that in his period the American theater, especially the musical theater, was then in its Golden Age in United States. It was an age of talented persons united in a confraternity of the theatrical arts. It has never been repeated. The Ziegfeld <u>Follies</u> helped this Golden Age to come about, in that many outstanding professionals with their glamorous, tear-dropping, laugh-bursting acts and tuneful melodies from other contemporary productions were given further recognition in the <u>Follies</u>. In a way, these guest attractions were like the educational and religious world - the loan of professors and their chairs or the preachers and their pulpits - all delivered a happy message to a wide, wide world audience. Truly the cream of the crop was represented each year and in turn each "full

---

[13]Drury, p. 184.

house" was in such demand by the theater loving public that some, like "Diamond Jim Brady", "paid $750 for a pair of tickets."[14]

The theatrical brotherhood was made up of many segments: the singer, dancer, actor, comedian and musician; the librettist, lyricist, and composer; the director, manager and technician. As in a kaleidoscope of changing colors and designs the memories of such artist-magicians are recalled: Jerome Kern, Victor Herbert, Sigmund Romberg, Richard Rodgers, Oscar Hammerstein, Moss Hart, Gene Buck, George S. Kauffman, Ring Lardner, Ira and George Gerswhin, Rudolph Friml, Irving Berlin, Otto Harbach, Jake and Lee Shubert, Jack Yellen, George M. Cohan, Channing Pollock, Fred Allen, Charles Dillingham and Joseph Urban.

There has always been a need for human entertainment, "something offering diversion or amusement." We know the nine Greek Muses, daughters of Zeus and Mnemosyne, with Apollo as their leader, offered the ancients a varied program. Calliope was the Muse of epic poetry and eloquence; Enterpe, of lyric poetry or music; Polydymmia of oratory or sacred poetry; Erato, of the poetry of love; Clio, of history; Melpomen, of tragedy; Thalia, of comedy; Terpsichore, of choral song and dance; and Urania, of astronomy. It is said that the Greeks claimed Sappho as "the tenth Muse;" she lived in the 600's B.C. and fragments of her actual poetry, such as a hymn to Aphrodite, are gem-like.

And so today we still have our hippodromes and coliseums thanks to the Greeks and Romans. Now in this late twentieth century we must not forget that just about fifty years ago there were other star-studded, gay and tuneful versions of the musical theater besides Ziegfeld's Follies; rivals perhaps, but all members of that brotherhood, and after all, "The play's "the thing"," even as interpreted in both the classical version and in modern slang.

Among such productions contemporary with Ziegfeld's Follies was the Hippodrome Extravaganza which continued from 1905 to 1922. This show was given at the Hippodrome Theater with an auditorium capable of seating 5000 persons and with a circus-like atmosphere. The Shuberts were the managers until 1914 when Charles Dillingham became manager. During the period of the Hippodrome, attractions such as Anna Pavlova, Annette Kellerman, Sousa and his band, Houdini, Toto, the Russian ballet clown, and the opera singer Orville Harrold were among the many artists.[15]

Other extravaganzas were George White's Scandals, Earl Carroll Vanities, Greenwich Village Follies, Irving Berlin's Music Box Revues and Shuberts' The Passing Show.

In fact, The Passing Show of 1894 was the forerunner of all these later extravaganzas, including the Follies. George W. Lederer took vaudeville and embellished it with bits of 1894 Broadway acts as well as burlesque and ballet. In 1912, the Shuberts, who envied Ziegfeld, picked up the old title, The Passing Show, and produced a rival extravaganza from 1912-1924 at the Winter Garden and had many of Flo's best talent.[16]

---

[14]Ewen, p. 593.

[15]Ibid., p. 230.

[16]Ibid., pp. 410-411.

Who were some of Flo's best talent who came from everywhere and "way back when?" The list must be abbreviated, the reader can supply the omitted favorites. There were Nora Bayes, Mae Murray, Eva Tanguay, Sophie Tucker, George White, Bert Williams, Fannie Brice, Dolly Sisters, Lillian Lorraine, Ann Pennington, W. C. Fields, Ed Wynn, Leon Errol, Marylin Miller, Will Rogers, Eddie Cantor, Raymond Hitchcock, Gallager and Shean, Paul White, Ray Dooley and Helen Morgan. Of these, Fannie Brice, Eddie Cantor, Leon Errol, Will Rogers, and Bert Williams were Flo's beloved friends.[17] They were all comedians.

In recalling these persons and their many, now nostalgic songs, one can almost hear the echoes as they continue to drift through the years truly as - "The Melody Lingers On." In a potpourri we hear "Oh What a Beautiful Morning," "Some Enchanted Evening," "My Man," "Second Hand Rose," "It Ain't Necessarily So," "Bali Ha'i," "My Heart Stood Still," "Embraceable You," "Why Do I Love You?", "Smoke Gets in Your Eyes," " I Told Every Little Star," "Play A Simple Melody," "Alexander's Rag Time Band," "God Bless America," "0h How I Hate to Get Up in the Morning," "Ah, Sweet Mystery of Life," "When You're Away," "The Way You Look Tonight," "With a Song in My Heart" and "A Pretty Girl Is Like a Melody". Perhaps this last title is what Flo Ziegfeld considered the epitome of his <u>Follies</u>.

It was not until 1949, seventeen years after Flo Ziegfeld's death, that Billie Burke published <u>With a Feather on My Nose</u>. While this is her autobiography, it also is her personal memoir of her husband, Flo Ziegfeld the man, as well as the showman. Surely, a woman as life partner should know the qualities of her husband better than any other associate. Her descriptive narratives are sincerely written and help the later reader to visualize this greatest showman of the twentieth century.

Here was his physical description:

> "...a man who was magnificently fashioned, lean-hipped, broad-shouldered, thin-waisted, and tautly muscled... Flo was an athlete of almost professional skill in many fields. Under the influence of Eugene Sandow ["the strong man"], he had learned to use bar bells and Indian clubs daily and to take a special delight in building a strong body... He was interested in every form of outdoor sport, was a skilled and enthusiastic horseman, a fancy ice skater, an expert gunman, and an angler of real prowess with either big-game fish or fighting trout... He was a dancer of notable grace, a boxer, and was one of the first men of his time to race high-speed automobiles. You must believe me: this was an exceptional man. These were some of the qualities that made him exceptional."[18]

Here were some intellectual descriptions:

---

[17]Burke, p. 243.

[18]Burke, pp. 149-150.

"...a man who had been given a classical education, who had heard the greatest music, had met celebrated writers, painters and musicians from childhood, but his taste in literature never included a classic. He never read poetry or quoted it... he was barely able to carry a tune. He rather croaked when he attempted to hum one of the great melodies he had driven composers frantic to get... but he did know when a tune was good, as the blazing list of his successes reveals."...

"He sought beauty everywhere. His love and devotion to his *Follies* girls was, for this reason, a special and outstanding thing, quite aside from whatever interest he might see in them as women. He groomed their beauty as a horticulturist tends rare orchids, gave each one of them great personal interest and affection."[19]

Now in this present day and age it is heart-warming to know that Flo Ziegfeld

"was... one of the first, to recognize and to appreciate the theatrical genius of the Negro race. Bert Williams was his star at a time when no other managers had promoted any Negro stars, and his presentation of Negroes in *Show Boat* needs no emphasis..."[20]

Billie Burke's summation of Flo's genius as a showman were his love of color, music, spectacle and fun which he was able to use as an artist -

"...a painter who starts drawing at some unexpected point, adding here, splashing color there, changing his mind, erasing, making a bold stroke here--and possibly entirely unable to explain in advance the sum total effect that he felt and aspired to."[21]

---

[19]Ibid., pp. 154-156.

[20]Ibid., p. 242.

[21]Ibid., p. 243.

7. Home of Flo Ziegfeld, Jr. While the author originally obtained this photograph Courtesy of Chicago Sun-Times, the Chicago Sun-Times informed the Editor that the photo is not attributed to one of their photographers, and attempts by the Editor to identify the source of this photograph have been unsuccessful.

8. Flo Ziegfeld, Jr. From: Cantor, Eddie and David Freedman, "Ziegfeld, The Great Glorifier. Alfred H. King, N.Y., 1934.

DR. EVARTS AMBROSE GRAHAM

The ethics for members of both medical and legal professions traditionally stresses refraining from undue secular, political or social publicity - that their success be known by their good works for the betterment and protection of humanity. There were many such professional men and women who had their beginnings in Brown School.

Dr. and Mrs. David W. Graham with their two sons, David and Evarts, lived at 672 Monroe Street, about a half block from our home. Dr. Graham was then a well-known surgeon and professor of surgery at Woman's Medical College and Rush Medical College. Both David and Evarts went to Brown School, graduating in 1894 and 1896, respectively, and were part of the neighboring young people gathering in nearby homes for evenings of music, taffy pulls and chatter. Both boys graduated from the Lewis Institute Academy and Princeton University.

Evarts Graham received his medical degree from Rush Medical College in 1907, interned at Presbyterian Hospital, was a Fellow at Rush Medical, Assistant Surgeon at Presbyterian Hospital and a student in specialized chemistry at University of Chicago. Here he met his future wife, Helen T. Tredway, a young chemist. He then became chief surgeon at Park Hospital, Mason City, Iowa in 1915-17.

With the coming of World War I, Dr. Graham served on the Emphysema Commission in Camp Lee, Virginia and at John Hopkins University; then he was overseas Commanding Officer of Evacuation Hospital No. 34, France. The world was stunned by the treachery of mustard gas poisoning inflicted on our soldiers and allies by the Germans with the disastrous aftereffects of emphysema of the lungs. It was then that Dr. Evarts Graham started his life's greatest work, medication and surgery of the thoracic cavity.

Upon his return to United States, he became Bixby Professor of Surgery at Washington University School of Medicine and Surgeon-in-Chief at Barnes Hospital and St. Louis Children's Hospital from 1919 to 1951. He then became Professor Emeritus of Surgery and Lecturer in Surgery at Washington University School of Medicine from 1951 to 1957 - his death.

It was for what he did for mankind that he was to be honored by hundreds of acclamations from all over the world. In layman's words, his first surgical removal of a cancerous human lung and the consequent saving of a life in the early 1930's was then as great a surgical accomplishment as the 1968 heart transplant by Dr. Christian Barnard in South Africa.

In a tribute to the memory of Dr. Evarts Graham, Dr. Alfred Blalock of Johns Hopkins University said:

> "The death of Dr. Graham has removed the most widely known and most influential surgeon in the world, but the influence of such a life and work will endure".[1]

---

[1] Graham, Evarts Ambrose, brochure, Washington University School of Medicine, Saint Louis, 1957. Permission Medical Public Affairs, Washington University School of Medicine.

Chancellor Ethan A. H. Shepley, Washington University, St. Louis, in the Memorial Service in Graham Chapel on the campus recalled on March 31, 1957, this remark made by Dr. Graham:

> "There is no greater satisfaction a teacher can have than to have his former students grow taller than he is, and that is what many of you are doing."[2]

---

[2]Ibid.

9. Dr. Evarts A. Graham. Courtesy Graham Family.

EDGAR RICE BURROUGHS

Another well known writer whose early antecedants were Brown School, although he did not graduate from there, was Edgar Rice Burroughs. He was born September 1, 1875, and died March 19, 1950. His childhood home was on Washington Boulevard near Robey Street. From Brown School he went to Harvard School, then to Phillips Academy in Andover, Massachusetts, and Michigan Military Academy at Orchard Lake, Michigan.

Always a restless youth, he would continue so for another fifteen years with mediocre jobs - a cattle-driver in Idaho, a dredge worker in Oregon gold territory, a railroad policeman in Salt Lake City.[1]

In an idle moment, while reading a pulp magazine, he decided he could write better stuff than that and wrote a series on life on Mars which he sold to Munsey Magazine. His principal works started with Tarzan of the Apes in 1914, for which he researched at Chicago Public Library while employed by Sears, Roebuck Company. When McClurg Company published the first Tarzan book in 1914, the flood gates opened. Argosy Magazine then accepted his series for publication.[2]

Isabelle Walker Meyer, when a student at Brown School, lived across the street from Edgar Rice Burroughs; he was then living on Park Avenue near Robey in the Hulburt home. Emma Hulburt had married Burroughs in January, 1900. Isabelle, then about eleven, was playing on the Hulburt front steps, when "Ed," as Burroughs was known then, came out. She told him she liked one of his stories which she had read in a magazine. Ed looked startled and said: "Do you read that stuff?" She assured him she really liked it and he asked her if she would like to read one of his manuscripts. She was thrilled, a live author lending her a book before it was published; it probably was Tarzan and the Jewels of Opar.

Another neighbor, from a little further west and who had gone to John Marshall High School, was Vincent Starrett. He was then a free lance writer and young critic of anything that came out of a bookshop or newspaper. He wrote of Burroughs:

"...I did not think highly of his masterpiece, so I never asked him about the genesis of Tarzan, later to be a matter of dispute. He (Burroughs) had no illusions about his books... and wrote his wild stories with a twinkle in his eye, knowing they would sell prodigiously whatever might be said of them by the critics."[3]

---

[1]Kimitz, Stanley J. and Howard Haycraft, Editors, Twentieth Century Authors, H. W. Wilson Co., New York, 1942, p. 227.

[2]"Obituary Notes," Publisher's Weekly, Vol. 157, No. 13, April 1, 1950, p. 1588.

[3]Starrett, Vincent, Born in a Bookshop, University of Oklahoma Press, Norman, 1965, p. 217. Copyright (c) Vincent Starrett, 1965, 1993. Permission of University Oklahoma Press, 2800 Venture Drive, Norman, Oklahoma 73069-8216.

A continuous succession of Tarzan descendants and their exploits followed down the years. They were seen and heard everywhere, in movies, comic strips, radio, television, and were translated into all European languages, as well as Oriental. He sold 25,000,000 copies of Tarzan books in fifty-six languages. His Mars books were not as popular.

At age sixty-six, still possessing that spirit of adventure which was expressed in his early life, as well as in his works, he witnessed the attack on Pearl Harbor and became a war correspondent for the <u>Los Angeles Times</u>.[4]

Edgar Rice Burroughs retired to Encino and a ranch in southern California whose post office was named Tarzana; it has since become the city of Tarzana. Here a complete office force conducts the many business facets of the Tarzan characters. Burroughs' writings, when produced in the three dimensional realms of Tarzan, became an industry rather than a literary profession.

At his death, he left fifteen unpublished novels and had just signed contracts for fifteen Tarzan motion pictures to be produced in the following ten year period.[5] While Tarzan and the Martian series were highly profitable as well as popular, mainly with juvenile readers and viewers, they are now becoming folklore and being re-appraised with more admirable and constructive qualities than earlier assessed.

---

[4]Kimitz, Stanley J. and Vineta Colby, Editors, <u>Twentieth Century Authors</u>, First Supplement, H. W. Wilson Co., New York, New York, 1955, p. 152.

[5]Ibid., p. 152.

10. Edgar Rice Burroughs, 1933. D.N. negative #A-3,271. Courtesy Chicago History Museum.

HELEN MORGAN

Brown School has provided many entertainers for the footlights, such as Lillian Russell, Glenn Hall, Harry Truax, Estelle Wentworth and Waterson Rathaker - all of an early vintage. There was also a late-comer, Helen Morgan. She was, in her short life, 1900-1941, to leave a mourning audience. Anyone who had ever heard her sing Jerome Kern's "My Bill" and "Can't Help Lovin' That Man," cannot forget the pathos of her voice. Claudia Cassidy said of her that she had something in her voice that was worth its weight in theatre gold: a note of authentic heartbreak.[1]

After school days she worked at various jobs, each a step in her climb to be a torchbearer. In Chicago, she worked as a sales clerk at Marshall Field's Loop Store, then in nursing, followed by posing for advertisements and modelling in Montreal. Here she was chosen "Miss Mount Royal."[2] Then on to New York, where Billy Rose recognized her singing potential, and Ring Lardner boosted her to the piano top where she could be seen as well as heard. This became her trademark, sitting on the piano. Years later, in a cartoon commentary, Dinah Shore is depicted as asking: "Ouch! Does anyone know what Helen Morgan did about slivers?!"[3]

Helen Morgan made her entry on Broadway in George White's Scandals of 1926. Jerome Kern, while casting for Show Boat, saw her sitting on the top of the piano singing a torch song, and chose her to play the part of Julia LeVerne in his Show Boat of 1927. The book and lyrics were by Oscar Hammerstein, based on Edna Ferber's novel of the same name. The music was by Jerome Kern, and the musical was presented by Flo Zeigfeld at the Zeigfeld Theater in New York. Here Helen Morgan as Julia LeVerne sang her heart breaking songs. "Bill," which she sang so feelingly, made her a star.[4]

When Edna Ferber heard the songs in Show Boat, especially "Old Man River," she said of the production:

""...the music mounted, mounted, and I give you my word my hair stood on end, and tears came to my eyes, and I breathed like a heroine in a melodrama," she had written.

---

[1]"Torchbearer's End," Time Magazine, October 20, 1941, p. 80.

[2]Ibid., p. 80.

[3]Santa Barbara News-Press, ""Name of the Game" Films An Unusual Series for TV," August 10, 1968, p. C-12. Quote comes from a cartoon-like capsule added onto a photo; the photo is located above the article's text.

[4]Ewen, David, American Musical Theater, Holt, Rinehart & Winston, N.Y., 1970, p. 473.

"This was great music. This was music that would outlast Jerome Kern's day and mine.""[5]

True to her prophecy, it has lasted, and Helen Morgan's lamenting voice has echoed through the years, even if only on an old Victrola record. Show Boat has been repeated even in late years. In 1966, it was performed at the New York Theater of the Lincoln Center for Performing Arts.

In 1929, Helen Morgan appeared in Sweet Adeline, a musical with book and lyrics by Oscar Hammerstein and music by Jerome Kern. As "Addie" she sang, "Why Was I Born?", "Here Am I," and "Don't Ever Leave Me."[6]

In 1931, in Ziegfeld's last Follies, Helen Morgan sang two numbers with Harry Richman, one being "I'm With You;" she also soloed in "Half-Caste Woman;" neither were her type.

In 1934, she played in Frankie and Johnnie as "Frankie." In 1935, Universal Studios made a motion picture of Show Boat.

Later, in New York, Helen Morgan continued singing her theme songs in her night clubs. They had such various names as "Chez Helen Morgan," "Helen M's Summer Home" and "House of Morgan."[7]

Helen Morgan flourished at the time of Texas Guinan, each with their own New York night clubs, once part of that gay period in New York's night life during Prohibition days. The styles of the two entertainers were different: Texas with her gay, "Hello Sucker" to each patron, brought an infectious happiness, even if only momentary; while Helen was demure and sad, which made her audience feel sentimental. Both girls sat on the piano top so they could be seen, as they were surrounded by a sea of faces.

Helen Morgan had one serious interest outside her music, her fish; she was a recognized ichthyologist and had many tropical fish in aquariums in her New York apartment.[8] She was married twice and had made and lost millions of dollars. She died in Chicago in October, 1941. Her death was as plaintive as her songs: she died in poverty.

---

[5]Ibid., p. 476.

[6]Ibid., p. 515.

[7]"Torchbearer's End," pp. 79-80.

[8]"Interesting People Ichthyologist," American Magazine, April, 1934, p. 31.

11. Helen Morgan in Flo Ziegfeld's "Showboat." Alfred Cheney Johnson, photographer. From: Cantor, Eddie and David Freedman, "Ziegfeld, The Great Glorifier," Alfred H. King, N.Y., 1934.

81

EDDIE FOY

Public school education in United States during the nineteenth century was often a come if you can or will type of instruction for the oncoming generations. Our national history of famous sons and daughters records incidents where a few years, even months, was all the formal education these patriots were given. To progress from log cabin to White House was cited as the latent power within the individual.

Brown School has had many such students; one was Eddie Foy. Just how many weeks or months he was privileged to attend is unknown. He was born Edward Fitzgerald in 1856 in New York City. His father died in 1863, having served in the Federal army. The family was desolate and Eddie at eight years was singing and dancing on the New York streets with a wandering fiddler.

The family moved to Chicago in 1865 where the boy sold papers, blacked boots along with other odd jobs while his ambition was to get into theatrical work since he had already known audiences and had rhythm in his soul as well as Irish wit. It was during these inexact years that Eddie Fitzgerald attended Brown School.

By 1872, still singing and swinging, he changed his name to Foy, Eddie Foy, and by 1878 in partnership with James Thompson, traveled to the far west mining towns with his song and dance. He then proceeded into minstrel shows in the eastern states where he began using a clown's face which became his trademark. From minstrels he progressed to comedy parts, being engaged by David Henderson in successful shows as Crystal Slippers, Mr. Bluebeard, Sinbad and Ali Baba. By 1894 he was to star in Off the Earth, Little Christopher Columbus, and The Stroller.

While playing Mr. Bluebeard in Chicago on December 20, 1903 at the Iroquois Theatre, fire swept the building and the audience panicked with blocked exits causing the death of nearly 600 people, many of whom died from suffocation rather than actual fire.

In Foy's later years, blest with seven chidren, he continued in vaudeville as Eddie and the Seven Little Foys. He died, February 16, 1928, one of Brown School's beloved alumni.[1]

---

[1]Editor's Note: A comprehensive biography of Eddie Foy was written by Armond Fields in 1999: "Eddie Foy: a Biography of the Early Popular Stage Comedian", McFarland and Co., Jefferson, North Carolina.

SAMUEL ETTELSON

Samuel Ettelson was born in Chicago, November 19, 1874, the son of Benjamin and Flora (Philipson) Ettelson, immigrants from Poland and Germany, respectively. Samuel Ettelson graduated from Brown School and West Division High School. He earned his law degree from Chicago College of Law in 1897, and had graduate study at Harvard Law School in 1903. While studying in Chicago, one of his jobs was on the staff of the catalog department of the Chicago Public Library. The library had migrated repeatedly for the first 24 years of its existence. This included a 11 year period when the library was located at City Hall, where Ettelson worked on the fourth floor.[1]

He became a member of the law firm, Schuyler, Jamieson and Ettelson and lived on West Monroe Street near Wood for some years. In 1906, he was elected to the State Senate from the third district and served in 1910 and 1914. In 1915, he became Corporation Counsel for Chicago under Mayor Thompson.

When Bobby Franks first disappeared on May 21, 1924, his father, Jacob Franks, called his friend Samuel Ettelson to help him find his son. After an unsuccessful search, they went to the police. After a ransom request was received by special delivery the next morning, Ettelson called his friend, the Chicago Police Department's chief of detectives. However, shortly after a phone call was received regarding ransom delivery, Jacob's brother-in-law verified that Bobby's body had been found in a culvert in the vicinity of Wolf Lake. While Bobby could not be saved, having been found dead before the phone call, unfortunately both Jacob and Ettelson forgot the address of the drugstore the kidnapper told them to go to, and thus the investigation was delayed.[2] A nephew of Ettelson, Bert Cronson, was assigned to the staff of Robert Crowe, the State's Attorney in charge of the investigation.[3] In the end it didn't matter: the perpetrators were identified. Thus Samuel Ettelson was involved in the tragic Leopold and Loeb kidnapping case through his friendship with the Franks family.

---

[1]Chicago Public Library, "The Development of a Central Library," History of the Chicago Public Library: Windows on Our Past; available from http://www.chipublib.org/003cpl/cpl125/central.html; accessed 1 March 2002.

[2]Bardsley, Marilyn, "Leopold & Loeb: Bobby Franks," *The Crime Library*; available from http://www.crimelibrary.com/loeb/loeb/loebmain.htm; accessed 1 March 2002.

[3]Bardsley, Marilyn, "Leopold & Loeb: The Investigation," *The Crime Library*; available from http://www.crimelibrary.com/loeb/loeb/loebinvest.htm; accessed 1 March 2002.

Early CPL, 1887   Chicago Public Library, Special Collections and Preservation Division

12. Samuel Ettelson (second from left). "Staff of the catalog Department in the library quarters at City Hall, ca. 1887. Left to right: Mr. Nyhuis, Chief; Samuel Ettelson, who later became Chief Corporation Counsel for the City of Chicago; Olaf, the office boy; Joseph McCarty; and Carl B. Roden, who later became Chief Librarian of the Chicago Public Library, 1918-1950." From: Chicago Public Library, History of the Chicago Public Library, Windows on Our Past, "Development of a Central Library," http://www.chipublib.org/003cpl/cpl125/central.html; accessed 1 March 2002. Scanned copy of photograph received from Early Chicago Public Library Archives, Special Collections and Preservation Division, Harold Washington Library Center, 400 South State Street, Chicago, IL. 60605. Courtesy Chicago Public Library.

CHAPTER TWO: OLD CENTRAL HIGH SCHOOL
AND ITS SUCCESSOR WEST DIVISION HIGH SCHOOL

OLD CENTRAL HIGH SCHOOL

Since 1839, Chicago had considered a high school; by 1856, when the city was nineteen years old, the Chicago High School was established and by 1878 was known as Central High School. It was a sturdy, ten room building costing $33,072. and was located on Monroe near Halsted Street. The school opened with 114 pupils equally divided between boys and girls; nine students were native Chicagoans, the others being from eastern states or foreign born. They ranged in age from twelve to nineteen years and lived in all sections of the city.

It is thought that old Central was the first co-educational high school in the United States. In Boston, there was a public Latin School in 1635 and an English School in 1821 for boys only; there was Central High School in Philadelphia in 1838 and the Academy of New York in 1849, both of which accommodated boys only.[1]

Admittance to Chicago High School was by entrance examinations in mathematics, history, geography and grammar. Three courses were offered, a three year General, a three year English-Classical and a two year Normal course which qualified graduates to teach in elementary schools. By 1866, subjects taught by a faculty of nine were Botany, Latin, French and German, Greek, Astronomy, Geometry, history, Cicero, [physical] Geography, mensuration [mathematics], political economy and natural philosophy.[2] By 1870, a four year curriculum replaced the three year courses.

A vignette describes the Chicago High School's earliest period with its aura of nostalgia:

> "The lofty rooms are heavy with quiet. In the long days of June and July the hot, fresh breath of the prairie blows in the open windows and the songs of birds float in the air. No telephone, no typewriter, no electric bells, no shouting from gym, no utilitarian sounds from shops, no automobile horns or clanging street cars interfere with concentration on Cicero's orations or the Odes of Horace.
>
> "It is a hushed zone of slates and sponges, where paper is precious and textbooks are cherished. The light clicking of slate pencils, the scratching of

---

[1]Pamphlets on Chicago High School, Chicago History Museum.

[2]Pamphlets on Chicago High School, Annual Examination of Classes of Chicago High School at the High School Building, on Monroe Street, between Halsted and Desplaines Streets, on Wednesday and Thursday, June 27 and 28, 1866. Dean & Ottaway, Prs., F38QC C33z, Chicago History Museum.

pens laboriously guided through lengthy longhand assignments punctuate the lagging minutes. A few students are memorizing entire chapters of different texts in anticipation of a formidable examination.

Someone pauses to wipe away perspiration and chase a recalcitrant fly..."[3]

Surnames of distinguished Chicago families, many now recalled in the city's landmarks, were alumni of Chicago High School and are briefly listed - Honore, Moulton, Swift, Peacock, Shipman, Revel, Palmer, Wolcott, Crane, Spaulding, McCormick, Stevens, Peck, Waller, Ryerson, Willard, Synon, Bigelow and Foley - the list could fill pages. There were two early superintendents of Chicago schools, Albert G. Lane and Ella N. Flagg (Young) who graduated from Chicago High School.

One of those early name bearers, Paul Shorey, Class of 1874, spoke for all these early students when he wrote as class poet:

"As they say that our blessings grow dearer,
    When fading forever away;
So our school and our schoolmates grow nearer
    Than e'er to our heart-strings, today."[4]

On January 7, 1874, the senior year of William Morton Payne and Paul Shorey at Chicago High School, the two friends started a school paper called The Lever. It was published weekly by these two editors who functioned under the title of "Gemini" and issued the paper from the mythical region of "Georgetown." It was all hand written in ink or pencil.

This publication as a weekly was probably the first of its kind in a Midwestern public high school and was more or less a "family affair" as the two editors gave vent to their more humorous and youthful side as well as encouraging their classmates to participate in this venture of journalism.

The editors in their opening number, Vol. 1, No. 1, gave a wordy but youthful editorial on their purpose and choice of title:

"On this solemn and joyful day we issue the first number of a journal destined in our opinion to become the organ of the west. After much meditation we have selected as a name a word highly appropriate, as expressing in the fullest manner the idea of power while the words of Archimedes ["Give me whereon to stand and I will move the world."] seem

---

[3]Pamphlets on Chicago High School, Author unknown, Chicago History Museum.

[4]Pamphlets on Chicago High School, "Farewell Poem" by Paul Shorey attached inside "Closing Examination" of the Chicago High School, at the High School Building on Monday, June 22nd and Tuesday, June 23, 1874, F38QC C33z, Chicago History Museum.

to be equally appropriate and fitting; as to the requisite--a place whereon to stand--we think that the present issue shows in the plainest manner that it is not wanting--Whether we retain it remains to our friends and supporters...

"...If some of the attempts at journalism of last year were so successful, what can we not expect from the Senior Class of Chicago High School, and more   especially, a class as talented as the Class of '74?"[5]

Among the contents of this new magazine were cartoons as well as "re-written" history such as the fable of George Washington and the cherry tree; there were dart-like articles such as "Grand Italian Opera," subtitled "Free Education" by Paul Shorey and dedicated to George Howland, the school's most loved principal. Today this writing might be classed as a forerunner of the "Mod" category.

The editorial in the second issue of The Lever, Jan. 13, 1874, was again flamboyantly youthful:

"When we issued our first number it was with uncertain knowledge of the result. We had been told that Journalism had run into the ground. And that there was a general dislike of anything of that sort. But the reception by Vol 1, No. 1 of The Lever has entirely reassured us and all things point to an era which in the history of Journalism shall out rival the Age of Augustus or of Louis XIV.

"Another week has rolled into the great flood of eternity. We have discussed questions of Political Economy, Exploderated [sic] under the guidance of soda fountain and smiled at the ghastly jokes of Wescott. We have endured all the trials and tribulations of an eventful week. And now again our paper appears, a messenger of light and joy.

"Whether we have any contemporaries we know not, we remember perusing a month ago the first copy of a quite credible sheet entitled the "Slocumville Gazette," whether it is still dragging out an existence or has given up the ghost we are unaware."[6]

This reference to "Slocumville" was a clever interjection, probably by William Morton

---

[5]The Lever, Editorial by William Morton M. Payne and Paul Shorey, Vol. 1, No. 1, Georgetown, January 7, 1874 (pp 15-17) (the author of the Lever accidentally dated issue No. 1 as being published in 1873 instead of 1874, but dated the next issue, No. 2, correctly with 1874), William Morton Payne Papers, Midwest Manuscript Collection, The Newberry Library, Chicago.

[6]The Lever, Editorial by William Morton M. Payne and Paul Shorey, Vol 1, No 2, Jan. 13, 1874, pp 45-46, William Morton Payne Papers, Midwest Manuscript Collection, The Newberry Library, Chicago.

Payne who had from Feb. 4 to June 10, 1873 edited a "Slocumville News." This editor as Wm. Rex commented in his first editorial:

> "...We hope soon to engage the most prominent authors of the country and intend making our paper one of the finest in the country. We have already engaged the following gentlemen, Jave Sextus, M. T. Jug, KookmacFlook and others..."[7] (All fictitious names, of course!)

The "Farewell Number" of The Lever issued in "Georgetown C.H.S. June 9, 1874" was completely hand written and is now quite uncipherable after a near-century. The mast head of this issue was like an illuminated page of a medieval manuscript both in color and lettering.[8] There were two later numbers, a "Reunion Number, Chicago, Dec. 29, 1874" and "Reunion Issue No. 2, Dec. 29, 1875."[9] These were probably nostalgic gifts to the old Chicago High School as both the twins (Gemini) were in their new life pursuits. Paul Shorey was at Harvard and probably home for the holidays while William Morton Payne was a busy librarian at the Chicago Public Library.

Letters that fall of 1874 indicated the two friends were very occupied but kept in touch with each other. Paul Shorey, a lonesome Harvard freshman, wrote from Billerica:

> "Dear Will... it has rained every day since I've been here. I don't think there is a sun in this heathen country... You must excuse a good deal of homesick talk... I have no one to pour it forth to but you... Everybody here laughs at the joyous look on my face when I got your letter. And my face was like the rising sun while I read it."[10]

Thus the pattern of this life long friendship would continue until death separated these two classmates of 1874, alumni of Chicago's oldest high school.

Their joint effort, The Lever which consisted of weekly papers about eight by fourteen

---

[7]Slocumville News, Vol 1, No 1, Feb. 4, 1873, by Wm. Rex - Editor [William Morton Payne], William Morton Payne Papers, Midwest Manuscript Collection, The Newberry Library, Chicago.

[8]The Lever, "Farewell Number" edited by William Morton M. Payne and Paul Shorey, Georgetown C.H.S., June 9, 1874, William Morton Payne Papers, Midwest Manuscript Collection, The Newberry Library, Chicago.

[9]The Lever, "Reunion Number, Chicago, Dec. 29, 1874" and "Reunion Issue No. 2, Dec. 29, 1875," William Morton Payne Papers, Midwest Manuscript Collection, The Newberry Library, Chicago.

[10]Paul Shorey to William Morton Payne, Billerica, Sept. 20, 1874, William Morton Payne Papers, Midwest Manuscript Collection, The Newberry Library, Chicago.

inches, and probably never duplicated, were retrieved undamaged after circulating among several hundred students and faculty. They were later bound in a hard cover and rested among the treasures of William Morton Payne for about forty years. Now these faded, crumbling and one time jolly souvenirs have been immortalized in microfilm preservation.

There was another proud first for Chicago High School. Probably the oldest literary society in a United States public high school was the Irving Society founded in 1857 at Chicago High School. The Society honored Washington Irving who in that period was a popular writer whose works appealed to young people because of their humorous satire.

The Constitution of the Irving Society, adopted in 1857, had two revisions: in 1868 and 1873. Probably, the changes in procedure in 1873 were the most important to the Irving Society since, by that time, the school had doubled in enrollment of students, all admitted by examinations, and many were gifted pupils; also the faculty had increased. This period might be called the Golden Age of Chicago High School.

The "Preamble." of the Irving Society's Constitution reads:

> "Believing that an Association for debate and other literary exercises affords opportunities for mental improvement not otherwise obtained, we do hereby organize ourselves into a society for mental improvement and mutually pledge ourselves to be governed by the following Constitution, By-Laws and Rules of Order."[11]

The Constitution was written under the rules established in Cushing's Manual of Parliamentary Practice (1844) and provides an insight into the economics of that bygone era. And while correct in every detail, today's reader can enjoy a smile over the serious attempts of the students. The "Order of Business." reads:

"1. Call to order.
 2. Appointment of Critic.
 3. Calling the Roll.
 4. Reading minutes of previous meeting.
 5. Propositions for membership.
 6. Voting for candidates.
 7. Reports.
 8. Literary Exercises. { Criticism, Paper, Declamation, Essay, Oration, Extemporaneous Speech.
 9. Extemporaneous Debate.
 10. Prepared Debate.
 11. Volunteered Discussion of Question.
 12. Miscellaneous Business.

---

[11]The Irving Society of the Chicago High School. Constitution. Chicago, 1873. William Morton Payne Papers, Midwest Manuscript Collection, The Newberry Library, Chicago.

13. Decisions.
14. Appointments.
15. Adjournment."

In the "Rules of Order." we read:

Rule 2. "When a member intends to speak on a question, he shall rise in his place and respectfully address the President, confine himself to the question, and avoid personality."

In the "By-Laws." in "Article II" we learn:

"Sec. 1. The initiation fee shall be twenty-five (25) cents.
"Sec. 2. The term dues shall be ten (10) cents, payable at the regular meeting previous to every regular election. Any member failing to pay the same shall not be permitted to vote.
"Sec. 3. Any member absenting himself from two regular meetings in succession shall be fined ten (10) cents, unless excused by the Society."

In the "Article I" of the "By-Laws." we read:

"This Society shall convene on the last day in each school week, fifteen minutes after the close of the afternoon session of the school, provided that the last two days in each school year shall not be considered a part of the term." [Shades of final examinations and graduations.]

In the Constitution, in "Article XI" in the "Miscellaneous" section, we read:

"Sec. 2. The Paper of the Society shall be called "The Echoes of the Irving.""[12] [No issues of that paper have come to light.]

With continuing growth on all sides of the city, auxiliary high schools offering two years of study were established as North, South and West Division High Schools. By 1880, these became four year schools and Central High School was abolished. The main reasons were that the old limestone building was too small and the region surrounding it was becoming heavily commercial as well as congested with struggling foreign-born families. It was Jane Addams and Ellen Gates Starr who saw the newcomers' plight and established Hull House in 1889 in the near neighborhood on South Halsted Street.

An affiliation with West Division seemed a direct extension of Old Central High School and for some years the alumni of both schools met in joint reunions. The secretary of the

---

[12]Ibid.

alumni association for many years was Lucy Wilson who had graduated from Old Central and would later become a beloved teacher in West Division and its successor, McKinley High School.

The last years of the relinquished school saw the building used as a warehouse by the Board of Education. In 1950, the structure, almost a century old, was demolished because it was in the path of a proposed northwest expressway.

Old Central was a rugged, built to endure structure. The earliest engraving of the building shows "Van Osdel & Bauman, Architects" under engraving of "Chicago High School Building."[13] It was built of "rubble limestone dressed square with rough face" and a slate roof. This building and Chicago Water Tower on North Michigan Avenue were contemporaries; both survived the Great Fire of 1871 because of their stone massiveness. The two buildings had Gothic elements in common; both had crenelated roof edgings. The effect on the Tower resembled a fortress, while the School had many turreted chimneys, each of which served a one stove heated classroom. The windows in both structures in their earliest period were composed of small diamond shaped, leaded panes. Expansive glass surfaces at the time were uncommon and costly. Today, in the Water Tower restoration, the amber tinted and leaded diamonds can be seen. This building, also in the path of progress, was saved by farseeing, patriotic citizens; Old Central was not so fortunate.

In the present metamorphosis of Chicago's old neighborhoods, the Circle Campus of the University of Illinois has been established on the South Halsted Street area. When the old brick Hull House on the campus was made a hallowed shrine and museum to a great woman, Jane Addams, both city fathers and planners began to understand that even stone walls have both use and personality and are cherished for ages to come.

Old Central, besides having famous graduates, had equally noteworthy teachers who helped mold those future illustrious city fathers, industrialists, professors, physicians and scientists. William Morton Payne wrote in a Chicago newspaper an article entitled, "Recalls Old High School." His estimate of the professors on the faculty were probably unbiased and mature since he wrote as one having been taught by as well as teaching with these "giants" of educators.

> "Men were sought for, not selected from applicants, and they were paid salaries which were, for that time, adequate to support a social position equal to that of men in the other learned professions."[14]

---

[13]School Report Chicago 1855-60, F38QB 1854-1860, First Annual Report of the Superintendent of Public Schools of the City of Chicago, Chicago. Democrat Book and Job Office, 45 La Salle Street, 1854, F38QB 1854 dup, Chicago History Museum.

[14]Payne, William Morton, "Recalls 'Old High School'," in Clippings from newspaper articles written by WMP, 1917-1918, William Morton Payne Papers, Midwest Manuscript Collection, The Newberry Library, Chicago.

Payne wrote of George Howland who was principal of Chicago High School

"in 1860, and remained in that position for twenty years. No other schoolman has occupied anything like the position of influence that he held in the community during those twenty years. A finished classical scholar and the embodiment of most of the other elements of the finest culture, he set a stamp upon the boys and girls of his teaching that was never to be effaced, and to which they paid grateful tribute all the rest of their lives."...

"George Philip Welles," who taught Latin, was at Chicago High School "until its doors closed" and then served "as principal of its successor, rechristened the West Division high school" "for nine years.

"Dr. Samuel Willard, a man of lovable disposition... taught history after a fashion that made its landmarks a part of the permanent furniture of his students' minds. His venerable presence (for he lived to be almost a centenarian) was like a benediction to his old students when they encountered him in later years.

"Henry F. Munroe, a humanist in the finest sense of the word, genial and inspiring, was also a pioneer botanist, and his love for the classics was divided with his love for the wild flowers."...

"Oliver S. Westcott... in his early teaching days trafficked with zoology... Marc Delafontaine... from France... was the instructor in chemistry."...

"These are but six of that remarkable group of men whose influence has made itself felt in the lives of thousands of Chicagoans..."[15]

Chicago High School had no large auditorium or gymnasium. Graduation exercises were held in churches such as the Tabernacle where many revival services were conducted. The Cyrus McCormick family frequently attended this church. Old Central's graduation exercises were held there in June 1879 which was the twenty-first anniversary of the school. In 1890 and 1892 the combined commencement exercises of all Chicago high schools were held in the magnificent new Chicago Auditorium.

---

[15]Ibid.

13. Old Central High School (Chicago High School). Board of Education Photograph, negative No. 2607a. Courtesy Chicago Board of Education.

CYRUS HALL McCORMICK II

Since Cyrus H. McCormick II was one of Chicago High School's ("Old Central's") illustrious alumni, and also of Brown School, his early history will be considered here.

The McCormick reaper was invented by Cyrus Hall McCormick and his brother, Leander, in 1831 at "Walnut Grove," Rockbridge City, Virginia; the machine's factory was established in Chicago in 1847. Cyrus Hall McCormick II was born in Washington, D. C., May 16, 1859, the son of Cyrus Hall and Nettie Fowler McCormick. He would spend most of his life in the Chicago area. It was evident that traditions of simple yet gracious living and a dominant religious faith would be stressed by these founding parents and expected of their children.

The mother and young Cyrus arrived by train from the east in the midst of the Great Fire of 1871 to make their permanent home in Chicago. The reaper factory was destroyed and the family took refuge on the West Side. Here Cyrus II, twelve years old, recalled standing in line for bread and blankets being given to the refugees at the old Third Presbyterian Church at Washington and Carpenter Streets.[1]

A temporary office of the reaper company was set up at 71 Ashland Avenue, while a new factory was built at Madison and the South Branch of Chicago River and the McCormick family moved into its new home on Fulton and Sheldon Streets. From here Cyrus went to Brown School from September, 1872 to his graduation in June, 1874.

Professional acclaim and its often aristocracy of wealth, creates inaccessibility to a great family's personal history. Also, time obliterates that human warmth which later readers seek in books, leaving merely cold facts to be found. To find a door left ajar is the biographer's greatest reward.

From boyish letters saved by motherly Nettie Fowler McCormick and Cyrus II's Journal kept during the Chicago High School days, one learns of the boy's aspirations and antics, as well as the high quality of education offered in Chicago's first public high school.

Most diaries of adolescent students record the main business of their lives - their schooling and friendships of both boys and girls; yet often bubbling over among these pages are bits of humor, naive philosophy and the evident influence of their parents' ideals. Young McCormick's Journal mirrored all of these. The pages written during the winter of 1875, his first year at Chicago High School, mention frequent ice skating days at the "Rink." This was probably a vacant low area on the near West Side which an energetic promoter flooded and whose icy surface he kept the ice clean and smooth while providing a place to put on one's skates and torch light for the evening session - all for a few farthings' admittance in the true Dickens' spirit.

On February 19, 1875 Cyrus wrote:

"Last night I went to the Rink. It was a benefit to the proprietors. They had fancy skating, also an imitation menagerie, elephants, monkeys, roosters, etc.

---

[1]Roderick, Stella Virginia, Nettie Fowler McCormick, Richard R. Smith Publishing Co., Rindge, New Hampshire, 1956, p. 97.

(Almost like a forerunner of the modern day "Ice Capades.") We have a short vacation now. No school on Monday because it's Birthington's washday."

"Went to the Rink this afternoon. Went home with Miss R. C., Miss Ella F., Miss P., Len Spoogle was along, too. Also Warren Salisbury."[2]

That March Cyrus recorded:

"...Mama has had trouble in getting me a bed long enough for me to repose my weary limbs on. Such is the disadvantage of being tall."[3]

He was then almost sixteen years old.

Yet as serious a student as he was, he had recorded:

"Hurrah! Today I went to school as usual. I got there at 8:15. The janitor said that one of the pipes had burst and so he was afraid he could not get up steam. Another boy and myself pulled two of the windows down and made the room very cold. When the teacher came, it was so cold he could not call school for 1/2 an hour. In a little while, the principal came in and said that the steam had to be shut off and so the scholars might go home. I got home at 10:30 a.m."[4]

In a letter to his mother in 1876, he gave his subjects and grades for September:[5]

"Eclogues (Virgil)	100	Scholarship	99.5
Spelling	100	Attendance	100
Aneid	99	Deportment	100
Lat. (in) Prose	98	General Average	99.5
Xen (ophon) Anal. (ysis)	95	Number in class	52
		Rank in Class	1"

In another letter to his mother, which has a most modern import, he wrote:

---

[2]Cyrus Hall McCormick Papers, State Historical Society of Wisconsin, Archives and Manuscripts. Permission Wisconsin Historical Society, 816 State Street, Madison, WI 53706-1482.

[3]Ibid.

[4]Ibid.

[5]Ibid.

"Would you believe it! The Chicago Board of Education passed a resolution a few days ago prohibiting the reading of the Bible and the Lord's Prayer in the public and high schools. I never heard of such a thing. We don't read the Bible or repeat the Prayer in school now. All we do is sing two or three songs."[6]

This was a fact; on July 13, 1875, the President of the Board of Education stated:

"We have demonstrated that there is a morality that can be well and profitably taught outside of religion... Our public schools are not places of religious instruction; this consideration has especial force in our schools where we have and always will have children of parents of all sects, creeds and shades of religion. Hence everything of a sectarian character or pertaining to religious beliefs, ought and must of necessity be excluded."[7]

This pronouncement met with considerable backfire from Chicago clergy, teachers and ordinary citizens. There was both protest against the ruling, as well as counter criticism of the protesters. That ruling continues today.

At the time only three clergymen were in favor of the Board's decision; one was Bishop Samuel Fallows. He said:

"The School Board is right... This is an America for all nations and all religions... In schools supported by taxes imposed on all, it is unfair to have religious observances not approved by all."[8]

Young McCormick was concerned early with his financial affairs. When twelve, he earned extra money by moving twenty-two tons of coal into the cellar from nearby. In an agreement with his mother, he, and not the coal man, was to earn fifty cents a ton; each day after school he reduced the coal pile. That eleven dollars, in addition to other earnings from errands and odd household jobs, reached $100.00 and was put in the bank. The bank failed a month later.[9]

In 1876 Cyrus became quite rhetorical in his descriptions in his Journal. At Thanksgiving he wrote:

---

[6]Roderick, p. 116.

[7]Chicago Board of Education, The 19th-22nd Reports, Year Ending July 25, 1875, p. 24. Permission of Chicago Public Schools, 125 South Clark Street, Chicago, Illinois 60603.

[8]Fallows, Alice Katharine, Everybody's Bishop: Being the Life and Times of the Right Reverend Samuel Fallows, D.D., J. H. Sears & Co., N.Y., 1927, p. 1.

[9]"C. H. McCormick Dies in 78th Year," Chicago Daily News, June 2, 1936, p. 1.

"Now I have a little time to take breath. As tomorrow is the day on which the festive byped of the gobbler kind is to grace the well stocked family board, that august and venerable assemblage, the Board of Education - how considerate they are - have determined after long cogitation... of the Pros and Cons to grant to the studious youth of the Garden City a brief holiday extending over the space of two days!"[10]

For this occasion he wrote two verses, the serious and not so serious:

"Let every son of Freedom
On this our festal day
Give thanks for many gifts to God
Who guides us on our way."

Ode to the Turkey:
"Cook it through tenderly,
Carve it with care,
Fashioned not slenderly
Plump and how fair."[11]

The two day vacation was put to good use:

"...Thanksgiving morning I spent in McGuise's blacksmith shop getting Princeton shod. Four new shoes and sharpened at that. Rode Princeton down to South Park [Jackson Park]. Air was cold but very bracing especially for toes. Mine got so braced up it took me 20 minutes to get them unbraced which isn't very agreeable."[12]

On Sunday, December 24:

"Went over with Mamma and Virginia in the sleigh this morning to the 8 o'clock meeting at the Tabernacle (Moody and Sankey Revival)..."[13]

On Christmas Day:

---

[10]Cyrus Hall McCormick Papers.

[11]Ibid.

[12]Ibid.

[13]Ibid.

"How soon it has come around again!... The all important questions - Has Christmas found me further on the road to eternal happiness than the last? I trust it has. When I ask myself the question, how much have I grown spiritually during the last year? I fear the answer must be, Not so much as I ought."[14]

In spite of earlier declaring a vacation for his "tired brain," on December 27 he wrote:

"This morning Howard Ross, Ed Adams and I start a course of Caesar reading to be continued during the two weeks of holiday. We expect to review the 5 Books in that time. During these two weeks the question as to my future course, either of study or work, will be decided. If I do not go to Princeton College, as I have always been intending, I think I should like to take a scientific course at Sheffield for two or three years."[15]

Father McCormick brought up his son with this ideal which was revealed in a later day:

"My father taught me that I must work out my own business salvation; that every man must carve his own way and by work and clear thinking earn his own station in business."[16]

Cyrus went on to Princeton University in 1879 and after two years entered his father's business, then called McCormick Harvester Machine Company. Upon his father's death in 1884, Cyrus became president; in 1902 the company became The International Harvester Company, with a capital stock of $120,000,000. He continued as president until 1919 when he became Chairman of the Board.

In brief mentions of his private pursuits, the identity of the man, little other than the son of the reaper's inventor, is revealed. After his wife's death in 1921, he established the Harriet Hammond McCormick Memorial - the Young Women's Christian Association Residence at 1001 North Dearborn Street. This building was recently sold and plans are for another building elsewhere in Chicago. This Y.W.C.A. served as a residence for students and employed women as well as a hotel for world-wide visitors to Chicago. It was not uncommon to meet many persons there in their native costume.

Also, as a memorial for his wife, he published her lectures and writings on Landscape Art: Past and Present. She was one of the founders of the Garden Club of America. There are many historical photographs in the volume including some of the McCormick estate, Walden, on

---

[14]Ibid.

[15]Ibid.

[16]National Cyclopedia of American Biography, Vol. D, James T. White and Co., New York, New York, 1934, p. 286.

Chicago's north shore. In these restful, unostentatious scenes, one sees qualities expressing the characters of Cyrus and Harriet McCormick.

In memory of their daughter, Elizabeth, who died in childhood, a section of the Junior Museum of the Chicago Art Institute was endowed. There, children enjoy hours of spontaneous appreciation of the fine arts and companionship of their contemporaries.

In November, 1932, at the Diamond Jubilee of Brown School, Cyrus H. McCormick returned for this ingathering of former students in the old, weathered brick building at Warren and Wood Streets. He was then seventy-three and one of the gracious hosts. Seeing old schoolmates again, from both Brown and old Central High Schools, he must have rejoiced that he could join them once more in a tribute to their alma mater. He died in Chicago on June 2, 1936.

WILLIAM MORTON PAYNE

For those readers whose family antecedents have included members who went to Chicago High School, or later, to West Division or McKinley High Schools, all can claim a beloved professor who taught consecutively at these three institutions for a period of forty-two years: from 1876 to his retirement in 1918. He was William Morton Payne.

Before his long career as a teacher, he had graduated from Chicago High School in 1874, and then joined his earlier mentors on the faculty in 1876, when he was eighteen years old. William Morton Payne was probably the greatest literary scholar that Old Central, or any of Chicago's public schools, ever produced.

He was born February 14, 1858 in Newbury Port, Mass., the son of Henry Morton and Emma (Tilton) Payne. He came to Chicago in 1868, and attended Chicago Academy on Wabash and Jackson. After graduating from Chicago High School, he was self-educated. He was assistant librarian at the Chicago Public Library from 1874 to 1876. This might be said to have been his university, since the world of books was there, and he drank deeply of "the Pierian spring."

During those forty-two years of patient, quiet teaching of science and world literature to thousands of young, receptive minds, he was also a literary editor of Chicago Morning Press, from 1884 to 1888, and of Chicago Evening Journal from 1888 to 1892; he was associate editor of The Dial from 1892 to 1918. As Mary Hastings Bradley, the writer and long time friend of William Morton Payne, said of him: "He was The Dial."

As a literary critic he was concerned with modern literature, especially poetry in English, French, Italian, German and Scandinavian languages. He translated Bjornson's Sigumund Slembe in 1888, and Jaeger's Henrik Ibsen in 1890. He was author of many literary text books, such as The Greater English Poets of the Nineteenth Century, 1907 and Leading American Essayists, 1909. He was author of The New Education, 1884, Little Leaders, 1895, Editorial Echoes, 1902, and Various Views, 1902. He edited articles in Warren's Library of the World's Best Literature and English in American Universities.

During the World's Fair of 1893, William Morton Payne was Chairman of the Philological Congress. He was lecturer at University of Wisconsin in 1900, and at University of Kansas and University of Chicago in 1904. He was an honorary member of Φ B K at Northwestern University, and received an L.L.D. from University of Wisconsin in 1903.

He was an active member of the Chicago Literary Club, the Twentieth Century Club and the Chicago French Club. To his friends and peers, he was the soft spoken gentleman; gracious, with a sense of humor which melted his serious, almost sad face. He remained a bachelor, living with his mother and brother, Henry, who was an artist. To many of his young students he remained an enigma. Yet at times their hero-worship of him was humanized by the professor's humor, with such quips as "Moonlight often saves on gaslight."

There were many European trips for this truly classical scholar. On some he joined Paul Shorey. Always, Payne was gathering new thoughts for his professional livelihood, as well as his inner life, the latter never completely revealed until his death.

Perhaps one of the last episodes in this serious man's life is the story told by Eulalie Walker, one of his students at McKinley in 1916. She, herself a spirited, beautiful, cherubic child, and later in the Ziegfeld Follies, was a tonic for this aging professor. A group had gathered at his home on Indiana Avenue for a class play rehearsal. During an interlude of that evening, Eulalie, as the ring leader, helped "short sheet" the professor's bed - a prank of young people, especially in freshman dormitories, which our readers may recall.

After William Morton Payne's retirement in 1918, he continued with his writing, chiefly editorials for Chicago Journal, which appeared regularly in 1917 and 1918.

Herbert and Mary Hastings Bradley were two of his closest friends. He often spent vacation periods at their summer home in Wisconsin; he was planning to join them there when suddenly he was overtaken by a stroke, and died July 12, 1919. His life's book was closed. Memorial services were held at the home of his dearest friend, Paul Shorey.

At this farewell Paul Shorey must have looked far back. Their friendship had been an idyllic comradeship; both men were brilliant students. The classical courses as taught then leaned heavily toward Greek and Latin, as well as to rhetoric and poetic composition. These two students had relished these intellectual pursuits to such a degree that they often spoke and wrote to each other in the classic languages as easily as in their mother tongue.

Paul Shorey was a fortunate student, whose financial background permitted him to continue a classical education, graduating from Harvard in 1878. He was then admitted to the Illinois Bar in 1880. Extensive study abroad followed, first at the University of Leipzig from 1881 to 1882, then the University of Bonn in 1882, the American School of Classical Studies at Athens in 1882-1883, and finally, Paul Shorey took his Ph.D. degree at Munich in 1884.

During all these collegiate years, the two scholars kept up their correspondence. In the meantime, financial help for William Morton Payne's college education was not available from his family. In spite of this misfortune, this student found a complete university education was possible for him in books at home. As Paul Shorey advanced, William Morton Payne did likewise, from many of the same books, which were in public and private libraries. The two scholars compared notes, perhaps only on postcards, as they pursued their goals.

Paul Shorey returned from Europe to become Professor of Latin and Greek at Bryn Mawr College from 1885 to 1892. President Harper called this classicist to the University of Chicago when it was founded in 1892 by its benefactor, John D. Rockefeller; Professor Shorey remained there until his retirement.

In the meantime, William Morton Payne had become a professor in the Chicago Public Schools, as described elsewhere in his biography, with his many honors and writings. To the very end these two men were an inspiration and a challenge to each other. Paul Shorey long out-lived his friend, dying on April 24, 1934.

William Morton Payne's life treasures were his many writings, especially poetry, and his methodical accumulation of souvenirs dating back to his hand written chemistry text; old high school programs, family photographs and letters - these made up his worldly estate. It was lovingly deposited in the Manuscript Division of Newberry Library by Mrs. Herbert Bradley. In turn, the treasures were precisely catalogued by Mrs. Jens Nyholm, Librarian.

Why such concern for the last mortal effects of a gentle schoolmaster, and the testament of his creative as well as ascetic life? A door had been left ajar; among his letters and editorials, were also sonnets and other verses, which he had written during more than a quarter century. Among them was <u>The Rosary of the Years</u>. Each year on April 19, he composed a memorial sonnet for the birthday of his youthful love, Mary, who died when eighteen years old and he was beginning his thirties. This life-long sorrow is the reason for the loneliness and sadness that seemed to remain with him all his years.

Many of the poems are so poignant and perfect in their expression that the reader feels the bond of sorrow is recalled which is part of all human lives. The poet and the reader also share in the renewal of faith, as Professor William Morton Payne speaks to his students and other friends:

I

My lady came with April to the earth -
  April, the month of suns and quickening showers,
  Resurgent life, and springing forth of flowers,
Yearning atonement for the season's dearth.
Wedded in her are tenderness and mirth;
  I see her ever as in rose-hung bowers,
  Linked in my memory with happy hours -
How may I fitly sing my lady's birth?

Eighteen her years of sojourn here below;
  Like jewels on a necklace strung, each one
  Makes fairer yet the life that was begun
In that auspicious April long ago.
Now by her grace my soul is made to know
  A joy undreamed, a crowning benison.

VII

"Month after month another year hath sped,
  And April airs again about me blow;
  Resurgent from its cerements of snow
Young spring once more arises from the dead.
With quickening showers the thirsty earth is fed,
  In tender hues the woods and meadows glow,
  Lush verdure greets my eye, and flow'rets show
How death by life at last is vanquish'ed.

Each year Spring thus renews earth's ancient grace
  Like springs agone, but far more fair and dear
  My lady's grace with each recurring year
Is shown, and bids my vagrant fancy trace

New signs of promise in life's horoscope,
Augured fulfilments of my fondest hopes."

XIII

My star of life sinks slowly towards the west,
  And vain it were to hope that all the joys
  Which made it shine so fair when at the poise
Of high meridian should endure - the zest
Which gave my days their savour, the confessed
  Hopes and ambitions; - still their sweetness cloys
  my memory; fond imagination's toys
They were, wherewith my dreams were richly blessed.

One blessing yet abides, its stedfast glow
  Pervading all the chambers of my heart
  Where else were chill; should once that fire depart
From its deep-hidden altar, I should know
That life itself were speedily to go
  To meet the Archer with his lethal dart.

April 19, 1912.

XX

The changing year hath brought to me rich store
  Of works and days, the garnered fruits of life,
  With manifold experiences rife,
And wisdom growing still from more to more;
And still the baffled spirit may outsoar
  Keen disappointment cutting like a knife,
  And prostrate hope, and failure in the strife, -
Of man's dim palimpsest are these the lore.

One joy unfailing still has been my lot,
'Neath cloudy skies or clear, whate'er the plot
  That destiny has woven; still my share
Has been the blessing of thy love, God Wot!
  A steadfast flame, a boon beyond compare,
  And all mischance it gives me strength to bear.

April 19, 1919.[1]

William Morton Payne was associate-editor of The Dial, from 1892 to 1918. Many of the authors who were reviewed each month were personally known by Payne, either through correspondence or actual meeting. Possibly no other literary critic of that period had as many doors opened to him; each meeting of minds was a thrilling adventure. One has only to peruse the many letters that Payne saved among his precious souvenirs to know his literary friends.

There was Brander Matthews, writer and professor at Columbia University, who with Payne expressed hope for a universal university:

> "...I note also in The Dial a hope that someday some of our universities will have great literary forms down through the ages - or words to that effect. Now this is what Woodberry & I are trying to do at Columbia. He has a course on Criticism from Aristotle to Coleridge, followed by a consideration of the great poems of the world; and I have courses on the Drama (from Aeschylus to Ibsen) and on Modern Fiction."[2]

In another letter, Brander Matthews writes:

> "...As you may suspect I am not wholly in accord with you. I rate Kipling (at his best) far more highly than you do - even as a poet. But I was staggered to note that you failed to mention Mark Twain, who seems to me, after allowing for all his limitations, one of the great masters of fiction. And this was Stevenson's opinion, confided once on the sole occasion when I had the good fortune of meeting him.
>
> "But I do agree with you in thinking that there is a lull just now not only in English literature as a whole (including American) but in French also."[3]

Payne's literary correspondents were as varied as the ingredients in a potpourri and as pleasant to recall. At random, these are a sampling: Matthew Arnold, Katherine Lee Bates, Hobart Chatfield-Taylor, Will Livingston Comfort, John Drew, Timothy Dwight, Charles W. Elliot, Alice Morse Earle, John Fox, Jr., Edward Everett Hale, Henry James, Joseph Jastrow, William Ellery Leonard, George Barr McCutcheon, Percy MacKaye, Harriet Monroe, William

---

[1]Poems, William Morton Payne Papers, Midwest Manuscript Collection, The Newberry Library, Chicago.

[2]Brander Matthews to William Morton Payne, New York, Feb. 18, 1894, William Morton Payne Papers, Midwest Manuscript Collection, The Newberry Library, Chicago.

[3]Brander Matthews to William Morton Payne, Narragansett Pier, R.I., June 26, 1908, William Morton Payne Papers, Midwest Manuscript Collection, The Newberry Library, Chicago.

Lyon Phelps, Charles E. Russell (AE), George Santyana, Beerbohn H. Tree - the list is only begun.[4]

In perusing the old <u>Dials</u>, one is impressed by the number of world famous writers whose works were reviewed through that quarter century. For William Morton Payne to have helped these ingenious thinkers with his sincere criticism, was a service to both author and the reader. A good example was Payne's review of a two-volume set of Matthew Arnold's <u>Poems</u>, some new, some old, published in 1884:

> "The volumes which contain the poems of Matthew Arnold are one of the priceless possessions of the English-speaking people.".....
>
> "A new poet is to the critic what a new plant or animal is to the naturalist: something to be carefully studied with a view to classification. It is at once asked, what are his affinities, his antecedents, his tendencies? And these questions must continue to be asked as long as he stands before the world as a giver of a new work."[5]

As to <u>Oliver Langston</u> by George A. Powles, who was Payne's fellow professor of English at West Division High School, the review was not promising:

> "We have here an intimate picture of provincial life, in which nothing is spared us of the pettiness and prejudice in religious and social matters, or of the ignorant materialism of the time and place."[6]

In Payne's appraisal of Brete Harte's <u>On the Frontier</u>, he wrote:

> "Mr. Bret Harte has drawn the one great literary inspiration of his life from his early experience of the rude conditions of pioneer civilization in the West. The most surprising thing about it is that this inspiration should last so long and still be so fresh; that many years spent amidst very different surroundings should have no power to weaken it, and that it should remain unquenched even by the life of the diplomatic service."[7]

---

[4]William Morton Payne Papers, Midwest Manuscript Collection, The Newberry Library, Chicago.

[5]Payne, William Morton, "The Poetry of Matthew Arnold," <u>The Dial: A Monthly Journal of Current Literature</u>, Jansen, McClury & Company, Publishers, Chicago, Jan. 1884, p. 221-2.

[6]Payne, William Morton, "Recent Fiction," <u>The Dial</u>, Chicago, Feb. 1, 1903, p. 89.

[7]Payne, William Morton, "Recent Books of Fiction" <u>The Dial</u>, Chicago, Dec. 1884, p. 206.

And so, Payne scrutinized each new or established author during his long period of editorship. Those giants, and a few who had yet to become tall in the coming years, amaze today's thinking reader. After perusing a partial roll call of these immortals, the reader may well ask how do we measure up today after a fifty year interval and an accelerated population growth? How do we measure the quality of the works of present day authors, not to mention the quantity?

Recall that Payne and Brander Matthews both agreed that in the early part of the century there was "a lull... not only in English literature as a whole (including American) but in the French also". Did that lull deepen?

Among authors and their works reviewed by Payne in The Dial in that early and long procession were: Edward Markam, Robert Herrick, Maxim Gorky, Thomas Hardy, Rudyard Kipling, Herbert Spencer, William Vaughan Moody, Kate Douglas Wiggan, William D. Howells, H. G. Wells, Israel Zangwill, Richard Harding Davis, Owen Wistar, George Barr McCutcheon, Booth Tarkington, Jack London, Upton Sinclair, Bliss Carman, Joseph Conrad, Thomas Bailey Aldrich, Henry Van Dyke, Edward Everett Hale, Helen Hunt Jackson, Alfred Tennyson and Robert Browning.

What of William Morton Payne, the prose writer? We have learned of him as teacher, poet and critic. An excellent example of his prose works is his address, The American Scholar of the Twentieth Century.[8] This was presented before The Phi Beta Kappa Society of Northwestern University on June 16, 1903, when Payne was elected to membership in this honor society. His theme was taken from Ralph Waldo Emerson's The American Scholar, an oration which Emerson delivered August 31, 1837 before The Phi Beta Kappa Society at Cambridge. In 1903, this revered author was being honored on the centenary of his birth.

Emerson's essays have been required reading for generations of students. Many an old graduate bored with world news, whether in print or on television, has fingered the open bookshelf and found there a volume of Essays and Poems of Emerson.[9]

Upon turning the pages of the once-underlined sentences of such essays as "The Over-Soul," "Self Reliance" and "The American Scholar," the world-weary citizen is still inspired:

> "All young persons thirst for a real existence, for an object - for something great and good which they shall do with their hearts."[10]

Yet, today, after seventy years, Payne's The American Scholar of the Twentieth Century, and after one hundred and thirty years, Emerson's The American Scholar, both suffer from changed opinion as to what defines a "scholar." Earlier a scholar was associated with the liberal arts:

---

[8]Payne, William Morton, "The American Scholar of the Twentieth Century," *The International Quarterly of New York*, Burlington, VT, Sept.-Dec., 1903, pp. 262-279, William Morton Payne Papers, Midwest Manuscript Collection, The Newberry Library, Chicago.

[9]Sherman, Stuart P., Essays and Poems of Emerson, Harcourt Brace, N.Y., 1921.

[10]Sherman, frontispiece (from Emerson's Journal).

literature, music and fine arts, natural sciences, social sciences and the humanities. Today's most dominant scholar is the scientist, both practical and theoretical, the engineer and the technician. All these scholars, including those of the liberal arts, have their place in this accelerating, inter-spatial world. Yet it would seem today, at least by popular acclaim, that the younger scholars choose Science as the campus king (queens are obsolete) and select a hero like R. Buckminster Fuller who "turns them on."

The liberal arts will survive in spite of their modern distortion, and Emerson will be read. Perhaps a new voice will define "The American Scholar in the Twenty-first Century." In Payne's time, The American Scholar had become known as the "intellectual Declaration of Independence." Today as one reads Payne's essay on Emerson, there is much that has been spared obsolescence, and is of the essence of our present day - human nature changes slowly.

"Many tongues and pens have united in paying tribute to Ralph Waldo Emerson... but the sum of our obligation to his memory has hardly yet been computed. It is comparatively easy to reckon up the influence of a thinker who has made definite contributions to the totality of human knowledge... We know pretty definitely what the world owes to such men as Adam Smith and Immanuel Kant and Charles Darwin. Their intellectual force is applied externally, so to speak, and its resultant is measurable. But Emerson was a thinker of different type, a philosopher whose principles defy formulation and whose ideas have neither logical development nor systematic arrangement. He was the preacher of a gospel, not the defender of a creed... His influence was... from within outwards, and its aim was a sort of spiritual regeneration rather than the modification of any particular idea or set of ideas. As he once said, "It is of little moment that one or two or twenty errors of our social system be corrected, but of much that man be in his senses." It was said with pregnant significance by Goethe... that "inner freedom" was the thing which men should, above all else, strive to attain... It will ever be to the glory of Emerson that he aided many thousands of his fellow countrymen to win this, the most precious of all spiritual possessions. By treating idealism as the natural atmosphere of the free soul, he responded to the deepest instincts of our nature... this nation was founded upon idealism, political, ethical and religious, and that it still believes in the sunlit peaks, however they may be obscured by the sullen vapors of these lower slopes upon which we grope from day to day. The time came, long before Emerson's own death when his gospel bore proper fruit, when his idealism became translated into action, and when it was seen, as Mr. Morley finally says, that his "teaching had been one of the forces that... nourished the heroism of the North in its immortal battle." Thus was Emerson's faith in the individual justified, and thus it will be justified many times over, if we give heed to his counsel... Henrik Ibsen, and his way of putting the matter is this: "Men still call for special revolutions, for revolutions in politics, in externals. But all that sort of thing is trumpery. It is the human soul that must revolt.""[11]

Payne reviewed the ideas of Emerson's address, preliminary to his own considerations for the twentieth century scholar.

Today, long after Payne's re-emphasizing of Emerson for the scholars of 1903, these same ideals are still bread-and-butter food for the emerging scholar, with ""the education of the scholar by nature, by books, and by action."" Strangely, there is even a hint of modernity in the wording of Emerson's cautionings. Of books, he admits their value but warns "against over-dependence upon them, lest "men thinking" become no more than bookworms. "I had better never see a book than be warped by its attraction clean out of my own orbit and made a satellite instead of a system."" Of action, Emerson wrote: ""The true scholar judges every opportunity of action past by, as a loss of power. It is the raw material out of which the intellect moulds her splendid products.""[12]

Payne recalls two hopeful trends voiced in Emerson's essay: first, "the entrance of democracy into literature," as shown in the works of Goldsmith, Burns, Cowper as well as "Goethe, Wordsworth, and Carlyle. The second was

> "..."the new importance given to the single person"... "For if the single man plant himself indomitably on his instincts, and there abide, the huge world will come round to him"... "This confidence in the unsearched might of man belongs by all motives, by all prophecy, by all preparation, to the American scholar. We have listened too long to the courtly muses of Europe.""[13]

Payne, in his suggestions for the scholar of the twentieth century, added that, in respect to education in Europe:

> "Many of our younger scholars are equipped at home with a training that means quite as much as any that the old world can give... American scholarship has its own peculiar coloring, no doubt, for it is the reflection of American activities and aims, but it can hold its own in any company."[14]

> "Every man is a "debtor to his profession," as Lord Bacon long ago reminded us, and the educational profession is one that has special claims upon the American scholar. No matter what his department of work may be, he is bound

---

[11]Payne, 1903, pp. 263-265.

[12]Ibid., p. 266.

[13]Ibid., p. 267.

[14]Ibid., p. 268.

to give his activity an educational turn, for this country, more fully perhaps than any other, accepts public education as one of the chief civic responsibilities... it would be unfortunate indeed if scholarship should become wholly divorced from teaching, or if the duty to impart should not remain closely allied with the duty to investigate."[15]

Payne as a teacher was disturbed about a new "sentimental pseudo-philosophy" being introduced in Chicago schools:

"The old and tried disciplines, whose effectiveness has been tested by ages of experience, are now forced to contend for supremacy with all sorts of upstart matters... Here, then, is a manifest duty of the American scholar toward his profession, to stand for a wise conservation in educational theory and practice...

"In the higher ranges of his profession, and in those which more immediately concern his personal occupation, the scholar has no clearer duty than that of standing for "Lehrfreiheit" in the most absolute sense. He must teach the truth as he sees it, and he must join with his fellow scholars in the determination that by every means in their power this freedom shall be kept inviolate."[16]

About materialism and wealth, Payne asked:

"Do we not as a people frequently set before ourselves for examples the men who have accumulated stories of wealth rather than the men who have accumulated stores of wisdom? Do we not sometimes even acclaim them as our leaders, forgetful of Jethro's ancient counsel, "Thou shalt provide out of all the people able men, such as fear God, - men of truth, hating covetousness"? ...That scholar is unworthy of his high office who joins in the querulous complaint... to the effect that scholarship does not command material rewards proportional to those won by other forms of endeavor. Are its own peculiar rewards to count for nothing then - its honors, its self-sufficing activities, its sense of esteem in which it is held by all whose approval is really worth having?"[17]

In a passage pertinent to world scholars of 1903, and earlier voiced by Emerson, Payne wrote:

"The rising tide of that movement which in the political sphere we call socialism, but which has many other manifestations as well, and which threatens

---

[15]Ibid., pp. 268-269.

[16]Ibid., pp. 269-270.

[17]Ibid., pp. 272-273.

109

to subdue the brightly colored world to a uniform hue of sober gray, constitutes one of the most insidious present dangers to scholarship. In the name of a social ideal almost wholly materialistic, and under the protection of a narrow interpretation of the utilitarian philosophy, this movement is everywhere seeking to weaken individual initiative and thus clog the feel of progress. Emerson apprehended this danger, and commented upon it... "Is it not the chief disgrace in the world," he said, "not to be an unit; not to be reckoned one character; not to yield that peculiar fruit which each man was created to bear, but to be reckoned in the gross, in the hundred or thousand, of the party, the section to which we belong..." It was an unerring instinct which led Emerson to put his finger upon this tendency, and mark it as dangerous to civilization... Huxley was the one who supplied us with a name... He called it regimentation by way of contrasting it with individualism... In view of the ever increasing encroachments of the method of regimentation upon our modern life, it seems to me that the duty of scholar is pronounced to take his stand in the defence of that individualism which was the core of Emerson's philosophy, yet avoiding the extreme of intellectual anarchy... or without clipping the wings of free thought."[18]

Is this not paralleled today (1974) in the scholarship of Alexander Solzhenitsyn?

In conclusion, William Morton Payne emphasized the need for the American scholar to have faith:

"Faith, that is, not in a creed or a body of doctrine, but in the validity of every fine, altruistic impulse, of every generous motion of the spirit. A faith that derives its sustenance from the contemplation of earth and sea and sky, from the forms of beauty created by architects and painters and musicians, from the inspired utterances of sages and prophets and poets. A faith that is proof against all frustrations and disappointments and disillusionments because it views all temporal phenomena under the species of eternity. A faith in the perfectibility of mankind... like that of Tennyson... from all the disheartening spectacle to man as he may yet become... -

""All about him shadow still, but, while the races flower and fade
Prophet-eyes may catch a glory slowly gaining on the shade,
 Till the peoples all are one, and all their voices blend in choric
Hallelujah to the Maker, "It is finished. Man is made!""""[19]

In closing his theme on faith, Payne, unknowingly, prophetically, wrote:

[18]Ibid., pp. 273-274.

[19]Ibid., p. 275.

"It is the highest duty of the American Scholar in our new century to uphold, not merely the faith in humanity... but also the special faith that to our own nation has been given the mission to lead the world toward a true conception of the fellowship of man, that the new world has, indeed, been divinely appointed "to redress the balance of the old."... For it must be confessed that democracy is undergoing a severer strain than was ever before imposed upon it, and it takes a stout faith not to quail under this trial... Robert Browning's last message to mankind teaches a lesson from which the poorest spirited may gain strength and courage...

> ""One who never turned his back but marched breast forward,
>   Never doubted clouds would break,
> Never dreamed, though right was worsted, wrong would triumph,
> Held we fall to rise, are baffled to fight better,
>   Sleep to wake.""[20]

William Morton Payne, a man "who never turned his back but marched breast forward," was indeed a true American scholar, or as Shakespeare wrote in <u>King Henry VIII</u>,

> "He was a scholar, and a ripe and good one
> Exceeding wise, fair spoken and persuading."

---

[20]Ibid., pp. 277-279.

14. William Morton Payne. Photo engraving honoring William Morton Payne. William Morton Payne Papers, Box 1. Photo Courtesy of The Newberry Library, Chicago.

ELLA FLAGG YOUNG

Chicago's most distinguished Superintendent of Schools was an alumna of the Chicago High School, Class of 1862; it is appropriate that her biography be given here.

Ella Flagg Young's life was influenced by her earliest years in Chicago's schools, namely Brown and Chicago High School. In the years to follow, all Chicago Public Schools would benefit from her indomitable and selfless fifty-three years as an educator.

Ella Flagg was born in Buffalo, New York, in 1845 and came to Chicago with her family when thirteen years old and ready for high school. She found that to qualify for entrance examinations, the candidate must have attended a Chicago grammar school for one year. She went to Brown School's highest grade for a few months and found it repetitious of past schooling and left. In 1860, she took the teacher's examination and passed, but was too young to be awarded a teaching certificate. In dismay, the superintendent asked her if she would like to enter Normal School, which she did. Upon completion in 1862, she first taught at Foster School and then became head assistant at Brown School for two years. It was here she realized her life's calling as a teacher of children, as well as of their teachers.

By 1865, she was selected as the first principal for the new practice school of the Normal School. The president of the board had high praise for this twenty year old when he said that Chicago Normal School was not excelled by any similar school in the country. In 1868, Ella Flagg was married to William Young, who died early in her teaching career.

Her next posts were as principal of Scammon School, and by 1879, principal of Skinner School where she taught until 1887. She then became assistant superintendent of Chicago Public Schools, under George Howland who served for thirty-four years.

From her beginning teaching at Brown and continuing, especially at Skinner, Mrs. Young's leadership and introduction of new teaching methods were outstanding. She created a school library, had reprints made of classics for supplementary reading, and offered "enriching materials" in such subjects as singing, drawing, clay modeling and gymnasium. Drawing was used for graphic recitation in many subjects. She encouraged mental arithmetic and discouraged homework. Penmanship was practiced with arm movements and prizes for such were awarded each year at Skinner. These efforts would all be far reaching and expanded in the years to follow. While her "severity was intellectual" she had great sympathy and humaneness for her pupils and teachers.

During her years as assistant superintendent from 1887 to 1899, sweeping changes were made in the school system. Classes were reduced from 70 children in a room to 54. Handwork helped to use the energy and capacity of children. She wrote:

"Drawing has given the children more means to express themselves... The aim of manual training is not to drive boys to trades - but to increase the value of their work in every department. Girls are not taught domestic arts in the public schools to train them for servants, but for the purpose of teaching them the value of food and hygiene".[1]

Political voices of dissension were heard throughout the years against such "fads," "mud pies," as paper cutting and clay modeling.

In 1895 when she was fifty years old, she began attending seminars at the University of Chicago under John Dewey in the Department of Pedagogy (then so called) or college for teachers. President Harper of the University offered her a full fellowship in 1899. This she could not accept, since she herself did not have a bachelor's degree. A compromise was an "associate lecturer in pedagogy"[2] and the opportunity to study that year for her degree in courses of philosophy and psychology and continue in Dr. Dewey's seminar. In 1899 Mrs. Young resigned after twenty-five years as a teacher and administrator.

There were six monographs published in 1902 by the University of Chicago Press. Mrs. Young co-authored three of them with John Dewey and authored three entitled Isolation in the School, Ethics in the School and Some Types of Modern Educational Theory.[3] Among items discussed were the dreariness of repeated drills for children, wasting their energy and the consideration of attention of children -

"...inattention was the child's attending to something else, or other directions, from those immediately apparent."[4]

Under ethics, the function of school was to help form character in children and to stress freedom and democracy in the classroom, as well as at home. William James called this movement at this new University of Chicago, "a new school of thought," while John Dewey said, "the school is not a preparation for life, but is life."[5]

Mrs. Young remained at the University until 1904, and after a year of European travel, became principal of the new Chicago Normal School on Chicago's south side.

In 1909, she returned to the Chicago public schools as its superintendent and retired in December, 1915. Some of Mrs. Young's reports during her superintendency were discussions on manual training, household arts, promotion and retardation, fresh air, physical education, athletics, school nurses, technical training for girls and morality considerations. During the last years of office, she found political interests so negative that many moves she made for public school welfare were blocked.

---

[1]McManis, John T., Ella Flagg Young and a Half-Century of the Chicago Public Schools, A. C. McClurg, Chicago, 1916, p. 91.

[2]Ibid., p. 110.

[3]Ibid., p. 111.

[4]Ibid., p. 113.

[5]Ibid., pp. 107-108.

There were, however, many altruistic voices and actions in force and in great concordance with Mrs. Young's programs. There were Jane Addams at Hull House, Amelia Sears in the social welfare agencies, Louise De Koven Bowen concerned with juvenile delinquency, and further away in Italy, Maria Montesorri - all seeking the child's best education for life. Citywide and nationwide, women were awakening to their rights of suffrage and becoming more informed on the conditions of their public schools and the works of elected public officials. In May, 1900, the National Congress of Mothers met in Chicago and Mrs. Theodore Birney was elected president - this was to become known as Parents and Teachers Association, or "PTA."

Upon Mrs. Young's retirement, she gave her books to the Chicago Public Library and her household goods to Mary Thompson Hospital. To the public, through the press, some of her closing words were:

> "I believe that every child should be happy in school... We have tried to recognize the types of mind as a mother does among her own children. We were losing many at the fifth grade. By letting them do things with their hands, we have saved many of them. In order that teachers may delight in awakening the spirits of children, they must themselves be awake... I want to make the schools the great instrument of democracy."[6]

On May 24, 1916, the Chicago Board of Education voted unanimously a resolution:

> "In humble acknowledgement of the unpayable debt of our citizens to the wisest, the greatest and most devoted teacher the schools of our city have ever known, this simple record of the official service and positions in public life of the first woman superintendent of schools of the City of Chicago, Ella Flagg Young, is spread upon the proceedings of this board of education."[7]

Ella Flagg Young died in 1918, aged seventy-three years. At her death, the Board of Education gave her a tribute which was presented to the Ella Flagg Young Club in May, 1921. A portion read:

> "Chicago has lost a great leader and the nation, an eminent educator, untiring in effort, original in planning, forceful in execution, Ella Flagg Young gave to Chicago a better school system and to the world, finer ideals. The thousands that she taught remember her with affection and devotion..."[8]

---

[6]Ibid., pp. 210-211.

[7]Ibid., p. 173.

[8]Chicago Board of Education, "Ella Flagg Young, An Appreciation," brochure, April, 1921, p. 13. Permission of Chicago Public Schools.

15. Ella Flagg Young. From: McManis, John T. "Ella Flag Young," A. C. McClurg & Co, Chicago, 1916, portrait facing page 214.

WEST DIVISION HIGH SCHOOL

The next stepping stone in public education for neighboring grammar school graduates was West Division High School. There were a series of locations for West Division after the parent school, Central High School, was abolished. The first West Division was at Aberdeen and Jackson (Skinner School) from 1875-1877. Several sections of its students were moved to Monroe and Halsted (Scammon School) to ease congestion. From 1877 to 1887 the "old" West Division, as it became known, was at Morgan and Monroe. This was a new fifteen room structure with steam heat which accommodated 945 pupils and cost $38,000.

The plans in 1886 for the next West Division High School costing $120,719.56 on a triangular lot at Congress, Ogden and Lincoln Streets, were for five stories. On the basement or lower floor, besides the Boiler, Engine and Store Rooms, were two sections labelled Girls' Play Room and Boys' Play Room. Here the students congregated at recess or in inclement weather; adjoining these sections were the toilets and lavatories labelled Water Closet in the plans.

On each of the first, second and third floors were eight class rooms. On the top story, termed the Attic Floor, was an Assembly Hall 58 x 115 feet with a stage. This type of school building design would be radically changed by the next generation of architects and engineers. Although earlier they had used all available space in the building, the location of the auditorium was the most dangerous place for the students.[1]

By 1887, this last and largest building for West Division was finished at Lincoln and Congress; it had twenty-four classrooms, an assembly hall, accommodated 1150 students and cost $132,000. West Division flourished here until 1901. While the last location had been a move in a westerly direction with the population flow, it was also in the heart of the expanding medical district, then commonly referred to as the "Latin Quarter," and was later to become the world's largest Medical Center. It was evident that the high school should be located elsewhere, further west, in an environment more suited to adolescent students.

In 1901, the West Division High School building was sold to the College of Physicians and Surgeons, later becoming part of the University of Illinois. For an interim of two years, while the new high school was being built, classes were held in temporary quarters of the old car barns at Western and Flournoy. In the meantime, West Division as a name would cease and the successor would become William McKinley High School.

West Division, as it had existed during its Congress and Lincoln location, was marked by a splendid spirit among students and faculty. The long tenures and the quality of the faculty, and the respect and love of the students was comparable to Brown School's family. Some of the teachers had taught at Central High; one was the beloved "dear Mr. Munroe," a "Mr. Chips" of his time. Also, a new pattern was growing; this high school was an island of interest to the

---

[1] Thirty Second Annual Report of the Board of Education, 1886. Committee on Buildings and Grounds.

young medical students, as well as a promising example of the very young "Gay Nineties" generation.

Voice was the school's monthly magazine, begun in early years, and continued by its descendant, McKinley High School. Both my sister Effie and Myrtle Reed (McCollough) were aspiring writers from Brown School, and editors of Voice. "Questions and Answers," a humor column, reflected the neighborhood attractions, such as: "Why do so many girls stroll down Harrison Street at noon?" Answer: "To keep appointments with the dentists."

The competing literary society was The Irving - Alphas were boys, Omegas, girls. They dueled as well as fraternized in debates, literary programs and social hours. This society was organized at old Central, and had a printed constitution as early as 1857; at that period, the Irving included only boys. Through the years of its existence, this debating club encouraged potential lawyers.

Athletics were quite developed, with football and baseball teams, which played such other high schools as John Marshall, Medill and Austin. This was a far cry from old Central days, where there were no competitive games. The first superintendent of the high school had stated: "The highest and most important objective of intellectual education is mental discipline."

There was a Girls' Athletic Association, and while they had gym suits of "full bloomers and blouse waist with a sailor collar of black, trimmed with orange braid," (school colors), the girls' favorite activity seemed to be rooting at the interschool boys' games. Girls and boys really do not change much in spite of clothes and hair styles.

If today's high school students think they have cause for youthful protest against school board and faculty rulings, or lack of equipment, let them scan the headlines of five Chicago Daily newspapers from November 12-14, 1895:

"Pupils are in Revolt" (Nov 12) and "Ridicule the Order" (Nov 13), Record; "Sedition in School" (Nov 12), Post; "Fuss in a High School," News; "To Burn a Teacher in Effigy" (Nov 13), Chronicle; and "School Trouble is Ended" (Nov 14), Tribune.[2]

These protests came from West Division High School students, whose school was then one of Chicago's most modern; yet, it had no gymnasium, cafeteria, nor a well equipped library. The students at recess, study periods and after school went across the street to Edward Speakman's store, where school books, candy and light lunches were sold. This store served as a gathering place for students to discuss their school activities and probably, to linger too long.

George M. Clayberg, the principal, issued orders that students found in neighboring stores during school hours would be suspended. Also, that students were not to loiter in these places after school hours.[3]

The students were defiant; their first reaction after school was to rush over en masse to Speakman's, let off steam, and chart their course. One ring leader, a senior in Latin, then a required subject for college entrance, spoke up in Sallust's manner:

---

[2]Chicago Public Schools, West Division High School, 1895, Chicago History Museum.

[3]Ibid., "Sedition in School", Post, Nov 12, 1895.

118

""Dost remember, noble Cassius," said one of the conspirators when school let out, "how on a raw and gusty day yon irate pedagogue did vent his spleen on the noble game of football?"

""The noble Brutus speaks truly," answered the lean and lanky youth who is known in the conspiracy circle as Cassius, "Forsooth," he added, "even owing to the tyrant's mandate must we forswear the honored name of our alma mater when contesting for superiority with other youths atween the boundaries of goal posts, and no longer as the West Division High, but as the Irving Football Club, may we don the armor of football players and cultivate our hair till it resembles the foliage of overgrown chrysanthemums.""...

""Shall we stand this? Have we no rights? Doth this bumptious pedagogue think, forsooth, that we are still in leading-strings, that we may be ordered home like yelping, yellow curs? Perish the thought!"

" Thus spoke the conspirator known as Brutus from a rostrum improvised from one of Speakman's lunch tables.

""Let him beware!" echoed the gaunt Cassius, flourishing aloft his [book of] Sallust as a double-headed battle ax in the direction of the red brick [school] building.[4]

Even the girls... echoed their sentiments, giving their names as Octavia, Flavia or Emilia. Outside on the sidewalks, the throng of boys and girls unable to get inside the store, vowed they would not "stand it, not in a thousand years."[5]

The protest continued for several days. The students' grievances concerning their lack of space for gymnastics, the principal's restriction on the Irving Literary Society and on the management of Voice, all merited further consideration. The older boys did acknowledge that there had been card playing on Saturdays at Speakman's, such games as "Old Maid" or "Big Casino."

The next proposed act of the insurrectionists was a plan to burn an effigy of Principal Clayberg.[6] However, the Tribune on November 14, reported there were no longer signs of revolt. The evening before, the assistant superintendent of schools, Mr. Nightingale, stated that the principal was acting on instructions from the Board of Education.[7]

George Clayberg continued his conscientious leadership of generations more of high school students. The school's athletics, Irving Society and Voice lived on. By 1897, the students' earlier revolt and their later petition to the Board of Education brought good results with a splendid new gymnasium and a regular physical education director.

---

[4]Ibid.

[5]Ibid.

[6]Ibid., "To Burn a Teacher in Effigy," Chronicle, Nov 13, 1895.

[7]Ibid., "School Trouble is Ended," Tribune, Nov 14, 1895

Speakman's Book Store grew too, with stores later at McKinley and Crane High Schools; the original Edward Speakman's book, candy and lunch counter became the Medical Book Company in the Medical Center, under Chester Speakman, the fourth generation owner.

Among old memorabilia are early numbers of Voice written shortly after the magazine's birth. A list of faculty, half of whom had taught at Old Central, were teaching the Class of 1885 at the W.D.H.S. of Monroe and Morgan Street period. In the photograph were: H. F. Munroe, James R. Dewey, Daniel F. Hicks, Franklin P. Fisk, George M. Clayberg, Mark Delafontaine, Herman Hausten and James F. Clafte - all wore full beards or mustaches.

Both faculty and students wrote for Voice. Professor George A. Powles wrote an article, "The Congresses and Man." He had attended the Congress of Religion and Philosophies at the World's Fair in 1893.

The class of 1894 seemed a very active class at W.D.H.S. That year a sorority called Alpha Psi was formed, probably the first sorority in a Chicago high school. Among other clubs was The Embers, literary-slanted for potential teachers.

In 1898 the Junto Club was formed; it followed a pattern set by Benjamin Franklin's Junto, which was to help his friends develop literary and forensic abilities through essays, debates and orations. West Division's Junto had no election of officers; instead each member held office in alphabetical order for a stated time. Membership was limited to fifteen boys. This club continued through the early years of McKinley High School's existence.

In the Voice of January, 1898, one of West Division's famous sleigh rides was reported in the Society Column. The editor, Mabel Darby, noted that all the bright and shining lights took the trip "...Wilcox the debater, Simon the lady killer, Badenoch the heavyweight... Boughton the poet, and many other prodigies and monstrosities of W.D.H.S.... Some evil genius had furnished about fifty horns making the night hideous until one of the party secured them all."[8]

In the progress of this journey to Humbolt Park, the driver's whip was lost and found, then the front truck on the sleigh broke and all passengers piled out into a foot of snow and strong wind. Next, because of a rut in the road, the sleigh tipped to one side and all were falling out into the snow when the "crew" applied the knowledge of physics and had their heavyweight classmate move to the other side; then he was placed in the center to maintain the ballast. In the course of these events, Miss Raymond, a faculty chaperon, had stolen all the noisy horns. After a tug of war with buffalo robes, two of which were torn in the pulling, the girls were kept from freezing. The trip was finally completed by midnight with no casualties. The junior poet spoke out "There never were girls like those of W.D."[9] Times change but the spirit of youth does not.

---

[8]Voice, McKinley High School, Chicago, January, 1898, p. 2.

[9]Ibid.

16. West Division High School. "April 30, 1889. West Division High School, Chicago: raising of the flag just presented to the school." "View taken from the corner of Lincoln and Congress Streets, at intersection by Ogden Avenue, looking eastward, down Congress." Courtesy Chicago History Museum.

121

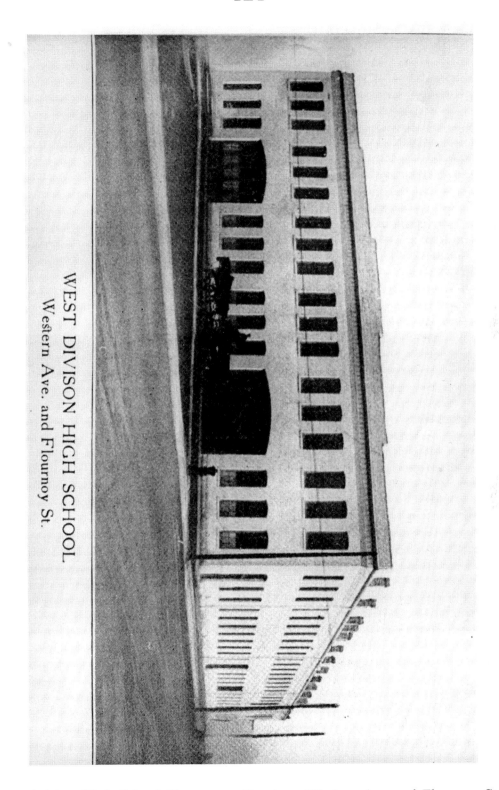

WEST DIVISON HIGH SCHOOL
Western Ave. and Flournoy St.

17. West Division High School Temporary Quarters, Western Ave and Flournoy St. School Photograph. Courtesy Chicago Board of Education.

MARY HASTINGS BRADLEY

One of the Mile Square's most famous members is Mary Hastings Bradley. From her childhood she was expressing her imaginative thoughts with her pen and has continued to do so most all her life as she travelled both the "high road and the low road" whether it was in England, Africa or Chicago.

She was born in Chicago, the daughter of William and Lina Richards Hastings; she has never divulged the date of her birth, the prerogative of many a woman. Her father died when she was a child and her mother remarried to Dr. Arthur Corwin, a professor at Rush Medical College. The family would make their home with Mary Hastings's grandmother, Mrs. Francis L. Richards on Ashland Boulevard near Van Buren, where Mary was born. Here young Mary had many friends in the neighborhood, the Pullmans, Owsleys, Harrisons, McLarens, Midgelys and others.

She graduated at twelve from McLaren School and while here won a prize from the Tribune for a pet animal story. Next she went to West Division High School where her literary trend continued to develop in her articles for Voice. Among old copies of Voice is an item on the Omega (girls) and the Alpha (boys) Irving Society of May, 1898. The subject of a debate was "Resolved that Hawaii should not be annexed." Hastings and Caswell were on the negative side and Boughton and Collins on the affirmative. The Omegas won the debate. Mary was active in Omega Irving, being its president one year. Among Mary's favorite teachers were Miss Lucy Wilson, William Morton Payne and Henry F. Munroe. Years later she wrote of them: "...they were finer than any I ever experienced elsewhere - even in Oxford."[1] The Union Park Congregational Church was where she attended from childhood into adult years. Her grandfather had been one of the founders.

Next, she graduated from Smith College in 1905 where she majored in English and was already writing for magazines. Then followed a trip to Europe with a cousin. They wintered in Egypt where Mary Hastings wrote two stories, "The Palace of Darkened Windows" and "The Fortieth Door" (these were published in book form in 1914 and 1920, respectively). These were a most auspicious introduction to her writing career as both stories were later made into a movies series. These brought to an American audience, the knowledge of the purdah system, the veiled and secluded women of Egypt.

That spring she went to Oxford University and worked in the Bodleian Library gathering material for her book, The Favor of Kings, which was a study of the period of Henry the Eighth and Anne Boleyn, the first beheaded woman in English history. Mary had the help of a tutor at Baliol College and also of the Earl of Dartmouth who made it possible for her to see the original manuscripts of the trial.

William M. Payne, editor of Dial wrote in his review of The Favor of Kings:

---

[1]Correspondence between Mary Hastings Bradley and the author, September 7, 1971.

"A fictional novel of Anne Boleyn in which "every recorded word of Anne's own writing... has been carefully weighed, and wherever possible, incorporated into the narrative... the feeling of romance is blended with the truth of history...""[2]

Payne then quoted the author's preface:

""I have tried to paint," says the author, "and to offer the Anne Boleyn of this story, a very human girl, gay and fearless who dared and lost so long ago and whose blood was the first of any woman to stain an English scaffold.""[3]

He prophesied of Mary Hastings Bradley:

"Much is to be expected from a writer whose first book exhibits such qualities as are to be found in "The Favor of Kings"."[4]

While she was writing this book she met her future husband, Herbert Edwin Bradley, a lawyer with the firm, MacChesney, Becker and Bradley. He was also a big game hunter, traveler and explorer. They were married in 1910. In 1915 their child, Alice Hastings Bradley was born. She was destined as a very young child to travel to the "ends of the earth" with her parents.

In 1921 and 1922 the Bradley family, including Alice, accompanied Carl E. Akley of the American Museum of Natural History, New York City, to Africa and the Belgian Congo for specimens of the mountain gorilla for exhibition in the Museum. This journey was described in On the Gorilla Trail, one of several books written of Mary Hastings Bradley's expedition experiences.

A very human incident is recorded. One of the natives with his chief visited the Akley-Bradley camp in Kissenyi, Belgian Africa. The native helper was entranced upon seeing little Alice Bradley with her blond curls and fair skin. He murmured, "Jesu Christ." The guide explained that the boy had gone to a Mission and seen a statue of an infant in a basket and who was called Jesu Christ. Alice became a living image to him since he had never seen a white child. The boy went out and returned with a gift, a little basket for the blond creature, also telling his interpreter that it was time for Jesu Christ to give him a gift. Little Alice gave the boy fourteen coins and he went away reconciled.[5]

---

[2] Payne, William Morton, "Recent Fiction," Dial, Chicago, June 1, 1912, p. 434.

[3] Ibid.

[4] Ibid.

[5] Bradley, Mary Hastings, On the Gorilla Trail, D. Appleton Co., N.Y., 1922, pp. 83-84.

Several other expeditions would follow, including another to the Belgian Congo in 1924; and an expedition to transverse the region west of Lake Edward in Sumatra and Indo-China for tigers in 1935; and a third expedition to Africa to study Pygmies and Mangbeton tribes in 1930-1931.

Needless to say these journeys inspired Mary Hastings Bradley to record them in writing. There was a series from 1926 to 1929 with such titles as Caravans and Cannibals, 1926, Alice in Jungleland, 1927, Trailing the Tiger, 1928, and Alice in Elephantland, 1929. The two "Alice" books were illustrated by Alice Bradley.

In studying the writing career of this author, her works fall into distinct categories. First, were her early Egyptian novels; second, her travels in remote parts of the world as Africa and historical scenes as Old Chicago Stories. Her third period was of magazine articles and mystery stories, some challenging the reader to be the detective. Such were Murder in the Family, 1951, Nice People Poison, 1952 and Nice People Murder, 1952.

Mary Hastings Bradley's last important book, I Passed for White, 1955, by Reba Lee as told to Mary Hastings Bradley, is probably true. While all names and places are fictitious, the facts are true. It touches upon a very sensitive and vital subject and concerns all people today, both black and white. The author in her preface presented this example "in the hope that it may lead to truer understanding and more kindliness in both white and Negro."[6]

This book has had continuous sales, and is still being published abroad. In 1972 Spain had brought out a second hardback edition of 80,000 copies.[7] Over fifteen years of readers' demands speaks well for the message in I Passed for White.

Mary Hastings Bradley is now living in retirement at her home in Chicago part time and her summer house in Wisconsin, and often winters in warm Mexico.

-----

[6]Reba Lee as told to Mary Hastings Bradley, I Passed for White, Longmans, Green, New York, 1955, Preface, unnumbered.

[7]Correspondence between Mary Hastings Bradley and the author, September 9, 1972.

MARY HASTINGS BRADLEY

18. Mary Hastings Bradley. From: "Prominent Women of Illinois, 1885-1932," Illinois Women's Press Association, Chicago, 1932, p. 47. Permission of IWPA.

126

MARY BARTELME

Judge Mary Bartelme was in the vanguard of voices in the early century speaking for Chicago's and Cook County's delinquent and impoverished children. Besides judges and clergy, there were kindred workers as Jane Addams, Amelia Sears, Julia Lathrop, Sophonisba Brechenridge, Edith Abbott, Louise De Koven Bowen and Ella Flagg Young. Incidentally, almost all were identified with the older sections of the west side.

Mary Bartelme was born July 26, 1866 of French parents, Balthasar and Jeanette (Hoff) Bartelme and lived in the neighborhood of Fulton and Halsed Streets. She graduated in 1882 form "old" West Division High School on Monroe and Morgan Streets. After private study and normal school training, she taught in Chicago's public elementary schools. Encouraged by Myra Bradwell, the first woman to be admitted to the Illinois bar, Mary Bartelme received her Bachelor of Laws degree from Northwestern university in 1894. She was appointed Public Guardian of Cook County in 1897 and served for sixteen years under four governors. In 1913, she was appointed Assistant Judge of the Juvenile Court under Judge Merit W. Pinckney. By 1923, she was elected Judge of Circuit Court and assigned as Judge of the Juvenile Court which she served until 1933.

Chicago's Juvenile Court was the first of its kind in the world.[1] Judge Bartelme's decisions in court attracted social and civic leaders from all over the world. Queen Marie of Romania in 1926 spent a day with Judge Bartelme in her courtroom. This judge's humane and maternal practices were both original and outstanding; being a woman she focused on the needs of young girls. Mary Bartelme felt that every girl upon being committed to a foster home was entitled to proper clothes and grooming and suggested that each girl be given a suitcase of clothes and accessories. At the time of Judge Bartelme's retirement in 1933, over 9,000 equipped suitcases were given to unfortunate children. From the beginning of her judgeship to her retirement, she had heard over 50,000 cases.

Among Mary Bartelme's personal and philanthropic efforts for dependent children, especially girls, was the giving of her Austin residence as a Mary Bartelme Club. As a result, more such clubs were formed in various sections of Chicago. It was said of her in 1927: "There is perhaps no woman in the world so widely known in juvenile service work or as deeply revered as Judge Mary Bartelme".[2] Her last years were spent in Carmel, California where a rose garden thrived under her loving care. She died July 25, 1954 at Carmel.

---

[1]Chicago Bar Record, "Judge Mary Bartelme," Feb. 1955, No. 5, Vol. XXXVI, The Chicago Bar Assoc., Chicago, IL, p. 232.

[2]Viewpoints, "Honored by Bench and Bar," Chicago, IL, July, 1927, p. 4. (McGraw-Hill, New York, in public domain.)

19. Mary Margaret Barteleme (1866-July 25, 1954). Courtesy Chicago History Museum.

LUTHER LOFLIN MILLS

The roster of lawyers coming out of the Mile Square is an impressive list. It included Luther Loflin Mills who was born September 3, 1848 in North Adams, Mass., the son of Walter N. and Caroline Mills. The family moved to Chicago where his father had a dry goods business, Mills and Co. After graduating in one of Brown School's earliest classes, young Luther became a prominent debater in old Central High School's Irving Society. Here he recited the orations of Daniel Webster and Patrick Henry; these may have helped him to become an effective speaker in his later practice of law.

After attending Michigan State University, where he was a member of Psi Upsilon Fraternity, he studied law under Homer N. Hibbard in Chicago and was admitted to the bar at age twenty-one. In 1876 he was elected to the office of States Attorney for Cook County and re-elected in 1880. He returned to private practice in 1884 in the firm, Mills, Gosham and Mills.

In 1876 he was married to Ella B. Boies and they would have four children. Mr. Mills was a Royal Arch Mason and member of Appolo Commandery. At his death the Academy of Natural Science in Lincoln Park was erected as a memorial to Luther Loflin Mills.

MARY SYNON

Mary Synon was an early student in the schools of the old Mile Square. Who's Who in Chicago and Vicinity - 1936 does not give her birth date; her parents were John Higgins and Annie Foy Synon and the family lived on the 600 (old number) block of Harrison Street near Ashland Avenue. Mary Synon went to Hendrick Grammar School and graduated from West Division High School on Monroe and Morgan Streets. It is probable that she also may have attended the Old Central High School as her name appears among a list of early students there. She received her B.A. degree from the University of Chicago.

She began her literary career as a Reporter for The Chicago Journal and was also a newspaper syndicate correspondent.

Among her published works are The Fleet Goes By, 1914; My Country's Part, 1918; The Good Red Bricks, 1929; and Copper Country, 1931. Besides, she contributed to many magazines. The Good Red Bricks concerns our old Mile Square and the author's vivid descriptions are very nostalgic for anyone who has ever been a part of that old region. Within this volume every sentence is a recollection, beautifully expressed, yet pithy with historic gems of days never to return. Leafing through this volume, here are some quotes:

"The stars came out on an April evening when pink clouds had hung over the roofs of the hospitals to the westward. Spring was in town, in the heavy fragrance of new-turned earth in little Union Park, in budding crocuses in the Gorman yard, in the eyes of students idling along the boulevard, in the quickened beat of the tambourines of the Salvation Army, in the throb of a hurdy-gurdy playing somewhere down Harrison Street..."[1]

"...they (a young couple) strolled to the West Town, that little theater which pioneered the neighborhood amusement palaces of the city, and groped their way to dim and shaky seats. A girl was playing heavily on an out-of-tune piano, and a man sang with a certain vivid lustiness which caught and held his audience. "That's Gene Gregg"..."[2]

This person was probably Gene Green in real life who once sang at these early movie theatres on Madison Street. In time, Gene Green moved on to greener pastures and plushier seats as "movies" became a huskier form of entertainment - but where the interpretive voices of both piano and singer would be needed until motion pictures had human voices and sounds in the moving picture reel - all made possible by Thomas A. Edison and improved upon by Lee De Forest.

---

[1]Synon, Mary, The Good Red Bricks, Little, Brown & Co., Boston, 1929, p. 6.

[2]Ibid., p. 14-15.

"At other times the West Side might be to her the great dynamo of the city's power, whirring, whirling in that ceaseless toil which was the city's birthright; the swarming hive of foreign hordes; the marketplace of vast farm lands she had never seen, although she heard the echoes of its epic in winds off the prairies, in creaking rumbles of freight-trains; the haven of derelicts, weaving in and out the swinging doors of..."[3]

Mary Synon's feeling for the power of sounds which through this one medium can describe an old neighborhood and its period of old landmarks is recalled later on in this book in Chapter Six: The Sights and Sounds, as are the sounds of New Year's Eve.

There were also descriptions of the (Cook) County Hospital area:

"...and the odor of iodoform, pouring over the neighborhood from the hospital chimneys..."[4]

"The crowds clanged in the treble, long processions passing, Indian file, Sunday after Sunday, to visiting hours at the County Hospital; the shadowy mob in the old baseball park down the street, faces uplighted under flaring gasoline torches at that ghastly October twilight..."[5]

"Over the river, beyond massed lines of fortressed factories, past lodging houses and thieves' market, lies a neighborhood, almost under the hulk of the huge hospitals, where once dwelt men and women whose faith and courage laid the foundations for a city that is. North and south through it runs the boulevard where old houses of bankers, senators, of judges and railroad builders hold now meeting rooms of the nation's organized toilers... Bisecting it, Harrison Street is a gray thoroughfare, its sagging sidewalks worn by the feet of tramping thousands on weary pilgrimages to the County Hospital, a dismal road to Jericho; but we who dwelt upon it in a time not so long ago knew it for more than its outward seeming.
"We know it for a street where children played and sang; where fathers brought home at the end of the day glimpses of the world at work; where mothers sewed, and mended - and baked and wove golden hopes for boys and girls; where old women sat at windows, and old men gossiped on the curbstones; where butcher, and grocer, and druggist, and doctor knew us all; where friendships were built, and sometimes broken; where beggars were fed; where lessons were lived and dreams born; where life was being painted on a canvas bigger than we who

[3]Ibid., p. 135.

[4]Ibid., p. 65.

[5]Ibid., p. 81.

were of its painters knew; where love, and hate, and joy, and sorrow stood in the wings; where youth had its fling; where some of us fought and failed, and others of us fought and won; where happiness came, and grief; and birth came, and death."[6]

"If life shall give us nothing else we have, at least, this knowledge for our pride: that we, the children of the good red bricks, have built our greater city."[7]

---

[6]Ibid., Prelude, p. viii.

[7]Ibid., Prelude, p. ix.

FINLEY PETER DUNNE

"There's a man that's known to all, a name of great renown,
   A man whose name is on the lips of everyone in town;
You read about him every day, you've heard his name, no doubt,
   And if he even sneezes they get the extras out.

For Mr. Dooley, for Mr. Dooley
   The greatest man the country ever knew,
Quite diplomatic and democratic
   Is Mr. Dooley - ooley-ooley-ooo."

Before my school days, I lustily piped the Dooley Song along with my sisters' college set whenever they gathered for a sing. The words were from the musical comedy, The Chinese Honeymoon in 1902.

"Mr. Dooley" was truly the man of the hour and appealed to all readers, especially students. The collegians, true to their alert and sympathetic interest in those who speak out on timely issues, worshipped this dart thrower.

Two schools, Scammon and West Division High School, shared a claim on this favorite pupil. Finley Peter Dunne, alias Mr. Dooley in later years, was born July 10, 1867 on Adams Street near Desplaines, across from St. Patrick's Church.

Young Peter was one of a large family, two of whom, Amelia and Charlotte, would influence his receptive years; other family members died young, as was the youthful mortality trend in that period, especially among immigrant families.

Amelia Dunne Hookaway, the eldest, would become a teacher and principal, distinguished in teaching children's dramatics and citizenship. Amelia Dunne Hookaway public school on south La Salle Street was named in her honor in 1928.[1] Charlotte, the youngest, was the mother-like sister, since the mother had died early in life; she kept a record of her brother's letters and acclamations.

Peter Dunne graduated in 1880 from Scammon School where Ella Flagg Young had been principal during his earlier grades. At West Division High School Peter was not an attentive student; he disliked Latin, mathematics and book sciences; he relished English and theme writing; this latter was already bristling with arguments. He wrote for the school paper, later to be known as the Voice; the editors thought some of Dunne's characterizations of teachers and students were libelous.

Peter with his friend, Arthur Pattison, published a hand-written paper, The Missionary, during one year for special readers. Besides school gossip, it contained serious political articles

[1]Chicago Board of Education Library.

which reflected Peter's father's ideas.[2] In the Irving Society, the literary organization originally formed in 1857 at Chicago High School, Peter let off some of his argumentive steam in debates. He graduated from West Division in 1884 and straightaway, at seventeen, headed for a journalist's career bereft of any further academic study.

He had been a constant reader of the classics since early childhood. Also, he had been an observer among his Irish neighbors - of saloons to storekeepers, fire departments, the courts, the adjoining Chicago River section as well as the downtown business quarter. At home his vociferous father and intellectual sisters all contributed to his evolving profession.

In June 1884 Peter became office boy for the Telegram until it was discovered he could write. A few months later his paper was the evening News, made famous by Melville Stone and Victor Lawson. Here Peter learned the rudiments of editorials as well as meeting top journalists. Continuing to climb, he joined the Chicago Times in 1888; by 1890, using a more distinguished name, Finley Peter Dunne, he became Sunday editor and a general reporter for the Chicago Tribune. A year later he joined the Herald where he knew many of the reporters and by 1892 he was editor of the Evening Post, owned by the Herald.[3]

It was in the Evening Post that Dunne started his Irish humor in editorials; here real events and persons, some with assumed names, were described in a conversational effect using Irish brogue. Such statements were often attributed to James McGarry who kept a public house near the Tribune office.[4] Dunne knew McGarry well, having been a patron of his bar since early journalism days. In the evolving Irish essays, James McGarry became Colonel McNeery, a saloon keeper who was Dunne's mouthpiece on a wide range of subjects. However, with the acclaim these articles were drawing with Colonel McNeery's wisdom, James McGarry felt personally ridiculed and told Dunne: "You can't put printer's ink on me with impunity."[5]

The anonymous Finley Peter Dunne immediately changed the locale from a Dearborn Street saloon to one on Archer Avenue; Colonel McNeery became Mr. Dooley. Then and there Archery Street and Mr. Dooley became the habitat and voice that would become know in Chicago and around the world for twenty years with the most human and humorous exploits of mankind.

Archer Avenue was situated in old Bridgeport, crossing south Halsted Street. The region had a large Irish population; "shanty Irish" because they lived in small houses and had vegetable gardens raising plenty of potatoes. The early stock yards and meat packing industry was centered in Bridgeport.

---

[2]Ellis, Elmer, Mr. Dooley's America: A Life of Finley Peter Dunne, Alfred A. Knopf, New York, 1941, pp. 113-114.

[3]Ibid., pp. 16-46.

[4]Ibid., p. 66.

[5]Ibid., p. 75.

It was also here that Tad Lincoln in 1866, as a very young journalist at Brown School with his Brown School Holiday Budget, had found Bridgeport news colorful and odorous with its neighboring Illinois (Drainage) Canal and the stock yards.

Finley Peter Dunne's friends were now mostly members of the Whitechapel Club, where complete freedom of expression existed and sometimes was rough on certain members. The club was made up of writers, reporters and cartoonists while their club room resembled a college fraternity den. Among the members were Eugene Field, John T. McCutcheon, Ralph F. Seymour, Brand Whitlock, Theodore Dreiser and George Ade. The latter described Dunne as having "scathing contempt for the self-seeking political bosses and the stuffed shirts of the millionaire aristocracy of their town."[6]

The awareness that Mr. Dooley expressed for the down-trodden poor, especially children, sums up some of Dunne's philosophy which echoed in the mutual thoughts of millions of his readers and was acknowledged in the pathos of a tear or the chuckle of a laugh.

By 1897 the old Chicago Journal was under new ownership and Dunne became the managing editor of this Journal. The Dooley essays were attracting nationwide attention, especially with the essay on Admiral Dewey's destruction of the Spanish fleet at Manilla. Also, Dunne's collected works appeared in Mr. Dooley in Peace and War. This was followed by Mr. Dooley in the Hearts of His Countrymen and Mr. Dooley's Philosophy.

After a climax of European travel, book publications and international fame, Finley Peter Dunne moved to New York in 1900, where he became editor of the Morning Telegraph, followed by becoming part owner and editor of American Magazine and later editor of Collier's Weekly in 1912.

The Dooley essays continued in many periodicals. While Chicago was where Mr. Dooley was born and Archery Street his home, the conversations were now addressed to a national audience; Chicago citizens and problems were replaced with national personalities and headlines such as war, woman suffrage and prohibition. Yet, throughout the years with over 700 dialect essays, one common theme remained, the common man. Dunne has been compared to Mark Twain and Will Rogers in their respect for the common man as well as in their greatness as sympathetic humorists.

Finley Peter Dunne died in New York City April 24, 1936; Chicago mourned for this son. On "Scribes Day," May 29, the Chicago City Council paid tribute to literary men and especially to Dunne; St. Bridget's Catholic Church on Archer Avenue celebrated a memorial mass; students from St. Patrick's School laid a wreath on the site of Dunne's birth place on Adams Street while a wreath was placed on the old West Division High School building by the Old Time Printers Association.[7]

Two quotes from Mr. Dooley are quite appropriate for this book:

---

[6]Adams, Franklin P., "Mr. Dooley," The New Republic, May 4, 1938, p. 391.

[7]Ellis, p. 286.

"The' further ye get away fr'm anny peeryod (history), th' better ye can write about it - Ye aren't subject to interruptions be people that were there."[8]

"D'ye think the colledges has much to do with the progress ie the wurrled?" asked Mr. Hennessey.

"Do ye think," said Mr. Dooley, "'tis th' mill that makes th' wather run?"[9]

---

[8]Ellis, p. 309; can also be found in: Dunne, Finley Peter, Mr. Dooley Remembers, Little, Brown, Boston, 1963, p. 307.

[9]Dunne, Finley Peter, Mr. Dooley's Opinions, Harper & Brothers Publishers, New York & London, 1906, "College and Degrees," p. 204.

20. Findley Peter Dunne (1867-1936). Courtesy of Chicago History Museum.

CHAPTER THREE: THE EARLY MEDICAL CENTER AND MEMBER ORGANIZATIONS

THE EARLY MEDICAL CENTER

The old medical district referred to as the "hospital section" or "Latin Quarter" by students and neighbors in 1900 was already a heavily concentrated part of Chicago's west side. At that period, the medical buildings with related professional and commercial establishments were located within an area roughly circumscribed by Congress, Ashland, Polk and Lincoln Streets. This compares to about one sixth of the area designated today for Illinois Medical Center.

Here were the Cook County Hospital complex, the Frances E. Willard Temperance Hospital and the Presbyterian Hospital. Also located here were Rush Medical College, the University of Illinois College of Physicians and Surgeons, its College of Dentistry, and the Illinois Training School for Nurses. Continuing were Chicago Medical School, Chicago College of Dental Surgery, Woman's Medical College, Chicago Homeopathic College and McCormick Institute of Infectious Diseases; as well as West Division High School and Marquette Grammar School - all were merged in a dense traffic of human activities. There was continual building of additions and interchange of older structures as new institutions joined the district.

The Victorian period of two theories of medicine, the allopathic and homeopathic, was coming to an end, while the recognition of the osteopathic would be the next encounter for the traditional medical profession.

Then as today, there were clustering, small, semi-medical institutions as Dr. L. Lindlahr's Sanitarium on Ashland Boulevard and Harrison, which in 1905 advocated "Nature Cure and Osteopathy." Dr. Clement Weirick, who received his medical degree in 1880 from Chicago Homeopathic College, was an early fighter with his clinic for narcotics victims who were a problem then as now. On Madison and Ogden was the Washingtonian Home (for alcoholics). It was organized in 1863 by Robert A. Law and members of the Independent Order of Good Templars, a temperance organization. In 1874, the wooden building used for this men's home, formerly the Bull's Head Tavern, was replaced with a brick structure. In 1920, the hospital for both men and women was merged in the hospital at Irving Park and Western and became known as the Martha Washington Hospital.

Scattered about the medical district were extraneous signs posted on empty-looking buildings which read, "Physical Culture Studio," "Swedish Massage," "Chiropractor - Spinal Adjustment," even a "Madame X - Palmistry." All these, presumably, were to catch the eye of the patient on his way to one of the dispensaries or clinics.

At this period, there were inferior medical schools or pseudo-medical schools, termed "Diploma Mills" in Chicago and elsewhere. Abraham Flexner, under the Carnegie Foundation for the Advancement of Teaching and the American Medical Association, made a nation-wide inspection and report of all medical schools.[1] In his report, the Chicago region was called "the plague spot of the country."[2]

Chicago's medical schools were not alone in their deficiencies; less than one third of the nation's medical schools were integral parts of universities. Private schools with third rate faculties and inadequate laboratory and hospital facilities made up the bulk of American medical colleges.[3]

Among the changing institutions in the old medical center was the Chicago Homeopathic College at York and Wood Streets which in 1905 reunited with the Hahnemann Medical College on the south side. This original school, functioning as early as Civil War days, was named after Dr. Samuel Hahnemann (1755-1843) of Germany. His theory was that symptoms of a disease were relieved by drugs which produced similar pathological symptoms in the human body and that these drugs were more powerful if given in minute doses.

In 1876 some of the faculty, headed by Dr. Nicholas Delemater, seceded and founded the west side college - the reasons being "to elevate standards and introduce a broader training in the basic medical studies."[4] Homeopathy was introduced into Cook County Hospital which conflicted with the allopathic system practiced there.

There were outstanding homeopathic physicians, as Doctors Davis S. Smith and George E. Shipman, founder of Foundlings Home and our own family doctor, E. C. Sweet of Monroe Street.

As a small child, I recall him dissolving one pin-head sized white pill in each of two full glasses of water, each with its saucer and spoon for a specified dosage. I surreptitiously took a generous taste of both potions and found them tasteless and most disappointing, as well as having no discernable after effects. One reason for the popularity of homeopathic medicine was due to Hahnemann's theory of reduced dosage, which earlier had been given in almost lethal amounts.

By 1922, homeopathy became an obsolete theory of medicine, just one of many, as men have searched through trial and error to heal mankind. In this period of great medical advancement,

[1]Arey, Leslie B., Northwestern University Medical School, 1859-1959: A Pioneer in Educational Reform, Northwestern University, Chicago and Evanston, IL, 1959, p. 211.

[2]Flexner, Abraham, "Medical Education in the United States and Canada: A Report to the Carnegie Foundation for the Advancement of Teaching," Bulletin Number Four, The Carnegie Foundation for the Advancement of Teaching, New York, New York, 1910, p. 216; also in Bonner, p. 109.

[3]Bonner, Thomas Neville, Medicine in Chicago, 1850-1950, The American History Research Center, Inc., Madison, Wisconsin, 1957, p. 115.

[4]Bonner, Thomas Neville, Medicine in Chicago, 1850-1950, The American History Research Center, Inc., Madison, Wisconsin, 1957, p. 63. Permission University of Illinois Press, 1325 S. Oak St., Champaign, IL 61820, publishers of the 2nd Edition in 1991..

as well as the relinquishment of out-dated medical theories, <u>Mr. Dooley</u>, West Division High School's hero, spoke out:

> "Father Kelley says th' styles in medicine changes like the styles in hats... He says that if they (doctors) knew less about pizen and more about gruel an' opened fewer patients and more windows, they'd not be so many Christyan Scientists. He says th' diff'rence between Christyan Scientists an' doctors is that Christyan Scientists thinks they'se no such thing as disease an' doctors thinks there ain't anything else. An' there ye ar're."[5]

In sensing the changes taking place in the old medical center in the early twentieth century, it is even more amazing to the lay reader to learn what constituted medical practice at the time when Rush Medical College and the City of Chicago received their charters from the State of Illinois' legislature in 1837. It is, also, humbly gratifying to learn what medical changes and discoveries were made later in the nineteenth century.

At the beginning of the nineteenth century, as well as centuries before, limited surgery and bone setting were performed using alcoholic intoxication, opium or hypnotism to dull the pain. By 1846 ether and chloroform had been discovered and these made internal and difficult surgery possible. Nitrous oxide had been found practical for dental extractions in 1844. It was Oliver Wendell Holmes (1809-1894), physician as well as author, who termed this "death of pain" anesthesia.

In the earlier centuries of medicine, the three mainstays of the medical practitioner were bleeding, emetics and purging. Today, the principle of withdrawing blood as a curative process seems as ridiculous as primitive man's belief that the blood letting released or exorcised the evil spirits from the body. The process of arterial bleeding was a controversial subject as to what was removed or how the patient was relieved. Moliere (1622-1673) wisely wrote in his <u>Le Malade Imaginaire</u>:

> "Nearly all men die of their remedies and not of their illnesses."

The bleeding process was as much of a ceremony as a technic, with special porringers or ornate bleeding glasses. Our first president, George Washington, probably was hastened to his death in 1799 by two consecutive blood lettings, which even a virile athlete would find debilitating today.

---

[5]Booth, E. R., <u>History of Osteopathy and Twentieth Century Medical Practice</u>, Quoted in Memorial Edition, The Caxton Press, Cincinnati, IL, 1924 (previously printed in 1905), p. 214.

Cryptic notations found in a prescription book at Fort Dearborn cited: ""Bled"; "Blister"; "Calomel xx gr.""[6] Besides Calomel, other common medicines were quinine, jalap (purgative) and opium. An echo from the Calomel age is an anonymous verse written in 1850:

"How'er their patients may complain,
Of head or heart, or nerve or vein,
Of fever high, or parch or swell,
The remedy is Calomel."

By the 1850's, leeches had been substituted for arterial bleeding; both seemed equally repulsive to the victim, fifty sucking leeches or fifty spurts of blood. These "worms" were sold in drug stores. For the modern generation, there is (or was recently) a thriving nest of these blood-thirsty creatures in a glass container on exhibit at Disneyland's "Old Drug Store."

Before the end of the nineteenth century, medical science had discarded such blood-theories and hematology had become a true science of the blood. The old theory was to be completely reversed; transfusions of whole blood or its plasma were given to help the patient recover.

Another less sensational revolution had started earlier in European medical centers and would thrive in America during the last half of the nineteenth century; this was the rise of eclectic medicine. Many doctors were prescribing less poisonous medicines. Some of these physicians would be termed "botanical" because they prescribed mild vegetable substances in place of poisonous drugs.

Housewives and gardeners have grown herbs for centuries; these simple and benign plants have demonstrated healing properties and probably did save lives which otherwise might have been bled, blistered or purged to death.

Because of the overwhelming increase of population in our large cities, especially of immigrant families living in poverty and showing malnutrition, scientists in the late nineteen hundreds began a study of foods to determine what essential elements were lacking in the diets of these citizens. The knowledge was evolving of chemical substances which later would be called vitamins by Casimir Funk in 1912. For a simpler identification of their long, technical names, they would be designated as vitamins A, B, C, D, E, and K. Here was some vindication for the botanical insisters who really dated pretty far back with the "Vittels and drink" and "An apple a day keeps the doctor away" - as well as those who were for laissez-faire: "Let nature take its course."

The late eighteenth century and all of the nineteenth century were in a period of great awakening for consideration of the welfare of man, his health, economy and happiness. The search was world-wide. The practice of medicine would branch out into many sciences - bacteriology, radiology, biology, chemistry, physics, psychology, physiology, pathology - the list is long. The newcomer, bacteriology, was the most spectacular since it was performing miracles with vaccines, antitoxins and various immunizing therapeutics arising from the knowledge gained in the specific identification of bacterially caused diseases. The other new

---

[6]Bonner, p. 11.

science, radiology, the use of roentgen rays or X-rays for diagnosis and the radioactive isotope for medical therapy, was still under much experimentation until the twentieth century.

Our physicians, surgeons and technical specialists who came out of the old medical center on Chicago's west side, or any of the great centers throughout the world, became indebted to many earlier as well as contemporary scientists who continually were widening the field for humanitarian studies and improvements.

Some of these names have become household words; the encyclopedia will give a quick, kernel history of them. In chronological order they are: Edward Jenner, 1749-1823; Charles Darwin, 1809-1882; Gregor Mendel, 1822-1884; Louis Pasteur, 1822-1895; Thomas Huxley, 1825-1895; Joseph Lister, 1827-1912; Robert Koch, 1843-1910; Wilhelm Roentgen, 1843-1923 and Sigmund Freud, 1856-1939.

Fraternities and sororities at the end of the nineteenth century were a rapidly expanding national adventure. They are classed as honorary, professional and social. These organizations have been censored as being undemocratic, sophisticated, discriminatory to race, color, creed and wealth, as well as causing unhappiness to ambitious students who were not selected. All these reasons have been valid on many college campuses. Honorary societies have remained exempt from most criticisms, and professional associations, such as law, medical or engineering, have been altruistic in their memberships. Their purpose is of a semi-social nature with the common bond of interest, professional studies or practice.

In the medical schools these men, past early collegiate years, were living on fixed and often meager incomes and coming from distant regions. They were needing a common meeting place to relax with their fellow students, as well as having comfortable beds and regular meals. Medical fraternities became a happy solution as many chapters of national organizations were formed in the Mile Square of the west side. Among the early chapters were those of Phi Rho Sigma, Nu Sigma Nu, Phi Beta Pi, Phi Delta Epsilon and Alpha Kappa Kappa.

Whenever a large desirable house was vacated by its owner because of death or moving to the suburbs, it was purchased, but more often rented, by a medical fraternity chapter. The quieter streets as Monroe, Adams, Jackson and Ashland were preferred because hospital congestion, even odor, was more removed. The hospitals at that period reeked with phenol, used as a disinfectant, and chloroform or ether from the operating rooms. When our neighbors, the Forbes family, moved away, their gracious fourteen room house became a chapter house identified by its Greek insignia on the front door. These medics were serious students with little free time, yet they were neighborly and all known by sight, if not by name.

The Presbyterian Hospital Training School for Nurses had their dormitory on Ashland and Congress; the Illinois Training School for Nurses was at 304 Honore Street. The women medical students found their refuge under the roof of Frances E. Willard Hospital or Mary Thompson Hospital.

The old Medical Center area is nostalgically described by Mary Synon in The Good Red Bricks. This writer had once known this region when she wrote:

> "April, coming to the West Side with spring song of hurdy-gurdys, with circus parade, with returning baseball players, with clattering hoof beats on the boulevard asphalt, and the long rows of pale men in wheel chairs on the sunlit

side of the County Hospital, brought with it wedges of wild geese the last herald of conflict."[7]

While with the coming of autumn the picture was not too changed:

"Other crowds clanged in the treble, long processions passing, Indian file, Sunday after Sunday, to visiting hours at the County Hospital; the shadowy mob in the old baseball park down the street, faces uplifted under flaring gasoline torches at that ghostly October twilight..."[8]

The Chicago Cubs' old baseball park was almost as well known in Chicago as the Medical Center; both were busy places but each with a different mission.

Just about the time that Dr. Daniel Brainard and his Rush Medical College were emerging in 1838 and Chicago was becoming a city with a chapter, so in Cooperstown, New York, Abner Doubleday was organizing the game of baseball. He laid out the rules which are essentially the same today as then. He later became a Union General in the Civil War; baseball became a popular recreation for the soldiers.

In Chicago the game caught on early in the vacant lots. One of the first baseball parks was located at Congress, Harrison, Throop and Loomis Streets, and was known as the West Side Park. Later, the open area where the present University of Illinois Colleges of Medicine, Dentistry and Pharmacy now stand was the Cubs Ball Park. These ten acres were bounded by Lincoln (Wolcott), Wood, Polk and Taylor Streets and was used for League games until World War I when the Medical Center began to expand. The Chicago Cubs found a new home at Wrigley Field at Addison and Clark Streets.

---

[7]Mary Synon, <u>The Good Red Bricks</u>, Little, Brown & Co., Boston, 1929, p. 184.

[8]Ibid., p. 82.

The Presbyterian Hospital Training School for Nurses.   Congress and Ashland Blvd.

21. Top: Illinois Training School for Nurses, circa 1900. Courtesy Chicago History Museum.
Bottom: Presbyterian Hospital Training Center for Nurses at Congress and Ashland Boulevards.
Source of photograph is not known to Editor.

22. Baseball Game, West Side Ball Grounds. The photograph shows the Cook County Hospital Chimney in the distance. The ballpark was located at Polk and Wolcott (Lincoln Street) Avenues prior to 1916. The photograph was reproduced from a post card circa 1909. Courtesy Ridgemoor Archives, Graphic Historical Collection, 4316 Meade Ave, Chicago, Illinois 60634.

THE UNIVERSITY OF ILLINOIS AT THE EARLY MEDICAL CENTER

Many of the early medical schools in Chicago began their pioneering stages in developed areas; their transfer to the west side took place after the Great Fire of 1871.

The University of Illinois had its beginnings of medical education with the Chicago College of Pharmacy organized in 1859 in downtown Chicago. Its first permanent building was at 465 State Street in 1884. In May 1896 it became the University of Illinois, School of Pharmacy. After several locations, the final move was made in 1915 when the University purchased the property on South Wood Street, formerly occupied by the Chicago Homeopathic College.

In the meantime pharmaceutical standards for both admission and academic courses were rising with the trends in all medical practices. By 1932 the name of the school was changed to College of Pharmacy which offered a Bachelor of Science degree in Pharmacy. In the next twenty years Master's and Doctor's degrees in Pharmacy would follow, while splendid new buildings would replace the earlier outgrown structures.

In 1881 the College of Physicians and Surgeons was incorporated, the parent of the present College of Medicine of the University of Illinois. The college was founded by five practicing physicians: A. Reeves Jackson, S. A. Williams, D. A. K. Steele, Leonard St. John and D. Warrington Earle. These men furnished the money to build a four story stone structure, modern in every detail, at the corner of Harrison and Honore Streets. Since this was a proprietary school, faculty members bought shares in this corporation. The college opened with 165 students and 21 faculty members. Dr. William E. Quine joined the faculty, becoming its president, and later, Dean of the College.

In 1893 the College erected the first laboratory building in Chicago for training medical students. In 1896 the old Post Graduate Medical School and Hospital nearby was purchased. On April 21, 1897 the College of Physicians and Surgeons became affiliated with the University of Illinois.

The expanding College next purchased the West Division High School in 1900 and a year later acquired the Illinois College of Dentistry; it was housed in the original College of Physicians and Surgeons building. The University Hospital was then built, which added 100 beds for clinical instruction. By 1902 the enrollment was over 700 students with a graduating class of 200.

However, the next ten years were lean ones, since the College received no state support, and had only the prestige of being part of the University of Illinois. By 1912 this relationship came to an end; the College re-opened as the old College of Physicians and Surgeons. This pleased no one; the alumni, the faculty and others secured every share of the original corporation stock and gave it all to the University of Illinois. State support was then assured; the scholastic admission requirements were increased; the title was changed to the University of Illinois College of Medicine. With state support, the old Department of Public Welfare and the University began a series of hospitals for the use of the College for its teaching and research.

The third college to become part of the University of Illinois was the College of Dentistry. Its history dates back to 1892, when it was known as Columbian Dental College until 1898; then it emerged as Illinois Dental College in the Chicago Loop. Next, it affiliated with the College of Physicians and Surgeons in 1901; when this College suffered from lack of funds in 1912, they sold this school of dentistry.

Again the faculty and alumni persuaded the University of Illinois of the necessity for dental education. The College of Dentistry was re-opened in October 1913, and moved back to the same quarters in the building at Harrison and Honore Streets, where it remained for the next twenty-five years. In the meantime, it was continually updating and growing, with advanced degrees being offered. By 1937 the College of Dentistry moved into spacious new quarters on Polk and Wood Streets.

An echo is heard in a solicited advertisement by the editors of Lewis Institute's Annual for 1904 to help defray costs of its printing:

> "The College of Physicians and Surgeons is situated in the heart of one of the greatest medical centers in the world; it offers clinical advantages to students which are unexcelled."

In 1905 the Illinois College of Dentistry had an advertisement in the Annual which read:

> "Located on the West Side, in the center of the greatest medical and dental community on earth. Honore and Harrison."

23. University of Illinois College of Physicians and Surgeons, Congress and Honore Streets. An earlier incarnation of the building was as West Division High School. Courtesy Chicago Medical Book Company, 7400 North Melvina, Chicago, Illinois 60648.

COOK COUNTY HOSPITAL

Chicago's old City Hospital and Dispensary dating back to 1837 served as a general charity hospital and was helped by private agencies such as Mercy Hospital and Rush Medical College faculty and students. It was located at 18th and La Salle Streets and in 1865 became known as Cook County Hospital under a Board of Supervisors with Rush Medical College and Chicago Medical College representatives and doctors without connections serving the institution.

In 1874 the County purchased a site on the west side bounded by Wood, Harrison, Lincoln and Polk Streets. Here, two central pavilions were built in 1876, and by 1881 the Illinois Training School for Nurses served the hospital. The medical staff continued to be supplied by the medical colleges and non-collegiate physicians chosen by the supervisors.

By the turn of the century in Cook County Hospital a visiting physician might be able to see more cases of diabetes, cancer or meningitis in one day than in a life time of practice in his home town. This was partly because of the coming of Christian Fenger, a Danish surgeon and pathologist, to Cook County Hospital in 1878. He is credited with having had the greatest influence on the development of surgery and general practice in Chicago.

Christian Fenger had an excellent medical training in Europe and experience in both the Danish-Prussian and Franco-Prussian Wars as well as having served on the Egyptian national board of health. At County Hospital Fenger's surgical skill attracted many promising surgeons and medical practitioners to study his surgical diagnoses and pathological methods. Among his students were John B. Murphy, William Mayo, Ludvig Hektoen, E. R. Le Count, H. G. Wells, James B. Herrick and Frank Billings.

Christian Fenger was a hard worker, carefully reviewing each step he would follow in surgery. He pioneered in Chicago the use of rubber gloves and changing from street clothes and shoes to special clothing in the hospital.[1] His personality showing friendliness, humility and integrity made him a beloved and revered person. Dr. Buford wrote of him:

"Christian Fenger was the greatest man I have ever known. He possessed so many admirable qualities that I am sorry every medical man of his time did not come to know him well, for a slight acquaintance was likely to create an erroneous impression of him."[2]

He was gruff and had a speech impediment.

---

[1] Christian Fenger and B. Holmes, "Antisepsis in Abdominal Operations, a synopsis of a series of bacteriological studies," Journal of American Medical Association, Chicago, Oct. 1, 1887, No. 9, pp. 444-470.

[2] Coleman C. Buford, "Christian Fenger: A Biographical Sketch," Bulletin of Society of Medical History in Chicago, March, 1913, pp. 196-202.

His student, John B. Murphy, became a world famous surgeon; William J. Mayo called him "the surgical genius of our generation." His surgical miracles were even greater than Christain Fenger's. Murphy was, however, egotistical and enjoyed his professional audiences as well as feeling no obligation to perform charitable service. In spite of these personal eccentricities, his professional record placed him among the greatest surgeons of all times.

Frank Billings, another student of Fenger, would become a builder of medical institutions, as well as serving the rich and poor alike. He helped build Northwestern University's Wesley Hospital; worked for the expansion of Rush Medical College and Presbyterian Hospital. Later, under William Rainey Harper, he created the University of Chicago's South Side medical campus. His contemporary, James B. Herrick, said of him:

"...the biggest, best balanced all round doctor we have ever known."[3]

There were other epoch making physicians and surgeons who contributed to County Hospital and other medical institutions in the old medical center. Among them was Nicholas Senn, who independently of Christian Fenger, saw the coming promise of clinical microscopy, animal experimentation and antisepsis.[4] Bertram W. Sippy, a specialist in gastro-intestinal disease is still recalled today in the Sippy tube for stomach exploration. James B. Herrick, who once lived in the old Mile Square and who studied at Rush and interned at County Hospital, left his mark with his research and practice in cardiology.

There was, however, dissension between the medical staff and the supervisors or the Board of County Commissioners, as they were to become known. A new board of medical practitioners was formed which included homeopathic physicians. Medical colleges had no official representation on the County Hospital staff. Professional unrest would continue for the next twenty-three years. By 1905 the Board of Commissioners placed appointments with their tenures to the staff on a civil service basis. Internships were for specified periods and filled through competitive examinations. Medical schools acquired representation; medical care for patients improved and the hospital became a teaching hospital.

By 1912 it was necessary to replace older buildings and enlarge the hospital; in 1916 over $3,000,000 were spent on new structures, increasing the number of beds to 2,700. By the 1950's Cook County Hospital complex had 3,400 beds. These would be included in the following hospitals: General, Men's, Children's, Psychopathic, Contagious Diseases and Tuberculosis Hospital. Other buildings added during that period were: Radiation Center, Fantus Out-Patient Clinic, School of Nursing, Karl A. Meyer Hall, Hektoen Institute and Cook County Graduate School of Medicine, as well as a morgue, main power plant and laundry.

---

[3]James B. Herrick, "Frank Billings," Bulletin of the Alumni Association of Rush Medical College, Aug. 1924, pp. 12-18. Permission Rush University Medical Center, Chicago, Illinois.

[4]O. J. Ochner, "Nicholas Senn, the Surgeon," Bulletin of the Alumni Association of Rush Medical College, Feb. 1908, pp. 4-13.

Unfortunately, Cook County Hospital, in its earlier history and less so through the later years, has been saddled by political influences. In spite of such, this hospital has become one of the largest general hospitals in the world and the largest for acute diseases in the United States.

Two early departments of Cook County Hospital should be described: The Hektoen Institute and the Cook County Graduate School of Medicine. The first named began as the John McCormick Institute of Infectious Diseases, founded by Harold and Edith McCormick in 1902 as a memorial to their son who died from scarlet fever.

The director was Dr. Ludwig Hektoen and the Institute was at 229 S. Hermitage. Interest was burgeoning in the study of bacterial and virus caused diseases. Dr. Hektoen trained many laboratory technicians in the new fields of blood typing, isolation of bacteria, the practice of immunization and early efforts in cancer study. Two workers, Doctors George and Gladys Dick, are best known for their researches on scarlet fever, its prevention, recognition and active treatment.

By 1941 the bankrupt Institute affiliated with Cook County Hospital as the Hektoen Institute of Medical Research, and in a new building, continues its dramatic battle with many diseases such as leukemia, pernicious anemia and cancer.

The second thriving department is the Cook County Graduate School of Medicine, one of the first such schools in the United States. It was founded in 1932 by Drs. Karl A. Meyer and Raymond McNealy. It is non-profit; the faculty are all from the hospital staff; the courses offered vary in length, from a few days or weeks, to a month's intensive study. The General Hospital of over 2,750 beds serves the graduate school with

> "the vast facilities and materials for intensive and practical continuing education in medicine, surgery and the specialties."[5]

Some of the divisions are: Gynecology and Obstetrics, Radiology, Anesthesiology, Orthopedic Surgery, Pathology, Internal Medicine, General Surgery, General Practice and Neuromuscular Diseases of Children. From this listing the lay reader glimpses the extensive knowledge and technics our medical scientists have reached; it is so in most arts and sciences. The wonder of it is that most all of these accomplishments of modern medicine have occurred in the life span of many persons living today - Dr. Karl A. Meyer witnessed most all of them during his half century at Cook County Hospital.

The original Illinois Training School for Nurses was organized in 1880 with such far seeing women as Sara Peck, Mrs. Charles Lawrence, Dr. Sarah H. Stevenson and Lucy L. Flower. This school worked under arrangement of the County Commissioners at County Hospital but had its own system of nursing which spread to fifty-four schools of nursing in the middle west over a period of fifty years.

In 1929 the school as it was originally known merged with the University of Chicago. The Board of Cook County Commissioners arranged to inaugurate its own Cook County Hospital School of Nursing, using the old facilities and faculties.

---

[5]"Cook County Graduate School of Medicine Incorporated Not For Profit Division of Pathology," Cook County Graduate School of Medicine, 707 South Wood Street, Chicago, IL 60612, 1969, p. 1, leaflet.

151

24. Cook County Hospital, looking south from Nurses Training School. Courtesy Chicago History Museum.

25. Horse Drawn Ambulance appeared in Centennial Issue of the University of Illinois at the Medical Center. Copy of print at University of Illinois, Illustration Studios; the negative #54-152 is in possession of the Armed Forces Medical Library, Washington, D.C. Courtesy of State of Illinois Medical Center Commission, 736 South Ashland Avenue, Chicago, Illinois, 60607.

26. Christian Fenger (1840-1902). Engraving by Henry Taylor, Jr., Chicago. Courtesy Chicago History Museum.

27. Nicholas Senn (1844-1908). Engraving by Henry Taylor, Jr., published by Beers & Co., Chicago. Courtesy Chicago History Museum.

RUSH MEDICAL COLLEGE

Rush Medical College is a landmark and the mother-institution for the old medical center; it was founded by Dr. Daniel Brainard in 1837, the first school for medical education in the State of Illinois. Rush was named after Benjamin Rush, the Revolutionary physician-patriot who was called the "Father of American Medicine."

Dr. Daniel Brainard, a graduate of Jefferson Medical College, came from New York to Chicago's frontier country, sensing the opportunities that were possible there. Judge Caton, a pioneer Chicago lawyer wrote in a letter:

> "Dr. Brainard rode up to my office on a little Indian pony... and asked my advice about commencing the practice of medicine in Chicago. I knew he was ambitious, studious and a man of ability and I advised him to go to the Potowatomi Camp, where the Indians were preparing to start for a new location west of the Mississippi River and sell his pony, take... a small table I had in my office and put his shingle by the side of the door, promising to aid him in building up a business."[1]

In 1837, Rush Medical College was conducted in a shed attached to Dr. Brainard's house where he was teaching anatomy and surgery to a few private students. By 1844, a permanent building at Illinois and Dearborn Streets flourished with faculty from distant communities and Dr. James V. Z. Blaney, professor of chemistry and materia medica, who already resided in Chicago.

The first annual announcement in October, 1843, proclaimed in part:

> "The trustees have determined to lay the foundation of a medical school whose means of teaching shall be ample in all the different branches, which shall be permanent and adequate to the wants of the community, and which shall in all respects advance the interest and honor of the profession".[2]

Rush prospered in both quality and number of faculty and students. Dr. Brainard, as president and professor of surgery, died suddenly of cholera in October, 1866; Chicago was in the midst of a cholera epidemic. Dr. James V. Z. Blaney followed as president of Rush.

---

[1]Richter, M. D., Richard B., "A Short History of the Medical School at the University of Chicago," Medical Alumni Bulletin, University of Chicago Medical School, Chicago, IL, 1967, p. 4.

[2]Council of the Chicago Medical Society, History of Medicine and Surgery and Physicians and Surgeons of Chicago, 1803-1922, The Biographical Publishing Corporation, Chicago, IL, 1922, p. 191.

The Great Fire of 1871 burned the college building to the ground. The faculty and students were then tendered the use of Cook County Hospital's clinical amphitheatre and dissecting room in the new buildings at Wood, Harrison, Polk and Lincoln Streets. The trustees and faculty realized the importance of being adjacent to this hospital and accordingly built their new structure in 1875, diagonally opposite the County Hospital at Wood and Harrison Streets.

In the interim of the college's beginnings and continuous growth into the twentieth century, there were many changes, all for altruistic purposes. Like a lodestar, the early faculty helped organize and staff Chicago's hospitals as the Chicago Hospital (the first city general hospital), Illinois General Hospital of the Lake (now Mercy Hospital), the first U.S. Marine Hospital, Chicago Eye and Ear Infirmary, the first Cook County and Presbyterian Hospitals.

In 1859, several of the Rush faculty, led by Dr. Nathan Smith Davis, founded the Chicago Medical College which later became Northwestern University Medical School. Rush founded the medical education at Lake Forest College, University of Chicago School of Medicine and the University of Illinois College of Medicine.

Among the increasing departments of Rush, dentistry was recognized and several of the faculty established the Chicago Dental Infirmary in 1882; this later evolved as the Chicago College of Dental Surgery.

In 1891, when the University of Chicago was founded, President William Rainey Harper had plans

"for an institution of a more comprehensive and higher type than had previously existed in this country."[3]

This would include professional schools such as of medicine. By 1898, Rush Medical College became affiliated with the University with two years pre-clinical work on the south side campus and two years clinical at the west side. In 1924, Rush became part of the University with its having now two campuses and the intention of Rush becoming a post-graduate school. By 1942, the agreements between the two schools of medicine were terminated, since the University wished to have its own complete medical school on the south side and the wish of Rush to continue under-graduate training and give service to the west side community through the original agreement with Presbyterian Hospital.

The College facilities were returned to Rush trustees and leased to Presbyterian Hospital which had served as the affiliated teaching hospital for the College. In 1942, the Presbyterian Hospital entered an agreement with the University of Illinois College of Medicine to teach undergraduate students; the hospital staff were given academic appointments on the faculty of the University's medical school, as well as certain faculty members being designated as Rush professors.

Who were some of the faculty and alumni of Rush Medical College who over its century of history were part of the old medical center on the west side, or serving in neighboring Chicago institutions, as well as their good works reaching out all over the world?

[3]Ibid., p. 196.

Today such names are remembered in educational memorials, text books, theories, technics, treatments, and above all, in the knowledge and inspiration given to their professional progeny. Lucien Price wrote:

> "What else are our hospitals, colleges, museums, laboratories, libraries and a host of other memorial foundations than the souls of those long since dead in the flesh, living on in the spirit of beneficent action..."[4]

There were surgeons such as Christian Fenger, Nicholas Senn, John P. Murphy, Arthur Dean Bevan, Dean Lewis and Dallas Phemister; physicians, as Frank Billings, James B. Herrick, George Dick, Ernest Irons and Bertram W. Sippy; pathologists, Fletcher Ingals and Ludwig Hektoen. The frontiersmen should be included too: Daniel Brainard, James Blaney, William Byford, Nathan S. Davis and James P. Ross.

Among our own from Brown School were Dr. Carl B. Davis, who received his degree from Rush as well as later serving on its faculty - on the surgical staffs of Cook County and Presbyterian hospitals and clinical professor at the University of Illinois. Dr. Roger T. Vaughan received his degree from Rush in 1903 and was surgeon at St. Luke's Hospital and later Professor of Surgery at Cook County Graduate School in 1932. There was Dr. Josephine Estabrook Young who received her degree from Woman's Medical College in 1896 and became Associate Professor of Medicine, Pediatrics and Neurology at Rush. In later years, she served as Assistant Director of the Orthogenic School for Retarded Children which is now affiliated with the University of Illinois.

One of the most famous graduates from Rush was Dr. Evarts Ambrose Graham. His biography is recalled here as a tribute to these Chicago Schools - Brown Grammar School, Lewis Institute and to those colleges which nurtured him (Book One, Chapter One, Number Eight).

In 1969 the Rush Medical College charter was reactivated and the Rush-Presbyterian-St. Luke's Medical Center was formed by the merger of the college with Presbyterian-St. Luke's Hospital and Central Free Dispensary. This merger was brought about by the accelerating need for medical care in Chicago's and the nation's increasing population. Likewise the goal of the reactivated College is to revive the original Rush philosophies while educating young physicians of the highest calibre for the nation's need of more physicians.

To further assist this rebirth of Rush Medical College, the alumni formed the Benjamin Rush Society to aid in providing financial support for the College. This keystone of giving by alumni and friends assures the College a strong base on which to plan and develop its curriculum of medical education on levels from undergraduate through postgraduate training.

During Rush Medical College's first hundred years from 1837 to 1942, 10,976 alumni received their medical degrees. By 1970, having progressed through the cycles of living and dying, the ranks numbered 350; yet through their indefatigable spirit there will be new leaven for the next century.

---

[4]Price, Lucien, Litany For All Souls, The Beacon Press, Boston, MA, 1945, p. 77.

A review of some of the "firsts" coming out of "old" Rush Medical College, which today continue as great milestones in medical history, lists members of Rush faculty who performed the first operation west of the Alleghenies in which chloroform and ether were used as an anesthetic.

Original research in the laboratories and clinics included the first description of sickle-cell anemia, coronary heart disease, and anatomy of the inner ear. Preliminary studies to the "blue baby" operation were performed at Rush and the Dick test for scarlet fever was developed by a husband and wife team on the faculty. In 1923 a Rush professor of surgery performed the first operation using ethylene-oxygen which became a common anesthetic until the 1950's.

28. Rush Medical College. Courtesy Rush University Medical Center, Chicago, Illinois.

THE PRESBYTERIAN HOSPITAL

In 1883, eight years after Rush Medical College had established its new buildings on the west side, it was evident that another general hospital, besides Cook County, was needed. Half of Chicago's population lived on the west side. Dr. Joseph P. Ross of Rush was the leading spirit in the founding of Presbyterian Hospital, he realizing its great potential as a regional general hospital as well as a teaching hospital for the College.

A charter was granted in July 1883 for which the application had stated in part:

> "We, the undersigned, being citizens of the United States desiring to form a Society, not for pecuniary profit... The object of the Society (the Presbyterian Hospital of the City of Chicago) is the establishment, support and management for an institution for the purpose of affording surgical and medical aid and nursing to sick and disabled persons of every nationality, creed and color."[1]

An agreement was reached with the trustees and faculty of Rush by which the site and their hospital building on which $25,000 had been expended were deeded on January 2, 1884 to the Board of Managers of the Presbyterian Hospital. At that time, it was agreed that the hospital medical staff would be nominated by College faculty and this faculty would have charge of clinical instruction given in the hospital. This policy has continued in the years which have followed.

The first Presbyterian Hospital was the Ross Building in 1884 with a capacity of 45 beds; in 1887, the Hamill wing was built, the cost of which was contributed by Dr. Ross and Cyrus H. McCormick, Jr. In 1889, the Daniel A. Jones Memorial Building was completed at a cost of $120,000, which at the time was considered the finest building west of the Alleghenies. By 1908, the Private Pavilion wing increased the beds to 435 and in 1912, the Jane Murdock Memorial replaced the original and now obsolete Ross and Hamill wings. Then followed the Sprague Home for Nurses and the Rawson Laboratory, the latter being a five-story building connected with the Senn Memorial Building.

With the merger of St. Luke's Hospital with the Presbyterian Hospital, resources and endowments were made more effective for both institutions. St. Luke's in its old South Side location was surrounded by a heavily congested industrial neighborhood and suffered from polluted air and noise as well as decaying conditions.

In late 1970 the combined hospitals had 836 beds and 66 bassinets. An additional 400 beds will be available in the new medical center while the hospital programs also include four million dollars worth of research each year.

---

[1]The Presbyterian Hospital of the City of Chicago, Bulletin, September 1936, No. 90, Chicago, IL, p. 5. Permission Rush University Medical Center, Chicago, Illinois.

The last merger, after Rush Medical College was reactivated in 1969, was the forming of Rush-Presbyterian-St. Luke's Medical Center. Strictly, this was not a merger since Rush has been affiliated with Presbyterian Hospital since this hospital was organized in 1883. As the great Illinois Medical Center District prepares for its phenomenal growth, three already amalgamated groups will function under their individual Boards of Directors yet within the purpose of the District. University of Illinois, Cook County Hospital, and Rush-Presbyterian-St. Luke's Medical Center, and the newer institutions in the Medical Center are another City of Hope for Chicago and the nation.

29. Presbyterian Hospital, about 1892-93 (dates of photographic firm of D. M. Morris & Co.). Courtesy Chicago History Museum.

WOMAN'S MEDICAL COLLEGE

The founding of Woman's Medical College came about in a circuitous manner. The Chicago Medical College had grown from a splintering of Rush Medical College, led by Dr. Nathan S. Davis in 1859, protesting certain defects in medical education and attempting to rectify these failings. This new medical school became affiliated with Northwestern University in 1870 and moved into its new building at Prairie and 26th Street, near Mercy Hospital.

Dr. William H. Byford on the Rush Faculty, and later of Chicago Medical College, specialized in obstetrics, gynecology and pediatrics - the welfare of women and children. In September, 1869, the faculty of Chicago Medical College "resolved that females be admitted to the College and graduation on precisely the same terms as males." Three women were in this first class; Mary H. Thompson, already a physician, "received the ad eundum degree at the end of the session." On reconsideration "the Faculty voted "that the matriculating officers matriculate no more female medical students...""[1]

Professor William H. Byford, the champion of the original measure to admit female students, straightway founded the Woman's Hospital Medical College and the two other women graduated from this school. This medical college for women was a hope realized for Dr. Mary Thompson and was made possible by medical men who were ahead of their times when women were considered the inferior sex. Today, women still fight discrimination in the professional and business world.

In the mid-nineteenth century the prevailing attitude, especially of professional men, toward women and their so-called inferiority was expressed by Dr. Alfred Stille in 1871:

> "...All experience teaches that woman is characterized by a combination of distinctive qualities, of which the most striking are uncertainty of rational judgment, capriciousness of sentiment, fickleness of purpose, and indecision of action, which totally unfit her for professional pursuits."[2]

Even President Nathan S. Davis of Chicago Medical College disapproved of women in medicine and described them "as a "few singularly constituted women"."[3]

The first women in the new medical school had their classes and home in Dr. Thompson's small hospital on Division at State Street. After the Fire of 1871 wiped out that building, the school resumed in a small hospital on Adams and Paulina. By 1884, the college now know as Woman's Medical College moved into a building at 337 South Lincoln Street, next door to the

---

[1]Arey, Leslie B., Northwestern University Medical School, 1859-1959, Northwestern University, Evanston and Chicago, IL, 1959, p. 118. Permission Northwestern University.

[2]Ibid., p. 120.

[3]Ibid., p. 119.

Frances E. Willard Temperance Hospital in the old medical center. Dr. Byford was still championing the cause of medical education for women, being both President of the Faculty and Board of Trustees until his death in 1890. Besides, he was teaching classes in gynecology at Rush, having a large private practice, and writing many medical publications which brought him national recognition.[4]

By 1892, the pioneering and solvent Woman's Medical College was renamed Northwestern University Woman's Medical School[5] while the Chicago Medical College was to become known as Northwestern University Medical School. In 1897, the old buildings of the woman's school needed extensive updating and the question of admitting women to Northwestern University Medical School was re-opened. The vote was against the union in medical education.[6] By 1902, the student enrollment of women had dwindled, since more medical schools across the country were becoming co-educational. The University then closed the Woman's Medical School and sold the property.[7] It was not until 1926 that Northwestern University Medical School admitted women students.

---

[4]The first medical book written in Chicago was by Dr. William H. Byford in 1864: A Treatise on the Chronic Inflamation and Displacements of the Unimpregnated Uterus.

[5]Ibid.

[6]Ibid., p. 121.

[7]Ibid., p. 122.

THE MARY THOMPSON HOSPITAL

The acceptance of women as medical students by our Chicago medical colleges in the mid-nineteenth century was not practiced. While schools of nursing had then become accepted by the medical profession, through the example of the lady with the lamp, Florence Nightingale, women physicians and surgeons were discriminated against. Around the Civil War period, there were only two hospitals in Chicago, one of which did not admit women patients and the other closed its door to women physicians and surgeons.

Among the pioneer Chicago women physicians and surgeons was Dr. Mary Thompson. She was born at Fort Ann, New York in 1829 and earned her Doctor of Medicine degree from the New England Female Medical College.[1] She came to Chicago during the Civil War and saw the great need of a hospital for impoverished women and children. Dr. Thompson's plea for such a hospital was answered by leading physicians and surgeons as well as helped financially by Chicago's prominent families.

In May, 1865, the Chicago Hospital for Women and Children was opened with Mary Harris Thompson, M.D. as resident and attending physician. The first frame building at Rush and Indiana Streets had fourteen beds and a dispensary. In the years from 1865 to 1873, the hospital occupied several locations, one being wiped out by the Fire of 1871. A large house at Paulina and Adams Streets was purchased, and by 1885 a five story brick structure, accommodating 80 patients and quarters for 22 nurses, was built on this site.

Upon the organizing of this hospital in 1865, it became the policy that the attending medical staff be composed of women physicians, while the consulting and courtesy staffs included men. In 1870, the Chicago Medical College conferred a medical degree on Mary Thompson, the only one ever granted to a women by this institution.[2] In 1870, the Woman's Hospital Medical College was organized and in 1874, a School of Nursing; all were under the roof of this hospital.

Upon the completion of this modern hospital at Paulina and Adams Streets, the Woman's (Hospital) Medical College moved to a house on south Lincoln Street in the growing Medical Center. In 1895, at the death of Mary Harris Thompson, the "lady doctor," the hospital's name became the Mary Thompson Hospital of Chicago for Women and Children.

By 1927, this hospital building was inadequate for the growing needs and a building fund of $500,000 was raised in a two week campaign headed by Judge Mary Bartelme of the Chicago Women's Court. In 1929, a new 150 bed, five story Mary Thompson Hospital was opened at 140 North Ashland Boulevard and considered one of the country's finest. It was a neighbor to the Spalding School for Crippled Children.

Now in its second century of benevolence, Mary Thompson Hospital has expanded again with a new addition increasing the bed capacity to over 200. At the dedication program for this new building on October 5, 1972, the spirit of Mary Thompson was evoked:

---

[1]Mary Thompson Hospital, A Century of Service, 1865-1965, Chicago, IL, Pamphlet, p. 3.

[2]Ibid., p. 8.

"One hundred and seven years ago, Dr. Mary Thompson lit the torch... she bore that torch aloft for many years... she passed it on to others, who in turn passed it on to us. This new building that we dedicate today bears witness that we have kept faith with Dr. Thompson."[3]

A message of the Hospital's Administrator, William Sanz, was most timely and oriented to the heart of the region which this hospital serves:

"Very few hospitals, after searching their souls, decided not to abandon their old neighborhoods. Of these few, still fewer have been able to maintain their former standards of excellence. Only one has actually expanded and modernized to become an even more effective health care resource to the surrounding neighborhoods ... Mary Thompson Hospital. As Administrator, I have the honor, on behalf of the staff, to congratulate the Board of Trustees and the Medical Staff for their courage, vision and determination in leading us to this new and higher plateau."[4]

In the years that have followed since this beginning in 1865, there have been many "firsts" for this crusading hospital. Under the Trustees of Chicago Medical College's guidance, it housed the first Woman's Medical College in the Midwest and Chicago's first School of Nursing. Under continued, inspired leadership, Chicago's first Mother's Milk Bureau was established in 1930; in 1943, the Midwest's first Cancer Detection Clinic; in 1946, Chicago's first Mental Hygiene Clinic for Working Women and in 1951, the Midwest's first Cardiac Kitchen.[5]

Many century old, ivy-covered institutions of learning and altruism have their traditions and legends intertwined in their formal history and Mary Thompson Hospital is no exception. The Legend of Donny Boy is symbolic and bespeaks of the great humanitarian spirit which is associated with this rugged and enduring institution.

The bronze statue of a small boy which stands over the fountain and greets those who enter the hospital lobby is Donny Boy. It is said that the sculptor of this cherubic work was once a very sick little boy named Donny, who was taken by his widowed mother to the Chicago Hospital for Women and Children, where the lady doctor and her nurses lovingly cared for Donny during his long illness.

Donny grew to manhood and became an artist. He married and had a little boy and girl, both of whom were born at the Chicago Hospital for Women and Children. These two children became models for two little bronze statues. In 1895, Dr. Mary Thompson died and Donny, now the artist and father, recalled the little hospital on Ohio Street and the loving care that Dr. Thompson and her staff had given him and his family. As a memorial gift to the hospital he gave the statues of Donny Boy and his sister.

_____

[3]Source is not known to editor.

[4]Source is not known to editor.

[5]Mary Thompson Hospital, p. 8.

30. Mary Thompson Hospital, 1909, 615 West Adams Street. Negative #54,474. Courtesy Chicago History Museum.

31. Mary Thompson Hospital. The photograph displays the hospital which opened in 1928 at 140 North Ashland Boulevard, Chicago, Illinois 60607. It is a member of the Welfare Council of Metropolitan Chicago. Permission of Zuno Photographic Studio, 1444 N. Milwaukee Avenue, Chicago, Illinois 60622.

32. Dr. Mary Thompson. Munsell & Co., New York and Chicago, photographer. Courtesy Mary Thompson Hospital.

170

THE CHICAGO FOUNDLINGS HOME

"Oh! teach the orphan-boy to read
Or teach the orphan-girl to sew."

Alfred Tennyson (1809-1892)
Lady Clara Vere de Vere

A century ago, hearts and minds of understanding individuals were sensing the wrongs being done to city children and those youngest, the infants. Then, more than a thousand babies a year were abandoned on doorsteps, many close to death from exposure. Dr. George E. Shipman, a practicing physician, and his wife opened the Foundlings Home in 1871, letting it be known:

"Those having babies which they wish to dispose, whether they are children of sin or poverty, have but to leave them in the basket at the home and they will be cared for. No questions will be asked or answered."[1]

The response was large with many babies as well as destitute pregnant women seeking shelter from the storm. In 1874, generous gifts made possible a large four-story Victorian brick building at 115 South Wood Street, two blocks from Brown School. The school and Home had a mutual kinship not only because of participation of the pupils in the Home's needs, but also due to Frances Shipman, eldest daughter of Dr. Shipman, who taught sixth grade at Brown School. One pupil, Gertrude Morgan White, recalled years later: "The dearest teacher I ever had was Miss Shipman."[2]

She taught in the early 1880's and left teaching to help her father with administrative duties. The Foundlings Home depended entirely on charitable contributions, and at times even food was a problem yet no one hungered. Miss Shipman was superintendent from 1903 to 1928 and had as her helper another Chicago public schoolteacher, Miss Kate Waterman. Upon Miss Shipman's death in 1928, Miss Waterman succeeded her as resident trustee, editor of Faith's Record and supervisor of adoptions - all in addition to her teaching, until her retirement in 1937. Each morning as I walked north to Brown School, I passed kind faced Miss Waterman on her way south to Marquette School where she was a much loved teacher in the third grade. The second generation of Shipmans was at Brown, Elizabeth Shipman, daughter of Dr. Shipman's son. She and I were both in the St. Cecelia Choir at the Church of the Epiphany.

As the Chicago Foundlings Home grew with the needs of Chicago, so also earnest doctors and executives have guided its administration, all, in a labor of love. One such person was Dr. Karl A. Meyer, president of the trustees. Early in his career as head of Cook County Hospital, he sensed the great plight of unwanted babies and unwed mothers, and for fifty years he served the Home with his professional and personal devotion. In 1959, the Home moved to its new location at 1720 West Polk Street in a modern, efficient building where the Maternity Home and Nursery have the advantages of the Medical Center and the Adoption Department completes the purpose of this new, yet old, Chicago institution.

---

[1]"The Chicago Foundlings Home," brochure, 1966, second unnumbered page.

[2]Correspondence between Gertrude Morgan White and the author.

Among those going to Brown School was Priscilla; her last name was unknown to fellow students, perhaps, she had none. She was almost totally blind and the cause was also unknown. She lived at the Foundlings Home, probably one of those unwanted and never adopted children of "sin or poverty." She was a smiling, attractive girl as she was seen walking in the neighborhood on Miss Shipman's or Miss Waterman's arm. At school she was a quiet, attentive student and read her lesson books in Braille.

The Foundlings Home was part of our family's interest almost from the time of its inception. Our great-aunt in Kenosha in 1880, subscribed to Faith's Record, the Home's publication for humanitarian appeal. Then, when the family moved to Chicago, only two blocks away from the Home, the younger generation became interested in its progress. As a small child, it was a happy experience on Tuesday, visitor's day, to be taken to the Home to see the babies, and when leaving having already hopefully picked out a new little sister. Also, it was a joy to see my own outgrown iron crib with new white paint and a dear baby soundly sleeping in it.

A demise in 1971 was that of the Chicago Foundlings Home, Chicago's oldest charity; it was exactly a century old. The closing of this institution definitely shows the sweeping social changes, not only in Chicago, but over the nation and the civilized world.

As a result of pregnancy prevention by the use of the pill, the number of babies born out of wedlock has been drastically reduced. Also, the acceptance of the unwed mother and her child in normal society is becoming more general. Because of these two factors, the number of infants available for adoption as well as the number of older children in orphanages, is decreasing each year.

This is a hopeful work of the future among the many discouraging symptoms of our times. The last mother left the Foundlings Home hospital in April, 1971; and the nursery closed in May. The new modern building in the Medical Center will be put to good use for other humanitarian needs. Unwanted babies of unwed mothers will not cease, but other benevolent organizations will serve them as the need arises.

And so to Dr. George Shipman and his helper wife, the founders of this most humanitarian refuge, and to Dr. Karl A. Meyer, President of the Board of Trustees as well as a generous donor of his professional services and gifts to this institution - your missions have ended in hopefulness for the coming generations. The original basket used to leave the unwanted babies in and displayed at the Home all through the hundred years as a symbol of its mission, is no longer needed.

Among the echoes from Dr. Shipman's Foundlings Home is that Mayor Carter H. Harrison and his wife were generous contributors to the Home, especially when it was established in the substantial brick buildings on South Wood Street. This was Mrs. Harrison's greatest object of her charity. Her mother-heart reached out to help save these unwanted babies while knowing the personal sadness of having lost most of her children in infancy. While out of the goodness of his heart, Carter H. Harrison during his tenure in office as County Commissioner of Chicago turned over his salary of three years' total to the Foundlings Home.[3]

The last chapter in the history of the century old Chicago Foundlings Home has now been written. In early 1972 it was sold to Rush-Presbyterian-St. Luke's Medical Center for use as a Mental Health Treatment Center. There is pressing need of this institution in the surrounding community with its contemporary drug involvement and the resulting mental disturbance.

---

[3]Abbot, W. J., Carter Henry Harrison: A Memoir, Dodd, Mead, & Co., New York, 1895, p. 61.

33. Chicago Foundlings' Home. Photographic print ICHi-38743, Foundlings Home, 15 South Wood St, Chicago, IL, April 20, 1959, Photographer: N.K. Benedict. Courtesy Chicago History Museum.

THE WASHINGTONIAN HOME

This organization, a hospital dedicated to the treatment of alcoholism, has existed since 1863. Like its neighbors, The Chicago Foundlings Home and Mary Thompson Hospital for Women and Children, it had its beginnings near downtown Chicago and would become established a few years later in the old Mile Square.

The "Washingtonian Home for the Cure of Inebriates in Chicago" was founded by the Grand Lodge of Good Templars and by 1867 was incorporated by the State of Illinois. The first president was Charles J. Hull, who later gave Hull House to Jane Addams.

The early preamble to the Washingtonian Home's Constitution read in part:

> "Whereas, ever since Noah entered into the Ark and became a husbandman and drank of the wine and was drunken... intemperance has spread its withering and blighting curse over every village, town and hamlet... and believing that... our fellow beings can be reclaimed, redeemed and regenerated... that the establishment of an institution... will result in vast good as a reformatory agency... we agree to be governed by (this) Constitution."

Mr. Robert or Rolls A. Law, a printer and member of the Independent Order of Good Templars, was the original organizer of the Washingtonian Home. As the institution outgrew its quarters on State Street, a new home was purchased in 1867 at Madison and Ogden Avenue, formerly the Bull's Head Tavern. By 1874 this frame structure was demolished and a five story brick building was erected. The main floors housed stores which brought in an income to the Home.

In 1882 the Washingtonian Home Association purchased ten acres and an old academy building in Lake View, then a country-like region. Here the Martha Washington Home for Women was established, the first of its kind in Chicago.

By 1920 both the men's and women's divisions were merged at the one address, 2318 West Irving Park Road. The old building on Madison Street was sold in 1925; this made possible the funds for helping to erect the Martha Washington Hospital, a general hospital. By 1957 a new Washingtonian Home was built serving as a modern hospital specializing in the care of the alcoholic. Both of these non-profit institutions continue to serve the Chicago area.

Through the years, since the Bull's Head Tavern was occupied by this humanitarian institution, the second and third generations continued to carry on the good works of the original helpers. Dr. J. Lawrence Rose was President of the Trustees in 1963. He, as a small boy, grew up in the old neighborhood and would later be a member of his father's company, Rose and Carter, jewelers and opticians on Madison Street, near Lincoln.

174

CHAPTER FOUR: DISASTER AND RESTORATION

THE GREAT FIRE OF 1871

"Blackened and pleading, helpless, panting, prone,
On the charred fragments of her shattered throne,
Lies she who stood but yesterday alone.

Queen of the West: by some enchanter taught,
To lift the glory of Aladdin's court,
Then lose the spell that all that wonder wrought.

Like her own prairies by some chance seen sown,
Like her own prairies in one brief day grown,
Like her own prairies in one fierce night mown.

She lifts her voice and in her pleading calls,
We hear the cry of Macedon to Paul,
The cry for help that makes her kin to all.

But happy with wan fingers may she feel,
The silver cup hid in the proferred meal,
The gifts her kinship and our loves reveal".

Bret Harte, October 10, 1871
"Chicago"[1]

Patrick O'Leary, his wife Catharine and family, living at 137 De Koven Street, were entertaining neighbors at a Saturday night celebration on October 11, 1871. About nine o'clock, a fire was seen in their barn and was soon out of control. The fire was supposedly caused by the O'Leary cow kicking over an oil lamp which ignited the straw. In more recent historical accounts, a few more accessories have been blamed for the fire. Harry B. Smith, the playwright, dramatically wrote:

"Mrs. O'Leary declared that the animal was maligned. She blamed the whole

---

[1]From The Great Conflagration by James W. Sheahan and George P. Upton, Union Publishing Co., Chicago, 1871, p. 364.

thing on Daniel Sullivan's pipe and the McLaughlins who occupied a part of the O'Leary home. Mrs. McLaughlin was giving a party that evening in honor of her cousin just arrived from Ireland, and there was a Hibernian wassail. A guest brought in some oysters. Milk was needed for an oyster stew and Danny Sullivan was delegated to milk one of Mrs. O'Leary's cows - she had six of them. The fire could have been confined to the stable; but unfortunately Sullivan had a wooden leg, and as he started out to give the alarm, the end of the wooden leg caught fast between the planks of the flooring and held Daniel a prisoner until the building was in a blaze. He shouted but the O'Learys and McLaughlins did not hear him. They had a fiddler at the party and everybody was dancing. Chicago is the only city ever destroyed by a wooden leg. These details became known during the official investigation."[2]

In two days, this holocaust swept over three square miles, from the western edges at Chicago River, north as far as Lincoln Park. Over $200,000,000 worth of property and 250 lives were lost and over 100,000 inhabitants were homeless.

The Chicago History Museum archives have photographs and drawings of the Chicago Fire, even a photograph of the O'Leary cottage, which ironically was spared. The stories of the fire coming from old news reports as well as family annals, have common facts of truth - that both man's greed and destructive spirit, as well as his unselfish compassion were then his prominent traits.

As the fire swept the downtown area and its concentration of stores, the fury of both fire and humanity was greatest there. The contents of dry goods and food supply companies were ravaged by the pillaging hordes and often carried to safely by the anguished owners. In the inhabitants' frenzy, as they pushed across the wooden and threatened bridges of Chicago River towards the lake shore's protection, they broke windows, tramped on books, oil paintings and china, which then had no foreseeable use. They crowded the saloons for liquor as long as it lasted to comfort their fears and hysteria.

The owners and employees of Field, Leiter and Company known to later generations as Marshall Field & Company, worked all night to save their most valuable merchandise. Later historians wrote:

> "From the top floor came bolts of Japanese silks, black satins, black velours, German Mantilla velvets. While four of the huskiest men stood guard at the front doors, the others lifted the bolts of cloth into waiting wagons. Whips fell, the wagons rumbled off to the lake shore, there to be met by other strong shouldered guards, to unload and return for more. Now came packing boxes filled with laces and heaps of Ristoni and Patli shawls, French

---

[2]Smith, Harry B., <u>First Nights and First Editions</u>, Little, Brown & Co., Boston, 1931, p. 37.

cretonnes, Biaritz cloth, Empress Sultana and Tibet scarves."[3]

But vandals were on the lake front too: Field and Leiter salvaged and repacked the merchandise into wagons and took it to Mr. Leiter's home on South Prairie Avenue where it was stored and guarded.

The Pinkerton Detective Agency worked day and night during the Great Fire. At that time the Agency was known as Pinkerton Preventive Police or just Pinkerton's Police. Notices were posted in the burned district which read:

> "Thieves and Burglars!... Any person Stealing or seeking to steal any of the property in my charge, or attempt to break open the Safes, as the men cannot make arrests at the present time, they shall Kill the persons by my order, no Mercy Shall be shown them, but Death shall be their fate.
> Allan Pinkerton."[4]

With the engines' failure in the city's water works on Michigan Avenue, the pumping of lake water stopped and the fire continued uncontrolled, reducing the heart of the city to a mass of ruins after the two days' inferno. Immediately, Joseph Medill, owner of the Chicago Daily Tribune announced: "Chicago Shall Rise Again." This became the city's watchword, and reconstruction began immediately.

One of Chicago's West Side neighbors, and a famous son, Hobart C. Chatfield-Taylor, witnessed the Great Fire of 1871, when, as a small boy living on West Washington Street, he watched

> "...the fateful night when the heavens to the south and east of us were reddened by fire and the bell on the stone Court-House across the river began to peal a frantic alarm. Then we rushed to our windows and house-tops, or into the flame-lighted streets, to gaze appalled upon the conflagration that was destroying the city.
>
> "Through the slums of the West Side, where it had started, its flames leaped from roof to roof, the impotent streams played upon it by the firemen evaporating in its inordinate heat. Fanned by the southwest gale, it quickly reached the river, where a blazing brand, carried by the wind to the opposite bank, fell, of all places, among wooden hovels near the gas-works. In vain the weary firemen lashed their horses across the bridges, for soon a mighty report stifled for a moment the roaring of the flames. The gas-works had exploded;

---

[3]Wendt, Lloyd and Herman Kogan, Give The Lady What She Wants!, Rand McNally Co., Chicago, IL, 1952, p. 106.

[4]Dedmon, Emmett, Fabulous Chicago, Random House, N.Y., 1953, p. 95 (from "Death Shall be their Fate", A Pinkerton broadside).

the South Side was ablaze, and except for the glare of the fire upon our window panes, we of the favored West Side whose houses had been spared were in darkness.

"Throughout an agonizing night we watched the business district burn, building by building, block by block, then saw the angry flames sweep northward. Above the roar of the fire and the crash of falling buildings we heard explosions of oil and chemicals, the bell on the Court-House tolling a knell, meanwhile, till with a mournful clang it fell into the relentless flames that were lapping the skies with their scarlet tongues.

"When the sun rose over the windswept lake, the devastated city and the blue sky above it were hidden from our sight by dense black smoke, cloud above cloud, with gleaming fire beneath it. In dismay we saw the flames rush northward in their fury to the water-works, the smoke above them filled with embers borne onward by the gale. To the southward we heard dull detonations and soon we knew that valiant "Little Phil" Sheridan had upon his own red-tapeless initiative blown up several blocks of houses with army gunpowder, to stop the southward progress of the fire. But all day long, and into the night as well, it swept on to the north unchecked, until arrested by the open expanse of Lincoln Park and a heaven-sent shower of rain.

"All day long too, the homeless trooped through our West Side streets, begging at our doors for food and shelter, - some grimly bearing their lot, others in tears, or frenzied with excitement. Over the few bridges that were still unburned they came, driving wagons filled with household goods, or trudging hand-in-hand with crying children, their backs bent to the weight of treasured objects, a baby's crib, maybe, or a family portrait. But some had only the rags they wore, and some were without sufficient clothes to hide their nakedness; for I remember that my mother stripped my last suit from my back to cover a shivering boy of my age, I being put to bed till clothing could be procured for me."[5]

Besides the hysterical and panic frenzies of the Great Fire there were the plain, everyday facts of living that had to be faced. Mrs. Joseph Frederick Ward in her "As I Remember It," graphically stated some of the problems:

"There was no credit for anyone, and it was astonishing how little money people had in their pockets. It was nearly a week before money could be obtained from the banks. We were not allowed to use kerosene and there were so few shops left unburned and so few candles in them that only four could be sold to one person. Our only water was brought in barrels from the lake.

---

[5]Hobart C. Chatfield-Taylor, <u>Chicago</u>, Houghton Mifflin Co., N.Y., 1917, pp. 60-64.

"When the vaults of the banks were opened, after four days' cooling, a large part of the bank-notes were found baked to a brown crisp. These were sent to Washington, where experts estimated their value and sent back new bills.

"The Horse Railway Company had built a new car-barn near 22nd and State streets. It had never been used, and there Field and Leiter opened a store. Mandel had a small establishment on 22nd Street, but no one bought anything except to make clothing for the sufferers. All the world rushed to our relief. Tents and, afterward, rows of wooden cabins were hastily put up; everything was done by widespread charity and sympathy...

"It was a strange winter. When we looked across the ruins and counted our losses, everyone joked; it was so great and universal a disaster, there was no other way to bear it. There were calico balls and all sorts of entertainments, all for the benefit of the relief and aid societies. I heard Ole Bull play in a hall on 22nd Street where the stage alone was lighted, and that with candles. It was a blessing to hear Ole Bull under any circumstances. With his grand figure, his noble head and beautiful white hair, he came forward, gave us a bow of old-fashioned courtesy and a benign smile, lifted his violin to his shoulder, laid his cheek against it, closed his eyes and filled the world with music...

"The work of clearing away and rebuilding was undertaken with great vigor and much good cheer. With that rebuilding my tale ends. Old Chicago passed in that smoke and flame and on the wings of that mighty wind, and it exists now only in the memories and hearts of those who loved her."[6]

The Carter H. Harrison family on Ashland Avenue, who lived across the road from the Pinkerton family, also watched the conflagration from their roof lookout or widow's walk. The center of the inferno was less than two miles away from their home.

After the fire had been quelled and the ashes cooled, young Carter and his small friends viewed the charred wreckage of the downtown buildings, as did other curious Chicagoans. Here, what was once a hardware store yielded treasures such as bullet molds, shot guns, a small cannon, knives, axes, hammers and chisels. While the extreme heat of the fire had destroyed the temper of these metals as well as the wooden handles and stocks, still they were a precious loot for small boys. These childish paraphernalia were kept hidden by the youngsters, except when playing soldiers and Indians with improvised forts on the wooden sidewalks in front of the Ashland Avenue home.

Carter H. Harrison II told a story of the Great Fire of 1871 as witnessed by his father. He, like so many thousands who owned property in the path of the fire, rushed to his

---

[6]Ward, Mrs. Joseph Frederick, "As I Remember It," (pp. 88-116) in: Kirkland, Caroline, Chicago Yesterdays: A Sheaf of Reminiscences, Daughaday & Co., Chicago, 1919, pp. 115-116.

holdings on Clark and Harrison Street - a five story brick hotel, and also some small frame buildings at Harrison and Pacifica. It was these smaller buildings which were in danger from the flying embers. The saloon-keepers of one building and a half dozen recruits formed a human chain to carry buckets of water from a hydrant to the second floor. Then word came ""There's no more water!"" The Chicago pumping station on Chicago Avenue had been made useless by the fire.

As new embers hit the roof father Harrison called for rags, a carpet or anything to smother the new flames. "A helper called out: " Here's a slop bucket, it may help. Hell! No! It's nothing but... and...!"" The father yelled back: ""Pass her up!... don't burn worth a cent!"" The "property was saved by a slop bucket of" unmentionables.[7]

A letter written after the Fire of 1871 by William Ogden, one of Chicago's pioneers, to his niece, Julia Wheeler, expressed for the millions of Chicagoans what they all felt so deeply -

> "Never before was a large and very beautiful and fortunate city built by a generation of people so proud, so in love with their work; never a city so lamented and grieved over as Chicago."[8]

Among the refugees was a nineteen year old schoolboy who had already fled bucolic Wisconsin to become an actor in Chicago. Here he was performing such roles as Richard III, King Henry IV, or appearing with the Genial Dramatic Club at Chicago's Athenaeum Hall, or at the New Chicago Theatre in Lady of Lyons. He was George W. Warvelle, future father of this book's author.

Lake Michigan's shore to the east had to be the fire's limit and here the boy gathered with his troupe which had been playing Shakespearian drama at McVicker's Theatre. He had dragged his trunk from their boarding house at Wells and Monroe Street to the beach refuge. There thousands of homeless people made their beds on the sandy, moist ground and stood in line for soup and bread.

This interruption ended his theatrical career and the boy returned to his home in Kenosha. In his pocket, he carried two souvenirs from the Great Fire's path of cluttered debris. Years later, his children saw these salvaged fragments which were always a good incentive for a story about the fire. One was a cluster of three tiny china dolls which had melted together with the glaze - all testifying to the great heat to which they had been subjected. The other item was a small crucifix, minus its rosary; this must have been silver-plated earlier, but through frequent use or the fire's scouring, was worn down to a verdigrised brass. These

---

[7]Harrison II, Carter Henry, Growing Up with Chicago: Sequel to "Stormy Years", Ralph Fletcher Seymour, Chicago, IL, 1944, p. 49.

[8]West, Mrs Frederick T., "Through a Child's Eyes," (pp. 216-236), in: Kirkland, Caroline, Chicago Yesterdays: A Sheaf of Reminiscences, Daughaday and Company, Chicago, 1919, pp. 231-232.

were things of no value only minutiae of suffering humanity and a young man's recollections.

When the young actor returned to Kenosha, he settled down to read the law in the offices of Head and Quarles, the latter becoming United States Senator from Wisconsin. The young man, George W. Warvelle, was admitted to the Wisconsin Bar in 1876 and also became editor of the <u>Kenosha Advocate</u> whose motto was: "For the right as we understand the right." He married Lydia Bangs - they had three daughters, and in 1881 he came back to Chicago, becoming a member of the Chicago, Illinois, and American Bar Associations.

By 1887, the family no longer commuted between Chicago and Kenosha, but settled in a Victorian stone house at 654 (old number; later numbering system: 1743) West Monroe Street, and the little girls, Effie and Florence, entered Brown School in the primary grades. Some years later two other children, Gerald and Marjorie would join this family.

At Haddock, Cox and Company at Wells and Washington, George W. Warvelle wrote his first law text during those days of a lean practice. This volume was to become the beacon for his legal career - <u>A Treatise on Abstracts and Examination of Title</u>, more frequently known as <u>Warvelle on Abstracts</u> or "<u>Abstractor's Bible</u>." It went through four printings, 1883, 1892, 1907 and 1920. In 1932, the author then eighty, was asked to update a fifth printing which was never completed. There were other volumes of legal studies by Dr. Warvelle which were used by the profession and law schools throughout the country for fifty years.

34. Chicago Fire Panorama. Gravure copyrighted by S. L. Stein Publishing Co., about 1892-93. Courtesy Chicago History Museum.

THE WORLD'S COLUMBIAN EXPOSITION OF 1893

"Make no little plans. They have no magic to stir men's blood and probably themselves will not be realized. Make big plans; aim high in hope and work, remembering that a noble, logical diagram once recorded will never die but long after we are gone will be a living thing, asserting itself with growing intensity."

Daniel Burnham[1]

Each century after the discovery of America in 1492 by Christopher Columbus, the world has paused to consider this event. Towards the end of the third century, our young republic became immersed in Columbian nomenclature. The feeling of debt to Columbus was profound, as well as resentment towards Americus Vespucius or Amerigo Vespucci, for whom America was named.

The name, Columbia stirred when King's (George III) College in New York became Columbia College and countries, cities, rivers, trees, ships, cultural and commercial organizations - all were given a Columbian prefix - even our then national anthem, "Hail Columbia, Happy Land." William Thornton, codesigner of our national capitol building, proposed in 1815 Outlines of a Constitution for United North and South Columbia.[2]

Why was this Western Hemisphere called America and not Columbia? The grade school child often questioned this and was never answered completely. Vespucci is known to have made voyages to this hemisphere in 1497 which were recorded in letters to friends. These letters reached Martin Waldseemuller, a cartographer of Saint Die in Friburg, Germany. He saw the rich material he could add to his world map. With no dictates from royal or legal authority, only his enthusiastic mind, he published the Cosmographiae Introductio quoting the Vespucci letters and the World Map of 1507. In the years that followed, the original letters and map were lost; the "Book of St. Die" lived on - the only printed clue to America.[3]

Later Waldseemuler saw the injustice done to Columbus and drew a map in 1513 omitting the word America and crediting Columbus. However, America, a gracious sounding word, had already spread over Renaissance Europe.[4]

---

[1]Dedmon, Emmett, Fabulous Chicago, Random House, New York, 1953, p. 301.

[2]Cleven, Andrew N., "Thornton's Outlines of a Constitution for United North and South Columbia," Hispanic American Historical Review, Vol. 12, 1932.

[3]Adams, Edward Dean, America and Americans, Brochure, New York, New York, 1926.

[4]Ibid.

In 1900, the long-lost Map of 1507 was found in Wurtemburg, Germany by Joseph Fischer, a Jesuit professor. He entitled the document <u>The Baptismal Certificate of the New World</u>. Time and the little evidence exonerates Vespucci of any deliberate naming of America.[5]

Columbus Day, October 12, is now a holiday in most states and school children have become more enlightened on their national and hemispherical history.

As the four hundredth year approached, there was restlessness as to where the Columbian anniversary should be celebrated. Forward looking Chicagoans, building a new city on the ruins left by the Great Fire of 1871, had visions, even then, for a World's Fair in 1892. Other American cities, such as New York, were interested in the Columbian celebration and some citizens were aghast that Chicago could have such pretension - a city just fifty years old. Mexico City felt the urge to honor the southern European, but the Fates gave Chicago the grand chance.

The passing of time, while it dims events and those who participated in them, also winnows out qualities of those leaders which earlier may have been only partially known to their contemporaries. Such is the history of James W. Ellsworth, one of the committee for creating the World's Columbian Exposition.

Mr. Ellsworth came to Chicago in 1869, being a coal mine owner and operator. He married Eva Butler in 1874. Both Eva and her sister Nellie were early students of Brown School and lived in the vicinity of Union Park Congregational Church where their parents, Oliver and Reforma Butler were members. James and Eva Ellsworth had two children, Lincoln and Clare. Their mother was to die in 1888 and the father to remarry in 1895 to Julia M. Fincke.

James W. Ellsworth worked for the civic betterment of Chicago during his residence there as president of the South Parks Board and in the promotion of the World's Fair. The early plan and suggested method of financing such a gigantic display was the work of a small committee of Chicago's leading industrialists and was spearheaded by James W. Ellsworth.

Daniel H. Burnham in later years remarked:

"I do not know who first advocated holding a World's Fair... Mr. Ellsworth, almost alone among the directors at the beginning, saw the vision."[6]

Mr. Ellsworth set before Frederick Law Olmsted, developer of the expanded L'Enfant plan for the City of Washington, his dream for Chicago's exposition with waterways, lagoons, promenades and classic buildings near the lake front in Jackson Park. An area of 600 acres with an outlay of $15,000,000 was suggested.[7]

---

[5]Ibid.

[6]Ellsworth, Lincoln, <u>Search</u>, Brewer, Warren & Putnam, New York, New York, 1932, Introduction, pp. 18-19.

[7]Moore, Charles, <u>Daniel H. Burnham</u>, Houghton Mifflin Co., New York, New York, 1921, Vol 1, p. 32.

However, earlier Ellsworth had not favored the project since he objected to fairs as they were usually conducted. Olmsted also at the first consideration was not interested in this gigantic promotion, but together the two men realized the great potential in such a world-participation project. It was rumored that Ellsworth's money made the Exposition possible. He had said that he "personally would see that the cost was met".[8] [9]

Frederick Law Olmsted was retained as Consulting Landscape Architech and the Chicago architectural firm of Burnham and Root was appointed Consulting Architect. Due to the early death of John Root, consulting architect for the Exposition, Daniel H. Burnham, as chief of construction, called upon the eastern architectural firm of McKim, Mead and White to carry on. These men were already expressing the Italian Renaissance in the millionaire colonies of the eastern states.

The Exposition directors determined that the plan should follow the Roman-Renaissance architectural style. There was both praise and adverse criticism of the buildings coming from contemporary architectural leaders who felt the buildings should express the new concepts for the twentieth century. The architects, most of whom had built on the fire cleared land around the Loop, were John Root, William Jenny, Dankmar Adler, Louis H. Sullivan, and Daniel H. Burnham. The buildings designed by some of these men in other cities would become known as the Chicago School of Architecture. What started out to be a neo-classic spirit for the World's Fair became even more neo - an architectural fantasia.

Chicago was building a new city as well as a fair grounds and there were valid reasons for many types of architecture. The World's Columbian Exposition was not ready until May 1893. When it did open, Chicago gave its guests a wide choice of spectacular sights.

Because of Chicago's swampy land, iron and steel skeletons with deep pilings were necessary for safe construction and having these firm foundations, buildings could loom to fantastic heights as well as having decorative details from street entrance to roof; these were the original sky-scrapers.

Visitors to the Fair saw these new tall buildings as Richardson's, Marshall Field Wholesale Store, Root's Monadnock Building, Burnham and Root's Masonic Temple Building, their Women's Temple (W.C.T.U.), and the Auditorium Theatre Building by Adler and Sullivan.

The Auditorium completed in 1889 consisted of the theatre surrounded by eight stone stories of offices and hotel. Besides its splendid acoustics, 4200 seats with unobstructed views, the enormous encircling arches - brilliant with gold design and thousands of lights - it rivaled anything to be seen at the Exposition, except, perhaps, the Transportation Building with its "Golden Door," also designed by Louis Sullivan.

The Masonic Temple, built in 1890, and twenty-one stories high, was the tallest building in the United States until 1900. It was situated at Randolph and State Streets and now long demolished. Built of iron and steel construction around a rotunda open from ground floor to the

---

[8]Ellsworth, Lincoln, Beyond Horizons, Doubleday, Doran & Co., Inc., New York, New York, 1938, p. 25.

[9]Lincoln Ellsworth later wrote: "The Exposition Company owed father something over $800,000, which he had advanced out of his own pocket. But as everybody knows, or did know then, the gate receipts paid everything off and even returned a profit to the stock holder" (Ellsworth, Lincoln, Beyond Horizons, p. 25).

skylights, this railed structure, like the Golden Gate Bridge, became a suicidal jumping off place. (One poor soul left his shoes in front of Room 1901, my father's office.) It became necessary to place metal mesh between the seventh and fourteenth floors to protect pedestrians on the main floor. It was from the top floors of this building that visitors viewed the early airplanes.

While the provocative architects were swayed by the dominating and functional forms of their own creations as well as professional rivalry, Augustus Saint-Gaudens, as the general director among sculptors for the Exposition, exclaimed to a board member:

> ""Look here, old fellow, do you realize that this is the greatest meeting of artists since the fifteenth century.""[10]

It was, and probably has not been duplicated since that civic effort of architects, landscape designers, sculptors and painters all working in a common effort.

Chicago's White City was a temporary fabrication as all world fairs seem to be; few leave lasting memorials. Wooden or metal frameworks covered with stucco and plaster, painted with a marbleized effect were quickly assembled and even more quickly demolished. Many structures while attempting a classic plan, were as diverse as the nationalities who furnished the exhibits. Henry Adams wrote:

> "Critics had no trouble in criticising the classicism, but all trading cities had always shown traders' taste... All traders' taste smelt of bric-à-brac; Chicago tried at least to give her taste a look of unity."[11]

Henry Adams was one of our scholarly critics of the Exposition, and while his remarks were written closely following his visit to the Fair, they have not become too obsolete for judging his reactions in this earlier time and place. Along with those millions of wide-eyes spectators, he, too, was being educated. He wrote:

> "Education ran riot at Chicago, at least for retarded minds which had never faced in concrete form so many matters of which they were ignorant. Men who knew nothing whatever - who had never run a steam-engine, the simplest of forces--who had never put their hands on a lever--had never touched an electric battery--never talked through a telephone... had no choice but to sit down on the steps and brood... The historical mind can think only in historical processes, and probably this was the first time since historians existed, that any of them had sat down helpless before a mechanical sequence.[12]

---

[10]Moore, Charles. Daniel H. Burnham; Architect, Planner of Cities. 2 volumes. Houghton Mifflin, Boston, 1921, Vol. I, p.47.

[11]Adams, Henry, The Education of Henry Adams, The Modern Library, Random House, New York, New York, 1931, 1918, p. 340.

[12]Ibid., p. 342.

"Did he himself quite know what he meant? Certainly not! If he had known enough to state his problem, his education would have been complete at once. Chicago asked in 1893 for the first time the question whether the American people knew where they were driving. Adam answered, for one, that he did not know, but would try to find out... Chicago was the first expression of American thought as a unity; one must start there."[13]

Another critic, Montgomery Schulyer, wrote:

"The landscape-plan is the key to the pictorial success of the Fair as a whole..."[14]

How true, with Lake Michigan and its shoreline, Frederick Law Olmsted's Jackson Park with its woodland of trees and vegetation plus the created waterways, promenades such as the Midway Plaisance, and the lighting effects of the new electricity - all must have created an unforgettable picture. Schuyler understood the hopes of the planners when he wrote:

"It is essential to the illusion of a fairy city that it should not be an American city of the nineteenth century... It is what you will, so long as you will not take it for an American city of the nineteenth century, nor its architecture for the actual or possible or even ideal architecture of such a city."[15]

Finally, the disputed evaluation of the Exposition can be resolved by Fiske Kimball's conclusion:

"True to the hopes of the designers, the classical buildings produced a cumulative effect of harmony and magnificence which was deeply stamped on the memory of the nation."[16]

The memory of the nation was composed of middle class Americans, few of whom had visited Europe or classic shrines. Some mid-westerners had been nurtured on Gothic and various eclectics of Queen Anne and gingerbread architecture. Some had come from small cities where the classic colonial and Greek Revival architecture had a tenacious hold. When visitors to the World's Fair returned to their home cities, it was evident that some would build their state capitols, courthouses and public buildings in the classic style.

---

[13]Ibid., p. 343.

[14]Schuyler, Montgomery, "Last Words About the World's Fair," Architectural Record, Jan-Mar, 1894, Vol. III, #3, p. 294. (McGraw-Hill, New York, in public domain.)

[15]Ibid., p. 300.

[16]Kimball, Fiske and George H. Edgell, History of Architecture, Harpers, New York, New York, 1918, p. 556.

Others recalled Sullivan's magnificent Transportation Building whose "Golden Door" entrance was to be mirrored in diminished proportions around the nation in commissions for small banks and mausoleums. Likewise, his skyscrapers would continue, as the Prudential Building in New York. In Chicago, his lavish detail for the Carson Pirie Scott & Co. Department Store would reach the saturation point for decorative design.

In the summer of 1893, among the series of congresses held at the Fair, was the World's Congress of Architects where the American Institute of Architects held its annual convention. At this congress, Louis Sullivan discussed "Polychromatic Treatment of Architecture." This may have been given as an enlightening as well as a justification of Sullivan's elaborate design and lavish color treatment of the Golden Door of the Transportation Building. This building's interior, however, was a huge, undecorated shed where both large and small mechanical exhibits were unable to be properly exhibited. George Davis, Director General of the Fair, also questioned whether

> "the expense of painting and gilding the exterior of the building was warranted when the best exhibits could not be used to create a corresponding effect inside."[17]

Sullivan's statement, occurring in his autobiography written a generation after the Fair:

> "The damage wrought by the World's Fair will last half a century... if not longer"[18]

could also be taken as an recrimination of his fellow directors and their architects of the Renaissance style as well as perhaps his own participation in his Transportation Building. Frank Lloyd Wright recalled:

> "The Transportation Building... cost him (Sullivan) most trouble of anything he ever did. He got the great doorway "straight away," but the rest hung fire. I had never seen him anxious before, but anxious he then was."[19]

Perhaps one reason why Sullivan's original Golden Door and its later models found such favor in United States was that they were a new inspiration for Americans although the source

---

[17]Crook, David H., "Louis Sullivan and the Golden Doorway," Journal of the Society of Architectural Historians, Dec. 1967, Vol. XXVI, No. 4, p. 251. Permission Society of Architectural Historians, 1365 N. Astor Street, Chicago, Illinois 60610-2144

[18]Sullivan, Louis H., The Autobiography of an Idea, Dover Pub., New York, 1956, p. 325. (Previously published in 1924 by Press of the American Institute of Architects, New York.)

[19]Wright, Frank Lloyd, "Louis H. Sullivan - His Work," The Architectural Record, LVI, 1924, p. 29. (McGraw-Hill, New York, in public domain.)

was very old. The origin being Islamic and used in designs for mosques, mausoleums or gateways to walled cities of Asia and Africa.

The memory of the nation did not forget the gay exhibits which behoove any county or world fair to offer - a carnival of Ferris wheel, side shows, music and libations. Chicago's show was considered with hurrahs by some and disgust by others. Not having been there myself, but hearing my parents' diluted stories suitable for a child's sophistication, I regretted being born too late for the Fair.

Our high school hero, Finley Peter Dunne's Mr. Dooley, was at the Fair. What was the opinion at the "Archery Street" address?

> "They tell me that (the Chicago Fair) give an impetus, whativer that is, to archytecture that it hasn't raycovered for yet. Afther th' fair, ivrybody that was annybody had to go live in a Greek temple with an Eytalian roof... But thim that wasn't annybody had f'rgot all about th' Court ir Honor, and whin ye say annything to thim about th' fair, they say: "D'ye raymimber th' night I see ye on th' Midway? Oh, my!"[20]

The Art Institute on Michigan Avenue was a part of the World's Columbian Exposition, although a distance from the Midway Plaisance; the building was completed in 1893 and the picture galleries were then in the initial state. The Art Institute served as the headquarters for the congress of nations, or more specifically, the World's Congress Auxiliary of the Exposition. The average person, among the millions from all over the world who attended the World's Fair, was unaware of this small but earnest gathering of great souls who spent their time at a "Summer University of the World." Just what was the purpose of this assembly?

> "The Auxiliary was planned to do for the mind what the other departments did for matter - to show the progress of the mind of mankind; to establish fraternal relations among the leaders of mankind; to review the progress already achieved; to state the living problems now awaiting solution and to suggest the means of further progress."[21]

Some of the subjects discussed were:

> "Education, Temperance, Moral and Social Reform, Labor, Literature, Law Reform, Commerce and Finance, Agriculture, Arbitration and Peace, Music, Art and Women's Welfare."[22]

Our neighbor, Bishop Samuel Fallows, was chairman of the general committee on Education.

---

[20]Dunne, Finley Peter, Mr. Dooley's Opinions, Harper Brothers, New York, N. Y., 1906, p. 45.

[21]Fallows, Alice Katharine, Everybody's Bishop: Being the Life and Times of the Right Reverend Samuel Fallows, D.D., J. H. Sears & Co., Inc., New York, 1927, p. 324.

[22]Ibid., p. 324.

Among other Congresses which became most vociferous for their causes were the suffragettes and the Labor Congress. In August of 1893 when so many workers had been laid off all over the country, the trade unions were demanding a program of public works. At one meeting held on the Lake Front to accommodate the crowd and mostly "to let off steam," 25,000 people gathered to hear Samuel Gompers of the American Federation of Labor, the single tax advocate, Henry George, and the railraod lawyer, Clarence Darrow.

There was the Parliament of Religions where religious congresses were held for seventeen days and discussed "the verities that united them, not the unessentials which divided them."[23] Here, if only briefly, was brotherhood where black and white, Jew and Gentile, Mohammedan and Evangelical experienced this common bond.

The Parliament of Religions was made possible by the gift of Daniel H. Burnham and other individual subscriptions. Burnham looked to this

> "religious congress "to bring about, if not a universal creed, certainly a universal code to morals, to be used as a standard by lawmakers, emperors, merchant-princes, clergymen and laymen; and to be fixed as the sun in the centre of our universe.""[24]

This World Congress had been under consideration as early as 1889 where a proposal was published in The Statesman titled "A World's Congress at the World's Fair."

> "The crowning glory of the World's Fair of 1892 should not be the exhibit then to be made of the material triumphs, industrial achievements and mechanical victories of man, however magnificent that display may be. Something higher and nobler is demanded by the enlightened and progressive spirit of the present age...
>
> "For such a congress, convened under circumstances so auspicious, would surpass all previous efforts to bring about a real fraternity of nations, and unite the enlightened people of the whole earth in a general co-operation for the attainment of the great ends for which human society is organized."[25]

The World's Congress Committee of 1892 was represented by Chicago's finest leaders, names still familiar after eighty years: Charles C. Bonney, Lyman Gage, Walter T. Mills, Rt. Rev. Samuel Fallows, D.D., William J. Onahan, John Mitchell, Ferdinand W. Peck, Rev. John H. Barrons, D.D., Julius Rosenthal and John Enander.

Under the watchword, Not Things but Men, the premise for the Congress consisted of eight themes, each of which had many facets. Basically they were:

---

[23]Ibid., p. 325.

[24]Moore, Vol. II, p. 165.

[25]Bonney, Charles Carroll, "Mr. Bonney's Proposal," The Statesman, A Monthly Magazine devoted to Problems of Practical Politics, Co-operative, Industry and Self-Help, The Statesman Publishing Co., Suite H, 78 La Salle Street, Chicago, Oct., 1889, Vol. VI, No. 1, pp. 1-3.

"I. The grounds of fraternal union in the language, literature, domestic life, science and art of different peoples.

II. The practicability of a common language, for use in the commercial relations of the civilized world. [Recall the attempts with later Esperanto.]

III. Educational systems, their advantages and their defects; and the means by which they may best be adapted to the recent enormous increase in all departments of knowledge.

IV. International copy-right and the laws of intellectual property and commerce.

V. Immigration and naturalization laws, and the proper privileges of alien governments and their subjects or citizens.

VI. The most efficient and advisable means of preventing or decreasing pauperism, insanity and crime; and of increasing productive ability, prosperity and virtue throughout the world.

VII. The international law as a bond of union, and a means of mutual protection; and the best means whereby it may be enlarged, perfected and authoritatively expressed.

VIII. The establishment of the principles of judicial justice, as the supreme law of international relations; and the general substitution of arbitration for war, in the settlement of international controversies."[26]

While some of these proposals seem hopeless for negotiation in a world as we know it today, still, if sections VIII and IX could have been more fully studied and understood by civilized, intelligent nations and their leaders - perhaps World Wars I and II would never have occurred. It is reasonable to believe that those efforts in 1892 made by educators, statesmen, clergymen and representatives of many professions as well as all races and most nations of the world were in that brief period, the genesis of the League of Nations, which was succeeded by the United Nations. Others have concluded that the World's Auxiliary Congress

"was a visionary and impossible project... We listened to them and applauded them, our duty done, took our gay way out to the radiant Fair where they rapturously followed."[27]

After the World's Fair, James Ellsworth helped persuade Marshall Field to endow the Fine Arts Building as the Field Museum of Natural History. In 1896, Ellsworth approached Daniel H. Burnham on creating a plan for the development of a parkway from Jackson Park to Grant Park. Mr. Burnham's plan was then shown to the city's entrepreneurs - George Pullman was willing to release certain riparian rights to pave the way while Marshall Field saw the

---

[26]Ibid.

[27]Calhoun, Mrs. William J., "The World's Fair," in Kirkwood, Caroline, Chicago Yesterdays, Daughaday & Co., Chicago, 1919, p. 296.

commercial advantages to the downtown district and Philip D. Armour prophesied that some day this plan would be accomplished.[28] It was, and has continued with greater improvements extending north of the Loop, as well as increasing the land area of the park by filling in the shore-line - all of which would have pleased James Ellsworth had he been living today.

There were three buildings left from the Fair for the next generation to see; the rest had folded their tents like the Arabs. The Fine Arts Building became the Field Museum of Natural History; the German Building became a refectory near the beach and the Chicago Art Institute has continued as a vital, sheltering building for the fine arts. As a little girl, a visit to the aged looking museum and several hours spent communing with Egyptian mummies, followed by an ice cream soda in the empty-looking and echoing German Building, was my limited vision of the once proud Exposition in Jackson Park.

The Chicago Art Institute's history began when the Art School was formed in 1866, later becoming known as the Chicago Academy of Design in 1882 and then the Chicago Art Institute, meeting in rented rooms until the building was ready. In 1897, the Alexander N. Fullerton Hall was built and in 1901, the Martin A. Reyerson Library was added. By 1904, under Director William R. French, the Art School had an enrollment of 2,500 students including day, evening, Juvenile Saturday School and summer sessions. My sister, Florence, graduated from the Normal Department in 1904, and among the faculty at that time were John H. Vanderpoel, Frederick W. Freer, Jannette Buckley, Louis J. Millet and Lorado Taft. J. Wellington Reynolds taught portrait painting around 1913.[29]

It was a great joy when I, too, went to Juvenile Saturday School in 1915-16, studying Decorative Design under Alvin Kramer. It was also fun to hold the tails of the lions which majestically stand guard at the Institute entrance. This has been a temptation for generations; so much so, that the bronze tails have become highly polished, while the manes keep a worthy patina.

A late student of the World's Columbian Exposition of 1893 judges Chicago's historic panorama to have been a splendid example of functioning committees with many individuals' dedicated services, as well as our country's appreciation of the world's cooperation and patronage in this our greatest international assembling of peoples and ideas. Every great event has to have some controversial estimate of its greatness as well as its weakness. No man is so universally grounded in all the aspects of the arts, sciences and philosophies that he can censure with any degree of finality the results of such collective participation.

Daniel A. Burnham felt that in one sense the Exposition of 1893 would "be the third great American event, comparable to 1776 and 1861. "In both these crises men came to the front and gave themselves up to the public...""[30]

---

[28]Kershner, Howard Eldred, The Ellsworth Family, National Americana Society, New York, N. Y., 1930, Vol. 1, p. 84.

[29]French, William R., Historical Sketch and Description of the Art Institute, brochure, Chicago Art Institute, Chicago, IL, 1904.

[30]Moore, Vol. I, p. 43.

35. Palace of Arts, World's Columbian Exposition of 1893, Chicago. It was also called the Fine Arts Building. During the interim period between housing the art collection at the exposition and the opening of the Museum of Science and Industry, this building was know as the Field Columbian Museum and Field Museum of Natural History. Courtesy Chicago History Museum.

36. Looking across the Court of Honor towards the Administration Building, east to west, during the World's Columbian Exposition of 1893. Courtesy Chicago History Museum.

37. Transportation Building Facade showing the Golden Doorway, World's Columbian Exposition of 1893. C. D. Arnold, photographer. Courtesy Chicago History Museum.

38. Relic of World's Columbian Exposition of 1893, currently located at Western Reserve Academy, Hudson, Ohio. Courtesy Western Reserve Academy.

39. La Rabida, World's Columbian Exposition of 1893. Courtesy Chicago History Museum.

CARTER HENRY HARRISON I

Citizens of Chicago, its old West Side, and in particular, a mile square of that region, are proud to claim two of Chicago's "first citizens" as having lived among them for a considerable period of time at 231 South Ashland Boulevard. They are Carter Henry Harrison and his son, Carter Henry Harrison II. It can be said that Chicago was most fortunate in having two such superior men for mayors of this city. Father and son, each elected for five terms; probably no other city in United States has ever had this distinction.

Besides their high degree of political acumen they answered the ideal description for an official of any high office whether federal, state or municipal. As leaders their assets were their interests in the common man, a trite but embracing title; their sympathetic knowledge of the foreigner who predominated in Chicago's population during most of these two mayors' years; their tact in dealing with corrupt political citizens, as well as with the under-privileged and ignorant poor, and in keeping the continued support of the upper class citizens, composed of professional and successful persons, many of whom belonged to the opposite political party of their leader.

At this late date it is pointless to review the political history of these two mayors; much has become obsolete with the vast changes in world environment, even since the death of Carter H. Harrison II in 1952 and more phenomenally so since 1893, the death of Mayor Carter H. Harrison.

Rather, we should learn from their records of leadership as well as their citizenship in Chicago, what intensely human, well-balanced and down-to-earth individuals they were. At the same time we catch glimpses of their old neighborhood as well as the larger area of Chicago itself.

In the ancestry of Carter Henry Harrison were such historic personages as the American Indians, King Powhatan and the princess Pocahontas; there was Robert Carter, rector of William and Mary College and a member of the House of Burgesses in Williamsburg, Virginia. There was the Benjamin Harrison family who bore that name for five generations and furnished two presidents of the United States. In the marriage of Anne Carter, daughter of Robert Carter to the fourth Benjamin Harrison the name of Carter Henry Harrison became a family name, both in the early South and later in Chicago.[1] This name carried on to Mayor Carter Henry Harrison's grandson who had four daughters - the end of a name's dynasty but not the proud members of the Harrison lineage.

Mayor Carter H. Harrison was born to Carter Henry Harrison and Caroline Russell Harrison on February 15, 1825 on a plantation near Lexington, Kentucky. The father would die when his only child was a few months old. The mother would raise the boy, giving him his early schooling as well as managing the family plantation.

Late in life Carter H. Harrison wrote a volume of his travels around the world in 1889 entitled, A Race with the Sun. In a few parts it was autobiographical and revealed pages from

---

[1]Johnson, Claudius O., Carter Henry Harrison I, University of Chicago Press, Chicago, 1928, p. 6.

his early childhood. As a child of three he visited his father's grave and recalled hearing his mother in prayer: "Thou has promised to be a father to the fatherless and the widow's God."

With tears on her cheek she said to her young son:

> "...his last words were for you: "Tell our child that an honest man is the noblest work of God. Teach him not to tell a lie"; and then he died."[2]

While Carter H. Harrison was still a child his mother wrote out the father's last wishes for her son and gave the paper to him. This family treasure was given by the mayor to his daughter for safe keeping. Under his mother's signature he had added a few lines of guidance for his own children. On his last campaign for mayor when sixty-eight years old, he recalled the precept - to be truthful, which he had learned from his mother.[3]

Young Harrison, after being tutored by his mother and later by Dr. Lewis Marshall, attended school in Kentucky and then entered Yale where he graduated in 1845. Upon his graduation he started to study law in Transylvania University but interrupted his training to help his mother on the plantation.

After her remarriage, he went abroad for two years in Europe and the Mid-east, taking notes as a thoughtful student. In 1855 he finally received his law degree and in the same year married Sophonisba Preston of Henderson, Kentucky. Included in their wedding trip was a visit to Chicago at which time it was decided this was the place in which they would finally settle. After selling the plantation property they came to Chicago in 1858.

Young Harrison's first pursuit was not establishing a law office but buying Chicago property. In a letter in 1856 he wrote:

> "I am about to purchase another piece of land, (the first being at Clark and Harrison Streets) about three miles from the centre of the city, but just in the suburbs, and the seller lets me have fifty-five acres of good land adjoining it, simply by fencing and paying taxes for six or seven years. On this I think I can make a very handsome thing by gardening on a large scale. As soon as I have got things in proper gearing I shall open my office and do the best I can for my clients, if I ever have any. On the five acres I shall build; and my wife may amuse herself raising flowers and bramah chickens."[4]

---

[2]Harrison, Carter Henry, A Race with the Sun, Dibble Publishing Co., Chicago, 1889, pp. 246-7.

[3]"Traits of Mr. Harrison, Unique Peculiarities That Marked a Many-sided Character," Chicago Times, Sunday, Nov. 5, 1893, pp. 4-5.

[4]Abbot, Willis, J., Carter Henry Harrison: A Memoir, Dodd, Mead & Co., N.Y., 1895, p. 48.

In 1857 with Henry H. Honore, his associate in investments, and several others, they bought forty acres of land from Madison to Harrison Streets and from Ashland (Reuben) to the west. Harrison in the meantime built a home on Hermitage and Congress (Tyler) in 1860. When the Honore family moved to Michigan Avenue in 1866, the Harrison family moved to this home at 231 South Ashland and would occupy it until the death of Carter H. Harrison in 1893.

In 1857 there had been a recession in Chicago and young Harrison had considered staying in Kentucky, but as skies cleared such a thought faded away. The next shadow was the Fire of 1871 followed by a recession in 1873. Harrison had now "hung out his shingle" of his law practice, specializing in real estate law and having many non-resident clients, especially in Kentucky. He also was being noticed for his civic activities as well as his reputation for speech making.

His first political position would be on the new board of county commissioners starting in December, 1871 with a three year term. In the spring of 1873 the family went to Germany; the two older children were in school there while Mrs. Harrison was seeking better health. She had lost six children in infancy or early childhood by 1873 and was expectant for another child.[5] In December of 1873 a daughter, Sophie Preston Harrison was born in Heidelberg, Germany.

In the fall of 1874 Harrison was elected to the Forty-Fourth Congress and by March of 1875 he went to Washington, his family still in Germany. Mrs. Harrison would die suddenly in September, 1876, and the sorrowing family returned to Chicago. Harrison would serve a second term in Congress and by 1878 retired with his family at the Ashland Avenue home.

It was not for long; by the spring of 1879 he was elected Mayor of Chicago on the Democratic ticket and would be reelected in 1881, 1883 and 1885. In 1887 Carter H. Harrison's second wife, Marguerite Stearns Harrison died and the mayor retired from politics, taking what might be called a sabbatical leave from 1887 to 1891. He went on a world tour lasting over a year and covering most all of the important countries and their cities. He took with him his younger son, William Preston and his friend John M. Amberg, both boys being in their teens.

All his life Carter H. Harrison had been an outgoing, observing person and enjoyed people of all stations in life. On this long tour he wrote:

> "I visit cities more to look at and into their people, than at and into their edifices and shows."[6]

This world voyage was recorded in letters and then published in book form as A Race with the Sun. While generally descriptive of persons and places, it also contained introspective thoughts of this extroverted man, especially since at this period he was relieved of political and possessive impulses which had ruled his younger years. Now in a relaxed mood he wrote:

---

[5]Ibid., p. 63.

[6]Ibid., p. 155.

"Reclining upon an easy chair... I watched the waves coming in from the east, and thought of my own native land and dear ones on the other side of the world. The waxing moon was climbing half-way up to its zenith, a dim, silvery spectre upon the hot, blue sky. It had been shining upon my own land but a few hours before perhaps and lighted up the faces of some of those who were so dear to me. As I looked, I almost fancied I could see them photographed upon its pale silvered plate.

"There in my west-side snow-mantled home were my children - my laughing little girl - a father's heart went out to enfold them. There were my good neighbors and true friends from all over the city. One by one they walked across the polished plate, and bent upon me a kindly look. Friends of every nationality, Teuton and Hibernian, Frenchman and Norseman. Bohemian and Dane, Italian and Swede, Christian and Jew, rich and poor. Ah! How I wish I could bid you pale moon to bear to them my own picture, looking as I feel, brimful of goodwill, and running over with kindly fellowship. To one and all I drink a cup as full as yon sea - a cup brimming over with affection."[7]

Although the Mayor had written that he visited cities to know their people and not the scenery, his writings were often minute details of scenery so as to portray a picture for his reader. In 1890 with his youngest daughter Sophinisba, they took a trip to the far western United States and Alaska which was recorded in A Summer's Outing and The Old Man's Story. The descriptions of Yellowstone National Park are timeless. The "Canyon below the Falls" scenes concur with the modern viewer's reaction:

"The rocks lift on either side in mighty buttresses like giant cathedral walls. Standing out before the walls are towers and pointed spires of the most artistic form. All painted in exquisite tints. The upper walls are of yellow and orange hue, with here and there towers and bulwarks of chalky white or of black lava over which is a film of venetian red... Had an artist tried to sell me a picture of these cliffs before I had seen them... I would have called him a fraud... I have seen now and then pictures which I considered daubs, which I now know did not overdo Nature in its freak rock-painting."[8]

Upon Mayor Harrison's return home from his travels he again put on his fighting armor at the request of his many political friends and probably, too, from his own restless urge. The Republicans had triumphed as mayors in 1887 with John C. Roche and in 1889 with De Witt C. Cregier. The newspapers of the ensuing period from 1889 to 1891 were strongly leaning to

---

[7]Ibid., p. 259.

[8]Harrison, Carter H., A Summer's Outing and The Old Man's Story, Dibble Publishing Co., Chicago, 1891, pp. 78-9.

the Republican party. In the election of April 7, 1891, Carter H. Harrison trailed as a Democrat Independent in third place.

At this uncertain point in his political career Harrison and his family purchased the Chicago Times, a Democratic newspaper. His reasons were that he had gone out of office in 1887 with a press united in opposition to him and he wanted to have a paper on which he could rely "through fair weather or foul" and he had said after his election failure - "Not a newspaper in Chicago is willing to set me right".[9] It was evident that this investment paid off in the 1893 election of Carter H. Harrison with an overwhelming majority over his opponents.

Willis Abbot who was editor of Harrison's Chicago Times defended his candidate in that last election of 1893. In part he wrote:

> "...If abuse could ruin a politician, Harrison would have been destroyed. If ridicule could have driven him out of town, he would have fled. Neither truth, decency, nor common sense was permitted by the editors of the opposite press to stand in the way of their malice... They demanded, rather than advised, the defeat of this man, held over the people the whip of the slave-driver rather than the torch of the guide... The subscribers of five to six morning papers saw Harrison daily described as an associate of gamblers, conscienceless politician, a weak-minded and insanely egotistic old man... "[10]

When the tirade of the press was at its worst, Harrison, his sons and editor did not fight back with abuse but rather printed excerpts from the Mayor's record of four previous administrations and forbid the printing in the Times of any abuse of the Mayor's opponents.

It was during those last days of Carter H. Harrison's life and those following his assassination that the once withheld sentiments of respect and honor now embraced him in both life and death. The Mayor's love of Nature was extolled as it reflected in his home on Ashland Boulevard. He prided himself on his luck with horticultural pursuits as well as the plain husbandry of his block square property, a veritable miniature of his Kentucky home's domesticity.

He loved animals, perhaps horses, the best. The Mayor and his saddle horse, Kate, became a Chicago legend; they were seen together so often - on the boulevards, on alley and street inspections, protesting throngs - he was on the job. It was written:

> "...between this horse and rider grew up the strongest attachment. He knew every trait and she seemed to respond with zeal and intelligence to his desires. When he returned home from his trip around the world, though he had been absent over

---

[9]Abbot, p. 147.

[10]Ibid., pp. 205-6.

a year, she recognized him, and in many ways displayed her delight at his return..."[11]

As one reads the various comments on Mayor Harrison one is most impressed by the interest shown in him by the average Chicagoan - whether it was as a father, neighbor or dignitary. It is recalled that when Princess Eulalie of Spain arrived at the railroad station for the World's Fair visit, the majestic formality of the occasion was made a delightful, relaxed experience for the welcoming crowd. As the Mayor arrived in his fine carriage and a silk "topper," the people went wild with cheers. The band was to have played "Hail to the Chief" but there was a quick shifting to the tune "Where Did You Get that Hat?" The Mayor was as thrilled as the audience and his hat would be long remembered.[12]

Yet the paths of glory lead but to the grave - hardly had the spectacular World's Fair had its day when the assassin, Patrick Prendergast, a disgruntled office seeker, shot the Mayor as he opened the door of his hospitable home at 231 South Ashland. An era in Chicago history had suddenly ended.

Down through the years, even as late as these 1970's, there are those who recall the sad day when Mayor Carter H. Harrison was assassinated. As a little girl, Mary Hastings Bradley has living at the home of her grandmother, Mrs. Francis Rickords, on Ashland Boulevard diagonally across from the Harrison home. Mayor Harrison had just stopped at the Rickords' home to talk with Mary's great-grandfather about the World's Fair happenings on that day and then had crossed the street to the Harrison house. He had only been inside his home for a short time when a shot rang out and was heard throughout the neighborhood. It would seem that the assailant had followed his victim's path to the door.[13]

> "Here we leave Carter H. Harrison I, known to all largely through his ability to advertise himself through his native and acquired dramatic characteristics: admired by all for his conspicuous courage. He was supported by the majority because he had no boss and would tolerate none, because of his capacity for friendship with every class, race and creed, because of his liberal views on social and political questions, and because of his frugality, integrity, and strict attention to the duties of his office. Although not a demagogue, he possessed superficial and well-nigh indispensable characteristics of the politician which, happily combined with more fundamental qualities brought him repeated triumphs at the polls, the final and most signal honor being his election as World's Fair Mayor."[14]

---

[11]"Traits of Mr. Harrison Unique Peculiarities That Marked a Many-sided Character," Chicago Times, Nov. 5, 1893, p. 22.

[12]Johnson, pp. 159-160.

[13]Correspondence between Mary Hastings Bradley and the author.

[14]Johnson, p. 287.

Carter H. Harrison.
age 55.

40. Carter H. Harrison I, age 55. Copy of photograph appears in: Carter Henry Harrison: A Memoir by Willis John Abbot, Dodd, Mead & Company, New York, 1895, opposite p. 112. Call Number E5 .H246. Photo Courtesy of The Newberry Library, Chicago.

THE VILLAGE SQUIRE, JAMES ELLSWORTH

"The facts of any life, if one can get at them, are always more interesting than anything the imagination can invent, though imagination must aid biography to achieve, if it can, that synthesis which is the aim of any art."

Brand Whitlock
Preface to La Fayette, 1929[1]

By 1900, James W. Ellsworth having given his energies to Chicago's cultural growth, now enjoyed an active retirement as a world citizen. He had homes in New York, the Villa Palmieri near Florence, Italy where Boccaccio wrote the Decameron and a Hapsburg castle at Schloss Lenzburg, Switzerland, once the home of Marie Antoinette. In 1907, he returned to his birthplace, Hudson, Ohio, part of the original Western Reserve Territory. Here in his ancestral home, he would house some of his treasures from his Chicago residence. He would, however, sell the bulk of his world famous paintings, Greek sculpture, rare Chinese porcelains and a Gutenberg Bible as part of the financial preparation for his next pursuit which would last until his life's end.

His affiliations covered a wide spectrum, from the Vasari Society of London, the American Association for the Advancement of Science, the Ayrshire Breeders' Association of Vermont to the First Congregational Church of Hudson, Ohio - truly an epilogue to his versatile life.[2]

Now he gave his attention to this rural, peaceful village of less than two thousand inhabitants. Western Reserve College had left its near century old campus in Hudson to become a University in Cleveland in 1880. Mr. Ellsworth restored the architecturally worthy buildings, most of which were of Greek Revival influence. The rehabilitated campus became Western Reserve Academy, a boys' preparatory school. At his death, Mr. Ellsworth would leave a $4,000,000 trust fund, as well as his accumulated Hudson land holdings to the Academy.

In the meantime, he had concentrated on village improvements - a new village green or Square with its clock tower; underground electricity for the entire community; municipal water works and sewerage system. In his enthusiasm for an English type village, he gave red clay tiles to those wishing a new roof. The result was that some century old, white frame houses sagged under the weight of their new roofs.

Among the conditions agreed upon between Mr. Ellsworth and the Village of Hudson, which was to be binding for a fifty year period, was that no intoxicating liquors, except beer, were to

---

[1]Whitlock, Brand, La Fayette, D. Appleton & Co., New York & London, 1929, Preface, p. ix-x.

[2]Kershner, Howard Eldred, The Ellsworth Family, National Americana Society, New York, New York, 1930, Vol. 1, p. 84.

be sold in the Village. This was a controversial issue and the Village voted three to one, to accept the reservation. The news was broadcast from Chicago to New York - "Town Banishes Rum for $250,000 Gift" headlined the New York World after the December 22, 1907 poll.[3]

Mr. Ellsworth's own estate, Evamere, honored Eva Butler Ellsworth, mother of their two children - all a distant echo from old Brown School where Eva Butler had been a student. The extensive acres had woodlands of sugar maples whose syrup rivaled that of Vermont; there were bridle paths; a duck pond where ice was cut in winter and stored;[4] there were stables, a carriage house, windmill and a lofty clock which chimed the hours. At the street entrance was a gatehouse of charming Shakespearian qualities and a red brick euonymus covered wall defined the property facing Aurora Street. If one looked north, east or south, there were Evamere's cattle farms, fields and orchards.

On the grounds of Evamere were two souvenirs from the World's Fair of 1893. One, a log cabin, stood near the mansion for many years; Mr. Ellsworth's and the neighbors' children played in it and called it "Daniel Boone's Cabin." It had been constructed and given to the Exposition by Theodore Roosevelt, known for his love of outdoor life. The cabin was called the Daniel Boone and David Crockett Log Cabin on the Wooded Island of the World's Fair. A long haired hunter was in charge of this exhibit.[5] It was here that the artists and authorities of the Fair sometimes met for discussions as well as revels.[6]

The other bulky souvenir was a gigantic gilded metal eagle which rested on a sphere. Originally, this eagle and its globe were held aloft in the right hand of the robed female colossal Statue of the Republic. Here in a commanding view of the Columbian Exposition buildings overlooking the Main Basin, Daniel C. French's great lady of the Exposition welcomed visitors from all over the world. This colossal statue was probably the largest ever erected in the United States, with the exception of the Statue of Liberty. Here in Hudson, Ohio, a portion of the golden arm with its globe and surmounting eagle were stored in a loft. Lincoln Ellsworth remembered as a lad that the lady's little finger was as tall as he was.[7]

---

[3]Waring, J. F., James W. Ellsworth and the Refounding of Western Reserve Academy, Western Reserve Academy, Hudson, Ohio, 1961, p. 15.

[4]The duck pond was originally called Evamere Lake and was used for swimming in summer and ice skating in winter, as well as ice for domestic use. The duck pond title lingered because among Mr. Ellsworth's live souvenirs from the Exposition, were ornamental poultry such as peacocks, swans and Muscovy ducks. Earlier, these had been the colorful accents in the White City's lagoons and canals.

[5]Ellsworth, Lincoln, Beyond Horizons, Doubleday, Doran & Co., Inc., Garden City, New York, 1937, pp. 3-4.

[6]Moore, Charles, Daniel H. Burnham, Houghton, Mufflin Co., New York, New York, 1921, Vol. 1, between pp. 56 & 57 (photo).

[7]Ellsworth, Lincoln, p. 32.

On Founder's Day in April, 1932, at Western Reserve Academy, this symbolic bird on its perch was displayed on the campus. The eagle appeared about twelve feet tall, while the globe may have been five feet in diameter. The total effect of this exhibit resting on its improvised platform, caused the students to comment on the size of the "egg" that the eagle had laid. In World War II, this relic of the World's Fair was donated to the war effort as scrap metal.

It was necessary in the preparations for the World's Columbian Exposition, to procure many foreign exhibits; James W. Ellsworth, as an individual, probably did more than any other person at that period in touring the world and influencing foreign nations to pledge exhibits.

The Spanish government sent two crosses from Santa Maria de La Rabida Monastery, which were used on the La Rabida Replica at the Exposition. At the close of this great happening, the grateful trustees gave one of the crosses to Mr. Ellsworth and presented the other to a Chicago museum. Mr. Ellsworth, in turn, gave his cross to Western Reserve Academy, where it was placed in the sanctuary of the old chapel which had been restored. At the Founders' Day observance in April, 1932, the service read:

> The cross is placed here as a symbol of <u>Faith in Ideals</u> in the hope that it may give assurance and courage to anyone struggling to realize a dream; and that those going from this school, may take with them the blessing of La Rabida."

The story of Christopher Columbus at the Monastery of La Rabida is an historical fact, though like many simple occurrences, it became enshrined in the fabric of tradition. It was at this monastery in La Rabida, in 1491, that Columbus, weary and discouraged in his search for ships and money for his expedition, begged bread and shelter for himself and little son, Diego. The prior, Juan Perez, had faith in Columbus and his vision. As the prior had been confessor to Queen Isabella, he secured the interview which eventually led to Columbus' discovery of the new world.

Before dawn on August 3, 1492, Columbus having made his communion at St. George's Church in Palos, boarded his flagship and the anchors of <u>Santa Maria</u>, <u>Pinta</u>, and <u>Nina</u> were lifted aboard.[8] A mile-and-a-half away at La Rabida, the friars were chanting the office of prime. Tradition says that Columbus, before setting sail, took his communion from the hands of Fray Juan at La Rabida. <u>The Admiral of the Ocean Sea</u> needed much spiritual help for his great mission.

The beneficence of Spain's gift of La Rabida Replica lives on today in La Rabida Children's Hospital and Research Center in a complex of modern buildings at East 65th Street and Lake Michigan.

In 1895 Senor Staud, the Spanish Consul in Chicago, began the care of sick infants of the poor in the building which Spain had built for the Exposition, the replica of the Monastery of Santa Maria de La Rabida at Palos, Spain where Christopher Columbus and his son had refuge and help.

---

[8]Morrison, Samuel Elliot, <u>Admiral of the Ocean Sea</u>, Little, Brown & Co., Boston, Mass., 1942, p. 158.

This original replica was used as a hospital until 1918 when new buildings were needed. Today, children from infancy to age nineteen are given diagnosis and treatment of major long-term health problems; originally, the control and prevention of rheumatic fever and rheumatic heart diseases were specialized in. Today there are three divisions, Medical, Research and Behavioral Sciences. Truly the spirit and guidance of La Rabida lives on.

It was my family's good fortune in later years, to live in Hudson near the old Ellsworth home and to own the little gatehouse; my sister lived there for a time after retiring from teaching at Lewis Institute. Our children, along with the Academy masters' flocks, some of whom lived in apartments in the old mansion, roamed the Ellsworth Woods, either on horse or foot and rested with picnics in the rustic shelter house on the creek. They played in the dusty carriage house and its horseless phaeton. They ventured into the barn where old, yellowed ledger papers, dating back to Mr. Ellsworth's coal mining days, fluttered in the drafty hayloft. Such was the pathos of Evamere, the end of an age.

Mr. Ellsworth's son, Lincoln Ellsworth, is most famous for his epochal polar flight, known as the Amundsen-Ellsworth Expedition in 1925 to the South Pole. Earlier, Lincoln had written his father for financial help on this momentous project:

> "When you stop to think that the majority of people look forward to the possession of worldly things... I do not wish worldly goods... I do want the opportunity to make good and satisfy my inward self along the line of endeavor I have chosen... No better opportunity than that of being permitted under such a capable master... as Captain Roald Amundsen".[9]

The contribution given by Lincoln Ellsworth's father made the polar flight possible and James W. Ellsworth died in 1925 unaware that his son was alive, since at that time he had been reported missing.

_____

[9]Kershner, Vol. II, pp. 58-9.

SOUVENIRS OF THE WORLD'S FAIR

After a visit to the World's Fair in 1893, my sisters, then in fifth and seventh grades at Brown School, carried home delightful souvenirs - small keepsakes, remnants of time and place.

Among their souvenirs were two identical miniature, silver tea sets, each consisting of a tray, teapot, sugar bowl, creamer and two cups with saucers. The tray, less than three inches long was a perfect copy of an old Sheffield tray with grapes and leaves around the border, handles representing curved stems while the center surface simulated a chased design. The teapot, only an inch high, was a graceful curved form with a spout that really poured and the domed lid was hinged to the pot. The other pieces were of the same motif and all truly, exquisitely fashioned.

I was allowed to play with these tea sets. With the passage of time and many little hands fingering these precious items, one complete set was lost. The remaining set survived with a tray, teapot and sugar bowl. Later it was considered an heirloom and rested under a glass dome.

About fifty year after the Exposition, I chanced to be in an antique shop in Hudson, Ohio. An old, but charming doll house with a mansard roof, dormer windows and remnants of a balcony stood before me. I opened the front to peek in; although it was in disarray with legless chairs and many years of neglect, I was entranced and thought of my own childhood doll house. Fingering the tiny furniture, I suddenly saw the exact duplicate of our heirloom tea set; this too, had survived with only a tray, teapot and sugar bowl. I wanted to buy the set because my two little girls would love to own it. The shopkeeper was adamant, the tea set could not be sold separately. It was decided that the little house should be bought, restored and sold later. So we took the doll house home with its precious tea set. The children loved every broken article in this quaint three story, six room house. Chairs and tables found their legs; collapsed drawers now fitted into Lilliputian walnut chests and canopied beds with pink covers and "roses bedlight" held small dolls while the tea set reigned in the dining room on a rosewood table and tiny birthday cake candles lighted the room. Sell the doll house? Never - the whole family loved it.

So the years passed - the story is not over. The little girls and their three brothers grew up and now have little girls who like doll houses. The little old house is still intact and grandchildren play carefully with these ancient toys. A year or two ago at Christmas time, I passed an antique store in Santa Barbara, in a twinkling of an eye saw the exact duplicate of our old doll house in the window. It had been carefully restored. In comparing notes with the dealer, we found the houses to be dated the same, around 1850; this one from London, mine from Philadelphia. There was little doubt, one craftsman made them both. I cast a glance at the price tag - it was almost twenty times more than had been paid for ours with its dusty clutter. Later, a New York interior decorator bought this second miniature house and said that she would never part with it, for she loved it very much.

Relative to old doll houses and old neighbors on Monroe Street, our next door neighbor of years ago, Ralph Wheeler, a graduate in Decorative Design from the Chicago Art Institute, was one of the designers and craftsmen for Mrs. James Ward Thorne's Collection of Miniature Rooms. This is now permanently exhibited at the Chicago Art Institute after its many exhibitions over the country. These precise and authentically detailed rooms of historic homes are so perfect that the viewer, like Alice in Wonderland, seems reduced to the size of these creature reproductions. In no sense can one feel it to be an exhibit of toyland, yet children and adults both appreciate these exquisite works of art.

Another World's Columbian Exposition relic has been rescued and is now at Vernon Park. In fact, Vernon Park has also been rescued and restored. Here stands a statue of Christopher Columbus within sight from the Illinois Medical Center and walking distance from the University of Illinois Circle Campus. Both the resurrection of the Columbian monument and Vernon Park are excellent examples of urban renewal.

Here around the original block square park those "good red bricks" of the sturdy, mid-nineteenth century houses have been cleaned and painted while the windows and porches are inviting with shining glass and fresh paint. Descendants of earlier Italian and French families now living in this neighborhood and the new-comers, many of whom are professors at the Circle Campus or medical associates from the Medical Center - all have realized the charm as well as the convenience of this old neighborhood. One of those is Leonard Currie, Dean of the College of Architecture and Art at the Circle Campus. His restoration of a century old large brick house and its coach house resulted in making three apartments with separate entrances yet retaining the original effect of the old mansion.

Many of these "old-new" homes look out from their small dooryard gardens to the grassy mall which has been widened by creating cul-de-sacs of some of the streets. The approach is named Columbus Plaza and here Christopher Columbus invites the walking visitor. A metal, nine foot, 14,000 pound statue of the explorer stands encircled above a pool and fountain which protect and beautify the pedestal. Columbus appears as if scanning the distant view.

This Columbus monument has a long and moving history, literally speaking. Originally, it was created by an American, Moses Ezekial, and cast in Rome for the Italian Exhibit at the World's Fair. After 1893 it was moved to the Columbus Memorial Building at State and Randolph where it occupied a niche until 1959 when this building was demolished. The homeless statue landed in a lumber-yard on the West Side.

Once a year the Italians of Vernon Park area, sometimes referred to as "Little Italy," hauled out the statue and placed it on a float each Columbus Day. It was the dream of many Italians and other patriots that this Columbus monument be placed in Vernon Park. Such was made possible by a fund of $75,000 and maintenance by the community. This Columbus Plaza was dedicated October 12, 1966; Stephen Roman was the architect.

The spirit of 1893 lingers on while the restored homes recapture the earlier charm of that neighborhood and where today the "French" Church of Notre Dame with its rare stained glass windows and the more recent "Italian" Church of Our Lady of Pompeii help to reflect the feeling of renaissance for the near West Side.

41. Cross of La Rabida. Courtesy Western Reserve Academy.

42. Christopher Columbus Monument, Vernon Park. Courtesy Chicago Park District.

BOOK TWO

IN MY DAY

Here, in this section of the book, its writer, Marjorie Warvelle Bear, joins the procession of those who once lived in "A Mile Square of Chicago." It was here she experienced her young life with its joys and sorrows. Much of the detailed history of our public and private educational systems during the pre-war years of the twentieth century was my own experience. I have a deep gratitude for the privilege of having been a student in Chicago's schools.

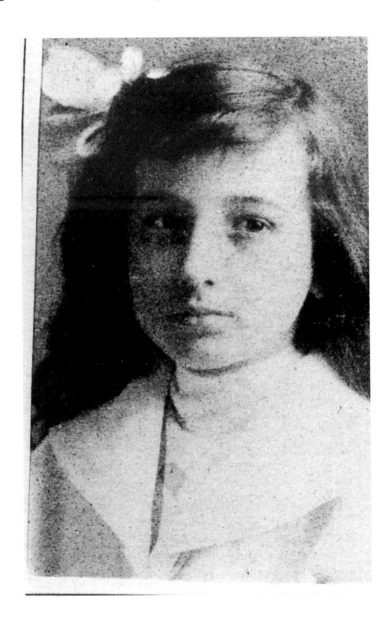

43. Marjorie Warvelle Bear, 8 years old (born July 28, 1897, Chicago, Illinois, fifth child).

CHAPTER FIVE: MY HOME

THE HOUSE WE LIVED IN

"Where we love is home,
Home that our feet may leave, but not our hearts."

Oliver Wendell Homes (1809-1894)

The old home at 654 West Monroe Street, Chicago, Illinois, was purchased in 1887 by George W. Warvelle for the sum of seven thousand dollars, plus the interest charges which were carried over for several years. It had been previously occupied, and at the time of purchase, was owned by the Van Vlissingan Brokerage Firm of Chicago. The street numbering of the house was later changed to 1743 West Monroe Street (between Paulina and Wood Streets).

At the time of purchase the location of the house was in a good residential section of Chicago. While there were some fine mansions on Washington Boulevard and Ashland Avenue where many of the wealthy pioneers of Chicago lived, such as Governor Carter Harrison, Potter Palmer and others, those on Monroe Street were substantial, pleasant neighbors with common interests, such as happy children and civic pride.

Putting aside such pretensions as pride, for the old house is now very old and decrepit, and the neighborhood a degenerated city street, let us try to recall in word pictures how the old house looked fifty years ago.

The house at 654 West Monroe Street, on the outside, looked just like its neighbor next door and many other houses for blocks around. It was a three-story, ten-room, white limestone front structure, less than thirty feet wide and seventy feet deep. Yet it was more than that, it was a home, just as all those other monotonous city houses were homes. An architectural historian would judge this house, and the thousands like it in Chicago and other cities, as eclectic, being composed of a diversity or conglomeration of architectural styles. A more sentimental but not distinguishing classification would be Victorian.

The lot (30' x 187') was somewhat longer than the average lots of the neighborhood, but the width was the prevailing, meager apportionment in the city planning. Needless to say, the house took up the entire width of the lot save for a narrow passage way for a service area to the rear of the building. On one side, the house had a common wall with its next door neighbor. It depended on its front and back, north and south exposures, for its air and light. Consequently, the house was only two rooms deep on all three floors. It contained ten rooms; there was the dining room, kitchen and servants' room on the first floor. At the rear end of the lower hall was the furnace. On the second floor was the front parlor, the back parlor or library, and a library bedroom. On the third floor were two large and two small bedrooms and one bath. There were lavatories in three of the bedrooms.

Even in inventory from childhood memory, there was much in those long-lived-in-rooms that could be called sentimental clutter, as well as uselessly ugly. Just as yesterday's long skirts appear ridiculous to us now, today's short hemlines will be equally ridiculous tomorrow and tomorrow's will return to the day before yesterday's length. It will be the same when our grandchildren toss out their parents' fit-your-spine chairs, spike-legged cocktail tables, cold gravel and plastic flower beds and non-private picture windows.

In memory many chairs were uncomfortable, the backs too rigid or the horsehair upholstery stuck one like needles; what use was a vis-a-vis, letter "S" chair, except to converse about, not in. A child delighted in one old marble topped walnut table whose pedestal base had wooden knobs which made imaginary faucets to be turned on for a soda fountain or a kitchen sink.

In the kitchen was an old-fashioned coal range with an oven, which was used both for cooking and for heating the first floor. A large gas range was used for the major cooking. Connecting the kitchen and dining room was a butler's pantry or cupboard. Six very large drawers held all the package provisions and bulky groceries, dish towels and mopping materials. Above, were doors opening on wide shelves which held all the china and glassware. There was just room for a narrow table and two chairs in this passage way. The children called it the "dining car,' and the space served as a "breakfast nook" for many years. Off the kitchen was a dark, large pantry which was used to store cooking utensils, the ironing board and utility articles. On the shelves were stored canned goods and jars of fruit. The kitchen opened out onto the back yard which was about one hundred feet in length.

The dining room bay of three windows was where mother kept her house plants. There were ivies, palms and geraniums the year round.

One distinct piece of furniture in the dining room was the sideboard. It was a ponderous structure made of rosewood and mahogany with an Italian marble top. Above were tiers of mirrors on either side of a large central mirror above which was a bas-relief in brass of birds on a leafy branch. In the base part of the sideboard were four drawers for table linens and silver. Under these were cupboard spaces for bottles and crockery. Father bought the sideboard in the early eighties from a friend who was moving away. He only paid a small fraction of the original cost which had been five hundred dollars. The dining room chairs were of mahogany, upholstered in dark wine-colored leather and matched well with the sideboard.

The large drop-leaf and extension table was always set for six. When death took the little son, Gerald Bangs, his chair remained there and his individual knife, fork and spoon, child size, were set in their habitual places, and for many years a small bowl of garden flowers at his place recalled his presence. The same was true when Florence Octavia passed on - her place remained waiting for her all these years. Recently, another generation has come to sit in the places of their elders, and the silver baby cups of Gerald now find a new purpose in the hands of these little grandchildren.

The front parlor had a regal appearance, and in its hey day was a perfect example of the best of the Victorian style. In the front bay of three tall windows were long, exquisitely fine, Brussels lace curtains hung on brass rings from shiny brass rods. The lace itself was a point design on bobbin net. The mantel piece was draped in a pale blue flowered silk, edged with ivory tassel fringe. Tassel fringe and ivory silk cords hung in festoons between the two connecting rooms. The drapes at the windows of the library were a pale Roman striped mohair extending to the floor. About the house, the shades were seldom drawn, usually the dark finished shutters were used instead.

The front parlor and the back parlor or library shared a Brussels carpeting; we walked in a flower garden as deep red roses with no thorns roamed among green and brown leaves of worsted pile. The sun had faded the design's sharpness and new colors appeared by way of spilt stains. This garden-like carpet gave way to modernization (large domestic rugs) at the time of the bathroom's renaissance.

A few pieces of furniture will be described because they were so typical of the front stone houses of that period. There was a double seat or lovers' seat with a matching single chair and a hassock, all of which were upholstered in a rich golden brocade trimmed with light blue velvet and cord and tassels. They were always kept covered with natural color denim slips and were uncovered only on state occasions and holidays. Several other Empire "lady chairs" and a horse hair rocker were always treated with extra concern, and little children did not sit on these chairs. There were several lovely tables and what-not which had belonged to "Auntie."

The walls were twelve feet high and an elaborate molded frieze of fruits and flowers in the center of the ceiling, where a bronze chandelier was suspended with five brackets. These held etched glass globes to protect the gas flames. Two other fixtures are recalled: the middle hall hanging opalescent globe resembled a lantern in Dicken's world; the lower hall had a ruby-red etched globe which in later years reminded one of the gospel hymn, Let the Lower Lights Be Burning, since the lower entry was used at night.

There were four fireplaces with marble mantels, a grey marble in the dining room and white marble in the two parlors and front bedroom. As one recalls these firesides, they were useful but their ornate Victorian designs were redundant with obscure forms and were not artistic compared to the fireplaces of the earlier American periods. One mantel was a mystery to a child who could not decide if the embellishments on either side were push button bells, or nipples of a lady's breast. On the other hand, they were well proportioned to the rooms and blended with their period, and were far more acceptable than the modern type of over-sized and ill-proportioned brick or stone fireplaces which frequently have a false front, that is, no chimney behind them. They may have a gas log or grate in them. All the fireplaces in the old home were used frequently, with the exception of the one in the front parlor. Since the two parlors opened in one immense room, one burning grate was enough. Both coal and wood were used, and these fireplaces were depended on to supplement the furnace heat which in very cold weather was not sufficient to heat rooms with twelve-foot ceilings.

One could observe many objects on the mantel top or its shelves on either side of a large mirror. There was a covered jar I always explored. It was cut from an alabaster step of our ancestor's home in England. He had conducted a boys' school in Headingley, and my grandmother brought this jar to America as a piece that would be forever England to her. Mamma kept dried rose petals in it and strangely, just opening the lid of this fragrant past led my way to other gardens and faces I was told about. There were a Sheffield silver candle snuffer and tray, an Italian molded china figurette of Mary and her lamb, an English ivory porcelain water pitcher depicting Paul Revere's Ride, and other vases of a later vintage.

In one corner of the room was a walnut whatnot, a "somewhat" to the children. Among the treasures, there was an inlaid tropical glove box of sandal wood with a secret opening and a rural scene made by artisans of Monrovia, Liberia and sent to our family as a token of esteem for the great-uncle who had died there while serving as United States Consul General, appointed by Abraham Lincoln. Resting on the top shelf was a jasper peace pipe carved by the Winnebago Indians; Papa said it breathed a peaceful blessing on our house because it had been smoked. Of all the curiosities most appealing to a child, was a sealed bottle with a cucumber filling the inside, except for some liquid to suspend the cucumber in its cradle. As a boy, Papa had grown the cucumber in the bottle tied on the vine. One can understand why this furniture was called a somewhat.

On subdued green walls, hung four large oil paintings of pastoral and nautical scenes known to me as the "cows in the meadow" and "ships a sailing." These were painted by D. F. Bigelow, a well-known Chicago artist in the 1890's. They were well executed and had an influence of Corot about them. They were in classic, heavy, ornate, gold-leaf frames and gave to the room a touch of Continental grandeur. The gold brocade armless sofa and chairs could feel at home in a modern interior. In the summer, they wore white denim slipcovers, a habit from Williamsburg homes, where people felt cooler sitting on cotton covers.

In the library, or back parlor, every inch of wall space, with the exception of the fireplace, was filled with tall glass-doored mahogany bookcases six feet tall or more. Every book had its place, and my father was able to lay his hand on any desired book. Woe to any one who misplaced a volume!

With a methodical index as well as a consideration of the artistic presence of the attractive bindings of many of his books, my father had classified and arranged the entire collection in sections, as for history, ancient, medieval and modern; for languages, Greek, Latin, French and German. Poetry and prose had various classifications. Encyclopedias and general reference books occupied a separate case, as did theological (including a rare Josephus) and legal reference books. Bound volumes of <u>Atlantic Monthly</u>, <u>Scribner's</u>, <u>Living Age</u>, and other magazines filled a large book case. "Old Books" had a nook of their own. Overflowing from the library, commoner books and texts found their way to the library bedroom which my father occupied for many years. In addition, there were book cases in the bedrooms.

Many of the books have no great value and are out of date; on the other hand, many are priceless, both from their rareness and from personal sentiment attached to them; quite a few, especially among the poetical volumes, are much sought "first editions" and would be a greedy find in the hands of the book collector or dealer in antique books.

My father had the nucleus of his library before he left Kenosha, Wisconsin, and while there had a book plate made for his volumes which read as follows:

"Library of George W. Warvelle,
Kenosha, Wisconsin.

"Neither a borrower nor lender be;
For loan oft loses both itself and friend;
And borrowing dulls the edges of husbandry.

Shakespeare."

Although the bookcases were enclosed, the key to them was always near; just the wish to read was the magic key for Open Sesame. No book was ever forbidden to be read after one had learned to read. Earlier, the child chose books known by their jacket or binding for the elders to narrate. Among the frequent requests were Sweet William and the fairy tales of Thumbelina and The Little Match Girl. The rollicking volume of James Whitcomb Riley's poems, especially, Little Orphant Annie, The Raggedy Man and Our Hired Girl were almost memorized. Eugene Field's The Land of Counterpane and Little Boy Blue were softly read since we had a brother, often sick in bed. It seemed that sad poems outnumbered the gay.

In one of my mother's well-worn books of her teaching days, was a certificate to teach in the third grade; in the volume were Thomas Hood's poems. The Song of the Shirt and The Bridge of Sighs, written of the poor in London or Leeds, seemed very real to me when we traveled on the elevated railroad to the Loop. We passed many children playing in the alleys and streets, while over-head were trolley-like clothes lines full of ghost-like garments drying in the dust and noise. On the crowded back porches of the flats, pans of red pepper paste had been set out to dry.

The library was the real living room of the house, and its heart was the fireplace where in most all seasons an evening cradle of glowing coals was enjoyed by both men and beasts, a cocker spaniel and an Angora cat. A broad, secure old clock passed away the minutes and chimed the hours as it sat on the mantel piece. In addition to the pictures, many of which were part of an early collection of steel engravings of my father, which hung on the library walls above the book cases, two hung over the mantel of Victorian white marble: the Virgin Mary by Sassaferrato and the Head of Christ by Guiodo Reni. Papa always called the fireplace the family altar. Other steel engravings were The Madonna Granduco and The Sistine Madonna by Raphael and The Madonna and the Angels by Murillo. There were several chromoes which had a great appeal for children. One was a robin's nest which had been rifled by a small boy; the sorrowing and dying mother robin lay near her three speckled eggs which had been strung on a sheaf of grain. A broken branch of apple blossoms completed the saga.

It was here, too, that my father had his visitors, frequently students from Chicago Law School where he was Dean, and later from De Paul University where he taught until the last years of his life. A newspaper obituary in November, 1940, reported that probably more law students had passed under Dr. George W. Warvelle's guidance than any law professor in the country - fifty years in teaching day and evening classes and almost as many in writing textbooks for his students.

The library was a sunny room with tall windows facing south, overlooking the backyard garden. There were sectional wooden folding shutters to reduce the glare. In the center of the room was an oval, leather-covered table with drawers and a green-globed student lamp. Surrounding the table were comfortable chairs; my father's chair was a Morris chair made popular in the William Morris and Pre-Raphaelite movement, and which in recent years both the arts and crafts as well as literature have tried to recall in this befuddled day of arts and literature.

As far back as I can recall my father was always revising his law text books for new editions. Such were Warvelle On Vendors, On Ejectment, On Real Property and On Abstracts. He was also creating new books or articles on allied subjects as "The Jurors and the Judge" published

219

in the <u>Harvard Law Review</u>, December 1909; or the book, <u>Essays in Legal Ethics</u> in 1902 which he prefaced:

> "I do not offer this book as a treatise on moral duties, nor do I assume the character of a teacher of morals. It purports to be, and is, nothing more than a series of brief suggestions relative to professional conduct, and as such it is submitted to those for whom the subject may possess interest."[1]

This book was in demand for over forty years. Ethics and principles of both jurisprudence and medicine change slowly but surely and with great concern since the two professions bear the responsibilities of life and death for a nation.

Besides my father's teaching, writing of legal works and partnership in the law firm of Warvelle and Clithero in Chicago's Loop, he had another abiding interest; he was a life-long Mason. Among his many Masonic writings were <u>A Compendium of Masonry in Illinois</u> compiled in 1887 and a charming book, <u>The Legends of the Saints</u> (1913) as related to Masonic ritual. In July, 1935, he was honored as holding the longevity record of a 33° Mason in both the northern and southern jurisdictions of United States. He became a 33° Mason September 18, 1888 in Kenosha, Wisconsin.

The greatest joy of my father's academic life was his teaching and the friendship of his young students. He always spoke of them as "my boys," perhaps with a fatherly longing, since his two sons had been taken in death, one at birth, the other in childhood.

During Dr. Warvelle's teaching days at De Paul University College of Law, there were two Red Letter Days which brought him great joy and remained with him until death. The first in 1913 was at the amalgamation of De Paul's chapter of Alpha Kappa Phi with Delta Theta Phi, national law fraternity.

Dean Emeritus, Francis X. Busch, of De Paul University College of Law and a former student under Dr. Warvelle, recalled that event:

> "...His address, delivered at the Chicago convention... served as an inspiration to the three fraternities who had the great task of consolidation before them.
>
> "There was never a doubt after that speech for whom "his boys" would name their chapter. The constitution (of Delta Theta Phi) prescribed that senates should be renamed after eminent jurists; and so in 1913, the Delta Theta Phi of De Paul University College of Law, faculty, alumni and students joined unanimously in naming the senate "Warvelle," a deserved tribute to a distinguished lawyer, erudite scholar and a great teacher.
> > ""And the Elements so mixed in him
> > Nature might
> > Stand up and say to all the world

---

[1]Warvelle, George W., <u>Essays in Legal Ethics</u>, Callaghan & Co., Chicago, 1902, 1920, Preface, p. vi.

This was a Man.""[2]

The second Red Letter Day was in May, 1929 when the Warvelle Senate presented to my father, at home in his library, a framed testament in honor of the Twenty-fifth Anniversary of Delta Theta Phi. A portion read:

> "...No words which we now utter, sir, can add to the honor intended to be bestowed upon you. No tribute which we now pay to you can equal the tribute then intended to be paid to you. No token of our affection we now offer you can equal the token of affection which your own boys then offered you.
>
> "Rather, Sir, this is an occasion when we can do no more than affirm what your own boys by their own action then implied and to express to you anew our admiration for your scholarly attainments, our gratitude for your assistance to the Fraternity and its individual members, our affectionate regard for you and our exultation in having you with us as one at this celebration..."[3]

The accolades have continued down through the years. In the December, 1962 issue of Summons, an article written for the Fiftieth Anniversary of De Paul University College of Law by the retired Dean Francis X. Busch, recalled the period when my father joined the faculty in the early 1900's.

> "...It was while the school was here (a temporary building at 301 East Erie Street) that Dr. Warvelle joined the faculty, teaching Legal Ethics and Real Property... Dr. Warvelle not only loved to teach; he loved the pupils he taught. Never was there a man more sympathetic to or understanding of the problems and frustrations of the law student; many an old grad looks back with deep affection to the Grand Old Man of the Illinois College of Law. It is indeed fitting that his name should be carried in honor of the Warvelle De Paul Senate of the international law fraternity of Delta Theta Phi."[4]

---

[2]Source not known to editor.

[3]The framed testament from The Delta Theta Phi Law Fraternity was signed by Fred J. Ploger, Dean of the Chicago Alumni Senate and dated Founders' Day, May 11, 1929.
In a letter dated September 20, 1972, Richard C. Groll accepted the Author's offer to present the original testament to the De Paul University College of Law where according to his letter the testament would be put on display in the law library. Permission Law Review, College of Law, DePaul University, Chicago, Illinois.

[4]Busch, Francis X., "A Look at the Law School," Summons, 50th Anniversary issue, Volume III, Number 7, De Paul University College of Law, Chicago, IL, Dec. 1962, p. 4. Permission Law Review, College of Law, DePaul University, Chicago, Illinois.

In February, 1972 Dean Richard C. Groll of the De Paul's College of Law wrote:

> "...Delta Theta Phi Fraternity still designates the De Paul Senate the "Warvelle Senate" ... several Faculty members remembered at some length about the splendid reputation that your father enjoyed within legal education. I thought that you would be interested in knowing that he is still remembered at De Paul."[5]

George William Warvelle, born May 3, 1852 at Kenosha, Wisconsin, died November 12, 1940 in Chicago, Illinois. In 1972, thirty-two years after his passing, there were older faculty and students of De Paul who remember him - so too, his last leaf on the tree - daughter and five grand-children and eleven great-grandchildren who carry on for the new day.

It should be noted that my father was a great student of the Bible. Psalm 27-4 describes his life:

> "One thing have I desired of the Lord, that I will seek after; that I will dwell in the house of the Lord all the days of my life, to behold the beauty of the Lord and to inquire in His temple."

---

[5]Correspondence between Dean Richard C. Groll and the author.

44. 652-654-656 West Monroe (old numbering system) in 1930. In a later numbering system in Chicago, the Warvelle home at 654 became 1743 West Monroe Street. The house originally had a white limestone front, which was later painted. The house was in the family until 1941.

45. George Warvelle, about 1904, while in his 50's and at the height of his legal practice. From M. H. Warvelle family album.

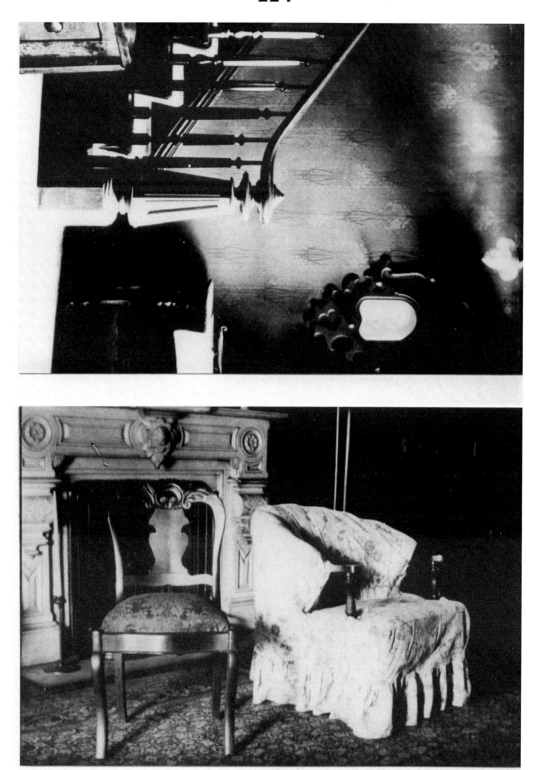

46. Hallway with newell post (top) and Front Parlor with mantel (bottom) (from MWB family album).

47. Living Room corner (top) and Library (bottom) (from MWB family album).

48. Dining Room with gray marble mantel (top) and bay window (bottom) (from MWB family album).

THE BATHROOM AND BEDROOMS

In 1900 the bathroom was modernized. The original plumbing and fixtures had been installed around 1880 and were then the best available for a house costing around $7000. Bathrooms and kitchens today have more overhaulings than other rooms and so it was in 1900.

Washbasins with hot and cold running water and flushing toilets have been in urban usage since Abigail Adams became mistress of the President's House in 1800. Benjamin Latrobe and Thomas Jefferson, while both had artistic and diplomatic minds, had engineering minds as well on this particular subject of domestic architecture. A century later, West Monroe Street homes were to have face-liftings, however it took another fifty years before such comforts reached the rural homes. Even today on back roads of isolated rural communities there can be seen a few old wells and pumps and "necessary houses;" this title was given by the powdered wigs of Williamsburg in 1700.

Looking back almost three quarters of a century, what were these old fixtures like that all the neighbors were discarding? In most of the Monroe Street houses the bathroom was on the top floor to take advantage of a skylight and be accessible to the bedrooms. The heavy glass panes of the skylight looked like a florist's greenhouse resting on the flat roof. The skylight was inaccessible for cleaning, and due to the city's winter soot, snow and bird droppings, required an annual scrubbing by a roofing company. After which the birds truly had a birds'-eye view of the private scenes below. The old bathtub, generous sized and deep, was made of soldered tin or zinc set in a box-like tongue and grooved, varnished structure. This matched the wooden dado about eight feet high around the room. The upper walls were painted a "sanitary," glossy white.

The "throne" was a large wooden tongue and grooved box-like affair with hidden pipe apparatus. On one side of the seat was a flat brass knob called a plunger; when pulled upward it released a stream of water and gravity did the rest. Mamma would call if the bathroom had not resounded with flowing water, "Did you plunge it?". Never, did you flush it. The washbowl in the corner was round marble encased in a circular tongue and grooved walnut cabinet to hide pipes and give storage space. Above hung a simple oval walnut framed mirror.

When modernization took place what were the improvements? The throne box disappeared and a white vitreous bowl with a golden oak seat and lid was installed. Overhead and behind on the wall was a golden oak box, big enough for a large cat's coffin and attached was a long pull chain with a golden oak handle similar to those on little girls' jumping ropes.

Next, the bathtub was removed and suddenly, the room seemed very large; it was never small. Resting on four white enameled ironclawed feet was a white porcelain bathtub with faucets marked H and C, as if one did not know, and a wire soap basket hung over the rolling edge of the tub. In earlier days one could sit comfortably on the flat wooden edge and dangle one's legs; now this was a cold, slippery edge. The washbasin, now an oval porcelain bowl had all exposed plumbing beneath, only the old mirror remained and previously hidden articles now rested on a new shelf; built-in medicine cabinets were still in the future.

Along with other plumbing renewal the first floor throne used by the help or "in a hurry" was replaced and two ceramic laundry tubs with useful covered working surface appeared in the kitchen. The marble washbasins with their cabinets remained in the bedrooms and did not seem obsolete.

As to the bedrooms - a bed is where one makes it, on the floor, on green grass, in a rocking chair, a crib or kind, strong arms; many are unspoken but remembered. The blankets were comforting, especially the "winter sheets" of cotton flannel augmented by the forerunner of electric blankets, a heated sad iron wrapped in woolen at our feet. Only a matter of a few jumps and one was on the warm, even hot, breathing register; here one could dress completely under a hot air ballooned nightgown.

The dresser or bureau looked like a sideboard with its array of matching painted china and abundance of silver articles with matching handles. Among those items were a buttonhook, shoehorn, nail file, nail cleaner, manicure scissors and a buffer. There was also a hairbrush, comb, clothes and hat brushes and hand mirror all in the same bulbous rose pattern. On either side was a covered china powder dish and a matching covered dish with a hole on top called a hair receiver. At the back of bureau top was a long pincushion full of interesting pins, some small ones with colored glass heads resembling dolls' or cats' eyes, others had stems long enough to be daggers; these were hat pins.

If one explored the generous top drawer there were other finds, a small alcohol lamp and its pronged curling iron. Pieces of paper were used to test the correct heat needed: if the paper did not burn it was the right temperature for hair curling. There was a large flat wooden box with a design burned into the top; pyrography was then one of the do-it-yourself crafts. In this treasure box of jewelry, genuine and otherwise, there were women's cuff links, a gold fleur-de-lis watch pin, a heart shaped locket, various school pins and souvenir buttons. There was one from "Brown School, '96" with an American flag, a momento from sister Florence's graduation and there was a "Re-elect McKinley" which the voters did in 1900.

49. Third Floor Bedroom (top) and Backyard facing garage and alley (with George Warvelle sitting in yard chair, 1940) (bottom) (from MWB family album).

THE BACK YARD

"I know a little garden - close
Set thick with lily and red rose,
Where I would wander if I might
From dewy morn to dewy night."

William Morris (1834-1896)

Fairies are my first recall of the back yard garden, perhaps because I had seen them in picture books, living among trees and flowers. Alura Kitty Goff age five, and myself age four, had seen evidences in our yard. They had poured water into nasturtium blooms which tasted good; along the brick path were lead pennies, who else could have left them? Surely not the roofer who had repaired a gutter the day before.

At twilight, the child ventured into the back garden to find a doll which must be brought in before heavy dew matted its golden hair. Suddenly she was aware, that this place where two children had played in the afternoon was now changed into another land. As she stooped to pick up the doll, dozens of soft, white stars brushed her face and arms, while an unknown fragrance was all about her. A child did not know that in the cool evening, certain flowers open like trumpets and exude a heavy perfume, as does Nicotiana. Close by, there was mignonette, scarcely noticed earlier with its humble blooms; now unbothered by ravaging bees, it too, was sending out a delicious smell.

As she clasped her doll she looked up, the moon was lighting her path. She was conscious of small shadows on the grass, little bugs jumping, as well as hearing crickets, and a sad mourning dove on a carriage house roof calling its mate.

As she approached the back stoop, still in this enchantment, a mouse scampered into hiding. She hurriedly opened and closed the back door. When she related her ecstatic experience to the receptive family, she realized there was one friend she did not hear, an owl. Such did inhabit the barn lofts in the neighborhood and were heard on moonlight nights.

Our city lot loomed large in childhood's memory, yet it was only thirty feet wide and one hundred and eighty-seven feet deep, including the ground covered by the house and shed. At the rear of the lot, a towering Balm of Gilead tree, a species of the cottonwood, gave pleasant shade. It was about three feet in diameter and probably well over a hundred years old. In spring, the cattails were a delight to the children. A common landscape was shared on one side with the Martin-Tyrell family of "Case and Martin Pies" fame, with no fence between the properties. Thus each enjoyed a wider expanse of garden view. In earlier years, the Martins had a greenhouse. A diary of winter 1897 records:

"Miss Martin's hyacinths are up two inches and there are large buds on the rose bushes."

This oasis shared by two neighbor families, was a haven of sunshine and flowers in the summer with its self-perpetuating garden. In the rear, under dense shade from adjoining carriage houses, there were rambling spreads of lily of the valley, which were full of fragrant blooms each spring. Each year at Memorial Day, then called Decoration Day, huge handfuls of these fragrant bells, France's symbol for love and remembrance, were gathered for the flower collection from Brown School students. The flowers to be placed on the graves of the Blue and Gray soldiers of the Civil War were brought in varying amounts, varieties and conditions. Mostly, they were purchased at local florists - three carnations, six red roses, bunches of violets and pansies. It is recalled of one child who brought a bunch of white clover blossoms and dandelions; all were soon withered but at the moment of picking, probably on a vacant lot, these golden and fragrant blooms must have been an experience of participation in loving remembrance.

There was a program and a song for this occasion found in the school's Corona Song Book. Tears were in the eyes and hearts, as the pupils sang:

"Cover them over with beautiful flowers,
Deck them with garlands, these brothers of ours,
Lying so silently by night and by day
Sleeping the years of their manhood away."

The lilies thrived for several generations with other city-hardy plants. Earlier, there were narcissus and Star of Bethlehem which originally had grown on Georgia Willimotte's grave in Kenosha. There were little perpetual pink rose bushes, peonies and annuals which seeded themselves each season, as petunias, bachelor buttons, pansies and sweet William. The rest of the yard was in grass with patches of clover. There was one patch which seemed to run to four leaf clovers for several years. Along a common border between the two yards there was a garden of perennials and annuals about eight feet wide and forty feet long. There were moss and cabbage (centifolia) roses, iris, lemon lilies, bachelor buttons and pansies. On the low fence next to Wheeler's yard were hollyhocks, golden glow, rampant morning glories, and old-fashioned hops vines. The vine had a leaf like an ivy, but was of very irritating texture and caused a skin rash. Mamma's house plants rested under a catalpa tree, one of five bought for a penny each, in one of Brown School's projects for neighborhood beautification and honoring Arbor Day. It was in this garden that a city child developed a love of the green world and its many families.

The backyard was a refuge for all, including cats and dogs. Behind the Balm of Gilead tree was an animal cemetery where friends of humble ancestry, but often noble qualities, were buried. Through the successive years, dogs, cats, their kittens, robins, sparrows, and broken dolls rested undisturbed.

It was under this friendly tree that the little girl, at times a lonely child, had the idea to create a miniature town, one that the dollhouse could be a part of. There were plenty of accumulated toys belonging to her and the invalid brother, such as iron wagons with horses, tiny wooden boats, small Noah's Ark animals, and an excess of tinware and small china tea sets. The doll house was already built out of two wooden orange crates which made four rooms. Then, with windows cut out and wallpaper from sample books, a respectable house for six inch china dolls was waiting for a town to live in. Why not build a barn, a grocery store, a lake, a park? She did; it was a happy contented summer. The miniature world continued to grow in her imagination where dried navy beans became eggs and cranberries, red apples for dolls. She decided to put in writing this world of fantasy. The manuscript read: "A Miniature World - Dedicated to the XYZ Club;" the club too, was imaginary. The carefully written article was sent to the Woman's Home Companion and after several weeks was returned with this letter which has been kept, if only for proof that a childhood had been lived:

"I have read over your story with so very much interest and pleasure, but am afraid I must disappoint you by saying I cannot find a place for it in Woman's Home Companion. It does show a great deal of promise and especially it is nice to think of the good times the XYZ Club must have had. It makes me wish I were a little girl, and I belonged to such a club.

I hope you will send me more of your work sometime, for I shall love to see it.

(Signed) Laura S. P. Paph
Editor, Children's Department"

In later years, and quite suddenly, as one of nature's ways to revive a neighborhood of decaying homes and dying trees, the Ailanthus tree, or tree of heaven, sprang up. In a single season, these palm or sumac-like trees could grow six or even ten feet tall. They were seen all over Chicago, in our back yard, in the alley, coming out of drainpipes, cellar window wells, under the "El." Easily transplanted, they were used on tree lawns where the original tree had perished. The tree of heaven was a blessing to city folk, in spite of what non-green thumb critics proclaimed, since it thrived so well in poor soil and sooty air. It is as though Nature took pity on the poor people of the slum districts of crowded cities, sending the fertile seeds of that luxuriant, sumac-like tree into the crevices of dingy buildings to hide them and make a green shelter. Just so, in the latter years, these trees by the dozen grew up in the old back yard, hiding ugly fences of the neighbors and the caving-in shed at the rear. In mature years, these trees recalled to me the invasion of golden sunflowers growing along the dreary roads of the iron and steel mills of Cleveland, Ohio. Also in the heavy growth of horsetails, Equisetum, seen along the tracks of the Chicago and Northwestern Railroad as I traveled into Wisconsin, where I was a university student.

In early college years, I returned to old Monroe Street and saw the dying trees there and in many sections of Chicago. My thoughts were these:

"We think those trees which die
In deluge, battle, drought or fire
Like noble soldiers fall.
Consider too, the doomed
which perish in the growth of cities.

In silent martyrdom,
They must endure throughout the years
The choking smoke, the strangling wires,
The stabs of nails, the bands of steel,
The gloom of walls and weight of stone.
While in this age-long suffering
The admiration of the poor
And the recollection of the old
Portray the only sympathy."

50. Backyard facing house (from MWB family album).

CHAPTER SIX: ONLY YESTERDAY

THE SIGHTS AND SOUNDS

"Her sights and sounds; dreams happy as her day"

> Rupert Brooks (1887-1915)
> The Soldier

"Such sights as youthful poets dream"

> John Milton (1608-1674)
> L'Allegro I, 121

"Reflection is to colours what echo is to sound"

> Joseph Joubert (1754-1823)
> Pensees

"Enable with perpetual light
The dulness of our blinded sight"

> Book of Common Prayer
> Ordering of Priests

In 1900, the sights and sounds that wafted down Monroe Street at most any hour of the day were for the most part agreeable to the eye and ear and heralded the needs of daily living. There were no panic provoking sirens; the worst were clangs made by foot pedals on fire engines and patrol wagons. Most sounds were human voices, bells, whistles, music, horses' hooves, rumblings of iron wagon wheels on uneven pavements and the periodic grind of passing trains on the elevated railroad.

The daily panorama was watched by small children imprisoned behind tall windows, pressing their noses on the cool glass. When the pane was frosty or steamed, they licked a peephole with their tongues in order to see and perhaps to imitate the hawker who called his wares.

The day began early when the slow and interrupted journey of the milk wagon, usually from Borden Dairy, echoed at the lower entry way. Around 1900, milk was measured and poured into waiting quart Mason jars. A few years later, the dairyman delivered bottled milk in Thatcher bottles. These had rubber stoppers controlled by spring locks. These bottles were used for other purposes, citrate of magnesia bought at the drug store or for homemade birch or root beer made with yeast.

The shout in the dining room would go up, "Cheer, cheer, the milk is here." Almost immediately, if not earlier, was the thud of the morning newspaper, The Chicago Daily Tribune. The day had now really begun with the aroma of coffee, milk in the silver mugs, bowls of hot oatmeal or better still, overnight cooked whole wheat grains. Cream of Wheat was soon to emerge, vitamins were unknown and oranges were not juiced.

Breakfast was hardly over, when a single chirp of a whistle announced the delivery of mail. The postman, fondly called the "letterman," did not seem to be molested by dogs as he came to the lower entry three times a day, at eight, eleven and three. His sack was heavy; he had no cart and wore the same grey woolen uniform summer and winter.

The next most regular person who served our needs was the iceman. By mid-morning several times a week, oftener if the window card was showing, a strong man carried a hundred pound slab of ice, securely clawed by bronze tongs on his leather-aproned shoulder. The icebox, seldom called a refrigerator, was in the lower hallway, not in the kitchen. The filled drip pan under the big golden oak, zinc-lined object was emptied on the grass or plants on the front lawn. Sometimes, if the weather was exceedingly hot, the ice wagon was emptied before all the customers had been served and a twenty-four hour wait often meant "turned milk" which was repulsive to city children. Outside, the cavernous wagon with its hanging scales and chipping hammers was a magnet for the neighborhood children who climbed in the truck and took slivers of ice to suck and "slither."

In the daily passing traffic were heavy moving vans and delivery wagons carrying wooden barrels, iron pipes or loads of coal. Most of the horses were a strong Belgian type and the drivers were strong too. The coal trucks carried six to ten tons of coal in bags or loose. In either case, the haulers already blackened from their loading process, shunted the coal down the shoot into the cellar. It was a noisy, grimy time for all. There could be several deliveries since three types of coal were used, large lump hard coal for the furnace, small egg for the kitchen range and semi-hard cannel for the four fireplaces.

The Railway Express wagon and Parmalee Transfer Company drivers carried heavy trunks in and out of three and four story houses. Light weight luggage was unknown; iron banded and nail studded wooden chests carried the wardrobes of those bound for summer resorts in Michigan as Charlevoix, Mackinaw or Saugatuck; in Wisconsin, it might be Sheboygan, Lake Geneva or Sturgeon Bay. Perhaps the luggage, especially in June and September, belonged to the college set nestled at Harvard, Princeton, Vassar or Smith. Nearby institutions seemed to require only a few suitcases.

About once a week, the street sprinkling truck would pass by. It was a huge wooden barrel-like tank which spread a fan-shaped spray of water in the center of the street, settling the dust and causing the accumulated horse manure to seek the gutters. Later these in turn were swept and the collected piles hauled away. Some garden minded neighbors who did not own manure producers, hurried out to get a scuttle full to spread on new flower beds. At each block's fire hydrant, the horses had a rest while the tank was being refilled.

There were pitiful sights and sounds, as well as pleasant ones, that the young mind and heart was to be subjected to. If he were a country child, he would have witnessed the squealing birth, possibly the conception, of pigs, lambs or calves and later, he was to shudder at the sight of dripping butcher-blood from the same, now mature animal. The city child was neither denied nor exempt from rubbings among his animal friends. To have witnessed the miracle of birth and heard the tiny cries from blind, pink bodies when a batch of kittens were born, was an incident never to be forgotten. Nor later, to see the aftermath of these now furry kittens lying half decapitated on the shed floor and not to understand why a tom cat should kill his own kind.

There was the child's hysterical scream as she rushed home, blurting through tears that dogcatchers had caught their dog and thrown him into a black wagon. The silence and absence in the succeeding days corroborated her anguish.

There were episodes when horses fell and children gathered to watch the snorting, dilated nostrils and heaving, gaunt ribs. It could be sunstroke or starvation. Sometimes a fallen horse, released from his wagon, was bleeding and the legs were limp, fractured from a misstep on uneven wooden blocks which paved Monroe Street before modernization with asphalt and concrete. The policeman would shoot the horse out of its misery, but the fly-ridden body might lay for several days while children passed by in sorrow.

As a child, I never experienced the sound of ships passing in the night, nor the fog horn's wailing. I do recall the distant steam locomotive whistles as they echoed in their corridors. It seemed that the sad, persisting cry of the ploughing train occurred when moonlight had invaded my bedroom; shadows quivered on the walls while the ruffled curtains moved in a rhythm of wind and sound. As oldsters and youngsters today attend the last runs and rites of vanishing steam locomotives and then listen to plaintive preservations on hi-fi, all are transported by the engine's rhythm and the whistle's voice on the wheels of time.

Other sights and sounds of a region south of Monroe Street were on Harrison Street, emerging at Vernon Park and leading to Cook County Hospital environs. Here these echoes have been captured by another writer, Mary Synon, who recalled them:

"Chimes that called and pealed and tolled, gongs that clanged and clashed and clamored, the bells of the West Side kept beating their brazen hammers of evangel on the white-hot forge of Sally Gate's sorrowing soul.

"From morning to midnight, from midnight to morning, fire gongs crashed out imminence of danger, patrol gongs clattered the nearness of crime, ambulance gongs claimed right-of-way for the dying. Slow bells knelled grief above the moaning of horns and muffled drums of Italian funerals, glad bells swung for wedding and festival. The sad bell in the tower of the Home of the Little Sisters of the Poor said Angelus over the old men and women in that high-walled haven of age and poverty. The great bell of Notre Dame bade the children of the inhabitants to fasts and feasts. Little tinkling bells of the Salvation Army begged remembrance for the city's derelicts. St. Jarlath's and Epiphany's to the northward, the Jesuit and the Lutheran to the southward proclaimed mass and matin, compline and vesper."[1]

Perhaps the clangs, gongs and toots best remembered by any Chicago childhood are those heard on New Year's Eve, if one could stay awake long enough to toot the little tin or cardboard horn with its wooden mouthpiece. Again, that clamor has been recalled:

"Somewhere to the southward a siren shrieked a shrill signal. From the street gongs banged, whistles blew, horns moaned. Shots flashed in staccato barking. Human cries wailed. A bugle called. Over the humming roar of the city rose a din of sound, sweeping, surging, in tremendous, terrible beat upon the house. Factories, engines, all the vast, chained, workaday power of Chicago swept up into a wild, demoniac, torturing voice, yelling its New Year's message in tearing might... From every street, every house, every throat rose voice until the city spoke with one great strident sky-piercing shout its work, and power, and pleasure, and speed and sorrow.

"Then, with glory of clamor, crashed the bells: bells of St. Jarlath's and Notre Dame; bells of the Jesuit and the Lutheran; bells of Epiphany; the bell in the Little Sisters of the Poor; bells of every creed joining in the one creed of triumph of man's soul over time and circumstance. Clanging high over whistles and horns, shots and cries, they rang out the old, rang in the new, rang out a year, rang in another, rang out a century, rang in another."[2]

---

[1]Synon, Mary, The Good Red Bricks, Little, Brown & Co., Boston, 1929, p. 235.

[2]Ibid., pp. 286-7.

51. Milkman's Wagon. Courtesy Chicago Public Library, Hild Regional Branch, 4536 Lincoln Ave.,
Chicago, Illinois.

52. Horse Drawn Fire Equipment, at Fire House on 83-85 S. Franklin Street (new number: 119 N. Franklin, still standing in 1957). Engine Company No. 40 and Hook and Ladder Company No. 6. Courtesy Chicago History Museum.

53. Police Wagon, 1905. D.N. negative #3714. Courtesy Chicago History Museum.

THE SMELLS

"They have ears and hear not; noses have they and smell not."

Psalms CXV, 6
The Holy Bible

"It smells to heaven -"

Shakespeare
Hamlet III-36

"Since when it grows and smells, I swear not of itself, but thee."

Ben Jonson (1573-1637)
The Forest IX, To Celia

"Life's sweetest joys are hidden
  In unsubstantial things;
An April rain, a fragrance
  A vision of blue wings."

May Riley Smith (1842-1927)
The Treetop Road

Besides the sights and sounds there were the smells that a youthful nose sensed and remembered. The most offensive was the nauseating odor from the Chicago Stockyards miles away on the south side of Chicago. When the wind was just right, an all-pervading invisible layer of air saturated with the smell of burnt flesh and bone cast a depressive pall upon city dwellers. Air pollution had begun early for this booming city which Carl Sandburg called "Hog Butcher for the World;" others called it a "Porkopolis."

Another unpleasant odor which emerged in the cool night breezes came from the chimneys of disposal furnaces of Cook County Hospital and its neighbor, the Presbyterian, while Mary Thompson Hospital only two blocks away from our house was, also, a contributor. An old photograph shows the latter in full action with its smokestack.

Commonplace objects, both odor and sight repellent to youngsters, were cuspidors, better described as spittoons. They were encountered in train stations, public waiting rooms, stores and even, homes. Today their titles have been changed and uses modified - ash trays have been elevated from the floor to cocktail tables and sand buckets adorn public buildings. Earlier, cigars, pipes and chewing tobacco were more common than cigarettes and definitely masculine in all categories. Later, pocket tissues replaced the scarce handkerchiefs and public expectoration became more refined as well as against the law and subject to a fine, if noted in public places. The evangelists of disease prevention also prevailed. While the pre-1900 students quoted, "Don't Spit Remember the Johnstown Flood," the next generation took up the cry, "Don't Spit Remember the Dayton Flood" (1913).

Another horrific smell and experience encountered by the small Chicago child was going through the tunnel under the Chicago River on a Madison streetcar. There was an abrupt entry into a black dungeon with sickening odors. All one could see from the car window was a black, oozing mud wall. The damp, putrid smell lasted only moments, which seemed never to end, until the streetcar climbed a hill into sunshine; the relief, almost a rescue from being buried alive, was shown as the little hand released its clutch on a protecting arm. An exchange of smiles closed this passage to and from a dark country and now we would soon wander into a world of brilliant light with color and sound at Marshall Field's Store.

Years later to drive through the Holland Tunnel under New York's Hudson River was slightly reminiscent of the old Chicago tunnel; yet that quality of tunnels still prevailed - the smell. That musty, earthy odor now coupled with exhaust gases still accompanies the calm, imprisoned humanity treading to higher ground beyond the river.

In a lesser degree, those childhood twinges and sniffs are still recalled when one walks down to the subway transportation in either Chicago or New York. That feeling of a dungeon and the always dank and humanly polluted atmosphere encounters one as all rush to make the express train to airier land.

There were odors that were not offensive even though they were from city industry. A flagrance happily relished and inhaled with gusto by the very young was the smell of baking bread, probably emanating from Wards or the "Butternut" bread factory. Later, these unwrapped five cent loaves of bread, when purchased at the grocery store, had lost that anticipated promise of home-baked bread.

Another pleasing odor to some was the aroma of roasting coffee beans at the distributing plants in the loop. However, the odor was upsetting to childish stomachs when riding on the elevated trains to downtown. Possibly the blame should not be put on the coffee odor; the grinding car wheels, sharp curves and fast moving scenery may have evoked those spells of butterfly stomach, common in childhood.

In everyone's memory there are certain treasured odors as well as tastes. Since a child's olfactory sense and taste buds are most acute in early years these sensuous experiences are not easily forgotten. An early memory, at three, was of being in large dimly lighted church for my baptism. The ceremony is not recalled but the dimness and the queer odor from the massive red sandstone walls, possibly the musty carpeting and wax candles, all created an odor, a "church" odor. It has been sensed in many churches and was a strange reaction upon visiting the cathedrals of Europe.

Another fragrance recollection is that of smelling a field of wild flowers, mostly sweet clover, for the first time. It was to a city child of five, almost an intoxicating sensation, akin to listening to a great orchestra and being lifted up for brief moments into a feeling of indescribable joy. The first occasion was the climax of a long streetcar ride west to the car barns. Here a suburban car took us to the "country" - open fields. One walked shoulder-deep in an ocean of blooming wonders - Decoration Day daisies, Queen Anne's Lace, sweet clovers and tasselled grasses. A lacy bouquet of these treasures was brought home; the perfume lingered and this fragrance memory grew secure for the years to follow.

The child did not know that this particular fragrance is one cherished by mankind and found in many plants. It is coumarin, found in clovers, honeysuckle, sweet woodruff or waldmeister and sweet grass used by the Indians; also it is found in vanilla and tonka beans. So it is not strange that two earliest memories should be a bouquet of sweet clover and a dish of vanilla ice cream. Shakespeare wrote: "A strange invisible perfume hits the sense."

The dish of ice cream recalls a first children's party at the Forbes' home, two doors away. About a dozen boys and girls in their Sunday outfits were roaming around the fourth floor ballroom. The large green felt billiard table was taken over by pint-sized little men while the girls admired themselves in a massive framed mirror reaching from floor to ceiling. I was still able to wear my baptismal dress of tiny tucks and fine embroidery. In a corner the grand piano sounded the call to games. Finally, the refreshments or "the party" began. Each child was served a molded rose shape of vanilla ice cream and Nabisco wafers. Today, this is still the easiest and best liked menu for children. To one little girl this was a taste of ambrosia, never to be forgotten. As the "Madeleine" wafer[1] was to Marcel Proust when "shifting and confused gusts of memory never lasted for more than a few seconds,"[2] so, too, that Nabisco wafer created a gustatory revelation to me both in its unique flavor and the pleasure of its crunch. The ice cream eaten then has never been duplicated except in the first brief mouthfuls when suddenly a delicious flavor is sensed and recalled. Prosaically one can explain that after a few frozen bites the taste buds are numbed. Hardly so; rather, these are the "gusts of memory" we chance to revive in those brief seconds.

Perhaps the most respected and anticipated smell was the aroma from the kitchen during canning season, at times so strong that the fruity and spicy odors were inhaled half a block from their source. In summer the successive quintessences of strawberries, raspberries, blackberries and Concord grapes, having perfumed the neighborhood, were captured in jelly glasses and rested on the table where they reflected through the paned window like parts of a stained glass chapel window. At summer's end, the full-bodied essence of tomatoes, onions and spices told the community that our season's supply of catsup, chili sauce, as well as watermelon pickles was being accomplished.

City folk, while they neither spun, wove nor butchered, did can and jam or bottle as the English-minded termed this age-old husbandry. In the 1900 era there were no electrically vented chimney drafts for kitchens, so the first floor windows and doors were opened to air out and cool that steaming, singing workshop of pots, strainers, jelly bags and paraffin. It was a practice indulged in by most of the neighbors; all were as busy as in a beehive. So true, that at the back stoop where baskets of peaches, pears and quinces awaited their futures, the neighboring bees, wasps and ants joined in this feast of odors and tastes.

---

[1]Proust, Marcel, <u>Rememberance of Things Past</u>, Vol. 1: <u>Swann's Way</u>, translated by C. K. Scott Moncrieff and Terence Kilmartin, Random House, New York, 1981, p. 48.

[2]Ibid., p. 7.

245

CANDY STORES AND BAKERIES

"Hear, Land O' Cakes and brither Scots"

        Robert Burns, 1759-1796

"Would you both eat your cake and have your cake?"

        John Heywood, 1497-1580

"There are marshmallows, gumdrops and peppermint canes -
With strippings of scarlet and gold"

        Eugene Field, 1850-1895

"What hymns are sung, what praises said
   For homemade miracles of bread"

        Louis Untermeyer, 1885-1977

"O God! that bread should be so dear
   And flesh and blood so cheap."

        Thomas Hood, 1798-1845
        The Song of the Shirt

"Honor bread, glory of the fields, fragrance of the earth, feast of life."

        Benito Mussolini, 1883-1945
        Proclamation, April 14-15, 1928

    Childwise, the most important store was the candy store. If the day was warm and our throats were dry that called for a visit to either Shannon's candy and ice cream store at the corner of Madison and Wood Streets or Robert Sawyer's drugstore across the street. Shannon's was a favorite for Brown School pupils; besides buying refreshments there, they bought school books and supplies.

Sodas and dishes of ice cream sold for five and ten cents. The soda fountain was more elaborate at Sawyer's with mirrors and shining faucets on marble walls. Here one could order phosphates, plain soda water, root beer, sarsaparilla and coca-cola, a new health drink which would become the familiar "coke" of today. At Shannon's one sat on the now traditional ice cream chairs - sturdy yet fragile looking seats with twisted wire backs and legs while the marble topped table had the same wire foundation.

The store's shelves were stocked with fancy candy boxes and apothecary type jars of stick candy. These were every flavor and color one could name - peppermint, spearmint, wintergreen, cinnamon, clove, lemon, lime, orange, cherry, chocolate, sassafras and sarsaparilla. The sticks came in three styles, a squatty, crunchy peppermint, then all flavors in sturdy, translucent slender sticks and the twisted, very slender opera sticks. Papa's treat was to let me choose ten varieties for ten cents.

Later Shannon's gave up the corner location and moved to smaller quarters on Wood Street nearer the school. Here they carried school supplies and the candy counter now sold only penny candies. Mrs. Shannon was a widow with two daughters and two sons, one of whom became a priest and editor of the diocesan paper The New World.

Penny candies are not a world unknown to children. Among popular items was the "fried egg in a pan," a doll-sized tin pan complete with spoon. The egg was yellow fondant with a glaze. The empty receptacles helped out in the doll house kitchen or for mud pies in the back yard. Then there were "all day suckers;" one of these hard black balls would last for hours if it was frequently removed and inspected for its change of color and flavor. There were about ten concentric coatings. At the core was a magic seed which was reported if planted would grow and produce more black balls. This was a coriander seed and usually eaten since it was easier and quicker to get another penny than to wait for a future crop.

There was the soda outfit, all for one cent, consisting of an envelope of sweetened, flavored powder which added to water made effervescent soda water (probably a fruit acid mixed with baking soda). A candy straw was provided which collapsed before the concoction was half consumed; also a small biscuit shaped candy completed this orgy. It was a nauseating combination and responsible for upset stomachs.

A new candy appeared following the advent of the teddy bear toy: chocolate teddy bears came in one, two or five cent sizes. All the traditional sweets were available at one cent prices as gumdrops, jelly beans, butterscotch, horehound and licorice drops - also licorice whips. Small candies as colored iced caraway seeds or "red hots" were sold by the measure, favorites then for playing doctor and nurse or decorating cookies. At Christmas time one could buy candy chains used to decorate the tree or just to chew the beads off of the string.

On walks one might stop at Bell's Candy Kitchen on Madison near Ashland. This large store had windows brimming with pans of fresh pulled taffy, peanut and coconut brittle, trays of heavenly opera caramels - delicately flavored strawberry, vanilla or chocolate fondant and the many varieties of chewy caramels. Chocolate creams and pastel colored bonbons were all hand dipped and hard to resist.

On Madison near Robey was Kehoe's Bakery. Such a fragrant welcome came from the constantly opening door that the aroma trapped us before we reached the store. Every kind of sweet roll and coffee cake was there, perhaps termed Danish pastry today. There were dozens of varieties of petit fours, ladyfingers, macaroons, cream puffs, tortes and charlotte russe - all were a child's dream of delight.

On coming closer to home we might stop at Naedelin's Bakery, earlier known as Ireland's on Wood Street near Brown School. Here the fragrance pouring out of the oven's chimney and the store's front door (it was a small but well stocked bakery) was heartier than that from Kehoe's; the specialty here was salt rising and sour dough bread - full bodied and crusty, relished by hungry folks, big and little. Today whether one thinks of this bread as emanating from California Gold Rush days, the immigrant delicatessens of New York or Chicago's early days with Mrs. O'Leary's cow troubles - all are correct, these sturdy loaves have been a sustaining daily bread.

54. Bell's Makers of Candies and Ice Cream, 1617-19 W. Madison Street.   Advertisement photograph of Jonas N. Bell, Inc., from McKinley High School *Voice*.

249

DRUGSTORES

"I do remember an apothecary
And hereabouts he dwells."

Shakespeare, 1564-1616
Romeo and Juliet

"Give me an ounce of civit, good apothecary, to sweeten my imagination."

Shakespeare, 1564-1616
King Lear

"Not poppy, nor mandragora
Nor all the drowsy syrups of the world,
Shall ever medicine thee to that sweet sleep
Which thou ow'dst yesterday."

Shakespeare, 1564-1616
Othello

"The miserable have no other medicine
But only hope."

Shakespeare, 1564-1616
Measure for Measure

"By medicine life may be prolong'd, yet death
Will seize the doctor too."

Shakespeare, 1564-1616
Cymbeline

"A merry heart doeth good like medicine"

Proverbs XVII, 22
The Holy Bible

"How'er their patients may complain,
Of head, or heart, or nerve or vein,
Of fever high, or parch or swell,
The remedy is Calomel"

Author Unknown (before 1853)

There were a goodly number of drugstores in the area whose proprietors' children attended Brown School and West Division or McKinley High Schools. The Arthur Bishop family of 677 Monroe first had their business at Madison and Paulina, and then at Ogden and Madison - totaling fifty years in the neighborhood. The children were Arthur, Edna, Mary and Henry. Merriman's Drugstore was at Ashland and Madison and their children were Esther and Fred who lived on Washington near Paulina. Other pharmacies (a word as little used then as apothecaries is today) were Thayer's, Haessler's, Horwitz's and Robert Sawyer's. Since the Sawyer Drugstore at Madison and Wood was nearest our home we usually traded there.

Of all the drugstores' window displays, those perennial, ornate glass bottles with sealed-off tiers of colored liquids are most remembered. They sparkled in sun or gaslight, in rainbow shades of red, orange, yellow, green, blue and purple. They appeared to children as giant perfume bottles. In the days of early apothecaries these "show globes" originally stored tinctures and alcohols.

As one entered Sawyer's store there was the immediate and familiar "drugstore odor." It was a lingering fragrance of cigars being lit at the perpetual gas flame which hung low over the tobacco counter and an indescribable "medical odor," seemingly of iodine, phenol and salicylic acid; this became stronger as one went to the rear where prescriptions were filled. In the glass cupboards one saw queer looking surgical instruments and rubber goods.

On shelves over the prescription counter were large bottles (termed apothecary jars today) some in cobalt blue, brown or milk glass to keep out light. Black and gold labels were molded on the glass. They had queer names which even then sounded like flower names and were familiar even in their Latin spelling. The one remembered from childhood was <u>Nox Vomica</u>, probably, because the word was disturbing, even in Latin.

In mature years the author acquired a collection of these jars from an old dissolving pharmacy; the labels seemed delightfully familiar. It is likely our old drugstores had the same titled bottles since pharmaceutical requirements for prescriptions were then limited and quite basic in their formulas; the age of chemical derivatives and synthetics had not yet arrived. A few such bottles may have read: <u>gum tragacanth</u>, <u>cornus Florida</u>, <u>P. valarian</u>, <u>angelica</u> (named for its angelic virtues), <u>cassia fistula</u>, nettles (must have been used to cause blistering), <u>passiflora incarnata</u>, <u>galium</u> (Our Lady's Bedstraw), <u>rheum</u> (rhubarb), <u>quercus alba</u>, <u>violae</u> and <u>rose otto</u>. These last two with <u>lavendula</u> were used in making the violet, rose or lavender toilet waters, commonly used in lieu of a bath or as fresheners, a polite interpretation of deodorizers. There were also bottles of <u>gaultheria</u> and <u>mentha peperita</u> used to disguise cough syrup or indigestion medicine.

On the lowest shelf were vessels needed in compounding, grinding and filling of gelatine capsules. Many of these mortars and pestles now rest in obsolescence except in the gourmet's kitchen or as decorative objects degraded to match or cigarette ash trays. In their useful day they came in all sizes and materials, from heavy white ironstone ware, clear glass, brass, bronze, iron and wood.

When prescriptions of pills or capsules in their little blue cardboard boxes or ointment in round tin boxes were all used as directed, these empty items were not discarded. They housed pins, pen points, thumbtacks, buttons or postage stamps. This was an age of thrift, few packagings were destroyed. Various strings were wound on spools or sticks, tinfoil was saved as well as reusable tissue and wrapping papers.

The prevailing newspaper advertisements of 1900 give some idea of the abundance of patent medicines. These were sold mostly in drugstores or directly from the compounder, never in grocery or mercantile companies; many of the drugs were bonafide, others, quackery of the most vicious type.

The common ailments of that age were phrased in different names than today yet were analogous to present day woes and worries which are thrown at us every fifteen minutes on television or radio. There was rheumatism, now embraced in its modern category, arthritis, and which uses aspirin or buffering compounds; earlier the affliction depended on wintergreen, both internally and externally. Catarrh, both "chronic, sneezing or ulcerative," today is pegged under sinus congestion or postnasal drip and drugs work so that one "can breathe again." In that earlier phase, hot lemonade or toddy and menthol salve did the trick. There was dyspepsia, which today is blanketed under upset stomach, heartburn, or indigestion, and is relieved by candy-like lozenges, still containing the time prescribed baking soda or "magnesia." Always there has been the "run down condition" whether it was spring or autumn, when tonics have been the biggest seller. Three favorites at the century's turn were "Vegatine," "Prunella" and "S.S.S. Compound." Most all tonics were heavily fortified with a strong alcohol base, in many cases the reason for its need and popularity; here a temperance worker had his excuse.

There was the plague common to men and beasts since recorded time, constipation, one word which has retained its universal name. While the animal chewed grass and man gulped castor oil, there was a new remedy, Cascarets. Here George Ade proved to be a superhumorist when he proposed to the medicine company who employed him: "They work while you sleep." Castoria, which "children (did actually) cry for" was an improvement on punishing castor oil. The last ailment, sleeplessness, which has been the torment of men since Caesar's time, is now elevated to insomnia and latest still, to "tension" for which physicians prescribe barbiturates. There are simpler medicines that make one sleep and sleep. In the older day a glass of milk or a nightcap of undiluted strength were the only help unless one possessed a loving bed mate or a book to read.

The householder living on West Monroe Street, like his faraway friend on Main Street in Minnesota, relied on the drugstore for help in his aches and pains. The use of home concocted remedies, the ingredients provided by the druggist or grocer, were as frequently resorted to as the "store bought" medicines. There was sassafras bark tea, herbal tisanes or sulphur and molasses for spring tonics; flaxseed and slippery elm emulsion for sore throats and onion and honey syrup for coughs. Ginger tea was for female cramps and senna leaves or dried rhubarb root eased intestinal passage. Asafetida, an ill-smelling gum in a small cotton bag, hung around a child's neck or chest to prevent catching diseases. There were children at Brown School who wore these amulets, relics of witchcraft doctoring. The necklace did keep the classmates at a safe distance from the wearer, simply out of its obnoxiousness. Another repellent, at least to the beholder, and perhaps a comfort to the wearer, was a woolen bandage saturated with mutton grease and worn on the neck or chest. Also, wads of camphor-saturated cotton in the ears helped to make the rooms in the lower grades redolent as well as stuffy and the visiting nurse respected the parents' efforts of prevention and cure.

In 1906 Louise De Koven Bowen helped form the Visiting Nurse Association which sent nursing aid to homes of Chicago's poor. Later, with the help of Jane Addams of Hull House, the visiting nurse became a part of the public school system. From 1907 on, the "nurse" was a common sight in Brown School as she made her scheduled rounds as in other schools. Her motherly and knowledgeable methods found children "coming down" with contagious diseases, malnutritioned, chronically ill or just overly dirty. Perhaps, some were suffering from pediculosis, a common plight of childhood. The body lice, like fleas, would pass from desk to desk, head to head, so it was a matter of inspection with a fine comb by protective mothers.

At this period it was a common sight to see yellow or red quarantine signs posted on front doors forbidding admission because of diphtheria, scarlet fever, typhoid or even, smallpox. Measles, chicken pox, whooping cough and mumps seemed to go unreported to the authorities. Frequently when the sign was removed, another took its place - a white crepe or spray of white carnations.

One shudders as one recalls the prevalence of contagious and infectious diseases which, especially in winter and spring, ravaged the school children. Many large families simply let their children be exposed to such diseases as measles, chicken pox and mumps just "to have it over with." Yet these, too, were serious diseases. Deaths from diphtheria, typhoid fever and two diseases often unrecognized, poliomyelitis and encephalitis, often wiped out families.

 Some familiar titles of drugs and medicines advertised in 1900 are recalled. With the crackdown by the Foods and Drugs Act on spurious and dangerous pharmaceuticals of every type, many were withdrawn; some became obsolete while others have proven their worth and continue today. Dandarine was for the woman who wanted waist-long hair and should have appealed to some present day moderns of both sexes. Lydia Pinkham's Vegetable Compound was slanted towards women and children and still endures spicy ridicule at campus frolics. Mother's Friend for the muscular comfort of the mother-to-be and Horlick's Malted Milk continues today for her child or those favoring a "body-builder." Listerine was easing throats and killing germs way back in the days of the father of antiseptic surgery, Dr. Joseph Lister, and continues today with a little more outspoken purpose. Now its advantages for combatting halitosis or outright "bad breath" are publicized by the voice and eyes of America. Smith Bros. and Dean's cough drops were sometimes smuggled as candy into Brown School classrooms and the teacher did not order them put on her desk or in the wastebasket. Topping the contents of the medicine chest for seniority is Squibb's Milk of Magnesia in its original cobalt blue glass bottle which also serves a useful purpose (ask any young bottle melters or oven plastics and glass bits crafters). Two other close contesters are Murine, once censored as being nothing but boracic acid which in 1900 sold for pennies per pound, yet still acknowledged the best eye aid, and Bromo-Seltzer, which still carries on after many balls are over.

THE GROCERY AND MARKET

"Grace is given by God, but knowledge is bought in the market."

Arthur Hugh Clough, 1819-1861

Around 1900, the expression "going to market" implied going to both grocery and meat market. While such markets continue today, they are the exception and have been replaced by supermarkets which supply all needs for pantry, cupboard and freezer as well as kitchen, laundry and bathroom, including the latter's medicine cabinet. To recall the grocery and market in 1900 may be nostalgic for some and a pleasant trip for young homemakers.

In these earlier food markets, the prices and qualities of food varied as did the service. Having found the one that suited the family's needs, it became "our store." There was little commercial advertising; one did not do much shopping around for special sales or "come on" items. One's grocer and butcher were trusted friends and knew their patrons' likes, dislikes and preferred brands. Possibly, the relation could be compared to the family doctor and his patients. A roll call of the neighborhood food stores would list Herron, Turner, Ahern, Palm, W. A. Stanley, Ryan, J. B. Warder and Kreuger. Stanley's was nearest our house and in the direction of Brown School so there were frequent errands there; besides, handsome McKinley Stanley, the teen-aged son, delivered the groceries. Most grocery stores offered charge accounts. At the time the bill was paid at Stanley's, one's patronage was acknowledged with a bag of hard candies for the children.

Stanley's was on Madison, a few doors east of Wood Street; it was a long, narrow store with the grocery department up front and the meat market toward the back. In mild weather, fresh produce was displayed outside the building; an awning kept excess sun or dampness from the fruits and vegetables. In seasonal order, one could see quart wooden boxes of strawberries, raspberries, gooseberries, currants, cherries, blackberries and blueberries. They were protected from insects, birds and fingers by a generous white mosquito netting. In larger square boxes would be peaches, apricots, plums, pears and California grapes. Oval wooden baskets offered Concord, Muscadine, Delaware and Catauba grapes. The small, red Catauba had a most elusive flavor and are now seldom seen.

These grape baskets fitted with wooden lids and sturdy wire or wooden handles were excellent for picnic baskets and came in several sizes. In this age of thrift, the wooden berry boxes and larger crates found many uses. The damaged, provided kindling for fireplaces and kitchen range while others became containers for nails, knobs, casters, odds and ends - all neatly assembled on my father's workbench in the shed or cellar. Here, too, were shelves for the fruit cellar where empty glass containers and Mason jars awaited their yearly turnover of preserves.

The broad windows on each side of the entrance into Stanley's store displayed fresh vegetables in season as lettuce, celery, green onions, radishes, peas, beans, tomatoes and carrots. All this fresh produce was brought in from the wholesale Water Street Market each morning.

On the left side of the center aisle were heavy wooden counters on which rested a red, painted iron coffee grinder, worked by hand, and a large roll of wrapping paper in its metal rack. Suspended from the ceiling were several cylinders of twine along with seasonal ribbons of flypaper and two bunches of bananas; one ready to eat, the other still green. At one end of the counter were wheels of cheese, cheddar and Swiss, covered with cheesecloth. The cheese was sliced to order and weighted on old fashioned Fairbanks scales nearby. In a glassed cupboard, fresh baker's bread, pan biscuits and store cake (often pound cake) were kept while the extra long loaves of French or Vienna bread rested outside, covered with the inevitable cheesecloth.

On the right side of the aisle were large coffee and tea canisters of black enameled tin with gold letters. There was Mocha and Java coffee and probably Columbian; the teas were in great variety, Formosa, Oolong, Japanese green, as well as Darjieling and Gunpowder. On the floor were bushel baskets of sweet and Irish potatoes, melons, squash, pumpkins and apples in season. Many of the apples were kinds rarely seen or grown now, as Baldwins, June apples, Greenings and snow apples. So-called Delicious apples had not been developed yet but would evolve as Stark's Delicious coming from a Missouri orchard.

Along the wall were covered bins of dried peas, navy beans, lentils, barley and rice. On the walls were shelves reaching almost to the ceiling and loaded with various canned and packaged goods including large cubicle tin cookie containers. Each had a window showing the contents which might be fig newtons, vanilla wafers, animal crackers, ginger snaps, five o'clock teas and graham, soda and oyster crackers; Nabisco wafers and "Educator Crackers" were sold in re-usable tin boxes.

Continuing on to the meat market where the floor was covered with sawdust, a wooden open counter displayed smoked hams, sausages, slab bacon and a hunk of dried beef which was sliced paper thin to order. All fresh meat was kept in the walk-in refrigerator. At holiday time, turkeys, geese and ducks hung for inspection in their cadaverous state with heads, feet and pinfeathers.

In the see-in icebox there were wooden tubs of butter, oleomargarine, lard and eggs. Whatever meat was requested was brought out in a carcass-sized portion and cut to order by the butchers. The meat saws hung in menacing fashion over the two chopping blocks. Under the counter were containers for suet, bones and trimmings which were sold to soap factories. Dogs, cats and birds could have complimentary meals for the asking, and children with a parent often were given a withered, pale frankfurter. Better still was to have a dill or sour pickle from the nearby open barrel. This with a crunchy peppermint stick stuck in it and sucked through was tops for any school child.

55. Turn of the Century Grocery. Courtesy Chicago Public Library, Hild Regional Branch, 4536 Lincoln Ave., Chicago, Illinois.

DRY GOODS AND VARIETY STORES

"The whole trade in the luxuries of life is brought into existence and supported by the requirements of women."

> Count Tolstoy, 1828-1910
> The Kreutzer Sonata

"The doll is one of the most impervious necessities, and at the same time one of the most charming instincts of childhood."

> Victor Hugo, 1802-1885
> Les Miserables

After candy and grocery stores, the children's next choice was the dry goods or variety stores. These were all on Madison Street - Haskett's at Ashland, Madigan's at Wood, Born's at Robey and Weinberger's at Hermitage; all had corner locations. The first three were typical dry goods stores - yardage, notions, trimmings, household linens and some clothing and best of all, toys at Christmas. Weinberger's had a little of everything for the household.

In this period there was not much choice in "store bought" dresses and coats in these small stores. Downtown department stores as Marshall Field, Mandel Brothers, Carson, Pire, Scott and Company or Stevens had wide selections while lesser priced outfits could be had at The Fair, Hillman's or the Boston Store (a wise crack of youngsters was of the man who was shot in the evening between Hillman's and the Boston Store).

Robert Haskett, his wife and child Grace, lived across the street at 649 Monroe; their store received most of our patronage for neighborly reasons. A child's mercantile episodes can neither be degraded nor satisfactorily inventoried as she shopped for a few yards of baby ribbon, embroidery floss and a new hoop or asked for samples of some admired cotton or silk cloth. On a shopping expedition one could pick up a complimentary copy of the latest McCall or Butterick fashion sheet. These illustrated patterns were cut out or copied for paper doll wardrobes.

The longed for visit to these stores was near Christmas, when toy displays crowded the windows and were touchable at counter's edge. Rows of bisque headed, flaxen haired, glass-eyed creatures with papier-mache jointed bodies, all cradled in flimsy boxes were inspected by both parent and child. The clothing on these dolls was monotonously the same, a cheap chemise relieved by a colored ribbon or lace edging; underneath were matching drawers and equally tawdry stockings and black paper slippers. Naked dolls were seldom seen, unless a few small bisque or china-headed, cloth bodied creatures filled with saw dust, remnants of an earlier Lilliputian age. Baby dolls with nursing bottles and character dolls were just beginning to be offered to the little mother. These lifelike toys were to start the procession of infantile robots who now sleep, drink, wet, cry, talk, crawl, stand or walk while the layettes and imported wardrobes of the early century have now run the gamut from diapers to ski pants.

Boys were not slighted; theirs was a world of wheels either mechanized or self-propelled. Among the bicycles were such models as the Soudan, Nile, Pyramid or Pirate as well as tandems and velocipedes. Just emerging was an automobile which emulated the brass trimmed horseless carriage, including a honking horn and concealed pedals. The Texas Flyer, hand propelled, was faster and there was always the red express wagon. Little girls shared in the wheel world with girl's tricycles and doll buggies. Some of these were replicas of their own baby carriages made with a woven reed body and waving parasol; there were English perambulators with folding leather hoods, black wooden bodies resting on high front wheels and small back ones. These, little mothers envied because only rich children seemed to own them.

For the very young, this was still the age of rocking horses; some were wooden, painted a dapple grey with a red harness; others more costly, had a velvet-like hide texture and strawberry roan color with real horse hair for mane and tail. Diminutive iron horses pulled milk wagons or farm carts of barrels or logs while red fire engines with hook and ladder trucks were ready for a call. Cast iron or wind-up locomotives complete with "overland limited" trains of coaches or freight cars traveled on small, dizzy, oval tin tracks. Building blocks intrigued then as now, and many games have remained perennial as authors, checkers, dominoes and jig-saw puzzles. Hardly a Christmas that Santa Claus did not leave us a cut-up United States map to reassemble and thereby absorb geography.

The breakthrough in animal toys came with the teddy bear, named after Teddy Roosevelt and his big game hunting. The little bear, a lovable, durable, plush-like being with snub nose and flat button eyes became available for many sized purses. Now several generations later, he is still a treasured bed-fellow and has not been exiled by the permissive thumb or blanket. With the success of the teddy bear, stuffed animals were to become a most demanded toy as dormitory friends. These friends were to see their greatest evolution in the Walt Disney characters.

Returning to Madison Street and Weinberger's variety store, it might be compared to a combination of a five and ten cent store (now almost an anachronism) and a bargain basement. Here one found all housekeeping needs - pots, pans, brooms, carpet sweepers, dust pans, laundry tubs, pails (wooden) and scrubbing boards. There were also garden tools and spring cleaning paraphernalia. One important article was the rattan battan (now an obsolete word and item) looking like a combination tennis racket and Eskimo snow shoe; this was a carpet beater. Floor coverings were taken up in the spring, hung on a supported clothes' line in the backyard and beaten in a cloud of dust, and then left to "purify" in the warm sun.

Other spring chores were calcimining the ceilings and varnishing the walnut woodwork; all this done by Mr. Dingman, house painter on Madison Street. The furnace was cleaned of clinkers and soot; registers and pipes were "blown" by McKinley Brothers. Then, there was the laundering of window curtains; these were ten foot lengths of Battenberg and Nottingham lace or Madeira embroidered muslin. After being hand laundered, they were dried on stretchers or ironed and the ruffles fluttered on a two piece fluting or crimping iron. Weinberger's sold most of this equipment.

Among all those counters in Weinberger's store filled with articles for the daily or seasonal chores were to be found oases of inexpensive toys for children. There were bargains in spinning tops, marbles, puzzles, iron banks, jumping ropes, tin buckets with shovels for the sandbox or seashore. Besides, there were ice or roller skates, small cast iron toy stoves, miniature weighing scales and Noah's Arks. If one looked carefully, one could find small bisque dolls with movable limbs, golden or brown hair, and eyes that moved. Many of these toys were from Nuremberg, Germany, toy center of the world. Even if one had only one or two pennies, it was possible to buy a whistle, pinwheel, rubber balloon or a white clay bubble pipe. Mr. Weinberger knew the selling power of toys even in a hardware store because he had a son and daughter, both at Brown School.

CHAPTER SEVEN: THE NEIGHBORHOOD

WALKS IN THE NEIGHBORHOOD

"All the walks one can take on foot around one's village: that is one's native
land.
Walks. The body advances, while the mind flutters around like a bird."

> Jules Renard, 1864-1910
> The Journal of Jules Renard

"Millions of unseen creatures walk the earth
Unseen, both when we wake and when we sleep."

> John Milton, 1560-1674
> Paradise Lost, Line 677

"For we walk by faith, not by sight."

> 2Corinthians V, 7
> The Holy Bible

"And seem to walk on wings and tred in air."

> Alexander Pope, 1688-1744
> The Iliad of Homer

At the turn of the century, walking was a healthy and instructive occupation in which
toddlers as well as elders participated. Children learned early to walk a six blocks' stretch
and its return which was the distance for many from their homes to Brown School.
Strangely, these walks offered as much provoking observation as did the walks proclaimed
by Thoreau. Both city streets and wooded paths enjoy the same sun, moon, stars, winds and
storms. The walk from Ashland to Western Avenue was a mile; various routes were used,
Monroe, Adams, Jackson, Warren or Washington Boulevard. Madison Street was seldom
taken, as the crowds and stores were distracting for an active pace and limited time

allowance.

What were the inspirations found on streets of houses, row on row, identical in structure and known by a number on the front door? These house fronts, their dooryard gardens and the homes within where friends lived, were islands of communication. Telephones were not yet common. The walk was usually in late afternoon or early evening; it was not unsafe to walk on city streets although children went with an elder.

Frequently the man of the house and his dog were seen; it could be Tarball, the black water spaniel next door, pulling on his master's rein, so anxious to explore for the thousandth time the cast iron horse-head hitching post. Earlier, the two Wheeler children, Virginia and Anabelle, with their governess had taken Tarball for his midday leg stretch. Two sailor straw hats with streamers flying, rested on the two heads respectively assigned. One had thick, taffy-colored braids reaching to her waist. The other had auburn, almost carrot-colored robust braids, also reaching to her waist. These could be an artist's subject for a sketch in color, form and action.

In summer, the air seemed clear and fresh with the smell of ozone in the lake breeze. Not so in winter, when chimneys bellowed out soot and gas from soft coal furnaces and treacherous glass-like ice on the sidewalks was covered with furnace ashes to help warn the unsure foot. It was on summer strolls that definite observations were pursued, casual perhaps, as seeing new geraniums in the window boxes or in the small front garden, neat round beds of pansy faces edged with sweet alyssum lace or sea shells.

For me it was a pleasure just to gaze upon the front lawn statues which overlooked small pools, some having fountains. These lead sculptures, cast from molds in many duplications, were the epitome of Victorian statuary, both for country estate or the town house. Two linger in memory. On Washington, near Ashland Boulevard, the lawn at the home of the H. M. Hooker family (paint manufacturer) had a large pool above which two leaden children were standing under an umbrella, which dripped rain into the pool. Another was on Adams, near Winchester; in the earliest days, the property belonged to the McMullen family of the Chicago and Alton Railroad. Later, the house was occupied by the Sears family, Amelia, Rose, and Sarah; Amelia was particularly well remembered as an early teacher at Brown School and later she became well known as a social worker in Chicago.

Here in Sears' yard, I saw a large ornate pool which had a solitary swan or goose-like bird spouting water. To a young child it seemed an anatomical distortion. A later owner of this property, William F. Conlon, said that the figure was a horse-like creature. By any name, it was true to the definition of allegory - an abstract or spiritual meaning in a material form.

The trees along the outer lawns were not uniformly planted as in later city development; each owner had planted his choice of tree. As city lots were narrow, some only twenty-five feet wide, that one tree was a treasured friend. While American elms were predominant, there were maple, ash, poplar and cottonwood trees. The last, referred to as "those dirty trees," were the children's favorite, as the catkin curls were gathered and made into silly wigs for "play shows."

On the equally small lawn or "front garden" between the sidewalk and the house, interesting plants were grown. Chicagoans, like contemporary New Yorkers, hungered for a few plants recalled from ancestral homes.

261

The scenery was more dramatic and splendid, some truly palatial on Ashland, Jackson and Washington Boulevards; all could be included in a circuit of the mile-square region. Here were expansive, velvet lawns with raised flower beds, some in geometric designs, others forming a clock dial or the American flag; hundreds of small bedding plants were used. It was in these gardens that many city children saw for the first time apples or cherries on trees, or were enveloped in the purple haze and perfume of towering lilac bushes.

There were other rewards for these tired strollers - "hikers" was a word not yet in use. Almost every block had at least one family known to the walking householders, some of whom they would visit. As the condition of the times was discussed, the youngest were having lemonade and cookies, operating wind-up toys, while a loving cocker spaniel kissed our cheeks, or a tremendous tiger cat brushed our knees with affection.

All children, except those who were crippled, walked to school. There were few bicycles used for school purposes; even carriages, and later automobiles, were infrequent. In 1901, the school board reported:

> "Chicago is the only city in the world where free transportation service for crippled children is an adjunct to the public school system."[1]

A photograph of the horse drawn "Children's Omnibus" accompanied the statement.

The Crippled Children's School, later to be known as the Jesse Spalding School for Physically handicapped Children, was next door to the Home for Destitute Crippled Children. This was a one hundred bed hospital, under the guidance of Rush Medical College, then part of the University of Chicago; this hospital was later moved to the midway campus at Billings Hospital.

The present extensive complex, usually termed Spalding School, is at Washington and Paulina and has a public school program from kindergarten through high school. It is

> "the largest of the four public Elementary Schools and the one High School operated by the Chicago Board of Education for handicapped children who, because of a physical or medical problem, cannot attend a regular school. The course of study is adapted to the needs of the child. Numerous special learning aids, modified methods and materials, specially trained teachers and individually designed devices give the child the best education possible."[2]

---

[1] 46th Annual Report of the Board of Education year ending June 30, 1900. Permission Chicago Public Schools.

[2] Editor's note: the source for this quote could be either a Chicago Public Schools bulletin or a paper entitled "The Early History of Spalding" which is prefaced with the following: "The following paper was prepared for an assembly of Parent Teacher Association members and friends by Rose Rudolph, Cecilia Foote, and Robert Underwood. The paper was presented by Robert Underwood, a senior student in the year 1948-49. The early history was

Having passed the Spaulding School and seen the children being lifted out of a conveyance by relatives or the children on their crutches waving goodby to their visitors - all brought a realization to each of the happy navigating and carefree walkers how very fortunate they were to be able to walk on two sturdy legs.

---

dictated personally by Rose Rudolph. Cecilia Foote contributed the information contained in Part II and supervised the writing of the paper by Robert Underwood." Unfortunately Part II of a copy of this paper found among the author's papers is missing, and the source of the quote remains uncertain.

CRIPPLED CHILDREN'S OMNIBUS.

56. Crippled Children's Omnibus. Appeared in "Annual Report of the Board of Education ending June 30, 1900," opposite page 40. Courtesy Chicago Board of Education.

A WALK ON ASHLAND BOULEVARD

When the oldster and the youngster, a fifty year old father and his six year old daughter, charted one of their frequent walks, it might be a leisurely stroll down Ashland Boulevard. Starting from their home on Monroe Street, they would go east to Ashland and then walk south to about Harrison Street. They would walk first on the east side of the boulevard, or avenue as it was more popularly known, and return on the west; or vice versa, it did not matter since in either case this walk might consume the sunny part of that afternoon, especially, if there were visits en route or chats with passing neighbors.

Sunday afternoon was a favorite time because one saw interesting horse-driven carriages and those without horses, which chugged along with beautiful brass lamps and honking horns. Even then, in 1904, there was an unrecognized prediction of traffic problems and pollution to come. There were often offensive gasoline fumes and smoke, oil droppings and sputtering engines, not to mention frightened horses and nervous children at the street crossings.

On the avenue there were well dressed pedestrians as well as leash-led dogs; these animals seemed to be fuzzy white poodles or punched-in-the-nose English bulldogs; and, occasionally, a red sausage dachshund. Even more engaging was the walking game of recognizing the houses of those who were living there or had lived there and now had either died or moved away to the suburbs; their spirits or their reputations seemed to linger in the old neighborhood. Houses, which may have had new owners, often were called by the earlier occupants' name, such as the home of "old Dr. So and So."

As we reached Ashland Boulevard we saw the new West End Woman's Club (1904) at the northeast corner of Monroe Street. It was a beautiful red brick building, with white trim and Colonial type of architecture, and was in a startling contrast to its brownstone Gothic or Victorian neighbors. A few doors away lived Mrs. Helen M. Waite, our beloved first grade teacher. We never chanced to see her at home, only at Brown School.

The next building we studied might be the Illinois Club, an inviting, glistening, white painted two-story building with a wide veranda and comfortable chairs for the members, all men. Here they could chat, smoke and watch the passing parade, if the day was mild. Approaching the northeast corner of Adams Street was where Dr. Truman Brophy and his family lived. He was Dean of the Chicago College of Dental Surgery founded in 1880 on Harrison Street in the old medical center. An advertisement in the 1904 Lewis Institute Annual stated that there were 2251 graduates. This advertising space was probably procured by junior Thomas Brophy, who was then a student at Lewis. Later this dental college merged with Loyola University in the old medical center.

At the southeast corner of Ashland and Adams was the Byzantine-Romanesque styled Episcopal Church of the Epiphany, built in 1885 and cherished by this walking family. Next door to Epiphany was the home of Mr. and Mrs. William J. Wilson; the house was a glistening castle-like structure. The Wilson family were generous donors to this church and eventually their home was given to Epiphany Church and was known as Chase House, honoring Bishop Chase.

The next house was the home of William Pinkerton and his family, son of Allan Pinkerton, founder of Pinkerton Detective Agency in 1850. William and Robert continued the Agency after their father's death in 1884.

Girls as well as boys were thrilled with the stories of Detective Allan Pinkerton: of how his cooper's shop in West Dundee, Illinois became a station of the Underground Railroad for the fleeing slaves; how Pinkerton discovered a band of counterfeiters and captured them; how he became the first detective on Chicago's police force. The most exciting was how in 1861 Pinkerton foiled a plot to assassinate Abraham Lincoln on his way to his inauguration in Washington, and how in the Civil War Pinkerton directed the espionage system behind the Confederate lines. After the war, the Agency guarded industrial property such as the Cyrus McCormick plant on the Chicago River; the Agency also protected strike breakers and spied on radicals.

William Pinkerton, in 1904, when asked how to stop an alleged crime wave, said:

> "The whipping post is the thing. Instead of regarding a bandit as a hero, the youth today would hardly look with admiring eyes upon a cringing, whining criminal who had been publicly flogged."[1]

The next house we passed was that of the beloved and well-known physician, surgeon and professor at Rush Medical College, Dr. James B. Herrick. Besides writing professional works, Dr. Herrick was interested in the medical history of Chicago. A daughter, Helen, graduated from Lewis Institute where Dr. Herrick served on the Board of Managers.

The intersection of Ashland and Jackson Boulevards presented a host of gracious homes and their owners. To the east on Jackson was the home of Mr. and Mrs. Edward Hines. This family had one of the pioneering lumber companies of Chicago. On the northeast corner of Ashland was the home of Mr. and Mrs. William James Chalmers, both of whom were peers in their respective interests. Mrs. Chalmers was Joan Pinkerton, daughter of Allan Pinkerton and sister of William who lived about nine doors away from the Chalmers' home.

In the society world Mrs. Chalmers represented the West Side, or more elegantly worded, she represented the West Division of the Chicago Blue Book in the Grand March of the Charity Ball given each year at the Chicago Auditorium. Mrs. Potter Palmer usually led the Grand March and represented North Division, while Mrs. Horatio O. Stone held forth for the South Division. On the more practical side, Mr. Chalmers was associated with a machine company which began as a small industry on Union Street and later would emerge as Allis-Chalmers Co.

On the southeast corner, the E. A. Robinson family had lived before they moved to the suburbs; Mr. Robinson manufactured furnaces. On the southwest corner, the John W. Midgley family was a happy household with three children, Arthur, Stanley, and Edith, who attended the public schools and then went on to Lewis Institute where they were active students.

The Reverend and Mrs. Theodore Morrison had lived about six doors south of the Midgleys' home. Rev. Morrison was the rector of the Church of the Epiphany from 1876 to 1899 when

---

[1]Ginger, Ray Altgeld's America, Funk and Wagnalls Co., N.Y., 1958, p. 215.

he was consecrated a bishop in the church he helped to build. He would return to Epiphany to preach in June, 1910 for the twenty-fifth anniversary of the laying of the corner stone.

Bishop Morrison's successor, the Rev. John Henry Hopkins was now living a few doors from where the Bishop had lived on Ashland. Rev. Hopkins was a handsome, tall man with black hair and searching dark eyes; as a child I loved him very much since I could recall when he baptised me at Epiphany Church.

On the northwest corner of Ashland and Van Buren, the John Owsley family had once lived. That house in its heyday is recalled by Mary Hastings Bradley who played with the orphaned grand-daughter, Alice Pullman Owsley. Alice's mother had been the bridesmaid for Mary's mother, so the two little girls felt a secret relationship. They often played in the fourth story ballroom of the Owsley house; here two hundred people could be accommodated for an evening dance.

At the northeast corner of Ashland and Harrison Street was the Lindlahr Nature Cure Sanitarium. In earlier days it had been the Michael McDonald home. It was said that he made his wealth as a gambler but the details were not discussed before children. The walking father summarized all of this with the statement that all life is a gamble.

This "home for the sick," as the children called it, was not welcomed by the permanent residents in the neighborhood. However, as one passed the old mansion with its generous sized green lawn and completely surrounded by an iron picket fence, one saw people playing croquet or just visiting in garden chairs; they seemed to be enjoying themselves.

The large fortress-like stone house had many semi-circular bays extending from the first floor to the attic story. There was a rounded cupola on the roof which added to its military appearance.

Dr. Henry Lindlahr, born in 1862, the early promoter of the Nature Cure Sanitarium, graduated from National Medical University, Chicago. This was a short-lived school, not recognized by the Illinois State Board of Health in 1909, and closed in 1914.

Dr. Lindlahr explained the purpose of this sanitarium to a prospective patient:

> "We combine in our work everything that is good in the natural methods of treatment, such as pure food diet, Hydrotherapy, Osteopathy, Chiropractic Massage, Medical Gymnastics, air and sun baths, Mental Therapeutics, Homeopathy, and non-poisonous herb remedies. By the judicious combination and application of these natural healing methods, we cure all forms of so-called incurable chronic diseases. Nature Cure knows incurable patients, but no incurable diseases. Any case may proceed to a point where cure becomes impossible, but if there is sufficient vitality to respond to our treatment and the destruction of the vital parts and organs is not too far advanced, a cure is possible."[2]

---

[2]Lindlahr, Henry, Letter written June 21, 1911, Records of American Medical Association, Chicago, IL.

The rates were $25.00 and up per week; this included board, room, daily treatment, and doctor's attention.

This was the age before the great advancement in modern medicine which followed World War I. These health resorts and spas were then the answer for those who could afford such periods of nature cure under authentic as well as pseudo-doctors. There were those who suffered from worrisome malaise; "nervous breakdown" was a popular diagnosis, while the conditions of personal ennui and marital conflict often went undiagnosed. For the terminal patient, perhaps the change of scenery and faces was a bit of temporary relief.

As Dr. Lindlahr grew older, his son, Victor Lindlahr, became manager of Nature Cure Sanitarium. He was not a licensed physician, only a holder of a "diploma mill" certificate, the scourge of the ethical medical profession in the early 1900's. Victor Lindlahr was, however, alert to the public's acceptance of so-called nature cures and self-administered medicine, "patent medicine," used in place of physicians' prescriptions.

After senior Lindlahr's death in 1924 and irregularities charged against the Nature Cure Sanitarium, it was closed. Victor Lindlahr transferred his residence to New York. Here he promoted patent medicines with several drug companies who manufactured Lindlahr's formulas. He also edited Journal of Living which was his advertising medium for these patent medicines and their manufacturers.

Next, he had a radio program in 1936, speaking as editor of Journal of Living; this advertised the magazine as well as giving him an opportunity to hawk his so-called nature cures, chief of which was "Serutan." Drew Pearson was sponsored by the promoters on television for this particular patent medicine.

Among a series of Lindlahr's patent medicines, which were curtailed by the Federal Drug Commission, was "V-Bev;" this was advertised in Lindlahr's magazine. This nostrum claimed relief of arthritis, nervousness, indigestion, sleeplessness, lack of energy, underweight, general rundown condition or associated with Vitamin B_1 deficiency.[3] Such was the pseudo-scientific hokum spawned on the troubled reader.

In the case of "Serutan," this patent medicine has had many bouts with the Federal Trade Commission, Food and Drugs Administration and the American Medical Association. The promoter, Victor Lindlahr and the manufacturers misrepresented this drug in advertisements in newspapers, periodicals, circulars and radio broadcasts. The principal components of "Serutan" - rice polishings and parts of psyllium seed - were not a cure for constipation as advertised, but rather an irritant for the intestines.[4]

"Nature's" spelt backward, probably now, has settled for less irritating ingredients as well as stating the limitations of this nostrum on the package. "Nature's" advertising was later blended into the tunes of champagne music on television.

---

[3]"Bureau of Investigation: Backward Goes "Serutan": Federal Trade Commission Calls Halt on the Advertising Claims," Journal of the American Medical Association, Vol 127, No. 12, March 24, 1945, p. 733.

[4]Ibid.

Like his father, Victor Lindlahr was a shrewd seducer with words. He could have been an auctioneer at a country fair or an evangelist at a rescue mission with his folksy appeal as he stumped for Geritol, his other money-maker medicine.

In 1950 Lindlahr ran a four-column advertisement in the Sunday edition of his old hometown newspaper, <u>Chicago Sun-Times</u>, with "A Frank Statement to Tired Men and Women Who are Over 35." He began by saying the odds were 8 out of 10 that when someone asks you how you feel, you answer that you are tired and without energy; and that you may conclude that you are getting to be old. His answer to this is that you should try a new method to invigorate your circulation in order to get your vigor back: take Geritol to obtain miraculous factors that promise to regenerate your blood. To get a supply for yourself, just send the attached coupon in.[5]

You, out there, have you just now become tired?

If one deviated from the straight walk down Ashland at Harrison and turned left, there was a short street called Marshfield Avenue. Here, on the next corner, was the home of Thomas Wilce, a well-known lumber merchant, in business with his brother George. What attracted children was a life-sized iron deer nibbling flowers in a colorful, rustic garden. He was what Santa's reindeer must have looked like, and children living on Marshfield Avenue, such as Eulalie and Valerie Walker and Mildred Clark, always passed him on their way to Marquette School.

Having walked as far as Harrison Street, with a short detour, the professorial father and his impressionable little girl crossed to the west side of Ashland and turned north to return home. On this boulevard, along with the temperance neighbors and friends of the then active Frances E. Willard, there were also those who enjoyed the philosophy of Omar Khayyam. My father often quoted:

> "How long, how long in infinite Pursuit
> Of This and That endeavor and dispute?
> Better be merry with the fruitful Grape
> Than sadden after none, or bitter, fruit."

At 369 S. Ashland, near Congress, Mr. and Mrs. Adolph Stein and daughter, as well as brother "Barney" F. Stein, received callers the first Saturday in the month.

Receiving days were then the accepted fashion of neighborly communication. Whatever day was listed in the Blue Book (issued yearly) was adhered to by both the householders and their visitors. On that day the presiding lady would be in her most attractive gown which her incoming guests might rival. Refreshments would offer hospitality from the heavy silver

---

[5]Lindlahr, Victor H., "A Frank Statement to Tired Men and Women Who Are Over 35," <u>Chicago Sun-Times</u>, Section Two, Sunday, August 29, 1950, p. 19. (Copyright ownership of ad content would belong to GlaxoSmithKline, owners of the Geritol Trademark, and/or Victor Lindlahr.)

service on the tea table while the friendly wine decanter stood close by. There was pink lemonade for very young callers.

Messrs. Adolph and Bernard Stein knew both the temper and taste of their quests since each brother had his own prosperous saloon on opposite sides of Madison and Paulina Streets.

The next home known to the walking family was that of Mr. and Mrs. John McLaren and their children, John Loomis and twin daughters, Grace and Jessie. The girls were childhood friends of Mary Hastings (Bradley) and the three would later attend the John McLaren Grammar School at York and Laflin Streets. Previously this was called Hendrick's School but since there were two schools with the name of Hendricks, the one in West Division district was renamed in honor of John McLaren.

He was born in Scotland in 1836 and came to United States in 1852; he served in the Union Army and later came to Chicago as a member of the John Mason Loomis Company, lumber merchants; McLaren later became president of Pere Marquette Lumber Company. He was a member of the Chicago Board of Education and a trustee of Lewis Institute, where both his daughters had attended. Jessie married James Simpson, president of Marshall Field and Co., and Grace married Philip Hosmer.

Next, we would pass the home of Mrs. Francis L. Rickords, Mary Hastings' grand-mother. After Mary's father, William Hastings, died and her mother remarried to Dr. Arthur Corwin, a professor at Rush Medical College, they made their home with Grandmother Rickords, and Mary grew up as a part of this neighborhood.

Next door to Grandmother Rickords was the Charles H. Thayer home. Mr. Thayer kept a drug store at the corner of Madison and Ogden in the Washingtonian Home (for Drunkards) building. As a pharmacist, Mr. Thayer probably filled many prescriptions for the patients who occupied the second and third floors of this building.

As we continued south on Ashland, we passed the Lee Borden home. This family was always described as "Bordens, the milk people." Everyone knew the Borden Milk Company wagon as it stopped each morning at daybreak and left milk and cream at the lower entrance door of hundreds of families in the neighborhood and later, all of Chicago. Henry Lee Borden and his wife spent their later years at the Ashland Avenue home. Previously they had lived in Texas and New York where the ancestor, Gail Borden, had invented the process of condensing or evaporating whole milk and his sons carried on the world famous industry. Borden's Condensed Milk, Eagle Brand, continues to be a family friend after more than a century.

On the northwest corner of Ashland and Congress was the home of Alfred Featherstone. The name always intrigued the youngest walker: how come a feather as heavy as a stone or a stone as light as a feather? Alfred Featherstone and Joseph Bromley had established a flourishing factory on the south side. They manufactured bicycles, velocipedes and baby carriages. Later they introduced pneumatic tires on their products, having a special arrangement with the English manufacturer, Dunlop. His famous advertisement at the beginning of the automobile tire age showed the sleepy, pajamed child with his candle saying: "Time to re-tire."

After Mr. Featherstone's death, his widow Ruth and son Edward continued living in the old home until it became the dormitory for the Presbyterian Hospital Training School for Nurses.

At the northwest corner of Ashland and Van Buren, the John Guy Owsley family had once lived. That house in its heyday is recalled by Mary Hastings Bradley, who played with the orphaned grand-daughter, Alice Pullman Owsley. Alice's mother had been a bridesmaid for Mary's mother, so the two little girls felt a secret relationship. They often played in the fourth story ballroom of the Owsley house; here two hundred people could be accommodated for an evening dance.

We were now approaching Jackson Boulevard, and looking westerly, we could see homes of my father's acquaintances, all judges. On the corner, Judge Christian C. Kohlsaat and his family occupied a large house for a large family: there were Philemon, always called "PB," Edward, Helen, Cora, Mary and Ernest. Most all of them went to West Division High School and Lewis Institute. "PB" Kohlsaat became professor of philosophy at Lewis and remained until the last days of the Institute. Judge Kohlsaat was a trustee of Lewis for many years.

Looking directly west down Jackson were the homes of Judges Richard S. Tuthill and Richard Prendergast, next door. Some of the young collegians in the neighborhood called this region "the Judges' Chambers." Judge Tuthill was the first judge to preside over the newly organized and built Cook County Juvenile Court and Detention Home at Twelfth Street and Oakley Boulevard. This juvenile court was made possible by the persistent efforts of such dedicated women as Louise De Koven Bowen and Judge Mary M. Bartelme.

On the other side of the Tuthill house, the family of Benjamin F. Ferguson lived for a period from 1885 to the late 1890's when the Fergusons, wealthy lumber people, moved to Massachusetts and gave the home to the Chicago Orphan Asylum. The old Ferguson house was very similar to the Featherstone house nearby; both exemplified the prevailing sturdy brick and stone, four story homes built in Chicago in the early 1880's.

In 1902 Dr. and Mrs. Arthur H. Brumback purchased the Ferguson house. They had lived in the neighborhood for some years on Loomis and Monroe and had considered this long empty house on Jackson as just right for their large family. They loved this four story, fourteen room structure with its leaded windows, parquet floors and onyx fireplaces.

Directly across the street on Jackson was the home of Mr. and Mrs. George J. Titus. He was an early printer, producing rare volumes as well as single page items. The home was full or rare antiques; in addition, there was a warehouse elsewhere of antiques which the daughter, Lina B. Titus Knox, watched over for many years.

At the time this youngster and her chronicler, her father, took those frequent strolls on the neighborhood streets, especially Ashland, the old Carter H. Harrison home at 231 South Ashland was no longer occupied by Chicago's first family; new homes occupied what was once a block square of Harrison property.

After the assassination of the five time Mayor Carter H. Harrison in October, 1893, happening at the close of the World's Fair, a pall of sadness enveloped the old homestead. The Harrison son and daughter, now grown, had their own homes to keep up as well as the management of the Chicago Times, a powerful voice at the time of the Pullman strike and panic of 1893.

The saga of the Carter H. Harrison family and their home on Ashland Boulevard has lived on in spite of change and decay. For years, the house remained a symbol of a family's stability as well as its political acumen.

This Chicago saga began in 1855 when Carter H. Harrison purchased land at Clark and Harrison Streets where he built a pension or family hotel. In 1858 he brought his family from Lexington, Kentucky to this building and here Carter H. Harrison II was born in 1860.

That same year the family purchased a piece of prairie land at Hermitage and Tyler Streets (Congress). Six years later they would move again to a block square bounded by Reuben, Jackson, Marshfield and Van Buren Streets. This property was the former home of the Henry Honore family who had moved to Michigan Avenue and a less rustic atmosphere where their two daughters, Bertha and Ida, respectively, met their future husbands, Potter Palmer and Col. Frederick Dent Grant, son of President Grant.

Reuben Street as a name did not appeal to the incoming Kentuckians who associated Reuben with a "Rube" or clodhopper. So the city fathers obliged with the name changed to Ashland Avenue. This made the settlers from Kentucky, such as the Walkers, Honores, Wallers, Moores, Winchesters, as well as the Harrisons, very happy.

Several generations later, those passing the old home at 231 South Ashland, including this youngest stroller, saw a stately home occupying a city lot. The house still had its widow's walk or lookout on the roof, the ornamental iron fencing, the hitching post, the carriage landing stone and the city lamp post.

We can visualize from Carter H. Harrison II's two autobiographies what that period was like when the Mile Square was still a prairie - a prairie which disappeared very quickly. The descriptions cover the two homes, the Hermitage and the Ashland Avenue. The first home was rustic in the true sense, on open prairie, a house without indoor plumbing and dependent on well and cistern water. Yet both homes possessed those homely industries and pastoral functions which today's children read about in books or see in museums.

Behind the Ashland Avenue house was the farmyard and agricultural area. Here the generous barn held horses, cows, and sometimes, goats, while the chickens had their hen houses. Even a wild doe roamed the acreage and young Carter once had a baby eagle. Peacocks had the run of the place, even of the neighborhood. Mary Hastings Bradley, then a very young neighbor, recalled chasing these peacocks with her little neighbor, Alice Pullman Owsley.

The seasonal vegetables and berry crops were grown and harvested and placed in jars in the cellars; this also included sauerkraut and wine. There was a smoke house where hams and bacon were sugar cured with hickory smoke after the southern tradition. The winter's supply of apples and nuts were stored in a locked room because of invasions by little two-footed raiders.

The Harrisons sold a corner of their land at Van Buren and Ashland to John Guy Owsley, which this new buyer found, when cultivated, produced an abundance of edible mushrooms. There was a secret for these sprouting fungi. Senior Harrison, for some years, had wagon loads of street dumpings put on his low areas to raise them to the street level. It was the practice of the city to have street cleaners sweep the debris, mostly horse manure, to the curbs where the collections were hauled away to a dumping ground. (See photograph of West End Woman's Club with street sweeping wagon around 1907.)

The John Owsley family would become life long friends of the Harrisons. The twin sons, Harry and Heaton, attended Bell's School with young Carter; later, Heaton would marry the Harrison daughter, Lina. The young Owsleys became owners of the St. Nicholas Manufacturing

Company, makers of Hibbard bicycles. When Carter H. Harrison II campaigned for Mayor of Chicago in 1897, he depended on the Owsley Brothers' bicycles to help him.

At that time cycling was as popular a sport as it is now in the 1970's, and young Harrison was an enthusiastic rider at the Century Club where he earned eighteen pendant bars for eighteen 100 mile stretches or centuries.

He donned an old grey sweater with his pendant bars and assumed a determined expression as he rode the latest Hibbard bicycle for a photograph. This was made into a campaign poster for the oncoming mayor which read: "Not the Champion Cyclist but the Cyclists' Champion."[6]

The autumn afternoon was growing chilly and there were still several blocks to go before we reached our home on Monroe.

At the northwest corner of Jackson and Ashland we passed the Nicholas E. Wathier home. Mr. Wathier had a jewelry store on Madison and Halsted, next door to the John M. Smyth furniture store and across the street from the William F. Conlon real estate agency. All three of these persons had their places of business for forty years at this famous corner. They also had lived as long in the West Division area. The Smyth and Conlon families, of Irish extraction, lived on Monroe and Aberdeen and had been a part of the neighborhood schools, including Brooks, St. Patrick's, St. Jarlath's and Lewis Institute.

The Wathiers were of French origin, having had an ancestor who fought in Napoleon's army and whose name is carved on the Arc de Triomphe in Paris. The Wathier daughters, Frances and Helen attended St. Jarlath's School and Lewis Institute.

At 201 South Ashland was a large mansion and its blending carriage house of rough hewn brown granite blocks. It was originally built for General Charles Fitzsimmons in the 1880's. The next owners were Mr. and Mrs. Charles H. Case who lived there from mid 1890's to 1917.

Inside the house, there were mantels of carved mahogany, built in book-cases of cherry wood and stained glass; the sliding doors between the large rooms were paneled oak; the windows on the circular bay were of curved glass which reflected the passing traffic in exaggerated forms.

Charles Hosmer Case was a fire insurance underwriter and a member of the board of the First National Bank. Both he and his wife were active in the Union Park Congregational Church and leaders in the temperance movement. Mr. Case served on the boards of the Newsboys Home and the Chicago Relief Society.

The Bernard A. Eckhart family were next at 187 Ashland. Mr. Eckhart owned the B. A. Eckhart Milling Company which to the younger generation meant the flour business. He was also on the Board of Trade and a trustee of Lewis Institute. Here the two Eckhart daughters attended the Academy. Dorothy married the Rev. Reginald Williams of Milwaukee and Hazel married a neighbor, Truman Brophy, Jr. who in turn became an executive in the B. A. Eckhart Milling Company.

A child's favorite of the big stone mansions was the home of General Charles Fitzsimmons at 161 Ashland, near Adams Street. The massive stone blocks which created the arched stone

------

[6]Harrison, Carter H., Stormy Years: The Autobiography of Carter H. Harrison Five Times Mayor of Chicago, Bobbs-Merrill Co., Indianapolis and New York, 1935, opposite p. 106.

driveway and enclosed porch, the occasional semi-circular windows appearing at ground level to attic, all gave the house a most indestructible and castle-like impression. The overhanging semi-circular bay was a child's dream of a perfect playroom.

General Fitzsimmons had served in the Civil War, being mustered out in 1866 with the rank of Brig. General. After coming to Chicago, the firm of Fitzsimmons and Connell was organized, contractors for public works, such as the Washington Street Tunnel and substructures of the bridges over the Chicago River in 1881.

General Fitzsimmons continued in his military interest, being appointed Brig. General of the First Brigade of the Illinois National Guard by Governor Collum. So there were two Civil War generals in our neighborhood, Bishop Samuel Fallows and General Charles Fitzsimmons.

The next house we passed might be that of the Charles Moody family of the Moody and Waters Pie Company, and lifetime competitors of Case and Martin Pie Company. Neighborhood youngsters jokingly asked: "Are all their pies made of the moody and watery stuff?" There were two Moody daughters, Helen and Marie, both of whom went to Lewis Institute. Mrs Charles Moody, Mrs. Edward Hines and Mrs. Trude Wiehe were sisters and lived within walking distance of each other.

We had now reached the corner of Ashland and Monroe; here stood the large and sturdy brown granite Fourth Baptist Church. It was truly a beautiful edifice on its exterior; to a child it seemed more like a castle than a church. Inside, the circular auditorium and its balcony echoed if the pews were not well filled. The baptistry behind the pulpit area was kept drained for safety reasons.

For many years Brooks School occupied the Sunday School rooms during the week days. Miss Brooks, who lived with her mother, Mrs. Charles Brooks, on Ashland near Jackson, directed Brooks School in this empty, echoing building.

Both the wanderers were now a bit weary as we passed the home of Jonas A. Bell at 131 Ashland. That name rang a bell! Just another block and we could enjoy a wonderful treat at Bell's Ice Cream store on Madison. So hurrying past the Third Presbyterian Church and around the corner on Madison we entered a sparkling ice cream palace. Here we had our favorite ice cream sodas; mine was a sarsaparilla; the day had been perfect.

As the years took their toll, Ashland Boulevard became known as "Labor Avenue" or "Union Row." Here were headquarters for many trade unions; the sturdy, generous sized stone mansions became offices. In time even these strongholds were not large enough for the unions' needs and were gradually demolished and replaced by modern office buildings using every square inch of the once green lawns. The old Fourth Baptist Church in its pivotal position at the corner of Ashland and Ogden was demolished. Here a large modern department store was built, Wiebolts, in the early 1920's. It, too, is now gone from this location.

57. Ashland Avenue, north of Adams Street, 1908. Courtesy Chicago History Museum.

58. West End Woman's Club, 1906, Northeast corner of Ashland Avenue and Monroe Street. Courtesy Chicago History Museum.

59. Ashland Ave from Adams Street (top); Washington Boulevard and Ogden Avenue (bottom). Gravures published in 1892; copyrighted by S. L. Stein Publishing Co. Courtesy Chicago History Museum.

60. Church of the Epiphany, Ashland Avenue and Adams Street. Courtesy Chicago History Museum.

61. Altar, Church of the Epiphany. K. Errol Wilson, photographer.

62. St. Cecilia Choir for girls; taken in front of Church of the Epiphany; Marjorie Bangs Warvelle is on far right of second row, with long curls and big white ribbon bow; Jessie Holmes is in front row just to right of center, and Polly Walker (of Ziegfeld Follies) is to her right; in addition, Evelyn Livingston, sister of Homer Livingston (future President and later Chairman of the Board, of First National Bank of Chicago), is in the picture (not identified) (from MWB family album).

63. Ashland Avenue. Source not known to Editor (possibly Courtesy Chicago History Museum).

64. Dr. James B. Herrick, circa 1888. Courtesy Chicago History Museum.

65. Carter Harrison Residence, 1907, Ashland Avenue. Courtesy Chicago History Museum.

66. Carter H. Harrison on bicycle. Carter H. Harrison IV Papers, 1637-1953, bulk 1840-1950 in Box 17, Folder 827, 1860-1953, 1890's (cycling). Photo Courtesy Newberry Library, Chicago.

67. Madison Street, 1906, east from Ashland Ave. Courtesy Chicago History Museum.

285

68. Fourth Baptist Church, 1906, Ashland Avenue and West Monroe Street. Courtesy Chicago History Museum.

NEIGHBORHOOD PARKS

"It was a saying of Lord Chatham, that the parks were the lungs of London."

> William Windham in a Speech in House of Commons,
> June 30, 1808

"You must not know too much, or be too precise or scientific about birds and trees and flowers and water craft; a certain free margin and even vagueness - perhaps ignorance, credulity - helps your enjoyment of these things."

> Walt Whitman, 1818-1892

Union Park had existed in name as early as 1850 when it covered a great land area. It was not then bounded or laid out; rather, it was virginal growth of native trees, prairie and swamp grass and snakes in the low places. It was known as Chicago's most beautiful park - the area extended as far east in its primal greenness as State Street. Its north and south extension was narrow. The majority of Chicago's population was on the West Side, and at this period, predominantly Scandinavian, German and Irish.

Before the decade was over the Chicago Theological Seminary and the Union Park Congregational Church had established buildings facing Union Park on Ruben Street, later to become Ashland Avenue. With other buildings near the park, this area became known as Union Square. A small square is what the spacious prairie park became.

Union Park is nostalgic to readers because many persons mentioned in this book have walked on that grassy area over its century of existence. Little Tad Lincoln lived near Union Park and passed daily through this greenwood on his way to and from Brown School in 1866-7. The daughter of one of Chicago's earliest settlers and a student at Brown, Frances Beaubien, enjoyed the rustic park as it appeared in the early 1860's.

The park appealed to writers and artists, too, and would find a place in their works. Mary Synon, an early graduate of old Central High School and author of The Good Red Bricks, walked over much of the old Mile Square and recalled the churches which looked out to Union Park. A later writer, Theodore Dreiser, lived near the park during his earliest years in Chicago. He would later use Union Park region as the opening setting for Sister Carrie, published in 1900. Here Union Park provided a sad and seamy narration.

An earlier description of this region, one of several that Chicago's first citizen, Mayor Harrison would write, recalled:

"While the band played, the fashion of the neighborhood paraded in fine array, some strolling, some driving slowly in wide, open landaus, the populace in the meanwhile looking on in rapt admiration. Union Park was the Bois de Boulogne of the West Side!"[1]

Mayor Carter H. Harrison II had his remembrances of Union Park which was near his Ashland Avenue home and where he played as a boy. The park then seemed large and had been given to the city by Samuel S. Hayes. The pond was large enough to have a few rowboats in summer and there were fish. Summer concerts were given by a military band which played popular Civil War songs. Near the bandstand was a stone bear pit with a caged cinnamon brown bear named Bob; he partly subsisted on peanuts.

My childhood romps in Union Park, this green world, began when my sisters took me in a baby carriage while they played tennis on the grass courts. As one progressed from apron strings, we neighborhood children spent many hours in all seasons at this playground. Sometimes we brought a picnic lunch hastily assembled in a paper bag: jam sandwiches, cookies and fruit. There was a water hydrant in the park. We sailed our boats, safely secured on a long string, in the lagoon; in winter we skated on the same lagoon with our double runner ice-skates and small boys played shinny with a tin can. In a few years we had progressed to the tennis courts and were learning correct strokes with hand-me-down rackets.

What impressed this city child most were the many shrubs and trees growing in Union Park as though God had planted them there. In later years it was my privilege to have among my teachers in landscape design such men as Frank Lloyd Wright, Lorado Taft, Jens Jensen and Franz Aust. Jens Jensen first made his reputation as a landscape architect when he created for Chicago's West Side such beautiful and restful scenery as in little Union Park and the magnificent Garfield, Humbolt, Douglas and Columbus Parks. Earlier, in 1869, Frederick Law Olmsted had created the city's circumferential system of parks and boulevards.

Only in the West Side parks did one observe such colorful bushes with their early flowerings and seasonal berries, all nonpoisonous for curious children and hungry birds. With common names known to us all, these hardy plants could be found - snowball bush, highbush cranberry, coral and snowberry, red-twigged and blueberried dogwood, pendulous bridal wreath, cinnamon scented flowering currant and most tempting of all, red-berried hawthorn. It was Jens Jensen who put them there in little Union Park for all to enjoy.

Lee De Forest, while living at his Aunt Hattie's home on Marshfield Avenue, enjoyed both Union and Garfield Parks. He expressed himself in poems about the beauty which surrounded him. In October, 1900, the young scientist, already tinkering with his famous Welsbach gas burner, and then unknown to the world at large, was one who came to Garfield Park on his bicycle and found a joy which he wrote down after the manner of Walt Whitman.

---

[1]Harrison, Carter H., "A Kentucky Colony," (pp. 162-178) in: Kirkland, Caroline (garnered by), Chicago Yesterdays: A Sheaf of Reminiscences, Daughaday and Co., Chicago, 1919, p. 177.

288

"Autumn Evening in Garfield Park."

"As I rode through the park at evening,
As I rode through the park toward the descending sun,
I breathed deep the fragrance of the Fall--
The breath of grass, new mown and dying in the autumn air;
The perfume of dead leaves dropping from the branches--
The dead leaves which rustled, ghostlike, as I rode over them--
The odor that rises with Autumn, from the decaying year.
I saw the soft light looming up from the golden lake,
And sifting through the drooping harp strings of the willows, bowed above the lake.
I saw feathery clouds, white in the sapphire sky,
And the white flotilla of swans, ebbing over the azure water.
From the rosy light into the dark shadows they glided,
Save where golden lances from the low-set sun flashed through the aisles of trees upon them.
All was beauty beyond man's expression,
Beauty that I cannot describe, nor that any poet can describe.
Such beauty can be told only by music,
Music such as the sun's fingers play on the strings of the willows,
As the wind breathes at evening and whispers to the branches;
Or as the twilight murmurs as it steals softly from the east;
Or as the songs of birds at morning or evening, in exquisite tone tints,
Plaintive calls, delicate twittering, an endless flow of lawless melody,
Rising in one voluptuous flood of mellow song.
Yet have I heard such descriptions in music which man has written--
Beethoven at times, and Wagner, and especially Mascagni, the Italian.
In the city and opera, and far from the beauty of the fields and sky
I have heard the tonal counterpart of all the glories of sight;
And I have blessed *Music*, because she alone could so describe my Paradise."

October, 1900[2]

There were two monumental statues in Union Park, one, Mayor Carter H. Harrison, by the sculptor Frederick C. Hibbard in 1907. The Mayor, having been a neighbor to Union Park, it was appropriate that his monument should be here. At the Ashland Boulevard entrance, the Mayor in his Prince Albert coat still looks out upon the city children today. At the opposite end of the area was the Haymarket Riot Monument, always called the "policeman's statue."

---

[2]DeForest, Lee, Father of Radio: The Autobiography of Lee De Forest, Wilcox and Follett Co., Chicago, IL, 1950, p. 470.

289

Sculpted by Johannes Gilert and subscribed by individual donation it was unveiled in 1889; the engraving read: "In the name of the people of Illinois, I command peace."

The Haymarket Riot at Randolph and Desplaines Streets occurred May 4, 1886, when a bomb exploded at a mass meeting of workers and where an anarchist demonstration was taking over. A force of over one hundred police were ordered to quell the rioting which resulted in seven police deaths. The statue of the city policeman in his helmeted cap and uniform was always fascinating to small boys; especially those who may have had a guilty feeling from small mischief or a sense of hero worship for a soldier they would like to become. In May 25, 1958, the monument was moved to Randolph and Kennedy Expressway, just two hundred feet from the original riot location.

If there ever was an example of hoodlumism and depravity it was the recent bombings of the old Haymarket Square statue on Kennedy Expressway.

The first of the recent bombings which felled the bronze statue occurred on October 6, 1969; the repair costs were $4,700.00.[3] The second blasting was on October 5, 1970; the repair costs were $8,000.00. In both instances members of the militant Weatherman groups proudly claimed credit for the explosions; the last party was presumed to have been female.

On January 5, 1971 the policeman dressed in his nineteenth century uniform was rededicated by Mayor Richard Daley who said this statue would always last as a important symbol of Chicago's ""I will spirit"." To all patriotic Chicagoans this became a dismal commentary on a times when Chicagoans cannot commemorate the lives of seven policemen, by erecting a statue to them, without the monument undergoing repeated attacks.[4]

It was now necessary to have a twenty-four hour police guard to prevent future vandalism. This dastardly act echoed from Chicago east to New York and west to San Francisco. It likewise stirred in the memories of many Chicagoans who had known this monument on its original site in Union Park. It way also have been recalled by those who were once small boys and climbed up on this monument and when up there felt like a midget since they could scarcely reach the policeman's hand for support in this precarious climb.

Finally in 1972 after police protection costing the City of Chicago $68,000 a year, the statue was moved inside police headquarters for final sanctuary. Here, like a family heirloom or revered image, it will rest in a friendly atmosphere.

In Garfield Park, of 187 acres, once called Central Park, and about two miles west of Brown School, one could explore great grassy meadows, gather acorns and maple wings. The lagoons were large and spanned by a bridge. On a summer's day, one could rent a rowboat for fifteen cents an hour, capable of holding a small family and lazily drift into vistas of wild-like impression. The gigantic conservatory was interesting in all seasons with a tropical room and flower shows; the chrysanthemum exhibit was perhaps the most spectacular. These have been continued on through the years. The play areas and service sections were all considered as well as the Pavillion and its refectory where organizations and schools could have programs and

---

[3]Felcher, Barry, "Bomb Haymarket Statue," Chicago Daily News, p. 1, October 5, 1970.

[4]Associated Press, "Chicago Cop Back on His Pedestal," San Francisco Chronicle, San Francisco, CA, p. 7, January 6, 1971.

dancing. In the summer, there were band concerts; here families relaxed under the trees with an evening picnic, while little children caught the drums' rhythm and the elders hummed along with the horns' melody.

In the coming years, with Chicago's increased population density, natural deterioration of plantings and greater need for assembling places, all Chicago parks were modified and simplified. One of Chicago's most outstanding developments has been the city and county green belt areas. In 1900, Jens Jensen advocated extension plans for the West Side reaching into the valleys of the Chicago and Desplaines Rivers and also, skirting Cook County as far north as Lake Forest and south to Hammond, Indiana. Today, access drives take city folk to these areas.

Recently, there appeared a poem by Ernest Kroll, Homage to Frederick Law Olmsted. It was he who designed the landscape plan for the Chicago World's Fair, Jackson Park and New York's Central Park, among others in the United States. Now, more than three quarters of a century later, comes this echoing tribute to this man and others who have made restful, green oases for our cities' millions. Jens Jensen's works can be evoked here too. A portion reads:

> "Not kingdoms or provinces, but city greens
> Dropped from his pocket where he stepped
> Across the continent, rallying life to catch
> A breath of air. It was there my parents, gasping--
> Dumped on a beachhead of the ghetto world,
> Set like the seal of disease on the wilderness--
> Dragged me, feet off the ground, to one of his
> Clearings wedged in the forest of man.
> It was there that I learned to breathe.
> It was there that I felt the shock of
> Marc Chagall, touching the earth of Provence,
> Not that, as for him, it suited ceramics,
> But that, for me, it suited existence.
> Oddly blessed, the devisers of parks,
> Not that they enter the Kingdom of Heaven,
> But that they establish, here, a plausible copy
> Without having glimpsed the original."[5]

Another park site, Hippocrates Park, is planned at the intersection of Ashland and Polk Streets. Here, the statue of Hippocrates, donated by the University of Illinois, will be placed, honoring the Greek physician who was born on the Island of Cos and who flourished from 460 to 370 B.C.

Hippocrates has been called the father of medicine. There at Cos, a school was formed around him since he labored to separate medicine from superstition and philosophical speculation. He believed that the then called four cardinal Humours were influenced by the

---

[5]Kroll, Ernest, "Homage To Frederick Law Olmstead", Saturday Review, p. 21, May 17, 1969.

outside forces and that <u>Humours</u> were glandular secretions; that the good of medicine was to build the patient through diet and by hygienic measures and not resorting to drastic treatment until necessary.

The <u>Hippocratic Oath</u> represented his ideals and principles and this continues today to be honored by the medical profession. The Oath follows:

> "You do solemnly swear, each man by what ever he holds most sacred, that you will be most loyal to the profession of medicine and just and generous to its members; that you will lead your lives and practice your art in uprightness and honor; that into whatsoever house you enter, it shall be for the good of the sick to the utmost of your power, you holding yourself far aloof from wrong, from corruption, from the tempting of others to vice; that you will exercise your art solely for the cure of your patients and will give no drug, perform no operation for a criminal purpose, even if solicited, far less suggest it; that whatever you shall see or hear from men which is not fitting to be spoken, you will keep inviolately secret. These things do you swear. Let each man bow the head of acquiescence. And now if you will be true to this, your oath, may prosperity and good repute be ever yours; the opposite if you shall prove yourselves forsworn."

69. Chicago Theological Seminary, 1906, across the street from Union Park, and next door to Union Park Congregational Church at Ashland Avenue and Washington Boulevard. Courtesy Chicago History Museum.

70. Union Park. Courtesy Chicago History Museum.

71. Carter H. Harrison, Sr. Monument, Union Park, south of Washington Boulevard. Frederick C. Hibbard, sculptor, unveiled June 29, 1907. Photograph 28062. Courtesy Chicago Park District, Administration Building, 425 East 14th Boulevard, Chicago, Illinois 60605.

72. Haymarket Monument at Union Park. Courtesy Chicago History Museum.

73. Union Park, circa 1864-1870. Courtesy Chicago History Museum.

297

THE CARRIAGE PROCESSION

"Carriages without horses shall go
And accidents fill the world with woe."

"Mother" Martha Shipton, 1488-1561
<u>Prophecy</u>

"The King in a carriage may ride,
And the Beggar may crawl at his side;
But in the general race,
They are traveling all the same pace."

Edward FitzGerald, 1809-1883
Chronomoros

"I can't afford a carriage
But you'll look sweet upon the seat
Of a bicycle built for two."

Harry Dacre, 1857-1922
"Daisy Bell" ("Bicycle Built for Two") (1892)

Sunday on Monroe Street was different than weekdays. At regular hours, bells from nearby St. Jarlath's, Church of the Epiphany and Fourth Baptist Church pealed the summons to worship and the mingling of their chimes seemed like a hymn, an unrecognized portent of ecumenical days to come. The traffic on both pavement and sidewalks was a relaxed procession of carriages and well-dressed pedestrians. The conveyances were carrying people to church, or on an outing to Garfield Park, Lincoln Park Zoo or the Field Museum in Jackson Park. The variety of vehicles seemed as assorted as today's parade of motorcars.

There was the sulky, a lightweight vehicle with two wire spoked wheels and hard rubber trees. The driver, wearing a gay ascot scarf gave his well-groomed horse a Sunday workout, out-passing the casual drivers going in his direction. The calash, single seated and two wheeled, had a black leather folding top similar to English perambulator hoods. Another single seated and four wheeled was the buggy, used by doctors and messengers. On our block, Doctors Fitch and Sweet used these for house calls. The coach was the commonest and most practical for families, being four wheeled, enclosed and weatherproof. Many of our neighbors owned such coaches. The shining black carriage awaited them at their front loading stone, being brought around by the coachman or the liveryman. A glance into the interior, after admiring the well-groomed horse with its brass or silver accented harness, showed a tufted plush or leather upholstery and often a small hanging vase of fresh flowers. Our immediate neighbors such as the Martin, Wheeler, Forbes, Krum, Benham, Haskett and Baker families, owned carriages. We neither owned a carriage nor a carriage house. We only had bicycles and a tricycle which were kept in a shed. Papa said when he bought the property in 1887 from the Van Vlissigan brokers, that he was the poorest man on the block.

If one strolled on Washington, Ashland or Jackson Boulevards, one could see a greater variety of carriages - aristocratic phaetons, surreys with fringed tops, and hackneys, the predecessor of taxicabs. Sometimes a cabriolet passed, with seats facing each other and a pedestal seat for the coachman who wore colorful livery. Gayest of all the conveyances were the tallyho coaches driven by a team of six horses and carrying thirty or more singing students; perhaps they were the graduating class from West Division or collegians from Lewis Institute. These coaches were rented from Hebard's at Winchester and Ogden Avenue. In winter sleighs were rented.

Monroe Street on Sunday, in winter, was not completely deserted. Surefooted horses drove exquisite, graceful cutters and sleighs built for two showing fur turbans and rosy cheeks above generous blanketing while bells on the horse's harness played in rhythm with his hooves.

Part of that succession of vehicles passing by the front windows were occasional funeral processions. The hearse had a symbolic message for the onlooker. If it was white, there was a child's coffin within this ornate glass frame; if gray, it was an adult, probably young, and black meant only the elderly. The religious affiliation was shown; in the center on both sides of the windows was either a crucifix for the Catholic, a star of David for the Jew and a non-describable fleur-de-lis or scroll design for the Protestant. There was, also, Masonic insignia. If the deceased had been a prominent person, sometimes the horses drawing the hearse wore embroidered or knotted coverings edged with tassels, remnants of an earlier age when royalty took the last ride, draped in a velvet pall and the horses regally covered. Frequently, the elaborate flower pieces were displayed in an open phaeton. This was before the days when affection and honor memorials could be living endowments and charitable gifts. It was the children's habit to count the number of mourners' carriages and to hold their breath during the procession, if possible.

Funeral tradition decreed the use of crepe or a spray of flowers on the front door of the home, and respectful silence was observed by the passerby. At the turn of the century, the funeral home or mortuary had not come into common use for the waiting period or where final services were held. The undertaker, as he was then called, might have his office in a hardware store or livery, as did Postlewait in the 1890's on Ogden Avenue near Van Buren. Funeral services were held in the home or at a church.

The neighboring carriage houses were interesting, especially for city children, many of whom had never seen a farmyard with its barns and stables. Wheeler's structure next door was a well managed part of an established household. On the ground floor was housed a carriage, a horse, its stall and needed supplies. Along one sidewall, completely incased by glass sliding doors, were shining harness and other equipment. On the second floor were living quarters for the coachman and his wife who assisted in the household.

The Forbes' carriage house was one of great interest to a little girl because a life-size lead horse's head always looked out at her from a simulated oval window on the second story. Years later, when the once little girl wanted this horse for her rustic homestead, the leaden and aged replica, being hollow, collapsed in the workman's hands as he tried to rescue it.

Even our shed should not be overlooked. In hot summer, it had a heavy, woody odor partly from workbench shavings and discarded furniture, such as one old horsehair chair with its innards pulled out by nesting cats and sniffing dogs. This once fine chair had elegant carved dogs' heads on the arms and paw-like feet for legs. However, Duncan Phyfe would never have claimed this Victorian half-breed. Yet to sit in that broken down chair in one's summer play seemed to cast a magic spell over a very young mind. Sometimes an uninvited tramp found a night's lodging in the shed and appeared next morning at the back door for a cup of coffee. Years later, the urge came to rescue that old mahogany chair; it was gone. Perhaps the tramp appreciated it, too.

Within a span of ten years, horses and their wagons and carriages were fast disappearing and shining automobiles (the word sounded like "oatmeals" to one at four) with big brass lamps and plump tires incasing wooden carriage wheels were being heard on Monroe Street. These self-moving objects were honking, sputtering, smoking and even "stopping dead" in front of our house. Children were getting their first automobile rides. Dr. Walter Fitch at 645 Monroe, probably had the first automobile on the block. On a free hour in summer, he would add an auxiliary seat to the rear of his one cylinder, one seated Brush and off the children would ride, in what in later years was termed a rumble seat (which this undoubtedly was). By 1912, the doctor had a Model T Ford. His oldest son, Franklin, who later was to follow in his grandfather's and father's profession, was then interested in fixing up an old car to make it run. In this case he used two Sears gas buggies to make one that worked. The other children, Edith May, Dorothy and Horatio, depended on this conveyance to get them to their summer cottage at Twin Lakes. They all graduated from Brown School, the girls from West Division and McKinley and the boys from Crane; all were later in the teaching profession.

Mrs. Albert Tyrell, our next door neighbor, had an early electric automobile, probably a Baker. The serviceman would deliver the car to the door and call for it later to return it to the service garage where it would be re-charged for the next trip. It was a truly beautiful coach of royal blue, outside and inside. We often went to Garfield Park and back which was the machine's limit. George Orseck of the high school group drove his father's Rambler open touring car. It was a gorgeous maroon, outside and inside, with a black leather top held in place with straps and big brass knuckles or buckles. This car was often loaded with eight crowded but gay occupants whose destination was Horwitz's drugstore at Madison and Lincoln, famous for its hot fudge sundaes.

With the advent of motorcars, Chicago's streets such as Monroe were modernized for this new traffic. The original paving of wooden blocks was replaced with asphalt and concrete curbing. It was an eventful time for young and old. Some thrifty neighbors took advantage of these old hunks of wood and carried them to cellars to burn later in fireplaces.

As the cracks between the asphalt and the concrete gutters oozed with fresh tar, small boys spied these penny size spots and found them chewable, a substitute for gum or flavored paraffin.

300

The tar fad passed after a few unhappy experiences since it discolored the teeth and fingernails, as well as being tracked in on the floors and ruining clothes.

There is one nostalgic sound which echoes through the years:

> "And sound of iron on stone
> And how the silence surged softly backward
> When the plunging hoofs were gone."

Walter De La Mare, 1873-1956
The Listeners

74. "Fashionable "Turn-Outs" in Central Park." Published by Currier & Ives, 152 Nassau Street, New York. A copy of the print appears in: Call Number: WING, fZ, 41225, C9367: Harry T. Peters, "Currier and Ives Printmakers to the American People," Doubleday, Doran & Co., Inc., Garden City, New York, 1942, Plate 45. Photo Courtesy of Newberry Library, Chicago.

75. Street Cars, 1906, Franklin and Madison. D.N. negative #50,842. Courtesy Chicago History Museum.

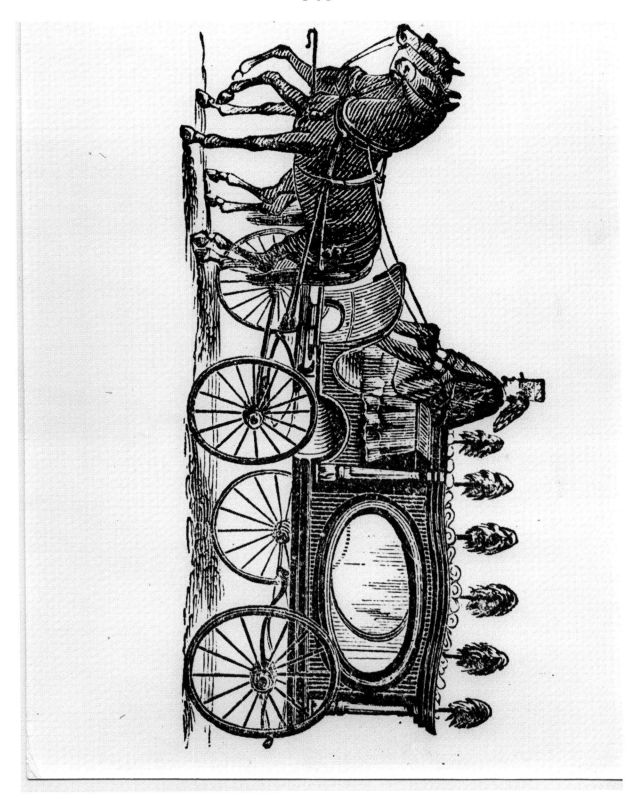

76. Horse Drawn Hearse. Photo Courtesy Newberry Library, Chicago.

77. "The Road,-Winter." Published by N. Currier, 152 Nassau Street, New York. Copy of print appears in: Call Number: WING, fZ, 41225, C9363: Russel Crouse, "Mr Currier and Mr Ives. A Note on Their Lives and Times," Doubleday, Doran & Company, Inc., Garden City, New York, MCMXXX, "Frontispiece". Photo Courtesy Newberry Library, Chicago.

742 WEST ADAMS STREET

While the largest mansions of the Mile Square were located on the boulevards, there were distinguished homes on other residential streets. Here, these costlier homes would relieve the monotony of the "row houses" - a plague of today as well as yesterday in the large cities.

A majority of these brownstone, white limestone, and brick houses of our period under study were similarly marked by the characteristics of style flourishing in the 1870's and 1880's. These could be classed as Gothic or Victorian; even these titles do not describe this period's houses, their exteriors, interiors or household furnishings. It might be said these row houses were simply "city-styled," in that one finds many common qualities in these homes which mushroomed in American cities during the mid-nineteenth century of population expansion.

Some architectural historians simply apply the title "Eastlake" to these many thousands of homes cut from the same pattern, the same solid furniture, the same butler's pantry and the same front steps.

Sir Charles Lock Eastlake (1793-1865), the English painter and art critic in his period of architectural history, advocated simplification or utilitarian principles of design such as "every article of furniture should, at first glance, proclaim its purpose." The drabness of the later London slums was the epitome of monotony.

In American cities where repeated duplication was practiced, houses did have distinct regional patterns as well as the earmarks of the local craftsmen. In comparing row houses of New York, Baltimore and Chicago, each had its own particular characteristics.

New York's row houses, more often composed of multiple flats than single dwellings, were four stories tall with the outside front stairs leading to the second story. These usually numbered from 10 to 14 steps, while the basement or ground floor entry was two or more steps down. In Chicago, the front stairs were often 16 or 18 steps high for the three story house while the ground floor entry was a few steps up. In Baltimore, the houses were either two or three stories tall and the outside stairs consisted of usually three steps leading up to the first floor. Baltimore's white stone steps have become collectors' items.

While many of the old mansions of our Mile Square have been mentioned in historical reviews, few have had architectural descriptions. In Chicago, a house at 742 (1938) West Adams Street, at the corner of Winchester Avenue and directly across from St. Paul's Reformed Episcopal Church, was one of a kind and had intriguing qualities as well as guessings about its heritage.

This house was built in 1879 by Colonel Joseph Hooker Wood, nephew of General Joseph Hooker of the Union Army. In 1938, Mr. and Mrs. William F. Conlon purchased the property from Mrs. Harry Waidener, one of the Colonel Wood's daughters. The Conlons restored the old mansion, its cottage and gardens.

Colonel Wood had a New York architect, whose name, unfortunately, seems to be lost, draw the plans for the house. The design of the house has been termed by several critics as Renaissance, even Dutch Renaissance, a form of the "Art Nouveau" practiced by a group of eastern architects. In New York at the period of this house the architects McKim, Mead and White as well as Richard Morris Hunt were reviving the classic spirit of Italy and France in their commissions for millionaires in the east. While Hunt's palatial buildings, such as the Vanderbilt town residence in New York City (1881), or "Biltmore" in Ashville, North Carolina (1895), were castles more lavish than their original inspirations found in France or Italy, this simplified, yet most comfortable Chicago residence, bore vestiges of the Renaissance impact, especially of Hunt's style.

As one looks at the attic story of this house there is a trace of Dutch influence as recalled in the facades of Amsterdam homes on the canals. There is also a marked incongruity in the front window structures, while an isolated corner with a stone railing attempts to merge the first and second stories as well as to compensate the entrance door. Yet the right side of this house is truly symmetrical and noble. Could this have been an early Hung design for a modest home?

Instead of stone, this twelve room three story house was built of Milwaukee cream brick, which when hand scrubbed forty years later, showed a patina reminiscent of the mellowed houses built of Wisconsin sandstone. Being brick, the use of corbelling marked the first story from the second, while more elaborate corbelling under the eaves of the roof was matched on the five chimneys, each of which had a monolithic coping stone on top.

The steep roof was of "peach blossom" slate with its accented ridge line terminating at the apex with an ornamental finial; a dormer window on each side of the middle chimney on both sides of the house complimented this roof design. On each side of the middle chimney on the first and second floors were windows recessed at a forty-five degree angle which gave the maximum of light between the three chimneys facing Winchester Avenue.

Above the entrance door was a transom and side panel of stained glass; also a transom was over the center drawing room window. In the center of the library chimney above the mantelpiece was a painted glass medallion depicting a Kate Greenaway scene. This rested in a leaded glass panel, two feet wide and six feet high, extending to the bottom of the ceiling's plaster cove. In this charming scene of an English garden, three little girls were running, followed by a fourth in their billowy and colorful dresses.

The entrance hall, stairway, drawing room and library were of cherry wood; this was a departure from the typical walnut or mahogany seen in Chicago houses of that period.

These were six black marble fireplaces in excellent simplicity of design. On the second floor were six bedrooms, varying in size, and three bathrooms. The latter number in that original period of plumbing was unusual in this size house. On the third floor was a well lighted ballroom which the Conlon family used as an extended library.

To the west of 742 Adams Street was a large garden area and the McMullin house. This, too, had been a charming Victorian home in its time and was occupied for a period by the Sears family. Rose and Amelia Sears were friends of the writer's family. It was here a small child came with her sister and gazed upon the spouting creature in the fountain of their sunken garden.

When the Conlons purchased this property, also in 1938, the McMullin house was demolished because it had been vandalized beyond repair. The old, stone cellar became a lily pond; the coach house was made into a recreation room with a chateau type fireplace. The sunken and terraced gardens were restored and colorful in all seasons. The fountain and its circular basin now had an Italian Bacchus pouring water out of his wineskin; the old spouting iron horse had been lost. A seven foot wall made from slab fragments and brick surrounded the gardens on all sides.

In 1967, this singularly beautiful home was sold and has since been demolished. This area now faces the twenty eight acre campus of a new Chicago City College, Malcolm X. College. As the remaining old row houses are demolished, plans are in progress for modern walk up apartments or townhouses to be built. Large cities as Chicago will always have row houses.

78. Colonel Joseph Hooker Wood Home, corner of Adams Street and Winchester Avenue, built circa 1879 (new numbering: 1938 West Adams; old number was 742 West Adams). The old number is designed in the stained glass over the front entrance. Colonel Wood was assistant to the president of the Chicago and Alton Railroad. Photographed May 1938 by T. Kaitila, 1309 W. Adams Street, Chicago, phone: Haymarket 0594.

CHAPTER EIGHT: SOCIETY AND COMMERCE
IN THE NEIGHBORHOOD

THE SOCIAL COLUMN

"There are only about four hundred people in New York Society."

"Interview with Charles H. Crandell"
<u>New York Tribune</u>, 1888.

    This expression became known as the title of the "400," or in slang, "the upper crust," meaning socially important persons in a particular city or neighborhood who were listed in a special publication. In 1879-80, a social directory was published which stated "who was who" among the leaders of Chicago and the title page read:

> "The Bon-ton Directory: Giving the names in Alphabetical Order, Addresses and Hours of Reception of the Most Prominent and Fashionable Ladies Residing in Chicago and its Suburbs".[1]

    The <u>Bon-ton Directory</u> flourished for only one year. The <u>Elite of Chicago</u> followed from 1880 to 1892. The chosen elite were not listed alphabetically; instead, the street address located them. Where one lived was as important as how one lived. By 1890, another social directory appeared, the <u>Chicago Blue Book</u>.

    The Preface to the original issue of <u>The Chicago Blue Book</u> in 1890 stated in part:

> "The title, "Blue Book," is simply a name given the work on account of its *blue* cover. It does not refer to blue blood, as many people suppose. Webster's definition of Blue Book is as follows: "BLUE BOOK–A parliamentary publication, so called from its blue paper cover, such being commonly used; *also, a book containing a list of fashionable addresses*." We do not claim the BLUE BOOK to be either a City Directory or absolutely an Elite Directory; neither is it issued as a book for financial business purposes; but simply, as it claims to be, a list of names of twenty-five thousand of the most prominent householders of

---

[1]Harris & Morrow, Bon-ton directory, title page, Blakely, Brown & Marsh, Chicago, 1879-80.

Chicago and towns in the vicinity, published in the most convenient form for social purposes."[2]

It was a yearly directory of outstanding and socially prominent citizens and continued until the need for more crucial printed matter during World War I, or perhaps lack of participation, curtailed publication in 1916. To be listed was an assurance of respectability, possibly renown, but usually signified affluence or influence in Chicago's growing sophistication.

Unlike the Chicago City Directory which was indexed alphabetically, but like its predecessor, the Elite of Chicago, the Blue Book listed names by street addresses in various sections of the city and suburbs. Of two neighbors, living side by side and good friends, only one might be listed in the "Blue Bloods." The 1900 directory listed 26,000 names. While such social directories are still being published in the United States, they are becoming obsolete because of snobbish evaluation; they are a remnant of British and European aristocratic traditions and not a sincere concept of American appraisal.

It must be acknowledged that any listed person's name, address or club affiliation was duly paid for by subscribing to the volume, just as modern professional directories are financed. From the Chicago Blue Book's inception to its demise, our family name appeared with an italicized receiving day *Wednesday*, indicating "at home" day for my mother. By early 1900's she had retired from such social preoccupation and was quietly and stoically living her days. Our parents' earlier years were socially busy but usually with an altruistic incentive.

Around 1900 there was little organized city relief as "Community Chest" to distribute aid to orphans, the elderly or the impoverished. The county had its hospitals, its farms, often called the "Poorhouse," while the orphanages and refuges for the insane were termed "asylums." All levels of Chicago's society working through social clubs, fraternal orders, church organizations and private individuals helped the local charities.

Chicago society engaged in a continuous marathon of charity balls - from Mayor Carter H. Harrison's sponsorship and Mrs. Potter Palmer's patronage to simpler affairs by sodalities and fraternal orders. In 1905 Mrs. Potter Palmer, now a widow, was busy running the Charity Ball which that year was for the benefit of indigent soldiers and sailors.[3]

Such charity balls could have both altruistic as well as political tones. There was the annual First Ward Ball whose directors were saloon keepers, gamblers, dive-keepers, madames of the brothels and owners of flop houses. They sold tickets at five dollars each to employees of the breweries, saloons, gambling dens and houses of prostitution as well as the various stores in the ward.

---

[2]The Chicago Blue Book of selected names of Chicago and suburban towns, The Chicago Directory Co., Chicago, 1890, Preface. F548 .22 .C5 v.1890, Harold Washington Library Center, Chicago.

[3]Ross, Ishbel, Silhouette In Diamonds, Harper & Brothers, New York, New York, 1960, p. 188.

Part of these proceeds went to so-called charity and part to the strong box in the custody of Hinky Dink Kenna, Bath House John Conghlin and First Search Tom McNally. Many who purchased tickets did so considering the time when they might need friendly help from these First Ward diplomats.[4]

Among other balls, where the five times Mayor Harrison made an appearance for political friendly reasons, were the pastry cooks and waiters union, the Pilsen Turners and the Chicago Hebrews annual ball. The mayor tells of being introduced to the dowager Mrs. Schlesinger of Schlesinger and Mayer. His escort announced: ""Mr. Mayor, I want you to meet the first lady of the ball."" Mrs. Schlesinger replied: "I am very bleased to meet you, Mr. Mayor, very bleased, and vich vamily of Mayers?""[5]

The occasion which eclipsed all degrees of balls was The Charity Ball, held each year in the winter season at the Auditorium. This was a civic promotion and proceeds helped various publicly supported institutions. While being glamorous with the presence of many heavily jeweled socialites, the Ball also counted on the support of middle class Chicagoans. Those persons who experienced the Grand March, or promenaded in the magnificent Auditorium Theater would be remembered in their family annals. For such an occasion, a special parquet floor was installed flush with the stage for dancing.

The expression and popular ditty in 1900, "Tara-boom-de-ay" was not entirely a college fraternity song. The name also described the massive jewelry worn from head to foot at the Charity Ball. There were the diamond and emerald studded tiaras, gold and jeweled necklaces or neck bands called dog collars and long strings of pearls - the size of birds' eggs, which might extend to the knees.

A sixteen year old wrote in December, 1896:

> "Mamma has had two dresses made at the dressmaker. One is brown silk, trimmed with velvet; the other is black satin with jet bead trimming to wear to the Ball. She is so busy preparing for the ball - so much fuss, worry and expense for just one night of pleasure; yet I am glad that they can go."[6]

At eighteen the same diarist went to the Charity Ball on her father's arm, substituting for her mother who was then a lady-in-waiting and had neither time nor interest in balls. At about four, this last arrival, chanced to explore in her big sister's wardrobe while she was at the University of Chicago, living in Green Hall. There were dainty white kid slippers; even my plump feet filled them except for length. In its protecting dust-cover, her opera cape hung; she had worn it to the Ball. It was white broadcloth with shouldering fringe of white, wavy hair from some

---

[4]Harrison II, Carter H., Growing Up In Chicago: Sequel to "Stormy Years", Ralph Fletcher Seymour, Chicago, IL, 1944, p. 201-2.

[5]Ibid., pp. 203-204.

[6]From Effie Warvelle's diary.

unknown animal, probably Angora goat fur or mohair. Social events at both Lewis Institute and the University called for simpler costumes.

Many of the social clubs of the old West Side were in the near neighborhood, easy to reach by foot or carriage. The Ashland Club at Washington and Wood Street was the oldest, being in existence in 1870. Senior Carter H. Harrison and his wife invited members of the club to a fancy dress ball and masquerade at the family home, 163 South Ashland in December, 1870.[7]

Another social note read:[8]

"Compliments of Mrs. Carter H. Harrison, 163 Ashland Avenue,
for
Friday Evening, February 17, 1871,
Soiree Musicale et Dansante
for the
Benefit of the Half Orphans' Asylum
Single Admission $1.00. One Gentleman and Two Ladies $2.00
Supper, If Wished, 50 Cents Each.
Please Present This Invitation at the Door."[9]

Coming down the years, our next door neighbor, Albert Tyrell was President of Ashland Club in 1905. In that year the Ladies Auxiliary presented a play, La Nuella de la Softera, at the clubhouse.[10]

The Bicycle Clubhouse at Adams and Wood Streets was thriving in 1890. In that year the Washington Cycling Club attempted to girdle the city on "high wheelers." Carter H. Harrison II, when running for mayor, was a bicyclist belonging to the Century Road Club. He had a poster made in 1897 showing himself in proper attire upon an Owsley make which read: "Not the Champion Cyclist but the Cyclists' Champion".[11] Besides bicycles built for two, they could range up to ten cyclers - Carter H. Harrison also headed such a contrivance.

The Fort Dearborn Club at Washington and Ashland was patterned like the Ashland Club with a Woman's Auxiliary and calendar of events.

The Illinois Club on Ashland between Monroe and Adams was a men's club where members could enjoy evening smokers and relaxing conversation. Monthly invitations were sent to

---

[7]Harrison, p. 53.

[8]Ibid., p. 53.

[9]Ibid., p. 54.

[10]Chicago West Side Historical Society.

[11]Harrison, Carter H., Stormy Years: The Autobiography of Carter H. Harrison Five Times Mayor of Chicago, The Bobbs-Merrill Co., Indianapolis and New York, 1935, opposite p. 106.

members' families for evenings of dancing and entertainment. It might be musical with members of the School of Opera of Chicago Musical College under the direction of Dr. Florenz Ziegfeld presenting Act II of <u>Martha</u> and Act II of <u>Carmen</u>. At Christmas season the members' children had an afternoon party while the young adults celebrated later. Our family participated in this Club's events. One youngster recalls wearing a much loved brown velvet dress trimmed with gold soutache braid.

Another club which would experience its greatest activity during the World's Fair was the Acacia Club at 105 Ashland, next door to the Third Presbyterian Church. It was incorporated in 1890 in anticipation of the Masonic visitors to the Fair and one of its objects was the establishment of a library. In a short time the club possessed one of the largest Masonic libraries in the world. My father was an early president.

However, with the inrush of visitors to the Exposition, the Club's resources were over-taxed by hospitality demands and debts until it was necessary to discontinue maintenance of the clubhouse and the library was transferred to the Oriental Consistory building while the Club continued on a less expensive basis.[12]

By 1895, this aftermath of debts was to be seen all over Chicago and a commercial depression would be felt by many individuals. The school girl's diary of December 21, 1896 states:

> "Today the National Bank of Illinois failed. Papa lost all his ready money. I don't know if I can go to college now."[13]

The West End Woman's Club was organized in 1892 and its clubhouse at Ashland and Monroe was built in 1904. While stressing cultural improvement for it members, it also worked for neighborhood betterment and was especially active with the problems of child delinquency. During World War I, the clubhouse became the neighborhood center for Red Cross workrooms. The signs of the times then became an assortment of stern facts. Mixed with the increasing number of signs reading "Furnished Rooms for Rent" or "Rooms for Light Housekeeping" and the usual ice card, were small flags with a red star on a white field. Sometimes there would be two or even three stars on the same flag indicating that sons or brothers were in the armed forces and probably, already "over there."

---

[12]The evolution of the national Masonic fraternity, <u>Acacia</u>, came about in 1894 at University of Michigan with a group of law students forming a Masonic club. This was followed by Acacia becoming a chartered national fraternity in 1904 at Michigan. The organization has grown from coast to coast in leading universities and stresses Masonic ideas and high scholastic calibre. Whether this Acacia was inspired by Chicago's Acacia club can only be conjectured.

[13]From Effie Warvelle's diary.

THE NEIGHBORING STORES

"Good will is the disposition of the customer to return to the place of business where he has been well treated."

U.S. Supreme Court

The nearby stores and their merchants of Madison Street and its crossroads, Robey, Paulina and Ogden, were all part of the Brown School shopping area. Sometimes it was necessary to go as far north as Lake or south to Harrison Street. The stores were sufficient for the contemporary needs and were forerunners of present day community centers in our staggered cities and suburban projects.

In that earlier day, stores grew as needed without much concern for qualities of charm and invitation (sales appeal) as used to identify each establishment. True, no stores of early 1900's greeted their customers with such signs as "Ye Olde" this or that - timepiece or hair piece, much less "At the Sign of" - the copper kettle or bluegoose, so reminiscent of early New England towns. The signs were just plain statements, Grocery and Market, Coal and Wood or Soo's Chinese Laundry.

There were additional aids to identification; interspersed could be seen ancient guild signs, even in the twentieth century. Each of the following objects are recalled on the block of Madison between Wood and Lincoln Streets and were duplicated on all business blocks in Chicago and other cities before the advent of electric signs.

There was a red and white striped barber pole in front of Harry Thompson's shop; a life-sized painted wooden Indian with a hatchet stood in front of a tobacconist shop. Later, this was known as Drell's Cigars; by then the Indian had fled or been captured by a wooden Indian collector who probably made a killing with his later sale of this coveted object. There was a hanging gold-painted and watch faced clock in front of Rose and Carter's Optician and Jewelry. There may have been a pair of giant spectacles suspended over an optical shop, but the exact owner is not recalled. The swinging open umbrella was rightfully waving over Krueger's Umbrellas, "Made and Repaired." A large golden mortar and pestle, the apothecary symbol, belonged to Sawyer's Drugstore, and a black wooden boot hung above Joe's Shoe Repair. This place of business was only five feet wide with cobbler's bench.

There were numerous small tailor and haberdashery shops in the neighborhood. One of the oldest was A. Marks, Men's Furnisher, on Madison near Wood. He had two sons who graduated from Brown School. Alfred, the younger, to whom the writer is much indebted, saw in his mind's eye after a lapse of more than fifty years, the location and owner of each neighboring store. Such recall could be termed periscopic, as each storefront fitted back into the 1900 scene. Near Mark's store, J. Krifka had a small glove factory and men's wear. Ellsworth Landon, Madison and Ogden, catered to the young crowd; a well dressed young man could have suits and coats to order from fifteen to fifty dollars. Other tailors on Madison were T. Teplitz,

Waters, Touchband and William Rueckoldt. When I left for college, one of these tailors made my first "grownup" suit.

Among other stores recalled were printing firms - Jacobus, Springs, and John W. Lupton & Co. The latter printed magazine materials such as the monthly Voice of West Division or McKinley and church periodicals as The Epiphany Star or The Welcome. Jacobus and Springs did special orders as programs, advertisements, political and greeting cards. Each Christmas Jacobus printed my sister's annual poem for that season. These continued for years and many students in her classes at Lewis Institute received them. At random is one as appropriate today as forty years ago, entitled, Peace:

> "Shepherds and wise men now
> Look up into the skies -
> O may there not again
> A wondrous star arise -
> A star whose holy light
> Shall help each man to see
> His brother's soul aright?"

There were two florist stores: Schiller's was on Madison near Oakley and Fisk's was on Ogden Avenue near Madison. Both these florists served the neighborhood for over twenty-five years.

Schiller's was a large establishment with double window displays which pictured the seasonal verdure along with the expected blossoms, always real; there were no plastic gardens then.

Fisk, the florist, was perhaps patronized more often by the school children. A purchase of three carnations or a bunch of violets received as much attention as if purchasing an orchid. The latter had little appeal to children, probably because the orchids had no perfume and because they could not be picked up and inspected before purchasing. As for the asking of their price that decision was seldom, if ever, reached.

Of the two photographic studios, Patterson and Schimmin on Ashland and Madison, made graduation, club and sports team groups for various schools. William Huzah, near Wood Street, specialized in family and personal portraits. Here one would see in his window, wedding, first communion or baby pictures. These last might be posed in long baptismal dresses or chubby nudes resting on white fur blankets. Even a little French poodle dog had his picture taken at Huzah's.

There were plenty of local theatres after "moving pictures" became a way of life in United States. Among the earliest of those on Madison Street were the Wood Street and the Ashland Theatres. The Ashland had assorted chairs for seats in the beginning and Gene Greene was the leading local entertainer in early vaudeville acts. From the earliest nickelodeons to the advent of sound pictures, "the piano player," frequently a woman, followed the celluloid action with appropriate accompaniment; it could be syncopated, pompous, sad or sentimental. The pianist often had to pick up suddenly with a "fill in" when the film reel snapped and was rewound.

Two other nearby theatres were the Lincoln and American. The latter was vaudeville and pictures; an electric organ replaced the piano.

The Flatiron Building was the pride of the neighborhood, being its tallest and finest office building. Where Madison, Ashland and Ogden converged, a triangular structure was erected in 1891 by A. J. Stone and was to be known as the Stone Building. However, the "Flatiron" title became its final, colloquial name.

Alfred Smith was the architect of this red stone, fireproof nine story structure costing $175,000. It housed doctors, dentists, lawyers, insurance and realtor companies. On the ground floor a bank had three existences under the names of Wendell, Reliance and People's National. There were a few stores facing the various streets as Leebrick's Shoes and a tailoring shop.

Among some of the professional offices were those of lawyer, Anthony Cremerious and two dentists, Dr. Arthur Somerville and Dr. Michlethwait - he was our dentist, with whom I had frequent appointments for a siege of orthodontia. Since this building had elevators like loop skyscrapers, the necessary visits were made interesting; the ride up and down from the seventh floor produced certain soaring and plunging sensations.

At the demolition of this fortress-like structure, the last owners of Youngsdahl's optometry and jewelry store, across the street, looked back fifty years (see old photograph) and also looked forward to a new day in Chicago's reclamation of worn-out areas. The old site received an historical tablet in 1936 - "Near this site was the first and largest bull and cattle market."

79. Speakman Book Store. Courtesy Chicago Medical Book Company, 7400 North Melvina, Chicago, Illinois 60648.

80. Flatiron Building, at Ogden Avenue and Madison Street. Courtesy Chicago History Museum.

NEIGHBORHOOD INDUSTRIES

Many of the Mile Square manufacturers served the medical profession and nearby hospitals. Three firms on Madison Street were De Souchet Oxygen Gas, Zieman Orthopedic Supplies and Gelder Mattress Company; Sleepwell Mattress Company was on nearby Ogden Avenue. Mattresses for hospitals were often for temporary use, pads filled with cheap cotton or excelsior and later destroyed. Two concerns which have served the Medical Center since pioneering days to the present are Chicago Medical Book Company and V. Mueller and Company, manufacturers of surgical instruments.

Speakman's medical bookstore has been a family managed concern for four generations, since 1865. It was originally located a stone's throw (next door) to West Division High School and at that time, also, was the high school book store. After the school building was sold to the College of Physicians and Surgeons, Speakman's business became known city-wide as the Chicago Medical Book Company. The business remained in the community until 1968, when larger quarters were established in northwest Chicago.

V. Mueller and Company was started in 1895 by Vinzenz Mueller. He had learned instrument making skills in the Black Forest region of his native Germany. Upon coming to Chicago he was inspired by the promising Medical Center with its new surgical technics and specialized instruments. He set up shop on Ogden Avenue near Honore Street and was helped by his wife. He designed his instruments under the best surgical advice and was a familiar figure in hospital operating rooms and medical libraries. In 1909, George W. Wallerick, an authority on electrical equipment, joined the company and the neighborhood workshops expanded. In 1955, V. Mueller and Company joined the American Hospital Supply Corporation as a wholly owned subsidiary.

Among other neighborhood industries were four cigar factories, all of whose owners' children attended the nearby public schools. In 1900, cigars and pipes were the most popular forms of smoking; cigarettes were frequently imported or smokers rolled their own, using papers and blended tobacco sold in small bags. These makings could be purchased where plug or chewing tobacco was sold. The "Bull Durham" bag was seen along with "Star" or "Five Brothers" chewing tobacco. The empty bags were perfect for children's marbles, jacks or pennies.

William D. Algeo and Company's cigar factory flourished next door to Adolph Stein's saloon on Madison and Paulina Streets. This company of less than a dozen employees handmade their complete productions. They had a retail counter and pool table in one corner of the factory; this was most convenient to the neighboring saloon patrons, especially, at Adolph Stein's place which had the extra inducement of free lunches. Brother Barney Stein's saloon across the street also benefited.

Tobacco used in cigar manufacturing came from Cuba and the central states. Wisconsin's seemed preferred. Extra crops were grown on small farms, even in suburban areas near Chicago. The routine day's work at Algeo's began with the bundles or "hands" of tobacco leaves being unpacked; they were dry and stiff and needed to be "cased" or immersed in water and shaken to be pliable. Then the central stem of each leaf was extracted or "stripped" by hand. The leaf then became a "filler" and a cigar shape was formed by hand or in a mold. The "binder," another leaf, was wrapped around the filler to further its shape. Then a "wrapper," a finer grade of tobacco, was put around the binder; the cigar was now finished. These cigars were then judged on color and shape and were sorted for boxing. Each was given its identification paper ring and packed in neat Cuban mahogany boxes.

These cigar rings were the manufacturer's only individual identification and were often decorated with cameo-like feminine faces and the trade mark or brand. Algeo's best was "La Flora de Algeo - all Havanna Cigar." Children prized these paper rings as well as the wooden cigar boxes which came in several sizes; they were perfect for dolls' trunks, sewing boxes or boys' treasure chests for trivia. The neighborhood cigar stands were seasonally solicited for these empty containers.

In early 1900's, a cigar maker's output could be 200 or 300 cigars per day and a fast worker earned around forty dollars a week - all hand labor.

The second local factory was located on Paulina and Jackson, and was owned by William Paley. This little company employed only about six workers but they were inspired. For their best cigar they chose the name of "La Palina;" this cigar would have a long life in the tobacco world. It has never been determined whether La Palina was named after Paley family or the birthplace of the cigar, Paulina Street.

A third factory was Wengler and Mandel on Madison between Lincoln and Robey, now Wolcott and Damen, Streets. Their two best known brands were "Tom Palmer" and "Tropics."

The fourth cigar factory was that of John B. Chiappe; it was located at 1912 Van Buren Street where he was in business for fifty years, closing in 1924. This was a Union Shop and known as "No. 11. 1st District of Illinois." There were about twenty men employed at prevailing union wages. This cigar factory, like the others, hand-made its cigars which were named Pour La Noblesse and Victoria Nobless. These were pure Havana tobacco and cost fifteen cents each. Their bands were plain maroon and gold with no crest. Victoria was a family name as well as that of a cigar since one of Chiappe's daughters was named Victoria.

Victoria Chiappe graduated from McKinley High School in 1919 and was a pretty as well as jolly minded student. So much so that two of her favorite teachers, Mr. Payne and Mr. Brimblecom, wrote on her Voice Annual flyleaf. Mr. Payne wrote:

"Now here's to Victoria Chiappe
Whose lessons were awfully scrappy
But whether her bit
Is a miss or a hit
The expression is equally happy."

In turn, "Brimby," referring to Victoria's earlier statement to him that in the next semester she was going to be a "devil," wrote:

"This year I intend to be regular - But depend on me, Vicky, I'll never give your secret away - the terrible awful secret will die with me."

Mr. Chiappe, one of those old school artisans, was dedicated to his business and made many trips to Cuba. A lucrative part of his business was selling to the various saloons, and when prohibition days came his business was hard hit; but with friends he survived.

Today cigar factories, like most types of manufacturing, are machine operated; there is little, if any, handwork. Now the literal definition of the word <u>manufacture</u> is almost obsolete - <u>to make with the hands</u>. Also, today, the old ways and old days of the arts and crafts which were mainly hand created or manipulated are being recalled in nostalgic literature as well as being re-created in workshops, classrooms and "where two or three are gathered together." Even some of the old industries such as cigar making are being re-valued and make interesting reading today. An article, "The Vanishing Chicago Cigar" by H. C. Mullins recalls:

"...the late 19th century when the whole world, with the exception of the English court, measured wealth, position, and gentility by the size of the cigar and the amount of smoke in a room at any given time."...[1]

"...Cigarmakers were once the aristocracy of the working classes. They were the highest paid workers of the time and, the legend goes, they could hire other men to read to them or violinists to serenade them while they rolled the tobacco leaf."...[2]

"...Who would ever remember Thomas R. Marshall, Woodrow Wilson's veep, had he not arisen one day on the Senate floor and uttered the ringing call that echoes to this day: "What this country needs is a really good 5-cent cigar"?"[3]

An industry which was a forerunner of prepared food supplies for both consumer and merchant was Case and Martin Pie Company, located at Lake and Wood Streets. Its chief rival was Moody and Waters, located outside our district. Both names were frequently confused as "Case and Moody" or "Moody and Martin." The Martin partner was our early next door neighbor on Monroe Street. These pie companies made only the conventional type pies which fitted into narrow shelved cupboards on their delivery trucks. The principal customers were wholesale buyers - restaurants, hotels, delicatessens and saloons (for free lunch bonuses).

Pies could be cheaply made and advantage was taken of assembly processing. Brown School children were taken on tours to this nearby factory and saw apples turning on spits as electric knives peeled, cored and cut them. On another moving line, the dough was being rolled and dropped on waiting pans where a press prepared a cradle for these waiting apples. Sweetened with sugar and spice, the pies moved to another track where they were capped, clipped and pricked and were headed for the ovens on long shovel-like arms. The pie factory had a good smell but that is all we ever were given, no tastes.

However, when a group of McKinley High School girls visited the Case and Martin Factory, they were each given a whole pie. Straight away they became known as the Eata Bita Pie girls.

-----

[1]Mullins, H. C., "The Vanishing Chicago Cigar," <u>Chicago Tribune Magazine</u>, October 29, 1972, pp. 24, 29.

[2]Ibid., p. 29.

[3]Ibid., p. 30.

PETER FAHRNEY AND SONS COMPANY

In that age of unrestricted manufacturing as well as fraudulent advertising of patent medicines, there were several such companies in the old Mile Square. There were good "money makers," totaling millions for their owners. While the manufacturer's intent was not necessarily to mislead ailing customers, there also were no stringent federal laws to protect these unwary and often desperate victims. Help did not come until the era in which the Federal Drug Commission and other authorities took over.

One such company which had several locations during its existence was the Peter Fahrney and Sons Company which prospered from around 1890 and continued until the 1950's. The last location or factory was at 2501 (new number system) Washington Boulevard. Peter Fahrney and his wife were listed in the 1890 Blue Book and by 1893 and after, there was a sizable family of Fahrney children and in-laws listed at 1074 Warren Avenue (old number system) which was near the factory on Hoyne and Washington. This patent medicine company was strictly a family run business passing to Ezra C. Fahrney after his father's demise. This was necessary to keep those secret formulas from being picked up by outside help. This was true also in the history of the Victor Lindlahr patent medicine described elsewhere in this book.

Among the Fahrney nostrums which had been under indictment by the Federal Trade Commission in 1942 were Forni's Alpenkrauter, Forni's Magolo, and Forni's Heil-Oel Liniment. The first item, Alpenkrauter, appeared under six other names according to the nationalities to which it was advertised. This was during the period of the immigration of many foreigners to Chicago area. Perhaps an expert can determine the nationality each of these items were beamed to: Hoboko, Novoro, Zokoro, Kuriko and Gomozo! Forni's Alpenkrauter, or whichever language version selected, was analyzed and found to consist of 14% alcohol, 13% sugar and a little laxative material. Not a bad drink for a "wino" or a self-protesting member of a prohibitionist family!

In 1942 the Fahrney Manufacturers agreed to the stipulation:

> "...to cease representing that the Alpenkrauter will regulate the bowels, relieve rheumatic pain, ward off disease and beneficially affect skin eruptions; that the Magola will neutralize acids in the stomach or be of benefit in diarrhea due to "summer complaint" and that the Heil-Oel Liniment is a competent treatment for severe burns, corns, calluses, or wounds from rusty nails, and may be used for backache with beneficial results..."[4]

Again in 1946 further stipulation was ordered on Alpenkrauter and its various other names:

---

[4]"Bureau of Investigation: Stipulations," Journal of the American Medical Association, Vol. 120, No. 6, p. 470, Oct. 10, 1942. Copyright © 1942, American Medical Association. All Rights reserved.

"...that in labeling and advertisements of its product, under whatever name, it will not fail to warn that the nostrum should not be used when abdominal pain, nausea, vomiting or other symptoms of appendicitis are present."[5]

A most detailed description of the patent medicine which paraded under its various nationality titles was on the label of Kuriko. A portion read:

"A Blood Purge that Acts on the Stomach, Liver, Bowels, Kidneys and other Emunctories of the Human Body.
　"Adapted for the treatment of blood and constitutional diseases, Constipation, Sick and Nervous Headaches, Liver Complaint, Bilious Disorders, Rheumatism, Gout, Dyspepsia, Indigestion, Erysipelas, Worms, Tape Worm, Neuralgia, Chills and fever, Scrofula, Pimples, Boils, Skin Eruptions, Ulcers and Sores, Pains in the bones, Piles, Kidney Complaint, etc."[6]

The directions for taking were even more detailed with advice on the bowel movements which might produce

"too great a drain on the system... may tend to weaken you... too small a dose may produce a slight griping".[7]

Dr. Peter Fahrney's name appears in the 1909 (Volume 2) edition of the American Medical Directory at Frederick, Maryland. He represented many legitimate physicians of his period who turned to commercial manufacturing and selling of particular formulae rather than remaining in so-called "private practice." An undated newspaper clipping recalled the Fahrney family in Hagerstown, Maryland:

"The Dr. Fahrneys have been practicing medicine and made a specialty of chronic diseases for over 100 years. I am working only with chronic diseases - bad kinds - difficult cases - and I diagnose your case before I treat you. If you have a trouble or a weakness or deformity, write me and I'll study your case and give you satisfaction".[8]

---

[5]"Bureau of Investigation: Stipulations," Journal of the American Medical Association, Vol. 131, No. 11, p. 938, July 13, 1946. Copyright © 1946, American Medical Association. All Rights reserved.

[6]American Medical Association Files.

[7]Ibid.

[8]Ibid.

In questioning old timers from the West Side of Chicago, another patent medicine factory was recalled. It was known to the neighborhood in the early 1900's as a liniment factory. This was the Gile Remedy Company located at 706-708 (old number system) Van Buren Street. An undated resume on a bottle of one of the best sellers informed the prospective buyer of Gile's Germicide:

> "A new discovery for all acute or chronic diseases of germ origin, internal or external.
> "A Magical Germicide, Antiseptic, Tonic and Blood Purifier all contained in one preparation.
> "Regular size bottles 50 cents each and $1.00 each.
> "The Gile's Remedy Co. 706-708 Van Buren St."

A report from the American Medical Association stated:

> "This purifier and remedy for a large number of pathologic conditions was declared false and fraudulent. In August 1928, no claimant having appeared, the judgment was entered and the court ordered that the product be destroyed." Notice of judgment 16079, Issued July, 1929.[9]

Patent medicines seem to live on; just turn on the radio or television and get a good dose of indoctrination of the contemporary products, many of which are continually under investigation.

---

[9]"Bureau of Investigation," Journal of American Medical Association, September 28, 1929, p. 1008. Copyright © 1929, American Medical Association. All Rights reserved.

THE AUTOMATIC TELEPHONE COMPANY
AND THE CHICAGO TUNNEL COMPANY

Around 1902, the neighbors, young and old, on the 600 block of Monroe Street (early numbering system) were curious about a new building on the northwest corner of Monroe and Paulina. The bronze plaque simply stated: Automatic Telephone Company. This was a one story brick building with a few translucent glass windows. No one was seen entering or were there sounds, or smoke from the chimney.

By 1905, there was a bustling new tenant, the R. E. Rappaport Luggage Company. (It is still in business at this location.) The school children still wondered what was the Automatic Telephone Company and where had it gone?

In the early 1900's, telephones were not the universal necessity they are today. Many homes on Monroe Street did not yet have telephones and depended on the drug store booth for making calls. It was difficult for children to reach the wall mouthpiece, as well as to make the operator understand the uncertain number they were calling, even though it had only two digits. Dr. Finch's number (kept on hand for emergencies) was simply West 41; years later, it became West 0041.[1]

The Automatic Telephone Company was an independent organization with a far-seeing idea of putting telephone wires and cables underground in a congested city. In 1901, tunnels were being dug in the downtown district. These were well constructed tubes, six feet wide by seven and a half feet high and horseshoe shaped.[2] One of these tunnel entrances was to be at the building on Monroe and Paulina which would probably house switchboards and life lines.[3]

However, the project, though being well built, proved too costly to be continued and was abandoned by the original Automatic Telephone Company. During this period, the downtown merchants considered the idea of tunnels connecting their places of business, to avoid the surface traffic. In 1903, the Illinois Tunnel Company was formed to take over the abandoned project and complete the tunnels for merchandise transportation, as well as sound communication.

The Chicago Subway Company joined to further the tunnel so that merchandise could be moved between railroad stations, terminals and other buildings. In 1904, the Chicago

---

[1]Schlaepler, Dorothy Fitch, 645 Monroe Street - The Fitch Family, Unpublished manuscript.

[2]Ford, Nancy, "The Railroad Under the Loop," Chicago, The Magazine of Mid-America, December, 1955, p. 24.

[3]Later research by the historian of the Illinois Bell Telephone Company and Mr. R. J. Greene of Staff Services of Western Electric discovered that an entrance to a tunnel was in the basement of the vacated building and was later walled up when the early project was discontinued.

Warehouse and Terminal Company was organized to build facilities for these stations, while the Illinois Tunnel Company continued work on the mainline tunnels. By 1909, the construction work by these companies was completed; the Illinois Tunnel Company was reorganized as the Chicago Tunnel Company in 1912 and finally in 1923, all participating members became the Chicago Tunnel and Terminal Company.[4]

This "Railroad Under the Loop" now had a coverage of 62 miles of 24 inch gauge tracks. They extended south to 16th Street, west to Halsted, north to Erie and under Grant Park to the Field Museum. There were eleven tunnels under the Chicago River at the depth of 60 feet. The rest were 40 feet below the streets. The materials and men reached the tunnels by elevators. The cars to be loaded, each capable of holding as much as a motor truck, were spaced two feet apart and pulled by a locomotive powered by its overhead trolley and capable of 35 miles an hour.[5]

At one time, these tunnel cars, besides carrying freight, also carried U.S. Mail, newspapers, coal, cinders, and trash from office buildings. The tunnels were neither damp nor airless; they maintained a 55° year round temperature and were so breezy that cool, fresh air service was piped to Union Station, Blackhawk Restaurant, Morrison Hotel, Edison Building and Mandel Brothers - all before the days of electric air conditioning.[6]

By 1930, the tunnel services were decreasing due to the increase in motor trucking of freight as well as U.S. Mail and the discontinuance of coal for fuel. The Chicago Tunnel Company suspended its last few operations in 1959 and the tunnels are no longer used for freight hauling.

This has been a journey outside of our Mile Square, yet the beginning of our path was at Monroe and Paulina Streets. Like the course of life, it has led far beyond the children's wildest imagination. Some of these children, truly, thousands of Chicagoans, never learned of this narrow gauge railroad existing for 62 miles under Chicago's Loop.[7] It was a rarity of its kind and one which old train and locomotive lovers should add to their data collections.

---

[4]Crittenden, H. T., "The Chicago Tunnel Company," Bulletin No. 59, of the Railway and Locomotive Historical Society, 1942, pp. 21-23.

[5]Ford, p. 23.

[6]Ibid., p. 24.

[7]Editor's note: In 1992 (Kendall, Peter, "Tunnel's vulnerability prompts deep thought," Chicago Tribune, June 6, 1999, Section 4, pp. 1, 3) an old service tunnel belonging to this system was breached during repairs to a wharf in the Chicago River. This resulted in the flooding of basement lower levels of many Chicago Loop stores and office buildings. Thus many not only in Chicago but around the world finally heard of this tunnel system.

81. Chicago Freight Tunnel, 1924. D.N. negative #77,911. Courtesy Chicago History Museum.

327

THE PEDDLERS

"Are there no beggars at your gate
  Nor any poor about your lands?"

Alfred Tennyson, 1809-1892

"Hark, hark, the dogs do bark
The Beggars are coming to town,
Some in rags, some in tags
And one in a velvet gown."

Mother Goose

"When I was a beggarly boy
  And lived in a cellar damp
I had not a friend or a toy
  But I had Alladin's lamp."

James Russell Lowell, 1819-1891

"Mark Haley drives along the street
Perched high upon his wagon seat;
His sombre face the storm defies
And thus from morn till eve he cries -
    "Charco! Charco!"
While echo faint and far replies -
    "Harko! Harko!"."

John Townsend Trowbridge, 1827-1916
The Charcoal Man

Some of the peddlers were seasonal; spring was welcomed with the flower vendor coming near Easter with his awning-topped open display wagon. It was full of potted blooming tulips, hyacinths, daffodils, Easter lilies, ferns, mother-in-law tongues, ivy and aspidistra. Later in May he came again. If the day was warm the horse wore a straw hat with his ears projecting and a lei of paper or feather flowers around his neck. He walked slowly while his master went from door to door. The offerings now were gay geraniums, daisies, pansies, ageratum and small rose bushes. Mamma hungrily bought all she dare with money she had saved for this feast of beauty. Truly the poem written by the Persian poet, Saadi, in the thirteenth century applied to her:

> "If thou of fortune be bereft
> And in thy store there are but left
> Two loaves, sell one and with the dole
> Buy hyacinths to feed thy soul."

A potted aspidistra on a small octagonal stool rested in the bay window of our dining room for a generation; later it traveled to Ohio for another generation and today descendants of those same roots grow joyously in a California garden.

The vegetable peddler, usually of Greek or Italian origin, passed by almost daily in mild seasons. While most neighbors bought from the nearby grocery stores, these transients did offer bargains, sometimes. One such pair of hucksters later rented the carriage house of the Forbes' home on Monroe. In the early morning, and at twilight, melodies from a music box drifted over the back yard gardens. Two repeated airs were Santa Lucia and Feniculi, Fenicula - a breath from old lands to these lonely immigrants.

Another wagon and its hawker was the ragman. He usually went down the back alley rather than the front street because materials he sought were stored near the back gate and also his rickety wagon and thin horse were not appreciated alongside waiting carriages. Besides, his heavy loads and overburdened horse might be reported to the police. The peddler's call was sharp and plaintive as he asked for "rags an' ol' iron" and the neighborhood boys quickly heard his call. They scurried to accumulations which might contain old iron water pipes, discarded gutters, rusty hinges, leaky skillets, brass bedsteads with broken springs, hampers of moldy rags and bundles of yellowed newspapers. The small boy might be richer by twenty cents; the rest was cunningly but pitifully classed by the dealer as trash hawling, which in truth it was.

Not all peddlers had horse-drawn conveyances; some had pushcarts. One which pleased the children was the popcorn and peanut man who appeared at dusk when he would find more patrons sitting on the front porches. His sputtering oil flame and insistent whistle was the signal for trailing children. However, the peddler's hands were often dirty and the popcorn could be also; we were allowed only the hot roasted peanuts packed in green and red striped bags with two twisted ear-locked ends; the cost was five cents.

The broom man appeared about twice a year, always in time for spring cleaning. He was heavily laden although his goods gave the appearance of lightness and fluffiness. Over his shoulder was a bundle of brooms; around his waist attached to a leather belt were various items. Towards the rear and sticking out were a bundle of feather dusters with wooden handles. On one side hung assorted sizes of whisk brooms used for many purposes - from cleaning toilet bowls and garbage containers to small clothes brushes. In this feathery garb the broom man looked like Mr. Chantecleer, himself; otherwise, he might be called a pre-Fuller Brush man.

From somewhere in his pack he would suddenly produce a child's sized broom; just big enough for when children played house or were responsible for a cleanup job after cutting out paper dolls or scrap-book making. These handy brooms cost only fifteen cents. One could become a good housekeeper as well as gardener with a rake, hoe and shovel of the same proportions as the broom. The garden tools were purchased at Wienberger's toy counter but Mamma always seemed to have a hidden supply of these little brooms. Papa liked them too, for sweeping stray ashes from the fireplace.

Among other self-propelled vendors was the scissor grinder. About once a month his tinkling bell was heard and scissors, knives, grass sickles, and hoes were gathered up and given a sharp, new life. As he treadled his grindstone with the water dripping from a suspended tin can, the children watched in awe as he wiped the blades and tested them on his fingers. Another pushcart peddler was the banana man with his large open tray of fruit, usually divided into hands of a dozen which sold for ten cents; they varied in quality and size. His call, made popular in recent years, was imitated by the children and sometimes made angry tradesmen.

It seemed the lower entry doorbell was always ringing. There might be a Greek or Italian carrying a huge wicker basket on his shoulder full of statuary; these were copies of famous sculpture and cast in plaster of Paris, papier-mache or possibly executed in alabaster. Many were hideously painted, especially, the blue veiled Mary and the bleeding heart of Jesus.

An occasional visitor, usually on Saturdays or Sunday mornings, was the balloon man, walking down the center of the street with a colorful cluster of round balloons quite high on their strings. Balloons were easier managed than kites but both were usually ill-fated, the balloons accidentally floating away and the kites caught on tree tops or telephone wires.

Many of the door to door peddlers could be classed as tramps from the expanding skid row, called Hobohemia by one social worker, at Canal and Madison Streets. They offered pencils, patent medicines, soap, perfume and shoe polish while a few self-proclaimed preachers called to save our souls and many just asked for a cup of coffee and a dime.

The most colorful transients who usually appeared in twos were the gypsies "doing" a block. The children gave the alarm and immediately found a hiding place where they could watch and hear. It was tradition that sometimes those red and multicolored petticoats hid kidnapped children. The waddling and swarthy gypsies bedecked with huge dangling earrings, chains of beads and a handful of playing cards for fortune telling, did do some business with the newly arrived Irish hired girls who may have recalled the lonely, outcast gypsies of Ireland.

Children were trained not to ring door bells of their friends' homes; rather they stood outside and called out names in a singsong fashion until a door or window was opened and a reply was given. Telephones were not used by children. Frequently at eventide when the national events had been relayed across country by telegraph, the youthful cry of the paper boy was heard with his "Extree, extree, read all about it." Extra papers usually brought bad news, seldom happy. In those years at the century's turn such news as the San Francisco earthquake, the Iroquois Theatre fire in Chicago, the assassination of President McKinley, and Robert Peary reaching the North Pole echoed in the youthful callers' voices.

As a prelude to night, in rain or snow, winter or summer, the lamplighter would come as he did all over the cities of the world and is so poignantly expressed by Robert Louis Stevenson in The Lamplighter:

"For we are very lucky, with a lamp before our door,
And Leerie stops to light it as he lights so many more;
And oh! before you hurry by with ladder and with light;
O Leerie, see a little child and nod to him tonight."

For us it was like a liturgical ceremony of lighting the Pascal candle as he lifted his long rod and turned on the incandescent filament gas burner protected in a heavy glass housing. A white light flooded the area and children chased or were followed by their clown-like shadows. The lamp post was the gathering place for flying moths as well as youngsters past the nursery stage; it was the goal for "Run my good sheep, run," "Red light" or the bellowed "Allee, allee, all in free" for hide and seek.

After the children's hour under the lamp post was over, one sat quietly on the front steps and looked up into the evening sky to locate the Big and Little Dipper, the evening star and to note the size of the moon, if it was visible.

Shooting stars were sometimes an extra spectacular. While the summer evening was still young, even for four year olds, the nostalgic sound of the organ-grinder would pervade the whole block and the family sitting on cushions would be regaled or put to sleep by the melodies churned by the hopeful grinder. After one or two selections the boy helper passed the hat. If the collection was sufficient there were encores; if not, the music maker sulkily pushed on to the next block and like the Pied Piper had a crusade of children in his train.

What were those then entrancing melodies ground out either in a stepped up presto or dragged as a largo, depending upon the urge left in the grinder's right arm or the sudden transference to his left arm? The sounds often seemed to vary from fortissimo to a fading pianissimo depending on the poetic temper of the tired pusher of sounds. The strains of Cavellera Rusticanna brought tears to a mother who knew it, not as the opera intermezzo, but the lamenting cry to the Virgin, "Mother, see my tears are falling - Thou has also sorrow known." The tune might be Mendelssohn's Spring Song, so appropriate for the season as well as a young, practicing pianist.

Besides the more frequent "piano wagon" grinder there were smaller performers such as the back carried grinding box which rested on a single stick support when played. The operator turned the crank with his right hand while his left held a generous leash on a monkey who passed a tin cup to the children's audience. Sometimes a lonely concertina or accordion, termed a "come to me, go from me" by the children, was heard or a harmonica, violin or an operatic baritone. All these musicians were from southern Europe, and while not able to speak English well, could speak the language of the heart and music.

82. Street Types of Chicago--Character Studies: Nice Feather Duster, 1891. Krausz, photographer. Courtesy Chicago History Museum.

83. Street Types of Chicago--Character Studies: Scissors!!, 1891. Krausz, photographer. Courtesy Chicago History Museum.

STREET TYPES OF CHICAGO--CHARACTER STUDIES

FROM FAR-AWAY DAMASCUS.

84. Street Types of Chicago--Character Studies: From Far-away Damascus, 1891.   Krausz, photographer. Courtesy Chicago History Museum.

85. Street Types of Chicago--Character Studies: Organ Grinder, 1891. Krausz, photographer. Courtesy Chicago History Museum.

SALOONS

"Indeed the Idols I have loved so long
Have done my credit in this world much wrong;
   Have drowned my Glory in a Shallow Cup
And sold my Reputation for a Song.

Would but some wing'ed Angel ere too late
Arrest the yet unfolded Roll of Fate
   And make the stern Recorder otherwise
Enregister, or quite obliterate."

               Edward FitzGerald, 1809-1883
               Rubaiyat of Omar Khayyam

Saloons were part of Chicago's commerce as well as its evil and should be acknowledged with honest recognition. Selling liquor is a trade as old as man's recorded history and has journeyed with him down the ages accompanied with both joys and sorrows. There probably will always be a tavern, pub or inn where for a coin one can know a world of cheer.

There were at the turn of the century on Madison Street on four blocks from Ashland to Robey, at least ten saloons occupying choicest locations, the corners. This predominance of saloons was not unique to this portion of Chicago but was evident in many sections of the city. Among these saloons, some gave free lunches, a few had pool tables, while others offered cabaret, often of licentious variety. It is apparent why this was such fertile territory for the Salvation Army, W.C.T.U. and Bishop Samuel Fallows.

Saloons by the very nature of their business were affiliated both psychologically and commercially with the red light districts of Chicago. Old Brown School neighborhood was no exception, although sections on the South and North Sides were more heavily trafficked. In turn, this was a part of a more vicious cycle - saloons, white slavery and corrupt politicians formed notorious and black pages on Chicago's reputation in the eyes of the nation. Names made infamous by ward bosses, cooperating saloon keepers and flophouse "residents" were family names as Hinky Dink Kenna, Bath House John Coughlin and Red Brennan.

By the upper grades, children had learned to walk on busy thoroughfares with miscellaneous traffic. The tether of parental restraint was relaxing; pupils had been cautioned on minding their own business and never speaking to strangers. Even so, the visit to Madison Street for a loaf of bread might include distressing sights and sounds. Frequently, the paddy wagon was heard clanging down the street to pick up an inebriate who had managed to go, or been pushed, through the swinging, shuttered saloon doors to the gutter, the traditional landing place, both in fact and fiction.

Following such a scene the Salvation Army moved to the corner. The group consisted of about six persons so as not to impede traffic. The men wore neat, blue uniforms and had ruddy, all-weather faces and husky bodies. The leader was armed with a Bible, while the rest of the men with trumpets or other horns were in tune with Lassies in blue outfits and red-ribboned bonnets. They heartily sang hymns of courage while beating the rhythm on tambourines. At intervals, a tambourine was passed asking for help in the Lord's work. As the leader preached salvation, he did not stress damnation and the songs echoed hopefully:

"Hark! The Savior's voice from Heaven
   Speaks of pardon full and free;
Come and thou shalt be forgiven;
   Boundless mercy flows for thee."

Or it could be:

"Sinner, how thy heart is troubled!
   God is coming very near;
Do not hide thy deep emotion
   Do not check that falling tear.
O be saved, His grace is free!
O be saved, He died for thee."

Soon the Army went on to the next target, another corner saloon. These were moving experiences for the innocent and debauched alike; more than one child had seen eyes oozing tears on unshaven, slobbering beards and dirty shirt fronts.

It was my good fortune to have known two of these Lassies whose fathers were connected with the West Side Citadel. At McKinley High School, beautiful Edith Story and Katharine Estill were two of my friends.

The neighborhood children did not differentiate as to whether these missionaries, at the frequent corner gatherings, were the Salvation Army or the Volunteers of America; they both marched down the same streets and offered the same help to down-trodden men.

The Volunteers of America is an offshoot of the original Salvation Army. The splintering in 1896 caused the English founder, William Booth, great sorrow when his son, Ballington Booth, seceded while serving in the United States where he formed the new organization.

General William Booth then sent his daughter, Evangeline, as Commander in America, which post she held until 1934 when she became General of the world-wide Salvation Army and returned to London, the international headquarters. During her years in America, Evangeline Booth became one of the world's most honored and beloved women. She and her Lassies are especially recalled for their services to the Doughboys in the A.E.F. of World War I, with their offerings of doughnuts and warm cheer. Evangeline Booth died July 17, 1950 in England, aged eighty five. She was a soldier in the Salvation Army from her birth to her "going to glory" - this expression is traditionally used in that organization in announcing a death.

There were other contemporary missionaries in less noticeable garb on Chicago's saloon corners - itinerant, self-appointed preachers or possibly they were disciples of Moody and Sankey who carried on after the Tabernacle Revival of 1876. There was preaching and singing, often accompanied by a small portable organ. These orators sometimes kindled fires of speech when hell and eternal damnation were described, yet their gospel hymns echoed in melody and rhythm, as well as with comforting words. There was Sankey's Harbour Bell:

> "But o'er the deep a call we hear
> Like harbour bell's inviting voice,
> It tells the lost that hope is near
> And bids the trembling soul rejoice."

Or it may have been:

> "Shall we gather at the River
> Where bright Angel feet have trod
> With its crystal tide o'er flowing
> Flowing to the throne of God."

One of the prime movers of the great temperance movement echoing around the world at the nineteenth century's end was Frances E. Willard. She lived in the Chicago area, first as a student at Northwestern Female College in Evanston and graduating in 1859. She taught until 1871, when she became Dean of Women's College of Northwestern University. In 1879, she was elected president of the National Woman's Christian Temperance Union and in 1881 became its worldwide spokesman.

There were many monuments to her while still living: the Frances E. Willard Temperance Hospital for Women and Children, at 343 South Lincoln, part of the early Medical Center; also the Women's Temple of W.C.T.U. at Monroe and LaSalle, designed by Burnham and Root in 1891, one of Chicago's earliest skyscrapers. It has been said that at the hospital no alcohol was used; acetone substituted for sterilization purposes. Frances E. Willard died in 1898 and her statue was placed in the Hall of Fame in the national capitol.

The world sweeping movement of evangelism coupled with the temperance crusades were brought close to our old Mile Square in the person of Bishop Samuel Fallows, who for half of his long, dedicated life was rector of St. Paul's Reformed Episcopal Church on Adams and Winchester.

Samuel Fallows was born in Lancashire, England in 1835 and came with his parents to Wisconsin in 1848. Five years later he joined the Methodist Church, and the following year was a licensed preacher. His earliest dream was "to preach the gospel to the masses." He graduated from the University of Wisconsin as valedictorian in 1859 and with intervening pastorates and a Master's Degree from Wisconsin, he would then serve in the Civil War in the Wisconsin Infantry and be brevetted Brigadier General of Volunteers "for meritorious service." After the war, he returned to pastorates in Milwaukee; became State Superintendent of Public Instruction

338

of Wisconsin from 1870-4; received an honorary Doctor of Divinity Degree from Lawrence University (College) and became President of Illinois Wesleyan University.

By 1875, he entered the Reformed Episcopal Church and became rector of St. Paul's Church in Chicago; a year later, he was elected Bishop of the Reformed Episcopal Church. He continued as rector of St. Paul's, with Chicago as his diocese in ecclesiastical terms, but in a larger sense, Chicago's and the whole country's "weal and woe" concerned him until his life's last day. His early life's dream of preaching the gospel to the masses was realized and broadened in a practical encounter with human welfare problems. While some of his efforts proved impractical, all voiced the needs of suffering humanity and were allied with the other social reform movements in Chicago and the country.

Among such endeavors, was the People's Institute founded in 1892 by Bishop Fallows. This was a community center, one of the first in the United States, and was a place where young and old, entire families, could come to enjoy good entertainments, athletic and patriotic events, undenominational services on Sunday, as well as the study of educational courses. This latter was one of the first in the country with the University Extension idea. The People's Institute was located at Van Buren and Irving Avenue in a substantial building with an auditorium seating 3,000 people who flocked to the Institute's meetings.

Jane Addams' Hull House, in the same period, recognized the need of a "coffee house" and gymnasium to combat the effect of the saloon hall which was the only place where an immigrant could celebrate social occasions such as weddings or christenings. Here at Hull House, young people's clubs could have dancing and refreshments, but nothing that would rival the saloon with its liquor.

The later development of refectories in our city parks, such as Garfield and Douglas on the West Side, helped provide places where dancing or programs and refreshments could be reserved for group celebrations.

By 1895, with the success of the People's Institute, Bishop Fallows considered a "portable People's Institute" which could function in a store on any street corner and become a poor man's club to compete with the saloon. His idea was based on the English Coffee House Movement with its hundreds of meeting places in England. The Bishop stressed that men being social animals needed a place to congregate; he saw the saloon as the only place a poor man could go to. It was his club room, labor bureau and his food supply when homeless or jobless.

The Bishop asked:

"What has the Church or the Temperance Movement to offer in a material way to compete with the saloon? Nothing... I believe such a work as this, if it proves successful, will be worth fifty years of purely intellectual temperance work."[1]

His plan was to organize a Home Salon with the best features of a saloon and the refreshments of a restaurant, including a non-intoxicating beer.

---

[1]Fallows, Alice Katharine, Everybody's Bishop: Being the Life and Times of the Right Reverend Samuel Fallows, D.D., J. H. Sears & Co., Inc., New York, 1927, pp. 328-9.

The Home Salon was opened in 1895 in the basement of a former saloon at 155 West Washington Street. It retained the original tall bar with foot rest and white aproned "beer slingers." The new temperance drink contained a small percent of alcohol. It was made from pure hops and malt and stored in kegs by a cooperating plant. Immediately the beer was called Bishop's Beer. The Home Salon flourished for a few years and was copied in other cities. However, the beer was difficult to keep stabilized at its temperance limit of alcohol and the temperance amount of capital involved could not compete with the plentiful dollars that the irritated breweries and liquor interests possessed for making war on this small competitor. So this experiment ended - mission incomplete.

Among Bishop Fallow's next adventures was his movement, Christian Psychology or Religious Therapeutics. This began suddenly in 1907, when he preached a sermon with that title. Immediately he was besieged by hundreds of Chicagoans seeking his help as a Faith Healer.

He quickly responded that he had no sympathy with any doctrine of healing which eliminated the physician.

> "What we want to do is to bring about this proper union, the doctor to aid the clergyman in correcting bodily evils and the clergyman to aid the doctor in putting the mind and spirit right... There are thousands and thousands of people who are suffering today from melancholia and hysteria, and that most common of human ailments with the uncommon Greek name, neurasthenia" (nervous exhaustion).[2]

While Bishop Fallow's ministry in the Christian Psychology movement was an age-old labor, still it aroused both doctors and clergymen to the problems of mental health; medical schools and theological seminaries improved their courses of study. The more humane treatment of animals and prison reform were influenced by this movement and continue so today.

The last years of the Bishop, while he was still shepherding at St. Paul's Church, were marked by his great patriotism and devotion to the dwindling Grand Army of the Republic. Many pupils from the neighborhood around Brown School and Lewis Institute recall that on Memorial Day, Bishop Fallows would gather with the soldiers in their old blue uniforms at the corner of Madison and Winchester to march two blocks to St. Paul's Church for a special service. One former student wrote:

> "When their leader would get them into something resembling a straight line, he would shout: "All right boys, let's go." ...They stepped off on command, many feeble and bent, some with canes, all eyes straight ahead, heads held high in pride and dignity."[3]

---

[2]Ibid., p. 366.

[3]Correspondence between Mrs. Dorothy K. Toms and the author.

In April 1922, he presided at the dedication of the Grant Memorial at Washington and in May was chaplain of the day for the Grand Army of the Republic at the dedication of the Lincoln Memorial at Washington.

Bishop Fallows loved his Alma Mater and the University of Wisconsin cherished him. The Alumni honored him at the 1918 Commencement as its oldest, living graduate; it was the Bishop's sixtieth anniversary. At the June 1921 Commencement, he told the flapper graduates that he liked their short skirts. He said:

"Women are not growing less moral, they are just beginning to enjoy their privileges. The short skirt is no lowering of standard."[4]

The news went over the country - "Bishop Fallow Approves of Short Skirts."[5]

In November of 1921, the Bishop returned to dedicate the Memorial Union on the campus, and the following June, 1922, spoke on "Value of Science" at the University of Wisconsin Commencement. This was his last return to his campus; Bishop Fallows died September 5, 1922.

Perhaps the best description of this radiant and magnetic person was given on Armistice Day, 1918, when Chicago went wild with joy. He had walked west on Madison Street to Oakley near his old home of thirty-five years on Monroe Street - here a mob stopped him, lifted him to a wooden soap box for a speech. A shoemaker friend who loved him recalled:

"The crowd lapped up against the Bishop like a sea. He stood above them and talked. His face was so joyful that it shone like a lamp, and the people looked up at him as they would at a saint."[6]

Unknown to me as a child, I later realized that my father throughout his life was a friend to down-trodden, discouraged men and more so, as age overtook him and decay claimed the old West Side. It had been his custom for many years of his disciplined schedule of reading, eating and exercising to walk the two miles to his law office in the Loop; in these morning walks as he approached the land of forgotten men, he learned firsthand the causes for their troubled lives. Liquor was their worst enemy.

The flophouse men at Halsted and Madison Streets were more numerous in winter months when jobs were scarce. They might be seasonal farm and dock hands, laborers from circuses, county fairs, racetracks or carnivals. Each autumn, they drifted on foot or freight cars along with perennial hoboes for their annual period of hibernation or job seeking.

My father's lifelong friend, Reverend Canon David E. Gibson, had walked among those men as early as 1894, helping with the city mission work of the Cathedral of S.S. Peter and Paul on

---

[4]Fallows, pp. 313-4.

[5]Ibid.

[6]Ibid., p. 404.

Washington Boulevard. Canon Gibson gave up an established photographic business to become a priest and founded the Cathedral Shelter which gave food, lodging and employment help to transient and homeless men.

In 1942, the Shelter was moved to the Church of the Epiphany at Ashland and Adams, and in 1958, the Halfway House for Alcoholics, founded by Reverend Joseph F. Higgins, was added to this refuge. The once proud church, capable of seating a congregation of a thousand, now reduced to mission status, still ministers to the neighborhood's many needs.

This magnificent Byzantine-Romanesque brownstone church, dedicated in 1885, is in need of repairs as it crumbles away. It is one of the few architectural landmarks left in the old Mile Square. Perhaps it can be saved "To the Glory of God;" this is engraved over the chancel. The Church of the Epiphany parish was organized in 1868 and built its first frame church on Throop Street facing Jefferson Park. The first service in this church was conducted by Bishop Henry John Whitehouse; today the vicar, Father Rempfer Whitehouse, a descendant of the early bishop, serves this mission, the Church of the Epiphany.

The widespread temperance movement[7] was not only endorsed by clergy, teachers and social workers but also by the medical profession. The latter saw and also helped these human wrecks of alcoholism in their worst and final stages. Dr. Nathan S. Davis, one of the early professors at Rush Medical College and a founder of Chicago Medical College, was a strict temperance advocate. He once said in a toast:

> "Pure water, Nature's universal antiseptic; it disorders no man's brain; it fills no asylums or jails; it begets no anarchy; but it sparkles in the dew drop, it glows in the peaceful rainbow and flows in the river of life close by the throne of God."[8]

---

[7]The temperance movement reached its climax with the Volstead Act of 1919 and its repeal, an anti-climax, in 1933. Two benefits from the temperance movement were government supervised liquor sales and protection of minors from liquor.

[8]Arey, Leslie B., Northwestern University Medical School, 1859-1959, Northwestern University, Chicago and Evanston, IL, 1959, p. 319. Permission Northwestern University.

86. "Veterans of Two Wars" (Bishop Samuel Fallows and a Doughboy), 1918. From: Fallows, Alice K. "Everybody's Bishop," J. H. Sears & Co., New York, 1927, facing page 366.

87. Bishop Fallows' Church: St. Paul's R. C. Church. Courtesy Chicago History Museum.

CHAPTER NINE: BROWN SCHOOL DAYS

THE PRIMARY GRADES

"We know how to find the pearl in the shell of the oyster, gold in the mountain, and coal in the bowels of the earth, but we are unaware of the spiritual germs, the creative nebulae, that the child hides in himself when he enters this world to renew mankind."

Maria Montessori, 1870-1952

How does one account for the hours in the day for school children? They are subject to the same joys and sorrows in which all ages participate - birth, deaths, the seasons, holidays, holy days and the ever changing sights and sounds. The five hours each day at their desks, plus comings and goings, are fourth of a day. With eight hours for sleeping, there are ten left for eating, playing, reading, dreaming, and most precious of all, just being part of a family. One must not overlook the bonus of Saturdays, Sundays and three month's summer vacation. The many outside interests of a schoolchild are as important to his total education as the grades he has stepped up to and the books he has mastered.

A child lives many lives. He is first an awakening body, member of a family; he goes to school, is part of a neighborhood which expands as he grows older and wiser, until he is called a citizen of the world. Having reached this stage, he tries to remember those earlier years. If he has climbed to eminence, these will be his memoirs; if only to the distinction of grandparenthood, these thoughts may be termed his second childhood. These, when the twinges of mind and body are removed, become an anticipated chapter in "Grandfather, tell me about when you were a little boy."

Besides eating, sleeping, and we hope being loved, that newly arrived child was reaching out with eyes, ears, nose, mouth and limbs - all suffced in the term, observing. In later years, he was seldom able to recall much of this rudimentary stage of accelerated mental and physical growth - termed infancy, so closely following his embryonic life. Even if bolstered by parental hearsay, there is little he can honestly claim. This stage cannot be measured in exact years or months. It would seem that "remembrance of things past" for most persons starts at the threshold of three, for many not until the fourth year.

These preschool and primary grade episodes are vividly remembered for a lifetime while later, more important events become veiled or completely erased. Perhaps, it is because our early memory's slate was clean; there had been no mistakes or sins to rub out, to try to forget. Innocence was natural, not feigned. Throughout the centuries wise men have noted that the years from birth to about six years are the most precocious, and many educators now advise formal education - reading, writing and arithmetic - to being when the child is "ready", not waiting until prescribed school age. The ecclesiastic for centuries has asked for the child until he is six, or was it seven?

Evolving records show that the plight of our children is in some cases improving, in others, worsening. The cry goes on - save the children, save the rivers, save the trees - not now so much, save the souls - all part of an encircling mandate, survival of the fittest.

In September, 1904, I entered Brown School, room 24, afternoon session, under the grandmotherly guidance of Mrs. Helen M. Waite. Upon our meeting she said, "Another little Warvelle girl has come to us." Eighteen and sixteen years earlier, my sisters Effie and Florence had Mrs. Waite in the primary grades. She was a smiling person with grey hair and the impression lingers that her clothes were grey.

Having qualified with a previous smallpox vaccination, I was assigned to a desk near the front and the blackboard. Here a series of colored pictures were posted from The Sun Bonnet Babies and the Overall Boys by Bertha Corbett Melcher. Already owning a pink denim sunbonnet and that very picture book, I felt at home with all these friends. Our Hiawatha Reader delighted me too, because at home there was a beaded apron and moccasins which had been given to my father by Winnebago Indians from Wisconsin.

The story hour and construction period were my favorites. The stories from Aesop's fables - the pathos of the dog in the manger and the lion and the mouse - could never be forgotten. During relaxation period, Mrs. Waite read from Kingsley's Water Babies; its musical flow entranced the children.

In construction work, sometimes it was paper weaving, making square mats with colored strips of paper; or folding paper to create baskets for candy or Mayday flowers. Other times it was paste work, making collages pertinent to the coming holiday, such as Valentine's Day or Washington's birthday. A dab of white paste, resembling cornstarch pudding, was doled out on paper resting over the empty inkwell. This paste had a delicious smell of sassafras or wintergreen and frequently I ate mine and would need more to finish the creation. The paste was child-proof, being gum arabic, water and fragrance (flavor). In later years I learned this was a common temptation; at least, it was not glue sniffing.

A child's progress was noted by stars pasted on spelling, arithmetic and writing papers. A gold star meant excellent, silver, good and no star might be passing or failure, the exact knowledge of which the beginner was spared. For excellence in drawing, Mrs. Waite gave a stick of peppermint candy which I frequently received.

The next year was room 21 under Mrs. Katharine Pyne. She perhaps, molded me more than any teacher in grammar school. She was tall with heavy blond hair, a young face and a determined voice. The three R's are dim in retrospect but the story hour is vivid. One story brought me to tears; it has been told to my children and grandchildren; the title and author are forgotten.

It is the tale of a faithful dog and his master who was traveling by horse carrying a message in his saddlebag to be delivered to the king in a far away country. At midday the rider dismounted and gave his horse and dog both food and water; then the rider ate and rested. Hours later, freshened and noting the lowered sun, the messenger started off at a gallop. The dog barked furiously, and bit the horse's legs as if to stay him. His master, who must go on, whipped the dog who still barked and tried to reach the man's legs. In desperation, and convinced that the dog had gone mad, the master shot the animal and sadly went on his way. Minutes later, he suddenly felt for his saddlebag; it was not on the horse. He hurried back to the resting spot; there lay his slain dog and nearby, the saddlebag - the same color as the fallen autumn leaves.

To Mrs. Pyne is owed a lifelong interest in the history of fine arts. It was her practice to introduce us to famous paintings and sculpture and their respective masters by displaying copies of one particular work each week. These prints were in sepia tones and known as Perry pictures. Happier still, we each made our own album, mounting these penny size prints. In a few months, a seven year old could recognize in a museum or illustrated book the works of these artists: Raphael, Da Vinci, Della Robbia, Rembrandt, Saint Gaudens, Gilbert Stuart and Praxiteles. The strange truth is that this knowledge, pigeonholed in a receptive young mind, has been retained for a lifetime. Incidentally, to a child's sensitive hearing and as yet unsure reading, Raphael's Sistine Madonna was to her the assisting madonna.

Since readers and workers of all ages need a recess or coffee break, so the children needed to recharge their batteries or let off steam. Recess period was similar to that in public and parochial schools today, except that the small, brick paved and fenced yard did not permit vigorous games. On spring days the boys were shooting or exchanging agate marbles while the girls played ball and jacks. In those games one could play alone or take turns at skill and speed.

The children moved about in this confining enclosure, and sometimes against rules, a few slipped away to Shannon's candy store to spend a few hot pennies. Sometimes as groups looked over the fence they heard passing pedestrians, probably foreigners, busily arguing with each other. The youngsters also started a conversation loud enough to distract the real linguists. What the children emitted was not pig Latin, but a spontaneous combustion of tortured syllables accented with frequent "spits and sputs" and tongues clicking in their cheeks.

Years later the writer met a talented, young African studying on a scholarship at a California university. She demonstrated in a lecture how difficult some of the tribal languages are. Her native speech required tongue clicks in the cheek, probably consonants. The childhood experiences in jargon was recalled and also the expression, "Tongue-in-cheek" which originated from another source.

Looking back as an energetic child, few gymnastics are recalled although "Physical Culture" was printed but never graded on the report card. The most strenuous exercises were done standing in the aisle beside our desks and doing routine set ups. At these times, windows were opened from the bottom as well as the top because fresh air was urgently needed.

The third grade was room 18 with Miss Maud Appleyard. She was a school friend of my sisters and a young teacher just as they were starting to be. She had dark brown hair and eyes and was lithe as an apple tree in this case. Again, there was an intriguing book, all about the Brownies by Palmer Cox. His Brownies became three dimensional in later years like Rose O'Neil's Kewpies, only the Brownies were more sprite-like and masculine in green and brown felt clothing which young minds pictured them as they climbed trees and painted the maple leaves in October.

Today the first order of the Girl Scouts are the Brownies. A later influence of Palmer Cox was seen in the Teenie Weenies of William Donahey. These little good-doers were loved by children. All these "people" have helped establish American versions of the Germanic gnomes and the Irish leprechauns, all healthy friends compared to some of the ugly creatures modern children are forced to associate with on television.

In the fourth grade, my teacher was Maude J. Black and she had black hair. That year is clouded because of a tragic happening; like a nemesis it removed the memory of happy and creative days which there must have been and left only a burned scar to recall. On a winter's day, a neighbor child and I played in the large front bedroom where a grate fire was helping a burdened furnace. Mother was downstairs at household tasks and I was to help care for my invalid brother. Unmindful that any urgency would occur, the classmate and I went to another room for extra toys. Suddenly my brother's screams were heard and rushing back we saw him standing in a pillar of blazes in front of the fireplace. Manna was there as fast as human limbs could lift one up two flights of stairs. She rolled him in a hearth rug, smothering the flames which had eaten through overalls and underwear. With the doctor's quick response, the child's life was saved; the lower half of his body had third degree burns and he would spend many months in bed. Remorse, almost too great a punishment for a child to bear, seared my soul each time I saw good Dr. Finch lift the blanket and remove the putrid bandages along with flesh that wasted away. Heart and body sick, I sought my pillow to weep for this only brother so dearly loved.

HALFWAY

"The chief cause of human error is to be found in the prejudice picked up in childhood."

Rene Descartes, 1596-1650

Now halfway through grammar school, students were learning more than the three R's; we were learning to be citizens of the world. What child has not written his address something like this: "John David Jones, 18 West Rosemary Lane, Chicago, Cook County, Illinois, United State of America, Western Hemisphere, the World!" There has been much written on school days in the little one room red schoolhouse in a bucolic setting with a steepled bell, potbellied stove, outside privies for boys and girls, the culprit's corner, the teacher's desk and her disciplinary procedures, as well as the sheriff's duties. The city child's version is not as often extolled, yet there was the counterpart of all these rural items.

At Brown School, the electrically controlled clanging bells rang inside and outside for beginning and ending of classes, as well as for recess and fire drills. There were times when the electrical impetus failed and a messenger brought the dismissal signal to the teacher. The steam heated radiators thumped and gurgled on extra cold days, and sometimes a boy was sent to the boiler room to report it was too cold or too hot in a certain room. The days of room thermostats had not yet arrived. By the twentieth century, the plant was developing a few cramps in its pipes.

Both the old and new buildings were equipped with fire escapes. These were cylindrical metal structures reaching to the roof with openings on each floor. The evacuation method was simple: the children sat down on the sloping metal floor and slid down the decline which had a center post to prevent colliding and at the bottom were ejected to the ground or into the janitor's arms - at least, the primary children were. It was always a lark to have fire drill which was usually at the end of a day, since the experience was too exhilarating to settle down to post-drill studies. The janitor took the preliminary ride sitting on mop rags to clean out the accumulated soot, dust and rust. Even then, the ride was hard on children's clothes. These old-fashioned fire escapes were used until the twenties when they were judged as fire traps rather than escapes.

The girls' toilet rooms on the basement level were rows of cubicles without doors; the dividing galvanized sides presented a continual study of pornographic words and drawings in spite of the janitor's weekly scrubbing. In all honesty, the children had a natural and curious interest in that subject matter.

The culprit's corner was the dressing or coat room. In this narrow room were pegs for the children's outer garments, while rubbers or overshoes were hopelessly mixed up by mischievous boys who were sent to this room "to think it over." Sometimes, coat pockets were explored by these offenders.

If the child's impudence frustrated the teacher's ability to maintain classroom discipline, he, sometimes she, was sent to the principal's office. There were times when corporal punishment was administered there. Next day, the culprit's desk might be vacant; he had been suspended and reinstatement came after confrontation with the parents.

In recollection these overgrown, unruly children, in kinder and diagnostic words, were often mentally retarded. Some occupied seats until old enough to leave school. Some of these students accounted for those coming under the Juvenile Protective Association.

Under the "El," it was dark and dismal, out of bounds for neighborhood children; the "bad boys" jail was there. This was the early Chicago Juvenile Detention Home located at 625 West Adams. Neighborhood boys had passed this house and seen frightened faces peering through iron-barred windows. Occasionally a "prisoner" escaped; word was flashed around the vicinity and all doors were securely locked.

The Home, in 1893, consisted of a large house and barn which was fitted with fifty beds. Boys stayed here while awaiting Juvenile Court hearing. These orphans of the storm were not always bad boys; they were waifs found all over Chicago in pool halls, cabarets, dance halls, vice dens, sweat shops, and most were neglected and ill-nourished. Between 2600 and 2800 children passed through this Home yearly.

The City allowed eleven cents per day per child for food. The Juvenile Court Committee composed of women delegates from various clubs visited the Home; they inspected the beds, tasted the food and heard complaints. One mother of a truant son reported worms in the soup - these were vermicelli noodles. An old rickety horse and omnibus transported the inmates to their fates.

One understanding social worker and friend to underprivileged children for three quarters of a century was Mrs. Joseph Tilton Bowen. She was more familiarly known as Chicago's first lady and is remembered in the Louise De Koven Bowen Center of the Juvenile Protective Association. She spent her energy and wealth helping Jane Addams at Hull House, beginning in 1894, and continually worked for social legislation. It was she who organized the first Juvenile Detention Home in the world, located in this original house on Adams Street.[1]

Today, when parents, educators and law enforcement officers are perplexed by the irrational conduct of young people, it should be noted that in 1900 the problem was also worrisome. However, the offenses committed then by these young people, most of whom could be classified as children, were not as disastrous and harmful as today's violent protests.

In that earlier day in Chicago, four-fifths of the children brought into the Juvenile Court were children of foreigners.[2] The crimes were not murders, conflagrations and bombings, but rather acts of parental rebellion, truancy and robbery. These children reflected the unadjusted,

[1]Bowen, Louise De Koren, Growing Up With a City, MacMillan Co., New York, New York, 1926, pp. 106-9.

[2]Addams, Jane, Twenty Years at Hull House, MacMillan Co., New York, New York, 1910, p. 303.

impoverished conditions of their home life and their parents' lack of education to earn a living and maintain a home conducive to wholesome development of their offspring.

One of the most important legislations of 1900 was the Juvenile Reform Law creating a Juvenile Court and providing a parole system and probation officers to over-see all truants. As part of this program, the Chicago Board of Education built the Parental School in 1901.[3] Here as the name implies, the young offenders were housed and the parents were instructed. The children under rehabilitation were given manual arts training and other constructive work along with regular school courses. In this project, "work with the hands," Richard T. Crane was a generous donor of tools and equipment for the establishing of manual training in Chicago's schools.

Some of the youths having problems were the newsboys and bookblacks; they were not protected by the Illinois Child Labor Act since they were merchants and not employees. As early as 1868, a home or refuge for these young boys was established and first known as the "Newsboys and Bookblacks Association." Its purpose was to "provide a good Christian Home for newsboys, bookblacks and other unprotected and homeless boys."[4]

In 1900, Abbie B. Champlin gave the organization her large home on Adams and Ashland in memory of her husband, William F. Champlin. The new name became Chicago Homes for Boys and while affiliated with the Episcopal Church, was non-sectarian. In 1914, the Home merged with the "Episcopal Church Home for Boys" and today is known as Lawrence Hall, 4833 North San Francisco Avenue. Since 1914, more than 10,000 boys have found a home at Lawrence Hall, Chicago's oldest home for boys.

---

[3]The Forty-Sixth Annual Report of the Board of Education, year ending June 30, 1900, Chicago, IL, p. 14.

[4]Source of quote is unknown to the Editor.

THE UPPER GRADES

"The years teach much which the days never knew."

Ralph Waldo Emerson, 1803-1882

In the fifth grade, Miss Katherine Bestel was our teacher. She was young, beautiful and a highly sympathetic person. The students adored her; in my idolization, I often walked past her home hoping to talk to her as a neighbor, not as a teacher; some children seemed to know about some of her romantic affairs. In her room we read a great deal of poetry, mostly from <u>Lights to Literature</u>. Poetry had now become a comforting subject to me because that January, 1909, my only brother had died at fourteen, a lifelong invalid. This first encounter with death was a crushing sorrow, the climax of a sadness I then had known all my young life.

This longed for son when about a year old had struggled out of his nurse's arms, falling down a steep flight of stairs, finally, hitting the angular newel post. With a fractured skull and damaged brain, the once happy, creeping baby was to become a hopeless but precious burden to his family. Brain surgery in the 1890's was not far advanced. Today it might have been different, as records of recovered brain and skull wounds of a half century's war casualties have proven. So a child had become stoic as she walked with his long-used buggy or watched at his side in the sunshine while passing children in their unintentional cruelty would sing out, "Margie's got a crazy brother." Inwardly only, I wept.

It was the custom in our construction work to make a memory book from a five cent ruled notebook. By turning the two end corners of each page inward to make a triangular enclosure and after cutting the outside cover to fit this new shaped volume, it was covered with a cloth binding. Then a stenciled design on the top cover completed the book. These little volumes were traded around at the end of the school year to teachers and classmates for farewell greetings, each message in its own compartment. Two messages are recalled; Christopher Vardis, a charming Greek boy wrote:

"Roses are red, violets are blue
No knife can cut our love - together."

and Miss Bestel sensing my recent sorrow, wrote Longfellow's lines:

"Into each life some rain must fall,
Some days must be dark and dreary."

In the sixth grade, Miss Lizzie Ryan was our teacher, a solid, business-like person, possibly with tinted hair. Textbooks were now reaching a sizeable weight to be carried home each day for homework. Geography interested me and we still read from the <u>Lights to Literature</u> series.

The arithmetic was by Luby and Touton and still my dreaded subject. In mature college years I learned that my future husband had been first, a student under Mr. Touton in Kansas City and then his helper, being paid to solve all the problems and list them for the answer page at the back of textbooks on beginning and advanced mathematics.

In this grade, a new writing method was introduced called <u>Palmer Method</u>, a system of relaxed fingers guiding the pen by means of a rotating wrist and forearm movement. Twisted and tortured finger writing was now to be obsolete. Each day we practiced concentric "Os" which lengthened into spiraling coils on lined "foolscap" paper. The straight lines needed for a t or p were first practiced into what looked like the waves of an electrocardiogram report. Each letter was studied - always preceded by the warm-up of "Ms and Os," jerks and coils. At the course's end a stamped diploma with the writer's name in Palmer Method script was awarded for a lot of pen pushing.

We used fine pointed steel pens and black ink in Palmer Method writing. Fountain pens were costly items and seldom used by children; besides, they were usually wide pointed. There were bound to be a few blots - ink dropped in its precarious journey from the inkwell on the upper right-hand corner of the desk to the extreme left-hand side of the paper where the movement began each time. Having had a blot, that sheet of paper was ruined for writing judging but when folded and pressed where the blot was and then opened - presto, a puzzle creation. What was it? It might resemble a bug, queer animal or flower. This was all before the days of psychoanalysts who now study such blot interpretations for behavioral quirks in their creator-artists.

In going through a few surviving fragments of childhood accumulations, there was a report card for the first five months in Miss Ryan's room. The method of grading in 1910 for grammar and secondary schools was: E, 90-100, Excellent; G, 80-90, Good; F, 75-80, Fair; and P, below 75, Poor. The subjects graded were English, reading, writing, arithmetic, geography, history, music, drawing and deportment. The teachers probably graded too generously in those days. Es were always in the majority for me, sometimes EE. Perhaps that extra E stood for effort or extra effort.

There were rewards for scholarship, perfect deportment and perfect school attendance. If a student qualified by some prevailing prerequisite, he was excused from the final June examinations. This meant a full holiday for lucky students. It seemed my childhood was healthy, deportment never under any indictment and most studies relished; I cannot recall having to take final examinations in grammar school.

Mrs. Sara G. Perce was our room teacher in seventh grade; she was handsome, well dressed and well liked. Both my sisters had her in the upper grades and loved her. The seventh and eighth grades were on the third or top floor and enjoyed a certain isolation from the lower grades. The students were experiencing a new procedure, the forerunner of modern junior high school. Here the students, already adolescent and aping high school students in dress, manners and social affairs, were now treated with a more adult approach. The students, while having a room teacher, were also taught by Miss Isabel Gould, Miss Elizabeth Sneed and Mrs. Josephine Kirkley Green. They circulated among the four rooms, each teaching a special subject. It is surmised this change was instituted by Superintendent Ella Flagg Young who had been recently teaching the newer methods in Chicago Normal School.

In the seventh and eight grades girls had domestic science and the boys, manual training. The girls learned sewing the first year by making, among other items, a white bibbed apron out of long cloth or muslin to wear in our course in cooking which followed. This apron was laboriously made and unmade, subject to much inspection for French seams, blind stitching, feather stitching and buttonholes. The boys were learning the rudiments of mechanical drawing in preparation for their pieces of furniture.

The cooking class is vividly recalled and some of the recipes practiced there have been used in the years which followed. Our basic equipment was already furnished in a deep drawer shared by two girls in the kitchen classroom. We provided only our bibbed apron, notebook and a pint sized covered tin pail. In this, we carried home delicious bits, as apple sauce, baking powder biscuits, Dutch apple cake, meat loaf, brown Betty, ginger cookies and a small loaf of yeast raised bread. As we walked home proudly carrying that little tin pail, we might pass some elder, also carrying a much larger tin pail. It could be a woman bringing fresh milk from a little milk depot on Paulina, near Adams. More often, it was a burly and shoddily groomed man carrying an already frothy and dripping pail of beer from one of the many saloons in the school district. He might have said, "You too, sister?"

In the seventh and eighth grades, we were concerned with debates as part of our Friday programs. In 1911 or 1912, I was privileged to have been in a debate: "Resolved, which has been most ill-treated, the Negro or the American Indian?" Today, such a debate would not be attempted. Over fifty years ago, this utterance caused soul-searching among these young debaters. Memory falters here; the question must remain, unresolved.

Again, as a child, I was to know the heartbreak of death when my sister, Florence Octavia, died in the spring of 1911 of diabetes. The medical profession of her day had not yet found the key to save lives from early death of diabetes. That miracle was to come nine years later with the discovery of insulin by Doctors F. G. Banting and C. H. Best.

Through the years I have grieved for her; she had been my mother-sister as had my sister Effie. Florence and I spoke the language of the fine arts; she had encouraged me with crayons, painting tablets, wonderful French pastels, water and oil paints, all purchased from Abbott's store on Wabash Avenue. As an art supervisor in the Illinois public schools, she gave me extra art textbooks such as the Prang series, monthly art journals as L'Illustration and the Craftsman. We went to many art exhibitions and on sketching trips to the sand dunes, south of Chicago. My earliest memories of her were, when as a student at the Chicago Art Institute, she took me to visit her classes, seeing the models posing for charcoal sketches, for oils or clay modelling of pre-sculptural studies. Naive and embarrassed to see the mature human form in its naked beauty, I was soon reconciled and saw as beautiful the human form in all its periods of life. It could range from the Holy Infant to the naked crucified Christ, from Michelangelo's David to the sensuous and heroic works of Rodin and the American contemporary works of Bela Pratt and Lorado Taft.

In the last heroic months she sensed her condition, declined all doctoring and lived by faith alone. She continued working on her trousseau, embroidering linens and painting a set of Haviland dinnerware. Then suddenly on a day in May, she was gone. The nurse who attended her in the one and final coma, remarked that she must have been invalided for some time - no, she had gone to her final bed only yesterday. Faith had given her strength to the very end.

Among the adolescent changes taking place, although we, as seventh and eighth grade students, were not conscious of this pattern, was the forming of little cliques or clubs. Earlier in the primary grades, we had chums among the girls, and to cement our friendship, we wore chum ribbons and tried to dress alike and wear our hair in the same style. In this new stage of friendships, there were boy and girl attachments and in larger groups; there were three types: boys and girls, all boys and all girls. This was perfectly normal with the grouping of those with like interests and social backgrounds. In many of these multiple associations there was one element in common, secrecy. Again, that was a normal tendency. Both grammar school and high school secret clubs were influenced by tales of mysterious ceremonies indulged in by older students in college fraternities and sororities. While most of these junior clubs were harmless gatherings, some proved disastrous in their attempts at sophistication with dangerous initiation rites, as well as silly snobbishness to non-members. In 1908, the Board of Education being faced with this growing tendency ruled that any student in Chicago Public Schools found belonging to such secret societies, termed Greek letter fraternities and sororities, would be suspended.

One group of about twelve girls did not fall in this pernicious classification; rather, it could be considered a most altruistic organization. It was called the "ABC's" - meaning Athletic Butterfly Club - a most ridiculous title, until it was defined. One of its chief purposes was to sew layettes for the Chicago Foundlings Home, as well as to be athletic and graceful as butterflies in our social lives!

Our two eighth grade teachers, Miss Sneed and Miss Gould, have lingered in the memories of their pupils since 1885. Dorothy Kent Toms recalls them as late as 1924, when these two fostering mothers, in the true sense, were still teaching at Brown School, as having been

> "...quite old... crowding eighty; their snow-white hair piled high on their heads, bespeaking a style of an earlier period. Each wore a little black velvet band around her neck with a cameo at the throat. Both were small of stature, but Miss Gould who used a cane, looked so fragile that one could easily imagine her becoming airborne in a gust of wind. Another teacher is recalled who taught sixth grade, a tall, angular, middle-aged woman of stern visage named Miss Steele. She was so unbending that I always thought she was aptly named. By the time I left Brown, Miss Neihaus was gone and in her place was Mr. Reed."[1]

---

[1]Correspondence between Dorothy Kent Toms and the author, February 20, 1970.

THE BOOKS WE READ

"The images of men's wits and knowledges remain in books, exempted from the wrongs of time, and capable of perpetual renovation."

Francis Bacon, 1561-1626
Advancement of Learning

The records of Chicago's Public Schools, tracing back to the earliest days of pioneering boards of education, are kept in printed and bound volumes. All financial transactions, building and maintenance reports, the listing of all textbooks approved and materials used, the names of teachers employed as well as moral issues considered - all are intact after a century and more of bookkeeping. Only missing are the names of millions of children who journeyed through those schools.

What were the names of those textbooks which introduced children to the school of life? To be sure, they were often portioned in sections to be tolerated by a child's concentration span. They were never expurgated nor adulterated. Around 1885 to 1896, the School Board affirmed the use of McGuffey's New Eclectic Reader, ranging through books one to five. These were used for several generations over a great portion of the country and there are those living today who were touched by the varied (after all, the books were eclectic) samplings in good literature. Today these volumes are collectors' items and still good reading. Other early textbooks were Cyr's Primer, Harper's Readers, Appleton's Readers, Robinson's Complete Arithmetic, Hooker's Book of Nature and Scudder's History of the United States.

A set of books fondly recalled was Lights to Literature for second through eighth grades, published by Rand, McNally Company. These volumes appeared in 1900 and offered participation in all types of literature - fiction, essay and poetry, gleaned from world sources - an updated "McGuffey" for that contemporary generation. Other readers of this same period were Stepping Stones to Literature, published by Silver, Burdett Company; Tarr and McMurray wrote the long used geography while Greene's History of the English People and Fiske's History of the United States were not considered obsolete after more than ten years of use.

"Listening books" were those read by the teacher to the pupils, especially those in the lower grades who had not yet mastered reading ability but understood all the spoken words. Usually these were read when the children's physical as well as mental energies were tired. Stories also were used as a collective reward for a room's excellent deportment or achievement. These special books might be Collodi's Pinocchio, Lewis Carroll's Through the Looking Glass, Mary Mapes Dodge's Hans Brinker; Or The Silver Skates, Robert Louis Stevenson's A Child's Garden of Verse, David Copperfield by Charles Dickens or the King Arthur Stories.

One child overheard the teacher's conversation to a student who was given special books with the reminder that they were "Fund Books." To innocent ears these sounded like "fun books" and should be pleasant reading. At best, such a book could only be an arithmetic, reader or speller loaned to the child unable to pay for new textbooks and would be returned to the school at the end of the year.

By 1911, almost a complete change of textbooks was in force and the new reader was Progressive Road to Reading for the first four grades. Enticing titles were not prevalent; a new method was introduced with more visual memory approach and less stress on phonetic unraveling of syllables.

Only in recent years have school libraries become a part of the public school building. Now well stocked libraries and reading rooms, many in separate buildings, are one of the advancements in modern education. Before the 1900's, grade school children were dependent upon either the luck of being born into a family with a home library or upon available collections in their respective classrooms.

At the century's turn, a change come about when the hunger for books and public libraries was of national concern. Andrew Carnegie in his essay, The Gospel of Wealth (1889) described rich men as "trustees of their wealth" and should administer it for the good of the people. In his later years, his life was dedicated to this principle and his public benefactions amounted to $350,000,000. Of this, $60,000,000 was given for public libraries across the country, in cities large and small, with the recipients maintaining well-chosen books housed in substantial buildings. When the Chicago Public Library at Michigan and Randolph was opened in 1893, both the building and its contents were considered one of the world's finest.

A public library branch was established on the ground floor of Lewis Institute in 1897. Being near Brown School as well as McKinley High School, this library served three schools, including Lewis Institute. After acquiring a library or borrower's card, each and all of the neighborhood students, both public and private, stepped into other worlds, reading their way into history, science, literature, fine arts, and for very young minds, the world of fantasy. Here was a treasure house for rich and poor. Grammar school children from the increasing foreign born families found a source where they could gather arm loads of books to take to book hungry as well as bread hungry households.

Again, the fostering mother, embodied in a book, was gently but firmly teaching her pupils. These young minds were protected through the library board's censorship of books which could be termed undesirable because of pornography, vulgarity, cruelty or violence. At that period, even the most sophisticated American writers were inhibited in their descriptions of morals and sex.

Every public school pupil in his eight years of grammar school would be touched by samples of the best English and American classics. What then was his extra curricular reading at the public library or school and home collections? Some students continued reading more standard classics while the very young were delving into Arabian Nights or Grimm's and Hans Anderson's fairy tales. A distinctly new version was Frank Baum's The Wizard of Oz. Older children read stories of fictional or historical national heroes. On the masculine side, Mark Twain's Huckleberry Finn and Tom Sawyer along with Stevenson's Treasure Island were in competition with Horatio Alger Jr.'s heroes of Sink or Swim, or Luck and Pluck. Such authentic heroes as De Morgan's Ethan Allen and His Green Mountain Boys or Thomas C. Harbaugh's Washington's Young Spy were samplings from these prodigious authors. For girls, Louisa May Allcott's Little Women, The Five Little Peppers by Margaret Sidney and The Little Colonel series by Ann Fellows Johnston were beloved; today they are almost obsolete. Later models for "girldom" have replaced them, much like character dolls change from year to year.

At nine, I was loaned a book, The Wide, Wide World by Susan B. Warner with the warning by the other nine year old that this was a "novel" and should be kept hidden. It was kept under the mattress and each early morning that summer, I limited myself to one chapter so my sadness could last longer. I wept regularly for Ellen Montgomery as this orphaned child rambled through the book's pages although her piety did not affect me. Nowadays it is hard to understand how this milk-toast novel could ever have been an adult best seller.

The popular children's books led into young people's ("teenagers" had not yet evolved) and mature reader's selections. Today many enumerated here would be considered saccharine by teenagers who have been subjected to television glamour and guns since kindergarten viewing age. There was John Fox Jr.'s The Little Shepherd of Kingdom Come and The Trail of the Lonesome Pine; Gene Stratton Porter's Freckles, Girl of the Limberlost, Laddie and Friends in Feathers; Kate Douglas Wiggan's Rebecca of Sunnybrook Farm and Zane Grey's Riders of the Purple Sage. The list could ramble on; the works mentioned were all instructional in disguised fashion. In Porter's books the world of moths, butterflies and birds was explored; in Fox's there was a brave study of "Appalachia" which is now being reappraised; Wiggan's title suggest rural consideration, and Zane Grey's narration heralded the trail to thousands of future cowboy and Golden West stories.

In the periodical section of the branch library could be quite a complete array of monthly magazines, more than half of which have perished in the years to follow. To name a few of the vanished: Littel's Living Age, Collier's, McClure's, Scribner's, American Mercury, Literary Digest, Woman's Home Companion, Life (satire), Judge, Harper's Weekly, Forum, and recently, the perennial Saturday Evening Post. Children lost friends too: St. Nicholas Magazine, Youth's Companion and American Boy.

The comic sections in the daily and Sunday papers were avidly read in the early century, just as today. In the Sunday two-toned "funnies" was "Happy Hooligan" who was what his name implies, a clowner; the squatty "Katzenjamer Kids" were always in trouble and poor Mamma Katzenjamer, when things got too noisy or little Fritz too naughty, would announce: "Enough is too much." "Buster Brown" and his dog "Tige," with round eyes, were law-abiding and preached a moral in disguise. Buster always wore a large white collar with a Windsor tie and his blond hair was Dutch cut. Both his hair style and clothes were worn by small boys but considered sissy after the first grade. Another cartoon was "Mutt and Jeff," a tall and a shorty who were buddies and each day discussed homemade philosophy.

One of the happiest recollections of the mystical season of autumn with "October's Bright Blue Weather" and the inevitable coming of a "long winter's nap," was a cartoon, Injun Summer, by John T. McCutcheon which originally appeared in the Chicago Daily Tribune.[1] It showed the old farmer and small grandson sitting in the twilight looking over the field of

---

[1]McCutcheon, John T., "Injun Summer," Chicago Sunday Tribune, October 17, 1937, Graphic Section, p. 1 (Copyright: 1912: By John T. McCutcheon. Reprinted here [in 1937] by general request.). Editor's Note: It is still seen in the Chicago Tribune in the 1990's.

shocked cornstalks. At this time of day and season, the cornstalks became tepees as the Indians returned for a harvest dance while red maple leaves floated to the ground - "That's the war paint rubbed off'n an injun ghost sure's you're born." This much loved cartoon continues to appear each year at the mystical time in the Chicago Tribune. John T. McCutcheon and George Ade in their youthful days ran a column in the Chicago Record, Ade with his pen writing humor and McCutcheon with his pen drawing humor. In later years he won a Pulitzer Prize for one of his famous cartoons depicting a Depression-era scene.

SOME BROWN SCHOOL FRIENDS

Lillian and Rose Sauer were daughters of a Bohemian family who lived in an apartment of a large five-story warehouse on Ogden Avenue; the father was in the moving and storage business. The girls were lovely as their names, golden haired Lily and a pink cheeked Rose. The mother spent her time in this cluttered apartment, either in the kitchen where she cooked their favorite Bohemian dishes or busy tatting another doily for the parlor, already full of doilies on the small tables where china-globed oil lamps rested. These lamps at the Sauer home had blushing roses, possibly lilies, painted on the white milk glass globes.

As to the piece de resistance in their culinary department, that was fried goose blood. At the holidays, Mrs. Sauer and her husband butchered their geese on the back porch or some better place and saved the drippings. The final result was a gourmet's recipe. At the time, the thought of such a dish was repulsive to me and yet in the light of other extras from butchered animals - brains, stomach linings, intestine skins, the "last to jump over the fence" as well as the blood-milk health drink - the Bohemian fried goose blood was as choice as Patie de Foie Gras. It was only that my childhood entrees had been limited to lamb, beef, pork or chicken dishes served as stew, steaks, chops or roasts.

The Collins family on Monroe, next to the "elevated," sold their home after Grandpa Collins died; he had fallen from a three story window, being dazed by the fast grinding train. The building and its adjoining twin were sold to the Benson family who made the structures into six apartments. The former owner's grandchild, Alura Kitty Goff, was my dearest friend; we were friends before I remember our becoming friends.

Among the new apartment occupants were the Carlson family whose daughters, Marian and Ruth, were luscious specimens of Norway's contribution to the American girl. Each Saturday, the Carlsons had mid-morning coffee and pastry. Tanta came from Humboldt Park area (then the Scandinavian section of Chicago) to enjoy the fresh brew, delectable torte or apple skivars and to be briefed on family happenings. I tried to time my visits to include Carlson's coffee hour since the invitation was always cordial. In a few years this family moved to Logan Square area; I missed this wholesome, close-knit family.

Another apartment family to follow had a daughter, Laura Fardette, whose aunt, a gracious person, lived with them. One Saturday morning upon visiting Laura, I found her alone with this aunt who then was having a convulsive seizure of epilepsy. Deftly and calmly, Laura, then eleven, leaned over the suffering body on the floor and held a spoon in the patient's mouth to prevent the tongue from being bitten during this tortuous period. And so, another lesson in life's school was learned by a little girl.

In this same building, a little four year old boy lived, named Herbert. His last name is forgotten, but not his head of heavy brown curls and his limpid brown eyes. He, true to the rummaging habits of childhood, came upon a loaded revolver in a bedside table drawer. Curious, he tried it; it worked and the beautiful child perished. All the neighborhood children wept as we passed his coffin where he slept in a white sailor suit and his dark brown curls.

At the corner of Monroe and Wood Streets in a three-story row house, early doomed to furnished room renters, lived Regina Ryan, an angelic looking child of around six. It was evident that much love and attention was given to this only child. She wore clothes I dreamed about - a little French blue coat, probably broadcloth, with matching leggings and hood. The coat collar, hood and muff were trimmed with simulated ermine (rabbit). If these had been genuine ermine, they could not have graced that little body more queenly, nor further delighted that adoring mother and pampered child. Yet they lived in furnished, light-housekeeping rooms and much of their family wealth probably was in that sweet blue outfit.

The picture of that little girl was never forgotten by the neighbor child and when her own girl child was born, that child too, had a blue outfit with rabbit fur which graced a little blond, brown-eyed queen. Again, there was an adoring mother and a pampered child.

There was the journey to the blacksmith's shop on Madison near Paulina Street. It was out of bounds for one little girl and her visit there was kept secret for many years, for fear of its punishable consequences.

Ogden Place was a short street running from Wood Street where the Foundlings Home looked out, to the side door of the Third Presbyterian Church at Ashland Boulevard. There were a few frame houses predating the Great Fire on this street; a colored family lived in one. I became acquainted in Brown School with one of their little girls; her name is forgotten but we often walked together to and from school. I do remember admiring her shining, unblemished bronze face - she did not have hundreds of freckles. She proudly showed me one of her hands; there were six fingers. This extra digit was pondered over for many years but not discussed.

Her father was a blacksmith at Carpenter's Blacksmith Shop; here the little neighbor and I went on an errand for her mother. While I was familiar with Longfellow's The Village Blacksmith, this actual confrontation was a blending of wonder, anguish and nausea. The hot belching forge, the powerful hammers swung to their anvils by two aproned but bare armed smiths, awed me. At this point, Longfellow's poem came alive; I had not yet pictured the horse. Now as he stood patiently, while the hot iron shoes were nailed into the cartilaginous hooves, I was trembling, almost weeping. Worse still, the stench of burning bone mixed with the accepted manure impregnation was truly sickening. The anticipated enchantment of the village blacksmith was lost for me. Perhaps, if the scene had been witnessed under a spreading chestnut tree - all would have been a place of wonder.

Across the street from our house, where the Benhams and their daughter Jessie had lived, the Flanagan family now occupied the house. They had a daughter with whom I played on Saturdays; she attended St. Jarlath's Parochial School at Jackson Boulevard and Wood Street. One day at her home, I noticed a bottle with a cross on it and I was curious. Where-upon Mrs. Flanagan picked it up and sprinkled water from it on my head saying, "This is holy water. Now I've baptised you a Catholic." I rushed home because I did not want to be baptised again, nor be a Catholic. At that time, I was not quite sure what a Catholic was; I knew we recited a prayer in church, "I believe in the holy, catholic church." Of course, good hearted Mrs. Flanagan assured me, "It would not really take," and my father, an Episcopalian, Mason and professor in a Jesuit University, advised me that it just might do me some good.

Two doors west of our house, the Daniel Gregory family and their daughter's family, the William Rodigers, lived for a generation. Then the household moved to the suburbs and the house at 660 Monroe Street was sold. The next occupants were Mrs. Wolff, a widow and her four children, ranging from preschool age to fourteen. Mrs. Wolff probably rented this ten room house from the new agent-owner. She was an immaculate housekeeper and appeared tired, thin and pale; the children were neatly dressed and well behaved.

Henry, the oldest boy, who should have been in school, worked for the Wrigley gum concern as an errand boy. He always had packages of gum to give or barter. Juicy Fruit gum at that time came in a single, divided bar wrapped in tin foil one broke or bit off a section somewhat in the fashion of taking a chew from a tobacco plug. Ethel, about ten, was my friend; she had little time to play as she helped her mother in the constant work of running a rooming house for men. Of the ten rooms in the house, seven were rented out. At that period in renting furnished rooms, the proprietor kept the occupants' rooms in order and made the beds, as in a hotel. In fact, such a rooming house could be compared to a second or third class hotel. While there were built-in lavatories in some of the rooms, one bathroom with tub and toilet served all the renters. Mrs. Wolff probably did the personal laundry for some of the roomers, as her ironing board seemed always in use.

The Wolff family had their apartment on the first floor. This consisted of two bedrooms: one was the once large dining room; the other, formerly a maid's room, had a shower, lavatory and toilet. The very large, sunny kitchen had room for both stationary laundry tubs and a generous dining corner. There was also a windowless pantry which probably combined for food, tableware and utility storage.

The furnace was at the back of lower entry hall; the coal was kept in a pit under the front stone steps while coal for the kitchen range was stored periodically in a frame, box-like structure in the backyard. In summer, when the stove was not used, this blackened coal house was cleaned by the children and became their playhouse. The backyard, while utilitarian with clothes line and wood pile, was green and possessed a spreading purple lilac bush, as well as a rift of lilies of the valley and a back row of hollyhocks.

OUR MUSICAL HERITAGE

"Music must take rank as the highest of the fine arts - as the one which, more than any other, ministers to human welfare."

Herbert Spencer, 1829-1903
The Origin and Function of Music

Music, mainly in the form of singing, was always a part of the public school curriculum and listed on the report card. The grade of the student's proficiency was not completely affected by his deportment; that, too was on the card. If the mark was less than E or G, it might mean tone deafness, inability to carry a tune, or in the upper grades, slowness to read and understand the musical score of a song. The Brown School 1900 vintage had no school band. There was a piano on each floor. Choirs, glee clubs and quartets were in full swing and a child learned early what his voice range was, whether first or second soprano, first or second alto, tenor or bass.

From the first day in Mrs. Waite's room we sang, "Good morning dear teacher, good morning to you" in answer to her salutation to us. Even if a child had no home exposure to music such as piano, gramophone, singing parents, Sunday School or choir experience, he would in his grammar school days become familiar with American patriotic songs, traditional hymns, carols, folk songs and some classic or operatic melodies.

Our first singing efforts under Mrs. Waite were primed by the pitch pipe. It was a mystery, how with one blow on the pipe, a sound would come out which the teacher hummed and like a lighted candle was passed to the students who joined her in humming. While there were a few discords from tone-deaf children, it was a swell of joyfulness. The pitch pipe continued in the upper grades, this time like the first violin's pitch for the orchestral instruments' tuning, as each soprano, alto and bass hummed his signal. Melody and rhythm flowed from the teacher's pitch pipe into her lifting, swaying arms, as well as an occasional cringe, as volume became over-powering or voices off key.

It was normal to have spontaneous mischief pop up in classrooms, especially when singing. It seemed to be tolerated by the patient teacher who probably, behind her stern face, was laughing inwardly. Teachers were and are, kind persons as well as humorous; their profession demands such. When the old song was sung, "How dear to my heart are the scenes of my childhood - The moss covered bucket which hung on the wall," a deep antiphon would slyly end the melody - "go soak your head in it."

Or, if having participated in a lugubrious hymn where the alto and bass echoed in measured tones, one deep voice would softly add, "You get your dominoes, I'll get my dominoes and we'll all play dominoes." It was evident the boy had known Gregorian chanting.

Musical mischief continued outside of school, as boys stopped on street corners to hear missionaries pouring out, "When the roll is called up yonder;" one falsetto voice would squeak, "I'll be there." Or if the hymn was "Brighten the Corner Where You Are," they would change the text slightly by adding, "There may be someone across that bar, so brighten the corner where you are." The import of Moody and Sankey revivals was still echoing down the streets of time even though the big tabernacle at Monroe and Franklin Streets had resounded thirty years earlier in 1876.

The home has always provided the balance of opportunities for musical and artistic appreciation. In our time period of consideration, family singing was a popular diversion, as well as piano duets and chamber music, where such training and instruments existed. Most homes on Monroe Street had a piano. A few had reed organs, and our next door neighbors, General Wheeler's family, had a pipe organ which the members played quite frequently. Even through the thickness of two stone or concrete walls, one listened to an evening of organ classics. They were diminished enough to be called background music and perfect lullabies for tired children, or for one who lay ill in bed.

There was evolving in group participation, two different and opposing styles. On one side was the singing and playing of old melodies, folk songs and classics, ages old and sentimentally loved. On the other side, quite new and disturbing to those who might have been grandparents in the early 1900's, was the advent of popular music. This American music still ebbs and flows and continues to be a profound subject for today's youth. It has had many names from Dixie music, ragtime, blues, jazz, swing, syncopation, boogie-woogie, rock and roll to soul music. Perhaps it is best to review the classic and sacred before the so-called profane, erratic and erotic.

After the Great Fire of 1871 and until the 1900's the West Side experienced its greatest growth, as was evidenced in the building of large churches by their prosperous and devout congregations. The immediate area around Brown School had a church for almost every two blocks of row houses. A quote of the times stated that for every 2000 persons there was a church and for every 200 there was a saloon. Even so, every denomination was represented; among the largest congregations were St. Jarlath's Roman Catholic, Fourth Baptist, Church of the Epiphany, Union Park Congregational, Jewish Zion Temple, Third Presbyterian, Park Avenue Methodist, St. Andrew's Episcopal and St. Paul's Reformed, usually referred to as Bishop's Fallow's Church.

Having been baptised and confirmed in the Church of the Epiphany, it was my church home under the guidance of Rev. John Henry Hopkins. It was a privilege to belong to St. Cecilia Choir which often augmented the boys' choir at festival services or substituted during their absence on singing tours. The boys' and men's choirs were trained under Mr. E. C. Lawton. His boys' soprano voices would have compared in quality with the Vienna Boys Choir of today. The church organ, one of the largest in Chicago, was under the direction of Mr. Francis Hemington; his organ recitals and choir oratorios were attended by the public for over twenty years.

It was at the Third Presbyterian Church where many school friends attended and the evangelical Sunday school singing was a new experience for me. "Work for the night is coming when man works no more" offered a philosophical meaning. In later years, the power of its melody and words seemed restated in Walt Disney's "Whistle While You Work."

Where the Church of the Epiphany had inspired with its choir and organ, the Third Presbyterian stimulated both old and new residents through its Sunday Evening Club. This was similar to the present organization in Orchestra Hall on Michigan Avenue. Thought provoking, non-political, non-sectarian speakers drew full audiences with such notables as Senator Borah and Dr. Frank Gunsaulus. At these services, anthems and oratorios were sung by a vested mixed choir. The minister, Rev. Martin D. Hardin, was determined to reach the transients who had no church home.[1]

Union Park Congregational Church, oldest of the neighboring evangels, had splendid men's, women's and children's choirs as well as a concert orchestra. In summer, the church had outdoor services which echoed throughout Union Park. The church has been noted for its work among young people, especially university students lodged in the neighborhood, including medical, dental and nursing students at the Medical Center.

In the unmissed absence of musical abundance as we know it today with television, radio and stereo, there was recorded music in its earliest wailing and grinding. First known as the gramophone, the Edison story is known to all.

Besides the neighborhood advantages, the City of Chicago offered much for a musical heritage. To have gone to a symphony orchestra concert, under the direction of Frederick Stock in Orchestra Hall, was to experience a life's preparation for musical appreciation. The first sound, as well as sight, of this great ensemble was one of bewilderment for the child who did not know about French or English horns, oboes, cellos, flutes or trombones. Yet the golden harp, kettle drums, cymbals and movements of the director were intensely watched while the overall blending of the orchestra engulfed the young listener in a new world. This would become more understood with successive performances.

One evening, in college years, the Chicago Symphony was playing in Milwaukee at the Auditorium. At a magic hour of ten, the clock in the City Hall tolled the hours in perfect rhythm and pitch with the music the orchestra was performing. These moments so moved the leader and his audience that at the finish he exclaimed that even the city's bells joined in a mutual affinity of sound.

The city child likewise had the advantage of the theatre, either musical or dramatic productions. Theatre going was not a common practice, at least for children; to have witnessed only a few choice theatricals was a privilege. In 1903, before starting to Brown School, I saw my first "stage show;" it was Victor Herbert's Babes in Toyland which made its premiere in Chicago rather than New York. This operetta has never been repeated and probably never will because of excessive and minute details which would be too costly today. It might also be boresome, even to young children who have had their fairy friends expelled from earth and must now look for planetary friends. Babes in Toyland was a kaleidoscope of colors and a symphony of sounds as Mother Goose characters, toys and even trees came alive. Today, "The March of the Tin Soldiers" survives at Christmas.

While in Brown School, I saw Maurice Maeterlinck's The Blue Bird at a Loop theatre. While this was not a musical in the true sense, the musical flow of the dialogue was full of harmony and mysticism as inanimate objects acquired voices. Years later, when I read L'Oiseau Bleu in college French, some earlier thoughts were clarified.

Again, an evening of songs sung by Carrie Jacobs Bond lingers. Her concert was given at the Third Presbyterian Church. She was then a young widow with a small son, and had come to Chicago to make her living, writing and singing her songs. These, which have always been

---

[1]Rev. Hardin, besides being a man of the cloth, was well grounded in politics and statesmanship, his father having been governor of Kentucky and his wife the sister of Vice-President Adlai Stevenson, the father of the late Adlai Stevenson.

nostalgic, were even more so as she sang them in her unaffected simplicity. So she continued on her way singing "When You Come To The End Of A Perfect Day" and "I Love You Truly" which were to bless the author all her life as Carrie Jacobs Bond became a successful songwriter.

When it came to the young people's choice of music, both vocal and instrumental, their's was of another world:

> "You call it a waste of time, this taste
>   For popular tunes, and yet
> Goodbye to care when you whistle the air
>   Of the song that you can't forget."

Guy Wetmore Carryl, 1873-1904
The Organ Grinder

Singing and whistling, the neighborhood young folks gathered to practice some new songs of the gay nineties at my sister's home. Some of the early favorites were Goodbye, My Bluebell, A Bicycle Built For Two, Come Josephine In My Flying Machine, and In The Shade Of The Old Apple Tree. The accompanying instrument besides the piano was a banjo, which served to add twangy rhythm to the popular melodies. In the years which followed as the new American music developed, rhythm was to become the dominant quality. Who were some of those experts in barbershop harmony and on a par with any of today? They may have been Helen Sullivan, Willie Best, John Smale, Annie Williamson, Louis and Lotta Krum, Fred Forbes, David and Evarts Graham and Kittie Kimball.

After going through harmony numbers as The Little Brown Jug, Where Is My Wandering Boy Tonight and There's A Tavern In Our Town, all were thirsty and hungry. In the dining room downstairs a collation of cheese fondue, Melba toast and hot chocolate would revive them. Encircling the table, each helped stir the chafing dishes heated with small alcohol burners. The white Haviland chocolate pot and its diminutive cups were filled many times. Eleven o'clock came too soon and the group left with the sound of "Merrily, we roll along o'er the deep blue sea" floating down the street on a warm summer evening.

Almost a generation later, when the little sister's group came, Mamma put some restricting ribbons on two antique chairs, as done in museums, since these chairs could not hold football players such as Oscar LeBeau, or "Molly," Frank Malloy or even the substantial but beautiful Clementine O'Connell. Among others in the group from Lewis Institute or McKinley, may have been Mabel Evans, Berte Hay, Fred Maxwell, Alva Marwood, Edward Fabel, Mildred Clark, Ivan Kingsley and the two Herberts, Spierling and Slusser.

The banjo was missing; a new "twanger," a ukulele took its place. What were some of the popular hits around 1916? There were I'm Sorry I Made You Cry, When You Wore A Tulip And I Wore A Big Red Rose, By The Light Of The Silvery Moon, Meet Me Tonight In Dreamland, The Curse Of An Aching Heart, Alexander's Rag Time Band and for double rhythm, Kitten On The Keys.

Refreshments were a platter of sandwiches, potato chips, chocolate cake and carbonated beverages. The closing hour was twelve o'clock and departure was a bit noisy as well as delayed due to cranking two Model T. Fords.

366

THE CLOTHES WE WORE

"This same Miss McFlimsey of Madison Square
The last time we met was in utter dispair,
Because she had nothing whatever to wear."

William Allen Butler, 1825-1902
Nothing To Wear

In winter, both boys and girls wore stocking caps of heavy knitted or crocheted wool ending with a tassel; the most popular color was red and the further the stocking hung down the back, the more esteemed it was, as well as pulled by teasing schoolmates. Scarfs to match were prized when long enough to wind twice around the neck or to cross the chest and tie in back. Mittens could match, too, in perennial red, either five-fingered, or the paw with a separate thumb. When a child started to Brown School, he was already informed on the importance of mittens from the tale of the kittens and, often, mittens were attached on a cord through the coat sleeves.

Coats for both sexes were often of blue wool chinchilla cloth, double breasted, lined with red flannel and using brass eagle or star buttons. One might wear a visored and ear-muffed cap to match the coat or a tam o'shanter. Heavy cotton leggings with unnumbered buttons impeded the child, and when wet, from snow mounds or rain puddles, were as uncomfortable as an infant's wet diaper.

Knickerbockers of blue serge and black full length ribbed stockings, held up by round garters, were quite standard for city boys. Shirts were blouse-like but Little Lord Fauntleroy fashions had long since passed. Long underwear was worn by both boys and girls in winter.

The period's styles for children were influenced by costumes worn by royal families in England, Germany and Russia. The military imitation was apparent for several generations in the overcoats and sailor suits for small boys and middy blouses with pleated skirts for girls. Several names for the feminine version were "Thompson" dresses and "Hofflin" middies, also "Norfolk" jackets for all children. These could be colored linen for summer and blue serge for colder weather. The insignia used were unofficial assortments of United States Navy symbols.

Schoolgirls of all ages wore jumpers or suspender skirts. Very small girls wore pinafores or aprons made famous by Alice in Wonderland, as illustrated by the British, John Tennial. For Friday's special programs one might wear a flowered wool challis dress with smocking and ribbons, reminiscent of storybook drawings of Kate Greenway and those later interpreted by Jessie Wilcox Smith in her paintings of children.

A white dress for many special occasions was appropriate from first grade through college days to that lived-happy-ever-after day and it's wedding dress. This white dress was often pique, embroidered linen, lace trimmed muslin, billowy organdy, China silk or creamy, featherstitched cashmere. Not to be overlooked were the accessories, hair ribbons, sashes and dainty slippers such as Alice wore when she experienced Through the Looking Glass.

While this attire would fit grammar school fashions, what were the rest of the family wearing? Strangely, dress lengths remained almost floor length for several generations. When costume design periods are studied, it is overwhelmingly apparent that through the ages full length, flowing costumes have been dominant.

So skirts were long and waists were small around 1900; a slender waistline might evoke more attention than a bosom or a limb. These waists, some no greater circumference than the owner's head girth, were not because of a generation of small women or malnutrition; rather they were achieved, molded and started early. The adolescent girl was wearing a "Farris waist" which too soon would change to a steel or bone ribbed corset, perhaps a "Dr. Warner." When strings were tightened regularly over the shaping years, a "wasp-waist" or an "hour-glass" figure could result. If overdone on the plump figure, an "Old Ironsides" might be produced. The brassiere was not in common usage - one might refer to a camisole; modesty was accomplished by a corset cover or chemise. Decollete was modestly assumed by the very young, while mature, firm bosoms might feel freer depth-wise.

The impetus for a grand style was emphasized by the social demands of Chicago's World's Fair in 1893. Had this not occurred, perhaps adolescent scholars would not have been rushed into adult fashions. Long skirts appeared on students when only fourteen years old at graduation from Brown School; skirts were then nearing ankle length. By high school days, they were touching the ground. One sister rebelled, as written in her diary of April, 1897:

> "I have my first long dress. Wore it Easter Sunday and I don't like it. Such uncomfortable things, twisting about your feet all the time and dusting the sidewalks. I am not going to wear it to school until the 12th of May. Then I will be classed as a young lady but I wish I was little again."

Women's fashions of this period were conspicuous for their preponderance of peplums, cascading trains, leg-o-mutton sleeves, over saturation with lace and tucking and the indiscriminate use of plumes and feathers in millinery as well as clothing, such as capes and boas. The Great White Heron, Snowy Egret and the Great Blue Heron were so depleted, that the government and the Audubon Society had to protect these beautiful birds from extinction.

What about the styles for men which have been traditionally conservative in civilized countries until the present day Hippie movement? In summer, the high school and college set wore white trousers and gay blazers - red, green or blue and white striped jackets. Bright banded straw hats and sporting canes were part of the ensemble. This happy style became a cliche in vaudeville and lives on in television wherever an atmosphere of the Gay Nineties is needed. Hats were always worn by men and were in constant process of being tipped in the presence of ladies. The hat might be a derby, fedora or the satin-faced stovepipe, depending on the formality of the occasion.

It seemed as though most all older professional men wore Prince Albert coats, so tenacious was the Victorian image on men's fashions. Full dress evening wear remained so stable in its style that it could be worn for a generation of formal wear. Moths claimed it sooner than usage.

A beard of some kind seemed to be the accepted and predominant feature of the male whether it was worn full or in its various abbreviations. These could be a Van Dyke, a mustache curled or twisted to points, a short "tooth brush" style or sideburns. Clarence Day's stage version of Life with Father captured all the Victorian elements of the age here studied. His "Father" could have been my father, so clearly did he return in my childhood memories of him.

It was the progress and change of the new century which would bring to the upcoming male generation such things as business suits, tan oxfords, striped shirts, four-in-hand ties, pompadours, close cropped hair, smooth shaven faces and evening wear in flattering tuxedos.

88. Lydia and George Warvelle with Florence and Effie. From MWB family album.

HOLIDAYS AND HOLYDAYS

From the first grade on, children participated in extra curricular activities such as observing the national or calendar holidays. Pledging allegiance to the flag had not yet evolved, although we were instructed in the history and use of the flag. Prayers or Bible readings were only occasional, as at graduation or Memorial Day exercises; when these were a part, they caused no outward or negative reactions. Catholic children of confirmation age were excused from classes for weekly instruction.

Washington's and Lincoln's birthdays were observed with proper recitations, songs and room decorations. On St. Valentine's day, each room had a valentine mailbox (usually an old hat box) with a slit in the top to collect cards which were sent to teachers and classmates. Comic valentines were forbidden, being too sophisticated and often vulgar. Popularity was judged by the number of cards one received, also their quality. A little girl is recalled who wished to be popular and for several days she put many valentines addressed to herself in the box. Later, when the teacher called her name from a succession of envelopes, she was very embarrassed. It was evident to all who the sender was.

Easter usually came during a spring recess period. If not, there was no special celebration except for the singing of spring songs. May Day was observed by making little paper baskets to hold spring flowers for teacher and mother, providing that day had not been eclipsed by moving week or spring vacation, which sometimes was the first week in May. The Fourth of July (seldom called Independence Day), while it occurred during summer vacation, was an insane celebration for children. The earlier era of parades, speeches and gatherings on the green had vanished.

For the city child, the day began at daybreak with "bombs bursting in air," giant firecrackers set off by neighborhood boys or resounding cannons from somewhere. The dog went immediately into hiding in the dark cellar. Shooting of firecrackers of all sizes, imported from China, continued all day. Younger, more timid children threw torpedoes on the sidewalk; these were explosive caps embedded in a bundle of gravel and wrapped in red tissue paper. The air reeked with gunpowder and punk smell. Punk, while used to light the weapons, also was wrapped in tissue paper and smoked by children. By noon, there were reports of neighborhood casualties, burnt fingers to tragic eye damage. Newspapers on July 5, listed the city's and nation's casualties; there were many deaths, usually children.

By evening, having spent every penny and shot every cracker, one sat on the front porch to watch the neighborhood fireworks display, fortunately managed by elders. There were skyrockets, Roman candles and fountains cascading from the sky after a sizzling entry; pinwheels and red or green flares illuminated half the block. Balloons were set off on their trip to the moon; the dark sky all over the city seemed full of these moving stars which children tried to count. The next morning, there was not a trace of a balloon to be seen; the dog emerged from the cellar and it was many years before this traffic in death was outlawed and a so-called "sane Fourth" was attempted.

The next holiday, important to school children, was Halloween. That such a day as All Hallow's Eve should through the filtering years become so dissipated of its original intent is poetically and religiously a loss to mankind. It was the eve of All Saints' Day recalling when a "multitude of heavenly hosts" clothed in white robes and with palms, rejoiced. The folklore power of the devil and the ghost still prevails in the modern celebration, much as the spirit of Mardi Gras for Shrove Tuesday is celebrated in France and other Catholic regions.

Halloween is sometimes remembered as a vicious day among grammar school children and Brown School was no exception. The traditional "must" was a bean shooter, a foot or more long, tin pipe-like stem with a wooden mouth piece. The ammunition was a bag of dried navy beans or peas which were fired from the mouth through the bean shooter to the intended target - a window pane, eye, pair of glasses or anywhere on the body. Most vicious of all, were soot bags made from flour or gunnysacks, and filled with ashes or soot. Armed with this weapon, the boy (never a girl) hid behind a building corner, or in the alley crossing and when the right victim passed by, hit her or him on the head. It was a frightening and damaging experience.

A minor trick (there were no trick and treat arrangements then) was the sticking of thumbtacks or pins in push button bells of apartment houses; the bells rang or buzzed until relieved of the pins. While not a common part of Halloween, like the costumes of modern beggar's night, there were some ghosts seen in sheets and fabricated skeletons roaming the streets. There was little classroom participation except for Jack-o'-lantern paper cutouts in the primary rooms. The story of Washington Irving's headless horseman in The Legend of Sleepy Hollow was read in the upper grades and appropriate for the day.

Thanksgiving Day and Christmas celebrations came in quick succession. For Thanksgiving observance, primary children decorated the windows with pumpkin and turkey silhouettes while older students, dressed as Pilgrims and Indians, visited the classrooms with a playlet. They carried pewter bowls of fruit, pumpkins, ears of corn and even a roast turkey; the last was papier-mache and kept for perennial use in the stage props' closet. The singing was joyous with the always loved:

> "Over the River and through the snow
> To Grandfather's house we go.
> The horse knows the way
> To carry the sleigh
> Through the white and drifted snow."

It was also prayerful as portions of this hymn recall:

> "Come, ye thankful people come.
> Raise the song of harvest home;
> All is safely gathered in
> Ere the winter storm begin.

...

First the blade and then the ear
Then the full corn shall appear;
Grant, O harvest Lord that we
Wholesome grain and pure may be."

Christmas exercises were held the Friday before the holiday vacation and were festive in their simplicity. Each room had a Christmas tree for which all the decorations had been made or donated by the pupils. There were tinsel-edged embossed cardboard creations; these might be angels, manger scenes or St. Nicholas which to some viewers might have been considered icons. There were freshly strung chains of popcorn, cranberries, or colored paper links, hanging gilded or silvered peanuts and emptied walnut shells, swinging gingerbread men and star cookies. If candles were there, they were never lighted because of fire danger. On the top of the tree was an angel or star, resplendent in rays of tinsel looking down upon enraptured children. This might be the only tree that some could call their own. The room teacher usually knew of her less fortunate children and informed certain parents who saw to it that baskets of cheer were delivered to those children's homes. This was way before the days of P.T.A. cooperation.

In primary grades, St. Nicholas (this title was used until Santa Claus replaced him) visited each room with his sack and pulled out the exact number of tarlatan stockings filled with nuts and hard candy (called kindergarten candy) for all. This was made possible by the children, each bringing a few pennies for the party. The pupils had made presents for their parents - blotters, bookmarks or calendars with a Perry print of a famous painting - perhaps Raphael's Madonna of the Chair. Carols were reverently sung by these young seekers - O Little Town of Bethlehem and Silent Night, Holy Night.

89. Walker Sisters: Christmas with Friends. Courtesy Valerie Walker.

FRIDAY AND SATURDAY

"Friday's child is loving and giving
Saturday's child works hard for a living."

Author Unknown

Friday in all grades was an easy, relaxed and happy day; teachers and pupils had worked hard the rest of the week. Besides Friday debates, spelling bees and construction work, there were special programs. Visitors, meaning parents, were invited. Brown School had no auditorium, so each room had its separate celebration. The children helped clean the blackboards; made sure all desks had no ink or pencil drawings or gum stuck under the desk top. They carried in extra chairs for the guests. Sometimes two rooms joined in the happening and then each desk held two students. The special program could be poetry recitations, carefully memorized, or short plays in costumes; or a distinguished parent or world traveler who gave a talk. Closing the Venetian blinds to create some degree of darkness, lantern projection slides might be part of the speaker's message.

In the primary grades, a child's birthday was often celebrated with the mother sending a cake large enough to serve the whole class. After being cut into thirty or more pieces, it was never enough to suit everyone. Also, in the lower grades a stereoscope was passed down the aisles, desk to desk, and each child had a view of some famous building or sculpture.

On these Friday afternoons, the girls often wore a Sunday or dressy outfit. That for some, included long, white stockings and high, black buttoned shoes. One little girl was allowed to wear white stockings only in summer and black the rest of the year; she coveted this luxury and was determined to be in style one winter's day. Before she left for school, she simply tucked her finely ribbed cashmere underwear into the high button shoes. It looked successful, until after a strenuous morning recess when the "stockings" became very baggy, having no garters. It was necessary to hurriedly change them for the customary black during the noon lunch hour at home. The excuse given to inquiring friends that afternoon was that muddy snow had splashed on them - two wrongs never did make a right.

As one looks back on such incidental matters, it is also remembered how charming these little girls were. To name a few scattered through the years and judged through the eyes of the contemporary child were Irene Descombe and her chum, Frances Cote; the girls dressed alike and these outfits were made by Irene's mother. There was Helen Frohmuth, with cornflower blue eyes and brushed finger curls, not corkscrew ones made by kid curlers or rags. There was Helen De Souchet with blond curls and crisp pleated skirt held up by suspenders over a ruffled white gimpe, as the blouse was called; her father had the oxygen supply store on Madison Street. There were Gertrude Jones and Lillian Kendrick, both with charming Dutch cut hair, who lived directly across from Brown; their homes, partly out of convenience, were a mecca for the young set. And dear Dorothy Rogers, who sometimes had to forego tomboy games because she had leakage of the heart; and Antha Cruver with a tantalizing lisp, whose father owned the Cruver Manufacturing Company nearby. I, myself, when young, had long, brown curls, big ribbon bow and many freckles.

Of course one remembers the boys who were handsome, though still in the gangling years; "nice looking" was the description used then. At random one sees Alphonse LaBelle, blond and rosy cheeked; Alburn Rector with shiny brushed pompadour; the quiet Irwin Brand. There was gentlemanly Barry Hodges; the girls' heartbreakers - handsome Merrill Smith and Edwin Stott who had the makings of diplomats.

The anticipation of a weekend free from school made one want to celebrate, to sing, or jump around. One could make candy if permission was given. In childhood's recipe book, there were three candies one could make, fudge, taffy and popcorn balls. All these required skill and, until in the upper grades, big sister assistance was needed. Fudge was first mastered and it had advantages: it could be made alone or with friends.

Popcorn balls and taffy, to be most fun as well as successful, needed in educator's words, group participation. The procedures were time consuming, so Friday or Saturday evening, when the kitchen had been cleared, was the best time. With a gang (this word was then in good repute) assembled for popcorn balls, one person would shell corn off the cob; another sifted it so that chaff would not burn in the popper. Turns were taken at pushing the popper, while a chief cook measured the ingredients and set them to cook on the gas stove. Someone prepared a large kettle to receive the white morsels and soon it was full. The hot glaze at the threading stage was poured on and stirred with a wooden spoon. Then all hands present and buttered, invaded the kettle and molded the balls. In no time, the tray was piled high, the utensils put to soak, all sticky hands washed at the kitchen faucet over the zinc covered sink (often called the "zink") and dried on a huge red bordered linen roller towel which hung on the back door. Then all found places to sit, either in the kitchen or the butler's pantry which was called the "dining car" since it was a narrow passage to the dining room. With chewing, crunching and laughter, the evening was over too soon.

A taffy pull needed almost the same requirements, a company of strong hands and hearts and an expert on timing the hardening stage. Having reached that stage and cooled sufficiently to pull, the hot hunks were portioned out. One could pull alone, or in a tandem of four buttered hands. Braids, looking like their namesakes, taffy colored braids, or figure eights were pulled out and set to cool. Again, there was chewing, crunching and laughter.

Saturday was a very busy day for all, including the pinafore-knickerbocker group. Brown School was out and Saturday could claim:

> "No more pencils, no more chalk
> No more teacher's sassy talk."

Many "kids" (a new slang word) were causing a sidewalk jam with their bicycles, tricycles and dragging red wagons which might hold a cat, dog, or small brother. Those who lacked these conveyances, had homemade contraptions such as a wooden apple box attached to a spare set of wheels. This congestion would worsen when little ladies appeared in long skirts, veils and unsteady high heels pushing doll buggies; in these might be a nest of kittens, or just dolls.

Traffic lessened as the day wore on. Some went shopping, others to practice or take piano or violin lessons. Frank Winter, an earlier Brown School graduate, conducted a violin school at 642 Washington. His fee was one dollar per half hour and his solo engagement for an evening of music was six dollars. Piano teachers usually came to the house and varied in quality and cost, some giving lessons for fifty cents each. Mr. Winter's wife, Grace, charged this amount.

There were dismal Saturdays when it rained or snowed and little scholars were forced indoors. On such days, the big iron kitchen range with its oven door open offered soothing heat, thawing out numb thumbs and damp, cold toes while we sat in round backed wooden chairs, nowadays called captains' chairs. Here on the stove's top griddle, one could push a wire corn popper and soon have hot buttered popcorn, also good for cold fingers and warm friends.

On snowy days after school or Saturdays, little folks were sledding, pulling each other, or sliding under one's own power. Boys had coasters and did "belly whoppers" and even hitched onto the rear of passing wagons. On the corner of Monroe and Paulina, the old First United Presbyterian Church had a wide approach of six stone steps. As the church was seldom used during the week or steps cleared of snow, they made a toboggan slide. One coasted down this bumpy slope across to the furthest curb. To make the trip more exhilarating, water was poured on the edges of the steps which froze to a hard finish. Little traffic passed on cold days and no accidents were ever reported. The tempting steps were later removed by the next congregation owning the building, the Mormon Church.

Corrine and Irene Johnson lived across the street and next door to their house was a large, weathered, frame house with an encircling Queen Anne porch and on the second story a projecting, tower-like room. The house was said to be haunted; it faced a corner lot. Probably in better days, its yard was lovely; now it was full of dandelions; the neighborhood boys played ball here. The vacant lot and the storybook house disappeared before 1906, when a one story building, known as Automatic Telephone Company, replaced another gathering place for city children.

Besides children busy at play, adults were busy at work in preparation for Sunday. Our hired girl had scrubbed the large kitchen floor whose maple strips seemed almost white; a few rag rugs were in vulnerable places. Next door at Wheeler's, the coachman was polishing the steel rails which completed the ornate iron bannisters on the front steps. At the Tyrell-Martin house, the hired girl on her knees scrubbed an eight foot square limestone slab of the short stairway leading to the first floor. In later memory, it was reminiscent of the old Baltimore doorways of scrubbed stone. Also, both Wheeler's and Martin's white stone carriage blocks were scrubbed and woe to any dog or child who set foot on them.

Our house had a low, twenty foot wide limestone wall in front of the inner lawn; this was scrubbed only occasionally because it was always in use by children, especially on Saturday and vacations. Here they sat to watch the passing parade, played school, store or circus on it. The lower entry made an excellent dressing room for between the acts, as well as a playhouse on chilly days.

The props and makeup for these spur of the moment shows and circus acts were ingenious, considering the age and experience of both announcers and performers. For the prima donna's regal beauty, there must be rouge, lipstick and eyebrow pencil. Where to find them? Such were not found on our bedroom dressing table; they were frowned upon as being used only by "low class" ladies.

Hurrying to the kitchen, perhaps one picked up a ripe red beet or fresh strawberries or even red currant jelly to rub on lips and cheeks - sticky, but pretty. One time, colored chalks from our school box were used with disaster, as the queen's blushes and the Indian's war paint did not wash off; cheeks became sore and the towels were ruined. For black needs, shoe polish or a piece of charred wood from the fireplace was handy. As for face powder, whether it was for the leading lady or the clown, flour was excellent for the complexion or a grandfather's white hair as well.

The wardrobe was never hard to find. In the perennial rag or rummage box, one found all accessories from old lace curtains for bridal veils to cast-off bibbed overalls for the farmer. Wigs were a problem; if time allowed one could be made of strands from the hemp twine ball, the same used for tying bundles or supporting morning glories. A few such locks under a hat or shawl did the trick. Sometimes there were fresh wood shavings from the shed workbench. These were perfect for blond ladies' curls.

Besides impromptu "shows" or theatricals with actors in costumes, the neighborhood children could assemble, on the spur of the moment, a band or orchestra. This concert might have been inspired by a recent band concert in the park or a passing parade. The instruments varied with the inspiration of the musicians, as well as the number participating.

Two children could make beautiful music together, each having eight empty, clean, jelly glasses and a teaspoon to play the do, re, me, fa, sol, la, ti, do of the scale. With a pitcher of water, they would create their scale tones by filling the glasses in varying amounts and then testing the tones which sounded. Someone would run in the house and sound middle C on the piano or just hum his own version of do, re, me. Assembling these orchestral masterpieces usually became an afternoon's absorbing occupation.

If the group was large and in a hurry for music, then assorted sizes of pots and pans and sturdy spoons, both metal and wooden, created percussion instruments. The violin or string section was, of course, combs covered with a piece of tissue paper to hum through. Additional sound effects were always possible with dinner bells, the baby's rattle, whistles and horns. The latter could be real or improvised paper tubes; there was the occasional jew's-harp, mouth organ, or toy drums. Often the musical program was simply singing with selections ranging from Mother Goose to popular songs, as well as patriotic and Sunday School hymns.

In hot summer, Saturday or any day, these twenty feet of low, stone wall were ideal for a lemonade stand. Here two orange crates, with a cloverleaf tea towel, stood in front of it while the sellers sat behind and the customers sat comfortably on either side, some dangling their feet - all, even the tall and hot passers-by, rested their feet. There were a few cardboard round fans (advertiser's compliments) to use while being refreshed. The refreshment source was the traditional large glass pitcher, sparkling with hunks (no cubes available yet) of ice, lemon rinds and outside condensation. This was surrounded by assorted odd glasses, mostly jelly containers, some penny size, others, two or five cent.

On the hidden shelves below were a saucer for a cash box, dish towels and extra sugar, in cast the brew was sour to some. Behind the wall was a dishpan of water, convenient for this bar since the used water and part empty glasses could be dumped on the grass at one's back. While Mamma worried over our sanitation, no epidemics were ever traced to this place of business.

As the day wore on, the supply tended to be diluted and finally was exhausted, as were the little peddlers. The saucer had become full of pennies. Who were the customers? They were the postman, iceman (who also contributed free ice), neighbors old and young, passing peddlers of uncertain origin, and a few non-paying customers who gave leg service by running home to fetch a piece of ice or an extra lemon. This age-old traffic in lemonade endures, but few with as convenient curb service, due to a low stone wall.

On spring or fall Saturdays, when there was garden clean up of leaves and fallen branches, some neighbors had small bonfires in their backyards. It was fun to gather loose bricks and stones to make a wall around the pile, or failing that, to dig a shallow pit and put the rakings in. Just before lighting the fire, some big Irish potatoes were buried in the pile. By the time all leaves were burnt and the ashes white, one took a shovel and lifted out the charcoal covered lumps. After penetrating a half inch crust, one found flaky, white baked potatoes, which after adding butter, had an undefinable flavor. While they were not hickory smoked, they were Balm of Gilead smoked and perhaps had a little tang of resin. Anyway, the cookout seemed as satisfying then as a modern day barbecue.

The advent of roller skates was a boon to youngsters. One could get most anywhere on roller skates in half the time it took to walk the distance. While there were bicycles for the older set, these vehicles were forbidden on city sidewalks; this ruled out the primary children. Roller skates could be used on sidewalks; however, cautious older pedestrians often wished these too were off the walks, especially when skaters performed in tandem, even foursomes.

When one was very small and a beginner, the "learning" pair of skates had wooden wheels. These became run down and wobbly after a few runs on granular sidewalks while older skaters objected to those unsure skaters blocking traffic.

Next came the skates of champions - ball bearing, steel rollers with secure ankle support, straps and clamps, the latter tightened with a key. That skate key, almost as crucial as the modern car key, locked and unlocked those skates on our shoes; it usually hung on a string around the neck of the skates' manipulator.

Roller skating was more comfortable on smooth limestone sidewalks. Concrete walks were gritty and noisy; the cracks between each section, after the skater had worked up speed, made noisy vibrations - so much so that the fast sliding skater thought he was an engine on a railroad track. Sometimes he carried a whistle on the key chain for just such occasions. Street crossings were a trial, especially if the pavement was not asphalt. Wood Street was brick paved and Ogden Avenue, besides having street car tracks, was paved with large stone blocks which had been eroded by iron wagon wheels into rounded sinkholes.

As one grew older, one traveled longer distances, away from Union Park to Garfield Park where there were unlimited numbers of tennis courts. While forbidden by most parents, some boys, even girls, would hitch a ride by holding on to the rear of a passing truck, either horse drawn or automobile, and then just slide along. There were unexpected pitfalls because the driver might turn a corner or the vehicle might suddenly stop and the "hitch-hiker" would get bumped, even fall and get raw knees, if nothing worse.

Roller skating was so popular with young people that roller rinks developed along with the contemporary amusement parks or permanent carnivals as "White City" and "Riverview Park." These commercial parks were tabooed in my upbringing as an environment not suited to very young children.

GRADUATIONS, AS THEY WERE

Commencement exercises at Brown School in my sisters' days were long sessions with instrumental music, singing, recitations, debating, the presentation of honors, medals and diplomas, oratory of religious significance as well as the speaker's address to the graduating class - all this on a sunny June morning.

Such was traditional for generations in both public and private schools throughout the United States. There was a reason. In the nineteenth century this event might be the only one that many graduates would participate in. So these exercises took on the dignity of college commencements which honor both students and faculty of a particular institution or alma mater. The teacher, from primary grades through college, has always been our alma mater, our fostering mother. This is affirmed by graduates of one room school houses to holders of doctor's degrees given by our proudest universities. Dr. Silas W. Mitchell wrote of his University of Pennsylvania:

> "Ave materna
> Loving and wise,
> The light of the ages
> Is bright in your eyes."[1]

Today, at colleges and universities, many oratorical frills and baccalaureate services have been shortened or eliminated. The complexities of modern living and learning allow less consideration of ceremony which has added personality and tradition to institutions of learning, be they as humble as the public elementary schools. So, too, the relationship between pupils and teachers has been modified. Is the efficiency of computer, television and ear phones replacing the personal guidance of the teacher?

Among those early honors for public school graduates was the Foster Diploma which had a long history. In 1856, Dr. John W. Foster gave the city one thousand dollars:

> "For the encouragement of scholarships and good conduct, and to excite a laudable emulation and appreciation among scholars of the public schools of Chicago."[2]

The interest from the fund was to be used for purchasing gold, silver and bronze medals or diplomas. As the school population increased, the pupils at the century's end received only

---

[1]Source is not known to editor.

[2]Superintendent's Report For the Year 1856, Chicago Board of Education. Permission Chicago Public Schools.

Foster Diplomas, but the honor implied was not diminished. By the early twentieth century these, too, were discontinued along with some liturgicals of preceding graduation ceremonies.

In the 1894 commencement from Brown School, Louise Krueger and Effie Warvelle were awarded Foster Diplomas. Effie also received the 1894 Chicago Daily News Patriotism Medal for an essay on <u>Prodeo et Patria</u>. This and her last medal of a fifty year alumni from University of Chicago have survived. She was also the Class Poet of 1894 and with her typical seriousness she wrote:

> "Dear Brown within thy sheltering walls,
> Thy well-known rooms and oft trod halls,
> We as thy children come no more;
> Farewell, for our school days are o'er.
> To higher realms on knowledge bent
> By thy kind hands we now are sent."

In 1896, Florence graduated from Brown without medals or extra diplomas but with a gay, vivacious spirit sparkling in her amber eyes and titian hair. Louisa May Alcott's poem written for her sister could describe Florence:

> "A child her wayward pencil drew
>   On margins of her book;
> Garlands of flowers, dancing elves,
>   Bird, butterfly and brook.
> Lessons undone, and play forgot,
>   Seeking with hand and heart
> The teacher whom she learned to love
>   Before she knew 'twas art."

She was Class Poet and her poem's title became the class motto - "I'll Stand True:"

> "In life's great school we cannot ask
> For help on our allotted task,
>   But each alone must bear her part
>   With courage firm and faithful heart;
> Yet naught shall come that we shall rue
> If only we shall all stand true."

That 1896 program listed seventeen numbers plus the class flower, a white carnation! There was the valedictory by Lucile Talbot, the class song by Ethel Shader, the debate: "Resolved - that the statesman who governs wisely does more for his country than the soldier who fights for it" (affirmative: Evarts Graham, Paul Fouke; negative: George Barrett, Edward Burrell). Besides, there were three adult speakers, two clergymen and the President of the Board of

Education - a sonorous sendoff into the wide world for a class of eighty-two adolescent graduates!

Graduation from Brown School in 1912, when the last Warvelle sister graduated, was still held in a crowded classroom. There was a moveable partition blackboard between two of the eighth grade rooms which made possible a larger room for assembly purposes. The years had simplified the ritual since my sisters' graduations. There were no printed programs, class officers nor poem, no honors awarded, declamations nor elocution. No special speaker or clergyman is recalled. There was glee club and class singing and a short address by Miss Niehaus, our principal, before she awarded the diplomas tied with brown and gold ribbons. The graduating class wore streamers of the same colors on their left shoulders. Each girl wore her prettiest white dress while the boys, too, were shining from their well-groomed hair to freshly polished shoes. The whole experience seemed blended in a quickly ending vision of colorful young people amid many bouquets of flowers. There were both happy and sad embracings as we left the old brick building into the warm June sun.

CHAPTER TEN: WILLIAM McKINLEY HIGH SCHOOL, FACULTY, AND SOME ALUMNI

WILLIAM McKINLEY HIGH SCHOOL

The last descendant of Central High School was William McKinley High School on Adams Street, between Seeley and Hoyne Avenues. The new school opened in September, 1904, in a splendid complex of classrooms, gymnasiums, laboratories, cafeteria and auditorium. The latter, jokingly called "Howling Hall," was dedicated to George Howland, early teacher at Central High School and later superintendent of schools.

The variety of subjects offered, especially for business education, reflected the guiding philosophy of Dr. Ella Flagg Young, who from her earliest teaching, advocated the building of sound bodies and equipping young minds to the best of their potential talents.

Many of the faculty who had taught at West Division continued in the new school with the same spirit and devotion known to earlier students. Among them were Mlle. Josephine Mack who taught French and was Dean of Girls; she was short of stature and temper, a Francophile who loved the Irish too. William Payne, called "Billy" behind his back, taught English and was an erudite person, having been a world authority on Shelley and other English poets. He had a Van Dyke beard, a balding head and appeared frail, yet his witty humor was very strong and his eyes twinkled at a student's excellent recitation.

There was Miss Sargent, who taught algebra and geometry; she was almost "a five by five" in her anatomical proportions, but her mind was sharp and oriented to the problem on the blackboard. Francis Brimblecom taught Latin; to him it was a second tongue; he spoke it so easily, while his blondish goatee seemed to jiggle in rhythm to the dead language meter. Then there was Cornelia Beardsley, a quiet voiced and most patient teacher of English.

Lucy Lamb Wilson, while teaching at McKinley for almost forty years, died in a traffic accident in May, 1925. After Brown School days, she graduated from old Central High School in 1880 and in thc ensuing years, was secretary of old Central Alumni and its successor, West Division. After her graduation from the University of Chicago, she would teach history until her untimely death.

As a teacher, she appeared substantial and plain in appearance and looked over her glasses for the pupil's answer. She was probably the most cherished woman teacher among students and alumni. She counseled them on the many school activities as Voice, the Irving Society and the need for a journalism course. She was never too busy to confer with troubled students who sought her personal guidance. It was a fact, disclosed at her death, that she had loaned, from her personal funds, the means for many students to continue their education. She had been called "Mother of McKinley."

Among Miss Wilson's personal files was a list of pupils having studied under her who had shown potential and later became prominent persons. Among such names listed were State's Attorney Robert Crowe, Judge Henry Horner of Probate Court, and later Governor of Illinois,

Judge Mary Bartelme, Harry T. Woodruff on the staff of the <u>Chicago Tribune</u>, and Samuel Ettelson, Corporation Counsel for Chicago under Mayor Thompson.[1]

There was George A. Powles, a beloved teacher of English who had two generations of daughters as well as pupils; Carrie was in my sister's class at West Division and Alice and Edith, in mine at McKinley. After thirty-seven years in 1927, at age seventy, George Powles reluctantly retired from teaching English - English literature, not a dull, rhetorical subject but full of human pathos and joy, poetry and mysticism.

In all those thirty-seven years, he had never been absent or tardy. Few students or faculty can match that record. Besides his academic teaching, he was continually writing several books, one such as <u>Oliver Langton</u>, and a host of poetry. Many of his poems were for his pupils in the <u>Voice</u>.

One other of those faculty who had also served at West Division was the principal, George Clayberg who retired in 1926 after a long tenure. Probably his greatest problems had been in the earlier school. He had a walrus mustache, bushy brows and seemed an impersonal, pre-occupied person. At least, he seemed so to freshmen and some thought his name just suited him.

There were three demises in the old Mile Square in 1954, not mortal deaths but passings equally as poignant to many thousands of Chicagoans since these obliterations were of the spirit and tradition: the spirit being an animating or inspiring principle such as pervades and tempers thought; tradition, the handing down of statements, legends, customs by words of mouth or practice.

In 1954, McKinley High School ceased to be; it was technically discontinued with valid reasons. McKinley High School's ancestry had begun in 1856 when Chicago High School was created and later would be known as old Central High School, as more schools were built to serve the expanding city - North Division, South Division and West Division High Schools. This last school would serve the west side students and become the direct descendant of Old Central, whose building by 1880 no longer would be used for students, becoming a warehouse.

By 1904, West Division faculty and students would move into a beautiful new home, McKinley High School; Chicago public schools no longer would be known by numbers or divisions, only by honored names.

Fifty years later, McKinley High School students, both boys and girls, would matriculate in Crane High School at Oakley Boulevard and Van Buren, formerly known as Crane Technical High School for Boys. The vacated building would become McKinley Upper Grade Center.

The second passing was the discontinuance of the Irving Literary Society, both Alpha and Omega, boys' and girls' sections. The Irving Society was organized at Old Central High School in 1857 and is thought to have been the first such literary society in an American public school.

The third death was that of the <u>Voice</u>, the literary publication begun in West Division's earliest years. It, too, was the first such publication in a Chicago public school. Both the Irving Society and the <u>Voice</u> were sponsored and guided by faculty members. Many famous writers,

---

[1]Memories of Miss Wilson Return on May 10 (1927), <u>Orange and Black</u>, McKinley High School, Chicago, IL, May 13, 1927, Vol. 6, No. 15.

as well as artists, had their first efforts published in <u>Voice</u>. To name a few, there were: Mary Hastings Bradley, Myrtle Reed McCollough, Judge Jacob Morton Braude, Samuel Raphaelson, George B. Petty, Milton Agar and Walt Disney.

Perhaps, considering the purpose of both classic and liberal arts studies which were basic requirements in both private and public education until recently and the role of the teacher as being a guide or counselor, this classic memorial written by the Roman poet, Juvenal, is the first century A.D., is prophetically nostalgic:

"Lightly lie the turf, ye gods, and void the weight on our grandsires' shades, and round their urn may the fragrant crocus bloom and eternal spring, who maintained that a teacher should have the place and honor of a revered parent."

90. McKinley High School, 2040 West Adams. A Chicago Public School photograph. Courtesy Chicago Board of Education.

91. Mlle. Josephine Mack, Professor of French, McKinley High School. From: *Voice*. McKinley High School *Voice*s Courtesy of Judge Jacob M. Braude.

92. Francis Brimblecom, Latin Professor, McKinley High School. From: *Voice.* McKinley High School *Voice*s Courtesy of Judge Jacob M. Braude.

388

93. Miss Lucy Lamb Wilson, Professor of History, McKinley High School. From: *Voice*. McKinley High School *Voice*s Courtesy of Judge Jacob M. Braude.

94. George A. Powles, English Department, McKinley High School. From: *Voice*. McKinley High School *Voice*s Courtesy of Judge Jacob M. Braude.

95. George Clayberg, Principal 1901-26, McKinley High School. From: *Voice*. McKinley High School *Voice*s Courtesy of Judge Jacob M. Braude.

JACOB MORTON BRAUDE

Jacob Braude knew early and exactly just what he wanted to be when he grew up. When he was a senior in 1914 at McKinley High School, a census of sorts appeared in the Voice Annual under the heading of "Wants To Be." Listed for his name was "Judge in a law court." That is exactly what he became for thirty-six years.

Judge Braude was born in Chicago in 1896 and graduated from Marquette School where he recalled being completely surrounded by the Medical Center buildings - Cook County Hospital directly across the street, College of Physicians and Surgeons to the right and Rush Medical College to the left - all on Harrison Street near Wood.

At McKinley, Jacob Braude was an earnest student in all of his studies, clubs and athletic activities. His dossier, that collection of school participations covering the four years of each student, was well rounded. He was Class Poet of 1914, and in the Senior Class Play; a member of Alpha Irving, Junto Club and Chess and Checkers Club; editor of Voice in 1913, and on the tennis and handball teams for several years.

He received his Bachelor of Arts Degree from the University of Michigan in 1918; Doctor of Jurisprudence from the University of Chicago Law School in 1920, followed by post graduate work at Northwestern University Law School. His early professional years were with appointments to the State of Illinois offices under Governors Henry Horner and Otto Kerner. In 1934, he was elected Judge of Municipal Court of Chicago and served four terms of office until 1956 when he was elected Judge of Circuit Court, where he was serving his last term at the time of his death, December 24, 1970.

His years were full of humanity's problems, especially Boy Problems. During much of his judicial career he presided over Boy's Court, dealing with criminal cases of boys from ages seventeen to twenty-one. His Boys' Court experiences involve a total of 25,000 cases. Like earlier Chicago leaders, Jane Addams, Amelia Sears, Ella Flagg Young and Bishop Samuel Fallows, Judge Braude was continually pleading for the children of the storm. He lectured extensively on Juvenile Delinquency and Adolescent Crime, as well as writing articles for national periodicals on his boys, for whom he said: "There is no such thing as a natural bad boy."[1]

Alongside the cares of judicial duties, he had a talent for humor, a helpful antidote for many in these stern days, and probably sterner to come. As a frequent after-dinner speaker, without his judicial robes, he accumulated hundreds of laugh-producing, icebreaker remarks and published these in Speaker's Encyclopedia of Stories, Quotations and Anecdotes in 1955, followed by a second encyclopedia in 1957 and Braude's Handbook of Humor For All Occasions in 1958. These are only a few of his many "happy" books, the last being a paperback edition, The Complete Art of Public Speaking.

---

[1] Source of this quote is not known to the editor. However, the author had known Jacob Braude who was known for making this statement.

96. Judge Jacob M. Braude. Courtesy Mrs. Jacob M. Braude (Adele Braude).

THE WALKER SISTERS

Two of the prettiest and gayest graduates from Marquette Grammar School, McKinley High School and Chicago Musical College were Valerie and Eulalie Walker. Born into a theatrical family, they were singing and dancing in Chicago theatres when they were seven and four, and would carry on in this tradition during a youthful part of their lives.

Valerie, the eldest, a brunette whose name suited her Spanish-like charm although her ancestry hailed from the British Isles, was the more serious minded of the girls. As a child, when the sisters were playing in Chicago theatres, Valerie would insist to her grandmother, who was their "stage mother," that she wanted to be a teacher. Later she did become a well known Chicago principal.

During the Walker Sisters' theatrical careers which were simultaneous with their educations, they appeared in road shows such as Her First False Step. While in Buffalo, Eulalie became ill and the Gish Girls took over for the Walker Sisters. Both Valerie and Eulalie were in silent movie productions made at the Selig Studios at Western and Irving Avenues. Such movies included The Wizard of Oz; Eulalie was "Dorothy" and Valerie, "Ozma." There was Cleopatra and Rostand's Chantecleer with a French pantomimist. Valerie was the favorite poulet.

Next came their summers in vaudeville circuit, and during the school year they sang and danced their way into many hearts at Chicago's well-known cabarets. Such were Boston Oyster House, Green Mill, Planters, College Inn and Marigold Gardens - all now vanished. The McKinley faculty would go back stage to congratulate their pupils, and incidentally, learn about make-up.

During the sisters' schooling years, they maintained top scholarship averages. Eulalie, Polly to her friends, graduated in three years from McKinley, while Valerie received her Bachelor of Music degree from Chicago Musical College at the same time she graduated from Chicago Teachers College at age eighteen, in 1914.

Valerie was married in 1916 to James F. Marshall who would perish in the 1918 influenza epidemic, leaving Valerie with an infant son. She went back to singing at night and teaching in the daytime. An incident occurred in her then extra busy life when a gossip-news hungry reporter emblazoned the headlines of a Chicago paper - "Pupils' Fathers See More Of This Teacher Than Their Children." Needless to say, the school's principal, as well as the retired superintendent of schools, defended Valerie's integrity.

In 1921, she married Dr. Frank Hoffmann, gave up the theatre, earned Bachelor of Science in Education and Master of Arts degrees at Northwestern University and became principal of Darwin School in Logan Square. Here she still helped with the school's stage productions. One which gave her great happiness was the annual Christmas and Hannukkah program. The Logan Square B'nai Brith gave a citation for this service towards brotherhood. Valerie is now retired and enjoys many visits with her son and grandchildren.

One of Valerie's most vivid memories of her early theatrical life is from Her First False Step when as a child she played the part of being in a cage with a real live lion. He was an old, tired and harmless animal and Valerie amused herself while in the cage scanning the audience to see if any women were fainting at the sight. This story continued to delight children of the next generation.

Eulalie continued in the limelight. She was blond, vivacious, with all the graceful attributes of femininity as well as voice. She had trained under Mrs. Letitia Barnum at Chicago Musical College. Among Eulalie's extensive theatrical appearances, in 1927 she was in Merry Malones with George M. Cohan in New York, and also in Melbourne and Sydney, Australia, where her singing of "The Easter Parade" is recalled. In Vincent Youman's Hit the Deck, a screen musical comedy starring Jack Oakie and Polly Walker, such songs as "Sometimes I'm Happy" and "Nothing Could Be Sweeter" are recalled. In 1926 it was Ziegfeld's Revue No Foolin' where Polly played the part of "Ellen Mackay." In 1924-25 she was in the Ziegfeld Follies.[1]

In 1935, Eulalie (Polly) married Dr. Frederick H. Moran; she forsook the stage, had a son, Bruce Walker Moran and lives with her family in Australia.

[1]Blum, Daniel, A Pictorial History of the American Theatre, 1900-1951, published by Greenberg, New York, New York, 1951, p. 181.

97. Eulalie and Valerie Walker. Courtesy Valerie Walker.

MILTON AGAR

Milton Agar was born in Chicago in 1893 and graduated from McKinley High School in 1910. He showed his musical and theatrical talent early when he wrote the scores for school productions such as My Sweet McKinley Girl. During his high school years, he was a piano player in the neighborhood movie theatres. This proved to be a preparation for correlating sound with silent action, even though at times it may have been monotonously repetitious.

In World War I, Milton Agar was with the United States Army Morale Department and wrote scores for musical comedies. Here again was a challenge; these helped the needs of the military, as well as widening the experience of the writer and composer for his later success. Among his earliest song hits was "Everything Is Peaches Down in Georgia."

In 1921 Bombo was a musical extravaganza by Sigmund Romberg which starred Al Jolson, while Milton Agar and Jack Yellen wrote the music and words for "Who Cares."[1]

In 1928 there was Rain or Shine, a musical comedy by James Gleason and Maurice Marks; lyrics by Milton Agar and Owen Murphy.[2]

In Chasing Rainbows (M.G.M. 1930), a screen play, Agar and Yellen wrote the well-known "Happy Days Are Here Again."[3]

Agar, Yellen and Borstein formed their own publishing house in 1922.

Later in Hollywood Agar wrote professionally for sound pictures such as King of Jazz, Chasing Rainbows and Honky Tonk. Among his many remembered songs are: "Happy Days Are Here Again," "Lovin' Sam," "Auf Widersehn, My Dear," "Crazy Words, Crazy Tune" and "If I Didn't Care." This last was made popular by the "Inkspots" quartet and has nostalgically lingered over the years.[4]

---

[1]Ewen, David, New Complete Book of the American Musical Theater, Holt, Rinehart and Winston, New York, 1970, p. 52.

[2]Ibid., p. 444.

[3]Ibid., 731.

[4]McNamara, Daniel Ignatius., Editor, The A.S.C.A.P. Biographical Dictionary of Composers, Authors and Publishers, 2nd Ed., Thomas Y. Crowell Co., Pub., N.Y., 1952, p. 5. Reprinted by permission of Mike Kerker, ASCAP-New York, One Lincoln Plaza, New York, New York 10023; 212-621-6000.

WALT DISNEY

A young genius who would come to Chicago and the old Mile Square was Walter Elias Disney. It would seem that in a short period of just one year his life's scholastic and pretechnical training would suffice to start him on a great adventure by the time he was eighteen years old.

Walt Disney was born in Chicago on December 5, 1901 at 1249 Tripp Avenue. His parents were Elias and Flora (Call) Disney and members of St. Paul's Congregational Church. The father was a carpenter who helped in the World's Fair of 1893 construction work and also built many houses in his own neighborhood.

When Walt was five years old the family moved to a farm in Marceline, Missouri. By 1910 they moved to Kansas City where the father had a Kansas City Star delivery service; both Walt and his brother Roy were delivery boys. Walt went to Benton Grammar School on the east side. In 1917 the family moved back to Chicago where the father was a maintenance man for a jelly factory located on Kedzie Avenue. Here young Walt worked after school peeling apples, nailing boxes and doing scullery work.

The Disney home during this miraculous educational period for Walt was at 1525 West Ogden Avenue near Madison Street. Walt went to McKinley High School as a freshman. There are many alumni of McKinley who remember Walt as a student there. The Disneys lived next door to the Crowther family on Ogden Avenue; Grace and Mary Crowther were friends of Walt and his sister Ruth; she used to practice on Crowther's piano. The girls and Walt walked a good six blocks to school each day, but Walt, then fifteen and bashful, preferred to walk behind the girls as they chatted within hearing distance from him. Walt's stern father practiced corporal punishment and this may have contributed to Walt's early timidity, but it had not harmed him in his later determined dexterity and creativeness.

Immediately Walt began his drawing profession at McKinley, becoming one of the artists on the staff for the school publication, Voice, the oldest printed magazine in Chicago's public schools. In seeing these fifty year old Disney drawings today, his composition ability is most apparent while his humor is his very own brand. Walt was generous with his drawings; across the classroom aisle from him, Rose Lipschuetz was to receive a drawing as a token of his admiration for her. Walt had many friends: the Youngsdahl family who had the jewelry store at Madison and Ogden, George Cooper, Jessie Howes, Evelyn Livingston and Walt's best friend, Russell Maas; all were McKinley students.

Of his many friends three stand out, Russell Maas, George Cooper and Walt's brother, Roy Disney. All three kept in touch with Walt through the years, perhaps Russell Maas was the closest, and they would be buddies in France later. George Cooper was a quiet person and a great confidant for Walt. Young Cooper kept a watchful eye on the boy's progress after he left McKinley High and often displayed the picture he carried in his wallet which Walt had given him.

In the meantime, George Cooper chose to work for the unfortunates in creating and managing a public library open both day and night in the old Halsted Street area where unfortunate transients from flop houses could browse. George in his study of humanity became a deacon in the Episcopal Church and sent all his personal belongings home to his mother's keeping. Among them was the prized Walt Disney picture. Somehow, as the belongings were distributed after the mother's sudden death, the snapshot of school boy Walt was lost, and George became a busy deacon at the Church of the Epiphany in the old Mile Square.

Of the later years of Russell Maas, it is told of one of their last visits together when Russell visited Walt in California. Here were two once poor, poor school boys - now they each had been successful business men and one had reached the millionaire's goal. Did it make any difference? No! Walt was still Walt and Russell was still the jolly Russell. While, of course, Roy Disney was always his young brother's confidant during those predestinating days in Kansas City, and later would be Walt's confidant in this huge Disney Land, which grew into the world's greatest amusement industry.

The expression "Life is earnest" truly fitted Walt Disney from his early searching days to his most creative career, which filled his life to the very end. Here in 1917 in Chicago, this boy worked twelve or more hours a day. Besides his high school classes he attended classes three nights a week at Chicago Academy of Fine Arts under the direction of Carl Wertz in the Willoughby Building. Here, young Disney studied from live models; in Kansas City at the Art Institute, he had attended Juvenile classes and drawn from plaster casts. His dream had started early. For cartoon technics at the Academy there was Leroy Gosset, a cartoonist on the Chicago Record; Carey Orr, a Tribune cartoonist, also taught there and made it possible for students to visit the Tribune's art department and watch cartoon making.[1] These technics were reflecting in Walt's cartoons for McKinley's Voice.

Besides day and night schools, Walt was earning his way. This meant work at the jelly factory, which was hard on artistic hands, or night watchman duty, which was not very restful. World War I was on and there were other jobs as the fury increased and young manpower left for "over there."

Walt, not yet seventeen, enlisted in the Red Cross Ambulance Corps along with his school buddy, Russell Maas. While the war had ended in November, 1918, there was still plenty to do over-seas; Walt spent eleven months in France. Business-like, he was sending home his pay and some of his luck in fellow gambling, so that later there would be funds for his life's work. While overseas, his active hands and humorous heart were busy with drawings on the sides of ambulances, foot lockers, helmets or camp posters.

Upon Walt's return to Chicago his father offered him a job in the jelly factory which he refused as he definitely wanted to be an artist. So the Chicago period was closed; school days were over and by eighteen years of age Walt was a commercial artist in Kansas City; an almost incredible life story would unfold from then on.

Walt Disney started with the idea of making motion pictures with a fresh cartoon for each movement of the character or object. He succeeded with his camera in making short animated cartoons which had a market in Kansas City. Soon the inspiration came - why use human

---

[1]Miller, Diane Disney, as told to Pete Martin, The Story of Walt Disney, Holt, New York, 1957, p. 41.

beings in cartoons, why not other characters as animals?[2] By 1923 Disney went to Hollywood determined to go into the motion picture industry.

From here on Walt Disney's life and works are so well known that the reader needs little retelling. Perhaps, a parade of some of his best loved characters or titles from cartoons and standard film productions which he created or revitalized will bring some nostalgic recall to many. This period starts with Mickey Mouse, the happy symbol for all Walt Disney Productions; it may be called a touchstone or good luck charm. The others fall in line in attempted chronological order; Silly Symphonies, Donald Duck, The Three Little Pigs, Snowwhite and the Seven Dwarfs, Ferdinand the Bull, Fantasia, Reluctant Dragon, Dumbo, Bambi, The Three Cabelleros, Cinderella, Alice in Wonderland, Sleeping Beauty, The Shaggy Dog, Darby, Toby Tyler, Babes in Toyland, Treasure Island and Davy Crockett.

We must not forget Walt Disney's early recognition of the nation's need for ecological awareness, as in Sea Island, Water Birds, The Living Desert and The Vanishing Prairie - all with superb regional scenery and animals in their natural habitats.

The creation of Disneyland near Los Angeles in 1954 as an amusement park was of the highest standards ever produced in America, as well as the dream of every child to visit. It was almost revolutionary when compared to the old tawdry, unsafe amusement parks which earlier young generations had known. Disney in the years which followed added new attractions but never has the standard of its moral, technical and creative qualities ever lessened. Closely following came the television program Walt Disney Presents every Saturday night, another beacon light for the nation's young audiences.

Before Walt Disney's death he had plans for a second amusement park in Florida. On October 1, 1971, this became a reality in Walt Disney World, near Orlando. It is a 27,400 acre park complete with five lakes, three golf courses, a 7,500 acre wildlife preserve, plus the town with its Main Street attractions and story book characters, not to mention all the rides and side shows.

The impetus of this organization, Walt Disney World, is so stupendous that the whole State of Florida has been given an incentive to clean up, paint up and be prepared to host millions of visitors, young and old, as they sight-see this whole wonderland state of Florida. A feeling of hope and happiness blots out some of the nation's depression in these befuddled days.

Walt Disney, self-educated, having only one year of combined high school and drawing instruction, possessed determination - a power of vision - which would lead him in all his pursuits. At his death he left a huge estate which would be the means for continuation of that vision. Half of his estate was

---

[2]Ibid., p. 74.

"to found a community of the performing arts - an institute where students could come as artists to learn from other accomplished artists in a less structured format than the university or the conservatory."[3]

Disney's heirs carried through his wishes, and thus was born the California Institute of the Arts. It is the most radical, large-scale experiment in the history of the creative arts,

"a school where musicians, film-makers, dancers, actors, painters, sculptors and designers interact and collaborate as part of their training."[4]

The campus of Cal Arts, as it is called, like Cal Tech, is thirty-five miles north of Los Angeles in Valencia, where a complex of workshops, studios, stages and galleries - all dubbed "Southern California Motel Modern" - accommodate 785 students and prominent faculty.

Cal Arts had an earlier period in 1955 when Chouinard Art Institute in Los Angeles was rescued from fiscal ruin by Walt Disney. Also, Los Angeles Conservatory of Music, founded in 1883, was in pecuniary trouble. The two schools joined forces, incorporating as California Institute of the Arts in 1961.

After Walt Disney's death on December 15, 1966, the new $28,000,000 campus of 600 acres was started. Dean Corrigan of New York University was to be president and chief administration officer and Dr. Herbert Blau of the Repertory Theatre of Lincoln Center was named provost and Dean of the School of Theatre and Dance.

By September, 1970 the faculty and students were ready but the Valencia campus was not, so temporary quarters were leased in the Villa Cabrini in Burbank.

As is the tendency in all advanced institutions today, especially, in such an arrangement as at Cal Arts, there was dissension among faculty and students which caused the Disney family great concern. After consultations of faculty, trustees and students, some of the "far out" actions were subdued. President Corrigan acknowledged "the program was too unstructured for new students who found freedom bewildering."[5]

After a year and a half on the Valencia campus the trustees were pleased with the student accomplishments. President Corrigan said that in music it was "equal to Juilliard, Eastman or Curtis;" in the theatre it was

---

[3]Gottschalk, Earl C. Jr., "Animating Disney's Dream," Saturday Review, January 29, 1972, p. 33.

[4]Ibid., p. 33.

[5]Ibid., p. 35.

""rich and exciting, similar in quality to NYU, Yale, and Carnegie Tech." Two of the three top prizes in the Los Angeles County Museum of Arts exhibit of young artists"[6]

went to Cal Arts students and the dance troupe won high praise at the Connecticut College annual dance festival. Corrigan summarized the situation:

"New York is the commercial capital of the arts, but the West Coast is the creative art capital. I believe the world is shifting from an East Coast - New York - Europe axis to a West Coast - Asian axis."[7]

Now, in the mid-seventies, the Disney traditions continue to expand. Having two successful Disney creations, Disneyland at Anaheim, California and Disney World, near Orlando, Florida, which children all over the world dream about seeing, there is now the possibility that such enchanted creations may be established in far-away Switzerland and Japan.[8]

In either case these Disney Lands would blend with the traditions and environments of those countries. Yet there would still be those American miracles of Mickey Mouse and his many friends, the junior episodes of space travel, and submarine adventure - all those magic exploits that the young in heart dream about. Just when such new developments will become a reality is unpredictable. Having had American scientists walk on the moon, those very young expect some equally thrilling adventures to evolve for them.[9]

Walt Disney in his theatrical profession was one of the most beloved and outstanding educators of young Americans of the twentieth century. Three universities gave him honorary Masters' Degrees - University of Southern California, Yale and Harvard.

Walt Disney died December 15, 1966. He is survived by his wife, Lillian Rounds Disney and their daughters, Diane, Mrs. Ron Miller and Sharon, Mrs. Robert Brown. A United States commemorative postage stamp was issued honoring this twentieth century genius. Today, Disneyland and Disneyland Presents,[10] the television program, now minus the presence of its beloved announcer, carry on, still maintaining the high quality always inherent in any Walt Disney production.

---

[6]Ibid.

[7]Ibid., p. 35.

[8]Editor's note: The openings of Disneyland in Anaheim, CA in 1955 and Disney World in Orlando, FL in 1971 were followed by Epcot Center and MGM in 1982 and 1989, respectively, in Orlando, Disneyland Tokyo in 1983 and Disneyland Paris in 1992 (World Book Inc., Vol. 21, Scott, Fetzer Co., Chicago, 1996, pp. 20-21).

[9]Robert Meyer, "Of Mice and Men," Mainliner, United Air Lines Magazine, March, 1974, p. 37-8.

[10]Editor's Note: The television show has been replaced by cable channels.

98. Cartoon by Walt Disney for Rose Slipschultz. From: McKinley High School *Voice*.

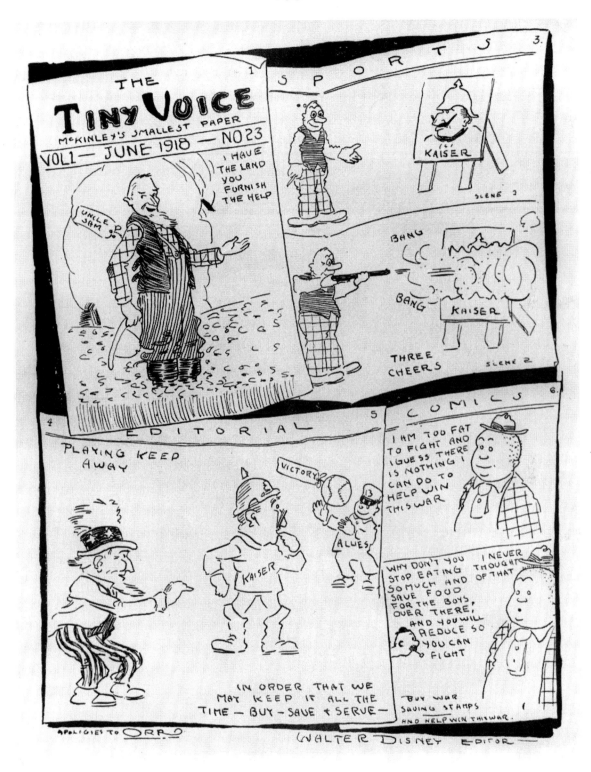

99. Cartoons by Walt Disney for "THE TINY VOICE, McKinley's Smallest Paper, Vol. 1--June 1918--No. 23." From: McKinley High School *Voice* (these also appeared in *Chicago American*, April 27, 1967).

GEORGE B. PETTY, JR.

George Brown Petty, Jr., Class of 1913 at McKinley High School, was an outgoing, talented student. In the 1913 Annual Voice's poll of "Why I Came to McKinley," George's answer was: "To sing and draw." That was an excellent epitome except that "and work" should have been included. He was born in Abbeyville, Louisiana, on April 27, 1894. The family moved to Chicago before George learned a southern accent and lived on Jackson Boulevard near Ashland. The father, George B. Petty, was president of the Progressive Portrait Company on Blue Island Avenue, and young George would learn many "tricks of the trade" from his father.

While at McKinley, he was staff artist for Voice. His figures then were mostly masculine for athletic events. He was on the basketball and track teams and is remembered as the school's first to jump over the bar with a body roll instead of a scissor's kick.

His first "Petty Girl" was not a drawing, but the lyric of My Sweet McKinley Girl for the 1912 Athletic Association Theatrical. The composer of the musical score was Milton Agar. The "Railroad Quartet" composed of Milton Agar, Rupert Purdon, Milton Zelotkoff and George Petty introduced the song hit. The chorus was:

"Girls from North Division
Girls from Englewood,
Girls from Wendell Phillips
Charm like no one could.
Girls from any high school
Keep me in a whirl -
But still you are my queen of queens
My sweet McKinley girl."

During these apparent carefree days, George was attending both Summer and Evening School at the Chicago Art Institute during the years of 1911 and 1912. The results of this art instruction were evident in his work on the Voice. For many years after the young artist had left McKinley, several of his drawings continued to be used in the Voice.

After high school days, George and his sister Bessie went to Paris to study. Bessie had graduated from McKinley and Northwestern University with honors and went on to the Sorbonne, the University of Paris; George entered the art school, Academe Julian. After an extended period abroad, he returned to Chicago and began his career in commercial art. He married Jule Donahue who became his first model for the evolving Petty Girl; later, when he was well established with studios in Northbrook, Illinois, his daughter Marjorie and son George became his models as well as critics.

The Petty Girl, a twentieth century girl, was to become as well known as the Gibson Girl of the gay nineties, yet they bore little resemblance to each other except that both were girls. This new creation was a blending of more erotic proportions than normal, and as such was appreciated by her admirers. Her limbs and torso were longer, bust more defined, shoulders broader and head smaller - today these qualities are associated with feminine fashion designs and sculptural studies. The old academic anatomical proportions had been the head as a ratio of one to seven with the rest of the body; Petty's ratio was about one to ten.

One of Petty's secrets for the success of the spicy personality and sex appeal of his girls was his technic of air brush painting. This put a third dimension on the girlish figure with accent in certain areas while the vibrant, clean colors produced sun-kissed tones. Besides her accentuated charms, she was happy and healthy looking. The poses, while voluptuous, could not be censored as indecent; she was often scantily clad but never obscene.

The Petty Girl was seen on calendars, in magazines such as Esquire and Life and various advertisements for beer and cigarettes. The wall calendars, issued each year with a girl for every month, provided the most popular pinup girl of the century, resulting in many later competitors. She was seen on walls in college dormitories, staid offices, over garage workbenches, ice cream parlors, and with our troops in Europe in World War II, as well as in jail cells and lonely lighthouses.

During those days of the 1930's and 1940's, George Petty's drawings were one of the few happy signs in American life which then was in a low key. First, there was a national depression with great unemployment and misery; then there were the devastating windstorms destroying thousands of acres of grain in the south central states; next came national Prohibition and the citizens' retaliatory attempts with home stills making "hooch," and finally, World War II was upon us with all its deprivations and a nation's sorrows.

In the bright side of that period was the Chicago World's Fair of 1933. Surprisingly, the Fair, even in the depths of the national depression, was carried over for a second year. George Petty's design for the official poster of the Century of Progress Exposition of 1933 in Chicago was chosen in a world-wide contest. It was a simple design - an Indian head with his feather headdress of 1833 and a classic feminine face of 1933 with an eaglet on her head while her hand beckons, Come! Chicago World's Fair.

During the years from 1936 to 1941, George Petty was an official judge for the Miss America beauty contest held in Atlantic City each September. He was always a good judge of bathing suit beauties since he drew them as advertisements for a leading bathing suit manufacturer for many years and the styles did change as more exposure was demanded on his models.

At the beginning of this century John D. Rockefeller gave an endowment of forty million dollars which was under the jurisdiction of the General Education Board of the Rockefeller Institute. The purpose: to promote education within the United States without distinction of race, sex or creed. This fund was used for various forms of education and carefully spent over a period of about forty years.[1]

In 1939 questionnaires had been sent to fifty-four of the country's leading art museums to ascertain their interest in collaborating with secondary schools in art education. As a result five museums were given a grant of $19,000 each for a three year collaboration project in the use of visual materials in education at the secondary level.

---

[1]Seybold, Geneva, compiler, American Foundations and Their Fields, Vth Edition, American Foundations Information Service, New York, 1942, pp. 84-85.

The museums chosen were: the Albright Art Gallery, Buffalo, N.Y., the Chicago Art Institute, the Cleveland Museum of Art, the Milwaukee Art Institute and the Museum of Modern Art, New York.[2]

Each of the five museums was chosen

> "because of some specific situation in the city or the school system or within the museum itself that seemed likely to provide marked variations in the conditions under which the experiment would be conducted. It was hoped that in this way several solutions might be found to similar problems."[3]

In the Chicago Project under the Chicago Art Institute and ten selected high schools there were some revealing preferences of the students over the three year period. With respect to paintings and their subjects, the students listed their preferences in this order:

> "landscapes, fashions, people, people doing things, and paintings that tell a story. Interest in subject matter decreased and awareness of aesthetic principles increased over the three year period."[4]

At the beginning of the testing 45 percent of the students indicated they had a favorite artist; by 1941 the positive response from these students had increased to 55 percent.

> "The favorite artist in eight of the ten schools tested was George Petty, and at no time was he given less than third place. The reasons given for this selection were: "It is so smooth, so slick - colors blend so well - looks real.""[5]

While most of these schools had murals and easel paintings by contemporary artists, at no time were there any other than Petty, Disney, Varga and Rockwell Kent mentioned as their favorites.[6]

This favoritism seemed to be contagious because the class of 1939 at Princeton University voted Petty's works first, Rembrandt's second, confessing a weakness for the Petty Girl.[7]

---

[2]Powel, Lydia, The Art Museum Comes to the School, Harper & Brothers, New York, London, 1944, pp. 5-6.

[3]Ibid., p. 6.

[4]Ibid., p. 64.

[5]Ibid., p. 64.

[6]Ibid., p. 64.

[7]"The Petty Girl, Triumph of Airbrush, is Feminine Ideal of American Men," Life, June 26, 1939, p. 34.

<u>The Art Museum Comes to the School</u> was a modern and generally successful experiment to integrate education in the related fields of art and their many contemporary forms with the guidance and inspiration found in the established art galleries of our country.

This was accomplished by means of exhibits held in the participating schools. The titles of projects studied were as youthful and modern as the students themselves. Examples were: "Ship models," "Streaming in Industrial Art," "Disney's Animated Cartoons," "Modern Housing Projects," "Contemporary Stage Design," "Art in Commerce," "Art in Home," "Oriental Arts and Crafts," "Athletics in Art," "Modern Textiles," "Modern Dress Design," "Functionalism in Furniture" and "Postimpressionist Painting."[8]

Simultaneously, efforts were made to introduce high school pupils to the conservative art galleries of the museums. Few of the above listed exhibits were to be found.

> "As a rule, wherever he looks, the same Madonnas and Romanesque carvings dominate the scene; the same dark-brown landscapes and solemn portraits; the same Greek vases and Chinese Buddhas. Fine as these are for the person of mature taste, they simply do not and cannot interest most high school students."[9]

This report was written in the World War II vintage. In the meantime the pendulum has flung to the extreme left of the dial for both young and mature artists while their works now hang in conventions alongside the galleries of the old masters. Today all galleries are visited and explored although the incentive for the students' visits may be the modern creations; still, the traditional works offer a quiet fascination which helps stabilize the questioning, unsure youth of today. This early project of the museum coming to the school continues to regenerate in these later years.

In those intervening years, while having plenty of poses waiting on his drawing board, George Petty became a big game hunter, going to Alaska and on African safaris in 1938. Among his trophies were a pair of elephant tusks weighing over two hundred pounds; lions, leopards and a rhinoceros were on his game list.[10]

In 1944 there was a sudden calamity, a casualty. Frank Walker, the United States Postmaster General, banned the Petty Girl from the mails! Was she obscene and were the school children, collegians or G.I.'s being demoralized?

George Petty recalls passing a second hand book store where there were two piles of old <u>Esquires</u> for sale. One pile was marked 15 cents each, the other 25 cents each. "Why the difference in price?" asked Petty. "The Petty Girl's been torn out," the dealer replied.[11]

---

[8]Powel, p. 152.

[9]Ibid., p. 153.

[10]<u>Life</u>, p. 34.

[11]Correspondence between George Petty and the author.

The Petty Girl became a live personification in 1950 when Columbia Pictures Corporation starred Joan Caulfield as The Petty Girl, based on an unpublished story of Mary McCarthy. The twelve months of a Petty calendar became twelve winsome varieties surrounding the Petty Girl.

Joan's qualifications, besides her glamorous self, were: height 5'5"; weight 110 pounds; bust 35-1/2"; hips 35-1/2"; hair honey blond and eyes blue. George Petty said that she was just what he meant all the time.[12]

Although there are at present Bunnies abounding in the glamorous Playboy Hotels, the original Bunny was the creation of George Petty and pictured in Life in June 26, 1939.

George B. Petty is still among us as his old patron, Esquire of October, 1971 invited the readers to a "Welcome Back to the 40's" by George Frazier.[13] Here all the nostalgic personalities and fetishes of that tragic period of the war years as well as the gay outposts are recalled. The Petty Girl swings across the magazine cover in her hammock of a two page spread while the viewer probably whistles or sighs. Inside the pages she chats gaily needing only her telephone.

Again in November, 1971 we find that haunting refrain, "One more tune, those good Old Forties' blues" in an article by Brock Brower[14] and the Petty Girl continues with her telephone ringing many old numbers.

Mr. Petty is now retired, living in California.[15] He mourns the fact that girls have slipped so far down on the list among the 150 million calendars now being circulated each year. When asked why that was the case, he indicated that everything must be shared with one's wife and children, so a man can no longer have his girl calendars.[16]

---

[12]Dimmitt, Richard Bertrand, A Little Guide to the Talkies, Scarecrow Press, New York, 1965.

[13]George Frazier, "Welcome Back to the Forties," Esquire, (A Special Eighteen Page Supplement) October, 1971, p. 98.

[14]Brower, Brock, "Play it Again, Sam, Bogie, Harry, Wendell and Claude," Esquire, November 1971, p. 120. Permission Brock Brower.

[15]Editor's Note: In an article published in 1983 (Derek Gill, "Was She Your Favorite Pinup?" Modern Maturity, June-July 1983, p. 77), Marjorie MacLeod, Petty's daughter, is quoted as saying that in 1973, not long before his death at 81, Petty, at the special request of Esquire's editors, painted one more Petty Girl: after cleaning out his airbrush, he drew her from memory, "but because it was now 40 years later, Dad painted her hair a dignified gray; and on her retrousee nose he placed a pair of granny glasses. The caption read, "When age shall this generation waste, the Petty Girl shall yet remain Man's friend.""

[16]"Where Are They Now?", Newsweek, January 4, 1965, p. 7. According to this article George Petty was 70 years old and living with his second wife (his wife Jule having died in Carmel, California) at that time.

100. Runner by George Petty. From: McKinley High School *Voice*.

101. George Petty at Easel. Used with permission of The Arizona Republic, Phoenix, Arizona.
Permission does not imply endorsement.

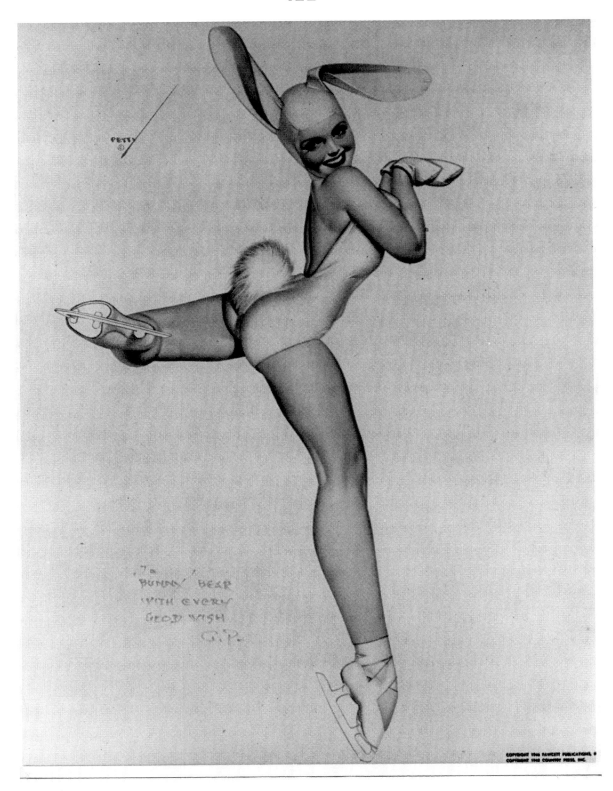

102. Petty Girl by George Petty sent "To Bunny Bear with every good wish G. P." Courtesy George B. Petty.

412

SAMSON RAPHAELSON

McKinley High School and its forebears seemed unusually productive of gifted students whose works blended with the allied brotherhood of musicians, singers, composers and writers. One student who would identify with the best in the field of modern light drama is Samson Raphaelson who graduated from McKinley in that famous class of 1914.

While at McKinley he showed his artistic leanings as staff artist of <u>Voice</u> as well as then being a literary contributor and member of the Irving Society, the debating club. The forecasting page for graduates in the 1914 McKinley <u>Annual</u> stated Samson intended to study illustrating. Like so many versatile artists he was then expressing his thoughts with both pen and brush. While the old maxim says the pen is mightier than the sword, one cannot declare it mightier than the brush. The pen became Samson's life vehicle for an amazing production of legitimate stage productions and motion pictures.

Samson Raphaelson was born in New York, March 30, 1896 to Ralph and Anna (Marks) Raphaelson. Young Samson and his family came to Chicago in 1907 and lived at 614 South Hermitage Avenue. His father was a designer and partner in a cap-making establishment.

After graduation from high school Samson had a trial and error period for several years working days at Sears and Roebuck as a correspondent, followed by a short period with City News Service. In the meantime at night he was writing short stories and getting them all back from the publishers.

One day he had a "personal letter of encouragement (but no purchase) from John M. Siddall, editor of the <u>American Magazine</u>."[1] Samson took the hint: more preparation - and crammed almost two years of college work in his freshman year at Lewis Institute under the kind, shepherding help of Dr. Edwin H. Lewis, head of the English Department.

Dr. Lewis was a patron saint for many Lewisonians. He had the uncanny power of sensing what his disciple or student needed most. Perhaps no teacher at Lewis was more loved and revered than Dr. Lewis. The professor saw promise in Samson's writing and he also noted that his student needed financial help. As in the case of an earlier promising writer at Lewis Institute, Arthur Krock, Dr. Lewis also gave Samson the editorship of the <u>Lewis Annual</u> which carried a stipend as well as being excellent training in publication management. While at the Institute, Samson added his bit of hero worship of Dr. Lewis in the 1914 <u>Annual</u> with this poem:

"A Free-hand Tribute to Doctor Lewis

> He is a big man -
> About six and a half feet
> In height and may be three or
> Four feet the other way.

---

[1]Correspondence between Samson Raphaelson and the author.

If he were as big as his
Heart he would have the United
States for a
Backyard.

He is a big man -
If he were as big as his understanding
He would live on 'Lympus

He is a big man -
If he were as big as
The gratitude of the hundreds
Whom he taught to
Love life he
Would straddle the world.

He is a big man -
If he were as big as he things himself little
It would take the light
Of the stars
A minute to reach him.

He is a big man -"

After his year at Lewis Institute Samson went to the University of Illinois and received his B.A. degree there in 1917. While at the University he married Rayna Simons who also graduated from McKinley; this marriage ended in an early divorce. Rayna became a Communist and went to China to work for that cause with the Soong sisters. Then on to Moscow where she was stricken fatally ill and was buried with Communist honors.

Vincent Sheean, then a young reported abroad, had tried to convince her to return to America, but without success. Her career is told in Vincent Sheean's Personal History.[2]

After graduation from the University, Samson plunged into his writing. He became an instructor in English at the University of Illinois in 1920-21. In 1927 he married Dorothy Wegman and there were two children, Joel and Naomi. Samson Raphaelson's works started with his short story writing in 1915; his legitimate stage play writing started around 1925 and led into screen writing by 1929. After a period abroad he settled in Hollywood where many of his films were reproduced.

---

[2]Sheean, Vincent, Personal History, Literary Guild, N.Y., 1934-35 (her name at this time was Rayna Prohme; her career is recounted from pages 192-398).

Among more than a score of his best known works, many of which were first played on the legitimate stage and then made into motion pictures, were The Jazz Singer, Lady in Ermine and Accent on Youth. The latter was included in The Best Plays of 1934-5 by Mantle Burns; also included were the Skylark, a novel, in the 1939-40 edition, and Jason in the 1941-42 edition. His Perfect Marriage, 1944, was included in Martha Foley's Best American Short Stories.

Other very successful works were his films of Trouble in Paradise (1932 - Paramount), Heaven Can Wait (1943 - Fox), Green Dolphin Street (1943 - M.G.M.), The Merry Widow (1952 - M.G.M.) and Hilda Crane (1956 - Fox).[3]

In 1956 Samson Raphaelson was visiting Professor of Creative Writing at the University of Illinois. While teaching this course in an informal procedure, a complete record was kept of this experiment and published in The Human Nature of Playwriting. In simple words his students were encouraged to use ideas for a play from their personal backgrounds. They were not attempting autobiographical studies but youthful experiences which could be elaborated into full multiple act plays.

Most were true life experiences of his students, some possibly exaggerated or consciously fabricated - hiding reality which could have become sparkling drama. In teaching his students of his own play writing he encouraged a confidential rapport among the students and the professor.

Samson Raphaelson is now retired, living in New York but still has his finger on the pulse of life and drama of today.[4]

---

[3]Rigdon, Walter, Ed., The Biographical Encyclopedia of Who's Who in the American Theater, James H. Heinman, N.Y., 1966, p. 761.

[4]Editor's Note: Samson Raphaelson died July 16, 1983. His obituary notice appeared in Contemporary Authors, Vol. 110, Gale Research Company, The Book Tower, Detroit, Michigan, 1984, p. 146.

415

PHYLLIS A. WHITNEY

The age-old tales of a fairy godmother or a guardian angel helping an orphaned child have appeared in folklore and classic literature through the centuries. In a philosophical definition, perhaps the "divinity which shapes our ends," or the genie, is a faith, a stroke of luck or just plain inspired perseverance. Under any title the literary success of Phyllis A. Whitney is that of "the orphan who made good."

Phyllis A. Whitney graduated from McKinley High School in 1924, then one of its honored students. Her earlier life is a complete story in itself. She was born September 9, 1903 in Yokohama, Japan, where her father, Joseph C. Whitney, was employed by an American steamship company, and her mother, Lillian Mandeville, went to Japan to marry him. Phyllis would be given the middle name of "Ayame," meaning iris in Japanese.

Perhaps this name had both a good as well as sad omen since this lovely flower, named after the Greek goddess of the rainbow and used for centuries by both the French and English in their heraldic fleur-de-lis, was also used by the Mohammedans as an expression of sadness in their cemeteries.

The Whitney family next lived in the Phillipines at Manilla. After seven years there, they moved to Kobe, Japan where Phyllis attended a Canadian Methodist school for foreign children. Next, the family moved to Hankow, China and the child attended a missionary school in the mountains above the Yangtze River. Her father died in Hankow and the mother and daughter returned to United States, living in Berkeley, California. Here the school girl had her seventh and eighth grades trying to compensate for her earlier schooling deficiency.

Their next move was to San Antonio, Texas where Phyllis had her first year of high school at Alamo Heights in 1921. Here she won her first silver medal in a state-wide essay contest and also a bronze medal for a declamation contest, the best in Bexar County, Texas. Her life then was on the upward swing until her mother died that year in Texas and the orphaned girl came to Chicago to live with her aunt, Mrs. Nagashio who had an ice-cream parlor, magazine and candy store on Van Buren Boulevard between Winchester and Lincoln[1] Streets. This location would begin the second chapter of an orphan's life which would be as full of surprises, some up, some down, just as the fictional stories she would later write for a national reading audience.

Here, living in the McKinley High School district, Phyllis began her sophomore year. She felt a sympathetic welcome there, a parental as well as scholastic interest by the faculty and a jolly, competitive friendliness among the students who then were predominantly Italian and Jewish at McKinley. Like earlier generations of West Division and McKinley students, she had those same perennial and beloved teachers as Mr. Brimblecom, Miss Lucy Wilson, Mlle. Josephine Mack and her favorite, Miss Mae Pruner, who taught English and helped Phyllis to start writing seriously.

Her home on Van Buren, a noisy commercial street, was in great contrast to her homes in the Orient where rainy seasons, typhoons, earthquakes, river travel in small boats and sedan

[1]Editor's Note: Lincoln was later renamed Wolcott.

chair rides up the mountains which were all part of her far east memories. Her more recent green vistas of California and Texas were also still vivid. Now on Van Buren, living in a small apartment of the store managed by her aunt, the "L," the elevated railroad, rumbled outside her bedroom window and the winters were cold and windy.

However, the candy, ice-cream and magazine store was well located to serve the students from the neighboring schools as Marquette and the medical schools. This store probably was to these persons what Speakman's Book Store in the neighborhood had been to several generations of students.

Among the neighbor students in Phyllis's generation was Victoria Chiappe whose father had a cigar factory across the street from the candy store. The girls would become intimate, life-long friends.

While at McKinley, Phyllis wrote for the Voice during her three years there, rising from contributor to Literary Editor and finally, Editor-in-Chief. In the 1924 Annual there were two of her stories, typical high school ideas of humor as "Mad Melody" by Willis Fitney. On the more serious side she was also Class Poet. In the Class Prophecy it was printed: "Phyl Whitney, author of genius and fame. Has added great prestige to her name." How true a prophecy!

Then followed a period of transition; there was no money for college. Phyllis worked in the juvenile department of the Chicago Public Library; later in Womrath's Library in the Stevens Building. She married George Garner, also from McKinley. In the meantime she continued sending in her efforts to good quality magazines, only to receive rejection slips. Her first break was a story for Chicago Daily News fiction section of the Sunday edition. Pulp and lesser publications began accepting her efforts and she was kept busy.

In 1941 her first book, A Place for Ann, was published; this was a novel for teenagers. Other books for the youthful world would follow. In 1947, Willow Hill won the Reynal and Hitchcock Award of $3,000 in the Youth Today Contest. This was one of the early books on inter-racial problems faced by young people. In 1963, another honor was the Sequayah Award of Oklahoma for the Best Juvenile Mystery of the Year, Mystery of the Haunted Pool. Mystery Writers of America give Edgars instead of Oscars; in 1960, Mystery of the Haunted Pool and Secret of the Emerald Star in 1964, received Edgars.

Besides stories for juveniles, Miss Whitney is probably best known for her adult Gothic novels. Such works refer to types such as the Brontes wrote in Jane Eyre and Wuthering Heights, also Rebecca by Daphne Du Maurier. Among Miss Whitney's Gothic novels are Listen to the Whisperer, Thunder Heights, Road to Manderley and Snowfire. She has written over fifty books and all but five are currently in print.

Time Magazine in 1971 had an article on the Gothic novel which today has many well known writers, many of whom have characteristics in common in their personal lives and also identify with the heroines of their books. First, their props or incentives in the novel are a naive girl such as a governess, nurse or secretary; then a ghostly or ancestral house, perhaps located in Wales, Scotland or Ireland, even in Greece, Lebanon or Australia. According to the writer, it is not as if these ingredients were conjured up with premeditation. Top genre writers, such as Phyllis Whitney and Victoria Holt, identified not only with their heroines, but also with their audiences. Thus it is not completely a coincidence that numerous writers of Gothic stories, just like the Bronte sisters, were the products of lonely, isolated childhoods which permitted ample time for fantasizing.[2]

Besides continuously writing during the earlier years, Miss Whitney was also teaching, first at Medill School of Journalism of Northwestern University in 1944-5 as instructor in children's writing, and then at New York University in the same subject from 1947 to 1958. She was also children's book editor for Chicago Sun from 1942-1946 and for Philadelphia Inquirer, 1947-8. In a word, this author has always kept young in heart. Mystery books in the juvenile field are her specialty and Gothic novels are a close runner up.

In private life she is Mrs. Lowell F. Jahnke. There are a daughter and three grandchildren. Our author lives with her husband on Jenny Jump Mountain surrounded by woodlands and with a view of the Delaware Water Gap. All of which has a mysterious ring and must be inducive for good stories, just as Washington Irving found Icabod Crane in Legend of Sleepy Hollow, somewhere in those magic mountains of our eastern states.

Perhaps the best story which has evolved in the fruition of this writer's life is that of the orphan child who through her good works has acquired thousands of younger brothers and sisters as well as many others among the older kinfolk.[3]

---

[2]Duffy, Martha, "On the Road to Manderley," Time Magazine, Book Section, August 12, 1971, pp. 95-96.

[3]Editor's Note: The 1993 edition of Gorton Carruth's Young Readers Companion, R. R. Bowker, A Reed Reference Publishing Co., New Providence, NJ, pp. 627-628, describes Phyllis Whitney as still actively writing; her most recent children's book is The Singing Stones, 1990, and is about a child psychologist's adventures in the Blue Ridge Mountains of Virginia.

103. Phyllis A. Whitney. Courtesy of Ken Bennett; © 1989 by Ken Bennett.

CHAPTER ELEVEN: NEIGHBORHOOD PRIVATE AND PAROCHIAL SCHOOLS AND OTHER PUBLIC SCHOOLS

EARLY PRIVATE AND PAROCHIAL SCHOOLS AND OTHER PUBLIC SCHOOLS

Through the years there were small private schools or classes such as kindergarten, dancing, painting (both oil and china) and music groups as well as more permanently organized grammar and preparatory schools. As more and better graded public schools were built, the private schools dwindled away. Brooks School had the longest existence.

Carter H. Harrison II recalled several of these schools where he spent brief interludes in his education. One was Miss Gregg's School for Girls on Sheldon Street where small boys would also be accepted; another, now nameless, was on Madison and Laflin. Then there was Bell's School at Sheldon and Lake Streets conducted by John A. Bell, a Scott, who believed strongly in corporal punishment:

> "...no morning was complete unless the rattan was wrapped around at least one youngster's legs."[1]

Here in this Dickensonian atmosphere, young Carter studied the three R's from 1868 to 1873. He noted that half of the boys who attended were discards for bad conduct from Brown or Skinner Schools.[2]

In fact, young Carter attended Brown School for a few weeks in 1868, but because he feared the sternness of the principal there he settled for Bell's School as the lesser of the two evils. Also, Bell's School was not far away from his country-like home at 163 Ashland Avenue where his father, the Mayor, and his mother, the "mayoress," entertained with a panorama of sights, sounds and good tasting foods.

Brooks School was founded by a one time Miss Brooks whose portrait hung for years in the classroom and suggested nothing of the glamorously feminine Miss Brooks as created for radio and television scholars. The building and staff accommodated about seventy-five students ranging from kindergarten through high school and existed for about forty years. Two of the faculty over that period were principals, Miss Effie A. Gardener and Miss Eugenia Chaffin. Brooks School occupied several locations over the years; one of the last was conducted in the

---

[1]Harrison II, Carter H., Stormy Years: The Autobiography of Carter H. Harrison Five Times Mayor of Chicago, Bobbs-Merrill Co., Indianapolis and New York, 1935, p. 20.

[2]Harrison II, Carter H., Growing Up With Chicago, Ralph Fletcher Seymour, Chicago, IL, 1944, p. 32.

Fourth Baptist Church at Ashland and Monroe.

Among some of the children living in the neighborhood over that span of years who attended Brooks School were: William and Ellen Conlon, Charles Anderson, Julia and Josephine Dole, Blanche and Charlotte Plamandon, Hazel Kircksberg, George Salisbury, the Wheeler children, Malcolm, Ralph, Virginia and Annabel; also, the Evans sisters, Ruth, Edith and Marian. This school was quiet and conservative with earnest students who had little communication with the public school pupils in the neighborhood.

There were three parochial schools in the Mile Square: St. Jarlath's on Jackson Boulevard and Wood Street, St. Patrick's Academy on Washington and Oakley Boulevards, and St. Malachy's, also at Washington and Oakley.

At first, St. Jarlath's School was under the Dominican Order of Sisters, some of whom were Sister Domitalla, Sister Phillipa and Sister Leo. Later, lay teachers augmented the faculty. At one period the student enrollment was near 800 students. As the congregation of St. Jarlath's Church decreased in these late years the school was closed and the parish dissolved. In September 1969, the Chicago archdiocese ordered the demolition of the beautiful eighty-five year old church and one more of the few remaining landmarks of the old Mile Square vanished; the reason given was that the buildings had "given way to the problems of age."

As the last material treasures of deceased persons are of interest to those who have come later, so the contents of the customary "box" entombed in the corner stone of St. Jarlath's were of interest to the later generations. Among the items, a copy of The Tribune carried news of 1869 which included drownings, murders, political news and advertisements. One of the latter items still brings a smile:

> "Many people think the delegates to the National Republican convention are coming here to nominate a candidate for the Presidency. The fact is that's only one of the things. The greatest thing is to rejoice over the grand success of the "Police Plug," a new brand of chewing tobacco."[3]

In the earlier years, from 1921 to 1968, a much loved priest served St. Jarlath's parish, Father Thomas Bernard O'Brien; he was also famous for his humor and was a true son of Ireland, being born in Tipperary. Father John Gallery, a later priest in a Chicago church and brother of Admiral Daniel Gallery, has in recent years been gathering all the anecdotes and witty sayings of the Venerable Father O'Brien.[4]

Among the many Mile Square pupils who attended St. Jarlath's school were Agnes Delany, Mary Baker and the two Wathier sisters. It was these sisters that Father Gallery approached for his O'Brien mission.

St. Patrick's Academy for girls and small boys was established in 1883 at Park Avenue and Oakley Boulevard in the St. Malachy's parish. Later in 1910, the Academy flourished at the

---

[3]Chicago Tribune, Vol. 23, No. 136, Saturday, Nov. 13, 1869.

[4]Correspondence between Father O'Brien and the author.

corner of Washington and Oakley in a woodland setting. This was now a boarding school for boys and girls in the grammar grades; day students were also accepted. The Order of the Sisters of Mercy was cloistered in the convent of this beautiful park-like region. Admiral Daniel Gallery was a student there and later at St. Malachy's. While the school was predominantly Catholic, there were also Protestant pupils. Among the latter was Isabelle Walker who fondly recalls both the Sisters and Daniel Gallery. St. Patrick's Academy was closed several years ago and sold to Rush-Presbyterian-St. Luke's Medical Center for the development of the Mile Square Medical Center, then located in temporary buildings. It is now demolished.

St. Malachy's School has a long and continuous history since 1884. It was first located at the corner of Western Avenue and Walnut Street where the church and rectory were built in 1882. In 1910 property was purchased at the corner of Oakley and Washington Boulevards, where a new St. Malachy's Church and School were built. In 1929 an addition to St. Malachy's facing Washington Boulevard was dedicated by George Cardinal Mundelein, Archbishop of Chicago. Until 1971 sisters formerly from St. Patrick's Academy taught at St. Malachy's School. Father Richard J. Ehrens is in charge of both the school and the parish church. The school is composed of 230 boys and girls from first through the eighth grade.

Two other grammar schools as well as Brown School served the Mile Square and beyond that area: Marquette School at Harrison and Wood and Grant School at Campbell and Monroe.

Marquette School, named after the explorer, Father Jacques Marquette, was built in 1879 and was surrounded by medical neighbors, Rush Medical College and College of Physicians and Surgeons being on either side of the school. A new Marquette School was built on the southwest side of Chicago and the old Marquette was disbanded as a public school in 1918. For a while the Illinois Emergency Relief Commission used the building as an infirmary. Later the building was razed to make way for the new Eisenhower Expressway.

Four principals served Marquette from 1879 to 1918: Frank B. Williams, George H. Rockwood, Charles W. Minard and Mary E. Tobin.

Grant School, named after General Ulysses S. Grant, grew with the increased population flow westward. The first building was in 1885 followed by two additions in 1913 and 1925. Its roster of principals from 1886 to 1956 have been: Mary E. Smyth, Sarah A. Kirkley (member of the Kirkley family also taught at Brown School), Marguerite L. O'Brien, Wilbur E. Wright, Sophia Schmidt, George Olson, Edna M. Siebert and Ione A. Foster.

While both Marquette and Grant were large buildings and built years after Brown School, neither had accommodations for teaching domestic science. Each week a class of girls from Marquette and Grant would have a long walk, almost a mile, to Brown School for the half day session in cooking class. On cold days this could be an ordeal but most of the time the girls enjoyed these brisk walks to Brown and back to their mother school. While there was some fraternizing with Brown School students, there were few opportunities as class periods were well regulated for all concerned.

CRANE HIGH SCHOOL

When the new structure at Oakley and Van Buren was built in 1903 it was first known as English High and Manual Training School; this insignia was engraved over the main entrance. The title was then currently changed to Richard T. Crane Manual Training School and in 1908, changed again to Richard T. Crane Technical High School. To all its students and friends the title would be shortened to "Crane Tech."

The parent and original school, English High and Manual Training School (for boys) was started in 1886 with classes in drawing held in the Chicago High School at Monroe and Halsted. By 1890 it was an independent school with classes in the old normal school building, part of Old Central, formerly Chicago High School; the principal was James E. Claflin.

At this period of American public school education, especially in the large cities, a great percentage of the pupils were foreign-born or first generation Americans and needed practical training in subjects which would help them in American industry. The classical training as given at Old Central High School in Greek, Latin and other languages, English literature, history and mathematics was not sufficient for these pupils.

The new school offered:

> "The three year course of study was to be confined to the English language, "half the studies to be purely mental and half to the education of the hand and the eye"... "the main purpose of the school is not the mere economic success of the pupil, but it is to employ these processes to build up in the pupils a manly, self-reliant character and a disposition to work, to render services to the community and to do it in an intelligent and manly way.""[1]

Crane Tech continued for fifty years under the successive principals, Albert R. Robinson, William J. Bartholf, Henry H. Hagen, Roy F. Webster, Leo R. Klinge, and Neal Duncan. In 1922 a new building was added to Crane on Jackson and Oakley.

By September 1954 Crane Tech became Crane High School at which time girls were first enrolled. With plans formed in 1971, Crane High School will be enlarged and be part of a new cultural educational-cluster concept for the Near West Side Area under the Board of Education and the Public Building Commission. This great wave of the future is discussed in a later chapter of this book.

---

[1]"Crane 6A Class to Give Dinner for Bartholf - Banquet is Testimonial to Long Service," Chicago Sunday Tribune, Metropolitan Section, W--, Sunday, December 15, 1929, p. 4.

104. English High and Manual Training School. The building in the foreground was the "original" building erected in 1903; the building of lighter construction was connected to it in 1922. A Chicago Public Schools photograph. Courtesy Chicago Board of Education Library.

HOMER J. LIVINGSTON, a graduate of Crane Tech

A neighborhood boy who "made good," as the cliche goes, and was an example of the time-proven maxim, "Where there's a will, there's a way," was Homer J. Livingston. In his continuous uphill climb he became the chief executive of the First National Bank and Trust Company of Chicago.

Homer J. Livingston was born in Chicago, August 30, 1903; his parents were John C. and Evelyn (Davis) Livingston; his sisters were Edith (Mrs. Carlson) and Evelyn (Mrs. George Hartford). The father was well known in the Mile Square, having a warehouse and moving business for over forty years on Madison Street near Damen.

The family's home for many years, until they moved to Austin, was on Washington Boulevard near Seeley; all the children went to Grant Grammar School and attended the Church of the Epiphany on Ashland and Adams. Here, Homer was in the boys' choir and an acolyte, while his sister, Evelyn, was in the St. Cecelia Choir for girls.

Homer graduated from Crane "Tech" in 1920. While there he played on the basketball team and was a fast player; so much so that he was nicknamed "Jupiter." Even in grammar school, Homer started earning his way, first as a delivery boy, and later working in a machine shop where he earned $10.00 a week for a ten hour day and a six day week.[1]

After graduating from Crane he worked days in the Post Office in the finance department while attending John Marshall Law School at night. In 1922, the turning point in his life was a telephone call from Edward Eagle Brown of the First National Bank to the dean of John Marshall Law School. The future chairman of the bank asked for a senior student to serve in the bank's law department on a temporary basis. The dean of John Marshall replied: ""The best man in the school is in the second year"... He was referring to" Homer Livingston.[2]

On December 26, 1922, the young law student was interviewed by Mr. Brown and was accepted ""on a temporary basis" at $100" per month. After that date his success story kept accelerating. In 1924, Homer Livingston received his law degree from John Marshall Law School and was admitted to the Bar in 1925; in 1930 he was the Bank's assistant attorney; in 1934, its attorney. He helped in preparing the Chandler Act, a federal law dealing with corporate reorganization, in 1938.[3] In 1944 he became counsel, and in 1945, vice-president, of the bank.[4] By 1950 he was president of the First National Bank and Trust Company of Chicago.

---

[1]"H. J. Livingston Dies at 66; Bank Figure," <u>Chicago Tribune</u>, Sunday, May 10, 1970, Section 1, p. 3.

[2]Ibid.

[3]Ibid.

[4]Ibid.

At that time, he was 46 years old, one of the youngest men ever to hold this post in a major banking institution. Ten years later he became chairman of the board.[5]

During these years he would often arrive at his well-appointed office in the old bank building at 6:30 or 7:00 in the morning. He said he needed only about five hours of sleep at night.[6]

Besides his professional life he served on boards of directors of other corporations.[7] Three of his altruistic interests were as trustee of the University of Chicago, as a trustee and treasurer of the Chicago Art Institute, and as director of the Chicago Boys' Club.[8] After his retirement in 1969 he had the satisfaction of seeing the new First National Bank Building completed - a six year, 110 million dollar project. It looms today as a glistening shaft or pillar on Chicago's skyline. The retired executive once wrote that while

"a banker's prime responsibility is to safeguard depositors' funds, changing times also required that banks become more extensive financial "shopping centers.""[9]

Homer J. Livingston died May 9, 1970; surviving him are his wife, Helen Henderson Livingston; a son, Homer, Jr., who is a vice-president of the First National Bank; two grandchildren and two sisters.[10]

---

[5]"Services Set Today for H. J. Livingston," Chicago Tribune, May 11, 1970, p. 41.

[6]Wiener, Leonard, "Homer Livingston mourned by Treasury chief," Chicago Daily News, May 11, 1970, p. 41. As published in the Chicago Daily News. Copyright 2005. Chicago Sun-Times, Inc. Reprinted with permission.

[7]Ibid.

[8]Chicago Tribune, May 10, 1970, p. 3.

[9]Wiener, p. 41.

[10]Chicago Tribune, May 10, 1970, p. 3; Weiner, p. 41.

105.   Homer J. Livingston, President First National Bank of Chicago.   Courtesy Homer J. Livingston.

CHAPTER TWELVE: LEWIS INSTITUTE, FACULTY AND DISTINGUISHED ALUMNI

LEWIS INSTITUTE AND ITS FACULTY

In 1896 a new educational institution, Lewis Institute, opened in the vicinity of the Brown School. It was a gift from the estate of Allen Cleveland Lewis, an early Chicagoan. The school was located on Madison Street between Winchester and Robey. It consisted of two connected five story stone structures, one devoted to engineering workshops and laboratories; the other housed an auditorium, gymnasiums, classrooms and laboratories. The ground floor had a branch of the Chicago Public Library and stores.

The original gift of Allen Lewis in 1877 was $550,000. The terms of the will were specific: the estate must increase to $800,000 before a school was built. In the lapse of eighteen years before charter and first building were in progress, the goal had doubled to $1,600,000. The nucleus of the original sum had been willed by his brother John in 1874. Both men had discussed their interest in the needs of boys who had to leave school at an early age to work. Allen Lewis made several trips to Europe to study school systems before making his will which proved to be written with caution and vision.

A school was created under able trustees which offered a two year college course leading to an Associate in Arts degree, a four year curriculum in Engineering and Domestic Economy leading to bachelors' degrees, and an Academy covering four years of high school. Besides, the will stipulated that opportunities for evening classes be made available to those employed during the day, and also that a free reading room be established for the public. The will stressed

> "courses of a kind and character not generally taught in public schools... studies that would be directly useful to students in obtaining a position or occupation for life."

In this respect, evening classes at Lewis Institute were the forerunner of adult education in United States. As well as helping a delayed occupational education, one could return to school for the love of learning.

The degree in Domestic Economy interpreted the will "...a school for respectable females," with courses in the arts and sciences in preparation for both homemaking and teaching. The course known as "Household Management" was found by the Home Economics section of the Bureau of Education at Washington to have been the first evolved and was taught at Lewis Institute in the early 1900's.[1] The School of Engineering had been specified in the will:

---

[1]Kaufman, Agness, "Lewis Institute," Illinois Technical Engineer, Chicago, Illinois, Vol. 12, No. 2, Dec., 1946, p. 18.

"the establishment and maintenance of a Polytechnic School, second to none, though in no way was this school to interfere with the school for females."

At this early period, Mr. Lewis envisioned a machine age forthcoming and left no restrictions on developing this school.

The trustees called upon such educational leaders as Dr. William Rainey Harper of the new University of Chicago and Dr. James Angell of Michigan to help select faculty for this last word in buildings and equipment. Dr. George Noble Carman became Director and Dr. Edwin H. Lewis was Dean, two of Lewis Institute's most beloved men.

In the school's second year, leaders met in the auditorium to establish educational standards which resulted in forming the North Central Association of High Schools and Colleges; Lewis was always on its accredited list. There were practical methods introduced: the lunch room was under the direction of home economics classes; a cooperative course for high school boys permitted them to serve as apprentices in industry. With a dedicated faculty of thirty five in 1897, it grew to over fifty by 1911. The two year college course is now considered to have been the first junior college in the United States.

As an Academy student at Lewis Institute, I recall exceptionally cooperative relations between classes and various departments. Two examples were from a physics class under Professor Wade. When the subject of light was studied, we each constructed a sundial with its gnomon; these metallic parts had been made in an engineering foundry course in sufficient quantity for our class. In the subject of electricity, after calculating the volts, watts and amperes, we wired a hot plate which rested in a glazed ceramic cradle, thanks to the pottery class in the art department. The little stove went through college dormitory days and even later warmed the baby's bottle.

Classes at Lewis were relaxed and friendly; some were conducted like round table seminars. Caesar was lively under beloved George Lee Tenney who was professor of Latin, director of glee clubs and director of men's athletics. (Imagine a public school teacher having three such assignments.) We explored Latin in its doggerel as well as Gregorian forms when we sang ancient carols and chorals. The association between collegians and academicians was tolerant and shared. The social life was gay and chaperoned under the then prevailing standards. There were fraternities and sororities which were under faculty advisors and most activities were after school hours. There was rivalry for scholastic attainment and each organization had an altruistic pursuit. There were well organized dramatic, science, literary, language and glee clubs. Sports including tennis, and inter-school football and basketball games followed the school year.

Many of the faculty gave all their teaching years to Lewis Institute. Among those were Director George N. Carman, Dean Edwin H. Lewis, Mlle. Lea De Lagneau, Hector Trowbridge, Fred Rogers, Warren Smith, George Tenney, "PB" Kohlsaat, Herbert Cobb, Marie Blanke, Charles Peet, John Smale, Jesse Owen and Agness Kaufman. These names were familiar to more than 100,000 students who had passed through the doorway marked Science, Literature, Technology.

All the Lewis Institute faculty meant "many things to many people;" perhaps the most outstanding professor over a period of forty years was Dr. Edwin Herbert Lewis. He was born in Westerly, R.I., November 28, 1866. He was educated in eastern schools and received his

Ph.D. in English from the University of Chicago in 1894. He taught at this university from 1893 to 1899; he then began teaching at Lewis Institute and continued as Dean of the Faculty until his death in 1938.

Besides being an author of many English textbooks, he wrote such novels as Those About Trench, 1916, White Lightning, 1923 and Sallie's Newspapers, 1924; he also had published poetry.

The relationships at Lewis Institute between faculty members and their students were sympathetic and reciprocal. One such incident was the lifelong friendship of Dr. Edwin H. Lewis and Dr. Ethel Percy Andrus. It began when she was a student at Lewis and received her Associate of Arts degree, followed by her Bachelor of Philosophy degree from the University of Chicago in 1903. She then returned to Lewis Institute as a fledgling instructor in English and taught until 1910. It was Dr. Lewis's inspiring example which led her to choose a teaching career. While at Lewis Institute, Ethel Andrus reflected that famous Lewis ardor in her teaching and student relations. In 1910, she and her family moved to California; in 1916, she became principal of Abraham Lincoln High School in Los Angeles, the first woman principal in a California high school. The 1916 Lewis Annual reported her as "the most popular teacher in California."

Through the years, there were honors and degrees for her; a Bachelor of Science from Lewis Institute in 1918; a Master of Arts in 1928 and a Doctor of Philosophy in 1930, both from the University of Southern California. Dr. Andrus carried on as an active alumna of Lewis Institute and friend of Dr. Lewis. It was the California alumni who presented to Lewis Institute, at the 1936 Alumni Reunion, a bronze replica of the distinguished Dr. Lewis. Ethel Percy Andrus wrote the verses for the occasion.

TO YOU, LEWIS INSTITUTE, GREETINGS!

"From California your alumni send you love
        And a gift, rich, rare and precious
Molded out of grateful pride and cast in bronze.

We send you now, as honoring ourselves
        A replica of Dr. Edwin Lewis, for forty years
Dean and Head of English in our school,
        Philosopher and author, artist in words and living,
Creative teacher, counselor and friend.

A kindly man, wise, sweet, gracious, human,
        He loved us, loved to know us,
Teach us, help us, comfort us in sorrow.
        Rejoice with us, make our trials his own.
Never did he find us commonplace and drab
        Or his day too crowded to be kind."

After her retirement from forty-one years of teaching the young, Dr. Andrus began a second career, that of organizing the potentials and opportunities for the elderly. In 1947 she founded the National Retired Teachers Association, "NRTA," and in 1958 founded the American Association of Retired Persons, "AARP," which today is known by most persons over sixty-five years of age. For twenty years, ending with her death in 1967, Dr. Andrus was the voice of these million membership organizations.

Among the great honors for this lifelong protege of Dr. Lewis is a living memorial built by these associations she founded and in partnership with the University of Southern California, a $5,000,000 research and training facility - the Ethel Percy Andrus Gerontology Center.

In Long Beach, California, in the Andrus Building, are the memorabilia of this founder; among them are letters from Dr. Lewis which Dr. Andrus treasured all her life, and the bronze bust of him given to her when Lewis Institute was no longer in existence.

Another faculty member of Lewis Institute was my sister, Effie Bangs Warvelle, who taught in the English Department for almost a quarter of a century, from World War I to 1939. Previously she had been a teacher of English in the high schools of Rochelle, Springfield, and La Grange, Illinois.

Effie B. Warvelle was a Chicagoan from her earliest years, having graduated from Brown School, West Division High School, Lewis Institute and the University of Chicago where she received her Ph.B. Degree in 1902.

Like her professor father, it could also be said of her that she loved her students and they loved her. The main subjects which she taught at Lewis were Freshman English and Shakespeare. Her early period was in the Evening School where she helped thousands of employed students, many of them foreigners, wrestle with the fundamentals of "writing readable English" in the required theme courses.

Dr. Edwin H. Lewis was head of the English Department just as he had been when she was a student in 1898. Lewis Institute was always like a large, devoted family and an exceptional school of altruism. There was banter along with helpful criticism among the faculty and students as they produced their works, some leading to publication, others just for self-expression.

My sister's brain children were her poems written from the time she was class poet in her grammar and high school days and her contributions to Voice, through her college and teaching period, and finally to her last years in retirement in Hudson, Ohio. Here she lived in a charming Shakespearian like gatehouse at the wood's edge; this had been part of the estate of James W. Ellsworth, also a former Chicagoan.

Through those cycles of years these thought treasures had accumulated, more than a hundred. Some are fragmentary lines, others in complete poetical forms and none in free verse. As in the collected verse of William Morton Payne, who had been Effie B. Warvelle's teacher at West Division, many of her poems are also predominantly introspective, nature loving and with a mystic sadness.

The quoting of poems can become as satiating to the reader as the over-indulgence in a box of candy - better to take a few nibbles from the whole and imagine the rest. Here follows a sampling:

431

"The Wind.

The wind is a questing thing,
Running through the skies;
Intimately touching
People's lips and eyes.

The wind is a questing thing,
Waking buds from sleep;
Struggling with the waves
To enter down the deep.

The wind is a questing thing
Infinitely old,
Seeking still a body
That can its spirit hold."[2]

"Word of Mouth.

A word
Came with a breath,
And it was heard.
One made it into life -
A word.

A word
Came with a breath
And it was heard.
One made it into death -
A word."

"Spring.

Come again the old, young spring;
Atom and star unfailing swing;
Earth returns her hallowed trust;
Blessed is the immortality of dust."

---

[2]Warvelle, Effie Bangs, "The Wind," <u>Contemporary Verse</u>, Philadelphia, January, 1921, p. 14.

There were many rollicking, happy verses appreciated by the very young, such as -

"On Drinking Tea.

O my mother and my father
        They both drink tea,
But there's never any served
        To my sister or to me.

We're not going to drink it
        Till we're quite grown up;
But our parents leave us sugar
        In the bottom of the cup."

"Poor Dog.

Today I saw somebody's dog
        That was so lonely, lean and sad,
I wonder if it could have been
        The one that Mother Hubbard had."

"Spend Not a Dream.

Spend not a dream
However wanted a thing may seem
Buy with labor; buy with gold -
Empty a purse of all it will hold,
But never let a dream be sold.

Cherish it deep -
Give it to your heart to keep;
For sometime it may prove to be
Life's happiest reality."

And finally, these few lines which mark her journey's end, Effie B. Warvelle died in February, 1954 in La Grange, Illinois:

"Afterward.

I shall be remembering
  The friendly star above my city street.
And I shall not forget
  The last green words
Of the farmer's winter wheat -
  The flowering of the skies -
O, there will be memories
  That will help my soul to rise."

"Karma.

All the chattels life gave to me
I can leave when I go to Thee
But that life that went through my heart
Until of my soul it became a part
O that I would bring to God."

Some years after Effie B. Warvelle's death, her sister Marjorie, now "the last leaf on the tree," was informed by several old family friends that Effie had planned to write a history of the old Monroe Street area. However, none of her recollections had been recorded except for inferences in her poetry. Is it not strange, that years later the same urge to record the old Mile Square scene for posterity should fall as a comforting mantle upon the mind and heart of the younger sister?

With the expansion of modern education, especially in science and technology, and the increasing financial struggle in small institutions, Lewis Institute and Armour Institute of Technology were consolidated in June, 1940, becoming Illinois Institute of Technology. IIT, as it is more familiarly known, carries on an educational tradition with its roots more than seventy-five years old. This modern complex of fifty buildings designed by the internationally known architect, Ludwig Mies van der Rohe, on a 120 acre Chicago campus, creates in the mid-west a young neighbor for both Massachusetts Institute of Technology and California Institute of Technology. The school's 1967 bulletin states on page 4 (in "Education at IIT"):

"The university offers both general and professional education programs on the undergraduate and graduate levels. It is coeducational and non-denominational and is organized as a private, not-for-profit institution, governed by a Board of Trustees consisting of approximately sixty leaders of industry, business and the professions.

"The academic organization of IIT consists of the College of Engineering and Physical Sciences; the College of Liberal Arts; and the Division of Architecture, Planning, and Design - plus the Graduate School and the Evening Division."

All of these objectives would have pleased the early founders and leaders as Philip D. Armour and Dr. Frank Gunsaulus; Allen C. Lewis and Dr. George N. Carman. Nor are the names of these early benefactors forgotten; they live on in grants and buildings. A nine-story student-staff apartment building of 96 apartments honors Dr. George Noble Carman in Carman Hall, while his painted portrait looks upon the young generation in the pleasant foyer.

After the merger of Lewis Institute and Armour Institute of Technology, Agness Kaufman, known to all who ever attended Lewis, wrote as one who had first been a student, then an instructor, and later on the administration staff, to acquaint those of IIT with its ancestry:

> "I have never known anyone who had a real and honorable part in this educational venture known as Lewis Institute, either as a student or as a member of the faculty or of the basement staff, who did not gain something fine from the contact, or who did not contribute something in the way of loyalty and devotion that was beyond price."[3]

That was indeed the epitome of Lewis Institute; where could one find a more understanding alma mater?

---

[3]Kaufman, p. 46.

106. Lewis Institute. Courtesy A. A. R. P., Andrus Building, 215 Long Beach Blvd., Long Beach, California 90802.

436

107. Lewis Institute, 1906. Courtesy Chicago History Museum.

LA MARCHE,   FINE ARTS BLDG.   CHICAGO.

108. Dr. Edwin Lewis. Courtesy A. A. R. P.

109. Dr. Ethel Percy Andrus. Courtesy A. A. R. P.

439

FANNY BUTCHER

Another pupil of the old Mile Square is three star Fanny Butcher (Mrs. Richard Drummond Bokum) who graduated from Brown School, West Division High School and Lewis Institute; this was followed with her Bachelor of Arts degree from the University of Chicago in 1910.

She was born in Fredonia, Kansas, February 13, 1888, the daughter of Oliver and Hattie (Young) Butcher. When a small child the family moved to Chicago and settled in the vicinity of Lake Street and Ashland Boulevard in an apartment with a view of Union Park and the Congregational Church, where Fanny attended Sunday School. The mother was burdened with domestic problems and the father had developed a chronic illness which changed his plans for art study abroad; when physically able he earned a living with his art works from which there was a meager income.

Fanny showed her great interest in books very early and taught herself the alphabet and the spelling of words from books she loved. Black Beauty was her first love and later she would write of the

"Five Little Peppers and How They Grew, a classic of the joys of poverty. I almost resented not being as poverty stricken as they, and how I longed for four other little Butchers to be poor with."[1]

The reader of Fanny Butcher's recent Many Lives - One Love will at once note that the volume is really two biographical studies or resumes; first, that of the author herself which is much too brief, especially of her younger, educational years; second, as a newspaper correspondent for the Chicago Tribune for over forty years she has written of the meeting face to face, mind to mind, probably, of more great authors of the world than any woman living today. These authors were mirrored or highlighted in brief but intriguing biographies. In the period that Fanny Butcher was with the Tribune, she served as many editors; besides literary editor she was at times columnist, society editor, assistant music editor, club editor, and even crime editor. Later in her travels abroad and about the United States she had occasions of meeting with many of the writers she had introduced or knew during her editorship years.

How did she become a writer? The secret was her diary which she began when thirteen years old and which through the years became her literary journal or notebook. Of her diary Fanny Butcher wrote:

""The way to learn to write is to write," and although what I put between the covers of the diary was twaddle, I did train myself to write sentences with a subject and predicate, properly punctuated. I never spilled over into sloppy

---

[1]Butcher, Fanny, Many Lives - One Love, Harper and Row, N.Y., 1972, pp. 14-15. Miscellaneous quotations from MANY LIVES - ONE LOVE by Fanny Butcher. Copyright (c) 1972 by Fanny Butcher. Reprinted by permission of HarperCollins Publishers Inc.

confidences to that captive listener, and as life became really exciting and there was something worth recording, I seldom took time to write down exactly what G. B. Shaw or T. S. Eliot or Richard Byrd or Lady Gregory or Jan Masaryk or hundreds of others had said."[2]

These revelations from the diary or journal are today like a meeting of Our Town by Thorton Wilder, whom Fanny also knew, and we are gathering again, even as the dead continue to speak through the pages.

We return to the early pages of the author's life. She mentions having only one dress and wearing a pinafore cover to school, and wearing the dress without the pinafore to Sunday school. Next, was the incident of her wishing for a white dotted Swiss dress with a pale blue satin sash to wear to a student's birthday party in the sixth grade. Such a dress was impossible with a sick father and a worried mother, but Fanny did not cry and went to the party in her plain dress. She had learned never to cry because of some forgotten infraction her mother had once said,

"You were an unwanted child, and don't you ever again do anything to make anybody not want you around and I will never let anyone say I am the mother of an only spoiled child."[3]

It is almost immediately that the reader senses the loneliness of this child. In the chapters on Fanny's grammar and high school education there is not one mention of her two schools' names, Brown School and West Division High School; yet she had many well know teachers in both schools and she probably graduated with honors. There is a brief mention of a copy of Barfussele, a book in German which was a class prize when she left the eight grade German class of Herr Bruno Kluge.[4]

There is not one incident of her years at West Division unless the fact that

"she walked a mile and a half to school each day, and home to lunch, which I often ate alone if my mother was at a luncheon party playing whist, and back to school and home again but I never felt alone. I had too many friends in books, too many thoughts skittering around in my head."[5]

This once young writer wrote to her correspondent that she had never written any articles for Voice, the high school magazine, the testing ground for many a hopeful writer whose name

[2]Ibid., p. 31.

[3]Ibid., pp. 14-15.

[4]Ibid., p. 18.

[5]Ibid., p. 16.

would become a voice heard years later.[6] All youth has its day dreams of future happiness and achievement as well as its whims of timidity and loneliness. All found a place in Fanny Butcher's diary.

Perhaps she thought there were so "many lives" to consider in her recent book and those persons and events concerned with Fanny's early schools were of interest only to a smaller audience, not a national or international. Such omission was the author's prerogative.

Chief of Fanny's dreams and hopes since early childhood was to go to college. Her mother

> "thought it all foolishness... that I ought to be earning my living... young ladies... didn't need a college education to be charming and to grace a home, which women were meant for anyway. Mother thought my idea of writing books was sheer selfish indulgence..."[7]

Fanny Butcher registered at Lewis Institute which offered a two year college program and a four year academy course. Here she found herself to be a student in Dr. Edwin Herbert Lewis's class in English. He was the peer of his profession - the teaching of English literature. Ask any Lewis Institute alumnus. Fanny wrote of him:

> "He looked incredibly like William Shakespeare, was a purist in words and loved and respected them the way an artist loves his colors or a sculptor his clay. Dr. Lewis was also that rarest of aristocrats of education, a born teacher."[8]

Good things began to happen. Mrs. French, a sister of Fanny's Sunday School teacher, had failing sight and arranged for Fanny to read to her for an hour five days a week at twenty-five cents an hour. Besides, this new kind of education was the switching point in Fanny's literary taste because

> "Mrs. French had the rare quality in readers of caring not only for what was written, but the way it was written."[9]

The reading matter was biography, autobiography and especially essays which delighted Mrs. French.

Later Fanny Butcher would write:

---

[6]Butcher, Fanny, in correspondence with Marjorie W. Bear, February 1, 1971.

[7]Butcher, 1972, p. 19.

[8]Ibid., p. 20.

[9]Ibid., pp. 23-24.

"Would I... have been so sure of the road to travel... if in my growing up I had not had Mrs. French and Dr. Lewis to give me eyes to see books as the sunshine of my often lonely childhood and adolescence and to cast their long shadows on my future?

If anyone person in my life did the most to make books the great love of my life, it was the gentle and sightless woman whom I needed infinitely more than she needed me."[10]

At Lewis Institute Fanny began to bloom. Here in this friendly atmosphere she made new friends and in 1908 when she graduated she belonged to the Collegiate Girls Club, the College Dramatic Club and the Girls Glee Club. Also, she was writing, expressing herself in both prose and poetry. In the 1907 Lewis Annual there was a beginner's story, "Jack Knott Meeker," while the poem, "On Reciting from the Chair, showed the influence of her master teacher, Dr. Lewis.

"Little thinks, in the chair, yon redfaced clown,
As he sits on the platform and looketh down,
For his soul is rattled with fear and alarm
As he gazes upon eyes that charm,
Deems not that he next must fill the chair
Nor knowest thou at what moment,
Thy voice for thy neighbor must be spent.
A speech is called for from each one
No one escapes. Oh, no, not one."[11]

After Lewis Institute Fanny Butcher's education at the University of Chicago was made possible by her own grit - correcting themes for Lewis Institute Academy students and reading to her blind friend Mrs. French, and spending four hours each day on a street car, elevated train and the rattling Illinois Central to reach the campus from her West Side home. Two kind friends provided the second year tuition and the experience of a year of dormitory life.

The years after 1910 were beginning to race - Fanny taught in the high school of Rolling Prairie, Indiana the year after graduation. It proved too vigorous and unhappy with unruly pupils; she realized that teaching would never be her profession. In the next interim she spent some weeks at the Bread Loaf Writers Conference offered by Middlebury College and then became involved in the newly organized Little Theater Movement in Chicago.

In the alumni news of the Lewis Annual of 1916, the reporter Winifred Bright interviewed Fanny Butcher after she had been on the Chicago Tribune staff for four years. She wrote:

[10]Ibid., pp. 23-24.

[11]Butcher, Fanny, "On Reciting from the Chair," Lewis (Institute) Annual, 1907, p. 176.

"I found her no austere highbrow, but a slip of a girl pounding the typewriter. So this was "Doris Blake!" I asked her how she came to be a writer and she said she always intended to write. What she liked about Lewis was being expected to become a writer. When she was a secretary to the Little Theater she kept on writing and one day (1912) the woman's editor of the Tribune sent for her, and she's been with the Tribune ever since. She invented the Tabloid Book Reviews, has done all sorts of special articles and now is Society Editor. Some day she's going in for fiction, and, says Miss Bright, "She will win in fiction because she is all energy and charm.""[12]

How very prophetic, Winifred Bright was. Fanny Butcher did write her book but it was not fiction; it was truth and "Truth is stranger than fiction." Many Lives - One Love was published in 1972 when the author was in her eighties. To note some of the sub-chapter titles tells us what is in this treasure house - "Chicago's Renaissance and Resurgence," "My Life Among the Poets," "My Life as a Galley Slave," "My Life in Business." This last was when she kept a book store, "Fanny Butcher Books" in the Loop, at the same time she was an editor for the Tribune. Curious passersby would inquire: "Is this a butcher shop?"[13] The shop was conveniently located and attractive in every detail but it was not a financial success. The owner tells us why:

"I found myself in the shop acting as guide, philosopher and friend, doctor, lawyer, employment bureau and purveyor of advice to the lovelorn. Helpless male customers gave me their entire Christmas gift lists to provide for, including, as well as books, jewelry, china... In my "spare time" I did their shopping and tied everything up gaily and of course charged nothing for the service..."[14]

Returning to the book's index there are so many spheres of interest, music, politics, crime, travels abroad, all part of Fanny Butcher's professional life. The last chapter, "Great Friends," named Edna Ferber, Willa Cather, Carl Sandburg, Sinclair Lewis, H. L. Menchen, Gertrude Stein and Ernest Hemingway.

Of these, Edna Ferber and Carl Sandburg were the closest, both of whom she knew for over fifty years. Narrowing to one, perhaps it was Carl Sandburg. In "A Tribute" to him she recalled

"those early timeless evenings... spent in my own little study under the eaves in my parents' home in what we called "The Garret"... From across the street came Lloyd Lewis, my contemporary... Sharing those hopes and dreams, although he was well our senior and had already seen them beginning to be realized in

---

[12]Bright, Winifred, "The Older Alumni," Lewis (Institute) Annual, 1916, p. 248.

[13]Butcher, 1972, p. 227.

[14]Ibid., pp. 229-230.

"Chicago," was Carl Sandburg, who, after their day's work on the <u>Chicago Daily News</u>, came home with Lloyd and over to my garret for long hours of talk.

"When <u>Smoke and Steel</u> was published Carl Sandburg wrote in my copy "For Fanny Butcher who heard many of these lines intoned before they were frozen in print," and that was literal fact, for Lloyd and I had heard them from his lips and scraps of paper. Often there came not only Carl the poet, but Carl the troubadour, complete with guitar eager to match folk songs with Lloyd... I always felt as though I were a kind of absorbent insulation - like the room in which Marcel Proust could work so happily and if I was the listener of the trio it was because nothing I would possibly have said could have rivaled their zestful talk."[15]

Carl Sandburg and his family who lived in Maywood were beloved by Fanny and her husband, Richard D. Bokum. Often the poet would spend the night at their home, sitting up very late with Mr. Bokum, while Fanny, who had retired for the next day's work, "found the morning light streaming in accompanied by distant waves of laughter."[16]

As the years have accumulated, so have the honors for Fanny Butcher. In her long dedication to the world of letters she was to witness and be part of that inspired period in Chicago's great literary <u>Renascence</u>. This term was emphasized by another Chicago contemporary literary critic, also schooled on the old West Side and a vocative writer, Vincent Starrett.

In 1952, she was the recipient of the Friends of Literature Award; in 1953 she was honored by the Friends of the Public Library for the work she had done for books in the Middle West. In June, 1964, she was cited as Communicator of the Year at the University of Chicago Alumni's eighth annual communications dinner at the Quadrangle Club. Her citation read:

"Her distinguished service to her profession, as a journalist, editor, and critic, has earned her a nationwide reputation as an outstanding woman in the field of communications."[17]

In October, 1964, she was honored at a literary tea and given a citation by the Alliance of Business and Professional Women. The program was "Books U.S.A., Inc., and Fanny Butcher

---

[15]Butcher, Fanny, "A Tribute to Carl Sandburg," <u>Journal of the Illinois State Historical Society</u>, Springfield, IL, 1952, Vol. 45, p. 390. Permission of The Illinois State Historical Society, 210 ½ S. Sixth, Springfield, IL 62701-1503.

[16]Butcher, 1972, p. 373.

[17]"Tribune Critic Honored by U. of C. Alumni, Fanny Butcher Given Communication Award" <u>Chicago Tribune</u>, Section 1, June 14, 1964, p. 16.

- Mrs. Books..."[18] Books U.S.A. may be likened to a Care program. One organization helps the physical needs while the other helps the intellectual needs of people where books are scarce.

Fanny Butcher is a member in the International P.E.N. Club, the Fortnightly, the Arts Club and the Scribblers.

Now in the 1970 decade she continues to keep a finger on the literary pulse as well as traveling and having reunions with many of her long time friends who are scattered from coast to coast, and keeps her residence in Chicago.[19]

[18]Powers, Irene, "Sunday Literary Tea Will Honor Fanny Butcher," Chicago Tribune, Section 2, October 9, 1964, p. 18.

[19]Editor's Note: Fanny Butcher (Fanny Bokum) died in May 14, 1987 in Chicago, Illinois (Contemporary Authors, Vol. 122, Gale Research Company, Book Tower, Detroit, 1988, p. 68).

110. Fanny Butcher. Courtesy of Fanny Butcher Bokum: "This is the last picture I had taken. Used it on a Christmas Card in 1965."

ARTHUR KROCK

The old Mile Square, which may be called an alma mater in the school of life for thousands of pupils, counts with pride, Arthur Krock, one of her favorite sons.

Probably, no other person knew as much as he did about modern American politics and Washington personalities. As a former correspondent and the Washington bureau chief for The New York Times, Arthur Krock had participated in the nation's political life for more than sixty years. He had known a dozen presidents of the United States and won four Pulitzer prizes.

He wrote three books dealing with the American political scene: In the Nation, 1932-1966; Memoirs - Sixty Years on the Firing Line (1968) and The Consent of the Governed and Other Deceits (1971).

Arthur Krock was born November 16, 1886 in Glasgow, Kentucky and would spend his childhood years in this rural community, living at the home of his maternal grandparents. His mother became afflicted with blindness after his birth and his father, a bookkeeper, left Kentucky with his wife for Chicago to a better position and access to a specialist, who, after five years, restored her sight.

Here, in Glasgow, relations between white and Negro populations were "courteous and considerate."[1] Some of Arthur Krock's "dearest friends" were Negro neighbors and the family servants.[2]

His education began early; he learned his letters at four and by seven "had developed a greed for reading." His grandfather Morris's library was the incentive that would lead him

"into writing as a profession because in those bookcases were standard works of great modern and ancient authors."[3]

In Memoirs he wrote:

"In this room I read, book by book, page by page, Thackery and Dickens and MacDonald, Dumas, George Eliot, Trollope and Matthew Arnold, Spenser, Shakespeare, Pope, Dryden, Spencer and Darwin, Kipling, Hardy and a host of others."[4]

Arthur Krock's primary schooling was in a frame building with two or three teachers where the three R's were learned by memory through repetition. The McGuffy Readers were the basic books.

---

[1]Krock, Arthur, Memoirs, Sixty Years on the Firing Line, Funk & Wagnalls, N.Y., 1968, p. 14.

[2]Ibid., p. 15.

[3]Ibid., p. 12.

[4]Ibid., pp. 11-12.

His secondary schooling started in the neighboring "misnamed" Liberty College where his mother had gone to school. Next, he joined his parents in Chicago and was enrolled in West Division High School. The high school was then in temporary quarters, being the old street car barn at Western and Flournoy, while the new successor, William McKinley High School was being built. The same faculty were teaching in the "barn" as had taught at the old West Division when it was located in the Medical Center, and they would continue in the new building, some, as long as forty years.

Arthur Krock recalled his teachers:

> "I well recall... Mr. Brimblecomb, straight out of Wessex and Thomas Hardy, was also a personal friend. Miss Wilson stimulated my natural interest in history. Mr. Payne was bearded, gentle and awesome because he wrote pieces for The Dial. He and Mr. Powles (like Brimblecomb, another Devon-Cornwall name) helped me to begin to try to write. Miss Mack (Mademoiselle) encouraged me to write a triolet in French... Mr. Clayburg I recall well and affectionately... with the benevolent attitude of the teachers [I] made it up pretty well."[5]

In June, 1904, he was stage manager and a character in the play, The Private Tutor, directed by Professor Rountree. For Class Day, Arthur Krock was Class Poet and wrote the words for the class song. Commencement was held at the Central YMCA since the school was in temporary quarters.

In the fall of 1904 Arthur Krock matriculated at Princeton University with the class of 1908. However, the promise of a loan for his college expenses did not materialize, and after one semester at Princeton, he returned to Chicago and enrolled at Lewis Institute. Here he could get an Associate in Arts degree and also manage financially with employment at Lewis while living at the home of his parents.

In recalling this period he wrote:

> "...I encountered one of the richest experiences of my life by attracting the favor of Dr. Edwin Herbert Lewis... He thought I was a promising student in his subject, English, and hired me to help grade the papers of his classes and take over a small freshman class in English poetry."[6]

Arthur B. Krock, as he signed himself at that time, was the editor of the 1906 Lewis Annual as well as a participant in it, since he was then a candidate for an Associate in Arts degree. He is seen in the oval frame on the Annual's pages as a handsome, serious young man with dark hair, a wing-tipped collar and four-in-hand tie. Among his Lewis Institute distinctions were Delta Sigma Fraternity (social), Parnassian Society (literary) and Assistant in English classes.

In a late recall (1971), he wrote of his Lewis Institute period:

> "Dr. Lewis... He was my patron and revered friend.

[5]Correspondence between Arthur Krock and the author, May 14, 1971.

[6]Krock, 1968, p. 25.

"I knew well and admired Dean Carman. Professor Tenney tried to make me a good Latin scholar, with the aid of Tacitus and Livy, but my rating was better as a member of his "glee club." I was also active in a debating society, the name of which I have forgotten. And my effort to make the football team at the weight of 130 pounds, stripped and wet, ended with a broken nose and a couple of very tender ribs."[7]

As one peruses the pages of the 1906 Lewis Annual there are several items identified only by "K." These were acknowledged by their author, Arthur Krock. Here is "Triolets," possibly the English version of the triolets he had written for <u>Voice</u> in Mlle. Mack's French class at West Division. In these verses the reader senses that ephemeral, mystic period of youthful searches:

"In Besancon, Hugo's town
I should see no houses old,
Nothing of quaint peasants brown
In Besancon, Hugo's town.
Only wreaths and wreaths cast down,
Sweet with human love untold:
In Besancon, Hugo's town
I should see no houses old.

II

In the towns of old Touraine,
Where was born the Romaune tongue,
I'd forget the zither strain
In the towns of old Touraine;
But the "Comedie Humaine"
I could read in old and young
In the towns of old Touraine
Where was born the Romaune tongue.

III

Now the fire is but embers,
Now the frail songs are all done.
Only he who writes remembers.
Now the fire is but embers -
All my Mays have been Decembers,
Phoebus only Phaeton,
Now the fire is but embers,
Now the frail songs are all done."

---

[7]Correspondence between Arthur Krock and the author, August 9, 1971.

Among other contributions, one again voiced the serious searching of time and place. "In the Pass at Jahil," a melodramatic poem about two lovers and the slayer of the beloved, these lines open the tragedy:

"Down through the passes to Kandahar
Went the hill-man, Singh, rejoicing:
Guided was he by the evening star,
And his own glad spirit's rejoicing."

***

"Suns have risen; suns have set;
They who played this scene are dust;
But the shed blood wanders yet,
Seeking vengeance as it must
Though its year is ages dead.
(Love's flower is white, Love's flower is red)."

***

In a more collegiate, humorous mood is "O Tempora! O Mores!" - mostly about the pitfalls of skipping classes at Lewis Institute. It shows that college humor of a few generations ago can still compete with the "hair" type of today.

The 1916 editor of <u>Lewis Institute Annual</u> wrote prophetically when he said:

"Art Krock edited the Annual in his day, and that is why he is the most remarkable journalist of his age in the country."

Immediately after graduation he took the first train to Glasgow, Kentucky where in his grandmother's home he could begin, cost-free, to search for a job in Louisville. The doors which had closed on his school days with such finality would reopen to great avenues of observation and writing. He began his journalist's career as a cub on <u>The Louisville Herald</u>.

During a period of about twenty years in Kentucky his reportorial assignments were with <u>The Herald</u>, <u>The Louisville Courier-Journal</u> and <u>The Louisville Times</u>. In addition, there were his friendships with a great editor, Henry Watterson and an advisor, Bernard M. Baruch.

In 1923 Arthur Krock entered New York City journalism where he wrote editorials for <u>The Evening World</u> during the absence of its editor, Walter Lippmann. Next, the young journalist became assistant to the paper's publisher, Ralph Pulitzer. While there were cross-fires, as in any office of young literary giants, Arthur Krock had among his associates, during his period with <u>The World</u>, such well-known writers as Allen Nevins, James M. Cain, Frank I. Cobb, Franklin P. Adams, Heyward Broun, Morris Markey, Deems Taylor, Lawrence Stallings, Maxwell Anderson and Alexander Woollcott.

In his assessment of The World, Arthur Krock wrote:

> "...the greatest increment of this opportunity was access to the joyous atmosphere that enveloped the daily business of producing The World."[8]

He also wrote:

> "For Ralph Pulitzer, as I intimately observed him from my post, had all the qualifications - character, courage, insight, and professional instinct - required to direct The World toward ever increasing excellence and financial stability. This was forestalled only by the power of the ghostly inhibition."[9]

At the demise of The World, Arthur Krock joined The New York Times in 1927 doing editorial work. In 1931 the Washington correspondent for The Times died suddenly and the director, Arthur Sulzberger, asked Arthur Krock to take over in Washington; he became bureau chief until his retirement in 1967 - forty years with this particular "firing line."

These years were not all spent on political or national assignments but were vibrant with human interests. The meetings with our chosen national representatives could be on Capitol Hill, the White House, the Metropolitan Club or in family retreats such as Kennedy's compound at Hyannis, or in London or Paris - Arthur Krock was there with his small personal notebook which has given to the world these factual memories. Truth is always stranger than fiction.

The best description of this forty year mission is described in the author's Foreword to his Memoirs:

> "The purpose of this book is to portray some of these men as I have known them in the context of great events - by watching them at work from a close point of vantage, and through intimate association... It is in broad outline the story of the revolutionary transformation of the American system of government in my time, an account of certain activities by the principal shakers and movers of this transformation, and a set of profiles of these personages."[10]

He also writes:

> "...I attribute my viewpoint and its concern largely to my experience as a first-hand observer of the men and events that have shaped our political system

---

[8]Krock, Memoirs, p. 72.

[9]Ibid., p. 73.

[10]Ibid., p. IX.

for the worse in the name of a "liberalism" both spurious of ancestry and destructive in practice."[11]

As <u>a voice of one crying in the wilderness</u>, Arthur Krock concludes his <u>Memoirs</u>:

"These are among my personal assessments of the consequences of the revolutionary political and social new American revolution. And from these consequences I have contracted a visceral fear. It is that the tenure of the United States as the first power in the world may be one of the briefest in history."[12]

A late nostalgic recall by Arthur Krock appeared in 1973, <u>Myself When Young</u>. In this small volume he gleans more memories of his Kentucky home and his early professional years. Here this work shows the universal longing or search for the youthful period we all experience but must soon leave. For many who are privileged to have a photographic memory, childhood and youthful scenes are deeply etched; while for others those pictures have faded with age.

To those who have experienced life either famously or infamously, death comes with finality to each and all. Arthur Krock died April 13, 1974 in his Washington home. He was eighty-seven years old. He is survived by his wife, the former Martha Granger Blair, a son Thomas Krock and two stepsons, William G. Blair and Robert H. Blair.

It has been said of Arthur Krock when he became chief of the <u>New York Times</u> Washington bureau that he demanded from his staff the same accuracy and enterprise that he practiced in his own career, or in his newspaper words:

""You've got to know as much about the subject you're handling as the men who are making the news. And for God's sake, try to keep it simple.""[13]

President Nixon eulogized Arthur Krock as a journalist of transcending integrity and judgment. He depicted Arthur Krock as one whose sense of perspective on, and understanding of, public affairs stood him well in his career as a correspondent and a commentator, and who was valued by many.[14]

---

[11]Ibid., p. X.

[12]Ibid., p. 416.

[13]AP, "Writer Krock of Times dies," <u>Chicago Daily News</u>, Saturday-Sunday, April 13-14, 1974, p. 26. Used with permission of The Associated Press Copyright (c) 2005. All rights reserved.

[14]AP, "Nixon Lauds Late Newsman Krock," <u>Chicago Tribune</u>, Section 1, Sunday, April 14, 1974, p. 38.

453

MAIN ROSSEAU BOCHER

Among others who passes through Lewis Institute's welcoming doors is Main Rosseau Bocher, professionally known as Mainbocher, America's foremost couturier and designer of women's fashions. He was born in Chicago, October 24, 1890, and lived on West Monroe Street near Western Avenue. His father, George Rosseau Bocher, was of French Huguenot ancestry and his mother, Luella Main Bocher, of Scotch and Irish. There were two children in this devoted family, Main and Lillian. The mother wanted her son to be an artist while the father wished him to be a musician and Main dreamed of being an opera singer.

Main Bocher attended John Marshall School which in the early 1900's was a combined elementary and high school. Here he was the musical member of the John Marshall debating team, playing piano selections from Ethelbert Nevin before the debates. During these early years, the family took walks in Garfield Park, a pastime for those not owning a carriage. Here the children, while studying the trees and greenery, munched popcorn.

His last two years of high school were at the Academy of Lewis Institute, where he graduated in 1908. Here he was encouraged to express his talents in dramatics, music and drawing. He belonged to the Academy Dramatic Club and appeared in several of its productions; he participated in the Annual Chorus and Glee Club's presentations such as The Bohemian Girl and Gilbert and Sullivan's Iolanthe. For the latter, he was the pianist. He drew many illustrations for the 1908 Lewis Annual; these had a hint of humor and the promise of his growing talent which would be expressed later in Aucussin and Nicolette which he illustrated in 1914 in London. While at Lewis Institute, he belonged to Pi Delta Koppa, a national academic fraternity which had a number of chapters in the far western states.

During these school days, he experienced three weeks of operatic atmosphere when he was hired to hold the stage curtain for the Boston Opera Company's stars on tour in repertory in Chicago. This memory was recalled years later with Mme. Alda of Rigoletto fame, when she and Main Bocher met at Lady Mendle's Versaille villa. He has described this episode of curtain pulling as nearly the most satisfying period he had ever known.[1]

The magic of the Auditorium's magnificence in 1908 entranced this youthful student as he acted as the costumed page to hold the curtain as each opera star appeared on the stage. Here, Main Bocher was experiencing the joy of being part of those great acts as the immortal music filled this palatial hall. Then, too, he was probably dreaming of the time when he would become an opera singer. Yet, in spite of the vicissitudes which would later befall him, this experience has remained:

"A thing of beauty is a joy forever;
Its loveliness increases; it will never

---

[1]Flanner, Janet, An American In Paris, Simon and Schuster, New York, New York, 1940, pp. 254-255.

Pass into nothingness."[2]

A year at the University of Chicago followed and the death of his father necessitated helping with the family income; yet Main Bocher continued his art education part time at Chicago Academy of Fine Arts. His next venture was New York City, where he worked for a lithographing company and attended the Art Student's League part time.

By 1911, the Bocher family sailed for Europe where Main would continue his studies at Konigliche Kunstgewerbeschule in Munich and later in Paris. World War I interrupted and after service with an American hospital unit, he enlisted in the Army's Intelligence Corps and was assigned as a plain clothes agent in Paris. Here he was able to carry on with vocal lessons under baritone Albers of Opera - Comique, while in government service. By 1921, after continued study with Mme. Valda of Paris, he was ready for his operatic debut. Suddenly his voice failed him completely, due to the strain of over-work and the door closed on a musical career.

After sketching fashions for Harper's Bazaar, he became Paris fashion editor of Vogue. By 1929, he decided that if he could select the winners in dressmakers' clothes, he could also design them. He incorporated a company known as Mainbocher at 12 Avenue George V, where for ten years his international clientele were among the world's best-dressed women. Among them have been the Duchess of Windsor, Constance Bennett, Kay Francis, Irene Dunne, Loretta Young, Claudette Colbert and Mary Pickford.[3]

In 1940, Main Bocher returned to the United States and established his salon in New York City at 6 East 57th Street, later at 609 Fifth Avenue. This was the first Haute Couture to come from Paris to New York, and as such, "out-Parised Paris."[4]

Mainbocher's precept in his world famous establishment has always been "to dress women as ladies." He has probably been the most successful of American couturiers because of his sensible, exquisite, durable and original costumes, not to overlook their elevated prices. Because of these qualities, and being enjoyed by women able to purchase such fashions, Mainbocher's designs are copied by garment manufacturers and eventually become available to the general public at more modest prices.

Among some of Mainbocher's "trade marks" or firsts, have been spectator sports clothes, the dressmaker suit, short evening dress, evening and costume decorated sweater, barearmed blouse for suit, dyed costume furs, the strapless bodice, cocktail suit and a jacket lining to match

---

[2]Keats, John, The Complete Poetical Works of Keats, "A Thing of Beauty is a Joy Forever" from Book I of Endymion, Houghton Mifflin Company, Boston, Cambridge Edition, The Riverside Press, Cambridge, 1899, p. 49.

[3]Ibid., p. 252.

[4]Current Biography, H. W. Wilson & Co., New York, New York, Feb. 1942, pp. 559-560.

blouse.[5]   One recent commentator wrote of 1970 fashions via a newspaper article title: "Mainbocher's Best Isn't Controversial; It's Remarkable."[6]

In Main Bocher's personal life, he still loves the musical world for his soul's refreshment. He also has always loved animals, particularly elephants and monkey friends in the zoos across the world. He probably met his first in Chicago's Lincoln Park Zoo. Strangely, his drawing for the Music frontispiece in the 1908 Lewis Annual was of an organ grinder and his small monkey; here was Main Bocher's subtle humor, as well as showing his thought for imprisoned animals.

Through the years, there have been designs for uniforms for Uncle Sam's Waves and Women Marines, Girl Scout Troop and the Red Cross leaders - besides nurses' uniforms for Chicago Passavant Hospital and Volunteer Aids at New York's Memorial Hospital - all with the compliments of Mainbocher.[7]

---

[5]Vogue, "Man Behind the Mainbocher Look," Vol. 137, June 1961, pp. 45-46.

[6]Morris, Bernadine, New York Times News Service, "Mainbocher's Best Isn't Controversial; It's Remarkable," Santa Barbara News-Press, Dec. 3, 1969, p. C-9.

[7]Editor's Note: In 1960 Main Bocher moved his couture "house to 609 Fifth Avenue where it existed until his 1971 retirement" (Milbank, Caroline Rennolds, Couture: The Great Designers, Stewart Datari and Change, Inc., New York, 1985, p. 426). Main Bocher died December 27, 1976 (The Almanac of Famous Persons, Gale Research, Detroit, 1998, p. 1098).

CHAPTER THIRTEEN: OTHER FAMOUS NEIGHBORS

CARTER HENRY HARRISON II

Our first native born Chicago mayor, Carter H. Harrison II, was born April 23, 1860 to Carter Henry and Sophonisba Preston Harrison in the Boardman House at Clark and Harrison Streets. The parents had recently moved from Lexington, Kentucky where their daughter Caroline (Lina) Dudley was born on March 28, 1857.

The Harrison family moved from their Hermitage and Tyler Street property in 1860, selling it to the Presbyterian Hospital and then purchased the Henry Honore home at 231 South Ashland, or Ruben Street as it was then called. Here young Carter would spend his early life.

His first school was Brown School; this was a matter of only a few weeks.[1] Next there would be several private schools. Carter attended John C. Bell's School on Sheldon "between Randolph and Lake Streets." Here corporal punishment with a rattan on the legs was an accepted course and Carter found many of his classmates to be students expelled from Brown and Skinner Schools. He attended Bell's School from 1868 to 1873;[2] then the family went to Germany as Mrs. Harrison's health was poor. They traveled leisurely, stopping in Heidelberg;[3] young Carter was impressed with the city's attractions and wrote his father:

> "...The largest barrel in the world, the great tun of Heidelberg contains 300000 bottles of wine. The Elector who had it built was a jolly fellow [-] he used to drink 18 bottles of wine a day...
>
> Your affectionate son
> Don't let anyone see this letter. CHH."[4]

The family settled in Altenburg where Carter entered the Gymnasium, living at the home of Professor Koepert of the Gymnasium, and Caroline, Carter's oldest sister, attended Gross Institute. Studies were serious and recreations were simple. For Carter, the latter was slanted towards adult participation, such as beer gardens and their music rather than athletics. Summers

---

[1] Harrison II, Carter H., Stormy Years: The Autobiography of Carter H. Harrison Five Times Mayor of Chicago, Bobbs-Merrill Co., Indianapolis and New York, 1935, p. 32.

[2]Ibid., p. 20.

[3]Ibid., p. 21

[4]Carter Henry Harrison II letter to his father, Heidelberg, August 11, 1873. Carter H. Harrison Papers, Box 9, Folder 527, Midwest Manuscript Collection, The Newberry Library, Chicago.

were pleasant with father Harrison joining his family in European travels. All this was interrupted in September, 1876 with the death of Mrs. Harrison, and the family returned to Chicago.

Upon Carter's return and three years schooling in Altenburg, there were serious problems for all the family: four motherless children, a national financial panic in process, father Harrison's finances affected, and his eldest son's future education to be determined.

At that period, entrance to West Division High School was by written examinations and the successful candidates' names were published. Young Carter who had taken the tests was not listed in the acceptances and father Harrison was embarrassed. In the meantime the president of St. Ignatius College on Twelfth Street was consulted and young Carter registered there in the "Class of 1st Humanities" - the equivalent of a college freshman.

The following week a letter from Superintendent Howland of West Division announced that Carter was admitted with advanced standing in Latin and Greek and could fulfill all requirements in a final high school year. The reason for the omission of his name from the earlier list was because all the applicants had come from district public schools and Carter was an outsider.

This was the turning point. Young Harrison chose St. Ignatius. He liked the "friendly attitude and surroundings at St Ignatius where the boys came from the plain classes."[5] Having been in a German school and worn German type clothes, he continued to wear them since at that period finances were tight and father Harrison was heedless of fashion. If West Division had been chosen and those clothes worn, Carter felt he would be conspicuous and laughed at by the girls and "gibed to the fighting stage by the boys."[6]

In 1877 he took the entrance examinations for Yale College and passed. Again there was the quandary, whether to enter Yale as a sophomore or junior or start as a freshman. His father advised him to start as a freshman; Carter decided to continue at St. Ignatius and entered the Philosophy or senior year in a class of two students. At that period he was a very bashful person and in his later years felt that while the socializing at Yale would have been helpful, still the rigid discipline, logical and analytical training at St. Ignatius were equally beneficial.

It was during these years at Bell's School and St. Ignatius College that Carter had his youthful fling in the old Ashland Avenue neighborhood. Being a city boy, unlike his father, he was never burdened with the tasks of a country boy, even though the Harrison land then covered a block square. Besides youthful sports, Carter had a broadening education in Chicago theatres of both the cultural and the baudy stratas. Among actors seen in his youth was Joseph Jefferson in The Rivals and Rip Van Winkle; later there were Edwin Booth in Hamlet and Ellen Terry as Portia and the memory of Adelaide Neilson for whom Carter "cherished the remains of a puppy love."[7] He had seen her first in Paris. His first view of Lillian Russell was when she played in

---

[5]Harrison II, Stormy Years, p. 29.

[6]Ibid., p. 30.

[7] Harrison II, Carter H., Growing Up With Chicago: Sequel to "Stormy Years", Ralph Fletcher Seymour, Chicago, 1944, p. 86.

a matinee at the Bijoux Opera House in New York in 1882 when he was a student at Yale. Only later would he learn that she was Nellie Leonard who went to Skinner School.

Young Harrison liked burlesque shows, Negro minstrels and traveling patent medicine shows as well as grand opera and orchestral music. He recalled his enjoyment of Gilbert and Sullivan's Pinafore which was given by the Chicago Church Choir Company, probably, at the Union Park Congregational Church. This had an interesting aftermath. With a group of his friends they were harmonizing a refrain one evening in Union Park:

> "Goodness me! Why, what was that?
> Silent be, it is the cat!
> It is the cat
> Sh-sh-sh! It is the cat."

Whereupon an Irish policeman stopped them - "Say! Wot do ye mean, insoolting the Police force hissin' a policeman like a bunch of geese? I've a good mind to run ye in!"

"All right run us in!" said young Harrison.

"That I will" said he; "Step along all of yez and be lively!"

As the trooping boys marched, Harrison had an idea and spoke out: "I wonder if Lieutenant Stanton will be around this late!"

"So you think to bluff me with knowing the Loot?" said the copper.

"Oh! No! But we are good friends, I am just wondering how the Loot'll feel when one of his cops runs in the son of the Mayor and his pals for no greater offense than singing a song from Pinafore."

The poor policeman wilted and apologized while the boys took pity and gave him saloon cigars which were bought with 5-cent bar checks.[8]

In those carefree days there was a small baseball park between Ashland, Jackson, Van Buren and Laflin Streets which was in use in 1868 with a grandstand seating two hundred people. On the Fourth of July every one drove out in their buggies to watch the Excelsiors and the Eurekas play, ending in a score of 98 to 87. Young Carter was paid a quarter to pass the lemonade to players and guests and also to chase the foul balls during the game.[9]

Too soon life became more earnest and Carter went to Yale Law School, receiving his degree in 1883. Here at Yale he had

> "a chance to enjoy at least two years with a flavoring of youth's most idyllic existence, the days of mingled duties and pleasures at a great seat of learning with the choicest of youthful companions and associations."[10]

---

[8]Ibid., pp. 98-99.

[9]Harrison, Carter H., "A Kentucky Colony," in Kirkland, Caroline, Ed., Chicago Yesterdays, A Sheaf of Reminiscences, Doubleday & Co., Chicago, 1919, pp. 169-170.

[10]Harrison II, Stormy Years, p. 33.

Carter H. Harrison II next settled in a law office in Chicago; attended to his father's properties with their rents and repairs; he watched over the old homestead on Ashland Avenue where Lina and the very young Sophonisba Harrison were awaiting the return of father Harrison and brother Preston from a trip around the world, later described in A Race with the Sun.

In December, 1887 young Carter married Edith Ogden of New Orleans and they would reside at 232 South Marshfield Avenue, near the old home, from 1888 to 1893. They would know the sorrow of losing their first born son. Later in 1890, Carter H. Harrison III was born, and a daughter, Edith Ogden Harrison, in 1896.

In 1891 father Harrison and his children had purchased the Chicago Times, a Democratic newspaper which would act as a voice in senior Carter H. Harrison's election for mayor. The paper had not been a paying investment and was sold after his tragic death, but not before it had been the only paper among five to speak up for the strikers and Eugene Debs, then president of the American Railroad Union, in the famous Pullman Company strike in 1894. Had the family not bought the paper until 1895 instead of 1891, the prosperous times, which began in 1896 following such events as the McKinley election and the gold finds of the Klondike with ensuing western development, would have resulted in advertising columns of Chicago merchants, then "the Times would have flourished like a green bay tree."[11]

Having sold the Times, what would Carter H. Harrison II do for a living? He was now thirty-five years old, a law graduate, but not practicing; he had been in real estate business which was not prospering, and in newspaper publishing which had been a failure. Having grown up in a political family and knowing political figures of Chicago, this second generation Harrison had the fever of politics in his blood or in his words -

> "the ambition some day to follow in the parental footsteps, to maintain the Harrison traditions of loyal public service."[12]

It happened that Governor Altgeld was campaigning in Chicago for his second term. Young Harrison had been honored to call the meeting to order and introduce Judge C. McConnell as presiding officer. At the close of the Governor's speech the Judge as well as Harrison and others of the committee escorted the Governor to his carriage. Within hearing distance of all, the Judge, with his hand on Harrison's shoulder, said:

> ""Young man, I am glad to have you enlisted in the cause. It was fine to have him open the meeting, Governor!" he added, [The Judge] turning to Altgeld "With his name a household word, the best loved name in Chicago, we are off with flying colors--our battle could not have started more auspiciously." ...Altgeld's sole response was a guttural: "Humph!"."[13]

---

[11]Harrison II, Stormy Years, p. 59.

[12]Ibid., p. 63.

[13]Ibid., pp. 66-67.

This was termed the "Baptism of Political Fire" by Harrison.[14] Traction problems[15] would concern the mayor from the beginning with his compelling the repeal of the Allen Law; his threatened veto of the Yerkes fifty year street railway ordinance and his securing the passage of the Mueller Law under which the final traction ordinance was passed.[16]

Today, the Mayor's early decisions are not easily understood. The days of traction, even by horse, and the various street-car systems, are obsolete as are the gas lighting problems for Chicago's streets. Street paving which abandoned cedar blocks for dressed granite stone or the forced abandoning of plank sidewalks and substitution of cement or cinder sidewalks in their stead - all seem very archaic today. Such miscellaneous improvements as providing free baths in the working men's wards or driving loan sharks out of City Hall - were considered accomplishments in the period of 1897 to 1905. Today we have our problems in the age of atomic energy and traffic pollution.

Yet by 1905 the mayor had

> "created a department of electricity and established the largest municipally operated electric light plant in the world. He was the first to officially suggest and plan for the utilization for city lighting purposes of the power developed by the Sanitary District. He created the Small Park and Playground Commission which planned the present system of small parks and playgrounds, as well as the Outer Belt Park System."[17]

Mayor Harrison related how, in his first year as mayor, many persons in high and low places approached him for a reward for their having supported him in the campaign for mayor. Among such was Judge Richard Prendergast who was baffled by the new attitude of City Hall when Mayor Harrison refused to compromise. The judge said: ""Tell me, for the love of God, who talks turkey for this administration?""[18]

---

[14]Ibid., p. 61.

[15]Editor's Note: Traction meant, in the lingo of the financial intelligentsia, street car (Harrison II, Stormy Years, p. 111).

[16]Editor's Note: Harrison earned a reputation as an honest reformer when he led the people "against powerful and unscrupulous utility corporations" and the men such as Yerkes who had used the streetcar and utility franchises to line their own pockets. He saw himself as part of the "first wash of the great wave of municipal and federal reform that was to assume tidal proportions under the turbulent aggressiveness of Theodore Roosevelt." (Harrison II, Stormy Years, p. 191.)

[17]"The Record of Carter H. Harrison as Mayor, 1897-1905," Pamphlet, Carter H. Harrison Papers, Box 1, Folder 32, Midwest Manuscript Collection, The Newberry Library, Chicago.

[18]Harrison II, Growing Up With Chicago, p. 208.

Mayor Harrison would have two separate periods as Mayor, 1897-1905 (four two-year terms) and 1911-1915 (one four-year term), totalling five terms. In the interim of these periods he would travel and spend much time with his family. His son Carter was a delicate child and the family spent frequent winters in Pasadena, California. While living in the West, the Mayor became interested in American Indian art and purchased many canvases. After his period of collecting American artists' works he became interested in European painters, mainly in Paris and Munich. With a planned budget and "an average flair for art values, and with an excess of energy" he acquired a collection of prevailing artists' works which were given to the Chicago Art Institute.[19]

His trips to various studios of his favorite painters, especially Lautrec, were one of the joys of his later years.

In the second period of Mayor Harrison's leadership from 1911-1915, Chicago had become a greater city and Harrison was still considered a great man for mayor, although the allegiance of the foreign-born was not as strong as formerly.

The chief adversary in the primary campaign was Judge Edward F. Dunne. Harrison's daughter, Edith Ogden, then fourteen, when asked if she was praying for her father's victory, answered:

> ""I started praying every night, then I suddenly remembered all those ten little Dunnes were doing the same thing; what chance had I against them? I just quit praying.""[20]

This last campaign "was a brutal fight."[21] There were insinuations against the candidate, from hypocrisy as to Catholicism, to "Back to Pasadena!" which Harrison defended for his son's sake and such did reach the public's heart.[22] Finally, on election day, Harrison held the plurality over Merriman, his final adversary.

What were the Mayor's problems to correct or institute in this period of his leadership? One was the clean-up, city-wide, of the vice dens with pressure on distillers, brewers and whiskey merchants as well as the demi-mondaines and their pimps, gamblers, prize fighters and sex perverts. The coup de tete was the closing of the Everleigh Club in October, 1911 for the duration of the Mayor's office. This red-light institution run by the Everleigh sisters was the most lavish and most widely advertised baudy house in the world.[23]

---

[19]Ibid., p. 332.

[20]Harrison II, Stormy Years, p. 269.

[21]Ibid., p. 282.

[22]Ibid., p. 286.

[23]Ibid., p. 309.

Among Mayor Harrison's remedial programs was the installing of modern sanitary plumbing in the run-down tenement houses on the lower north, south and west sides of Chicago where there were antiquated privies, out-houses and "hopper closets." While these improvements were needed, they also worked financial hardships on the property owners and hence unpopularity for the Mayor's actions.

Next, under the Department of Health, new, stricter regulations also created enemies for the mayor -

> "Pasteurization [of milk] was one of the outstanding good things I secured for my city, yet while the citizens at large gave me scant credit, the milk dealers organized into a solid phalanx for my defeat."[24]

The same attitude was reflected in bakeries and butcher shops which protested the ordinance providing clean, sanitary surroundings. Likewise, in the new movie industry, where shabby structures with no thought of sanitation or fire safety sprang up as "movie theatres," the owners protested the needed requirements. Club-women joined in this reform; and "an ordinance was passed creating a board of movie censors."[25]

Among the great public works underway or projected near the end of the Mayor's last term were:

> "the Municipal Pier... the Clarendon Bathing Beach...; the Contagious Disease Hospital...; [the modernized] Union Station...; the new bridges at Monroe Street and Kinzie Street... the marvelous Michigan Avenue improvement. These were largely the children of my brain, the crystallization into tangible form of dreamings over a long period of years. What more natural than a keen ambition to be on the job when they finally would be rounded into full fruition?"[26]

It is a matter of history that Carter H. Harrison II lost in the primary election in 1914 and William Hale Thompson won the final election as Mayor of Chicago.

When World War I was in progress, Carter H. Harrison, being beyond military age, joined the American Red Cross and was stationed in Tours, France where in his own words:

> "I practically lived the day-light hours on the front seat of a Ford one ton Camionette serving twelve A.E.F. hospitals situated from one to thirty-five miles from town. No lights. No windshield..."

---

[24]Ibid., pp. 342-343.

[25]Ibid., p. 344.

[26]Ibid., pp. 344-345.

He recalled the churches of St. Etienne and Rheims; of the latter, this priceless art so mercilessly damaged - but under moonlight:

"Oh! The glamour of moonlight! I shall carry the memory of it even into the other world!"[27]

Upon his return to Chicago and during his long retirement years, he continued living in the city on the north side - never in the suburbs; he loved Chicago. It was here he received the Legion of Honor at the Alliance Francais of Chicago and where he would be an active member the rest of his days.[28]

The following years were rich in world travels for Mayor and Mrs. Harrison. In 1921 - it was a summer in Europe, then on to Indian, Burma, China and Japan. Another world trip occurred in 1923-4 where in Saigon the mayor heard tales of wild animal hunting in Annan for tiger, wild boar, barking deer and greatest of all, sabadang or gaur. In 1925-6 this hunt was accomplished even to the gaur; while a voyage to the Nile to compare the monuments of Egypt with the Kmer ruins of Angkor completed the saga of the wanderings.

The Harrisons continued living in Chicago where their children, Carter III and Edith Harrison Manierre and their respective children, four daughters of Carter III and two sons of Edith, kept their grandparents abreast of the times. Inwardly, perhaps, the retired mayor wished that there was a Carter H. Harrison IV to carry on the historic name, so much a part of Chicago.

In Carter H. Harrison's last days he was busily getting his house in order - the many papers of his long and productive life were then being assembled in the archives of Newberry Library for posterity's treasures.

At that time Amy Nyholm was the librarian in the Manuscript Division and had the happy honor of working with Mayor Harrison who was then in his nineties. She wrote a Position Paper in the "Work to be done notebook" - The Carter Harrison Collection.

"Mr. Harrison was as bright as a bird, quick, sharp, perceptive and totally candid. He was greatly fascinated by the whole process of getting his life work in chronological order... He would come in every day and sit beside me, taking an interest in everything I did... Salty, witty, merry - I found him utterly captivating... If he missed a day because of the severe facial neuralgia he suffered from, he would return, notice I had used that day to catch up on all other work streaming in at the time, "You didn't work on me yesterday, did you? I see now I can't ever be absent again." He had Stanley Morison's, which means Sherlock Holmes', brilliant, sharp powers of penetrating acuteness. I was his willing slave. Times like that in one's life are forever remembered...

[27]Harrison II, Growing Up With Chicago, p. 349.

[28]Ibid., p. 348.

"I was never to achieve my hopes for the Harrison addition work (after his death)... Unfinished things... so deeply frustrating... Perhaps I should remember one of Harrison's favorite phrases. He would come back literally staggering after a bout with his neuralgia and say, "Another lost opportunity. But I have to remember every one of my days has been twice as good as anyone's. So I'm the winner in the end"... I loved him dearly."[29]

Carter H. Harrison died in Chicago on Christmas Day, December 25, 1953, age 93.

A letter written April 30, 1966 by Carter H. Harrison's daughter, Edith Harrison Manierre to the Associate Director of Newberry Library, Mr. James M. Wells, reveals much of the inmost character of this great man, much of which was unknown to his associates as Mayor of Chicago.

"...I feel called upon to say my father was a dreamer, a man who loved music and the arts. His light reading consisted always of poetry or Sophocles, Aristotle... his integrity was his great virtue... his exaggeration would be to belittle what he had done rather than enhance it. He was not a shrewd business man.

"...An incident during Franklin Roosevelt's first administration... He phoned my father and offered him the ambassadorship of either France or Germany. We urged Father to accept, and he must have been tempted but he said that he must refuse as he didn't have enough money to do the job properly, and he phoned the President back within six hours to tell him of his decision. He then accepted the Internal Revenue job solely because it gave him an income...

"...A truly great man who undoubtedly started too young on his career. He was "wet behind the ears"... However, a true politician would have dropped his dreams and quickly adjusted to the situations as they appeared. Certainly he could have been President instead of Wilson, most certainly he would have been at least a senator or governor if he had been more worldly with the powers that be. He also, would have died a rich man, rather than a poor one.

"There are many more incidents to prove these points. He was shy and retiring, a man who loved his home, the woods, the mountains, the sea. Up to the end he went to the symphony, and sat entranced at the opera and ballet. One of his greatest interests was the Art Institute... His innate good taste and knowledge must have been born in him, for he had no formal training.

"And finally, a man who every night of his life before retiring, read a chapter in the Bible. He gave the best he had and expected the best in return..."[30]

---

[29]Amy Nyholm. "The Carter H. Harrison Collection - A Position Paper," Work to be Done Notebook, Chicago, 1950. The Newberry Library, Chicago.

[30]Edith Harrison Manierre. Letters to Mr. James M. Wells, April 30, 1966, Nov., 1966. Accession File, Carter H. Harrison IV Papers, Midwest Manuscript Collection. The Newberry Library, Chicago..

In a second letter by Mrs. Manierre in November, 1966, she repeated some of her earlier conclusions but also had further statements of her father's very human elements.

> "...His name was needed at a critical time, he had power, and position sort of thrust upon him, all at once, before he worked up to it... rather he went in at the top... his party must have thought that because of his youth he would be an easy one to influence and mold into the form they wanted. They were to find that was not the case. He went on to become Mayor of Chicago many times, but his integrity, his love of the true and beautiful remained his ruin and at the end he was defeated by his own party who had never been able to sway him - he had been thrown into a political and competitive field, very material; he had been an idol of the people and for some years this had kept him in power but eventually the machine put him out.
>
> "He was at the end of his career as much a dreamer, an intelligentsia as he had been at the beginning."[31]

One thing his daughter as well as friends could never quite understand was the paradox of the Mayor's great love of animals and yet he relished hunting wild animals all over the world. While the carcass of such an animal could be used for food for the native inhabitants, still he treasured the hide and horns.

In our correspondence Mrs. Manierre mentioned that her father had been a great conservationist and how much he loved the isolated summer home on Lake Superior which even today is untouched by civilization, one having to drive ten miles to a telephone.[32]

Man is a complex being and as Emerson said:

> "Man is a bundle of relations, a knot of roots, whose flower and fruitage is the world."

[31]Ibid.

[32]Correspondence between Edith Harrison Manierre and the author.

111. Carter H. Harrison, II (1860-1953). Bust portrait probably made by Moffett Studies in 1911. Courtesy Chicago History Museum.

LEE DE FOREST

There were those who lived in the Mile Square for only brief periods of their lives, yet in those magic years were touched by the gifts of genius. These favored persons' achievements would encompass the whole world with new dimensions of sight and sound.

Lee De Forest, who gave the world radio and television, as we call these miracles today, first came to Chicago in 1893 as an eager student ready for Yale and equally as eager to see the World's Columbian Exposition. Here as a chair-pusher at the Fair, and boarding at his Aunt Hattie's home on the old West Side, Lee De Forest drank deep of the Fair's Pierian spring. His diary recorded:

> "I don't waste time or money in the Woman's or State Buildings or the Midway Plaisance, but study machines, engines, models almost entirely, and learn a great deal that will be of use to me."[1]

When his chair-pushed patrons asked him what exhibits they should visit, he steered them to Machinery Hall and if they insisted on seeing the Streets of Chicago, he too, enjoyed the hootchy-kootchy dancer. He took one night off in that short and thrilling summer to go uptown to the Auditorium where he bought standing room to see the spectacle "America." The magnificence of the theatre and it stupendous productions left him with a dream to return to Chicago.

This boy, then from Alabama, where his father was president of Talladega College, a Congregational missionary school for Negroes, went on to Yale. Here he graduated from the Sheffield Scientific School and also received his Ph.D. degree from Yale in 1899 at age twenty-five. He wrote a prophetic sentence in his diary in 1898 regarding his need for continued mathematical studies:

> "Then I can expect to deal intelligently with light and wave phenomena along which lines I see lies the great future of electronic advance."[2]

---

[1] De Forest, Lee, <u>Father of Radio: The Autobiography of Lee De Forest</u>, Wilcox and Follett Co., Chicago, IL, 1950, p. 62. Follett Educational Services indicated they sold publishing rights in 1983, most likely either to Allen and Bacon or New Win Publishing, both of which said they did not buy the rights. According to the Copyright Office web site, copyright was renewed by Lee DeForest 23May78 (RE-33-300); attempts by the Editor to locate copyright holder were unsuccessful.

[2] Ibid., p. 87.

His doctoral thesis pointed in the direction that his life's work would follow: "Reflections of Hertzian Waves from Ends of Parallel Wires."[3]

Lee De Forest returned to Chicago the fall of 1899 and was employed by Western Electric Company and lived at the home of his aunt. His first work was hard and greasy but promotion to the Telephone Laboratory came soon, his goal at that period. Again his diary reads prophetically:

> "What finer task than to transfer the sound of a voice of song to one a thousand miles away. If I could do that tonight."[4]

Work at assigned routine was followed but every spare moment, lunch periods and evenings of study - all were spent on the evolving "Responder" as De Forest called his first wireless detector. Leaving Western Electric, he became assistant editor of Western Electrician. He took a furnished hall bedroom on Washington Boulevard near where Ed Smythe of Western Electric roomed. Together they would be a team on many experiments. One was with the Welsbach gas burner.

This "flickering Welsbach burner" was in Lee De Forest's hall bedroom at 380 (old number) Washington Boulevard, near Troop Street in 1900. Many of the near neighbors were doctors or professors at Rush Medical College. Among them were Doctors G. W. Reynolds, J. S. Young, W. L. Noble, Z. P. Hanson, G. Van Zandt, J. H. Plecker and W. W. Dresden.[5]

Welsbach burners were in common usage in gas lit homes in the Mile Square as elsewhere around the early 1900's. These gas lights gave a brilliant white light from a filament mantle and were controlled by a pilot light. If comparison could be made today, the Welsbach might be compared to the brilliance of a 150 watt light bulb, while the ordinary gas jet might provide the equivalent of a 25 or possibly a 40 watt light.

In the notebook that De Forest kept of all his experiments, this one would become "highly significant historically." The Welsbach gas light was turned lower than the maximum brilliancy; the voltage coil was operated about twelve feet from the flame and the spark gap was one eighth inch long. Portions of the gas mantle burned immediately with a brilliant whiteness and the light responded to the making and breaking of the induction-coil circuit. The current for this was from two cells of storage battery; the interrupter was of the hammer type.

---

[3]Ibid., opposite p. 102.

[4]Ibid., p. 104.

[5]Mary Hastings Bradley recalls that Lee De Forest visited her step-father, Dr. Arthur M. Corwin at their home on Ashland Boulevard in hopes of interesting the doctor in De Forest's electro-magnetic work on the Welsbach gas jet - in other words, seeking financial help. She wrote: "It would have been a very good investment for my father - much better than he always made for himself. Dad never could resist a plantation in Peru or some ridiculous invention." (Correspondence between Mary Hastings Bradley and the author.)

At that time, De Forest and Smythe theorized that this phenomenon was a new influence of electromagnetic waves upon heated gases and/or incandescent particles. The notes explained in part:

> "...the expansion of the cylindrical body of heated and highly sensitive gases within and about the mantle, this latter serving merely as a holder to keep gases spread out in their most sensitive positions. The electrification of these gases by passage of a Hertzian wave may cause expansion and force the heated gases down the cooler and dark portions of the mantle, as we noticed to be the case."[6]

After further examinations with a Bunsen burner gas flame, De Forest "was convinced that this action existed, and firmly resolved to find it when opportunity offered."[7] Professor Clarence Freeman of Armour Institute allowed De Forest use of the laboratory in return for taking care of the apparatus and assisting students in laboratory work. The editing of Western Electrician was discontinued and De Forest taught two nights a week at Lewis Institute to help his meager livelihood. Ed Smythe, his brother, and De Forest moved to "Armour Flats" on the South Side; the midnight oil burned in the laboratory or the flat as the Responder demanded. De Forest studied the action of his Responder under the microscope. His description is both scientific and poetic for the lay reader:

> "Minutest particles, all but invisible, were seen torn off from metal electrodes under the stress of that wondrous electric force and, floating in the fluid there, move across to the other electrodes. Tiny ferryboats they were, each laden with its electric charge, unloading their etheric cargo at the opposite electrode and retracing their journeyings or, caught by a cohesive force, building up bridges... By pontoon bridges thus established, the current passed until the Hertzian waves arrived. Then all was commotion and change. Tiny bubbles of hydrogen appeared among the particles and... broke or burst apart the bridges, while the click in the telephone told the ear that the eye beheld the rupture of the current flow. But these little pontoon ferrymen instantly reformed to build new conducting paths... the local currents re-establishing, the ether waves breaking up its highways of passage... a veritable tempest in a microscopic teapot. By such observations, the actual explanation of my Responder's action became clear."[8]

It was now time to test the transmission process outside of that lone room in Armour Institute. From the top of Lakota Hotel, a half mile away from the Institute laboratory, De

---

[6]De Forest, p. 114.

[7]Ibid., p. 116.

[8]Ibid., p. 119.

Forest with his telephone receiver awaited the message from Smythe. Suddenly, the agreed signal sounded which -

> "seemed the sweetest music ever heard by man!... In the mystery of its transmission through that dark void, silently, invisibly, timelessly, I felt for the first time the presence of another world than I had known, the ether realm, to thought boundless, to the soul inspiring and to life infinitude."[9]

The next step was to transmit from a greater distance. Ferdinand Peck, one of the godfathers of the World's Columbian Exposition, as well as builder of the great Chicago Auditorium Building, granted permission to place the antenna on the top of the Auditorium tower. With Smythe at the key at Armour Institute four miles away, the signals were transmitted clearly and distinctly to a room at the base of the Auditorium.

Next, Professor Freeman had a friend with a yacht on Lake Michigan who arranged for the transmitter to be place on board. De Forest waited on the four mile crib with his Responder while the yacht with its spark coil and tall antenna disappeared over the horizon.

Again, the message came through as so movingly expressed by De Forest:

> "There was coal and fire on board, a whirling generator, a few wires - and the indestructibility of energy. I heard the voice of that inert carbon's chemical potential, translated through the heat into electric current, and carried by the wires to the spark coil, and through its spark again transformed to the silent and intangible waves from the antenna wires. And they rushed out to me, those etheric pulsations, infinitely rapid, and to all the wide horizon, the potential of coal, bound there inert for centuries, now liberated and seeking another resting place. The Responder heard them in their journey, caught the silent vibrations, and translated them into sound. So I harkened, and a great awe stole upon my heart, as I gazed across the silent waters toward that speck beyond their rim and heard the message from the Deep."[10]

The Chicago press heralded this great event, the <u>first attempt</u> in America to send dots and dashes by wireless. It was now time for the young inventor to move on to New York City to establish his brain-child as an American and financial industry, as well as to create an improvement on the Marconi wireless system which had been discovered two years earlier in Italy by Guglielmo Marconi.

The rest of Lee De Forest's life was filled with greater discoveries and inventions. The length and power of wireless communication increased and the United States military forces were the first to install the De Forest radio system on land and sea in 1903.

In the meantime, in 1903, De Forest was definitely determined to resume investigations of the gas-flame detector of wireless signals which he had observed with the Welsbach gas burner

---

[9]Ibid., p. 121.

[10]Ibid., p. 122.

mantle back in Chicago hall bedroom days. He sought a means to heat incandescent gases by electric current. "An incandescent lamp (tube) containing a carbon filament and a small platinum plate, exhausted to contain the optimum amount of gas," was made to specifications and became the first vacuum-tube detector to make use of two local sources of electric current. Again, a third or control electrode, a bent grid of platinum, was added to the lamp. This was the first three electrode vacuum tube - the Audion. It was patented January 15, 1907.[11]

This invention of the Audion tube ushered in the electronic age and made possible transcontinental telephony, both wire and wireless; created the foundation for radio, sound pictures and television. It has been written of this invention by Lee De Forest:

> "...so outstanding in its consequences that it almost ranks with the greatest inventions of all time."[12]

Of his life's work, Lee De Forest wrote:

> "Unwittingly then had I discovered an Invisible Empire of the Air, intangible, yet solid as granite, whose structure shall persist while man inhabits the planet; a global organism, imponderable yet most substantial, both mundane and empyreal; fading not as the years, the centuries fade away - an electronic fabric influencing all our thinking, making our living more noble.
> "For this, my life has been rich indeed!"[13]

In closing his autobiography De Forest[14] returned to the beginning of his miracle:

> "Alexander Graham Bell once said to Helen Keller: "It is not you but circumstances that will determine your work." Save in the one chance instance of the flickering Welsbach burner in Chicago, I cannot say that in my case his statement was true. In spite of circumstances, always unfavorable, I hewed out the way I had mapped for myself - against poverty, despite adversity, cynical skepticism, and endless discouragement, and without adequate tools, financial or other."[15]

---

[11]Ibid., pp. 213-214.

[12]Rabi, Dr. I. I., Nobel prize winner, quoted in Invention and Innovation in the Radio Industry, Rupert MacLaurin, MacMillan Co., New York, 1949, p. 70. Considered fair use by Simon and Schuster.

[13]De Forest, p. 466.

[14]Lee De Forest died July 22, 1961 (Colliers Encyclopedia, Vol. 8., MacMillan Ed. Co., New York, 1991, p. 31.)

[15]De Forest, p. 466.

112. Lee De Forest at State Street Wireless in 1902. Courtesy History San Jose. 1650 Senter Rd., San Jose CA 95112; 408-287-2290. Photo Collection # 2003-1-736.

473

DANIEL V. GALLERY

The old Mile Square can respond in some degree of recall on almost any event or personality that a late inquirer might be seeking in Chicago's first century of recorded history.

Militarily it is represented by such men as Brig. General Samuel Fallows of the Civil War period; Brig. General Nathan William MacChesney who served in three wars, Spanish-American and World Wars I and II; and such an admiral as Rear Admiral Daniel V. Gallery, United States Navy, Retired, who served in the Navy since his Annapolis days to his retirement in 1960; he is still concerned about his fatherland. His career has been a true drama, greater than any fictional sea story could produce.

Daniel V. Gallery was born July 10, 1901 at 49 Macalister Place which faced Vernon Park at the eastern edge of the old Mile Square. His parents were Daniel Vincent Gallery, a lawyer, and Mary Onahan Gallery. They had four sons and a daughter, Daniel, William, Philip, John and Margaret.

Vernon Park in the early 1900's was to the Gallery family and its grandsire, William J. Onahan, a hallowed, as well as a healthy, playground for this robust family of the Catholic faith. Here, William J. Onahan had received Notre Dame's Laetare Medal and had been made a "Camerari di Caba y Spada" by Pope Leo XIII, the highest honor the Pope can bestow on a layman; this grandfather was also a close friend of Archbishop John Ireland. Of the Gallery sons, three would become Admirals of the United States Navy while the youngest, John, would become a beloved priest of the Church.

Like many neighborhood communities of our large cities, Vernon Park was cherished and recalled by those who once lived there. A nostalgic novel, The Good Red Bricks by Mary Synon, recalls Vernon Park as

> "...that little square set in among wide-lawned, high-chimneyed houses, with the wall of the Convent of the Sacre Coeur for background of its budding trees..."
> "...the high steps of the big brick Byzantine structure known to the neighborhood as "the French Church," where every day in the week men and women of older races, habitants from Canada, sons and daughters of Italy, came to pray under the great gilded dome upholding the shining statue of the gracious Lady of Mercy."[1]

After kindergarten days at Notre Dame Church, Daniel V. Gallery went to St. Patrick's Academy at Oakley and Washington Boulevards for the first six grades. The school was conducted by the Sisters of Mercy: Sister Margaret was the Mother Superior; Sister Ambrose taught elocution; Sister Cecelia (most appropriately) taught piano; and the third grade teacher was Sister Rose, a real Irish Rose. Among some of his Vernon Park and St. Patrick's Academy friends were Raymond T. Way, Tony Caliento, Donald Brennock and Isabelle Walker. The last

---

[1]Synon, Mary, The Good Red Bricks, Little, Brown & Co., Boston, 1929, pp. 28-9.

named recalls Daniel Gallery as thin, with red hair and freckles, a serious face with intense eyes.[2] Even his later photographs confirm this memory.

The seventh grade was skipped and Daniel finished the eighth grade at St. Malachy's School which also was on Washington and Oakley. The Admiral in his inimitable way recalls his religious education and affiliations:

> "I attended a Catholic school, of course... On Sundays I distributed my patronage about equally among the Jesuit [Holy Family], French [Notre Dame] and Italian churches, all right in our neighborhood. I belonged to a Boy Scout troop that met in the First Congregational Church [Union Park]. And finally I joined a gym class at the Hebrew Institute... Vernon Park... wearing a miraculous medal around my neck. There I began learning how to wrestle, and ten years or so later I went to the 1920 Olympic games at Antwerp on the U. S. wrestling team."[3]

> "I used to draw pretty well when I was a kid, so my mother enrolled me in a Saturday morning class at the Chicago Art Institute. I went into it thinking I would get to draw nekkid wimmen from life models, but that illusion was soon shattered. All we drew was bowls of fruit and stuff like that. So I shifted to clay modeling."[4]

The next schooling was two and a half years of high school at St. Ignatius at Twelfth and Blue Island Avenue. The Latin, Greek and ancient history which the Jesuits taught were not so much needed as a grounding in mathematics in preparation for Annapolis which the boy's father chose for Daniel's career.

After special tutoring and having just turned seventeen, Daniel V. Gallery entered the Naval Academy at Annapolis in August, 1917. He has never regretted the choice. The West Side saga was now over and from then on the future admiral could say with Thomas Paine, My Country is the World.

It started with European duty on the Pittsburg in the Mediterranean's calm waters; next it was in the Pacific Fleet on the Idaho, still in calm waters. This was followed by Flying School in Pensacola in 1926 and three years of Navy Post Graduate School in aviation ordinance engineering.

By 1941 this naval aviator, now a commander, was sent to London as a naval observer. The R. A. F. was fighting the Luftwaffe as it blitzed London, Coventry and elsewhere while the

---

[2]Correspondence between Isabelle Walker and the author.

[3]Gallery, Daniel V., Rear Admiral U.S.N. (Ret.), Eight Bells, And All's Well, W. W. Norton & Company, Inc, New York, 1965, pp. 22-23. With Permission of Harold Matson Co., Inc., 276 Fifth Avenue, Suite 903, New York, NY 10001.

[4]Ibid., p. 23.

German U-boats sunk the Allied ships protecting the food supply for all the battles of Britain and France. In quick succession came the Day of Infamy: Pearl Harbor was attacked by the Japanese on December 7, 1941.

Commander Gallery was then ordered to Iceland to command the Fleet Air Base at Reykjavik. Here in Iceland, the natives were five percent pro-Ally, five percent pro-German and most of the rest did not care who won if only we could let them alone.[5] In this frigid world with its limited creature comforts, the Allies carried on their convoy escort missions determined to sink the enemy's ships and U-boats. The Battle of the Atlantic was the worst in 1942 when 7,500,000 tons of ships went to the bottom. By 1943 the tide of the Battle of the Atlantic turned in favor of the United States naval aviators with their destroyer escorts and Allies sinking around 300 U-boats and their crews.[6]

The next command for Daniel V. Gallery, now a Captain, was the Guadalcanal, a new ship honoring the marines who fought and died at Guadalcanal. Although made in the west by Kaiser, the ship did not remain in the Pacific but joined the Battle of the Atlantic, where "before Germany collapsed in May of '45, 328 more ships, totaling over 1 1/2 million tons, and 402 more U-boats would go to the bottom."[7]

On June 4, 1944, the task force commanded by Captain Gallery and five destroyer escorts captured the U-505 submarine and were awarded the Presidential Unit Citation for the daring exploit. This was the first U.S. Navy capture of an enemy war vessel on the high seas since the War of 1812.

This was also the greatest day of Captain Gallery's naval career. Later he philosophized a bit over this event and called to mind the old saying, "Opportunity knocks but once." Opportunity had knocked for him and his Guadalcanal task force when the U-515 and U-68 were captured; but then the crew did not have time to answer the knock at the door (the subs were sunk). The door, in turn, prompted the Captain to recall the philosophy of West Division High School's hero, Finley Peter Dunne and his Mr. Dooley who said:

> "...on some mens dures (doors) it [opportunity] hammers till it breaks down the dure and thin it goes in an' wakes him up if he's asleep, an' iver aftherwards it wurrks f'r him as a night watchman."[8]

This was the way Captain Gallery thought opportunity had worked for him. For some time he had considered the daring plan to capture a U-boat intact. Such a prize would benefit the Allies in learning of the U-boat's equipment and documents on board. A plan to capture such was prepared "to bring it back alive."

---

[5]Ibid., p. 125.

[6]Ibid., p. 136.

[7]Ibid., p. 158.

[8]Ibid., p. 184.

When one of the Guadalcanal's destroyer escorts, the Chatelaine, sighted the U-505 near Cape Blanco in the region of the Canary Islands, it immediately set off the depth charges whose detonations threw geysers into the air. The fighter planes overhead radioed, "You struck oil! Sub is surfacing."

The other escorts, Pillsbury and Jenks and the two "Wildcats" overhead fired a non-destructible barrage aimed not at sinking the U-boat but preventing its crew from managing the deck guns. The commanding officer of the U-505 believing his U-boat had been mortally damaged by the depth charges brought his ship to surface to permit the crew to escape. Immediately the escorts, Chatelaine and Jenks picked up the crew while the Pillsbury's boarding party went down the hatch of the U-505. It was deserted and there was water coming in through an opened eight inch sea strainer; the cover was near by and this was the only valve the Germans had opened in their haste to abandon ship.

The U-505 was towed away to Port Royal Bay, Bermuda with the aid of the Guadalcanal with the fleet tug Abnaki and the tanker Kennebec to provide fuel. With the capture of the U-505 all persons participating in this action were sworn to secrecy for the duration of the war. The Germans thought the U-505 had been sunk.[9]

At the end of the war, the U-505 made a tour of our eastern cities for U.S. Savings Bonds drives and then was tied up in the Navy Yard at Portsmouth, Virginia. For a while the U-boat was a white elephant - whether it should be scrapped or towed out to sea and sunk. When Chicago learned the story of the U-505 and that a native Chicagoan had been in command when it was captured, the Navy was asked if the U-505 could be brought to Chicago for a war memorial.

This was finally made possible by an act of Congress, $250,000 in monetary gifts and services and a long voyage of 3,000 miles via St. Lawrence Seaway and the Great Lakes to Chicago, arriving on June 26, 1954.

There was another feat, the overland journey of 800 feet from Lake Michigan's shore to the Museum of Science and Industry at 57th Street and Lake Michigan in Jackson Park. Here the U-505 rests in a cradled platform on the east side of the Museum. The submarine is 252 feet long, 22 feet wide amidship and the conning tower rises to the height of a three story building.

Inside the visitor sees the actual working compartments: The After Torpedo Room (Crew Quarters), Maneuvering and Electric Motor Room, Diesel Engine Room, Control Room, Radio Sound Rooms, Galley, Officers' Wardroom, Petty Officers' and Chiefs' Quarters and the Forward Torpedo Room (Crew Quarters). Today, more than a quarter of a century later, this U-505 exhibit still awes a thoughtful audience.[10]

The true significance of this memorial today is not that it is a trophy of war, but rather a silent and sad symbol of remembrance for the loss of 55,000 Americans who went down in ships, fighting against great odds to unmarked graves in the deep ocean. There are "No Tomb Stones on the Sea." Today as movies of this mortally unhappy saga are viewed, very young

[9]Gallery, Daniel V., Rear Admiral U.S.N. (Ret.), The Story of the U-505, 1955, 1969, Museum of Science and Industry, Chicago, pp. 8-10.

[10]Ibid., pp. 18-30.

hearts - tomorrow's burden bearers - are sadly questioning the future for themselves and their unborn children.

In 1944 Daniel V. Gallery was ordered to duty in the Plans Division of the Deputy Chief of Naval Operations (Air) in the Navy Department of the Pentagon. Then followed a period with the Pacific Fleet on the <u>Hancock</u>, a much larger carrier ship than the <u>Guadalcanal</u>; this was after the Japanese had surrendered as the result of the A-bomb. The next jump was promotion to rear-admiral and commander of Carrier Division 16 in the period of demobilization.

By 1947 it was the Pentagon again as Assistant Chief of Naval Operations for Guided Missiles - a door opening into that scene of the future which in time would become the headache for all humanity.

After the crescendo of World War II the process of returning "to normalcy" was difficult for any normal person. The almost unfathomable magnitude of technical discoveries and inventions in all sciences and industries for altruistic purposes was on the plus side of the war's aftermath.

On the other side was the sickening disclosure of the annihilation of millions of European Jews in Germany's gas chambers. There was Russia's renunciation with its withdrawal from the Western World as a friendly nation; hidden behind the Iron Curtain, Communism was pursued in its most cruel form by the dictator, Joseph Stalin.

These, plus United States' original A-Bomb and the next, the proliferating offspring produced to keep up with the Russian Joneses were and are causes enough for any alert American to voice his opinion on; even if people who live in glass houses should not throw stones at another. Criticism keeps the nation's arteries from hardening.

It was in these later assignments of Admiral Gallery when he sat in a swivel chair more than standing on the deck, that he became a writer. Most authors write on what they know from experience and observation, except for novelists who can ad lib most any situation, true or false. Non-fiction can stir up a hornet's nest causing a few stings for the subject written about and its author.

Among Daniel V. Gallery's controversial writings published in <u>Saturday Evening Post</u> were "An Admiral Talks Back to the Airmen" and "Don't Let Them Scuttle the Navy;" a third followed in <u>Collier's</u> "If This be Treason."

While spilling out serious articles as well as humorous, salty volumes, their author was Commander Carrier Division, flagship <u>Coral Sea</u> of the Sixth Fleet in the Mediterranean. The Sixth Fleet and the Seventh Fleet in the Far East with their amphibian and carrier task forces are ready to go into action instantly on orders radioed from Washington.

The Sixth Fleet ranged from one end of the Mediterranean to the other - the dream of any traveller - as cities of the ancient world were visited by the <u>Coral Sea</u>: Gibraltar, Nice, Aran, Naples, Liverno, Catania, Palermo, Athens, Istanbul and Crete. In Rome the Admiral paid his respects to Pope Pius XII; in Athens he dined with the King and Queen of Greece; the Duke of Edinburgh, now Prince Philip, was on active duty in the Royal Navy and commanded the frigate <u>Magpie</u>.

The two commanders spent an evening together and the Admiral mentioned that he had spent some months in Loch Ryan in Scotland and while there had taken a run over to Annie Laurie's hometown - the name of which failed him. And the Duke replied with an "Oh yes,... ah... er...

um." He did not recall the town either.[11]

Finally after each of them humming "Dum. Dum. Dum's braes are bonnie" and most of the primer, the bottle of Scotch, had disappeared, "the Duke banged his fist on the table and said, "I've got it... Maxwellton!"" So Annie Laurie was toasted and the men went back to their respective flagships.[12]

The next command was the Hunter-Killer Force, Atlantic Fleet. This was an important command as the Russians were building an extensive submarine fleet.[13]

By 1952 there was a change in pace with the Admiral reporting to the Naval Reserve Air Station at Glenview, Illinois (north of Chicago) as Commander, Naval Air Reserve Training. Glenview is the empire for the twenty-eight naval air stations scattered over the country. Also it is the realm of the "weekend warriors," Naval Reserve Aviators who spend one weekend each month flying service-type airplanes so that in case of need they will be ready to go into operating squadrons upon recall to active duty.

The period at Glenview was fruitful in many ways. Here the Admiral's family would join him. In 1930 Daniel V. Gallery had married Vera Lee Dunn of Fremont, Nebraska and there were three children, James J., Daniel V. III and Beatrice Constance. It was while he was stationed here that the U-505 was brought to Chicago for its final destination. It was also in Chicago, his old hometown, where the Admiral had enjoyed baseball since his Vernon Park days. Then, he went to the old Chicago Cub Park located at the rear of the old Medical Center. Here he had sold score sheets for the games. Now, he could see the White Sox games and such players as Casey Stengal, Whitey Ford, Dizzy and Daffy Dean as they played in the new Comiskey Park.

In December, 1956 Admiral Gallery reported for duty in San Juan, Puerto Rico as Commander, Carribean Sea Frontier; also he was Commandant of the Tenth Naval District and Commander, Antilles Defense Command, a joint command of Army, Air Force and Navy. Besides he was task force commander in the Atlantic Fleet chain of command and Senior U.S. official in the area. Because of Puerto Rico's Commonwealth status, he had diplomatic as well as military duties.[14]

Since this was a region of powder kegs such as Haiti, Cuba, Santo Domingo, Panama and Trinidad, the Navy had to be ready on short notice to evacuate Americans if necessary. One such person was Vice-President Richard Nixon during his goodwill trip to South America when he was forced to escape from Venezuela to San Juan.

Here in these Carribean waters, Admiral Gallery had the privilege of bringing baseball participation to the younger generation of these excitement prone natures; this was Little League Baseball. With the help of the lady mayor of San Juan, Donna Felicia, Rotary and Lions Clubs

---

[11]Gallery, 1965, p. 241.

[12]Ibid.

[13]Ibid., p. 244.

[14]Ibid., p. 260.

plus generous citizens, twenty Little Leagues were formed in Puerto Rico. This assignment as commissioner of Little League Baseball for Latin America paid off in many ways.

Most of the boys came from slum areas and by 1960 there were eighty teams in Latin America learning to know each other in the visiting teams. While there was some grief in the management of adolescent activities as anywhere, it was rewarding when the shoe shine boys saw the Admiral in his official car and would yell out, "Almirante Golarre".[15]

Another "soul" job was that of manager for the world's only all-American steel band. A steel band is a musical group whose instruments are made from empty oil drums which produce musical tones as well as rhythm. These steel drums originated in Trinidad where the natives have rhythm and harmony in their souls but little money in their pockets to buy bonafide instruments.

The West Indian boys found that by grooving, tempering and tuning the drum's top, a range of an octave and a half was possible. An array of twenty-one drums is a good steel band with the possible array of five and a half octaves of accurately tuned musical notes.

When Maestro Pablo Casals, one of the world's great musicians who lives in Puerto Rico, first heard the All-American steel drums perform, he was ecstatic when they played "Poet and Peasant Overture" and "Brown Skin Gal;" the latter truly belonging to Trinidad's waterfront.[16]

Since Admiral Gallery's retirement in 1960, an officer on duty now may be asked: "Do you know Dan Gallery?" The answer is apt to be: "Sure. He's the guy who started that steel band in San Juan."[17] As for this originator, he now lists West Indian steel bands as one of his avocations along with baseball and cartooning. Probably, his true avocation or calling is now his writing.

Through the years he has written many articles and short stories for the country's leading magazines; also motion pictures and television scripts on naval subjects. His five best known books are Clear the Decks, 1951; 20,000,000 Tons Under the Sea, 1956; Now Hear This, 1965; Eight Bells and All Is Well, 1965; and Stand By-y-y to Start the Engine, 1966. Eight Bells is his autobiography. All these writings are true experiences and persons expressed in sailor's language; they are non-technical, animated by jolly as well as serious moods but with the humorous predominant. As I remember one newspaper, the Cleveland Plain Dealer, once reported: "Dan Gallery is an Admirable Admiral."[18] [19]

---

[15]Ibid., p. 272.

[16]Ibid., p. 273.

[17]Ibid., p. 275.

[18]Editor's Note: much of the material in this chapter came from Daniel V. Gallery's Eight Bells And All's Well .

[19]Editor's Note: Daniel Gallery died January 16, 1977 in Bethesda, MD (Contemporary Authors, Gale Research, Detroit, Vol. 69-72, 1978, p. 260).

480

113. Admiral Daniel Gallery. Courtesy Admiral Daniel Gallery, U. S. N. Ret.

BOOK THREE

TODAY AND TOMORROW

482

TODAY AND TOMORROW

"Everyman's work whether it be literature or music or pictures or architecture or anything else, is always a portrait of himself, and the more he tries to conceal himself the more clearly will his character appear in spite of him."

Samuel Butler, 1835-1902
The Way of All Flesh

Many of the chapters in Book Two are candid resumes of one student's life and times as she progressed in that process called education for life or growing up in Chicago. These experiences were neither exceptional nor highly eventful; many of the scenes recalled may be familiar to the reader. In this present era of unrest, uncertainty and unhappiness, perhaps such recollections may present a relaxing interim as our mutual affiliations are reviewed.

At the present time, hardly a week goes by that the reader does not see in the newspaper, magazine or best seller some mention of nostalgia, a wistful word coming from the Greek nostos - return home - plus the -algia, hence homesickness. The American Heritage Dictionary defines the word: "A longing for things, persons or situations that are not present."[1] Among writers who have recently explored this melancholic affliction, which today seems to have reached epidemic proportions, is Loudon Wainwright who wrote a recent editorial: "Home is where it used to be." He wrote that nostalgia is basically an expression of hopelessness; after all, when something is gone, it's gone. But he said that we can surely use the word in other ways. One might say that nostalgia, when used in modest dosages, can dispel transient gloom, make memory more acceptable by smoothing over the truth, and help one's ego to construct and maintain a satisfactory self-image. Then again, a bit of longing for the unrecoverable, or a tear shed in longing for absent things, can help ward off dwelling on a future which has only one unsentimental and predictable conclusion[2]

William Zinsser has written of his teaching in the Indiana University Writers' Conference in 1968. He found that his students were not boys and girls of college age, and that rather than aiming them to the future, the task is to utilize their memories of the past. Their memories were of an America that no longer exists but in the minds of those who lived through it. The stories

---

[1]Definition as listed by author but quoted from an earlier, unidentified edition. The current edition has the definition listed on p. 1202 as follows: "a bittersweet longing for things, persons, or situations of the past". American Heritage Dictionary, Copyright (c) 2000 by Houghton Mifflin Company, Boston, New York. Adapted and reproduced by permission from The American Heritage Dictionary of the English Language, Fourth Edition.

[2]Wainwright, Loudon, "Home is where it used to be," Life Magazine, February 19, 1971, pp. 77-78.

have appeal because people can see themselves in many of them. While these memoirs seem to be but nostalgic longings for a simpler time, they also are attempts to locate our roots, and to give permanent form in written words to values they once believed to be true, values that gave continuity to our country.[3]

---

[3]Zinsser, William, "The Memoir Bore," <u>Life Magazine</u>, August 23, 1968, p. 12A.

484

CHAPTER FOURTEEN: THE TWENTIETH CENTURY OF CHANGE

In the ensuing years, with the population increase of both foreign-born and native citizens, the encroaching industry and the natural deterioration of property, Monroe Street homes like those in other Chicago areas began a decline which continues to the present day.

The tenement districts further east in the regions served by Hull House had been the result of over-crowding by the clustering ethnic groups in the small frame houses as well as in larger structures. The conditions which developed further west on the west side had other causes.

Primarily, the cause was the pernicious invasion by furnished rooms for light housekeeping. Here in formerly large, one family residences, now multiple families lived, often a family to a room. This original large room could become two rooms by using makeshift dividers while the adjoining clothes closet became a kitchen. A ten room house could hold ten families.

The once neat curtained windows, now often without screens, were opened wide in the summer to admit air to these cluttered, crowded rooms; the curtains waved in the breeze and milk bottles or food containers rested on the window sills in lieu of an ice box. Smoke and smells of food cooked on a two-burner gas or kerosene stove ushered forth, as well as sounds of a blaring phonograph or voices of angry arguers and often, wailing children.

The persons who lived in these rented rooms for light housekeeping were generally a shifting population. There were exceptions of honest, unfortunate families with as many diverse backgrounds as reasons for their present circumstances.

As for the manager of such a tenement and the later owner of this property who rented it to the landlord or the landlady, both parties saw the possibilities of maximum income with the minimum of capital investment for either furnishings or remodelling.

Once this trend started on a block in a neighborhood of single family dwellings, nothing could reverse it. Fewer families purchased these old homes for their individual use and with each ensuing owner, the value of the house decreased, although the land value in many cases increased due to the incoming industrial or commercial enterprises in the neighborhood.

There were many of the earlier and older residents who continued living in these roomy, old houses, and still do today in all sections of Chicago. Perhaps comfort, inertia and memories are more desired than fashion, modernity and flexibility. Nor are all of those latecomer transients undesirable; after all, they too, are subject to joy or sorrow, good health or pain, elation or depression, sympathy or aloofness.

William Morton Payne wrote, in one of his many editorials of 1917-8, his version of the old West Side's decay:

> "It was the lure of the lake [Michigan] which first drew away from the West Side those human elements which had counted for so much in the development of the city. To its attractive power was added the reenforcement of what an English writer calls the "desert of uncertain values which calls itself society". It

became "the thing" to have a house on Rush street or Prairie avenue, and those who set the social pace turned their thumbs down when pleas were made..."[1]

This statement is borne out with the insidiously similar circumstances in many cities located near a lake, river or ocean front. During that earlier Victorian age when the blame for many sentimental as well as physical illnesses was attributed to the "damp night air" and the "chilling, unhealthy breezes," townspeople did not build their permanent homes at the water's edge, nor did they open their bedroom windows at night. In summer, the lakes or rivers were considered as enjoyable to look at, fish in, sail on or swim in, but not suitable to live by for all seasons.

In my own family history I recall that the name of the street in Kenosha, Wisconsin, which was closest to the beach of Lake Michigan was called "Mechanics Street." Was this a verdict from "the desert of uncertain values which calls itself society?" A few small frame cottages and their garden plots, including that of my grandparents, were there on this street; it was not considered "desirable" property. However, one far-seeing institution chose to build its campus, in the early 1860's on that land. Perhaps because the land was cheap or offered as a gift to this school under the auspices of the Episcopal Church. This was Kemper Hall, a girls' boarding school, which until today looks out on Lake Michigan, and the once humble Mechanics Street became Durkee Avenue, named after a favorite Wisconsin son. The street is comparable to a Lake Shore Drive or Michigan Avenue.

So it is now in our cities, small or large, that the (damp) night air and the (chilly) lake breezes are now treasured restoratives for both soul and body. So much so that in cities such as Chicago, tremendous skyscraper apartments vie with each other for a whiff of that tangy breeze or a glimpse of open blue space where sky and lake seem one.

Mr. Payne continued his editorial (which now is somewhat out-dated):

> "The exodus [from the West Side] began, and it has continued ever since. The old mansions crumbled away, the old gardens withered, and the old avenues ceased to know the concourse that had once made them so brilliant.
>
> "The West Side was once the Chicago of churches and homes and the homely pieties. It is now [1918], in large measure, the Chicago of flats and slums and factories and seething caldrons of the melting pot. But it still has oases in which something of the old character remains. And a newer West Side, grown up in the region where men used to shoot prairie chickens, holds out a new promise for the future, and may yet again make the now despised section the throbbing heart of the true Chicago, as it was fifty and more years ago."[2]

---

[1]Payne, William Morton, "The Old West Side," editorial written for the Chicago Journal, 1917-1918, William Morton Payne Papers, Midwest Manuscript Collection, The Newbury Library, Chicago.

[2]Ibid.

Since William Morton Payne's appraisal and prophecy which was written more than a half a century ago, two more generations of change have taken place on the old West Side. A chronology of this section of Chicago, and duplicated in many other large cities of our country, began when the American pioneers came to this region as the founding fathers; next came the industrial middle class families with their ambitions, ideals and hard work; then followed the continuous pouring in of European immigrants with their determined drive to better themselves and give their children "book learning." This great invasion of struggling humanity continued until World War I when the peak of the Russian Jewish refugees was reached.

With each of these succeeding waves of human occupancy in Chicago, the earlier generation moved on to greener pastures and new homes while the late comers took over the vacated homes. As the years portrayed this evolving panorama of Monroe Street or any street in the Mile Square, the later inhabitants, whether young or old, were not completely aware of this neighborhood's transition. The evolving pattern, in whatever period it had been experienced, was tolerated by the new neighbors though not always accepted nor desired.

During World War I, cities such as Chicago were emptied of their young manpower who were sent "over there" to "make the world safe for democracy." Northern industry encouraged the southern Blacks to fill the new vacancies. These already impoverished people started what would become the greatest immigration of the twentieth century in the United States. This migration reached its peak after World War II. Whole neighborhoods, especially on the West Side of Chicago, changed from a white to a black population.

Now, we all stand facing today's scene and tomorrow's dream. Immediately, we are aware of the extreme desolation; houses with tottering stairs and boarded up windows; whole city blocks which have been demolished and are now bleak with emptiness and blowing debris - all waiting for a transformation which had been promised, at least on drawing boards, by federal, state and city authorities. The wheels grind slowly.[3]

One sees, in the old Mile Square, the earlier attempts by these authorities to provide living space for the incoming families in the Henry Horner Homes project. It has been proven in other American cities, as well as Chicago, that these huge, factory-like, high-rise, densely populated, noisy, hazardous structures are frequently not conducive to the well-being of their occupants.

The present trend in multiple housing is for sections of dwelling units or town houses and walk-up apartments as well as high-rise structures to be combined in a park-like region with special parking and recreational areas. The privacy of the townhouse has a popular appeal with its dooryard green area and a street tree.

---

[3]Eventually such downward trends can result in new construction and the preservation of what little is left of the old. For instance, 30 mansions were renovated in the 1500 block of Jackson Boulevard, the only block east of Ashland still preserving the character of turn of the century. This block is directly adjacent to the Mile Square, between Ashland and Liflin. (Brochure: "Jackson Boulevard District," Commission on Chicago Historical and Architectural Landmarks, Chicago, IL, Feb., 1976; "Work to restore West side homes: 30 mansions on Jackson to be saved," Urban Renewal Review, Department of Urban Renewal, City of Chicago, Vol. 14, No. 1, March 1975, pp. 1-2.

Under the Department of Urban Renewal of the City of Chicago, the city is divided into designated areas which have been surveyed and studied as to population statistics, the existing land use as to residential and non-residential, and the feasibility of redevelopment. The Mile Square area falls mainly in the <u>Central West</u> section and part of the <u>Near West Side</u> section.

The peak of the migration is now over, although the crowding, gang feuds, bombings, burnings and murders continue. Black and white neighbors are sadly but surely learning that both must have respect for each other, for their family cultures, their deep emotional feelings, and their search for a livelihood and human happiness. Such hopes resolve upon the solution of the hackneyed but true acknowledgement of <u>Man's inhumanity to man</u> which Robert Burns wrote: <u>Makes countless thousands mourn</u>.

THE RESTORATION OF THE CHICAGO AUDITORIUM[1]

The most resounding echoes, both literally and figuratively, from Chicago's great Columbian period when it was feverishly building, were heard when Adler and Sullivan's Auditorium Theater was being restored and re-opened to the public on October 31, 1967. This, probably, is the most memorable happening in Chicago's cultural and civic restorations in the last half of the twentieth century. This magnificent creation was one of the greatest attractions for visitors to the World's Columbian Exposition and now will continue as a heritage for all Chicagoans, all Americans.

The Auditorium's history reads like a biographical novel, not of a person but of a most animated, captivating building. Here was a structure conceived by a Chicago businessman, Ferdinand E. Peck, to possess a theatre seating four thousand people, a hotel with four hundred rooms as well as business offices. This was the greatest civic project in America since the founding of Washington, D.C. The early cost estimate for this building was $1,500,000, but the final total in 1889 was $3,500,000.

In 1890, the Chicago Auditorium Association issued a descriptive book on this monumental theatre-hotel-office building.[2] In a forthright manner it stated:

> "Almost every visitor to Chicago... is impressed with the massiveness of the stone work... In this feature it resembles the colossal edifices of the past, reared by Roman skill and magnificence. But in its interior the Auditorium is very distinctly of the Nineteenth Century... Internally it is American, and one may go further and say Chicagoan. For in its internal construction, this city has been forced by circumstances to abandon old ideas, and to create systems for itself."
>
> "...Perhaps the grandest of all its many remarkable features is the fact that it is fireproof... This edifice is probably the most thoroughly fire-proof structure of the kind in the world."[3]

---

[1]Editor's Note: While the Chicago Auditorium was not in the old Mile Square, its impact on the whole of Chicago and therefore on the Mile Square itself was felt to be so great by the author that its inclusion, just as the inclusion of topics such as the Chicago Fire and the Exposition of 1893, was justified.

[2]Auditorium, copyrighted by E. S. Hand, Exhibit Publishing Co. of New York, Philadelphia and Chicago for Chicago Auditorium Association, 1890, Copy in Chicago History Museum Library, Chicago, IL.

[3]"The Auditorium As It Was," The WFMT Guide, Pub. by WGN Continental FM Co., 221 North LaSalle Street, Chicago, IL 60601, April 1969, p. 4. [The article indicates that the material taken from pages 4-8 is quoted from an 1890 Chicago Auditorium Association book on the building. The Editor assumes it is from the book "Auditorium" listed in footnote 2.]

"There are in this theatre... only 40 boxes all told, with chairs for 200 people. This was the president's [of the Auditorium Association] idea, for he has no belief in privileged classes..."...[4]

"Occupants [of the gallery] have all the comforts of the people in the parquet circle and boxes. They see as well; they hear as well; they have the same admirable sea of light descending on them in floods; they have their coats, hats and wraps checked for them by attendants as obliging; and they have the same luxurious foyers with delightful fireplaces, comfortable chairs, thick soft carpets, and retiring rooms elegantly furnished... The general view, however, is not so fine as from the topmost seats of the grand balcony, where the eye is in line with the brilliant frescoing of the proscenium arch, and where the whole admirable system of lighting presents itself to the eye at a glance. Sit, good reader, on the seat that pleases you in the top row..."...[5]

"...This Auditorium would be applied to many uses--political and trade conventions, concerts by mannerchors and choral associations, and monster orchestras, mass meetings, lectures, operatic performances of every kind, balls, promenade concerts, charity fairs, etc., etc."[6]

The theatre was designed to convert into a smaller theatre as well as to expand. In addition to its usual 4000 non-box seat capacity, it could accommodate an addition 1000 on the stage, as was done during the dedication ceremony in 1889.[7] Or one could board over the entire parquet seating to create a flooring for 12,000 people during a convention.[8] This was all planned by the genius of mechanics, Dankmar Adler.

The acoustics of the Auditorium created under Adler's skill became the most technically perfect in the world and probably remains so today. In 1960, Cornelia Otis Skinner spoke a few lines from Shakespeare on the musty old stage and for those brief moments her voice carried to every corner of the Auditorium - there were no microphones or loudspeakers. One of the

---

[4]Ibid., p. 5.

[5]Ibid., p. 6.

[6]Ibid., p. 8.

[7]Ball, William, "Restoring the Auditorium," Talmanac, Talman Federal Savings & Loan Association, 5501 S. Kedzie Ave., Chicago, IL, Nov. 19, p. 5 (according to http://www.conway.com/ssinsider/bbdeal/bd010212.htm, accessed 18 March 2002, Talman Federal Savings & Loan was acquired by ABN AMRO).

[8]Auditorium, p. 132.

greatest reasons, acoustically, for the restoration of the theatre is that the audience can hear the great musical works in their full perfection, sounds <u>that cannot be adequately recorded</u>.[9] Live music is heard unadulterated by modern technics such as are now necessary at Lincoln Center in New York, our most modern of performing centers.

One must go back through those magic years, recalled now by grandparents and dusty pages from 1889 to 1929, when Chicagoans, rich and poor, had the privilege of listening to the great personages of the world for as little as fifty cents each, in that congenial, as well as comfortable, peanut gallery.

When the Auditorium opened on December 9, 1889, it was dedicated by President Harrison with these words:

> "I wish that this great building may continue to be to all your population that which it should be, opening its doors from night to night, calling your people away from cares of business to those enjoyments and entertainments which develop the souls of men and inspire those whose lives are heavy with toil; and in this magnificent and enchanting presence, lift them for a time out of dull things into those higher things where man should live."[10]

Also, that opening night, Adeleni Patti sang her famous rendition of "Home Sweet Home." Years later, my mother recalled to me how hauntingly beautiful Patti's singing was. Through the years came Strauss and his Vienna Orchestra in 1890 and Admiral Dewey was greeted at a Navy Ball. In 1890 and 1892, the combined Chicago high schools' commencement exercises were held in the Auditorium - what a thrilling send-off into the wide, wide world. The Auditorium's years which followed are headlines with such names as Melba, Lillian Russell, Caruso, Galli-Curci, Pavlova, Chaliapin, Max Reinhardt's <u>The Miracle</u>, Sarah Bernhardt and Mary Garden. When very young, I recall Mary Garden as she appeared in her gown of a thousand mirrors. With the lights in the proscenium and the twinkles on her gown, the eyes of the beholder were truly dazzled.

The years sped on; Sullivan's marble floors, mosaic friezes, delicate leafy stencils, golden sculpturesque cast iron railings and newel posts - all became dulled; the red velvet upholstery and carpeting, threadbare - all in the process of neglect and aging, common to both persons and buildings.

Under a new syndicate ownership, plans were afoot for a modern building to replace the Auditorium. Headlines of the <u>Chicago Tribune</u> on February 16, 1923 read: "Plan to Raze Auditorium as Obsolete." The United States Supreme Court halted such action.[11]

---

[9]Ball, p. 28.

[10]Terry, Walter, "Chicago's Auditorium Theater Reborn," <u>Saturday Review</u>, Vol. L, No. 47, Nov. 25, 1967, p. 81.

[11]Ball, p. 15.

491

In the meantime, Samuel Insull's millions were to build a new opera house on South Wacker Drive in 1929, convenient to the railroad stations where Chicago's suburbanites entrained each day. The hust office building like "...a gigantic throne with its theaters squeezed under the seat,"[12] opened with the Chicago Civic Opera Company being transferred to this new theatre. This was the nemesis of the Adler and Sullivan Chicago Auditorium.

In hastened decay, the old Auditorium existed on a variety of programs, motion pictures, popular shows, the last one being Hellzapoppin in 1941. During World War II, the U.S.O. Center used the large stage as a bowling alley. After that the theatre went dark and the doors were locked.

Samuel Insull's Civic Opera House became obsolete in less than ten years. From the beginning, its acoustics and sight lines were poor. The patrons of the opera no longer used trains to the depot area on the Chicago River. Automobiles with convenient expressways led to beautiful Michigan Avenue with its increasing attractions.

In April 15, 1945, Roosevelt University was founded in Chicago as an urban university in the Loop. Mrs. Eleanor Roosevelt dedicated the new school

"...to the enlightment of the human spirit through constant search for truth; and to the growth of the human spirit through knowledge, understanding and good will."[13]

Classes met in a rented building until the University's president, James Sparling, saw the great and almost immediate potential in the empty Auditorium Building, so centrally located at Michigan and Congress. By 1947, Roosevelt University moved in as the owner of this aging yet still robust structure. Hotel rooms became classrooms and the thriving student body helped their alma mater with the general housecleaning.

The old theatre was left untouched; President Sparling hoped that somehow the theatre could become Roosevelt University's gift to the city. Finally, after years of soul searching by many altruistic individuals, it was resolved that Roosevelt University could give the right to restore and operate the Auditorium tax free and rent free to a non-profit, tax-exempt and independent body organized solely for this purpose. On February 18, 1960, such a decision was carried out.[14] The trustees of Roosevelt University and the new organization, the Auditorium Theater Council, have a mutual contract which benefits both participants. Mrs. John V. Spachner became the dedicated and infatiguable chairman of the Auditorium Theater Council.

After a seven year fund raising of $2,225,000 spear-headed by Mrs. Spachner and some of the urgent restorations started on the theatre under Harry Weese, the architect in charge, the Auditorium once more became, in terms of opera and music, the greatest room to be found

---

[12]Ibid., p. 20.

[13]Source of quote unknown to Editor.

[14]Ibid., p. 21.

492

worldwide[15] - bar none, on October 31, 1967. These words by Frank Lloyd Wright had been said with nostalgic pride as he showed visitors the building undergoing resuscitation. He had been a fledgling architect of eighteen in the firm of Adler and Sullivan.

On the night of the Auditorium's rebirth, President Johnson's message was:

> "Louis Sullivan, one of the nation's greatest architects, created in the Chicago Auditorium a landmark of modern architecture whose significance reached far beyond our own shores. Your restoration efforts deserve the highest commendations from all Americans... your action should serve as a model for assuring that our finest architectural heritage will be preserved to inspire man everywhere."[16]

There is still much to be done before the Auditorium may be called restored and to do so is costly.

> "Today the materials [alone] would cost well over $20 million... but the figure is meaningless. The imagination of Adler & Sullivan, the skills of the workers, the irreplaceable marbles can have no cost put on them. The Auditorium is more a spiritual investment than a monetary one. Yet it takes more than spirit to recreate the unique beauty of this theatre, so the Auditorium Theatre Council continues as it has for 11 years, persistently struggling to bring the theatre back to its former magnificence..."
>
> "They've come so far, and done so well the question isn't *whether* they will succeed, but *when*."[17]

The Parthenon at Athens created in 438 B.C. with its majestic Doric columns and the Gothic Notre Dame Cathedral of Paris begun in 1163, with its flying buttresses, rose window and watchful gargoyles are two treasure of assembling places. Can not America preserve one of its own? Truly, man shall not live by bread alone, but by every word of God.

---

[15]Bruckner, D. J. R., "Rebirth of Great Theater After Generation of Idleness," Los Angeles Times, Calendar, Sunday, October 29, 1967, p. 51.

[16]Terry, p. 82.

[17]Kelson, Allen H., "The Auditorium As It Will Be," The WFMT Guide, WGN Continental FM Co., Chicago, April, 1969, p. 16.

114. Auditorium Hall, View From the Balcony, probably taken about 1895. Courtesy Chicago History Museum.

VICTOR HERBERT ELEMENTARY SCHOOL, CREGIER VOCATIONAL HIGH SCHOOL, AND IRVING VOCATIONAL GUIDANCE AND EDUCATION CENTER

The Victor Herbert Elementary School, one of Chicago's finest, was built in 1961 and named after the beloved American musician, conductor and composer, Victor Herbert. In keeping with the Board of Education's policy of naming new schools after famous persons who were an inspiration to children as well as contributing to the betterment of Chicago, the nation and the world, Victor Herbert was an excellent choice.

He is remembered for his operettas such as <u>Babes in Toyland</u> and <u>Naughty Marietta</u>, while his cherished songs such as <u>Ah, Sweet Mystery of Life</u>, <u>Gypsy Love Song</u> and <u>Kiss Me Again</u> live on for each new generation to enjoy.

Among other persons honored in recent years by Chicago schools have been Katharine Lee Bates, a college professor and author of our national hymn, <u>America the Beautiful</u>; also Kate Douglas Wiggin, a pioneer kindergarten teacher and author of two perennial favorites, <u>Rebecca of Sunnybrook Farm</u> and <u>The Bird's Christmas Carol</u>. Sharing a double title for a school are the two brothers, William James and Charles Horace Mayo, Surgeons. As famous doctors and founders of the Mayo Clinic they advanced the technic of surgery for the medical world.

The Victor Herbert Elementary School located on Monroe Street between Seeley and Hoyne Avenues and adjacent to William McKinley Junior High School, is a beautiful three story building accommodating 1140 pupils from kindergarten through sixth grade. The pupil average is 30 per room. There are 35 rooms besides a large gymnasium with a full sized basketball court which is shared with the Park District recreational program. The gymnasium also serves as an auditorium with a stage and chairs which are stored in carts under it.

Among the various rooms are a Headstart room, two kindergartens, a well-stocked library, an instrumental music room, reading laboratory and six classrooms used in special education for Educable Mentally Handicapped and Social Adjustment. Mr. Robert W. Mollendorf is principal and Vivian E. Lites is assistant principal of this progressive system of public education at Victor Herbert School.

Two other schools should be mentioned in the study of this neighborhood's modern schools, since they show the comprehensive consideration that Chicago's Board of Education and the city's educators have for the welfare of every pupil in the public school system. Both these schools, Cregier Vocational High School and Irving Vocational Guidance and Education Center, are located in the Illinois Medical Center District.

The De Witt G. Cregier School, now known as Cregier Vocational High School, located at Wood and Grenshaw Streets, is a 32 room structure built in 1914 and with an addition in 1957.

495

Originally a junior high school, it later served as an elementary and in 1957 became a vocational high school.[1]

Under the supervision of Herbert J. Schiff, the principal, the precepts of this much needed school are in full action:

> "Cregier Vocational High School offers an individual the necessary training, help and preparation needed to make him employable to the extent of his ability. Cregier advocates full development; hence the academic, social and physical, as well as vocational, are stressed."[2]

Among the courses offered are printing, machine operation, upholstering, auto mechanics, electricity, woodworking and architectural drafting. Any of these skills with the fundamental academic studies and pleasures of school days should prove the school's maxim - "Study to learn... learn to earn." Today Cregier has 800 pupils and 45 teachers.[3]

The other school, Washington Irving School, located on Lexington and Hoyne Avenue, was built in 1884, with an addition in 1912. This elementary school now serves as a Vocational Guidance and Education Center serving elementary pupils over fifteen years of age.

This new method in public school education was started in 1962 after success in earlier experimental programs. The General Superintendent of Schools stated that pupils in elementary schools who are over fifteen years of age have educational and vocational as well as social and physical needs different from those of younger pupils. These needs should be met by grouping such pupils together and providing them with a program of education tailored to their needs. Such school groups have been established in various parts of Chicago with pupils from as many

---

[1] Editor's Note: Subsequent expansion of the University of Illinois Hospital appears to have moved Cregier Vocational High School to 2040 W. Adams St., Chicago, IL 60612. Eventually it was closed in 1995.

[2] Source of quote unknown to Editor.

[3] Editor's Note: According to Janita Poe ("Adventures in Education," Chicago Tribune, Section 4, Sunday, September 15, 1996, pp. 1, 3), like many attempts at improving the learning experience, Cregier Vocational High School ended up being "one of the abysmal schools that helped give Chicago its national reputation as an educational disaster zone." It underwent a multimillion-dollar renovation converting it into the Cregier Multiplex School, a "result of the Chicago Public Schools' effort to explore desperately needed academic reform by encouraging the creation of small schools that try experimental approaches to learning." However, "...many of the experimental principles employed at Cregier - greater student autonomy, less rigid instruction - seem to go against the major focus of academic reform in the system at large, which is shifting back to textbooks, drills and "back-to-basics" tracking." According to Michael Klonsky of the University of Illinois at Chicago, ""what's important is that you have schools with committed teachers and well-organized, clear plans for instructors."" Time will tell if this new attempt at reform will work.

as six elementary schools attending the designated Vocational Guidance and Education Center. In the case of Irving School, pupils from McLaren, Gladstone, Irving and Jefferson School, all attend Irving School.

115. Victor Herbert School. A Chicago Public Schools Photograph. Courtesy Chicago Board of Education.

WILLIAM McKINLEY UPPER GRADE CENTER ELEMENTARY SCHOOL

This school is an example of the modernized system in elementary education in Chicago's public schools as well as elsewhere in United States. Schools given over to the exclusive education of seventh and eighth graders were evolving early in the twentieth century, as was the separation of high schools into junior and senior high schools.

The old McKinley High School's past history is well known; the McKinley Upper Grade Center Elementary School, established in 1954, is a new school using the old McKinley building and its equipment for the present purposes and programs.

Older generations of McKinley alumni as well as other grandparents, aunts and uncles will be surprised at what is provided for the last two years of elementary schooling today. In 1971 this school had 1092 pupils with a classroom ratio of 24 pupils. Recall, if you can, those years in public school education when the classroom had 30 or 50, even 70 pupils per teacher!

There are the principal, Mr. Charles Pace, and two assistant principals; among the teachers there are 55 regular teachers, one master teacher, three counselors, one speech teacher and four special education teachers for 57 special education pupils. Among others serving McKinley School are an attendance officer, school dentist, school nurse, and three secretaries. About 800 lunches are served each day.

Among the special programs for pupils are Spanish classes, home economics, instrumental music with instruction in horn and string instruments, and a school chorus. There is a wood shop, plastic shop and business education. The pupils have their student government, school paper and basketball team. Truly a full choice for seventh and eighth graders, offering some courses heretofore available only at high school level.

MALCOLM X COLLEGE

Institutions known as two-year or junior colleges are less than a century old. Lewis Institute of the Mile Square is thought to have been the first college in the United States conferring an Associate in Arts Degree. Junior colleges for public schools were one of Supt. Ella Flagg Young's plans for continuing education after high school graduation.

By 1911 the first junior or Chicago City College was formed in Crane Technical High School with twenty-eight students. This would become the nucleus of the present system of City Colleges of Chicago as well as the first home of the emerging Malcolm X College.

Until July 1, 1966, the junior college system was part of the Board of Education.

"On that day the Board of Trustees of Junior College District No. 508... became operative under the 1965 Illinois Public Junior College Act. This law transferred control from the common school board to the state system of junior college districts. Today the Board operates Amundsen-Mayfair College, Bogan College, Kennedy-King College, Loop College, Malcolm X College, Wright College and TV College."[1]

The City Colleges of Chicago are unique in both their past development and their present twenty-first century approach. A brief resume of their purpose, which applies to all colleges including Malcolm X, is quoted from the 1970-1 Catalog:

"The City Colleges of Chicago are public, community colleges. As open-door educational institutions of higher learning which provide services needed by individuals and the community, they serve the community in a multitude of ways by being the focal point of interest, a place where ideas generate, and where a welcome sign is extended to those who wish to learn. They are aware of change and modify programs to match new requirements and opportunities as they arise in our metropolitan cities...

"To keep ahead of changing times, each college of the City Colleges of Chicago which are accredited by the North Central Association of Colleges and Secondary Schools, offers more than a hundred programs and other learning opportunities designed for the individual.

"Many kinds of students with different motivations and objectives are blended within the College, one of the largest community institutions in the nation. There is a full time faculty of 1,160, a student body of 36,000. There are plans for new college campuses to serve the educational needs of 100,000 persons by the 1980's...

---

[1]City Colleges of Chicago Catalog, 1970-71. Permission of City Colleges of Chicago, 226 W. Jackson Blvd., Chicago, Illinois 60606-6998.

"In this atmosphere of learning, four areas of educational progress are offered:

"1. The Colleges provide two years of higher education which may lead to the Associate of Arts Degree or Diploma and enables a student to attend a senior institution and earn additional degrees.

"2. The Colleges provide a student with up to two years of specialized education which may lead to an Associate in Applied Science Degree or Certificate and prepares him for immediate employment.

"3. The Colleges provide background courses of study for the student who needs to increase his skills and knowledge for college work as the initial step in boasting his educational and employment opportunities.

"4. The Colleges provide a person with an opportunity to update and upgrade himself in a program offering community services and adult continuing education.

"Each student who seeks to enrich himself educationally is respected for his views, his ambition and his abilities. Counselors help him. Faculty work with him. Programs have been developed to fit the needs of the individual who is seeking a total personal involvement as he begins his college career..."[2]

In the beginning of junior colleges in Chicago, Crane Junior College, as well as later schools, had ups and downs due to two World Wars and a national Depression. Crane College was active in the high school quarters from 1911 to 1932; during that period more than 28,000 students earned college credits. After the Depression closing, Crane College re-opened in 1935 in rented buildings. In 1954 classes were resumed in Crane Tech building. In 1969 the college was threatened with loss of accreditation and placed on probation.

It was then that Dr. Charles G. Hurst, Jr. was called to serve as its president and to help the ailing institution. He immediately placed the college in a separate building at 1757 W. Harrison St. in the Medical Center. The name of the college was changed from Crane to Malcolm X, honoring the slain black civil rights worker.

Dr. Hurst instituted courses dealing with issues of law enforcement and problems in urban education. He allowed his students college credit for self-taught subjects and business experience. He advised extra counseling for students unable to meet class standards or allowed them to discontinue a prescribed course temporarily. He dispensed with failing grades. Unwed mothers who could not afford baby sitters brought their children to class while the lecture notes were taken.

Some of the administrators in the community service lacked for educational preparation; an office worker may have had a penitentiary record or is a present drug addict who is now under

---

[2]Ibid.

methadone treatments - yet all are functioning. Dr. Hurst indicated that they were establishing a new model for education in the urban environment.[3]

On June 2, 1970 the first annual commencement was held by Malcolm X College at the Church of the Epiphany on Ashland and Adams, where its members had extended the invitation, since the College had no auditorium space. Here with room for a thousand persons to assemble, a joyous evening with singing, commencement address, presentation of candidates for degrees, and awarding of honorary degrees marked the first milestone in the history of the new Malcolm X College.

Perhaps, the most meaningful expression on this occasion was the audience singing the Black National Anthem, "Lift Every Voice and Sing," written by James Weldon Johnson in 1900.

> "Lift every voice and sing
> Till earth and heaven ring,
> Ring with the harmonies of Liberty;
> Let our rejoicing rise
> High as the listening skies,
> Let it resound loud as the rolling sea.
> Sing a song full of faith that the past has taught us,
> Sing a song full of hope that the present has brought us,
> Facing the rising sun of our new day begun
> Let us march till victory is won.
>
> Stony the road we trod,
> Bitter the chastening rod,
> Felt in the days when hope unborn had died;
> Yet with a steady beat,
> Have not our weary feet
> Come to the place for which our fathers sighed?
> We have come over a way that with tears have been watered,
> We have come, treading our path through the blood of the slaughtered,
> Out from the gloomy past, till now we stand at last
> Where the white gleam of our bright star is cast.
>
> God of our weary years,
> God of our silent tears,
> Thou who has brought us far on the way;
> Thou who has by Thy might
> Led us into the light,
> Keep us forever in the path, we pray.

---

[3]Rankin, Deborah, Associated Press Writer, "Hurst's Vanguard Ideas Open Educational Field," ChicagoTribune, Section 10, Sunday, July 25, 1971, p. 6.

Lest our feet stray from the places, Our God, where we met Thee,
Lest our hearts drunk with the wine of the world, we forget Thee;
Shadowed beneath Thy hand, may we forever stand.
True to our GOD, true to our native land.[4]

In the meantime the new Malcolm X College Campus was being built at its location bounded by Adams Street, Wood Street, Van Buren Street, and Damen Avenue. Here on these 23 acres, the main building at 1900 W. Van Buren Street was completed after three years and dedicated on April 13, 1971 by its president, Dr. Charles G. Hurst.

On that morning the students and faculty entered the new building, assembled in the large auditorium, where President Hurst dedicated the building to

> "...the community - all black people and all people who support the black cause.
> "All we've had was spirit, now we have the assets of a beautiful new campus and we have the technology we need to be innovative."[5]

This building, the first structure planned, designed and built for junior college use in Chicago and costing twenty-six million dollars, is indeed a monument of enduring qualities. It is probably one of the largest and most advanced type of school structures in United States. Built of steel construction with window-glass walls, this three story, three city blocks long building has a total inside capacity of 521,000 square feet and is capable of accommodating 10,000 students.

This giant "think factory," as it is sometimes referred to, is a city within a building, with twenty-seven distinct and functioning departments. Those occupying the greater space are Administration and Counseling, Allied Health, Biology, English, Lecture Halls, Library and Audio-Visual Rooms, Maintenance and Service, Physical Education (includes swimming pool), Physical Science, Social Science, Speech and Drama, Student Union (includes food center) and Student Lounges.

Those occupying less space but equally as important are Architecture and Engineering, Art, Business, Child Care Center, Campus Nurse, Data Processing, Foreign Languages, Humanities, Locker Rooms, Mathematics, Music and Nursing.

The open landscaped campus has parking space for the students; the playing fields and swimming pool are open to the community.

On June 3, 1971 Malcolm X College celebrated its commencement on the new campus. It was planned to be held on the college plaza; because of threatening weather the event was held in the ground floor gymnasium. There was no traditional "Pomp and Circumstance" processional as the 219 candidates for Associate in Arts Degrees marched in wearing black

---

[4]James Weldon Johnson called it "National Hymn for the Colored People of America." His brother John Rosamond Johnson put the poem to music.

[5]Source of quote is not known to the Editor.

robes with red and green tassels and no mortar boards. Syncopated rhythm of African drums, the Malcolm X Band, psychedelic lights and dancers in black and traditional costumes ushered in this new baccalaureate of sight and sound.

Above the speakers' rostrum hung a red, black and green flag, the "Black Flag." President Hurst presided in a flowing pink gown. As of a year before at the College's first commencement held in a neighborhood church, the audience joined in the joyous singing of the Black National Anthem, "Lift Every Voice and Sing," and there was more music and poetry than formal addresses.

Of the 217 graduates, more than 100 received the Associate of Arts Degree in Nursing, which Dr. Hurst said was the largest class of nursing graduates in Chicago's history. That truly is "a first" for Malcolm X College's history in the making.

Colleges and universities have handed down through the years, even for centuries, their own individually recognized traditions of scholastic and intramural achievements. With time and circumstance, these have also changed through the years. For the most part these have been white institutions, as we speak of white and black education today. Now, as new predominantly black institutions are being formed, it is their prerogative to initiate life-styles or traditions relating to their African history or to form original patterns such as are evolving at Malcolm X College. Dr. Charles G. Hurst has said that although Howard University could not become a Harvard University, Malcolm X was already a great Malcolm X because it reflected the resourcefulness and real needs of black people. He indicated that the black community needed builders who could make a reality of self-determination.[6]

Among the remedial programs that Malcolm X College is participating in, is an extension program with the Illinois State Department of Correction at the Illinois State Training School at St. Charles, Illinois. Those inmates released on parole can continue their education at Malcolm X.

Students at Malcolm X College, which is adjacent to Illinois Medical Center, realize the great opportunities for service in this great humanitarian project as well as the means of earning a good livelihood. With the Circle Campus of the University of Illinois, also nearby, it has been made possible for serious students in technical curricula to register concurrently on the two campuses.

Among the many courses offered by the City Colleges of Chicago leading to an Associate of Arts degree or Certificate, and others leading into advanced training, are: Dietetics, Dentistry, Medicine, Pharmacy and Nursing. Others are Allied Health, Operation Room Technology, Inhalation Therapy, Radiologic Technology, Bacteriologic Technician, Histologic Technician, Medical Assistant, Medical Technologist and Prosthetic Orthodontics.

It seems almost predetermined that Malcolm X College will become vitally associated with this great Medical Center; the College has already evidenced this with having the largest class of nursing graduates in Chicago history; this was in 1971 and with a predicted doubling of enrollment of all students within a few years, what will the harvest be?

---

[6]"Monument to Blackness," Newsweek, August 2, 1971, pp. 47.

504

By 1972 Malcolm X College with its steady enrollment of students was on its way to a planned 10,000 student enrollment goal and with the general acceptance of the president, Dr. Charles G. Hurst, all spoke well for this new institution which already was creating national acclaim. In 1972 a visiting committee from Yale College, the Yale Mid-Careers Fellows Program in City School Administration, had reported:

> ""In the short history of the Institution's existence, much progress and success is evident. Much of this is directly attributable to the dynamism, the charisma, and the insights of its leader, Dr. Charles Hurst.""[7]

This young pioneer in collegiate education likewise had a sympathetic interest in the welfare of young children in Chicago's depressed Black areas. He organized a Malcolm X Educational Foundation for which a million dollars was approved by the former Governor Ogilvie of Illinois. This educational foundation was not connected with Malcolm X College and money from this fund was not used to benefit Malcolm X College directly, but rather to "serve as a tool for community rehabilitation on the financially depressed West Side."[8]

This grant was cancelled by the State Department of Children and Family Services, being considered a mismanagement of college funds and failing to report certain income. Dr. Hurst resigned as President of Malcolm X College, becoming President Emeritus for the balance of the college year.

Earlier a group of recognized Black community leaders and some Malcolm X students visited the office of Mr. Oscar E. Shabat, the Chancellor of the City Colleges -

> "...who questioned whether Hurst's praiseworthy, innovative educational ideas, as they were actually being implemented, were helping or hurting the West Side ghetto students who so desperately needed the prized educational opportunity that Malcolm X was created to offer.
>
> "The statistical and substantive answer, which would have been published by the board if Hurst had not stepped out, was that all too often the school's educational programs--under Hurst's chaotic administration--were failing to help the very students who needed them most.

---

[7]Simon, Roger, "Yale Report on '72 Visit Hails Malcolm X Hurst," Chicago-Sun Times, May 7, 1972, p. 13. As published in the Chicago Sun-Times, Inc. Copyright 2005. Chicago Sun-Times, Inc. Reprinted with permission.

[8]Hasman, Karen and Charles Nicodemus, "Malcolm X Foundation's $1 Million Grant Canceled," Chicago Daily News, Feb., 3-4, 1973, Section 1, p. 1. As published in the Chicago Daily News. Copyright 2005. Chicago Sun-Times, Inc. Reprinted with permission.

"Which was the real tragedy of Malcolm X College."[9]

Mr. Ewen Akin was appointed to head Malcolm X College. Previously, he was vice-president of academic affairs at Kennedy-King College. He graduated from the University of Illinois in 1951 and received his Master's degree in physics from De Paul University in Chicago in 1958. In assuming his new assignment Mr. Akins said: "This job can only be done with the cooperation of the students, community and staff..."[10]

President Akin faced some immediate problems. First, the student enrollment in the College had a sharp decline from in the 6,000's to the 4,000's in 1973, while all other City Colleges showed an increase. However, the peak enrollment had been in 1971 when over 7,000 students entered the new mammoth structure of glass and steel on 1900 Van Buren Street.

Mr. Shabat had several reasons for the exodus from Malcolm X -

"First, you must remember," he said, "with Hurst there was a tremendous charisma, a great deal of promise..."

"...Mr. Akin has not the personality Hurst had, but he is more deliberate" and a "much better administrator."...

"Hurst "had his part to play," said Shabat. He brought the school "a sense of identity... Unfortunately a lot of students left."" [11]

President Akin is optimistic for the future because Malcolm X has superior facilities and ""the ability to do things no other college could."" As to the students, they ""are as good as any I have seen.""

Dr. Hurst, on the other hand believed the college to be ""headed towards mediocrity"" and ""being run by marginal people""; also he thought of the students simply becoming nurses and technicians, a ""supply warehouse for major hospitals."" [12]

Dr. Hurst is still energetic, ambitious and continues to direct his brainchild, "The Malcolm X Educational Foundation" from his office at 230 N. Michigan Avenue, and from the foundation's office at 5412 W. Madison. Now he is planning a new "national college of urban sciences"; this will "be a private school with a $2,000 annual tuition" and will grant degrees

[9]Nicodemus, Charles, "The Tragedy of Malcolm X College," Chicago Daily News, Saturday-Sunday, Feb. 3-4, 1973, p. 13. As published in the Chicago Daily News. Copyright 2005. Chicago Sun-Times, Inc. Reprinted with permission."

[10]Jack Houston, "People - The New President of Malcolm X," Chicago Tribune, Section 2, Sunday, Feb. 4, 1973, p. 7.

[11]Case, Ellis, "Malcolm X College - Will Black Flag Fly Much Longer?" Chicago Sun-Times, Dec. 17, 1973, p. 30. As published in the Chicago Sun-Times, Inc. Copyright 2005. Chicago Sun-Times, Inc. Reprinted with permission.

[12]Ibid., pp. 30, 32.

"from PhD's on down" to lesser ones. He hopes to start the enrollment in late 1974 "with 250 students" and by the end of five years to have a 2,000 enrollment. The tuition costs will be helped by private industry and there will be no college building, classes being held in private industry buildings, churches and public facilities.

The school is "to operate on a passing through affiliation with Antioch College in Ohio." The teaching staff will be the best qualified that Dr. Hurst can find. He will remain separate from the school and will continue to work on the Malcolm X Education Foundation for the under-privileged in Austin and the Cabrini-Green area.[13]

Dr. Hurst is a modern example of Robert Browning's lines from Asolando:

"One who never turned his back but marched breast forward,
Never doubted clouds would break,
Never dreamed, though right were worsted, wrong would triumph,
Held we fall to rise, are baffled to fight better,
Sleep to wake."

---

[13]Case, Ellis, "Remember Dr. Hurst? He Has a New College in Mind," Chicago Sun-Times, Dec. 16, 1973, p. 9. As published in the Chicago Sun-Times, Inc. Copyright 2005. Chicago Sun-Times, Inc. Reprinted with permission.

FABIAN BACHRACH

116. Charles G. Hurst, Jr., first President of Malcolm X College (1969-1973). Fabian Backrach, photographer; Chg7703x8Hurst (Permission of Bachrach Photographers, 410 Boylston Street, Suite 2, Boston, Massachusetts 02116-3823; 617-536-4730). Courtesy Malcolm X College, 1900 West Van Buren Street, Chicago, Illinois 60612.

117. Malcolm X College. Courtesy City Colleges of Chicago, 226 W. Jackson Blvd., Chicago, Illinois 60606-6998.

THE WHITNEY M. YOUNG, JR. MAGNET HIGH SCHOOL

A plan on the drawing board of the Chicago Board of Education in the early 1970's was known as "The Cultural Educational Concept for the West Side." This subject, even then, seemed truly projected to the twenty-first century of education in the Chicago public schools. By September, 1975, this new proposed educational possibility had become a reality in the construction of the Whitney M. Young, Jr. Magnet High School. It is located in the area bounded by Ashland Boulevard on the west, Monroe Street to the north, Loomis to the east, and Van Buren to the south.

This school will be a magnet for students from all over Chicago; it is convenient to the West Side Medical Center, the University of Illinois at Chicago Circle, the Eisenhower Expressway, and CTA Rapid Transit; as well as near Crane High School. The Crane High School structure built in 1922 is being rehabilitated with a new addition and the 1909 building has been demolished since it was obsolete. Crane High School will also serve this Magnet School.

What is the Magnet Concept? It is best summarized in the description given in an early brochure:

> "Whitney M. Young, Jr. Magnet High School, one of Chicago's finest new educational facilities, promises to be among the most exciting schools in the country. The first high school designed specifically as a magnet school will attract students of all races and ethnic backgrounds from throughout the city. Magnet programs in the physical sciences, medical sciences and performing arts in addition to the innovative and extensive program for the hearing impaired provide unique educational opportunities for all students at Whitney M. Young.
>
> "The Chicago Board of Education, Park District, and Public Building Commission take great pride in presenting this exceptionally fine school facility to the students of Chicago."[1]

All three buildings are connected on the second level with iron bridges that give completely enclosed passage between them. Thus the three Units, Academic, Physical Education and Fine Arts become one diversified complex with convenient car parking space.

The Academic Unit contains the facility on the first floor for the 650 adolescent hearing impaired students. Here an extensive diagnostic and exploratory area for vocational activities are included. The central administration and community use facility is also on this floor.

The second and third floors of the Academic Unit are used by the four units or "houses" of 500 students each. Each house has an academic area, a dining and lounge area and counselor areas.

---

[1]An introductory diagrammatic "flyer" of four pages published by the Chicago Board of Education in 1975. Permission Chicago Public Schools.

The second floor contains the main Library Resource Center. The third floor contains the extensive Science Center.

To the east of the Academic Unit, with the ease of the bridge entry on the second floor, is the Physical Educational Unit. On the first floor are two large gymnasiums for boys and girls with a capability of being combined to form a field house for the Chicago Park District use. The boys' gym contains a competition basketball court with seating for 2000 persons. A two-story "core" contains locker and storage rooms. The six lane Olympic size swimming pool has a three meter and a one meter board. There is also a large exercise and gymnastics room. The upper part of the gym contains locker rooms and seating space.

Crossing the bridge or walk to the south of the Academic Unit is the Fine Arts Unit. Here,

> "the fine arts building contains areas for painting, sculpture, performing arts, music and the technical and applied arts. The first floor is devoted to the Fine Arts, Communications, Technical and Industrial occupations... The focal point of the first floor is the large space for the performing arts with unique details and capability of proscenium arch, thrust stage or theater-with-in-the-round productions."[2]

In closing this description of this most original educational complex in America, Superintendent James E. Edmonds said:

> "We feel the school is potentially the most exciting and innovative secondary school in urban America. We intend it to be just that... This school can fulfill many of our dreams, bringing together students from a wide range of social and ethnic backgrounds who have diverse academic abilities, interests and talents."[3]

In planning this new educational venture there were many social and academic rules to be considered. First, was the nationality make-up of students. For the September, 1975 opening, this was proposed:

---

[2]Ibid.

[3]Ibid.

	9th Grade	10th Grade	Total	%
Black	200	200	400	40%
Caucasian	200	200	400	40%
Spanish Surnamed	50	50	100	10%
Others	25	25	50	5%
Principal's Option	25	25	50	5%
Total	500	500	1000	100%

"The academic makeup of the student body was proposed to be 80% or more at the average or above as determined by the city-wide testing zones, the sex ratio to be balanced to the extent possible.

"The academic makeup of the student body be constituted that 80% or more is the average or above in ability as tested by scores. It will be processed by computer using established parameters of residence, race/ethnicity, academic ability and grade placement to determine the actual mix of selected students for enrollment.

"Eligibility - All students will be selected from those who express interest by making application for admittance. The educational programs of the Whitney M. Young Jr. Magnet High School will be made available to students throughout the city."[4]

There are two zones for student selection purposes. Zone I includes a section of Chicago south of Kinzie Street, between Western Avenue on the west and the Loop (which it includes) on the east. The student percentage in Zone I is 25%. Zone II includes the entire city of Chicago, exclusive of Zone I. Here the student percentage is 65% and the Principal's option is 10%.

In the Hearing Impaired Center only, a third Zone encompasses the entire Chicago Metropolitan Area.

When this school reaches its full enrollment possibilities there will be 2000 regular students, 650 in the hearing impaired section, all in a building complex covering 395,000 feet.

The name which this school honors has a familiar ring to the average white person, yet to the colored population that name is better known and appreciated. Whitney M. Young, Jr. is known

---

[4]Ibid.

as the inspired developer of the National Urban League, truly the voice for the colored population of United States. He would become the executive director of the National Urban League and traveled all over our country with his inspiring mission.

Whitney M. Young, Jr. was born in Lincoln Ridge, Kentucky on July 31, 1931, where his father was the president of Lincoln Institute, a boarding school for black children and his mother was also a teacher. After graduation from high school Whitney went to Kentucky State College where he received his Bachelor's Degree in 1946. He next enrolled in the University of Minnesota and received his Master's Degree in Social Work in 1947.

Then on to Omaha, Nebraska where the Omaha Urban League was active and Whitney M. Young became its leader. His last big advancement was to become the director of the National Urban League in New York City. From then on he was crusading in various parts of the country. At the same time he met in conferences with our national leaders as President Nixon and President Johnson, also corporation leaders from General Motors, The Ford Foundation - Whitney M. Young covered the United States with his crusade for Black Americans in the National Urban League. Through his books, To Be Equal and Beyond Racism, plus a syndicated column, he emphasized his central themes.[5]

In one of his many exhorting talks he was addressing the white man:

> "Personally, I am not a non-white, but I'm not a fool either. I can count. I know you can't fight a tank with a beer can or destroy a regiment with a switch. White racists are not afraid of our firepower but they are afraid of our brain, our political and economic power."[6]

While on a visit to Logos, Nigeria, at the conference group of leaders sponsored by The Ford Foundation to increase understanding between Africans and Americans, which included Ramsey Clark, former United States Attorney General, a group went swimming for a bit of relaxation. While in the water, Whitney M. Young suddenly drowned and resuscitation efforts failed. This was on March 12, 1971. He was 49 years old.

Slowly but surely his message to the world continues to spread. This Whitney M. Young, Jr. Magnet High School is a living memorial to him with his "educational program on the basis of democracy," adding as he wrote, "for the white people."[7]

---

[5]"Whitney M. Young, Jr. Dies on Visit to Lagos," New York Times, March 12, 1971, p. 41. Used with permission of The Associated Press Copyright (c) 2005. All rights reserved.

[6]Ibid.

[7]Ibid.

CHAPTER FIFTEEN: THE ILLINOIS MEDICAL CENTER DISTRICT

THE ILLINOIS MEDICAL CENTER DISTRICT TODAY

"I hold the unconquerable belief that science and peace will triumph over ignorance and war; that nations will come together, not to destroy but to construct; and that the future belongs to those who accomplish most for humanity."

Louis Pasteur, 1822-1895

The science of medicine, as well as all science and industry, took a great leap forward after World War I when the incentive was to prepare for a bright new world, so needed and longed for. The pendulum of men's energies moved from destruction to construction; then the pendulum swung backward in World War II and since has wavered all over the world. Nations continue to build and destroy, to heal and to kill - all in such great proportions that the world is in a stalemate between the forces of good and evil, peace and war - all because of <u>man's inhumanity to man</u>.

In the rise of the Illinois Medical Center District, commonly called the Medical Center, is to be found one of the finest expressions of man's humanity to man.

Here is a community which has professional and financial help from federal, state, county, city and private sources and has demonstrated that such a confraternity of dedicated individual groups can achieve a monumental, integrated, diversified and, above all, a humanitarian community for the sick in body and mind, be they rich or poor, American or foreigner. It is a city within a city; a haven where medical scientists, nurses, technicians and serious students work around the clock.

In 1941 the Illinois General Assembly created the Illinois Medical Center District, covering a tract of 365 acres. This area is bounded by Ashland Boulevard, Thirteenth Street, Oakley Boulevard and Eisenhower Expressway. Future expansion of land west and south of this area has been considered.

These considerations determined the location of the Illinois Medical Center District: first, it already had great hospitals and medical schools established there; second, the area is in the exact center of Chicago's population; third, the existing need for the re-development of the Near West Side, which is a blighted area. The Medical Center has its master plan in process of wide scale revision while the Chicago Plan Commission and the Department of Urban Renewal have each made correlated studies for the adjacent area known as Central West.

The Medical Center has become the anchor around which the re-development of the Near West Side has been planned. One sees another area of the west side, a mile east, where the new University of Illinois Circle Campus has recently been created and is flourishing both academically and civic-wise. That old neighborhood of Jane Addams' Hull House has become a living and expanding memorial to the greatness of its first benefactor, Jane Addams.

By 1946 the Illinois Medical Center District took on an improved architectural appearance with its new or restored buildings and a more attractive "front door" approach. The Convalescent Park established in 1910 was rejuvenated with new green plantings and on June 12, 1946 the Pasteur Memorial monument was re-dedicated in this park. Likewise, it was appropriate to have the title of Convalescent Park changed to Pasteur Park in 1951.

Originally, in 1928, the Pasteur Memorial was erected in Grant Park by the Pasteur Memorial Association headed by Dr. Frank Billings. The Pasteur bust was created by the French sculptor, Louis Hermant and cast in bronze.

Louis Pasteur was one of the great benefactors for mankind in conquering disease by his discovery of microscopic bacteria which are the causes for many infectious diseases. From then on the science of bacteriology expanded at an accelerating pace and initiated the age of vaccines and antitoxins with the resulting saving of human lives and increasing the span of human life.

Today the Illinois Medical Center District, after its third of a century of existence, has among its great hospitals, Cook County, Rush-Presbyterian-St. Luke's Medical Center, Veterans' Administration, University of Illinois Research and Educational, Department of Public Health Hospital and Clinics, Illinois State Psychiatric Institution and Illinois Pediatric Institute, all creating an in-patient capacity of approximately 7,000 beds.

Today, besides the University of Illinois Colleges of Medicine, Dentistry, Pharmacy and Nursing, there are its Illinois Graduate School of Medicine, the Library of Medical Science, the Medical Research Laboratory and the School of Associated Medical Sciences.

Among other affiliated institutions in the Medical Center are the Chicago Medical School, University of Health Sciences, Cook County Graduate School of Medicine, American Society of Clinical Pathologists and the Benjamin Goldberg Research Center.

Other structures recently completed in the Medical Center are Cook County Juvenile Detention Center - Juvenile Courts Building and the Children and Family Service Central District Office Building; the University of Illinois Administrative Office Building, Phase I and II of the College of Dentistry Building, and the Medical Research Laboratory Addition; also there is the Temporary Child Care Facility of the Department of Children and Family Services of the Department of Public Health, and the General Services Building of the Department of Mental Health.

Perhaps the greatest impetus of the 1970's is the reactivation of Rush Medical College and its incorporation into Rush-Presbyterian-St. Luke's Medical Center. This is described elsewhere in this book.

Since so many of the Medical Center's institutions are growing at such a phenomenal pace, it becomes apparent that the existing land allotment may not be sufficient for its future purposes. The Medical Center Commission, as it charts its course for each biennium, must consider its objectives in terms of fifteen years of projected activity. This organization could become so over-extended that its original purpose would be endangered. The Commission's leadership has initiated plans to convene

"all the interests and organizations in an effort to identify common goals... and
co-ordinate the activities of more than 40 separate entities in some kind of joint
planning effort... Economy can be the keynote... of those facilities which can be
shared by all organizations in the District."[1]

These suggested facilities are: additional steam and refrigeration services, purchasing and
stores, laundry, medical library, computer center, clinical laboratories, therapy services,
continual educational programs, auditoriums, automobile parking facilities, day care center -
pre-school nursery, hospitals and nursing homes and security systems.

One must not over-look the relationship between the Illinois Medical Center and the other
great medical centers located in the Chicago region. Among the best known are the University
of Chicago Medical Center on the south side, a generously endowed private institution; the
expanding Northwestern University Medical Center on the lower north side, also privately
endowed. Both of these institutions had their earliest development in the old west side hospital
region and many of their medical faculties had their training at Rush Medical College.

Loyola University Medical Center in Maywood, Illinois was located in the Illinois Medical
Center District until 1969 when its schools of medicine and dentistry joined forces with the
Veterans' Administration in creating the Hines-Maywood complex. Here, too, is a most needed
humanitarian effort for the care of the nations's military veterans. All of these great medical
centers are allied and have reciprocal relations in their common cause.

Individual cities over the nation and their collective hospitals are joining in programs of
sharing to meet the economic squeeze put on both large and small establishments. How much
more so is such a plan needed for the survival of the world's largest medical center?

The national unrest of underprivileged citizens, both black and white, the increasing poverty
in large cities and the resulting miseries of the sick poor are over-taxing both public and private
hospitals. There has been outspoken criticism in our large cities, including Chicago. This is all
the more reason why state, county and city should coordinate their efforts of public health
within the Illinois Medical Center. The Commissioners have pledged that

"problems encompassing the co-mingling of public and private efforts, political
as well as non-political, though seemingly unsurmountable, must be resolved."[2]

The longer the vacillation in these uncertain times, the stronger the tide rolls toward
socialized, governmental medicine and the vision of the good Samaritan fades away.

---

[1]Illinois Medical Center Commission Release, May 12, 1970, Chicago. Reprinted with
permission of Illinois Medical District, 600 South Hoyne Avenue, Chicago, Illinois 60612.

[2]Illinois Medical Center Commission, Statement by the Commission Concerning its
Objectives for the Ensuing Fifteen Years for Incorporation in the 1971 Medical Center Study
Report, To Mr. Joseph Anselmo, Chicago Plan Commission. Reprinted with permission of
Illinois Medical District, 600 South Hoyne Avenue, Chicago, Illinois 60612.

There is, in all this present gloom, a candle being lit in the medical community. As the medical profession progresses into the future, it is recognizing the needs for discussions relating to medicine and religion.

The world has had a century of miraculous medicine with its disease preventing and curing vaccines and anti-toxins. Equally miraculous has been the skillful surgery for the whole body, from brain to Achilles heel. Now another century has started with new hearts, kidneys or other organs, both human and mechanical, replacing damaged or diseased originals. Such "machine medicine" is causing much soul-searching among the medical profession, the clergy and the laity.

The Rev. Paul B. McCleave, director of the Department of Medicine and Religion of the American Medical Association has stated:

> ""Almost every state has a statute saying that when a man's heart stops beating, he is legally dead... But now, with plastic hearts, when does a man die? When he forgets to plug in his batteries?""[3]

Internal prosthesis, the surgical replacement of human organs, is still experimental, especially with heart transplants. The secret of the body's acceptance or rejection must still be found.[4]

Obstetrics also is changing with the creation of human life, the "test-tube baby," outside the human mother's body. This fertilized, developing ovum or embryo is returned to gestate in the original donor's womb or transplanted in another mother who is unable to conceive - at present only theoretical.[5]

Such questionings among the medical profession and the clergy have brought about a mutual program. In September, 1961, the American Medical Association established the Department of Medicine and Religion. There is an advisory committee of ten physicians and ten clergymen to give counsel to the Board of the A.M.A. and Department of Medicine and Religion.

---

[3]Malcolm, Andrew H., "Problems of a 'Machine Medicine': Power of Life and Death: How Is It To Be Used?" The National Observer, Monday, September 5, 1966, p. 12. Reprinted with permission of Dow Jones & Co., Inc.; permission conveyed through Copyright Clearance Center, Inc.

[4]Editor's Note: By 1996 hundreds of transplant operations have made the concept routine; now there are experimental transplants from other species, raising new dilemmas, such as the possibility of spreading viruses from baboons to humans.

[5]Rorvik, David M., "The Test-Tube Baby is Coming," Look, May 18, 1971, pp. 83-88. (Editor's Note: By the 1990's such children are already a fact, with new ethical issues arising, for instance, when a doctor used his own sperm to inseminate his patients' eggs.)

517

The concept for health care today is that man is a whole being. His health is affected by physical, spiritual, emotional and social factors, and in ill health he requires total care and treatment. The faith of the individual is a vital factor in total health.[6]

The goal of the American Medical Association is to cross all faith lines in developing dialog between the two professional groups. Resource information in manuals, films and programs is channeled through a state committee to County Medical Societies which implement the programs of local clergy.

Located in the Illinois Medical Center, the Bishop Anderson Foundation, established twenty or more years ago, is pioneering in its dialog between medicine and religion. Dr. Joseph Davis, former president of the Foundation, remarked:

> "With all the specialization in medicine today, there's a channel driven between the physician and patient. No longer is the doctor a father-confessor who knows the entire family. Now he just looks at you and puts in a heart valve... This new dialog will for instance let a Catholic doctor know how a Jewish patient views death and burial or how some groups look at blood transfusions... we're not trying to change anyone's mind, just to exchange view."[7]

Paul Tournier had also written on the issue that:

> "...We shall have to resolve to study man, not merely from the outside, through scientific investigation, but also from the inside, through intuitive knowledge, through the spiritual communion which establishes a person-to-person bond between the physician and his patient."[8]

This foundation attempts to serve a community of 25,000 persons including patients, professional students and staff. Recreational opportunities such as tickets to the symphony or theatres are sponsored ""to let the students see that the world still sings.""[9]

Help for married students with children is considered in Laurence Armour Day School, and it also serves as a training ground for student nurses while doctors see through one way windows how healthy children behave as compared to their sick small patients.

---

[6]American Medical Association, The Physician, The Clergy and Whole Man, Chicago, Pamphlet.

[7]Malcolm, p. 12.

[8]Tournier, Paul, The Whole Man in a Broken World, Harper and Row, N. Y., 1964, pp. 62-63. Quotation from THE WHOLE PERSON IN A BROKEN WORLD by PAUL TOURNIER and TRANSLATED by JOHN & HELEN DOBERSTEIN. Translation Copyright (c) 1964 by John Doberstein. HarperCollins Publishers Inc.

[9]Malcolm, p. 12.

Other church sponsored organizations are serving the Medical Center, one being the Cardinal Stritch Foundation and its Newman Club; this building was completed in 1965.

Here at this great Medical Center with its daily routine, life coming and life going, physicians, surgeons, nurses and unseen workers all have experienced what Pasteur put in these words:

> "My philosophy is of the heart and not of the mind, and I give myself up, for instance, to those feelings about eternity which come naturally at the bedside of a cherished child drawing its last breath. At those supreme moments there is something in the depths of our souls which tells us that the world may be more than a mere combination of phenomena proper to a mechanical equilibrium brought out of chaos of the elements simply through the gradual action of the forces of matter."[10]

---

[10]Pusey, William Allen, Louis Pasteur, Pasteur Memorial Committee, Chicago, 1928, Pamphlet.

118. Aerial Photograph of Illinois Medical Center District (pre-1974). Brandt & Associates, photographers (9265-7), 9344 N. Drake Ave., Evanston, Illinois. Permission of Brandt & Associates Ltd Photographers, 148 Algonquin Road, Barrington, Illinois 60010.

COOK COUNTY HOSPITAL TODAY

This venerable Chicago institution dating back to 1837, and known by early names as City Hospital or Charity Hospital, has had many periods of despair. Such discouraging causes were: being over-crowded with patients; inadequately supplied with hospital materials; using out-dated medical equipment; having insufficient and inefficient hospital help, and being subjected to unethical political practices. Hospitals all over our country have experienced some of these same conditions, so Cook County Hospital is not an exception.

County Hospital had been increasingly burdened with these deficiencies and by 1970 had reached a climax of crucial desperation. Over-worked staff doctors, residents, interns, nurses, and technicians in the County's obsolete buildings sounded the crisis alarm. News reporters, with their often gory and yellow journalism, informed the Illinois citizens of this problem-plagued county institution.

At the end of 1970, after some resignations and political over-hauling at the hospital, Dr. James G. Haughton became the executive director of Health and Hospitals Governing Commission of Cook County and also, director of County Hospital. At this time, he termed the hospital "a big sea of mismanagement."

Beside this "big sea," he faced hostile members of the hospital staff, a hospital on probation, and the threat of possible loss of County's most precious asset, the periodic certification by the Joint Commission on Accreditation of Hospitals which would be determined in July, 1971.

It was necessary for the entire force of workers at Cook County Hospital, including the house staff, resident physicians, interns, registered nurses, nurses in training, technicians, aides, office workers, janitors, and the many unseen employees, as those in the kitchen - all to work as a team with their director, Dr. Haughton, to restore a very sick hospital.

They were successful; the accreditation was heralded in the Chicago papers to the relief of worried citizens. On August 23, 1971, Chicago Tribune with super-sized headlines reported: "Accredit County Hospital."

Reassured, Dr. Haughton said:

> ""The dedication and teamwork that the drive for accreditation demonstrated was highly gratifying... I am confident that if we all continue our work with the same commitment, we will be able to achieve our ultimate goal of making Cook County Hospital the finest health-care facility in the nation.""[1]

Dr. Haughton is a man for the twenty-first century. He is a black man, born in Panama and formerly an executive with the Health Department of New York City. In this new Chicago position, he is the highest paid public official in Illinois.

For those who do not know about Cook County Hospital, it is a predominantly black hospital with a few Puerto Ricans and whites. The black people come to County Hospital for two reasons: first, it is always accessible, a huge emergency building with 1,800 beds where no one,

---

[1] Yabush, Donald, "Vital Test Passed," Chicago Tribune, Section 1, August 23, 1971, p. 1.

rich or poor, is turned away. The blacks, quite often, are not poor. Second, no doctor's admission card is necessary as in a private hospital. A third reason, perhaps, is often the particular location of County; it is in a black neighborhood, the Near West Side, and not too far for some to reach the hospital on foot; some come from distant sections of Chicago.

For the most part, those who come to County are emergency cases. There are other hospitals in this Medical Center region where the black person can be a private patient, if he so desires. Rush-Presbyterian-St. Luke's Medical Center, next door to County, the new Mile Square Health Center, and the University of Illinois Hospital serve the neighborhood.

Dr. James G. Haughton and Dr. Harry Elam, Director of the Mile Square Health Center, share the same philosophy of medicine as the reactivated Rush Medical College seeks to instill in their young doctors who prepare for the twenty-first century.

There was dissension between the new director with his dynamic plan and the medical staff and professional workers which continued to impede the already burdened hospital's progress. Dr. Haughton resigned as Director of County Hospital and remained in his pivotal position as Director of the Health and Hospital Governing Commission of Cook County. Dr. David M. Greeley became the new superintendent of County Hospital.

A solution is in progress for this troubled giant of a hospital. A plan was prepared by Hiram Sibley, professor of health and director of the Center of Patient Care and Community Health at the University of Illinois Medical Center. This plan could be used in other large cities which are experiencing the same crisis as Cook County Hospital.

> "The plan calls for distributing County's patient load--which totaled 56,838 admissions last year [1971]--among new and existing hospitals, university medical centers and health clinics located in regions of the city where the majority of the County's patients reside."...
>
> "If fully implemented, the phaseout could take 10 years and would require an estimated $200 million in renovation and new construction of hospitals earmarked to receive County's patients."...
>
> "Sibley proposes a series of alternative methods for redistributing County's patients, based on a detailed study of the present utilization and bed capacities of 34 Chicago hospitals graphically suited to absorb part of the patient load.
>
> Hospitals which would receive a majority of the load include The University of Chicago Hospitals and Clinics, Mount Sinai, Chicago Osteopathic, Mercy, Michael Reese, Presbyterian-St. Luke's and The University of Illinois Hospitals."[2]

The alternative plans are for construction of new small hospitals or modernized older structures in various sections of Chicago. The goal

> "...is to provide quality comprehensive health care to County's patients in the neighborhoods where they live.

_____

[2]Pearre, James, "$200-million Project: Plan County Hospital Phaseout," Chicago Today, April 24, 1972, p. 3.

"It isn't reasonable for a person who lives on 111th Street to have to travel 14 miles and spend a day going to County Hospital to see a doctor for 15 minutes," he [Mr. Sibley] said."[3]

Dr. James G. Haughton as Director of the Health and Hospitals Governing Commission of Cook County stated:

"The basic information in Mr. Sibley's report is quite sound. We don't propose to make any recommendations at this time, but it may be only a matter of months before we can."[4]

When asked if County Hospital might be closed, Dr. Haughton noted that

"...700 of County's 1800 beds are needed to serve residents of the West Side"...
""The issue of how those 700 beds will continue to be provided is a separate one and remains to be resolved...""[5] [6]

---

[3]Ibid., p. 16.

[4]Ibid.

[5]Ibid.

[6]Editor's Note: Regardless of individual good intentions, over two decades later this matter has yet to be resolved; the top of the front page headline of December 2, 1994 (Late Sports Final edition) in the Chicago Sun-Times reads: "New County Hospital Gets Go-Ahead" (by Jim Merriner, pp. 1, 12). It appears the state regulators finally gave the go-ahead, subsequent to the County Board's granting of a "certificate of need" on June 22, to build a new hospital to replace the 82-year old, 918 bed hospital at 1825 W. Harrison, with a 464 bed building for an approved $551.6 million in construction, and $37.5 million in major medical equipment, costs. Meanwhile, an opponent, Republican Commissioner Richard A. Siebel, estimates the final cost with interest on construction bonds would be $1.5 billion and sees no need for a new hospital with 7,500 empty hospital beds in the Chicago metropolitan area. However, outgoing County Board President Richard J. Phelan considered leading the fight for a new hospital "among "the most important things I've done in life"." Jim Merriner also reported Phelan to have "said that "610,000 medically indigent people in Cook County" depend on County Hospital for health care" and "that "operating a new, smaller hospital would save taxpayers $440 million in the first five years, vs. operating the existing facility."" Merriner also reported "the next step is for the County Board to hire an architect." [As published in the Chicago Sun-Times, Inc. Copyright 2005. Chicago Sun-Times, Inc. Reprinted with permission.] Finally, the new John H. Stroger, Jr. Hospital of Cook County opened on December 12, 2002 (https://cookcountygov.com/public_hosp.htm; accessed 9 November 2004). It is located at 1901 W. Harrison Street in Chicago. With 1.2 million square feet and 464 beds, it cost over $623 million (http://www.co.cook.il.us/agencyDetail.php?pAgencyID=53; accessed 9 November 2004).

523

DR. KARL A. MEYER

It is an honor to have personally known Dr. Karl A. Meyer as one as one who had lived in this Mile Square neighborhood where he acquired his training in the Medical Center and where he gave more than fifty years in treating the ill and teaching the young.

Dr. Meyer received his medical degree in 1908 from the University of Illinois College of Medicine. At that period, the school was called the University of Illinois College of Physicians and Surgeons and occupied the vacant West Division High School Building. He was born September 28, 1886 in Gilman, Illinois and had his early education there. After graduation from the University of Illinois College of Medicine, he served an Internship of eighteen months at Cook County Hospital and later became a Resident in Surgery under Doctors Carl and Joseph Beck.

In 1914, Dr. Meyer became Medical Superintendent of Cook County Hospital, which position he held until 1967. He began teaching at the University of Illinois College of Medicine in 1914, becoming Professor of Surgery in 1923. In 1926, he taught at Northwestern University Medical School, becoming Professor of Surgery in 1945, and later Emeritus Professor of Surgery.

In 1932, Dr. Karl A. Meyer and Dr. Raymond McNealy organized the Cook County Graduate School of Medicine, one of the first such schools in United States. At that time, Dr. Morris Fishbein, editor of the Journal of the American Medical Association, belittled the new short courses in medicine given by this new school. Cook County Graduate School of Medicine was twenty-five years ahead of its time, as now most all medical schools offer these short, refresher courses. These concentrated programs took the place of traditional study in Vienna, where in the early century medical men took post-graduate work.[1] Through the years, Dr. Meyer kept a watchful as well as proud eye on this school whose students are drawn from all over the world.

Besides his professional life, he had for over fifty years a dedication to and affection for the Chicago Foundlings Home. As president of trustees of this century old charity, he regularly looked in on the sick babies and mothers. Greatest of all, he found his three wonderful children there, a son and two daughters, whom Dr. and Mrs. Meyer adopted. They are now grown and have their own children; all were a joy to this great humanitarian.

Dr. Meyer had many honors such as serving as a trustee for the University of Illinois for eighteen years, vice-president of the Illinois Medical Center Commission, secretary of the International College of Surgeons of which he was one of the founders, a Fellow of the American College of Surgeons and past-president of both Chicago Medical Society and Chicago Surgical Society. The Karl A. Meyer Hall, opened in 1953, part of the expanding Illinois Medical Center, is a residence home for the interns and residents in the Cook County Hospital.

---

[1]Cook County Graduate School of Medicine, Chicago, Illinois, 1969, Continuing Education Courses.

As a member of the Board of City Colleges of Chicago he watched the development of Malcolm X College.

In 1967, when Dr. Meyer reluctantly resigned from the leadership of the Cook County Hospital, he said:

> ""It is because I dearly love Cook County Hospital, its staff, its residents, its interns, its people, and all that it symbolizes--and all that it is--that I make this decision at this time..."
>
> "I have held the torch of healing and hope, and I feel that the time has come to pass this responsibility on to younger hands. A great trust was mine and I have fulfilled it with the very fiber of my being"."[2]

The resignation was painful for him as it is for most great humanitarians. At that time Cook County Hospital, like many other large city charitable institutions today, was suffering from political issues as well as insufficient funds and excess patients. This stormy condition continued to be a problem at Cook County Hospital.

Dr. Meyer continued seeing his private patients in his Michigan Avenue office, having Cook County Hospital conferences and enjoying his twelve grandchildren and three great-grandchildren. He was a life-long advocate for temperance and non-smoking.

Death comes to all: on January 6, 1972, Dr. Karl A. Meyer died in Chicago at the age of 86. He was active in his office practice until December, 1971. Burial services were held in Gilman, Illinois where Dr. Meyer was born and near his refuge at the Kam Lake farm house. A painting of this peaceful scene hung in the doctor's Michigan Avenue office and it inspired him on those busy days of his dedicated life.

At the death of a great man his stature grows, almost to giant proportions when a life's works are recalled. Here was a man who in his medical profession of a half century is reported to have performed more than 100,000 surgical operations. One consisted of a complete resection of a patient's stomach when such an operation was unknown forty years ago, and the patient lived for twelve years after the surgery.

"Mr. County Hospital," as he has been called, was proud of the Cook County Hospital's accomplishments such as the first blood bank in 1925, the pioneering use of X-ray for diagnosis, the first trauma unit for accident victims, and the finest burn units in the country.

Mayor Daley said of Dr. Meyer,

> ""He brought the finest medical aid to all citizens and created one of the finest teaching hospitals in the nation"."[3]

---

[2]Kotulak, Ronald, "County Hospital Pioneer: Dr. Karl A. Meyer Dies at 86," <u>Chicago Tribune</u>, Section 1, January 7, 1972, p. 3.

[3]Ibid.

RUSH-PRESBYTERIAN-ST. LUKE'S MEDICAL CENTER

At the beginning of the twentieth century Rush Medical College, Presbyterian Hospital and St. Luke's Hospital were each an individual organization devoted to the humanitarian pursuit of "healing the sick." Today, in the 1970's, they are united as a collective instrument for a more efficient effort in serving mankind; their combined facilities and assets under a board of trustees have become known as Rush-Presbyterian-St. Luke's Medical Center, situated in the Illinois Medical Center.

On June 11, 1971, Dr. James A. Campbell, Sr., president of Rush-Presbyterian-St. Luke's Hospital Center and Albert B. Dick III, chairman of the board, announced a $91,000,000 expansion program is scheduled for completion by 1975. This construction expansion exceeds the total value of all the present facilities.

Included among the buildings will be patient care towers housing 400 beds and support facilities; the Johnston B. Bowman Health Park will provide nursing and convalescent home accommodations for the elderly; and the academic building for Rush Medical College; a garage with 1500 car capacity. Besides additions to the physical plant, there will be three endowments: six million dollars for basic sciences, seven million for clinical science and six million for student and special programs.

A health care insurance plan for the Center's employees, called Anchor Organization, will provide physicians' visits and basic health care to any premium holder.

The Rush-Presbyterian-St. Luke's program could serve as a prototype of a national health care system since it will combine into one system all local health organizations - this could serve a million to one and a half million persons and would utilize all resources.

At the core of the subsystem will be the acute care referral hospital which will be linked to a network of community hospitals in the inner cities as well as suburbs. These community hospitals will also be linked with a medical college, a research institute, and special facilities for the aged, health maintenance organizations, neighborhood health centers and physicians' offices.

This great medical movement is in action in many large cities although perhaps not as fully augmented as this proposed plan. In Chicago, among such other progressive medical centers, are the University of Chicago Hospitals and Clinics and the Northwestern University-McGaw Medical Center. It is hoped that construction of the Rush-Presbyterian-St. Luke's Medical Center will be completed for the bicentennial year of 1976.

In speaking of the prototype basic unit for a national health-care system, Dr. James A. Campbell said:

"As will be the case at Rush-Presbyterian-St. Luke's the medical center of the future will have at its core an acute care referral hospital. The referral hospital will be linked with a network of community hospitals, a medical college, a research institute, special facilities for the aged, plus pre-hospital health care facilities, including doctors' offices, health maintenance organizations, and neighborhood health centers. The medical center of the future will not simply be a collection of old institutions in a single geographic area; it will be a better way of providing health care to the people."[1]

Rush Medical College was reborn at Rush-Presbyterian-St. Luke's Medical Center. Rush University was created in 1972 to grant undergraduate and advanced academic and professional degrees as M.D. and Ph.D. A second college for nursing and allied health sciences has been activated and a third is being organized for graduate work and research.[2]

The construction of the first new building was begun in the Medical Center on November 15, 1973 - a sixteen million dollar structure for Rush, the first since its establishment 136 years ago. This new structure bridging Harrison Street on Paulina Street will permit the school enrollment to increase to 440 students by June, 1976 when the building will be completed. In the meantime in the 1970's, twenty-two million dollars have been expended to modernize existing facilities.

Dr. James A. Campbell, President of Rush-Presbyterian-St. Luke's Medical Center said of the new project:

"The new academic building permits us to see more clearly the role our educational programs must have in the orderly development of a cooperative comprehensive plan for service, directly and indirectly, to some one and a half million people in northern Illinois.

"The new building stands as a gateway not only to our present campus, but to the entire Medical Center District and the city. It provides for scholarship under modern concepts of instruction and investigation yet remains tied to service and patient care. As important as it is to students, it is just as important to the medical staff and faculty which carry the patient responsibility as well as the principal obligation of instruction."[3]

---

[1]News Rounds, Rush-Presbyterian-St. Luke's Medical Center, Vol. 9, No. 7, July, 1971. Permission of Rush University Medical Center, Chicago, Illinois.

[2]Editor's Note: The Medical Center became the Rush University Medical Center in 2003 (Wikipedia, "Rush University Medical Center," http://en.wikipedia.org/wiki/Rush_University_Medical_Center; accessed 6/3/2007).

[3]News Rounds, Rush-Presbyterian-St. Luke's Medical Center, Vol. 11, No. 11, Nov. 15, 1973. Permission of Rush University Medical Center, Chicago, Illinois.

RUSH MEDICAL COLLEGE TODAY

The fall of 1971 marked the beginning of the "new," reactivated Rush Medical College with an entering class of ninety students. The major goal of Rush is a revival of its philosophy to educate family physicians; in this age of specialized medicine, Rush will support the medical profession by training physicians or clinicians with the emphasis on patient care.

Presbyterian-St. Luke's Hospital which has been affiliated with Rush since its earliest days, accepted the challenge of reopening Rush Medical College because of a strong base support for research and education made possible by a program of endowed chairs. This is the only hospital in the country to establish an endowed chair program. As such it has attracted doctors renowned in their fields to fulfill the provisions of these endowed chairs - which is to achieve outstanding medical education and research leading to better care of patients.

Private citizens and leaders in Chicago have felt that research into major human diseases and the training of clinicians to treat these diseases, important enough for their financial contributions; they have been generous. The reopening of Chicago's oldest medical school has been an incentive to expand these endowed chairs into professorships for the new medical students; there are now twelve such professorships.

Rush faculty in 1970 consisted of 78 professors, 93 associate professors, 121 assistant professors and over 100 instructors; in addition to the Rush Medical College dean, there are four associate deans. Members of the hospital staff have accepted professorships with Rush; also, chairmen of scientific and medical departments at the hospital administer the corresponding departments at Rush. In this way total integration of patient care, learning and research functions will be achieved.

To accommodate the first class since 1942, two floors of Schweppe-Armour Hall had been renovated to provide study carrels for each student. In addition to laboratory and class room facilities, students receive training in physicians' offices and other hospitals in the community. The Rush Medical Library, which continued as a "living" library during the past 29 years and is used daily by medical students and hospital staff, has been enlarged with an additional floor for book space and study facilities.

Future plans include the Rush Graduate School of Health Sciences and Rush School of Allied Health Sciences. In the meantime the integration of Presbyterian-St. Luke's Hospital and Rush Medical College through the endowed chairs and professorships will continue with research into human disease and provide practicing physicians to the people of Illinois.

At the one-hundredth commencement of Rush Medical College on June 6, 1974, in Orchestra Hall, sixty-one Rush Medical College students took the Oath of Maimonides, accepting the responsibility of the medical profession. This oath, so very old and yet so vibrant and modern in today's interpretations, was first spoken by Moses ben Maimon, a Spanish-Jewish scholar and philosopher who flourished from 1135 to 1204.

Still echoing through the centuries - now more than eight centuries - this legacy of a devoted humanitarian who helped suffering mankind to the best of his knowledge when both medicine and surgery were in the primitive stage of development, continues to be the voice for the medical profession today:

"Almighty God, you have created the human body with infinite wisdom. You have chosen to watch over the life and health of your creatures. I am about to apply myself to the duties of my profession. Support me in these great labors that they may benefit mankind.

"Inspire me with love for my art and for your creatures. Do not allow thirst for profit, ambition for renown and admiration, to interfere with my profession, for these are the enemies of truth and can lead me astray. Preserve the strength of my body and soul that they ever be ready to help and support rich and poor, good and bad, enemy as well as friend. In the sufferer let me see only the human being. Enlighten my mind that it recognize what presents itself and that it may comprehend what is absent or hidden. Let it not fail to see what is visible and permit it the power to see what cannot be seen, for delicate and indefinite are the bounds of the great art of caring for the lives and health of your creatures. Let me never be absent-minded. May no strange thoughts divert my attention at the bedside of the sick, or disturb my mind.

"Grant that my patients have confidence in me and my art.

"When those who are wiser than I wish to instruct me, let my soul gratefully follow their guidance; for vast is the extent of our art.

"Imbue my soul with gentleness and calmness.

"Let me be contented in everything except in the great science of my profession. Never allow me the thought that I have attained to sufficient knowledge. For art is great, but the mind of man is ever expanding.

"Almighty God! You have chosen me to watch over the life and death of your creatures. Support me in this great task so that I may benefit mankind, for without your help not even the least thing will succeed."

THE MILE SQUARE HEALTH CENTER

This Chicago neighborhood health center is one of the most promising and effective medical care projects to evolve out of the National Economic Opportunity Act of 1964 which establishes grants to finance "experimental approaches that give promise of increasing the effectiveness of local anti-poverty programs."

In 1966 the Section of Preventive Medicine, Department of Medicine of Rush-Presbyterian-St. Luke's Hospital, developed a program under its administration for specifically organized teams of medical, paramedical and trained lay personnel which would provide a new type of community care program and be family (household) based.

This program comprises three echelons of care. First, is that represented by the public health nurse and community trained health aides; these visit the homes, evaluate their health needs and are the ongoing health advisors to these families.

The second echelon of care is the Mile Square Health Center which provides ambulatory care services. Here, lay personnel from the neighborhood, paramedical technicians such as X-ray and laboratory, and nurse's aides assist the physicians and nurses.

The third echelon of care is by Rush-Presbyterian-St. Luke's Hospital where cases needing more extensive diagnostic evaluation or immediate hospitalization are entered.

By March, 1967, a three story building at 2040 Washington Boulevard had been rehabilitated sufficiently to be opened to the community under the able direction of Dr. Harry P. Elam.

The Mile Square Health Center after only four months had registered over two thousand indigent families needing medical help. The public health nurse, acting as the family counselor had been accepted and welcomed by the patients visited. It was found that priorities had to be established for the families of new-born, pre-natal patients and families with multiple problems.

By 1968 the Health Center at 2040 Washington had rendered in depth services to over 10,000 of the neighboring population and it became evident that the facilities were becoming cramped in every respect. There was also need for more professional help in mental health and social work.

Expansion of service to this community was now reaching the 20,000 mark and a new, modern Mile Square Health Center was in process of construction on Washington Boulevard, near the old building, between Damen and Hoyne Avenues on land owned by Rush-Presbyterian-St. Luke's Medical Center. This is part of the tremendous, humanitarian and far reaching plan of this institution.

By 1973 the Center moved into its new spacious building, costing two and a half million dollars. It is ultramodern, fireproof, window-less on the street side; it accommodates a steady flow of patients with its examining and treatment rooms, laboratories and dental offices. The staff had increased to 339 including professionals and members of the community.

To further the Center's system of family health care, teams were organized. A team consisted of internists, dentists, pediatricians, social workers, nurses and other supporting personnel serve a census tract of 1,500 to 2,000 families. Specialty teams provide obstetrics, gynecology, mental health care, ophthalmology and optometry services on the referral from the primary teams.

Besides these teams there are dental and medical examinations for school children, screening and counseling for glaucoma, sickle cell anemia, lead poisoning, venereal disease and drug abuse.

All these humanitarian activities are under a Board of Directors numbering twenty-four men and women, the Administration Officers, F. Daniel Cantrell, President and Alvin R. Levitas, Administrator, and five Chiefs of Service in Obstetrics/Gynecology, Internal Medicine, Dentistry, Mental Health and Pediatrics.

The continuing history of The Mile Square Health Center is truly dramatic in its humanitarian involvement. The community which is served has about 23,000 low income residents whose only emergency room had been at Cook County Hospital. The Mile Square Health Center was committed to a program of comprehensive family-centered maintenance. This institution grew from 3,463 patients in 1967 to over 20,000 patients in 1972, almost the entire Mile Square's population.

THE CHICAGO MEDICAL SCHOOL

The Chicago Medical School is a robust newcomer to the Medical Center. After the old Frances E. Willard Temperance Hospital in the Medical Center ceased as a teaching hospital it was purchased by the Chicago Medical School in 1930. This school was founded in 1912 and then known as Chicago Hospital College of Medicine and was located on South Rhodes Avenue; in 1915 the name was changed. In 1917 Jenner Medical College closed its doors after a twenty-four year existence and its faculty and students transferred to Chicago Medical School.

From 1932 to 1966 Dr. John J. Sheinin was Dean; the school flourished and by 1948 had full accreditation by the American Medical Association. In 1960 a modern eleven story structure was built on Ogden Avenue in the Medical Center; in 1967 an agreement was made with Mount Sinai Hospital for the primary base hospital for the school. Third and fourth year students train at Cook County Hospital and other facilities in the Medical Center.

In 1967 the concept of a University of Health Sciences was established with the founding of a School of Graduate and Post-Doctoral Studies and School of Health Related Sciences - all sponsored by Chicago Medical School.

Since its establishment in 1912 as a privately supported, independent institution, it has graduated over 4,200 physicians.

119. Chicago Medical School, formerly Francis Willard Hospital. Courtesy The Chicago Medical School, 2020 West Ogden Ave, Chicago, Illinois 60612.

120. The Chicago Medical School, 1969. Courtesy The Chicago Medical School, 2020 West Ogden Ave, Chicago, Illinois 60612.

CHAPTER SIXTEEN: MY COUNTRY IS THE WORLD[1]

Watchman, tell us of the night
What the signs of promise are."

Thomas Paine, 1737-1809

The last quarter of the nineteenth century was dedicated to a humanitarian problem which would carry on into the twentieth century. This was the acclimation of foreigners, many of whom were impoverished and uneducated families coming from Europe to American cities. Many of these foreign families pulled themselves out of their Slough of Despond, namely, degradation, embarrassment and helplessness. Besides their own innate ability and determined grit, they had the help of understanding teachers, social workers and clergy. Many of those immigrants became our country's distinguished citizens.

Today, the needy are no longer predominantly foreign-born. The Negro population has moved from the rural south to northern cities; white families from Appalachian worn-out mining districts have come to the cities; while Mexicans and Puerto Ricans wander across country searching for a better manana.

Many of the present inhabitants in our Mile Square of Chicago, as well as in other sections of the city, may be compared to the country's earlier immigrants. Their problems are the same: the need for skills to earn a decent living and education for the complete family, so they may all enjoy a good life.

This generation of Chicago's immigrants, especially the young, can apply themselves with all their mind, heart and soul to the challenge as well as the privilege of a thorough education. The world needs them as teachers, doctors, nurses, technicians in all sciences and industries as well as writers, poets, artists, and philosophers. The doors are wide open through college and right at the doorstep.

At the advent of the twentieth century, Thomas J. See, formerly an astronomy professor at the University of Chicago, wrote a prophetic editorial, "The Passing of the Century."[2]

"The century has witnessed the growth of public sentiment towards reform in social and political spheres of activity and of a sympathy with the poor and oppressed which has busied the most alert minds with plans for alleviating their condition. Standing upon the threshold of the twentieth century it looks as if it would be the century of humanity and a keener realization of the brotherhood of

---

[1]"My Country Is the World," Thomas Paine, 1737-1809.

[2]See, Thomas J., "The Passing of the Century," The Chicago Tribune, January 1, 1901, A Century of Tribune Editorials, Books for Libraries Press, Freeport, N.Y., 1947, 1970, p. 71.

man. This will be a grander achievement than the discoveries of science or the triumph of art."[3]

This generation of American students of both college and high school age are experiencing unforeseen trials in their education. Yet the stamina of youth and each individual's inmost assurance, a still small voice, leads him on. The ferment of the times and the student's innate knowledge of his coming leadership sobers even the cocky college freshman. Young scholars today seem to have lost some of the joyous spontaneity once associated with that period of search in the fields of serendipity.

We see them as they appear on the campus or city streets. Both boys and girls, men and women are frequently conspicuous with their long, flowing hair and blue jeans apparel as they parade among the older population who might include their mothers. They, too, had once protested with bobby socks, shorn hair and scarlet lipstick. At heart, they were, and are, all the same, simply displaying their youthful independence. The pot must not call the kettle black.

Instead, each young soul has become the Ulysses as he continues on his life's journey, so well voiced by Tennyson:

"The lights begin to twinkle from the rocks;
The long day wanes; the slow moon climbs; the deep
Moans round with many voices. Come, my friends,
'Tis not too late to see a newer world.

* * *

It may be that the gulfs will wash us down;
It may be we shall touch the Happy Isles.

* * *

...that which we are, we are;
One equal temper of heroic hearts,
Made weak by time and fate, but strong of will
To strive, to seek, to find, and not to yield."

Many students today are finding a mutual philosophy in the works of Kahlil Gibran, the Syrian poet and artist. These lines may provide a bridge to the future:

"Peace be with you, years, which disclose
what the years have hidden!
Peace be with you, ages, which restore

---

[3]"The Passing of the Century," Chicago Tribune, Editorial Sheet, January 1, 1901, p. 18.

what the centuries have destroyed!
Peace be with you, time, which moves
with us into the perfect day!

* * *

Peace be with you, lips, that you utter peace
The while you taste the bread of bitterness!"[4]

A poem, written in the spirit of the Christmas season but applicable to universal time and place, appeared a few years ago in a household magazine. Here are a few stanzas from "What Shall We Give the Children?":

"In the long twilight of the
year, the faces of the children grow luminous.
Rosy with cold, arabesqued
with snowflakes, leaning into the wind, or drowsing
before the fire, their eyes large, they
look and listen, as if they glimpsed the peripheries of miracle
or heard a soundless music in the air. From the innocent
kingdom of implicit belief to that uncomfortable
arena where the implacable mind battles the
intractable heart, the
faces of children at Christmas are lighted
with visions of things to come.
What shall we give the children?
It seems certain that they will travel roads
we never thought of, navigate strange seas, cross
unimagined boundaries, and glimpse horizons beyond our
power to visualize. What can we give them to take
along? For the wild shores of Beyond, no toy or
bauble will do. It must be something more, constructed
of stouter fabric discovered among the
cluttered aisles and tinseled bargain counters of experience,
winnowed from what little we have
learned. It must be devised out of responsibility
and profound caring - a homemade
present of selfless love. Everything changes but the
landscape of the heart.

---

[4]Gibran, Kahlil, <u>Prose Poems by Kahlil Gibran</u>, "My Birthday," Tr. Andrew Ghareeb, A. A. Knopf, 1934, New York, New York, pp. 40-42.

What shall we give the children?
Attention, for one day it will be too late.
A sense of value, the inalienable place of the individual
in the scheme of things, with all
that accrues to the individual - self reliance,
courage, conviction, self-respect, and respect for others.
A sense of humor. Laughter leavens life.
The meaning of discipline. If we falter at discipline,
life will do it for us.
The will to work. Satisfying work is a lasting joy.
The talent for sharing, for it is not so much
what we give as what we share.
The love of justice. Justice is the bulwark against violence
and oppression and the repository
of human dignity.
The passion for truth, founded on precept and example.
Truth is the beginning of every good thing.
The power of faith, engendered in mutual trust. Life without
faith is a dismal dead-end street.
The beacon of hope, which lights all darkness.
The knowledge of being loved beyond demand or
reciprocity, praise or blame, for those so
loved are never lost.
What shall we give the children?
The open sky, the brown earth, the leafy tree, the golden
sand, the blue water, the stars in their courses,
and the awareness of these. Birdsong, butterflies, clouds and rainbows. Sunlight,
moonlight, firelight.
A large hand reaching down for a small hand, impromptu
praise, an unexpected kiss, a straight answer.
The glisten of enthusiasm and a sense of wonder. Long days
to be merry in and nights without fear.
The memory of a good home."[5]

Perhaps, this history of A Mile Square of Chicago, as we have looked back, and now as we look forward, may be summarized in a single sentence. This source comes from the National Trust for Historic Preservation; an altruistic organization devoted to the preservation of historic American buildings and to the memory of those persons who built these structures or were persons of esteem who once lived in these now historic buildings.

---

[5]"What Shall We Give the Children?" by the editors of McCall's Magazine, The McCall Publishing Co., Dec. 1964, p. 92.

Tony P. Wrenn wrote:

> "History is really the stuff of all men's lives, inalienably woven into the places they lived, the paths they walked, the activities they pursued, and the scenes they loved."[6]

---

[6]Wrenn, Tont P., "Conservation, Preservation and the National Registry," Historic Preservation, Vol. 18, No. 4, National Trust for Historic Preservation, Washington, D.C., 1966, p. 169.

BIBLIOGRAPHY

Abbot, Willis John, <u>Carter Henry Harrison</u>, Dodd, Mead & Co., New York, 1895.

Adams, Henry, <u>The Education of Henry Adams</u>, The Modern Library, Random House, New York, 1931.

Anderson, Nels, <u>The Hobo - The Sociology of the Homeless Man</u>, University of Chicago Press, Chicago, 1923.

Andreas, Alfred T., <u>History of Chicago from the Earliest Period to Present Time</u>, Vols. 1, 2, 3, 1884-1886.

Andrews, Wayne, <u>Architecture, Ambition and America</u>, The Free Press of Glencoe, Collier-MacMillan Ltd., London, 1964.

Angle, Paul M., <u>The Lincoln Reader</u>, Rutgers University Press, 1949.

Arey, Leslie B., <u>Northwestern University Medical School, 1858-1958</u>, Northwestern University, Chicago & Evanston, 1959.

Barnhart, Clarence L. and William D. Halsey, <u>New Century Cyclopedia of Names</u>, Appleton-Century Crofts, Inc., 1954.

Bayne, Julia Taft, <u>Tad Lincoln's Father</u>, Little Brown & Co., Boston, 1931.

Bishop, Glenn A., <u>Chicago's Accomplishments and Leaders</u>, Bishop Pub. Co., Chicago, 1932.

Brown, Frances Fisher, <u>The Every Day Life of Abraham Lincoln</u>, Brown and Howell Co., Chicago, 1913.

Bogan, Louise and Elizabeth Roget, Editors and Translators, <u>The Journal of Rules Renard</u>, George Braziller Inc., Pub., New York, 1964.

Bonner, Thomas, Melville, <u>Medicine in Chicago 1850-1950</u>, The American History Research Center, Madison, WI, 1957.

Booth, E. R., <u>History of Osteopathy and Twentieth Century Medical Practice</u>, Memorial Edition, Cincinnati, 1924.

Bowen, Louise de Koven, <u>Growing Up in the City</u>, MacMillan Co., New York, 1926.

Bradley, Mary Hastings, On the Gorilla Trail, D. Appleton & Co., New York, 1922.

Bradley, Mary Hastings, Old Chicago Metropolis, D. Appleton & Co., New York, 1933.

Braude, Jacob Morton, Braude's Handbook of Humor for All Occasions, Prentice-Hall Inc., Englewood Cliffs, N.Y. 1958.

Brooks, Noah, Washington in Lincoln's Time, The Century Co., New York, 1895.

Burke, Billie and Cameron Shipp, With A Feather on My Nose, Appleton-Century Crofts Inc., New York, 1949.

Burke, John, Duet in Diamonds: the Flamboyant Saga of Lillian Russell and Diamond Jim Brady in America's Gilded Age, G. P. Putnam & Sons, New York, 1972.

Butcher, Fanny, Many Lives - One Love, Harper & Row, New York, 1972.

Canton, Eddie and David Freedman, Ziegfeld, The Great Glorifier, Alfred H. Kind, New York, 1934.

Casson, Herbert N., Cyrus Hall McCormick, A. C. McClurg & Co., Chicago, 1909.

Chatfield-Taylor, Hobert C., Chicago, Houghton-Mifflin Co., Boston & New York, 1917.

De Forest, Lee, Father of Radio, The Autobiography of Lee de Forest, Wilcox & Follett Co., Chicago, 1950.

Dedman, Emmett, Fabulous Chicago, Random House, New York, 1953.

Dreiser, Theodore, Sister Carrie, World Publishing Co., New York, 1900.

Drury, John, Old Chicago Homes, University of Chicago Press, Chicago, 1941.

Dunne, Finley Peter, Mr. Dooley's Opinions, Harper Brothers, New York, 1906.

Dunne, Philip, Mr. Dooley Remembers, Little Brown & Co., Boston and Toronto, 1963.

Eaton, Leonard, K., Landscape Artist in America, The Life and Work of Jeus Jensen, University of Chicago Press, Chicago, 1964.

Ellery, Eloise, Brissot de Warville, A Study in the History of the French Revolution, Houghton Mifflin Co., Boston and New York, 1915.

Ellis, Elmer, <u>Mr. Dooley's America, A Life of Finley Peter Dunne</u>, Alfred A. Knopf Inc., New York, 1941.

Ellsworth, Lincoln, <u>Search</u>, Brewer, Warren & Putnam, New York, 1932.

Ellsworth, Lincoln, <u>Beyond Horizons</u>, Doubleday, Doran & Co., Inc., New York, 1937.

Evans, William A., <u>Mrs. Abraham Lincoln</u>, Alfred A. Knopf, New York, 1932.

Ewen, David, <u>Complete Book of the American Musical Theater</u>, Henry Holt & Co., New York, 1958.

Ewen, David, <u>New Complete Book of the American Theater</u>, Holt, Rinehart & Winston, New York, 1970.

Fallows, Alice Katharine, <u>Everybody's Bishop</u>, J. H. Sears & Co., New York, 1927.

Flanner, Janet, <u>An American in Paris</u>, Simon & Schuster, New York, 1940.

Frantz, Joe B., <u>Gail Borden Dairyman to the Nation</u>, University of Oklahoma Press, Norman, 1951.

Gallery, Adm. Daniel V., U.S.N. Rtd., <u>The Story of the U-505</u>, Museum of Science and Industry, Chicago, 1955, 1969.

Garrison, Fielding H., <u>Introduction to History of Medicine</u>, W. B. Saunders, Philadelphia, 1929.

Gernon, Blaine Brooke, <u>The Lincolns in Chicago</u>, Lincolnian Pub. Co., Fort Wayne, Indiana, 1934.

Ginger, Ray, <u>Altgeld's America</u>, Funk & Wagnals Co., New York, 1958.

Hamilton, Charles and Lloyd Astendorf, <u>Lincoln in Photographs</u>, University of Oklahoma Press, Norman, 1963.

Hamilton, Henry Raymond, <u>The Epic of Chicago</u>, Willett, Clark & Co., Chicago, 1932.

Harrison, Carter H., <u>Stormy Years</u>, Bobbs-Merrill Co., New York, 1935.

Harrison, Carter H., <u>Growing Up with Chicago</u>, Ralph Fletcher Seymour, Chicago, 1944.

Hayes, Dorsha B., Chicago, Crossroads of American Enterprise, Julian Messner Inc., New York, 1944.

Helm, Katharine, The True Story of Mary, Wife of Abraham Lincoln, Harper and Brothers, New York, 1928.

Hewitt, Barnard, Theatre U.S.A., 1668-1957, McGraw-Hill Book Co., Inc., New York, 1959.

Johnson, Claudius O., Carter Henry Harrison I, Political Leader, University of Chicago Press, 1928.

Jones, Howard Mumford and Richard M. Ludwig, Guide to American Literature and Its Background Since 1890, Harvard University Press, Cambridge, 1890.

Jordy, William H. and Ralph, Editors, Montgomery Schuyler, American Architecture and Other Writings, Harvard University Press, Cambridge, 1961.

Kerstner, Howard Eldred, The Ellsworth Family, Vol. I, 1930, Vol. 2, 1931, National American Society, New York.

Kimball, Fiske and George H. Edgell, History of Architecture, Harpers, New York, 1918.

Kimitz, Stanley J. and Howard Haycroft, Twentieth Century Authors, H. W. Wilson Co., New York, 1942.

Kirkland, Caroline, Chicago's Yesterday's, A Sheaf of Reminiscences, Daughaday & Co., Chicago, 1919.

Koestler, Arthur, Arrow in the Blue, MacMillan Co., New York, 1952.

Krock, Arthur, Memoirs - Sixty Years on the Firing Line, Funk & Wagnalls, New York, 1968.

Krock, Arthur, The Consent of the Governed and Other Deceits, Little Brown & Co., Boston, 1971.

Lewis, Lloyd and Henry Justin Smith, Chicago, The History of Its Reputation, Harcourt, Brace & Co., New York, 1929.

Luthin, Reinhard H., The Real Abraham Lincoln, Prentice-Hall, Inc., New Jersey, 1960.

Masters, Edgar Lee, The Tale of Chicago, G. P. Putnam's Sons, New York, 1933.

Mayer, Harold M. and Richard C. Wad, <u>Chicago, Growth of a Metropolis</u>, University of Chicago Press, Chicago, 1969.

McCormick, Harriet Hammond, <u>Landscape Art, Past and Present</u>, Charles Scribner & Sons, New York, 1923.

McGiffert, Arthur Cushman, Jr., <u>No Ivory Tower, The Chicago Theological Seminary</u>, University of Chicago Press, 1965.

McManus, John T., <u>Ella Flagg Young</u>, A. C. McClurg Co., Chicago, 1916.

McNamara, Daniel I., Editor, <u>The S.C.C.A.P. Biographical Dictionary of Composers, Authors and Publishers</u>, Thomas J. Crowell, Co., New York, 1952.

Miller, Diane Disney, as Told to Pete Martin, <u>The Story of Walt Disney</u>, Henry Holt & Co., New York, 1956.

Moore, Charles, <u>Daniel H. Burnham, Architect, Planner of Cities</u>, Volumes I and II, Houghton Mifflin Co., New York, 1921.

Morgan, Anna, <u>My Chicago</u>, Ralph Fletcher Seymour, Chicago, 1918.

Morrell, Parker, <u>Lillian Russell, the Era of Plush</u>, Random House, New York, 1914.

Morrison, Samuel Eliot, <u>Admiral of the Ocean Sea</u>, Little Brown & Co., Boston, 1942.

Powell, Lydia, <u>The Art Museum Comes to the School</u>, Harper & Brothers, New York & London, 1944.

Quaife, Milo M., <u>Che Cagou, From the Indian Wigwam to Modern City</u>, University of Chicago Press, Chicago, 1933.

Ralphaelson, Samson, <u>The Human Nature of Playwriting</u>, MacMillan Co., New York, 1949.

Randall, Ruth Painter, <u>Mary Lincoln</u>, Little Brown & Co., Boston, 1953.

Rigdon, Walter, Editor, <u>The Biographical Encyclopedia and Who's Who of the American Theatre</u>, James Heiseman, Inc., New York, 1966.

Roderick, Stella Virginia, <u>Nettie Fowler McCormick</u>, Richard R. Smith Co., New Hampshire, 1956.

Ross, Ishbel, <u>Silhouette in Diamonds</u>, Harper & Brothers, Pub., New York City, N.Y., 1960.

Rowan, Richard W., The Pinkertons, Little Brown & Co., Boston, 1931.

Sandburg, Carl, Abraham Lincoln, War Years, Vol. IV., Harcourt, Brace & Co., New York, 1926.

Sandburg, Carl, Mary Lincoln: Wife and Widow, Harcourt, Brace & Co., New York, 1932.

Seldes, Gilbert, The Stammering Century, Harper and Row, New York, 1965.

Shackleton, Robert, The Book of Chicago, Penn Publishing Co., Philadelphia, 1920.

Sheen, Vincent, Personal History, Literary Guild, New York, 1934-5.

Shephard, Jean, The America of George Ade, G. T. Putnam & Sons, New York, 1960.

Smith, Alson, J., Chicago's Left Bank, Henry Regnery Co., Chicago, 1953.

Smith, Harry Bache, First Nights and First Editions, Little Brown & Co., Boston, 1931.

Sullivan, Louis H., The Autobiography of an Idea, Dover Publications, New York, 1956.

Synon, Mary, The Good Red Bricks, Little, Brown & Co., Boston, 1929.

Toffler, Alvin, Future Shock, Random House, New York, 1970.

Tournier, Paul, The Whole Person in a Broken World, Harper & Row, New York, 1964.

Waring, J. F., James W. Ellsworth and the Refounding of Western Reserve Academy, Western Reserve Academy, Pub., Hudson, Ohio, 1961.

Whitman, Walt, Complete Prose Works, Small, Maynard & Co., Boston, 1898.

Whitehead, Alfred North, Adventures of Ideas, MacMillan Co., New York, 1933.

Wilson, Charles Morrow, Black Africa in Microcosm, Harper & Row, New York, 1971.

Young, James Harvey, The Toadstool Millionaires, Princeton University Press, New Jersey, 1961.

BROCHURES AND PAPERS

"A Century of Tribune Editorials, 1847-1947," <u>The Chicago Daily Tribune</u>, Chicago, 1947.

Adams, Edward Dean, <u>America and Americans</u>, New York, 1926.

Brown, William H., <u>Biographical Sketches of Some of the Early Settlers in the City of Chicago</u>, Fergus Printing Co., Chicago, 1876.

"Chicago High School Papers," Chicago History Museum Library.

"Cook County Graduate School of Medicine," <u>Continuing Education Courses</u>, Chicago, 1969.

<u>Cyrus Hall McCormick Papers</u>, State Historical Society of Wisconsin, Archives and Manuscripts, Madison, Wisconsin.

"Ella Flagg Young. An Appreciation." Chicago Board of Education, Chicago, 1926.

<u>Evarts Ambrose Graham</u>, written for Washington University School of Medicine, St. Louis, MO, 1957.

"First Annual Report of the Superintendent of Public Schools," Chicago, 1854, Chicago History Museum Library.

French, William R. <u>Historical Sketch and Description of the Art Institute</u>, Chicago Art Institute, 1904.

Nyholm, Amy, Position Paper on the "The Carter Harrison Collection," Newberry Library, Chicago.

Schaefler, Dorothy Fitch, <u>645 Monroe Street - The Fitch Family</u>, unpublished.

<u>William Morton Payne Papers</u>, The Newberry Library, Chicago.

MAGAZINES AND PERIODICALS

Bonney, Hon. Charles Carroll, Judge L.D. Thoman, Rev. David Swing, E. Nelson Blake, Thos. B. Bryan, Rev. P. S. Henson, and Rev. John Henry Barrows, "A World's Congress at the World's Fair: A Symposium," The Statesman, Vol. VI, No. 1, Chicago, October, 1889, pp. 1-5.

"Bureau of Investigation," Journal of American Medical Association, Vol. 127, No. 12, March 24, 1945, p. 133.

Burnham, Daniel H., "Lessons of the Chicago World's Fair," The Architectural Record, 33, 1913, pp. 35-44.

Cleven, Andrew N., "Thornton's Outlines of a Constitution for a United North and South America," Hispanic American Historical Review, Vol 12, 1932, pp. 198-215.

Crook, David H., "Louis Sullivan and the Golden Doorway," Journal of the Society of Architectural Historians, Vol. XXVI, No. 4., December 1967, pp. 250-258.

Kroll, Ernest, "Homage to Frederick Law Olmstead," The Saturday Review, May 17, 1969, p. 21.

Payne, William Morton, "The American Scholar of the Twentienth Century," The International Quarterly, Burlington, Vermont, December 1903, pp. 262-279.

Schuyler, Montgomery, "Last Words About the World's Fair," The Architectural Record, Vol. III, No. 3, Jan-Mar 1894, pp. 291-301.

Sheehan, John F., "Medical Schools and Veteran Administration Hospitals," International Medical Digest, Harper & Row, Hagerstown, MD, Vol. 85, No. 2, February 1969, pp. 53-54.

"The Chicago Medical School," International Medical Digest, Harper & Row, Hagerstown, MD, Vol. 84, No. 12, December 1968, pp. 552-553.

Wright, Frank Lloyd, "Louis H. Sullivan - His Work," The Architectural Record, Vol. LVI, No. 1, July 1924, pp. 28-32.

Wrenn, Tony P., "Conservation, Preservation, and the National Registry," Historic Preservation, Vol. 18, No. 4, National Trust for Historic Preservation, Washington D.C., July-August, 1966, pp. 164-169.

NEWSPAPERS

"Well Known Names in List of Brown School's Early Pupils," Oak Leaves, Oak Park, IL, June 28, 1945, pp. 9, 11 (from "The Austinite", Harriet N. Dunn).

Gilbert, Paul T., "Old Chicago Comes to Life Once More in Beaubiens' Tales, The Chicago Sun -Times, May 20, 1945, p. 21.

Morris, Bernadine, "Mainbocher's Best Isn't Controversial; It's Remarkable," Santa Barbara News-Press, California, December 1969.

Pearre, James, "Plan County Hospital Phaseout," Chicago Today, April 24, 1972, pp. 1-3.

Rusk, Howard A., M.D., "A Void at Christmas," The New York Times, December 26, 1965.

Toms, Dorothy Kent, "Your View of the News," Chicago Daily News, January 26, 1970.

Yabush, Donald, "Vital Test Passed," Chicago Daily Tribune, August 3, 1974.

WISDOM

Once all the paths of life
Had many a curve and bend,
And all the distances were blue with dreams.
At each quick turn a glad surprise
Awaited eager, visioning eyes.
But now -- white in the light of the sun,
The paths make straight - every one
Straight to the journey's end.

Effie Bangs Warvelle

121. Marjorie Warvelle Bear, from the 1960's. From MWB family album. The McAllisters, 1811 State Street, Santa Barbara, California, photographer.